GLOBAL POLITICS

SEVENTH EDITION

James Lee Ray

Vanderbilt University

HOUGHTON MIFFLIN COMPANY   BOSTON   NEW YORK

Sponsoring Editor: *Melissa Mashburn*
Assistant Editor: *Lily Eng*
Project Editor: *Elena Di Cesare*
Senior Production/Design Coordinator: *Jennifer Waddell*
Senior Manufacturing Coordinator: *Marie Barnes*
Marketing Manager: *Sandra McGuire*

Cover design by Judy Arisman

Cover image by Steven Hunt. *Flat Global Network Map.* The Image Bank

Library of Congress Catalog Card Number: 97-72534

Student Text ISBN: 0-395-87251-0

123456789–VB–01 00 99 98 97

Contents

Part II
INSIDE STATES: THE IMPACT OF INDIVIDUALS,
GROUPS, AND ORGANIZATIONS

Part V
INTERNATIONAL ORGANIZATIONS AND
TRANSNATIONAL ACTORS

10. Coalitions, Alliances, and Economic Communities

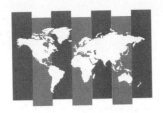

Maps

Preface

The seventh edition of *Global Politics* retains the three major themes of its predecessors. First, it provides a basic understanding of the history of the international system from the First World War to the present. Second, it explains current issues and crises in the global political system that are likely to have the greatest impact on its future. Finally, it discusses the possibility of discovering patterns in the foreign policies of states, and the behavior of individual leaders, multinational corporations (MNCs), and international organizations, as well as in the operation of the global political system. In short, *Global Politics* strives for the development of all three themes—the historical, the contemporary and policy-oriented, and the theoretical or systematic—and emphasizes the extent to which they complement one another.

FEATURES OF THIS EDITION

The seventh edition benefits from the input of at least two hundred new sources and deals with most of the dramatic recent events and contemporary trends in international politics. These analyses and discussions are based in part on pedagogical improvements incorporated in every chapter. The "Policy Choices" feature, new for this edition, analyzes key contemporary issues—such as dealing with ethnic grievances and handling international aggression—in terms of alternative options, complete with specified advantages and disadvantages, in a way designed to evoke debate both among students and between students and their instructor. The seventh edition also highlights important terms in **bold** print and provides a list of those key terms, at the end of each chapter, along with a systematic summary of the material presented in the chapter.

Following is a list of some of the more specific modifications and additions in the seventh edition:

- Chapter 2, "The Modern Era," contains an updated discussion of recent economic and political trends in the international system, introductory remarks about recent contributions from feminist theorists, and comments about neoliberal institutionalism, a topic also discussed in more depth in Chapter 12.
- Chapter 3, "The Public, Ethnicity, and Special Interests," includes a new analysis of the role of public opinion in foreign policy making, introduces the concepts of "two-level games" and "audience costs," and presents new material on the varied roles public opinion plays in several different democratic political systems.
- Chapter 4, "Making Foreign Policy: Bureaucrats, Diplomats, Leaders, and Logic," contains an updated discussion of decision-making theories, as applied to events leading up to the Persian Gulf War. It also includes a new analysis of a political forecasting model that has proved substantially successful in making accurate predictions about literally thousands of issues over the past twenty-five years.
- Chapter 5, "States, Nations, and Power," contains a revised section on the evolution of states, focusing on their historical competition with other types of entities, such as city-states.
- New in Chapter 6, "Comparing States and Foreign Policies," is an updated analysis of the democratic peace proposition, which evaluates the argument that democratic states are more peaceful than their nondemocratic counterparts and are less likely to fight each other, combined with a review of the recent debate over the quality of the evidence regarding that proposition.
- Chapter 7, "Interdependence Among Rich States: West-West Relationships," covers the impact of globalization on countries' domestic economies, including that of the United States, and reviews the possibility that the increasing integration of the world's economy exacerbates economic inequality within the United States and elsewhere.
- Chapter 8, "Rich States and Poor States: North-South Relationships," evaluates the latest developments in the debate over the relevance of the experience of the export-led economies of East Asia to that of developing states in other regions of the world.
- Chapter 9, "East-West Relationships: The Emerging Post–Cold War Era," presents a more detailed treatment of contending points of view regarding how and why the Cold War came to an end and who deserves the credit or blame; it also discusses the relevance of that debate to an evaluation of theories of international politics.
- Chapter 10, "Coalitions, Alliances, and Economic Communities," examines the most recent arguments regarding the question of whether, and how far, NATO should be expanded and explores the likely fate of the common currency in the European Union.

- Chapter 11, "Universal International Organizations," includes a new section on the utility of peacekeeping operations sponsored by the United Nations and considers possible ways in which the organization could be reformed.
- Chapter 12, "Ethics, Law, and International Regimes," reviews the debates over economic inequality in the world and examines causes and possible cures; it also offers a new evaluation of the role of nongovernmental organizations (NGOs) in providing foreign aid, as well as a discussion of the debate between neoliberal institutionalists and neorealists on the role of "regimes" in the international system.
- Chapter 13, "Transnational Actors: The Wave of the Future?" now contains an extended section on the role of MNCs in developing countries, including comment on controversies regarding the alleged abuses by corporations including child labor, as well as a new section on the World Wide Web addressing the potential threat of "information warfare" and the issue of whether the United States needs to develop a "cyberforce" to supplement the protection provided by its army, navy, and air force.
- Chapter 14, "The International System, the Balance of Power, and War," includes a revised section discussing the implications of the democratic peace proposition for analyses focusing on the whole international system, and summarizing the debate between critical theorists and neorealists regarding anarchy and recent trends in the polarity of the system (uni- versus multipolarity).
- Chapter 15, "The Future of the Global Community," reviews the latest evidence on global warming, analyzes the track records established by prominent "pessimists" and "optimists" in their recent predictions concerning various global crises and issues—such as population growth, depletion of natural resources, and global warming—and discusses the implications of these track records for evaluating the credibility of various sources of information about these issues.

Also for the seventh edition, John Kroll has carefully revised and rewritten the *Instructor's Resource Manual with Test Items*. The manual includes chapter summaries, chapter objectives, classroom activities, further readings, essay questions, and multiple-choice tests. Kroll also provides addresses for numerous useful sources of information on the World Wide Web and discusses a simulation of international crises that could be integrated into a course on international politics. *A Computerized Test Item File*, available for IBM and Macintosh computers, is a computerized version of the printed test items in the *Instructor's Resource Manual* that allows professors to create customized tests by editing and adding questions.

ACKNOWLEDGMENTS

Students from all my courses have made the largest contribution to this book. J. David Singer's influence on my thinking is reflected on almost every page. The following people provided extensive, detailed, and helpful comments on the first draft of this edition:

Glenn Palmer, State University of New York, Binghamton
Roy Licklider, Rutgers University
William P. Avery, University of Nebraska, Lincoln
Randolph Siverson, University of California, Davis
Michael Sullivan, University of Arizona, Tucson
Donald L. Hafner, Boston College
Richard Stoll, Rice University

This edition might have been even better if I had followed every one of their suggestions, but it clearly benefited from the ones I did accept. Any flaws or errors that remain are, of course, my responsibility. My wife, Cam, and my sons, Alex and Nicholas, lived through the process with me, for which they deserve my gratitude—and everybody else's sympathy.

J. L. R.

GLOBAL POLITICS

GREENLAND
(DENMARK)

80°

ALASKA
(U.S.)

CANADA

60°N

UNITED STATES

40°N

ATLANTIC OCEAN

Azores

Midway Is.

Bermuda

WESTE
SAHAR
(MOROC

Hawaiian Is.

MEXICO

BAHAMAS

CUBA

DOMINICAN REP.

Virgin Is.

JAMAICA HAITI

BELIZE
HONDURAS

Puerto Rico

20°N

ST. CHRISTOPHER AND NEVIS
ANTIGUA AND BARBUDA
DOMINICA
BARBADOS

CAPE
VERDE

GUATEMALA
EL SALVADOR

NICARAGUA

ST. LUCIA
GRENADA

ST. VINCENT AND
THE GRENADINES

GUINEA-BISSA

PACIFIC OCEAN

COSTA RICA

TRINIDAD AND TOBAGO

GUYANA

PANAMA

VENEZUELA

FR. GUIANA

COLOMBIA

Equator

SURINAM

0°

Galapagos Is.

ECUADOR

WESTERN
SAMOA

PERU

BRAZIL

TONGA

BOLIVIA

20°S

Easter Is.

PARAGUAY

CHILE

URUGUAY

ARGENTINA

40°S

Falkland Is.

160°W   140°W   120°W   100°W   80°W   60°W   40°W   60°S

2

80

RUSSIA

FINLAND

ESTONIA
LATVIA
LITHUANIA
BELARUS

UKRAINE
MOLDOVA
ROM.
BULG
MAC.
GEORGIA
TURKEY
ARMENIA
CYPRUS
SYRIA
AZERBAIJAN
LEBANON
ISRAEL
IRAQ
JORDAN
KUWAIT
EGYPT
SAUDI
ARABIA
YEMEN
OMAN
UNITED
ARAB
EMIRATES

KAZAKHSTAN

UZBEKISTAN

TURKMENISTAN
KYRGYZSTAN
TAJIKISTAN

AFGHANISTAN

IRAN

PAKISTAN

BAHRAIN
QATAR

MONGOLIA

N. KOREA
S. KOREA
JAPAN

PACIFIC OCEAN

PEOPLE'S REPUBLIC OF CHINA

NEPAL
BHUTAN
BANGLADESH
INDIA
MYANMAR
(BURMA)

TAIWAN

LAOS
THAILAND
VIETNAM
CAMBODIA
(KAMPUCHEA)
PHILIPPINES

Mariana
Islands
Guam

Wake I.

Marshall
Islands

CHAD
SUDAN
ERITREA
ETHIOPIA
DJIBOUTI
SOMALIA
CENTRAL
AFRICAN REP.

UGANDA
KENYA
RWANDA
ZAIRE
BURUNDI
TANZANIA

SRI LANKA

MALDIVES

BRUNEI
MALAYSIA
SINGAPORE

Belau

Caroline Islands

KIRIBATI

NAURU

SEYCHELLES

INDIAN OCEAN

INDONESIA

PAPUA
NEW
GUINEA

SOLOMON IS.

TUVALU

MALAWI
ZAMBIA
COMOROS

VANUATU

FIJI

ZIMBABWE
MADAGASCAR

MAURITIUS

AUSTRALIA

New Caledonia

BOTSWANA

MOZAMBIQUE
SWAZILAND
SOUTH
AFRICA
LESOTHO

ABBREVIATIONS

AUS.	AUSTRIA
BEL.	BELGIUM
B. H.	BOSNIA AND HERZEGOVINA
BULG.	BULGARIA
CR.	CROATIA
CZ.	CZECH REPUBLIC
DEN.	DENMARK
HUNG.	HUNGARY
LUX.	LUXEMBOURG
MAC.	FORMER YUGOSLAV REPUBLIC OF MACEDONIA
NETH.	NETHERLANDS
ROM.	ROMANIA
SLK.	SLOVAKIA
SLN.	SLOVENIA
SWITZ.	SWITZERLAND
YU.	YUGOSLAVIA

NEW
ZEALAND

°E   40°E   60°E   80°E   100°E   120°E   140°E   160°E

PART I

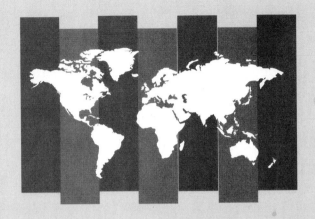

Historical Background

CHAPTER 1

The Historical Setting

The major purpose of *Global Politics* is to help the reader understand world politics today and tomorrow. The process begins in the first two chapters with a discussion of yesterday's world politics, for several reasons. First, today is, and tomorrow will be, unique. In fact, because of the demise of the Soviet Union and the end of the Cold War, one might get the impression that world politics has changed so fundamentally that the history of the global political system is irrelevant to an understanding of its future. It is true that the dramatic transformation of global politics in the 1990s has produced events and trends that are unfamiliar even to professional observers who have become accustomed to startling political surprises since the Second World War. This book will focus intently upon many of those unfamiliar events and trends. Still, even the revolutionary developments of the last decade of the twentieth century have not made the present entirely incomparable to the past. Although the statement that history repeats itself is an oversimplification, it is not completely false. Recurring patterns are clearly visible in the historical record of the global political system. History often provides situations that are comparable in important ways to those that create today's headlines. To achieve the best possible understanding of today's headlines—and tomorrow's—it is important to be knowledgeable about comparable past situations.

The second reason this book begins with a discussion of history is that, at least until recently, global politics has been dominated by nation-states and the people who control them. These people, whether official decision makers or powerful behind-the-scenes operators of various kinds, have had an important characteristic in common. They have been (and are), with some exceptions, steeped in the history of their respective countries and, to a lesser extent, of world politics. The decisions they make and the policies they formulate have been shaped, often in obvious and predictable ways, by the lessons they draw from history. Any fruitful attempt to understand their decisions and policies must involve not only a knowledge of history but also a knowledge of how history has been interpreted by the most important scholars and leaders in the world.

A third reason for beginning *Global Politics* with a brief historical analysis is that it provides a basis for interpretation and evaluation of the chapters that follow. In those chapters, we examine the various actors, organizations, and other social entities that play important roles in global politics. Chapters 3 and 4, for example, deal with the impact on foreign policies and international relations of individuals and groups inside states. In Chapters 5 and 6, our focus turns to states themselves. The succeeding chapters analyze relationships among various *categories* of states (rich with rich in Chapter 7, rich versus poor in Chapter 8, and East versus West in Chapter 9) and interaction within international *organizations*, such as political coalitions, economic communities, and the United Nations (Chapters 10 and 11). Chapter 12 is devoted to a discussion of the role of ethical principles and international law, which (together with international organizations) sometimes provide the bases for "regimes," or what might be broadly defined as communities of interest among nation-states. Chapter 13 focuses on organizations whose members and activities are found in several different states but which are not themselves formally affiliated with the governments of states. Multinational corporations, some groups engaged in international terrorism, and Amnesty International are examples of what are often referred to as transnational organizations. Chapters 14 and 15 take a comprehensive look at the international system as a whole. Finally, Chapter 16 analyzes the relationship between historical and scientific studies of global politics. The discussion of the recent history of world politics in the first two chapters provides a general background for examples that are referred to or discussed in more detail in those chapters that deal with the various important actors and entities in the global political system. The historical information also should enable the reader to recall and examine specific examples supporting (or refuting) the general points discussed in the later chapters.

A final reason for beginning with a historical overview is less important but deserves mention. It was not possible to write such an analysis without revealing personal biases and some ignorance. Aggressive, intelligent readers will want to keep these shortcomings in mind as they begin evaluating the material on the following pages.

THE EMERGENCE OF THE CONTEMPORARY INTERNATIONAL SYSTEM: TOWARD THE FIRST WORLD WAR

The international political system of the nineteenth century, after the Napoleonic Wars of 1803 to 1815, was relatively stable. One source of continuity in the century was the consistently important role played by Great Britain. If Britain was not always clearly the most powerful state, it was never very far from being so. Most British people who thought about such things assumed that the twentieth century would be no different. Britain's power and security rested first on its navy, which dominated the seas the world over and made any attack across the English Channel very unlikely to succeed. The second solid basis for Britain's nineteenth-century security was its manufacturing ability.[1] Britain was the workshop of the world and, with its navy ensuring access to the world's markets, seemed to have no reason to fear dramatic change.

In retrospect, it is easy to see that the beginning of the twentieth century brought several developments that would be detrimental to Great Britain (see the map on page 5). Probably the most important was the increasing power of three states. To the west, the United States was already superior to Britain in economic productivity and would soon surpass Britain in military strength as well. In the east, Japan was proving to be a major power in wars against China and Russia, making it very difficult for Britain to maintain its customary domination of the seas in that area. Most ominously, Germany began to challenge Britain's ability to preserve a balance of power on the European continent.

Great Britain accommodated the rising power of Japan by signing an alliance with that country in 1902, an unusual step for the British, who had traditionally avoided firm commitments of this kind. Britain's foreign policy had for several centuries been based on a perception of itself as the balancer in a balance-of-power system that was especially applicable to relations among the major powers of Europe. To make the system work, the British believed that they must avoid tying their hands prematurely and that they should become involved in interstate conflicts only after it became clear which state posed the greatest threat of dominating the European continent. Britain would then join the alliance that formed against that state.

---

[1] "So long as Great Britain as an industrial nation had no equal, it was the most powerful nation on earth, the only one that deserved to be called a world power" (Morgenthau and Thompson, 1985, p. 138).

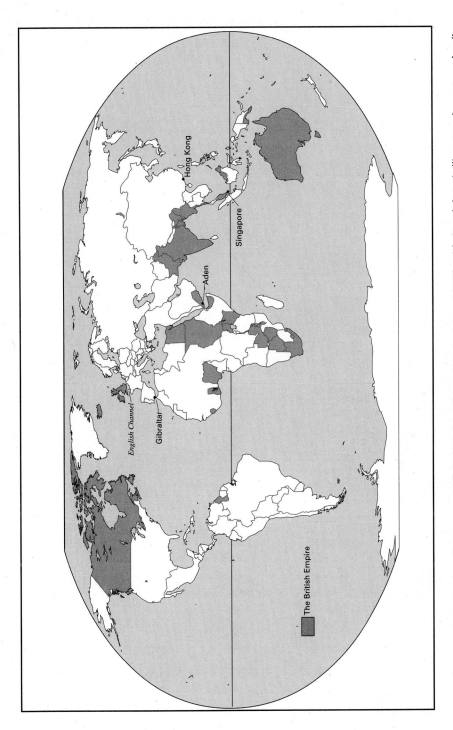

Great Britain, the Nineteenth-Century World Leader Great Britain (circa 1900) with its globe-girdling empire, was a leading international power for most of the nineteenth century.

Despite that policy, for some time the British were unconcerned about the rise of Germany. Otto von Bismarck, chancellor of the German Empire from 1871 to 1890, had long followed a policy of keeping the German navy small, and as long as Germany maintained that policy, it did not seem threatening. In fact, at the beginning of the century the British, because of colonial rivalries, tended to regard the French with more suspicion than they did the Germans. The suspicion was sufficiently strong that for a while the British were inclined to come to an understanding with Germany and perhaps even to become aligned in some way with the Triple Alliance of Germany, Austria-Hungary, and Italy (Haigh, 1973, p. 67). But this inclination was wiped out by a combination of French conciliation and German belligerence. The French agreed to give the British a free hand in Sudan and Egypt in return for the British giving the French a free hand in Morocco. Meanwhile, the Germans made it obvious that they intended to build a navy that might challenge Britain's control of the seas. The result of these two developments was the Entente Cordiale between Britain and France in 1904.

A shared suspicion of the Germans was the basis of this agreement. France had suffered a stunning defeat in the Franco-Prussian War some thirty years earlier. Out of that war had come a united German state that became increasingly threatening to France. French leaders took several steps to deal with this threat. In 1894, France entered into a military alliance with Russia. By 1899, that alliance was strengthened by an agreement stipulating that France would come to the aid of Russia if Russia were attacked by either Germany or Austria-Hungary, while the Russians would come to the aid of France if France were attacked by Germany. By 1907, the Entente Cordiale had—with the inclusion of Russia—become the Triple Entente. The entente was faced with the Triple Alliance of Germany, Austria-Hungary, and Italy. But France had arranged an ace in the hole within this structure of alliances. In 1902, France and Italy came to a secret agreement in which each promised to remain neutral if the other were attacked. This was one reason why Italy did not join its allies when the First World War began in 1914. (See the map on page 7 for countries' alliances and cross-alliances.)

After a number of international crises over the next decade, that war was ultimately sparked on June 28, 1914, when a Serbian nationalist, apparently hoping for the liberation of fellow Slavs under Austrian rule,

Choosing Sides in the First World War   ▶

In the First World War, the Central Powers of Germany, Austria-Hungary, and Bulgaria faced the opposition of not only the Triple Entente (Great Britain, France, and Russia) but also their several allies, such as the United States.

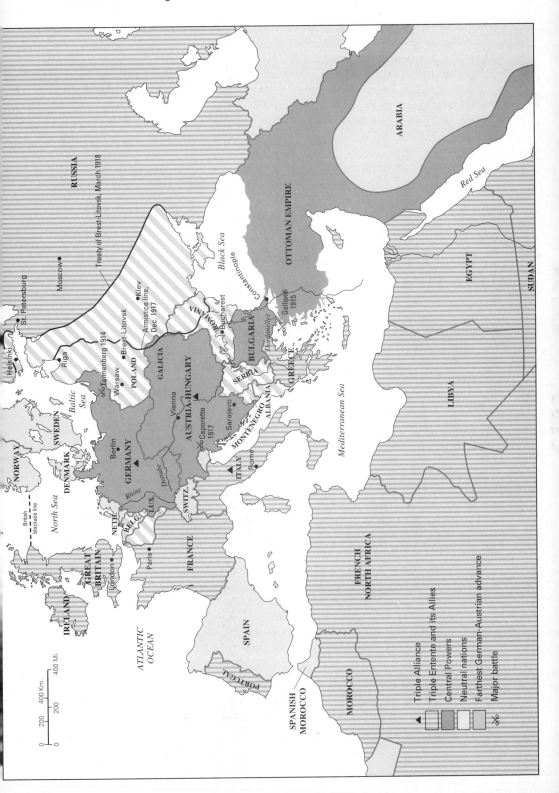

Treaty of Brest-Litovsk, March 1918

RUSSIA

Moscow●

●St. Petersburg
Helsinki●

Riga●

●Kiev
Armistice line, Dec. 1917

●Brest-Litovsk

○Tannenberg 1914
Warsaw● POLAND

GALICIA

ROMANIA

Bucharest●

Black Sea

Constantinople

OTTOMAN EMPIRE

ARABIA

Red Sea

EGYPT

SUDAN

Baltic Sea

SWEDEN

NORWAY

DENMARK

Berlin● GERMANY

Vienna●

AUSTRIA-HUNGARY

▲Caporetto 1917

Danube

Rhine

Sarajevo●

SERBIA

BULGARIA

Dardanelles

Gallipoli 1915

GREECE

ALBANIA

MONTENEGRO

ITALY▲ Rome●

Mediterranean Sea

LIBYA

North Sea

British blockade line

GREAT BRITAIN
London●

IRELAND

NETH.
BELG.
LUX.

SWITZ.

FRANCE
Paris●

ATLANTIC OCEAN

SPAIN

PORTUGAL

SPANISH MOROCCO

MOROCCO

FRENCH NORTH AFRICA

▲ Triple Alliance

Triple Entente and its Allies

Central Powers

Neutral nations

Farthest German-Austrian advance

�֍ Major battle

0   200   400 Km.
0   200   400 Mi.

assassinated Archduke Franz Ferdinand, heir to the throne of Austria-Hungary. Austrian leaders had long been concerned about separatist movements in their empire, and they were determined to strike back at Serbia, a nation that, in the Austrian view, sympathized with and supported these movements. Austria's determination was heightened when Germany, on July 5, assured Austria of support if conflict with Serbia brought Austria into conflict with Russia. Austria delivered an ultimatum to Serbia on July 23, to which Serbia made a very conciliatory reply. Even so, on July 28 Austria declared war on Serbia. By August 6, 1914, France, Great Britain, and Russia were at war with Germany and Austria-Hungary. The Allies were later joined by Japan, Italy, and the United States, while Bulgaria and Turkey fought on the side of the Germans and the Austrians.

Alternative Explanations

How could a small conflict between a small country such as Serbia and the declining Austro-Hungarian Empire lead to a war involving all the most powerful nations in the world? Possible answers to this question fill many volumes, and only a few can be discussed here. One prominent answer emphasizes the importance of the system of **alliances** that existed at the time of the quarrel between Austria-Hungary and Serbia. Germany, of course, was allied with Austria-Hungary, one reason that Germany became involved in the conflict immediately. Russia was not formally allied with Serbia; rather, the Russians became involved in the conflict as defenders of pan-Slavic nationalism and because of a fear that Austria-Hungary would, if not checked, dominate an area that lay in the path of a possible Russian outlet to the sea. Russia *was* allied with France, though. The Germans knew this and had for years assumed that if they became involved in a war with Russia, they also would have to fight France. Finally, Great Britain was allied with France and Russia. Although Britain's alliances did not require going to the aid of Russia and France in the event of war, there is little doubt that their existence made it more likely. Thus, one can see sense in the argument that the conflict between Austria-Hungary and Serbia was transformed into a major conflagration by the complex interlocking system of alliances built up by the major powers.

Another explanation of the outbreak of the First World War emphasizes the importance of military technology and the **bureaucracies** that administered the technology. Generals of the time, for reasons to be discussed later, were convinced that **rapid mobilization** of forces would be crucial in determining who would win the next war. Accordingly, in Germany and Russia particularly, but also in Austria-Hungary and France, the armies made elaborate plans to ensure rapid mobilization.

After Austria-Hungary attacked Serbia, Russia mobilized. Germany did not respond immediately; Kaiser Wilhelm sent a telegram to his cousin Nicholas, the Russian czar, requesting that he show some sign of good faith that would allow the kaiser to avoid issuing his own mobilization orders. The czar canceled a general mobilization order and substituted an order for partial mobilization. But the Russian military bureaucracy would not respond to a change of plans. The generals feared the consequences of trying to convert to partial mobilization once general mobilization had been initiated. Czar Nicholas then became convinced that such a sudden change of plans might throw his military organization into chaos, and he reinstated the original general mobilization order.

When Kaiser Wilhelm realized that Russia was not going to pull back from its general mobilization, he and his advisers decided that they must proceed quickly with their own. But because the German army was aware that France and Russia were allied and because the German generals assumed that the Russian army would take longer than the French army to mobilize effectively, the German plan called for mobilization and attack against the French first. The French would be quickly defeated, and the Russians could be dealt with in turn.

So, even though the Russians were responding to the threat from Germany's ally, Austria-Hungary, the German war plans called for an attack against France. At the last moment, Kaiser Wilhelm was led to believe (with help from the British) that France might be kept out of the war, even if Germany became involved against the Russians. Therefore, Wilhelm decided that, to give France a chance to stay out, Germany ought to turn its troops around and attack Russia instead. But the German generals were as reluctant as the Russian generals to change their plans at the last moment. Helmuth von Moltke, the German chief of staff, reportedly broke down in tears at the suggestion that such a thing might be attempted.

The fact that Austria-Hungary and France also had rapid mobilization schedules, an important element in the pressure on Russia and Germany, adds strength to the argument that the state of military technology and the bureaucratic organizations administering it were important causes of the war. With all sides so intent on rapid mobilization, had the assassination of Archduke Ferdinand not taken place, some crisis was bound to lead to war sooner or later.[2]

---

[2] Jack Levy (1986, p. 195), in an analysis of such theoretical ideas regarding the onset of the First World War, refers to the "common argument that in 1914, the military preparations of the great powers acquired a momentum of their own, that because of rigid military plans each step led inevitably to the next, that the serious threat of mobilization of one great power essentially forces certain other powers to mobilize, and that mobilization itself inevitably led to war."

Another explanation of the outbreak of the First World War was offered by Lenin in 1917. Lenin believed that **capitalist states** were necessarily **imperialistic** to ensure access to markets, fields of investment, and raw materials. All the important capitalist states in the world were in constant competition to establish imperialistic bases. Such competition led to instability, Lenin argued, because of the operation of what became known as the **law of uneven development.** The capitalist states might approach some clear definition of their respective spheres of influence, but that delineation would eventually become unsatisfactory to those states that were growing more rapidly than others. Dissatisfaction on the part of the up-and-coming states, according to Lenin, would lead to war and did lead, in his view, to the First World War. The spat between Austria-Hungary and Serbia served as an excuse to engage in a battle that the major capitalist powers were intent on for more important reasons.

Additional plausible explanations of the onset of the First World War have been numerous and diverse. Some scholars blamed the Great War on **German militarism.** Other writers blamed the **munitions makers** in all the countries involved. The **bipolarity** of the international system in 1914, the press in most European countries, and an **arms race** involving the navies of Great Britain and Germany were thought to be crucial factors by various analysts. The controversies regarding these various theories continue in scholarly books and journals even today (Oren, 1995; Levy, 1990/91; Stevenson, 1988; Sagan, 1986; Wohlforth, 1987). Continuing interest in the First World War as a monumental struggle that had a momentous impact on global politics for most of this century keeps these controversies alive. Also, that war, as well as the factors and crises that produced it, has been a crucial source of theoretical ideas in the field of international politics, and a source of examples in support of those ideas. As we shall see at several points in later chapters, differences in the processes leading to the First and Second World Wars have played a key role in producing contrasting notions about how global politics works. Those notions focus, for example, on the impact of governmental decision-making organizations, alliances, and arms races.

Effects of the War

Perhaps the most important impact of the First World War on international politics was the **weakening of Europe.** The European states had been in unquestioned command of the global political system up to 1914. By 1917, one important European state (Russia) was on the verge of dropping out of the war, and the rest were locked in a seemingly endless stalemate. It took a non-European state (the United States) to break the deadlock. By then, the Austro-Hungarian Empire had been destroyed and Germany, Britain, and France severely damaged.

The Russians had had their revolution, in no small part another effect of the war. It might have occurred in any case, but the war made the inefficient and outmoded aspects of the czarist regime more obvious and subjected the Russian people to such hardships that they became less tolerant of the government's inadequacies (Pipes, 1990). Alone among the major combatants, the United States emerged more powerful than it had been at the beginning of the war. It was in fact, according to many tangible indicators, already the most powerful state in the world (see Chapter 6). The First World War significantly enlarged the role of the United States in the global political system.

Another important impact of the war involved the realm of political ideas. The war had been fought, according to Woodrow Wilson, the leader of its most powerful victor, to make the world safe for **democracy.** It had been won, as no one could fail to notice, by the more democratic states (the United States, Great Britain, and France), while the nondemocratic states (Germany, Austria-Hungary, the Ottoman Empire, and Russia) had fallen to pieces. The war served to enshrine the intertwined (but not synonymous) values of democracy and **national self-determination;** and the other side of that coin was the beginning of the delegitimization of empires. Empires were antidemocratic, and national self-determination was viewed as democracy on the level of international politics. It was, therefore, to be cherished and protected.

Finally, any discussion of the effects of the First World War would be incomplete without an emphasis on the extent to which it created conditions conducive to the next world war. In addition to the lasting hatreds it created (or reinforced), the First World War had several important effects on the international economic system that shaped the process leading to the Second World War. The United States emerged, by a considerable margin, as the most important economic unit in the world, and Great Britain, France, and Germany became dependent on it. Furthermore, the war (and perhaps the provisions of the peace treaty) devastated the German economy in a manner that paved the way for the appearance, and later the success, of Adolf Hitler.

THE FIRST WORLD WAR AND THE STUDY
OF INTERNATIONAL RELATIONS

A widespread U.S. view is that the discipline of international relations was created by Americans as a result of their experience in the First World War.[3] This view might be criticized for its ethnocentrism. "Scholars, soldiers and statesmen have, in fact, speculated about the relations between states since the modern state emerged four or five centuries ago" (Knutsen, 1992, p. 1). Even before then, such scholars as Thucydides, Kautilya, and later Machiavelli made important contributions to serious thought in the area of international politics. One analyst of the history of ideas about international relations argues that "Kant is the greatest of all theorists of international relations" (Brown, 1992, p. 14). Still, before the First World War, nearly all ideas about the global system were neatly filed away in a box for international law, diplomatic history, or the parent discipline of political thought itself. After 1918, however, a generation of scholars and writers, appalled by the horrors of the conflict just past, began to scrutinize interstate politics in systematic terms (Pettman, 1975, p. 2). "World War I . . . did not so much give birth to International Relations theory as give the tradition a major jolt, a new emphasis, a higher popular profile, a new self-consciousness, a mission and a new direction of development" (Knutsen, 1992, p. 2).

Many writers, such as Brierly, Eagleton, Lauterpacht, and Potter, continued to write about international relations in terms of international law and organization. But others, analyzing the causes of the First World War, broke from this tradition and attempted to bring a knowledge of political, historical, economic, demographic, and geographic factors to their understanding of foreign policies and international politics.[4] All were most concerned with steps that should be taken to avoid another world war. And many were influenced by the American president who had guided the United States through the First World War. "Woodrow Wilson," according to former Secretary of State Henry Kissinger, "originated what would become the dominant intellectual school of American foreign policy." According to this dominant school, "peace depends above all on promoting democratic institutions. . . . Conventional American wisdom has consistently maintained that democracies do not make war against each other" (Kissinger, 1994, pp. 44, 33.)

By the 1930s, a split emerged between (1) those who advocated reliance on ideals, moral principles, international law, international organizations, and the "world court of public opinion" and (2) those who were basically suspicious of idealistic principles as guidelines for action in international politics and stressed instead the importance of power

---

[3] For example, Fred Warner Neal and Bruce P. Hamlett (1969, p. 283) state that "international relations is an American invention dating from the time after World War I when the American intellectual community discovered the world."

[4] Two famous examples are Schuman (1933) and Dunn (1937).

and conflict. The best-known analysis of the controversy between the **idealists** and the **realists,** as they became known, was written by Edward H. Carr (1939). This debate came to dominate the study of international relations in the United States after the Second World War.

POSTWAR SETTLEMENTS

In the months immediately following the First World War, idealists appeared to have more influence on the conduct of international relations, thanks largely to a very powerful advocate of their views, Woodrow Wilson.[5] Wilson was anxious to move beyond the days of balance-of-power and sphere-of-influence politics, which he saw as the dangerous kinds of principles that had led Europe to near total collapse. The major instrument through which such principles would be replaced was an international organization, to be called the League of Nations. As the president of the strongest victor in the war, Wilson provided the major impetus behind the creation of such an organization, but there was widespread agreement on the need for such a body. Many European leaders were of the opinion that "the war came into being largely by default, because the forces of negotiation and peaceful settlement marshalled against it suddenly collapsed" (Sweetser, 1920, p. 5, cited in Claude, 1964, p. 40). In short, the war occurred because the leaders had had no time or place to talk things over when the crisis began. The League of Nations would provide the opportunity for a cooling-off period that would have crowned with success the efforts to avoid the Great War.

Beyond that very general conception of the League, though, there lay important areas of disagreement among the victorious powers. One area became obvious when the disposition of Germany's colonies was discussed. Wilson wanted to make these colonies the common property of the League and have them administered by small nations. Britain, along with its dominions Australia, New Zealand, and South Africa, wanted to annex the colonies outright. A compromise was accomplished whereby the British dominions obtained the territories they desired under a loose mandate from the League. In fact, the distribution of the German colonies followed closely the provisions of the secret treaties concluded among the victorious European powers during the war. In adhering to the treaties, based on old sphere-of-influence ideas, the British and the other European powers demonstrated that their view of how international relations should be conducted in the postwar era was

---

[5] "Wilson's visionary hopes dominated the new discipline of International Relations in its first years" (Knutsen, 1992, p. 191).

perhaps not as revolutionary as idealists such as Wilson might have hoped.

The French were even less idealistically inclined than the British. In an important sense, France had been the real loser in the war. It had lost 10 percent of its active male population, the highest proportion of any of the major participants. France had mobilized 8,410,000 men to fight the Germans. Of that number, 1,355,800 were killed; 4,260,000 were wounded; and 536,000 were taken prisoner. All these categories together accounted for 73 percent of the total number mobilized. Also, the largest and most dreadful battles had been fought on French soil. The additional deliberate German destruction meant that fully a third of France was devastated. Almost 300,000 homes had been destroyed and some 3 million acres of land made unfit for cultivation (Shirer, 1969, p. 114).

Finally, the French treasury had been emptied, and its war debts were staggering. France suffered more than Germany in many ways, and its leaders were absolutely desperate to assure their people that they would never have to battle the Germans again. Their major concern was that Germany be kept under control, and they were not willing to rely on Wilson's idea of collective security without a solid base of concrete force behind it. "There is an old system of alliances," French premier Georges Clemenceau had said before the Paris Peace Conference, "called the Balance of Power—this system of alliances, which I do not renounce, will be my guiding thought at the Peace Conference" (De Conde, 1963, p. 474).

In pursuit of security against Germany, the French proposed the establishment of an international peace force. Wilson rejected the proposal on the grounds that once the facts of a dispute had been made clear by such an august body as the League, world public opinion would be sufficient to deter aggression. The British shared some of Wilson's optimism regarding world public opinion, but they had a more practical reason for being opposed to an international peace force: they needed all of their armed forces, in particular their navy, to defend the far-flung British Empire. Therefore, the French proposal to put some teeth into peace-keeping mechanisms to be established by the League was a failure (Northedge and Grieve, 1971, p. 150).

The French also wanted to take all of Germany's land west of the Rhine, an area containing some five million people, and create one or two republics that would be under French control. Wilson considered this notion a violation of the principle of self-determination. The peace conference came perilously close to breaking up over this point, but the French lost this argument, too. Germany was allowed to keep the Rhineland, although it was to be permanently demilitarized to about fifty kilometers east of the Rhine.

Another, eventually crucial, disagreement between Wilson and Britain and France concerned the matter of reparations. Before the peace conference, Wilson had promised Germany that it would suffer no punitive damages. Germany had signed the armistice on condition that the Allies would ask for payment only of damages to civilians and their property. But the British and the French wanted to make Germany pay the whole cost of the war. This intent was understandable, since the British and the French had suffered much more from the war than the Americans. Realizing this, and despite his reservations, Wilson agreed that Germany should be made to pay for pensions to disabled Allied soldiers and their relatives. The definition of civilian damages that Germany had agreed to pay was expanded considerably, and an increase of about 100 percent in reparations resulted. The debate over the justice of the reparations became a key element in Adolf Hitler's rise to power.

Having failed in their attempts to have an international peace force established and to have Germany dismembered, the French were particularly intent on forcing Germany to pay extensive reparations—more extensive, as it turned out, than the British and the Americans were willing to agree to. The French had to give in again; the bill ultimately presented to Germany was not as large as the French wanted. And by the end of 1920, Germany began to default on payment of even this reduced bill. Much to its chagrin, France could not even get London and Washington to put pressure on Germany to pay the reduced reparations. After about a year of bickering with its erstwhile allies, France decided to move on its own. In 1923, having waited until the Reparations Commission had officially certified that Germany had defaulted on payments, the French president sent troops to occupy the Ruhr Valley, the industrial heart of Germany.

The invasion did not work out well for France, partly because of opposition from the British. Britain's foreign policy after the war reflected a desire to adhere to the basic assumptions on which its prewar policy had been based. It wanted to preserve a balance of power on the European continent, and in the 1920s there was only one clear threat to that balance. Germany had been defeated and humiliated. Russia was still trying to recover from a revolution and a civil war. Only France was threatening, and the British treated France as a threat when its troops occupied the Ruhr Valley in 1923. They therefore joined the Americans in condemning French aggression.

The Germans adopted a policy of passive resistance in the Ruhr so that the French had problems getting the mines and the mills there to produce. The invasion also helped bring on a disastrous round of inflation in Germany, the effects of which were felt in France when the value of the franc dropped alarmingly (Knapton, 1971, p. 487). The invasion evoked sympathy for Germany, and in 1924 an American banker named

Charles G. Dawes persuaded the Reparations Commission to accept the Dawes Plan, a series of bank loans that allowed Germany to make some payments on reparations that were reduced by the terms of the agreement. France enjoyed some residual benefits of the Dawes Plan, but in the end France, as a result of all the financial wheelings and dealings between the Allies and Germany in the 1920s, received from Germany only enough to pay 20 percent of the cost of rebuilding its war-torn regions. Germany, on the other hand, actually came out ahead. Germany borrowed more from U.S. banks than it paid in reparations, and those loans were never repaid (Shirer, 1969, p. 150).

GERMANY AND ADOLF HITLER

At the eleventh hour on the eleventh day of the eleventh month of 1918, the armistice that ended the First World War went into effect. Three days earlier, a new German republic, replacing the old Hohenzollern dynasty, had been proclaimed. It could not have been born at a less propitious time. Within a matter of seven months, the new government, led by the Social Democrats, was faced with the responsibility of signing the Treaty of Versailles. The publication of the treaty in Germany in May 1919 caused an outcry throughout the country. Mass meetings were organized, the provisional president of the republic called the terms "unrealizable and unbearable," and the German delegate to Versailles called the treaty "intolerable for any nation" (Shirer, 1960, pp. 57–58).

Yet what choice did the new government have? Could it resist the demands? There was reason to believe it could, because the German army had been far from total defeat in November 1918. "The German army capitulated when it still occupied scores of square miles of enemy soil. It marched home as an integrated force" (Northedge and Grieve, 1971, p. 207). In view of this, the provisional president asked Field Marshal von Hindenburg if military resistance was possible. He replied that it was not. The new government took him at his word, and the German legislature accepted the peace treaty by a large majority.

Hindenburg's decision was wise, because the Americans were in command of the situation. Even if the Allied troops in the field could not have crushed the Germans, the troops and artillery yet to be deployed by the United States were an obviously insuperable barrier to further German resistance. But the myth grew in Germany, a myth Hitler would later use to advantage, that the German army had been stabbed in the back by the new democratic republic. The first basis of the myth was that the German army had not been destroyed physically at the end of the war. Also, after the crucial days had passed, the leaders of the German army forgot, conveniently or not, that they had sought an end to the war and had told their government that resistance was useless. For example, almost exactly one year after the armistice, Hindenburg himself testified to a committee of inquiry that the German army had been stabbed in the back.

This (imaginary) stab was especially hard for the German people to accept because of what they considered the unreasonable demands of the Versailles treaty. It took land away from them. Seven million people were no longer living under German sovereignty. Germany was virtually disarmed. Article 231 of the treaty held Germany responsible for the war. But the provision of the treaty that had perhaps the most lasting impact concerned reparations. The exact amount was not stipulated in the treaty, but the Germans were to make a preliminary payment of $5 billion between 1919 and 1921. That gave some indication of what was to come. Then in April 1921, the Allies presented Germany with a total reparations bill of $33 billion. By that time the German mark had begun to fall in value. It was normally valued at 4 to the U.S. dollar, but by the end of 1921 it had fallen to a value of 75 to the dollar.

That was merely the beginning of the most spectacular inflationary spiral in the history of the industrialized Western world. In 1922, the value of the German mark fell to 400 to the U.S. dollar, an inflationary rate of around 500 percent for one year. By the beginning of 1923, it took 7,000 marks to buy a dollar's worth of goods. When the French occupied the Ruhr Valley, the value of the mark dropped to 18,000 to the dollar. By July, it was 160,000 to the dollar; by August, 1 million to the dollar; by November, 4 billion. From then on, the value of the mark compared to the dollar had to be calculated in the trillions. It took a wheelbarrow full of money to buy a loaf of bread, assuming either were to be found.

This was the scene in Germany when Hitler made his first marked impression on the body politic. He staged what became known as the Beer Hall Putsch, a ludicrously premature attempt to begin his ascent to power in Germany. He was arrested, tried, convicted, and sentenced to five years in prison on April 1, 1924.[6] A normal man would have been discouraged, but Hitler was neither normal nor discouraged. He spent his time in prison dictating a book (*Mein Kampf*) that described in some detail his plans for the establishment of a "thousand-year Reich."

In time, Germany recovered from its economic problems, and things began to go well for the country both domestically and internationally. On the international scene, Germany signed an agreement with the other isolated state in the global political system, the Soviet Union, in 1922 at Rapallo, Italy. The treaty provided Germany with several benefits, but perhaps the most important effect was on Germany's relationships with Britain and France. Both states saw that Germany was no

---

[6] He became eligible for parole in six months and was released after only nine months in prison.

In the early 1920s, inflation in Germany was so severe that people, such as this German woman, used their paper money for fuel in their stoves and fireplaces. SOURCE: The Bettmann Archive.

longer isolated, and they did not want it to join forces with the Soviets. In 1925, the European allies proposed guarantees of the borders between Germany and its former enemies on the west. On the one hand, the French and Belgians were guaranteed support by the British and Italians in case of an attack by Germany. On the other hand, agreements signed at Locarno in Switzerland, also in 1925, protected Germany from a French reoccupation of the Ruhr, from which French troops had withdrawn in 1924. The symbolic importance of the Locarno treaties was that they marked the end of Germany's isolation from the West.

Domestically, the German economy began an impressive recovery, due in large part to a flow of U.S. capital, used to pay reparations and renew Germany's productive capacities. Unemployment dropped, wages rose, and neither Hitler nor his Nazi Party was prominent.

But the importance of the U.S. economy to German prosperity was soon to become forcefully apparent. In fact, Great Britain and France as well as Germany had become heavily dependent on the United States economically. In the 1920s, U.S. investors and Wall Street banks poured money into Germany, which used much of it to pay reparations to Great Britain and France, which in turn used that money to pay their First World War debts to the United States. This interesting arrangement was, perhaps, harmless enough until the **stock market crash** in 1929, when the supply of money in the circular flow from Wall Street and other sources in the United States suddenly stopped. Then the Germans could no longer pay their reparations, which meant that Great Britain and France could not pay their war debts. The only possible alternatives for the Germans, the British, and the French were to default on their debts or to increase their exports to the United States in order to accumulate dollars to pay the debts. President Herbert Hoover and the Congress moved to eliminate the second possibility (and to ensure the first) by putting the **Smoot-Hawley Act** into effect in June 1930, raising U.S. tariff rates to their highest point in history. "Over a thousand economists had pleaded with the president not to sign the bill, pointing out that higher rates would hamper foreign exports, block collection of the war debts, invite foreign retaliation, and embitter foreign relations. The predictions proved true" (De Conde, 1963, pp. 559–560). At least as important as the domestic impact was the international effect of the increased tariffs. "The atrocious Smoot-Hawley tariff of 1930 . . . more than any other act of policy, spread the Depression to Europe" (Johnson, 1983, p. 246).[7]

The effect of the **Depression** on German electoral politics was immediate and dramatic. In 1928, before the crash, the Nazis had received

---

[7] This is a predominant opinion, but Susan Strange (1985, pp. 239–240), while acknowledging that "conventional wisdom" asserts that high tariff barriers prolonged the Depression and spread its impact around the world, argues that the evidence actually indicates that "tariffs, though substantially raised, had made surprisingly little difference to the volume of trade, or its direction. . . . It was just that as markets shrank, politicians everywhere were under pressure to handicap foreign producers against domestic ones. Yet the handicaps actually did little to alter the pattern of trade flows."

Adolf Hitler, shown here in an official photo taken in Berlin in 1936, rose to power in Germany when economic problems made Germans desperate for strong leadership. SOURCE: UPI/Corbis-Bettmann.

810,000 votes and elected 12 of their members to the Reichstag. In the September 1930 elections, after millions of people had been thrown out of work and thousands of small businesses had failed, Hitler's party won almost 6.5 million votes and 107 seats in the Reichstag, thus becoming the second largest party in the legislature. The Communist Party in Germany also gained as a result of the Depression. Although its gains were not as spectacular (from 3.2 million votes in 1928 to 4.6 million in 1930), its rise undoubtedly smoothed the way for Hitler in the years to come.

By 1932, the Nazi Party was the largest single political party in the country. In January 1933, Hitler was named chancellor. On March 27, 1933, the German legislature passed what was called the Enabling Act, which served as the formal basis for the establishment of Hitler's dictatorship. He never received a majority of the votes, but a single party rarely does in a multiparty system of the type Germany had at the time. The Nazis used terror and intimidation, there can be no quarrel about that, but they also attracted millions of uncoerced voters.

The expectations of many German voters that Hitler could help solve their economic problems proved to be warranted. The economic policies of Hitler, based on large-scale borrowing for public expenditures that were principally civilian in the early years, worked well and quickly. "The result," as one well-known economist has pointed out, "was a far more effective attack on unemployment than in any other industrial country. By 1935, German unemployment was minimal" (Galbraith, 1975, p. 274).[8]

So Hitler came to power in part because many Germans hoped (correctly, as it turned out) that he could help them with their economic problems. He also appealed to Germans of all classes because of his denunciation of the Versailles treaty and his condemnation of the Jews and because he was an alternative to the assumption of power by the Communists.

JAPAN, ITALY, AND GERMANY: CHALLENGES TO THE STATUS QUO

Scholars of international politics will always vividly view the 1930s as notable for the successful challenges to the international status quo mounted by Japan, Italy, and Germany. Let us take a look at the assertive policies adopted by each of these dissatisfied major powers.

Japan

The first challenge to the status quo was made by Japan when it invaded Manchuria in 1931. Japan was a rapidly growing power in the decades before 1931, taking advantage of the First World War to acquire several German colonial outposts and to extend its economic and political privileges in China. Perhaps even more important, Japan dramatically increased exports to the Asian markets that were cut off from their traditional European suppliers by the war. By the end of the war, Japanese strength had become so apparent that it was accorded Great Power status at the Paris Peace Conference.

---

[8] Galbraith is not, as anyone familiar with him would know, an apologist for Hitler. "The notion that Hitler could do no good," he points out, "extends to his economics as it does, more plausibly, to all else" (p. 275).

All did not go well for Japan at the peace conference. The Japanese government insisted on the inclusion of an article in the League of Nations' covenant committing the League to the principle of racial equality. Great Britain and its dominions opposed the plank, mainly because Australia's domestic laws prohibited the immigration of Asians. Wilson, rather than see the League fall apart over this issue, felt it necessary to rule against the article on racial equality in his position as chair of the League of Nations Commission.

This ruling was not the end of international racial discrimination against Japan. In 1920, the platforms of both the Republican and Democratic parties in the United States had Asian exclusion planks. California, soon joined by Arizona, Washington, and Texas, passed laws that forbade Japanese from owning or even renting land. In 1921, the U.S. Congress passed the Emergency Quota Act, which cut off Japanese immigration into the United States entirely. Such discriminatory policies on the part of the most powerful nation in the world, in addition to the lack of commitment to racial equality in the covenant of the League of Nations, were not calculated to increase Japan's respect for the international status quo.

Even so, the early 1920s were good years for Japan, both economically and politically. But in 1927 Japan began to have domestic economic problems that were soon exacerbated by the onset of the Depression. The reaction of all the industrialized states to the Depression, as we have seen, was to throw up high tariff walls to protect jobs. Japan was hit hard, since it was particularly dependent on international trade.

While Japan was feeling the pressure of the high tariff barriers around the world, China began an effort to recover Manchuria, which it considered Chinese territory in spite of important Russian and Japanese influence in the area. Japanese interests were quite extensive; Manchuria accounted for some 40 percent of Japan's foreign trade and investment at the time (De Conde, 1963, p. 526). In reaction to the increased flow of Chinese people into the area, as well as anti-Japanese propaganda and incidents, the Japanese army took matters into its own hands. In 1931, manufacturing an incident involving the dynamiting of a Japanese-controlled railroad track, the army moved to clear Manchuria of Chinese troops and establish complete control.

The League of Nations urged China and Japan to restore normal relations. It took great pains to avoid taking sides on the issue, despite the rather obvious nature of Japan's aggression. A commission was formed to go to East Asia to study the matter, but it did not issue a report until one year later, and the League did not adopt the report until February 1933, almost a year and a half after the Japanese invasion. The report was not one-sided. It did call for an autonomous Manchuria under the control of China, but it also contained safeguards for Japanese interests there. However, when the report was adopted, the Japanese delegation walked out and announced that Japan was resigning from the League. Earlier, the Japanese had set up the puppet state of Manchukuo, officially recognizing it in September 1932 (Reischauer, 1964).

The incident set an unfortunate precedent for the League, and the United States did not help the situation. Speeches were made and warnings were given, but it was obvious to the Japanese, especially since the U.S. had never joined the League, that American resistance to Japan's actions would go no further. Needless to say, words alone did not cause the Japanese to withdraw from Manchuria.

Italy

The next challenge to the League of Nations' collective security came from Italy, which, like Japan, emerged as a modern nation-state relatively late (in 1861) and engaged in several foreign adventures in the first decades of its existence. Italy joined Germany's Otto von Bismarck in a war against Austria in 1866 because Italy wished to acquire Venetia, an area on Italy's northern border controlled at that time by Austria. In 1895, putting into action the idea that Italy, like other European states, deserved to have an African empire, the Italians attacked Ethiopia. To everyone's amazement, especially the Italians', Italy lost. In 1911, Italy attacked Turkish holdings in Tripoli (later Libya) for the purpose of taking them over. This effort was successful. Fortunately for Italy, it decided not to join its German and Austrian allies in the First World War and instead ended up fighting on the side of the Allies. For its contribution to the Allied effort, it expected much more in the way of territorial rewards from the Paris Peace Conference than it actually received.

In 1922, Benito Mussolini came to power. He benefited almost immediately from the general worldwide economic advance, and by 1929 he could claim that he had saved the lira, put an end to inflation, and reduced unemployment. However, Italy, like Japan, suffered from the Great Depression. "The underlying immobility and rigidity of the Italian economy under fascism was to prove a matter of first-rate importance for the world. The international Depression deprived fascism of its only real claim to material success. As the world began to go under after 1929, the fraudulence of Mussolini's claims to have found the secret to prosperity were stunningly revealed, and the security of the regime was accordingly endangered" (Dugan and Lafore, 1973, p. 80).

By 1935, Mussolini was ready, the necessary incidents had been engineered, and Italy once more attacked Ethiopia. The League of Nations responded, initially, with surprising forcefulness. Italy was officially branded the aggressor, and the League voted to institute an embargo of arms, ammunition, and implements of war against Italy. But this embargo was never effectively enforced. First, the League failed to classify oil, coal, and steel as implements of war. Furthermore, the United States refused to cooperate with the League in imposing effective sanctions. Britain and France, the most important states within the League, were apparently motivated by the fear that strong action against Italy might drive Mussolini into the arms of Hitler. They still hoped at this point that Italy might be an ally against Germany if the need arose. So Britain allowed all the Italian military forces and equipment to pass unchallenged through the Suez Canal. Franklin Delano Roosevelt was unwilling to go against the tide of isolationism in the United States to cooperate with the League in opposition to Italian aggression.

Not surprisingly, the Italian venture was successful. By June 1936, Ethiopia was defeated, and Mussolini proclaimed it an Italian province. In December 1937, Italy followed Japan in resigning from the League of Nations. Mussolini continued his aggressive policies by annexing Albania in the spring of 1939. "The action was a sort of trivial recapitulation of the Ethiopian venture . . . [It] was explicitly designed to show that Italy's capacity for annexing foreign states was as great as Germany's" (Dugan and Lafore, 1973, p. 339).

Germany

If Mussolini killed the League in Ethiopia, Hitler buried it, along with the Versailles peace treaty. First, he violated the disarmament provisions of the Versailles treaty. Then, in March 1936, he occupied the Rhineland, which according to the peace settlement was supposed to be a demilitarized zone. At this early stage, Germany's military strength was quite modest, and it is clear that Hitler would have had to back down in the face of any substantial resistance. But he met virtually no resistance at all. The German troops "simply marched in behind blaring bands—there was no battle order whatsoever" (Shirer, 1984, p. 242).

In 1938, Hitler officially incorporated Austria into the Third Reich. Later that year he began to demand a solution to the "problem" involving the people of German ethnic background who lived in a part of Czechoslovakia known as the Sudetenland. At a meeting in **Munich** in September, the British and the French gave in to Hitler's demands, under threat of military action, and Czechoslovakia was forced to cede to Germany 11,000 square miles of territory containing all the fortifications in the Czech defense line. The loss of territory left the country helpless. By April 1939, Hitler had absorbed the rest of the Czechoslovakian state into his empire. Yet Hitler was still not satisfied. There was one more territorial change that he considered necessary. On September 1, 1939, Germany attacked Poland in an effort to bring about that change, and the Second World War was under way. Even then, Hitler might have been stopped with relative ease if Britain and France had taken advantage of an opportunity to launch a vigorous counterattack following their declaration of war.[9] Instead, Poland's Western European allies chose to sit idly by, beginning what became known as the "Phoney War."

Factors Leading to Appeasement

The attempts by status quo powers such as Britain, France, and the United States to deal with the aggressive policies of those major states opposed to the international status quo in the 1930s were based on a policy of **appeasement,** that is, conciliatory compromises offered in the hope that the aggressors would be satisfied and thus cease their aggression. The obvious failure of this policy gave appeasement the bad name that it still has. Why did the Japanese, Italians, and Germans meet with only feeble resistance for so long? Perhaps the most important reason was the impression made by the First World War on the leaders and the people of those states that might have defended the status quo. Britain and France in particular had suffered horrendous losses in the First World War, and none of the changes demanded by the three opponents of the international status quo seemed important enough to warrant the risk of another such horrifying experience. The First World War, many concluded, had been brought about largely by a regrettable lack of patience on the part of the national leaders of the time. None had really wanted war, yet they had somehow stumbled into it. The lesson learned was that such catastrophes might be avoided if leaders would only be flexible and compromise.

The role of the United States in the international politics of the 1930s also must be emphasized. The First World War had been brought to a conclusion because the United States had contributed its strength to the Allied coalition. The peace settlement was constructed on the assumption that the United States would be one of its principal guarantors. But the United States refused to join the League of Nations, refused to sign the Versailles peace treaty, and withdrew militarily from the international stage onto which it had entered so dramatically. The defenders of the status quo that resulted from the First World War were left in a weak position, and they knew it. Their policies reflected that weakness.

The impact of the Great Depression should not be overlooked. Its effects on Japan, Italy, and Germany seemed to be quite the opposite of

---

[9] "For once he embarked on the Polish war, the cards would be decisively stacked against him for three to four weeks; he stood to lose everything if the French and the British counter-attacked against his weakened western defense" (Kimche, 1968, p. 85).

its impact on France, Britain, and the United States. The former states reacted to the Depression by pursuing more active foreign policies; they appeared to believe that a solution to their domestic economic problems could be found through foreign conquest. But the Allied powers responded to the Depression by turning inward, concentrating on domestic economic problems, and avoiding entanglements in foreign affairs.

In France, for example, economic catastrophe seemed to inflame relations between the Left and Right. The Right took to the streets, and the Left won electoral victories. In 1936, the Radical Socialists, Socialists, and Communists formed the Popular Front, which scored a substantial victory in the elections of that year. The Popular Front put fear into the hearts of many conservatives. The fear reached such heights that it led some of the French to sympathize more with foreign leaders than with their own government. "Better Hitler than Blum" (Blum was a leader of the Popular Front) was a slogan that succinctly expressed the opinion of a significant segment of French voters, who saw in Hitler someone who would protect their property from the Communist elements of the Popular Front.

"Better Hitler than Stalin" was another slogan that symbolized a serious problem for the Popular Front. Efforts to strengthen the French bond with the Soviet Union met with bitter opposition from those who feared the Communists in France would be strengthened as a result. France did ratify a pact with the Soviets, but the French never cooperated with them in ways that would have made the alliance militarily significant. Class divisions, focusing on the Communists, tormented France up to the moment of the German onslaught.

Strategic thinking in the French army was dominated by generals who had become heroes in the First World War. What they had learned in the First World War was that strategy based on an all-out offensive had led to catastrophe. In contrast, a defensive strategy, such as that used at the Battle of Verdun, had been successful. The French generals were convinced that none of the technological developments since Verdun had destroyed the legitimacy of that lesson. French strategy against a possible German attack was to be based on an impenetrable defense, the **Maginot Line.** Criticism of this strategy, especially in the military, was rare. One cogent voice did go against the tide of French military thought. It belonged to a rather obscure lieutenant colonel named Charles de Gaulle.

"To the everlasting credit of . . . the leading generals of the French army it must be said that one of the reasons for insisting on the defensive . . . was their determination to spare French blood in any future war" (Shirer, 1969, p. 182). Partly because of terrible losses in the First World War, France entered the Second World War with an available pool of military recruits roughly half as large as that available to the Germans. Reliance on the Maginot Line led France to defeat. The French could easily have prevented Hitler from reoccupying the Rhineland in 1936, but they were by then already in an overly defensive frame of mind. They could have discouraged Hitler from ravaging their eastern allies, such as Czechoslovakia, but what good would their Maginot Line do them if they left it behind to launch an attack against Germany in retaliation for German aggression in Eastern Europe? In the end, the Germans used modern, mechanized warfare to go around and over the Maginot Line.

In Britain, the Depression had driven a Labour government out of power in 1931, and it was replaced by a national coalition consisting of the three major parties in Britain: the Labour Party, the Conservative Party, and the Liberal Party. The coalition fell apart when the Labour Party, torn by internal dissension, left the government. The Conservatives effectively ruled the country in the remaining prewar years, and the leaders of the Conservative Party adopted an unwavering policy of appeasement. Neville Chamberlain is most clearly associated with the policy, but it should be remembered that he had great popular support in Britain and that it is unlikely that any prime minister who had adopted a much different policy would have lasted very long.

Chamberlain became prime minister in 1937. In 1938, Germany's military expenditures were roughly five times larger than Britain's. Chamberlain's deal with Hitler at Munich won for him a tumultuous hero's welcome when he returned to Great Britain. As late as April 1939, both the Labour and the Liberal parties voted against the introduction of conscription, thus reflecting the determination of many Britons to avoid war at any cost.

One reason the British and French lacked conviction regarding any attempt to resist Germany involved their guilt feelings about the Treaty of Versailles. Hitler had, of course, denounced it as grossly unfair, but his opinion was shared by influential, thoughtful people in Britain and France.[10] Thus, when Hitler began to challenge various provisions of the treaty, enthusiastic defenders of it were hard to find.

---

[10] Perhaps the most influential was John Maynard Keynes in Great Britain. His *Economic Consequences of the Peace,* published in 1920, argued that the economic demands on Germany were unreasonable and did not serve as a sound basis for a peaceful settlement. The book was widely read and its thesis accepted by many. Keynes's arguments were not effectively countered until after the Second World War. See Etienne Mantoux (1952). More recently, historian Gerhard L. Weinberg (1988, p. 176) has noted that "the peace treaty of 1919 is increasingly seen as far more favorable to Germany than either German propaganda or subsequent popular views in the United States and Great Britain have pictured it."

Finally, there is a tendency to forget the strength of the political arguments with which Britain and France were faced at the crucial meeting with Hitler in Munich. The territory that Germany demanded contained some 2,800,000 people of German extraction, compared with only 800,000 Czechs (Shirer, 1960, p. 421). National self-determination was a principle much revered in the aftermath of the First World War, and Hitler seemed to have it on his side in his quarrel with Czechoslovakia. Furthermore, the First World War had been precipitated by resistance to just such nationalist aspirations. To argue that such leaders as Chamberlain were extraordinarily stupid or cowardly is an overly simple and misleading explanation of the agreement arrived at in Munich.[11] Chamberlain was reacting in a reasonable manner to historical forces and to his interpretation of history only too recently past.

On the occasion of the fiftieth anniversary of the Munich agreement, at least some historians were inclined to argue that it was not, as has been almost universally believed, so obviously a mistake. For example, historian Gerhard Weinberg (1988, p. 178) pointed out that Canada, Australia, and South Africa had all made it absolutely clear that they would not go to war alongside Britain over the Sudeten German question.[12] He also observes that recently revealed documents show that Winston Churchill, although at the time a critic of Chamberlain's policies, told a Czechoslovakian leader that he would probably have followed policies similar to those of Chamberlain if he had been prime minister. Finally, it is especially interesting to note that in later years, Hitler himself felt that he had made a mistake at Munich, one so serious that it cost him victory in the Second World War. "He had been trapped in a diplomatic maze . . . and could not find the exit to the war that he sought. In the last months of his life in 1945, . . . he . . . asserted that his failure to begin the war in 1938 was his greatest error, contributing to the eventual collapse of all his hopes and prospects" (Weinberg, 1988, p. 172). So, ironically, while Chamberlain has so far been, and is likely to continue to be, remembered as the leader whose weakness and appeasement policies made the Second World War inevitable and needlessly

---

[11] One contemporary analysis of "Munich's Lessons" argues that "simplistic images of Neville Chamberlain as umbrella-toting . . . utopian . . . must be rejected. . . . The Prime Minister's misperception has often been exaggerated by historians: almost since Adolf Hitler's accession to power, Chamberlain had harbored suspicions of the 'Fuhrer' and of Germany" (Beck, 1989, pp. 169, 173).

[12] Weinberg emphasizes the future importance of getting troops from these countries into the war by pointing out that on the first occasion in the Second World War in which a British army decisively defeated a German army, at El Alamein in 1942, the majority of the divisions in the British Eighth Army came from the Commonwealth countries (p. 178).

difficult, Hitler apparently went to his grave remembering him as a clever opponent who outfoxed him diplomatically, causing him to delay the onset of the war to a time when Hitler could not win it.[13]

THE EMERGENCE OF THE BIG TWO: THE SECOND WORLD WAR

The Second World War was the most lethal international conflict in the history of the world. It set the stage, so to speak, for international politics for the rest of the twentieth century.

The Nazi-Soviet Pact

One of the crucial turning points in the process that led to the Second World War involved a contest between Germany and the Western democracies of Britain and France for an alliance with the Soviet Union. Britain and France, once Hitler had taken over Czechoslovakia, both pledged to protect Poland from the same fate. It was clear that Britain and France could use Soviet help to dissuade Hitler from whatever aggressive designs he might have.

From the beginning, the Western powers seemed to have a better chance than the Germans of obtaining the Soviets' signature on a treaty. Ideologically, the British and French democracies were hardly compatible with the Soviet Union, but neither were they so unremittingly hostile as Nazi Germany. And the Soviet Union had an old score to settle with the Germans. When the Soviets dropped out of the First World War, their departure was formalized by the Treaty of Brest-Litovsk, which they signed with the Germans. Lenin was desperate to get out of the war at the time, and the terms of the treaty reflected his desperation. Russia gave up 32 percent of its population, or 56 million people. The territory Russia lost contained 73 percent of its iron ore, 89 percent of its coal, and 33 percent of its railway mileage. In addition, Russia agreed to pay Germany an indemnity of 6 billion marks. Thus, in the 1930s the Soviets felt that some revision of boundaries and

---

[13] For a similar revisionist view of the Munich agreement, see Richardson (1988, pp. 284–316). Richardson declares, for example, that "Chamberlain does not provide the classic instance of misperception of the adversary's intentions, as has so often been asserted. . . . Rather, the premise of British policy in 1938 was that Hitler's intentions were uncertain, and that in the light of this uncertainty, the particular issue at stake—the future of the Sudeten Germans—should not constitute the *casus belli*" [that is, the circumstance which serves as the justification for war] (pp. 306–307).

Germany's Hitler and the Soviet Union's Stalin signed a nonaggression pact in 1939, giving Hitler confidence that he could attack Poland without becoming involved immediately in a two-front war. SOURCE: Stalin: Pierre Vauthey/Sygma, Hitler: The Bettmann Archive.

spheres of influence was desirable. Hitler did not seem likely to allow such revisions; perhaps with the help of the Western powers, the Soviets could bring them about.

Despite the advantages the British and the French had, the Germans won the contest. In August 1939, a **nonaggression** agreement, the **Nazi-Soviet Pact** was announced. What brought the two dictatorships together? In retrospect, Hitler's motives were quite obvious. Given his actions during the war, one may surmise that he never gave up his idea of acquiring *Lebensraum* (living space) in the east. And he knew that his planned attack on Poland might involve him in a war with Britain and France, especially if the two could count on a Soviet ally. Once the Nazi-Soviet pact was signed, Hitler did not have to worry that his attack on Poland would lead him into a two-front war, and he could hope that without a Soviet ally, Britain and France would refrain from serious opposition to his Polish venture. Even as he signed the pact with the Soviets, Hitler almost certainly knew that he would someday violate it.[14]

---

[14] "Never forget," Hitler (1925, 1943, pp. 600–661) had written, "that the rulers of present-day Russia are common, blood-stained criminals; that they are the scum of humanity . . . these rulers belong to a race which combines in a rare mixture, bestial cruelty and an inconceivable gift for lying."

The motives of Stalin, who rose to power after Lenin's death in 1924, are not quite as easily discerned as Hitler's. It is clear that Stalin was reluctant to sign a pact with the Western powers because he was not at all sure that they would abide by it in the event of a German attack on the Soviet Union. He suspected that both Britain and France might be happy to see the Nazis and the Communists engage in prolonged bloodletting. Furthermore, France and Britain were unable to get Poland to agree to allow Soviet troops onto Polish soil if Germany attacked Poland. This heightened Stalin's suspicions that the pact proposed by the West was a ruse designed to bring about war between Germany and the Soviet Union. Finally, Stalin, like Hitler, was worried about a two-front war. Germany's ally, Japan, was much on Stalin's mind as he signed the pact with Hitler.

Some argue that Stalin signed the pact with the idea that Hitler would get involved in a war with the Western powers first, thus ensuring that when he turned his troops on the Soviets, the West would be irrevocably committed against the Germans. Stalin may have had that in mind, but there is an obvious flaw in this argument. If Stalin calculated that the pact he had signed with Hitler would ensure that Germany and the democracies were at war by the time Germany attacked the Soviet Union, Stalin should have expected Hitler's attack. But according to every available indicator, Stalin and his army were caught entirely by surprise when the German attack came in June 1941. Possibly what surprised Stalin was the timing of the attack rather than its occurrence. Still, the fact that he was so surprised by it lends credence to the argument that Stalin hoped his pact with Hitler would allow him to stay out of the war altogether.

Germany's Attack on the Soviet Union

If Stalin's plan was to stay out of world war, it seemed to work for a while. By agreement, both the Germans and the Soviets moved against Poland, which ceased to exist as an independent entity. Despite their failure to obtain Soviet allegiance, the British and French decided that they could not tolerate another Hitlerian adventure and declared war on Germany. Hitler's initial successes in the ensuing months were spectacular. It took him a little over two weeks to defeat Poland. Denmark, Norway, Belgium, the Netherlands, and, most surprisingly, France fell in quick succession. After one year of fighting, Hitler seemed invincible and well on his way to adding Great Britain to his list of victims. But Great Britain's resistance proved more substantial than Hitler had planned and may have influenced him to make the decision that ultimately led to disaster. He decided to attack the Soviet Union.

To some extent, the decision was a strategic gamble on Hitler's part. His idea was that, once he had defeated the Soviet Union, he could turn the full force of his military might against the British, thus finally accomplishing the victory that so far had eluded him. But the importance of these more or less rational calculations can be overstressed. At bottom, Hitler's decision to forsake his attack against the British seems to have been an ideological one. Fifteen years earlier in *Mein Kampf* he had written:

> And so we National Socialists take up where we broke off six hundred years ago. We stop the endless German movement toward the south and west of Europe and turn our gaze toward the lands of the East. . . . When we speak of new territory in Europe today we must think principally of Russia and her border vassal states. Destiny itself seems to wish to point out the way to us here. . . . This colossal empire in the East is ripe for dissolution, and the end of Jewish domination in Russia will also be the end of Russia as a state (cited in Shirer, 1960, p. 796).

Hitler's attack on the Soviet Union, like Napoleon's on Russia in 1812, was a disaster. The Soviets managed to hold off the German onslaught until the harsh Russian winter became an ally of sorts to the Russian army, disrupting Germany's lines of supply and subjecting German troops to cold temperatures and other weather conditions with which they were not equipped to deal. That alone might have been enough, in the long run, to be Hitler's undoing. But just about the time the German troops began to have trouble in the Soviet Union, one of Germany's allies took the step that ensured the premature dissolution of the so-called thousand-year Reich.

Pearl Harbor

The Germans did not have previous knowledge of Japan's attack on Pearl Harbor, nor did they approve of it. Rather, they had hoped that Japan would be menacing enough to keep the United States out of the war. They did give assurances to the Japanese government that if it became involved in a war with the United States, it would have the support of Germany. But these assurances were apparently calculated only to encourage the Japanese to assume a menacing posture toward the United States, not actually to attack it.

Despite their renowned zeal for combat, the Japanese did not feel that they could defeat the United States, march into Washington, D.C., and dictate peace terms to their liking. They did, perhaps, underestimate the military potential of the United States, but not to such an extent. Japan's leaders knew they needed a new source of oil, especially after the United States put an embargo on U.S. oil exports to Japan in August 1941. The most convenient alternative source for the Japanese was the Dutch East Indies (now Indonesia), but to capture these oilfields, the Japanese fleet

The Japanese attack at Pearl Harbor in 1941 surprised the U.S. forces and sank or severely damaged 5 battleships, 3 cruisers, several smaller vessels, as well as 177 planes. Shown above are the *West Virginia* and the *Tennessee* shortly before they sank. SOURCE: U.S. Navy Photo.

would first have to neutralize the Philippines, at that time a U.S. colony. The Japanese idea was to deliver a punishing blow to the United States at Pearl Harbor, then resist the U.S. counterattack so vigorously and persistently that the United States would tire of the struggle and allow the Japanese to keep the gains in China, Southeast Asia, and Indonesia that they felt were necessary to sustain the Japanese economy. From the Japanese point of view, the United States had for years expressed unreasonable opposition to their economic and political expansion in East Asia, and there is little doubt that many Japanese sincerely felt that the slogan "Asia for Asians" accurately expressed the laudable goal of their country's policies.

The Japanese plan, of course, did not work. The productive and military power of the United States eventually overwhelmed Japan, especially when the Americans added nuclear weapons to their arsenal. Similarly, the Germans, having already suffered a grievous blow in the

Soviet Union, found themselves totally unable to withstand the combined weight of the Russians from the East and the Americans from the West. By the end of 1945, both Japan and Germany were occupied countries. (Italy had fallen in 1943.)

The Impact of the Second World War

Aside from the total defeat of the three challengers to the international status quo, probably the most important impact of the Second World War on the global political system involved the subsequent emergence of two **superpowers,** the United States and the Soviet Union.[15] When Germany attacked the Soviet Union in 1941, there was a widespread expectation that Soviet resistance would be short-lived. When these expectations were proved wrong and the Soviets defeated the Germans, their true strength came to light and was perhaps even exaggerated. The performance of the United States in the war made clear the identity of the other superpower.

The emergence of the **Big Two** was especially dramatic in comparison with the fate of Europe. The fall of Europe had begun in the First World War, but this fact was at least partially hidden by the withdrawal of the United States into isolationism and the revolution in the Soviet Union. After the Second World War, the only European state with credible pretensions to Great Power status was Great Britain. The weaknesses of Germany, Italy, and France were apparent to everyone. But within two or three years of the war, Great Britain's pretensions were shown to be unwarranted. It was no longer able to fulfill its previous global responsibilities: by 1947 India had gained its independence, to be followed by Ceylon (now Sri Lanka) and Burma (now Myanmar), and British withdrawal from Greece and Palestine. Europe, the center of world political power for at least three hundred years, gave way to the Big Two.

SUMMARY

It is important to begin the study of global politics with a review of contemporary history for several basic reasons. The first is that understanding the past is a key to understanding the present, as well as cultivating an ability to anticipate the future. The second is that key decision makers in the global political system are often affected by their perceptions of history. Finally, the historical knowledge will enable

---

[15] Writing around 1835, Alexander de Tocqueville in *Democracy in America* forecast that Russia and America seemed "marked out by the will of Heaven to sway the destinies of half the globe" (cited in Paul Kennedy, 1987, p. 95). While an admirable prognostication, it may have turned out to be an underestimate.

readers to evaluate the ideas on international politics presented in the following chapters.

The bases for the modern international system were laid in the First World War, which arose out of a confrontation between Germany and Austria-Hungary on the one hand and Russia, France, and Great Britain, on the other. Its outbreak has been blamed on alliances, the bipolarity of the international system, rapid mobilization schedules, capitalist imperialism, the media, and arms races. The war served to enshrine democracy and national self-determination as values in international politics. It weakened the major powers of Europe. It also inspired the creation of the modern field of international politics in the United States.

In the interwar period, France was intent on crippling Germany so that it could never rise again. This effort failed, partly because terrible inflation at the beginning of the 1920s, coupled with the Great Depression in the late 1920s and early 1930s, helped created conditions favorable to Adolf Hitler's rise to power. Italy and Japan joined Hitler's Germany in an assault on the international status quo in the late 1930s, which was met mainly by a consistent policy of appeasement on the part of the status quo powers. This assault was halted only by the Second World War, which weakened Europe further and led to the emergence of the United States and the Soviet Union as twin superpowers.

KEY TERMS

alliances	national self-determination
bureaucracies	idealists
rapid mobilization	realists
capitalist states	stock market crash
imperialistic	Smoot-Hawley Act
law of uneven development	Depression
German militarism	Munich
munitions makers	appeasement
bipolarity	Maginot Line
arms race	Nazi-Soviet Pact
weakening of Europe	superpowers
democracy	Big Two

SOURCES

Al-Marayati, Abid A., et al. *The Middle East: Its Governments and Politics.* Belmont, Calif.: Duxbury Press, 1972.

Beck, Robert J. "Munich's Lessons Reconsidered." *International Security,* 14 (Fall 1989), 161–191.

Brierly, James L. *The Law of Nations.* 2nd ed. New York: Oxford University Press, 1936.

Brown, Chris. *International Relations Theory: New Normative Approaches.* New York: Columbia University Press, 1992.

Carr, Edward H. *The Twenty Years' Crisis, 1919–1939.* London: Macmillan, 1939.

Claude, Inis L. *Swords into Plowshares.* 3rd ed. New York: Random House, 1964.

De Conde, Alexander. *A History of American Foreign Policy.* New York: Scribner's, 1963.

Dugan, James, and Laurence Lafore. *Days of Emperor and Clown.* Garden City, N.Y.: Doubleday, 1973.

Dunn, Frederick S. *Peaceful Change: A Study of International Procedures.* New York: Council on Foreign Relations, 1937.

Eagleton, Clyde. *International Government.* New York: Ronald Press, 1932.

Galbraith, John Kenneth. *Money: Whence It Came, Where It Went.* New York: Bantam, 1975.

Haigh, Anthony. *Congress of Vienna to Common Market.* London: Harrap, 1973.

Hitler, Adolf. *Mein Kampf.* tr. Ralph Manheim. Boston: Houghton Mifflin, 1943. (First published in 1925.)

Johnson, Paul. *Modern Times.* New York: Harper & Row, 1983.

Kennedy, Paul. *The Rise and Fall of the Great Powers.* New York: Random House, 1987.

Keynes, John Maynard. *The Economic Consequences of the Peace.* New York: Harcourt, Brace & Howe, 1920.

Kimche, Jon. *The Unfought Battle.* New York: Stern & Day, 1968.

Kissinger, Henry. *Diplomacy.* New York: Simon & Schuster, 1994.

Knapton, Ernest John. *France.* New York: Scribner's, 1971.

Knutsen, Torbjorn. *A History of International Relations Theory.* Manchester: Manchester University Press, 1992.

Lauterpacht, Hersch. *The Function of Law in the International Community.* New York: Oxford University Press, 1933.

Levy, Jack S. "Organizational Routines and the Causes of War." *International Studies Quarterly,* 30 (June 1986), 193–222.

Levy, Jack S. "Preferences, Constraints, and Choices in July 1914." *International Security,* 15 (Winter 1990/91), 151–186.

Mantoux, Etienne. *The Carthaginian Peace.* Pittsburgh: University of Pittsburgh Press, 1952.

Morgenthau, Hans J., and Kenneth W. Thompson. *Politics Among Nations.* 6th ed. New York: Knopf, 1985.

Neal, Fred Warner, and Bruce P. Hamlett. "The Never-Never Land of International Relations." *International Studies Quarterly,* 13 (September 1969), 281–305.

Northedge, F. S., and M. J. Grieve. *A Hundred Years of International Relations.* New York: Praeger, 1971.

Oren, Ido. "The Subjectivity of the 'Democratic' Peace: Changing U.S. Perceptions of Imperial Germany." *International Security* 20 (Fall 1995), 147–184.

Pettman, Ralph. *Human Behavior and World Politics*. New York: St. Martin's Press, 1975.

Pipes, Richard. *The Russian Revolution*. New York: Vintage Books, 1990.

Potter, Pitman B. *An Introduction to the Study of International Organization*. 3rd ed. New York: Appleton-Century, 1928.

Reischauer, Edwin O. *Japan: Past and Present*. New York: Knopf, 1964.

Richardson, J. L. "New Perspectives on Appeasement: Some Implications for International Relations." *World Politics*, 40 (April 1988), 284–316.

Sagan, Scott D. "1914 Revisited: Allies, Offense, and Instability." *International Security*, 11 (Fall 1986), 151–176.

Schuman, Frederick L. *International Politics: An Introduction to the Western State System*. New York: McGraw-Hill, 1933.

Shirer, William L. *The Rise and Fall of the Third Reich*. New York: Simon & Schuster, 1960.

Shirer, William L. *The Collapse of the Third Republic*. New York: Simon & Schuster, 1969.

Shirer, William L. *The Nightmare Years: 1930–1940*. Boston: Little, Brown, 1984.

Stevenson, David. *The First World War and International Politics*. Oxford: Clarendon, 1988.

Strange, Susan. "Protectionism and World Politics." *International Organization*, 39 (Spring 1985), 233–260.

Sweetser, Arthur. *The League of Nations at Work*. New York: Macmillan, 1920.

Weinberg, Gerhard L. "Munich After 50 Years." *Foreign Affairs*, 67 (Fall 1988), 163–178.

Wohlforth, William C. "The Perception of Power: Russia in the Pre-1914 Balance." *World Politics*, 39 (April 1987), 353–381.

C H A P T E R 2

The Modern Era

The focus of this chapter is the history of global politics since the Second World War. The development of the study of international politics during the same period is also analyzed.

AFTER THE SECOND WORLD WAR

The Origins of the Cold War: Conflict Over Eastern Europe

It was inevitable, at the climax of a gigantic struggle such as the Second World War, that the settlements and agreements arrived at by the victorious coalition would shape the primary conflicts in the years to follow. No matter what these settlements contained, some of the involved parties would be dissatisfied, and their dissatisfaction would form the basis of future conflicts.

Perhaps the most heated and important conflict in the months immediately following the war involved Poland and the rest of the Eastern European countries. (Since the end of the Cold War, these are more commonly referred to as East-Central European countries. See the map on page 39.) Great Britain, after all, had resorted to war in the first place to ensure the existence of an independent Poland. Roosevelt, after the

Squabbling over Eastern Europe after the Second World War ▶

An important basis for the Cold War developed as the Soviets moved into the power vacuum in Eastern Europe that was left after German troops retreated at the end of the Second World War.

United States entered the war, was anxious to protect the interests of the Poles at least partly because of a desire to avoid alienating an important voting bloc in the United States. So both countries began to press the Soviets about the future of Poland well before the Soviets had established their presence in that country. Conflict centered first on what government-in-exile would be recognized as the official representative of Poland. The British and the Americans favored one group in London, while the Soviets set up another more to their liking. The Soviets had several reasons to be suspicious of the Poles in London. In the years following the First World War, when the Soviets were weak and unable to resist, Poland had taken territory the Soviets considered their own. Later, many of the elements represented in the government-in-exile in London had refused to agree to allow Soviet troops on Polish soil in the event of a German attack, thus throwing an important roadblock in the way of the movement that might have resulted in an alliance between Great Britain and France on the one hand and the Soviet Union on the other. Mutual suspicions between the Poles in London and the Soviets were solidified by a controversy surrounding the discovery in 1943 by German soldiers of a mass grave for Polish army officers in the Katyn Forest. The Nazis accused the Soviets of these mass executions, while the Soviets blamed the Nazis. (The Soviets, under Mikhail Gorbachev's influence, accepted the blame for the massacre, or, to put it more accurately, admitted that Stalin probably ordered it done.) The Polish government-in-exile in London seemed to believe the Nazi charges against the Soviets. If there had ever been any chance of compromise between the Poles in London and the Soviets (and it is not clear that there was), this incident certainly undermined it.

The future of Poland and other Eastern European states was one of many topics discussed at a 1945 meeting of the Big Three (Roosevelt, Stalin, and Churchill) at **Yalta** in the Russian Crimea. One result of this discussion was that Stalin was persuaded to "endorse a **Declaration on Liberated Countries** which promised free elections and other democratic practices and liberties" in Eastern European countries that were at the time the site of Red Army victories over the Nazis (Calvocoressi, 1991, p. 231). Roosevelt's acceptance of this promise was to provoke controversy in the years following the war because Stalin, from the U.S. point of view, did not keep his promise. Elections were not held in Poland until 1947, and even then they were not what the Western powers considered the free and unfettered elections that had been promised in the declaration.

Critics of Roosevelt have argued vociferously that the U.S. president must have been incredibly naive to accept Soviet promises with regard to Eastern Europe after the Second World War, and that his acceptance paved the way for a Communist takeover in these countries. In support of such critics, it must be said that there is good evidence that Roosevelt was more optimistic during the war about the prospects for U.S.-Soviet postwar cooperation than subsequent events proved was warranted. But it is important not to overlook the basic, if obvious, fact that at the time when Roosevelt accepted Stalin's pledge concerning free elections in Eastern Europe, the Soviet Union had troops there and the United States did not. A refusal by Roosevelt to accept Stalin's word on the matter might have put a serious strain on a coalition that was never entirely solid. Roosevelt was particularly concerned that the Soviets join the United States in the upcoming assault on Japan, which, in the days before an atomic bomb had been successfully exploded, was expected to be very difficult. In retrospect, of course, we know that the United States did not need help against Japan. But Roosevelt did not have the benefit of hindsight.

In any case, the Soviet "satellization" of Eastern Europe was an important step toward the Cold War with the United States. But the view that the Cold War was a result of aggressive Soviet actions in Eastern Europe and elsewhere is hotly disputed. Several U.S. writers, for example, argue that Soviet policies in Eastern Europe were essentially defensive and that it was U.S. hostility toward the Soviets that was primarily responsible for the onset of the Cold War (Kolko and Kolko, 1972; Horowitz, 1965; Alperowitz, 1965). This controversy essentially turns on the question of which country took the action that first precipitated the Cold War conflict. Defenders of U.S. foreign policy point to the Soviet Union's refusal to remove its troops from Iran in 1946 as the precipitating event. Revisionists may point to some earlier occurrence. For example, when Italy surrendered unconditionally in 1943, "America and Britain, having won the Italian war, handled the capitulation, keeping Moscow informed at a distance. Stalin complained . . . . [But] Roosevelt . . . had no intention of sharing the control of Italy" (Schlesinger, 1967, p. 32). Discussion of the "who did what first" question, carried to its logical extreme, leads one side to emphasize the hostility of Bolshevik propaganda against the Western nations from the earliest days of the Russian Revolution and the other to point out that several Western nations invaded the Soviet Union in an attempt to dismantle the revolutionary government in the years when it was struggling to survive.

The origins of the Cold War are examined more closely in Chapter 10. Let us conclude this discussion with reference to an important attribute of the structure of the international system after the Second World War. By the end of 1945, only one country in the world was strong enough to pose a threat of any kind to the Soviet Union, and that was the United States. Conversely, the only country in the world strong enough to resist the U.S. will in any part of the globe at that time was

Communist Party Chair Mao Zedong announces to the world the founding of the People's Republic of China, October 1, 1949. SOURCE: Eastfoto.

the Soviet Union. The development of a Soviet atomic bomb in 1949 exacerbated the tensions inherent in such a situation. Perhaps the Cold War was not inevitable, but given the structure of the international system at the end of the Second World War, it was a probable development, regardless of which country was more aggressive or hostile to the other. Like two scorpions in a bottle, they were bound to become highly suspicious of each other.

Civil War in China: The Victory of Mao Zedong

The conflict over Eastern Europe was mainly the result of the fact that German power had been crushed in that area, thus creating a **"power vacuum"** into which the Soviets entered despite the resistance of the

Americans, the British, and at least some groups in the Eastern European countries. But Eastern Europe was certainly not the only sector of the globe where such a vacuum had been created by the Second World War. A broadly similar process took place in China. The Japanese had taken over large areas of that country during the war, pushing the Nationalist government of Chiang Kai-shek farther into the hinterland. As Chiang retreated, he became progressively more isolated from his more moderate sources of support and increasingly dependent on the more conservative classes. In the meantime the Communists, under Mao Zedong, took advantage of the Japanese invasion to strengthen their organization. The Japanese tended to concentrate on the cities as they took over Chinese territory, leaving the peasants in the countryside more or less on their own. The Communists moved into this vacuum, organizing the peasants, carrying out some land reform measures, and generally strengthening this important part of their power base.

When the Japanese evacuated the country, the stage was set for the culmination of the struggle between Mao and Chiang. Mao might have been successful eventually without the inadvertent aid of the Japanese, just as Lenin could conceivably have carried off his revolution even if the Russians had not experienced the disaster of the First World War. But there is little doubt that the Japanese invasion and evacuation created a fluid situation in China, of which Mao took good advantage. Despite considerable financial aid and free advice from the United States, Chiang was unable to quash the Communist rebellion, and in 1949 he was forced to flee to the island of Taiwan. The People's Republic of China was proclaimed on October 1 of that year.

The Korean War

Just as in China, the defeat of the Japanese created conditions conducive to conflict in Korea, which had been formally annexed by Japan in 1910. In the final days of the Second World War, the Soviet Union and the United States came to an agreement that the Soviets would accept the surrender of the Japanese troops to the north of the thirty-eighth parallel, while the Americans would accept a similar surrender south of that parallel. The agreement was carried out by both sides without serious problems. But problems were soon to develop. The Americans and the Soviets ruled their zones separately, and by 1948 North Korea and South Korea had become two separate nations, in fact if not in theory. Border tensions between the two halves were constant; each side threatened to liberate the other, and while the Americans armed the South, the North received military aid from the Soviets.

Finally, in June 1950, North Korea invaded South Korea.[1] The motives for this invasion have been the topic of lively speculation. There is widespread agreement that the North Korean government was heavily influenced by the Soviets, and therefore that the Soviets must have known about and approved the North Korean invasion plan. But why? At the time, the Americans and the Western Europeans were fearful that the attack was a diversionary tactic adopted by Stalin to pin down the United States in Asia so that he could move against Western Europe. Later, with the benefit of hindsight and knowledge of the conflict between Communist China and the Soviet Union, some observers surmised that the Korean War was Stalin's scheme to get the United States and the Chinese into a prolonged land war in Asia, thus weakening both. In his memoirs, Nikita Khrushchev insisted that the invasion was the brainchild of North Korean premier Kim Il Sung, who managed to convince Stalin that the South Koreans would greet the northerners as liberators, thus ensuring an easy, quick victory for the North (Barnet, 1971, p. 274). Stalin also must have been influenced by the announcement by Secretary of State Dean Acheson on January 12, 1950, that Korea was outside the defense perimeter of the United States. He was, finally, justifiably confident that the North Koreans would be able to defeat the South Koreans unless the latter got outside help.

Whatever the motivation, the attack by the North Koreans met with immediate success. With the U.S. and South Korean defenders rapidly reaching desperate straits, the United States urged the United Nations to resist the invasion. The success of this effort was ensured by the great influence of the United States in the United Nations and by the absence of the Soviet Union from the U.N. Security Council. (The Soviets were temporarily boycotting the council to protest its exclusion of China.) Eventually the United States and sixteen other nations sent additional troops to Korea and managed to halt the progress of the North Koreans.

In fact, the success of the U.N. forces (of which the U.S. contingent was by far the largest)[2] was so substantial and relatively easy that it brought about a change in U.S. policy in the middle of the war. When the intervention began, Acheson had explained that the U.N. troops were in Korea "solely for the purpose of restoring the Republic of Korea

---

[1] This version of the event is accepted by most Western sources, although the North Koreans claimed that they were responding to an attack by the South, and one well-known Western journalist argues that the United States was at least partially responsible for the onset of the Korean War (Stone, 1952).

[2] The majority of troops opposing North Korea, though, were South Korean. In the entire war, the United States suffered 54,000 battle deaths, while the South Koreans lost 415,000 (Small and Singer, 1982, p. 92).

to its status prior to the invasion from the North" (*Department of State Bulletin*, 1950, p. 46). But as the U.N. forces moved up the peninsula, the temptation to bring about a more permanent solution to the problem posed by the North Korean government proved decisive. Instead of merely pushing the North Koreans back into their own territory, the U.N. troops moved to unify all of Korea by force. The risk that China would enter the war was accepted willingly by General Douglas MacArthur, who commanded the U.N. forces. The U.S. government and MacArthur were sure that the Chinese would not intervene, despite Chinese warnings to the U.S. government (using Britain, India, Sweden, and the Soviet Union as intermediaries) that they would not allow the U.N. troops to eliminate the North Korean government next to their border (Whiting, 1960, pp. 108–109).[3]

But the Chinese did intervene, with immediate and dramatic success. Only after many months of hard fighting were the Chinese forced to halt their advance. As the war dragged on, its unpopularity in the United States grew, and the election of 1952 resulted in the victory of Dwight Eisenhower, who promised to end the conflict. The new president did manage to bring about an armistice, partly by threatening to use nuclear weapons, which ended the fighting in July 1953 but did little or nothing to solve the problems that had fueled the conflict in the first place.

The Beginnings of War in Vietnam

Yet another area where Japanese withdrawal left a vacuum to be filled was Indochina, more specifically, Vietnam. Before the war, Vietnam had been a French colony. It remained officially so (but under the pro-Nazi Vichy regime) even during the Japanese occupation. Vietnamese nationalists, known as the Vietminh, had staged uprisings against the French before the Japanese arrived. The Japanese, after their arrival, cooperated with the French in an attempt to stamp out the Vietminh. Finally, in March 1945 the Japanese staged a coup against the French and took formal control of the country. This coup presented the Vietminh with an opportunity, since the Japanese had never had the chance to develop a police apparatus as efficient as that assembled by the French. By September 1945, the Vietminh were in effective control of the country and issued a declaration of independence.

The reign of the Vietminh was short-lived. At the Potsdam Conference, the United States, the Soviet Union, and Great Britain had agreed that Southeast Asia was within the British sphere of influence, and thus

---

[3] President Harry S Truman may have exaggerated the extent to which the U.S. government relied on the advice of General MacArthur concerning the possibility of Chinese intervention in the war (Manchester, 1978, p. 585).

the British were given the responsibility of establishing law and order in the area. But in Vietnam the British were to share that responsibility with the Chinese. For this purpose, the former French colony was divided at the sixteenth parallel, with the northern part of the country becoming the Chinese zone and the southern part becoming the British zone. The Chinese and the British interpreted their mandates to restore law and order in dramatically different ways. The Chinese recognized the de facto Vietminh regime. The British, anxious to establish the principle that prewar colonies be returned to their rightful owners, set about dismantling the Vietminh regime in the South to transfer control of that area to the French. They did this with the cooperation of Japanese troops who were still in the country.[4]

The French began to have problems with their rebellious subjects in Southeast Asia almost from the moment they reassumed control of the area. For the first few troubled years after the war, the United States opposed the efforts of the French, viewing them as dedicated to reimposing an outdated colonial regime and regarding the Vietminh, on the other hand, as fighters for national liberation. As late as 1947, President Harry S Truman was so opposed to French policy in Vietnam that he insisted that U.S.-produced propellers be removed from British aircraft sent to French troops there (Stoessinger, 1993, p. 81). This attitude was to change quite rapidly without any essential change in the war taking place in Southeast Asia. In 1948, tension between the Soviets and the Americans increased dramatically. In 1949, China came under Communist control. By 1950, the Americans had come to see the French as defenders of the "free world" and the Vietminh as agents of a worldwide Communist conspiracy. Accordingly, the U.S. government began to support the French military in Vietnam economically, and by 1954 the United States was paying between 50 and 80 percent of the cost of the war against the forces of the Vietminh.[5]

The British Retreat

The British were not defeated in the Second World War, but it soon became obvious that they had been severely weakened politically and

---

[4] General MacArthur, in Tokyo at the time, was outraged by the use of Japanese troops against the Vietnamese people. He stated, "If there is anything that makes my blood boil it is to see our allies in Indochina and Java deploying Japanese troops to reconquer the little people we promised to liberate. It is the most ignoble kind of betrayal" (Isaacs, 1965, p. 46).

[5] For the lower estimate, see Farley (1955, p. 4). The higher figure is given in Hammer (1954, p. 313).

economically. As a result, they were forced to pull back from areas of the world where they had previously exerted influence or control. Further vacuums were created, and none was filled without conflict. In February 1947, Britain announced to the U.S. government that it could no longer support the government of Greece, then under attack by rebels, some of whom were Communists. Truman decided to take over British responsibilities there, but the decision concerning Greece was embedded in and overshadowed by a decision of much wider application—the decision to institute the policy of **containment.** Henceforth, Truman announced, "It must be the policy of the United States to support free peoples who are resisting attempted subjugation by armed minorities or by outside pressures" (Koenig, 1956, pp. 296–301). If this did not mark the beginning of the Cold War, it was at least an official pronouncement of it.

At about the same time, the British also decided they could no longer hold on to their colony of India. They pulled out in 1947. During their rule, they had managed to keep the lid on the conflict between the Hindu majority and the Muslim minority, even though they did nothing to bring about harmony between the groups. When the British left, having established two separate nations (Hindu India and Muslim Pakistan), the lid flew off and the pot boiled over. These nations fought two wars over disputed territory (Kashmir); and in 1971 a Pakistani civil war led to Indian intervention, a third bloody Pakistani-Indian war, and the creation of a third nation, Bangladesh.

Finally, in 1948 the British pulled out of Palestine. This area had been the scene of civil strife between Jews and Arabs from the time the British had been given a League of Nations mandate to rule the region after the First World War. After the Second World War, the Jews were anxious to proclaim an independent state for themselves, and the Arabs were equally anxious to prevent them from doing so. The British found themselves unable to mediate this conflict. So they simply announced that they were withdrawing their troops in May 1948. When they did, the Jews proclaimed the state of Israel, the Arabs tried to crush it, and the Israelis won the ensuing war. That war turned out to be only the first round of the prolonged Arab-Israeli conflict, which erupted into actual warfare several times in the ensuing forty years, most notably in 1956, 1967, 1973, and 1982.

The fact that bloody conflict and violent political strife still occur virtually on a daily basis in Kashmir and the Middle East almost fifty years after the British relinquished their imperial control over those areas has sobering implications, perhaps, regarding the demise of the Soviet empire in the contemporary era. Disintegrating empires typically leave bloody problems of long duration in their wake. How long will it take to bring political order to lands recently liberated from the Soviet empire?

The Hungarian Crisis

By 1955, the first of the several power vacuums discussed in this chapter—Eastern Europe—had been thoroughly filled by the Soviet Union. But in 1956, the ties between the Soviet Union and the Eastern Europeans began to weaken dangerously, that is, from the Soviet point of view. One event that accelerated this process was a secret speech given by Khrushchev in 1956, in which he criticized Stalin and Stalinist policies in harsh terms. The contents of the speech became known in Eastern Europe, where hope arose that a denunciation of Stalin might be a signal of renunciation of Stalinist control over Eastern Europe by the Soviet Union.

Workers' riots in Poland in June 1956 led to some limited measures of independence for that country. In October, a more uncompromising rebellion took place in Hungary, aimed at the elimination of the domestic Communist regime as well as escape from the Communist international bloc. The Hungarians' pleas for help went unheeded by the United Nations and the United States; the Soviets invaded Hungary and crushed the rebellion.

Neither the United States nor the Soviet Union escaped from this crisis unscathed. Soviet protestations that they were merely trying to save the Hungarians from reactionary capitalist elements were undoubtedly sincere in some measure, but their actions spoke louder than their words. Whatever the motivation, Soviet actions in Hungary appeared imperialistic, and the Soviet reputation as the leader of the anti-imperialist forces suffered accordingly. The reputation of the United States was not helped by the fact that President Eisenhower and Secretary of State John Foster Dulles had in the past proclaimed their intent to "liberate" the captive peoples of Eastern Europe. Their reaction to the pleas from Hungary during the Soviet invasion, limited to denunciatory speeches, revealed the emptiness of earlier rhetoric.

Despite the embarrassment suffered by both superpowers as a result of the rebellion in Hungary, the crisis marked an important turning point in the Cold War. Wisely or not, the United States had never clearly accepted the Soviets' firmly defined **sphere of influence** in Eastern Europe. The Eisenhower administration had emphasized this attitude with talk of rolling back the Iron Curtain. But when the United States stood by passively while the Soviets reestablished their control of Hungary, the U.S. government implicitly accepted the fact of Soviet hegemony in Eastern Europe, however reluctantly.

THE SOVIET UNION AND CHINA:
THE "MONOLITH" BEGINS TO CRUMBLE

Although the Soviets had felt it necessary to crack down on dissident elements in Eastern Europe, the general trend during Khrushchev's reign was toward liberalization and increasingly visible breaks in monolithic communism. After the Hungarian rebellion was put down, things were relatively quiet in Eastern Europe. In contrast, on the Soviets' other flank the Chinese showed increasing signs of dissatisfaction with the Soviet leadership of the Communist bloc. The alliance between the Soviets and the Chinese in the early 1950s had, in retrospect, several powerful forces working against it. First, there is the simple geographic fact that the Soviet Union and China shared the largest common border in the world. Second, the Soviet Union and China were two of the most powerful states in the world. These factors alone would seem likely to lead to mutual distrust, regardless of the personalities or historical events involved. Then, too, relations between the Chinese and Russian empires had been unfriendly from the sixteenth century on. And the fact that the Chinese have for centuries regarded their country as the "Middle Kingdom"—that is, at the center of the civilized world and surrounded by "barbarians"—must have made it difficult for them to accept another country's leadership even under the best of conditions.

By 1956, doctrinal disputes between the Soviets and the Chinese began to arise. Perhaps the most important one concerned the adaptation of Marxism-Leninism to the advent of nuclear weapons. At the twentieth Party congress in 1956, in the same speech in which he denounced Stalin, Khrushchev announced that there was no inevitability of war between the Communist and capitalist worlds. From Khrushchev's viewpoint, this modification of Leninist doctrine was a reasonable compromise in the face of possible nuclear destruction of the world. To the Chinese, it smacked of inadmissible timidity.

In October 1957, Mao Zedong made a speech at an international Communist conference in Moscow in which he emphasized dogma. He talked of the "east wind prevailing over the west wind" and insisted that even if the capitalist imperialists did plunge the world into nuclear war, only they would be banished from the face of the earth; the socialists would survive. About a year later, the Chinese began what appeared to be an attempt to take over the offshore islands of Quemoy and Matsu. From the Chinese perspective, the Soviets refused to back up these efforts with sufficient vigor. Convinced, perhaps, of the recklessness of their allies, in June 1959 the Soviets renounced an earlier agreement to help the Chinese develop their own atomic weapons (Stern, 1974, p. 134).

Sino-Soviet relations deteriorated rapidly from that point, and by the time of the Cuban missile crisis in 1962, the two countries were verbally tearing each other to pieces. (After the Soviet Union backed away from confrontation with the United States over Soviet missiles in Cuba, the Chinese accused the Soviets of "adventurism" and "capitulationism.") At bottom, though, the dispute between the Soviets and the Chinese was probably at least as much territorial as doctrinal. In 1964, Mao Zedong said, "There are too many places occupied by the Soviet Union. . . . The Soviet Union has an area of twenty-two million square kilometers and its population is only 220 million. It is about time to put an end to this allotment" (Stern, 1974, pp. 139–140).

SPUTNIKS, KENNEDY, AND VIETNAM

Soviet Success in Space

In October 1957, the Soviets launched the first human-made satellite; they followed it one month later with a satellite some six times heavier than the first. The space program of the United States had literally not yet gotten off the ground. The Americans had plans to launch a satellite, but the one they were about to send off weighed only 31 pounds, 153 pounds less than *Sputnik I* and more than 1,000 pounds less than *Sputnik II.*

The Soviet follow-up to these stellar accomplishments was to assume a bolder stance in the Cold War. Khrushchev, for example, began to put verbal diplomatic pressure on West Berlin, threatening to give East Germany control of supply routes to the city unless the Western powers removed their troops. The U.S. reaction bordered on panic: smug confidence that U.S. technological superiority in the world was unquestionable was replaced by fear that the country had fallen behind the Soviets in several strategically crucial areas. An extreme but instructive example of this fear was voiced by George R. Price, a physicist who had worked on the development of the atomic bomb for the United States in the 1940s. He was so impressed with the launching of *Sputnik I* that he predicted, "Russia is going to surpass us in mathematics and the social sciences. . . . Unless we depart utterly from our present behavior, it is reasonable to expect that by no later than 1975, the United States will be a member of the Union of Soviet Socialist Republics" (Cerf and Navasky, 1984, p. 260). The sputniks were also to have an important impact on presidential politics, because they provided a basis for the myth of the missile gap. John F. Kennedy ran for president against Richard Nixon with a promise to get the country moving again, claiming that the Eisenhower administration had allowed the United States to fall behind the Soviets in developing and producing intercontinental ballistic missiles (ICBMs). The charge may have seemed credible to some voters because of *Sputnik I* and *Sputnik II*.

Kennedy's Defense Strategy

Curiously, once Kennedy was elected, his defense strategy did not focus on missiles. (This may have been partly because Kennedy's secretary of defense concluded that no missile gap existed.) On the contrary, Kennedy tried to make the defense posture of the United States less reliant on missiles. Eisenhower and Dulles had decided that the United States could not, and did not need to, compete with the Soviet Union in maintaining large infantries. They concluded that the United States should rely heavily on missiles and nuclear weapons, in order to confront any Communist move anywhere in the globe with the threat of **massive retaliation.** (The policy was advocated on the grounds that it would provide more "bang for the buck." See the cartoon on page 52.) After Kennedy was elected, he concluded that this policy was insufficiently flexible. He feared that there were many kinds of subtle yet effective probes the Communists could make for which the threat of massive retaliation was not credible. The subtle kind of probe that worried him most, apparently, involved Communist-organized subversion and guerrilla warfare in Third World countries. Such efforts could not be countered with nuclear weapons, because the destruction caused by these weapons would be out of proportion to the nature of the threat; and in any case, guerrillas were hard to locate and separate from the local civilian population of the country being defended. To combat the threat of such subtle probes, Kennedy developed a more flexible defense posture that relied on techniques more appropriate for counter-guerrilla warfare, among them the creation of units such as the Green Berets.

Two Cuban Crises

The Kennedy administration's thousand days were marked by several dramatic events in the realm of international affairs. One involved the invasion of Cuba at the Bay of Pigs in 1961. The plan for this invasion originated in the Eisenhower administration shortly after Fidel Castro assumed power. The invasion was carried out by a small number of Cuban exiles who were financed, organized, and led into combat by agents of the Central Intelligence Agency (CIA) (Etheredge, 1985, p. 20). It was assumed that the invasion would spur massive numbers of

Cubans who were opposed to Castro to active rebellion. It did not, because there was poor coordination between the invading forces and the Cuban anti-Castro underground, and almost certainly because there was less opposition to Castro than the CIA supposed. The total failure of the invasion was assured when President Kennedy decided not to approve overt and substantial support for the effort by the U.S. Air Force.

The Bay of Pigs fiasco, along with the construction of a wall between East and West Berlin by the government of East Germany, set the stage for the Cuban missile crisis in 1962. The Soviets had hoped to slip missiles into Cuba secretly, for reasons that are still not totally clear (see Allison, 1971, pp. 40–55) but are easier to surmise now following two much later meetings (in Cambridge, Massachusetts, in October 1987 and in Moscow in January 1989), involving many who took part in the decision-making processes on both sides. At the latter meeting, President Kennedy's secretary of defense in 1963, Robert McNamara, admitted, "if I was a Cuban and read the evidence of covert American action against their government, I would be quite ready to believe that the U.S. intended to mount an invasion" (Allyn, Blight, and Welch, 1989/90, p. 145). In fact, one U.S. government memorandum, dated February 1962 and signed by the chief of operations, specified that Castro should be ousted, by military force if necessary, by late October 1962. An official military history of the crisis asserts that orders were given to prepare an air strike against Cuba two weeks before the Soviet missiles were discovered there. "Although operational plans . . . are not conclusive evidence of political intentions, they are nevertheless strong evidence of the worst possible case, and were apparently interpreted by Cuban and Soviet intelligence as reflecting a policy decision of the Kennedy administration to invade Cuba and to overthrow Castro" (Allyn, Blight, and Welch, 1989/90, p. 146).[6]

In any case, the United States discovered the missiles as they were being built and put a blockade (called a "quarantine") into effect to prevent the Soviet Union from delivering more missiles. In the end, the Soviets backed down, turning around ships headed for Cuba with additional missiles and agreeing to remove those already in Cuba. Although neither the American people at the time nor any others outside high government circles in the United States and the Soviet Union were aware of this secret arrangement, "it appears . . . that the withdrawal of [American] Jupiter missiles from Turkey in the spring of 1963 was indeed part of a private deal that led to the withdrawal of the Soviet missiles from Cuba in November, 1962" (Allyn, Blight, and Welch, 1989/90, p. 165).[7]

Kennedy might well have firmly resisted this Soviet move in any case, but his opposition was stiffened by the fear that, having denied air support to the Bay of Pigs invaders and having failed to take effective action against the construction of the Berlin Wall, he could not acquiesce in the secret shipment of missiles to Cuba without leading Khrushchev to believe that the United States would not actively resist other bold moves on the part of the Soviets. In the words of one retrospective analysis of the Cuban missile crisis, Kennedy and his advisers "were deeply concerned to avoid a precedent whereby the Soviets believed they might deceive the United States and then escape unpunished when caught in the lie. . . . If the United States failed to stand up to Khrush-

---

[6] At the 1989 conference in Moscow, several Soviet participants who were in a position to know, including then foreign minister Andrei Gromyko, insisted that at the time the decision to send missiles to Cuba was made, "fears of an American invasion were in fact uppermost in Khrushchev's mind" (Allyn, Blight, and Welch, 1989/90, p. 139).

[7] These missiles were obsolete and had already been slated for removal before the missile crisis began.

chev in such a blatant case of deception, what gamble would he try next?" (Blight, Nye, and Welch, 1987, p. 176). Khrushchev put the best possible light on the affair, arguing that his primary aim was the defense of Cuba and that since in return for the removal of the missiles he had obtained a promise from the United States not to attack the island, his aim was accomplished. "The Cuban missile crisis has assumed genuinely mythic significance. . . . [It] represents the closest point that the world has come to nuclear war" (Blight, Nye, and Welch, 1987, p. 176).

The Growing War in Vietnam

While the attention of Americans was focused on more dramatic events such as the Bay of Pigs invasion, the Berlin crises, and the Cuban missile crisis, quieter but important developments were taking place in Vietnam. Kennedy inherited from the Eisenhower administration a commitment to the government of Ngo Dinh Diem in South Vietnam that already involved the presence of some 1,000 U.S. advisers in that country. When Kennedy's aides recommended that he send 8,000 military troops to Vietnam, he instead sent 15,000 more advisers, who were supposed to avoid actual combat. They did not seem to help the situation substantially, and Kennedy became increasingly convinced that nothing would unless Diem, the Catholic leader of a predominantly Buddhist Vietnam, was replaced. The U.S. government looked the other way when a coup d'état in South Vietnam resulted not only in Diem's removal from office but also in his death.

Unfortunately, from the U.S. point of view the removal of Diem did not stabilize the government of South Vietnam. Instead, a seemingly never-ending series of generals succeeded Diem, and the situation deteriorated further. When Kennedy was assassinated three weeks after the death of Diem, Lyndon Johnson was faced with a problem in South Vietnam that he ultimately found insoluble. Kennedy's role in the process that created this problem for Johnson should not be overlooked, but neither should it be forgotten that when Kennedy died, only about 70 of the 17,000 Americans in South Vietnam had been killed.

Johnson delayed any serious increase in U.S. involvement during the election year of 1964. Then in 1965 he became convinced that some forceful response to the deteriorating situation in South Vietnam was necessary, and committed large numbers of U.S. combat troops. That was the beginning of the escalation by the United States and counterescalation by North Vietnam that ended in disaster for Johnson. His military advisers would request additional troops, and Johnson would grant only half the number requested, feeling that he was following a wise, middle-of-the-road course. The air force would submit an ever-expanding list of targets in the North to be bombed, and Johnson would trim that list at least partially, again feeling that his strategy was a moderate, reasonable one. The problem was that no matter how strongly Johnson resisted the pressures from the military, the escalatory trend continued. It reached the point where the army wanted one million soldiers and Johnson could barely hold the line at 550,000. The reaction from the North Vietnamese was always the same: no movement toward the bargaining table, which the Americans were trying to bring about, and counterescalation through infiltration of more men and supplies into the South. Finally, in March 1968, following months of domestic unrest in the United States and precipitously falling ratings in the public opinion polls, President Johnson announced that he would not seek reelection. At the same time, he announced that he would dedicate the remaining days of his term to an intensive effort to bring peace to Vietnam. At that moment, a prediction that Johnson would not be successful in his effort and that the next president would not be able to accomplish peace within the span of a full four-year term would have struck most Americans as unreasonably gloomy and pessimistic.

DÉTENTE AND TRIPOLARITY

President Nixon did manage to get a peace settlement, but only after incursions into Laos and Cambodia, a bombing campaign against North Vietnam unprecedented for its scope and intensity, and the deaths of thousands more Americans and Asians. The prolongation of agony on all sides seemed especially pointless, from the U.S. point of view, when Saigon was taken by Communist forces little more than a year after the peace settlement.

But Nixon was nothing if not a paradoxical man. While he fought the war against the small Communist nation of North Vietnam to its bitter conclusion, he took significant steps toward improving relationships between the United States and the leading Communist nations: the Soviet Union and China. Rapprochement with China was particularly dramatic and significant because formal diplomatic communication between China and the United States had been almost nonexistent for more than two decades. What brought about the sudden improvement in relations between Nixon, known for his rigid, vigorous anti-communism, and the leaders of China and the Soviet Union?

One factor may well have been the flexible position Nixon found himself in during the early 1970s. His personal anti-Communist stand was, of course, unquestionable. Probably even more important was the solid anti-Communist reputation of Nixon's Republican Party. The flexibility that this reputation gives Republican presidents generally was revealed when President Eisenhower accepted a peace settlement in Korea that might have been impossible for a Democratic president in the days of the anti-Communist scare (publicized most dramatically by Senator Joseph McCarthy) to accept.

Eisenhower also stood by while the Soviets crushed a rebellion in Hungary. In contrast, Kennedy authorized an invasion of Communist Cuba shortly after the beginning of his administration and exhibited more determined resistance to Communist activities in South Vietnam than Eisenhower had ever mounted. President Johnson escalated the anti-Communist crusade in Vietnam dramatically and staged an invasion of the Dominican Republic in opposition to a Communist threat of dubious validity (Lowenthal, 1972, p. 155). In short, when Nixon became president, he was not at all vulnerable to the charge of being soft on communism, and this may have eased the way for his move toward détente.

But almost certainly the most important factors contributing to the improvement in relations both between the United States and the Soviet Union and between the United States and China were the continuing conflict between the two Communist states themselves and their rising military-industrial might. As Henry Kissinger (1979, pp. 693, 746) observed in his memoirs, "China's cautious overtures to us were caused by the rapid and relentless Soviet military buildup in the Far East. . . . That China and the United States would seek rapprochement in the early 1970s was inherent in the world environment." The conflict between the Soviet Union and China led both countries to fear isolation from each other and from the United States. This made both amenable to any move by the United States to improve relations. In turn, the United States could not view the rising power of these two great Communist states with equanimity, especially if there were to be continued antagonism with them. From the viewpoint of the United States, the logic of the saying, "If you can't beat 'em, join 'em" was apparent in this situation. The pressures on the United States, the Soviet Union, and China would have exerted their force regardless of the preferences and idiosyncrasies of their particular leaders. This does not mean that the structure of the international system in the 1970s made détente inevitable, but it certainly did increase the probability of such a realignment in the relations between the United States and the Communist states.

THE REBIRTH OF THE COLD WAR

The latter half of the 1970s was marked by what some observers referred to as a rebirth of the Cold War. Some foreign policymakers in the United States were undoubtedly put into a belligerent mood by the fall of Saigon to the Communists in 1975. This mood was not improved when in the same year Angola achieved independence from Portugal in an armed struggle joined by Soviet-supported Cuban troops.

Still, Jimmy Carter came into the presidency in 1976 vowing to cut defense expenditures. He left that post in 1980 in the wake of a campaign based on the promise of significant *increases* in the defense budget, as well as condemnations of his Republican predecessors for allowing previous budgets to shrink to dangerously low levels! Obviously, something had happened to change Carter's view of relations between the United States and the Soviet Union rather drastically. The election of 1980 resulted in a victory for Ronald Reagan, who was even more enthusiastic than Carter about strengthening the country's defenses. Many U.S. voters, apparently, were more concerned about the Soviet threat and less concerned about escalating defense budgets than they had been not too many years before (Kriesberg and Klein, 1980).

Perhaps the increasing distance in time from the painful experience of Vietnam made Americans more inclined to flex their military muscle. Also, perhaps, the mass exodus of "boat people" from Vietnam and the fact that Communists were killing one another in great numbers, both in civil conflicts and in international wars (between Vietnam and Cambodia and between China and Vietnam), led some Americans to conclude that the people of Southeast Asia would have been better off if the United States had won the war in Vietnam. In any case, the natural result of such a conclusion would be reduced guilt feelings about that war and a greater propensity to build up and rely on military strength.

Events in Iran also had an important impact on American perceptions about the U.S. role in the world. First, in January 1979 the shah of Iran, who the CIA had played a crucial role in restoring to power in 1953, was deposed, to be replaced by a revolutionary government headed by the Ayatollah Ruhollah Khomeini. The shah had been one of the more reliable allies of the United States in a strategically important area of the world for almost two decades. His fall contributed to an impression that the United States was losing its grip on the drift of world affairs. That impression was reinforced when another longtime ally, Anastasio Somoza, was overthrown in Nicaragua in July 1979 by a coalition of forces that contained some undeniably anti-American elements. Finally, of course, U.S. feelings of impotence were heightened dramatically when, after Iranian "students" took ninety people hostage in the U.S. embassy in Teheran in November 1979, the U.S. government could not secure their release for 444 days.

One can argue persuasively that none of these problems was created by military weakness on the part of the United States, and one can claim even more convincingly that significant increases in nuclear capabilities were irrelevant to their solution. But when the Soviet Union invaded Afghanistan in December 1979, proponents of such arguments were quite noticeably rare. President Carter announced that the invasion had been an important educational experience for him with regard to his attitude about the Soviets. He retaliated by imposing an embargo on grain shipments to the Soviet Union and boycotting the 1980 Olympics in Moscow. He also declared that the invasion of Afghanistan had created the most dangerous threat to peace since the Second World War.

In retrospect, that invasion can be seen as the beginning of a period of tense relations between the United States and the Soviet Union. Antagonism between the Americans and the Soviets was fueled by actions on the part of both superpowers that may well have been defensive from their respective points of view but looked aggressive to their counterparts. The operation in Afghanistan itself, from the Soviet vantage point, was meant to protect socialism in that country and perhaps to stem the tide of Islamic fundamentalism so visible in Iran and so threatening to continued control of Islamic elements in the Soviet Union. Unrest in Poland was a clear threat to Soviet national security, and if the Soviets urged Polish head of state General Wojciech Jaruzelski to declare martial law in 1981, even with implicit threats of invasion, that was, they thought, their business and their right. (Nevertheless, the United States imposed economic sanctions on both Poland and the Soviet Union.) When in 1983 Soviets shot down a Korean airliner filled with civilian passengers as it flew over Soviet territory, the Soviets claimed that they were protecting themselves from a provocative spy mission. Americans viewed the act as barbaric. In the atmosphere created by that incident, the United States began to deploy new intermediate-range missiles in Europe in 1983, and the Soviets broke off arms talks with the Americans.

From the Soviet point of view, in the early years of his administration President Reagan was unpredictable and often aggressive. He significantly increased U.S. defense budgets, even in the face of massive budget deficits. He ordered an invasion of Grenada in 1983. He waged "covert" war against the Sandinista government in Nicaragua. Perhaps of greatest concern to the Soviets, he insisted on pushing ahead with the development of the **Strategic Defense Initiative (SDI)**, or "Star Wars," designed to prevent nuclear war by providing the technological means to knock incoming missiles out of the air before they hit their targets.

In the atmosphere created by such policies, one prominent specialist in U.S. foreign policy concluded his book-length 1983 analysis by pointing out that President Reagan had not been able to slow, much less halt, the arms race; find a basis for genuine détente with the Soviets; bring about a liberalization of Eastern Europe; force the Soviets out of

Afghanistan; or bring stability to Central America. "The Cold War continue[s]," this volume emphasized, "more expensive and more dangerous than ever" (Ambrose, 1983, p. 417).

THE END OF THE COLD WAR

It is instructive to remember, perhaps, in the light of some pessimism about the post–Cold War international political scene, how grim international politics looked by the middle of the 1980s, and how much change occurred (mostly for the better) in the ensuing decade. By the end of 1988, the United States and the Soviet Union had agreed for the first time to dismantle a whole category of nuclear weapons, in an agreement formalized in the **Intermediate-Range Nuclear Forces (INF) Treaty.** That was widely expected to be a first step toward a Strategic Arms Reduction Treaty (START) that would call for significant reductions in strategic weapons by both superpowers. President Reagan had several cordial summit meetings with Mikhail Gorbachev in Reagan's last months and years in office. The eight-year war between Iran and Iraq finally ended in 1988. The Soviets pulled their troops out of Afghanistan. The Cubans pulled their troops out of Angola. The Sandinistas in Nicaragua lost an election and allowed a peaceful transfer of power to their opponents.

One area of the world where problems were definitely not resolved as the Cold War came to an end was the Middle East. Iraq's attack on Kuwait in August 1990 evoked what turned out to be a furious counterattack by an American-led coalition whose activities were sanctioned by the United Nations. The attack quite efficiently achieved its primary goal of evicting Iraq from Kuwait. But the stunning defeat of Saddam Hussein's military forces did not remove Hussein from power. The war left Iraq economically devastated and created something on the order of five million refugees, many fleeing possible retaliation by Hussein. The Persian Gulf has certainly not seen the last of conflict and instability. The war did seem to create some movement toward a peace conference to address the Arab-Israeli conflict, and in fact ultimately a tentative peace agreement between the Israelis and the Palestinians was hammered out in 1993. At this writing, however, the implementation of that agreement is proving difficult, to say the least.

There is little doubt that the most dramatic political events in the late 1980s and the first half of 1990s took place in the Communist world. A decade of reforms in China culminated in massive pro-democracy demonstrations in Beijing in the spring of 1989. Those demonstrations were firmly repressed, and many of the leaders of the

The young man standing in front of Chinese tanks on Tiananmen Square became symbolic of popular resistance to the Chinese regime during demonstrations there in June of 1989. SOURCE: Reuters/Bettmann Newsphotos.

prodemocracy movement were jailed or executed. But as a result of reforms instituted in the late 1970s and early 1980s, in the wake of the crackdown at Tiananmen Square, China's economic output and exports grew faster than either India's or the Soviet Union's and even more rapidly than those of the well-known economic superstars in its neighborhood—Taiwan, South Korea, Singapore, and Hong Kong.

The story in the rest of the Communist world (when it was Communist, and afterward) was virtually the mirror image of that in China: economic reform and impressive economic achievements in China coincided with (in spite of, or because of?) political retrenchment and a vigorous battle against political liberalization by the Chinese leadership. In Eastern Europe, and especially in the Soviet Union, dramatic strides toward political liberalization and democracy coincided with equally dramatic economic deterioration. Mikhail Gorbachev came to power in 1985 and put into effect his policies of **perestroika** and **glasnost**—the former referring to market-oriented economic reforms, the latter to political reforms in the direction of greater "openness" and democratization. The political reforms certainly did decrease autocratic controls, but the economic reforms never achieved anything like the Chinese successes.

Gorbachev instituted an equally profound revolution in foreign policy, especially in Soviet relations with its erstwhile "satellites" in Eastern Europe. "In 1989," according to one historian, "while the nations of Western Europe celebrated the bicentenary of the French Revolution, the nations of Eastern Europe reenacted it" (Howard, 1989/90, p. 17). In that year, a long process of liberalization in Poland culminated in open parliamentary elections, with the anti-Communist coalition led by Solidarity winning ninety-nine out of one hundred seats in the Senate. As the *Los Angeles Times* (December 17, 1989, p. 1) observed in the wake of the 1989 revolution in Eastern Europe, "It took 10 years in Poland, 10 months in Hungary, 10 weeks in East Germany, and 10 days in Czechoslovakia." By the end of the year, the Ceausescu regime in Rumania had also been overthrown. By 1991, even the long-isolated regime in Albania was liberalizing in various ways.

By the end of 1989, the Soviet Union and its allies in the Warsaw Pact had explicitly renounced the Brezhnev Doctrine, in which the Soviets reserved the right to intervene, militarily if necessary, to save a fellow socialist regime from being overthrown (as happened in Czechoslovakia in 1968). By October 1990, East and West Germany were unified in one Federal Republic of Germany, and in 1991, the Warsaw Pact was officially disbanded.

Political reform in the Soviet Union came to a screeching halt in August 1991, when a group of high-level conservative Communists in the Party, the army, and the KGB (the CIA's Soviet counterpart) deposed Mikhail Gorbachev and began to restore the old system. But Boris Yeltsin, a reformist leader who had withdrawn from the Communist Party and established legitimacy by winning a free election for the presidency of the Russian Republic, took the lead in resisting the "putsch," which collapsed under the combined pressures of popular resistance and its leaders' incompetence and indecision. By the end of 1991, not only was the Communist Party of the Soviet Union deprived of its power; the Soviet Union itself dissolved, to be replaced by its constituent, formerly "Soviet Socialist" republics.

Despite the fact that they were marked more by economic setbacks than impressive economic achievements, political reforms in the Soviet Union and Eastern Europe seemed to have a kind of demonstration effect, encouraging emulation around the world.[8] Throughout the

---

[8] For evidence that regime transitions are not independent events—that is, that transitions tend to diffuse from one country and region of the world to others—see Starr (1991).

1980s, military dictatorships were replaced by more democratic regimes in Latin America.[9] In Asia, outside the People's Republic of China, a trend toward democracy in the 1980s and early 1990s was visible in Taiwan, South Korea, the Philippines, Nepal, Mongolia, and Bangladesh. In 1991 one informed observer in Africa declared that "after decades of unspeakable repression at the hands of authoritarian regimes, Africans stand at the threshold of a new epoch. Across the continent, millions are demanding freely elected legislators, an independent judiciary and an accountable executive" (Mutua, 1991, p. 13). The Middle East has not been fruitful ground for democratic reforms, but even there, Turkey and Pakistan moved in a democratic direction in the 1980s, King Hussein of Jordan instituted a series of liberalizing reforms, the newly unified Yemen showed some signs of moving in a pluralist direction, and Algeria's socialist regime moved toward multiparty elections (which were, however, postponed indefinitely in 1991).

Overall, from the early 1970s to the early 1990s, the number of democratic states in the world increased from about forty to almost eighty, with another forty or so moving in a democratic direction. In 1973, about half the people in the world lived in states with regimes that could be classified as "free," or "partly free." By 1991, that proportion had increased to a little over two-thirds (McColm, 1991, p. 6).[10] Even before the revolutions in Eastern Europe in 1989, Francis Fukuyama (1989, p. 4), in a widely publicized article, concluded that "what we may be witnessing is not just the end of the Cold War, or the passing of a particular period of postwar history, but the end of history as such: that is, the end point of mankind's ideological evolution and the universalization of Western liberal democracy as the final form of human government."

RECENT TRENDS

There are several reasons to suspect that this conclusion was premature, as Francis Fukuyama himself is aware:

---

[9] "Since 1979, the politics of Latin America have been transformed by the longest and deepest wave of democratization in the region's history" (Remmer, 1990, p. 315).

[10] These estimates by Freedom House in New York are not beyond dispute, but by the early 1990s, the notion that there was in place a global trend toward democracy was quite widely accepted. Samuel P. Huntington (1991a, p. 12) for example, noted that "between 1974 and 1990, at least 30 countries made transitions to democracy, just about doubling the number of democratic countries in the world."

> The end of the cold war has brought about a remarkable consensus
> between former hawks and doves . . . to the effect that the world has
> become a much worse place since the demise of the Soviet Union . . .
> Now, about four years later, we see that the world is not progressing
> toward the "global village" but retreating into atavistic tribalism, whose
> ugliest expression is the "ethnic cleansing" witnessed in Bosnia
> (Fukuyama, 1994, p. 25).

The bloody, seemingly endless dissolution of Yugoslavia and the
murderous war among the Serbians, the Croats, and the Muslims did a
lot to diminish post–Cold War euphoria. Literally for years, the international community, whether in the form of the United Nations, NATO,
or the European Union (previously known as the European Community)
seemed impotent and sometimes incompetent in the face of intermina-
ble warfare between and within the republics in the former Yugoslavia.
Finally, in 1996 peace was established in Bosnia based on an agreement
hammered out in Dayton, Ohio (and so labeled the Dayton Accords). On
the one hand, it should be noted that as a result "the killing has stopped
and the separation of forces has proceeded . . . " (Lampe, 1996, p. 73). But
on the other, there are apparently firm grounds for pessimism about the
political future of Bosnia. The Dayton Accords "institutionalize and
strengthen the power of Bosnia's nationalist parties and their Commu-
nist-type bureaucracies and militaries and do little to nurture a rebirth
of the war-shattered moderate political middle ground. This flaw . . .
could well lead to renewed conflict after NATO's 60,000 peace enforcers
depart . . . " (Landay, 1996, p. 66).

What made the ethnic strife in the former Yugoslavia especially
disheartening was that such conflict was not at all isolated to the
Balkans. Ethnic groups in South Africa, Burundi, Rwanda, India, Egypt,
Mexico, and Azerbaijan also engaged in brutal conflict, just to name a
few of the countries struck with this plague. Ethnic strife played a key
role not only in the dismantling of Yugoslavia but also in the breakup
of the Soviet Union, as well as Czechoslovakia, and was tearing at the
seams of Canada and India as well. Although ethnic conflicts seem to
have increased in number and intensity since the end of the Cold War,
the data on which Figure 2.1 is based suggest that what has occurred is
no more than a continuation of a trend that has been in place for some
time. "Since the 1950s all forms of [ethnic] conflict have increased
markedly. Nonviolent protest has more than doubled in magnitude (up
230 percent from 1945 . . .) and violent protest has increased fourfold (up
420 percent from . . . 1950–55). Rebellion also has increased almost
fourfold (up 360 percent from 1950 . . .)" (Gurr, 1993, p. 100). The role
of ethnic groups and ethnic conflict in global politics will be discussed
in more detail in Chapter 3.

Figure 2.1   Global Trends in Minority Conflict, 1945–1989

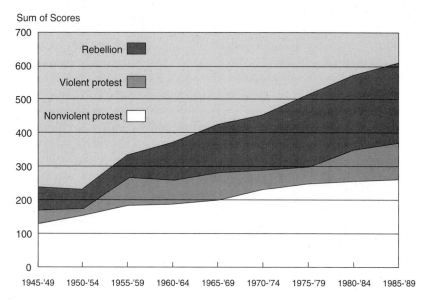

SOURCE: Gurr, Ted Robert, *MINORITIES AT RISK.* Copyright © 1993 by the United States Institute of Peace. Used with permission.

Another disturbing source of pessimism in the post–Cold War era involves political and economic developments in Russia. Boris Yeltsin disbanded the Russian parliament in 1993, and he ultimately found it necessary to use military force against his opponents in that body to keep it disbanded. A new parliament, however, was elected toward the end of 1993, and Boris Yeltsin himself did manage to win reelection in the summer of 1996.

Ethnic strife in many countries, political unrest such as that in the former Yugoslavia and the former Soviet Union, as well as the desire of poor people in poor countries to find employment and better lives elsewhere are among the most important factors contributing to another pervasive fact of life in the global political system of the 1990s, that is, refugees and migrants. By 1993 there were an estimated 44 million refugees in the world (Lewis, 1993, p. 1). As recently as the mid-1970s, there were only about 2.5 million refugees. From 1989 to 1994, the number of refugees in the world rose from about 15 million to 23 million (Kane, 1995, p. 133) (see Figure 2.2). The influx of immigrants into the United States reached about 1 million in 1993, an increase of 40 percent over 1987. There are about 25 million foreign-born persons in the United States today, whereas there were only 14 million in 1980

Figure 2.2 Official Refugees Worldwide, 1960–1994

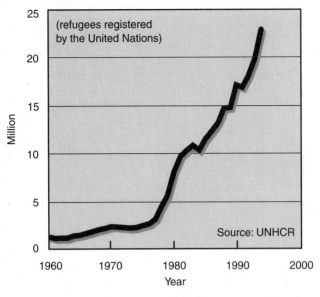

SOURCE: From *State of the World, 1995: A Worldwatch Institute Report on Progress Toward a Sustainable Society* by Lester R. Brown, et al., eds. Copyright © 1995 by Worldwatch Institute. Reprinted by permission of W. W. Norton & Company, Inc.

(Clad, 1994, p. 142). "The impact of immigration into the United States is intensified by its pace. Almost one-half of immigrants in the United States today were not here a decade ago" (Passel and Fix, 1994, p. 155).[11] But immigration is not an issue only in the United States. "West European governments are now more determined than ever to keep the foreigners out, and they are beginning to use regulations, deportations and gunboats to do so" (Nelan, 1993a, p. 38). Specialists on migration have concluded that "migration pressure is much higher today and increasing, both because the demand for migration has been increasing and because the supply of migration opportunities is much more restricted. . . ." (Brubaker, 1991, p. 946).

Amid the turmoil of the 1990s, the global trend toward democracy that by some measures reached a peak immediately after the end of the Cold War came to an end. Actually, the number of formal (or ostensible) democracies, with at least the trappings of democracy in terms of elections, continues to grow. "By the beginning of 1996, the number of

[11] "In 1989, the Census Bureau forecast a U.S. population of 300 million by 2050, but in 1993 it changed its mind. After factoring in high immigration rates, the estimate rose to 383 million" (Clad, 1994, p. 142).

countries meeting at least the requirements for electoral democracy had increased to 117. . . . The number and percentage of democracies in the world have increased *every* year since 1990" (Diamond, 1996, p. 26). However, if we look a little below the surface of these statistics and focus on regimes with the substantial political and civil rights usually associated with democracy, a different picture emerges. "The 1991–92 period seems to have been the high-water mark for freedom in the world. Since 1991, the proportion of free states has declined slightly, and since 1992, the proportion of 'not free' states has jumped sharply" (Diamond, 1996, p. 28).

Such reversals have occurred before. Samuel Huntington (1991b) points out that there was a long wave of democratization from 1820 to the 1920s, with the creation of twenty-nine new democracies. That wave was reversed in the twenty years from 1922 to the 1940s, when the number of democracies in the world was reduced to twelve. There was a second wave of democratization after the Second World War, with some twenty-four countries becoming democratic up to 1962. Then, from the early 1960s to the mid-1970s, the number of democratic countries was again reduced. The world may now be in the initial stages of a reversal of the third wave of democratization, which occurred roughly from 1973 up to the early 1990s. (Some of the implications of this trend for global politics will be discussed in Chapter 6.) The "end of history," to repeat, looks farther away, perhaps, than it did a few years ago.

As the author of "The End of History" points out, "At any given historical moment there are always ominous clouds on the horizon" (Fukuyama, 1994, p. 28), and clouds of that character certainly are visible as the twenty-first century approaches. But the current global trends away from democracy and toward increasing political chaos, military conflict, and economic misery in so many countries are not necessarily permanent or irreversible. Nor is it necessarily the case that the predominant political trends in the post–Cold War era are in fact toward chaos and a revolutionary new international political order. "Common wisdom" suggests that the end of the Cold War and the collapse of communism have brought the collapse also of the international order that emerged after the Second World War. But perhaps

> the common wisdom is wrong. . . . The end of the Cold War was less the end of a world order than the collapse of the communist world into an expanding Western order. . . . The United States built and then managed the containment order for 40 years, but it also built and continues to enjoy the rewards of the old liberal democratic order. America is not adrift in uncharted seas. It is at the center of a world of its own making (Ikenberry, 1996, pp. 79, 91).

In distinct contrast with this view is the idea that "the image of an emerging homogeneous, universally Western world—[is] misguided, arrogant, false and dangerous." According to this idea, Western values, and major powers committed to those values such as the United States, are in the process of becoming less influential. "As Western power recedes, so too does the appeal of Western values and culture, and the West needs to accommodate itself to its declining ability to impose values on non-Western societies. In fundamental ways, much of the world is becoming more modern and less Western" (Huntington, 1996, pp. 28–38).

THE STUDY OF WORLD POLITICS AFTER THE SECOND WORLD WAR

The reaction of scholars to the Second World War was quite different from the reaction to the First World War. After the First World War, the idea that world government, or at least some form of strong international organization, was essential to preserve international peace was very popular in academic circles. The Second World War, as well as the death of the League of Nations, seemed to indicate to most scholars that the approach taken after the First World War, involving reliance on the League of Nations and measures such as the Kellogg-Briand Pact of 1928, which "outlawed" war, had been too idealistic. Successful foreign policy, according to this train of thought, must be built on a **realist** appraisal of the world. People hunger for power, and the primary goal of those who make national foreign policy is to serve the national interest defined in terms of power.

The Central Role of Realist Thought

The chief advocate of the realist theory of international politics was Hans Morgenthau. His classic text, *Politics Among Nations* (1967), contains a thoughtful explanation of his theory, which many teachers and students of the post–Second World War era (the first edition was published in 1948) found convincing. But critics pointed out that states and their individual leaders have many important goals in addition to the national interest defined in terms of power. For example, an increase in the defense budget of a state may increase that state's power, but if it sparks an arms race, it may also decrease its security. Decision makers (at least in some cases) are aware of such a possibility, and they do not always seek to increase a nation's power when confronted with such a choice.

Decision makers also often become painfully aware of a choice between guns and butter; they may devote more resources to military equipment or consumer goods, but not both. They may opt for the latter, even if that decreases the power of their state, because they feel it necessary to keep themselves in power. In other words, they act not in the national interest defined in terms of power but in their personal interest defined in terms of their own political survival.

Another reason it may be misleading to assume that national leaders will *always* act in the national interest defined in terms of power is that very few interests are truly national in scope. Virtually every foreign policy decision hurts some people and benefits others. If the military budget is increased, that may well mean that there is less money for social welfare programs or education. A large military budget also can lead to inflation, which is particularly detrimental to people on fixed incomes. War helps weapons manufacturers and may even protect the security of all those who are too young or too old to fight. But it hurts all those young men who are unwillingly drafted to serve in the military, and it leads to the deaths of many of them. Similarly, if national leaders decide to raise tariffs against foreign imports, protected manufacturers and workers will be happy, but consumers will pay higher prices.

So it is clear that realism is not beyond criticism. But it is also true that "for over 2000 years, what Hans J. Morgenthau dubbed **'Political Realism'** has constituted the principal tradition for the analysis of international relations in Europe and its offshoots in the New World" (Keohane, 1983, p. 503). Three fundamental assumptions of realism are widely shared in the field. They are that states are the most important actors, that they seek power, and that they pursue their policies in an essentially rational manner, calculating costs and estimating benefits, typically in a logical fashion.

Studying World Politics Scientifically

Beginning in about the late 1950s, another controversy began to compete for attention with realists and their critics (some of whom were labeled **"idealists"**). This new controversy focused on the question of whether it is possible, or desirable, to develop a scientific study of world politics. Those who were convinced that it is were sufficiently numerous that the next decade saw a growing number of articles and research projects in world politics based on **scientific methods** (or, as some would insist, allegedly scientific methods).

Is it possible to study world politics, or human behavior in any context, scientifically? The answer depends, of course, on what is meant by science. Generally, those who have tried to develop a science of world politics are aiming to discover patterns in the making of foreign policy, the behavior of various social entities in the global political system, and the operation of that system. Any study that aims to discover such patterns and is based on reproducible comparisons is, in this author's view, scientific. **Reproducible comparisons**—the heart of the scientific method—are based on procedures so clearly defined that any qualified scientist, in addition to the original researcher, can carry them out and come up with the same results.

The steadily increasing amount of research in world politics that has been based on such procedures makes it progressively more difficult to argue that it is impossible to apply scientific methods to this field. Many still believe, though, that scientific methods will not produce findings of real interest to scholars of world politics. Is it not true, for example, that the behavior of different people, since they vary so significantly in background, beliefs, and character, is essentially unpredictable?

Accurately predicting people's behavior is certainly difficult, but it is not impossible. One can confidently predict, for example, that most people will stop at stop signs, flee burning buildings, and come in out of the rain. On a more significant level, researchers have found that in several countries wealthy people are more likely than their poorer fellow citizens to vote for conservative political parties.

The basic social scientific assumption is that similar people under similar circumstances will behave in similar ways, and this assumption is borne out in an increasing number of studies of world politics. Even so, exactly which similarities in people and circumstances are crucial to explanations of behavior in the context of world politics is not a question to which there are a great many answers. But there are tentative answers, some of which are discussed in the following chapters. Although some of these answers are based on too few cases or are defined with insufficient clarity to inspire great confidence, they provide some evidence in favor of the scientific argument that people's behavior in the context of world politics is, within limits, predictable.

International Political Economy and the Future

The debate between realists and idealists dominated the field of international relations in the 1950s, and the controversy between scientists and traditionalists held center stage in the 1960s. But a growing emphasis on international political economy was the hallmark of the 1970s. One reason for this was the U.S. experience in Vietnam. To many people inside and outside the United States, official explanations of U.S. policy with regard to the war in Vietnam were not convincing. But even though the official reasons for its actions seemed less than compelling, the U.S. government showed great determination in Vietnam, spent billions of dollars, sacrificed thousands of American lives, and provoked serious domestic unrest. Why?

Many (predominantly young) scholars in the United States and elsewhere concluded that the real reason, as opposed to the stated reasons, for American zeal in Vietnam involved the economic interests of the United States. Vietnam itself was of some economic value to the United States and was of even greater value to an important U.S. ally, Japan. More important, according to this argument, U.S. officials—and the business interests they represented—were concerned that if the liberation movement in South Vietnam was successful, others would be sure to follow, cutting off ever-greater areas of the globe from business interests in the United States and other important industrial states of the free world. Foreign markets, fields of investment, and sources of raw materials are absolutely essential to capitalist economic systems, and the U.S. government realized this. These kinds of concerns accounted for the determination the government demonstrated in Vietnam.

The plausibility of this argument inspired several books and articles that analyzed U.S. foreign policy from this point of view (Magdoff, 1969; Kolko, 1969; Fann and Hodges, 1971). It also led to a reanalysis of relationships between the United States and Third World countries and made many North American scholars receptive to what was basically a creation of Latin American economists: **dependency theory.** The major tenet of this theory is that economic contact between Third World countries and rich industrialized countries—whether in the form of international trade, foreign investment, or foreign aid—works to the disadvantage of Third World countries and will continue to do so until the international economic and political system in which these activities take place is radically altered. Chapter 8 analyzes the validity of theories that U.S. foreign policy (and the foreign policies of capitalist countries in general) is dedicated primarily to protecting the interests of expansive U.S. capitalism, as well as dependency theory as it applies to Third World countries.

The politics of international economic relationships among the major industrialized powers of the world also received increased attention in the 1970s. While dependency theorists focused on the relationship between rich and poor countries, those who concentrated on interactions among the richer countries spoke of economic **interdependence.** Again, events involving the United States played an important role in this development. Until the 1970s, the United States had occupied an obviously dominant position in the international economic system. By 1971, however, Western Europe and Japan competed with the United

States on much more equal terms economically. Problems in the U.S. economy, stemming in part from the Vietnam War, reinforced the trend away from U.S. dominance. When President Nixon announced in 1971 that the United States would no longer automatically convert dollars into gold, the whole international economic system set up after the Second World War was suddenly deprived of one of its basic supports. When the Organization of Petroleum Exporting Countries (OPEC) successfully quadrupled the price of oil in 1973, the system was shaken to its foundations once again. Rather suddenly, international economic transactions and problems that had previously seemed wholly technical and mostly apolitical became highly visible and of great concern to political leaders in all the industrialized countries. These shocks to the system also highlighted the interdependence of the economies of the richer countries. It became obvious that political and economic decisions in one industrialized society could have dramatic consequences for all the others (Keohane and Nye, 1977). In short, rules and customs involving international economic issues that had previously been relatively clear and established became open to question in the 1970s. The questions had to be answered in a process that was obviously political. It is no wonder, then, that in the 1970s political scientists and scholars of international relations turned their attention to international political economy. (Current relationships among the wealthy industrialized states are discussed further in Chapter 7.)

A related development in the study of world politics involved an emphasis on the importance of various kinds of nonstate institutions and organizations in the global political system. The interdependence of states discussed earlier seemed to undermine the sovereignty of nation-states and so, perhaps, made nonstate actors seem more important. Or perhaps it was the threat of nuclear war and the realization that states now commanded sufficient power to destroy the world that gave new impetus to an old idea—that is, that a world organized and dominated by states is a dangerous place. Dissatisfaction with states was reinforced by the realization that states are ill equipped to handle such global crises as the depletion of natural resources; the pollution of the world's atmosphere, rivers, lakes, and oceans; inequalities in the distribution of wealth; and the population explosion. This dissatisfaction with states and the simultaneous realization that "state-centric" theories of world politics have for some time masked the importance of other types of political entities led to increased interest in nonstate actors, such as intergovernmental organizations, multinational corporations, subnational "liberation" groups, and other transnational organizations (Mansbach, Ferguson, and Lampert, 1976; Ferguson and Mansbach, 1988). Although the continuing impact of nation-states on global politics is reflected in the pages that follow, the emergence and increased importance of nonstate actors is also discussed (with special emphasis in Chapter 13).

Future Directions for the Study of Global Politics

The last ten or fifteen years have been paradoxical for the global political system in many fundamental respects, and the seemingly contradictory trends that have emerged probably account to some important extent for the flowering of several diverse theoretical approaches to the study of international politics. The rebirth of tension between the United States and the Soviet Union in the late 1970s, for example, probably helped rekindle interest in the traditional issues of war and peace, international conflict, and national security. Realism, surviving a decade of attack in the 1970s from neo-Marxists and interdependence analysts opposed to state-centric approaches, staged a comeback. In *The War Trap*, Bruce Bueno de Mesquita (1981) posited that a nation's decision makers act in a rational, "realistic" fashion according to a few relatively simple rules, especially when making choices regarding the initiation of international war. His evidence, as discussed in Chapter 4, seems to indicate that national leaders have rather consistently behaved as if they make decisions based on those rational, utility-maximizing rules.[12] One important basis of what has come to be called **neorealism** was the *Theory of International Politics* by Kenneth Waltz (1979). While Morgenthau's realism stresses human nature as the origin of the characteristic behavior of nation-states, Waltz emphasizes the anarchic structure of the international system—that is, the absence of a central governing authority. We discuss Waltz's work in more detail in Chapter 13.

Another potentially beneficial development in the academic field of international politics that became more visible in the late 1980s was the "genderizing" of international studies. Politics in general, perhaps especially international politics, as well as the academic study of those topics, has always been male dominated. A U.N. study released in the early 1990s reported that fewer than 10 percent of the world's parliamentarians are female (Howe, 1991, p. 4). A perusal of the names of the foreign ministers and defense ministers in all the states of the world in the 1990s will show that only a few are female; also, only a very small

---

[12] This "rational choice" model of outcomes of international conflicts is expanded considerably in Bruce Bueno de Mesquita and David Lalman (1992). One of its modifications emphasizes the role of domestic politics, as well as regime types (e.g., democratic versus autocratic), in a way that is quite contrary to traditional realism, or neorealism.

minority of ambassadors to the United Nations are female (Central Intelligence Agency, 1996; United Nations, 1996).

In addition, discrimination against women, in part because they make up half the human race, is arguably the single most profound human rights issue in the world today. "In most developing countries women work an average of 12 to 18 hours a day—as opposed to 10 to 12 for men—in their multiple roles as caretakers, educators, health promoters, and income earners" (Jacobson, 1991, p. 10). Women do about two-thirds of the work in the world but receive less than one-tenth of the income and own less than 1 percent of the world's property (Alexandre, 1989, p. 6).

"IR," one feminist scholar notes, is "implicitly wedded to an unacknowledged and seemingly commonplace principle that international relations is the proper . . . place for people called men" (Sylvester, 1994, p. 4). By "IR," she quite clearly means "international relations" as a social, economic, and political activity in the "real world," as well as the academic study of such activities. Recently, women have begun to have their say about theoretical issues in the academic field of international politics (Elshtain, 1987; Enloe, 1989; Tickner, 1992; Sylvester, 1994; Whitworth, 1994). What they have to say is not easy to describe or categorize in a simple and definitive way.[13] One obviously fundamental difference among feminist scholars of international relations (and other disciplines) involves the question of whether or not women are different from men in essential ways that will affect their contributions to politics, as well as their academic studies of it. **Essentialists** argue that women *are* essentially different from men in ways that will constitute an important basis for the value of their contributions to politics and to ways of thinking about it. Liberal feminists, on the other hand, tend to focus on "women being not-different from men, and, therefore, entitled to men's rights" (Sylvester, 1994, p. 39).

Many feminist scholars have joined a broader intellectual revolt against "mainstream" thought in international relations known as **postmodernism.** Postmodernism has come to the international relations field from its origins as a form of literary criticism. In the postmodernist view, most work on international relations is dominated by the idea that there is a "singular, stable knowable reality"; postmodernism stresses that instead "reality is in a perpetual state of flux—of movement, change and instability." Western, "scientific," or "modern" ideas about reality are rejected by postmodernists as "narrative fiction." Postmodernists, some of them female and/or feminist, focus on "decon-

---

[13] Sylvester (1994), for example, in her discussion of the "palette" of feminists, discusses empiricists, liberals, stand-pointers, radical feminisms, cultural feminisms, feminist postmodernists, postmodernist feminists, and socialist feminism.

structing" this narrative fiction, revealing the hidden assumptions and tacit meanings in mainstream international relations theory. They tend to agree that much international relations theorizing, especially realism or neorealism, is based on masculine assumptions and reasoning of which its supporters may be unaware but in any case do not acknowledge. According to postmodernism, a "deconstruction" of the "great texts" in the international relations field will reveal that women have been "systematically omitted in the quest to represent elite male experience and images of reality, as reality per se. . . . The result is a Tradition and a discipline, and indeed a whole International Relations community, that has rendered women invisible. . . ." (George, 1994, p. 26).

Meanwhile, the field of international relations in the 1980s and the 1990s has also seen something of a rebirth of the 1950s debate between realists and idealists. Now the debate is between neorealists and **neoliberal institutionalists.** From the institutionalist point of view, there are important anomalies in international politics that cannot be accounted for by realism or neorealism. Among the more important of those anomalies are "the increasing salience of economic interdependence and the apparent tendency of democracies to behave differently in foreign policy than authoritarian states" (Keohane, 1993, p. 271). Certainly one of the ways in which democracies "behave differently," as was widely noted in both academic and policy circles in the 1990s, involves the fact that they have never, or at worst only rarely, fought international wars against each other (Russett, 1993; Ray, 1995). Perhaps the rapid changes of the 1980s and 1990s account for change, diversity, and some confusion in the academic field of international relations as we approach the twenty-first century. The 1980s began with the reputed rebirth of the Cold War; but by the middle of the 1990s the Cold War had ended and the Soviet Union had disappeared. In some circles there was even nostalgia for the allegedly simpler and more tranquil Cold War days.

What will happen next? Will the rest of the twentieth century bring as many surprises and rapid changes as the 1980s and early 1990s? Will scholars of international politics be able to help us anticipate, or at least understand, the changes that occur? There is a clear danger that having (perhaps) overreacted to détente between the superpowers in the early 1970s and then swung back too much in response to the increased tension between the superpowers in the 1980s, the discipline will succumb in the 1990s or in the new millennium to what appear now to be the rather faddish preoccupations of the 1970s. More optimistically speaking, perhaps diversity within the field of international politics is needed to cope with an increasingly interdependent and rapidly changing global political system and the flood of information that is now available about those changes. In any case, the goal of the chapters that follow is to provide an introduction to the most important recent developments in the field of international politics. Perhaps they will enable readers to decide for themselves the extent to which the diversity in that field is a source of debilitating confusion or, rather, one of healthy competition from which may emerge a better understanding of the increasingly well-integrated, but possibly more dangerous and certainly more pervasive, global political system.

SUMMARY

After the Second World War, a disagreement between the Soviet Union and the United States formed an important basis for the beginning of the Cold War between what became known as the two superpowers. Power vacuums created by the process of fighting the Second World War created disputes that often led to violent confrontations elsewhere, for example, in China, Korea, Vietnam, and the Middle East.

By the 1960s, the hitherto monolithic (in appearance, anyway) Communist world began to disintegrate; the Soviet Union and China became vigorous enemies toward the end of that decade. Not coincidentally, relations between the Soviet Union and the United States improved when the Soviet dispute with China became even more serious at the beginning of the 1970s. But "détente" between the United States and the Soviet Union did not survive the Soviet invasion of Afghanistan in 1979. The Cold War was reborn.

However, after the Cold War ended (again) around 1989, a period of euphoria following that development was replaced by some anxiety over ethnic violence, massive movements of immigrants, and sufficient instability of various kinds to make the Cold War days in some ways look less complicated, and even desirable.

After the Second World War, the academic study of world politics was dominated by an approach known as realism. In this realist view, the world is dominated by nation-states that calculate their interests in a rational way and are primarily concerned with national security. The 1960s produced analysts who were dedicated to studying world politics scientifically. The first end of the Cold War, in the 1970s, encouraged the analysis of economic issues by dependency theorists as well as by those who emphasized economic interdependence. In short, international political economy received more attention than the traditional issues of war and peace. The rebirth of the Cold War in the 1980s brought back realism in the form of neorealism. The end of the Cold War seems to have encouraged increased diversity in theoretical approaches to international politics, with feminists, postmodernists, and neoliberal institutionalists (among others) competing with neorealists to provide persuasive and instructive interpretations of past events, an understanding of current events, and some ability to anticipate future developments in the global political system.

KEY TERMS

Yalta
Declaration on Liberated Countries
power vacuum
containment
sphere of influence
massive retaliation
Strategic Defense Initiative (SDI)
Intermediate-Range Nuclear Forces
   (INF) Treaty
perestroika
glasnost

realist
political realism
scientific methods
reproducible comparisons
dependency theory
interdependence
neorealism
essentialists
postmodernism
neoliberal institutionalism

SOURCES

Alexandre, Laurien. "Genderizing International Studies: Revisioning Concepts and Curriculum." *International Studies Notes,* 14 (Winter 1989), 5–8.

Allison, Graham T. *Essence of Decision.* Boston: Little, Brown, 1971.

Allyn, Bruce J., James G. Blight, and David A. Welch. "Essence of Revision: Moscow, Havana, and the Cuban Missile Crisis." *International Security,* 14 (Winter 1989/90), 136–172.

Alperowitz, Gar. *Atomic Diplomacy.* New York: Random House, Vintage Books, 1965.

Ambrose, Stephen E. *Rise to Globalism.* 3rd ed. New York: Penguin Books, 1983.

Barnet, Richard J. *The Roots of War.* Baltimore: Penguin Books, 1971.

Blight, James G., Joseph S. Nye, Jr., and David A. Welch. "The Cuban Missile Crisis Revisited." *Foreign Affairs,* 66 (Fall 1987), 170–188.

Brubaker, Rogers. "International Migration: A Challenge for Humanity." *International Migration Review,* 25 (Winter 1991), 946–957.

Bueno de Mesquita, Bruce. *The War Trap.* New Haven, Conn.: Yale University Press, 1981.

Bueno de Mesquita, Bruce, and David Lalman. *War and Reason.* New Haven, Conn.: Yale University Press, 1992.

Calvocoressi, Peter. *World Politics Since 1945.* 6th ed. New York: Longman, 1991.

Central Intelligence Agency. *Chiefs of State and Cabinet Members of Foreign Governments.* Washington, D.C., 1996.

Cerf, Christopher, and Victor S. Navasky. *The Experts Speak.* New York: Pantheon Books, 1984.

Clad, James C. "Slowing the Wave." *Foreign Policy,* No. 95 (Summer 1994), pp. 139–150.

Diamond, Larry. "Is the Third Wave Over?" *Journal of Democracy,* 7 (July 1996), pp. 20–37.

Economist, June 1, 1991, p. 9.

Elshtain, Jean Bethke. *Women and War.* New York: Basic Books, 1987.

Enloe, Cynthia. *Bananas, Beaches, and Bases: Making Feminist Sense of Alternatives.* London: Pandora, 1989.

Etheredge, Lloyd S. *Can Governments Learn?* New York: Pergamon Press, 1985.

Fann, K. T., and Donald C. Hodges, eds. *Readings in U.S. Imperialism.* Boston: Sargent, 1971.

Farley, Miriam S. *United States Relations with Southeast Asia with Special Reference to Indochina.* New York: Institute of Pacific Relations, 1955.

Ferguson, Yale H., and Richard W. Mansbach. *The Elusive Quest: Theory and International Politics.* Columbia: University of South Carolina Press, 1988.

Fukuyama, Francis. "Against the New Pessimism." *Commentary,* February 1994, pp. 25–29.

Fukuyama, Francis. "The End of History?" *The National Interest,* No. 16 (Summer 1989), pp. 3–18.

George, Jim. *Discourses of Global Politics: A Critical (Re)Introduction to International Relations.* Boulder, Colo.: Lynne Rienner, 1994.

"The Global Migration." *Parade Magazine,* October 17, 1993, p. 19.

Gurr, Ted Robert. *Minorities at Risk: A Global View of Ethnopolitical Conflicts.* Washington, D.C.: United States Institute of Peace, 1993.

Gwartney-Gibbs, Patricia H., and Denise H. Lach. "Sex Differences in Nuclear War Attitudes." *Journal of Peace Research,* 28 (May 1991), 161–175.

Hammer, Ellen J. *The Struggle for Indochina.* Stanford, Calif.: Stanford University Press, 1954.

Horowitz, David. *The Free World Colossus.* New York: Wang & Hill, 1965.

"How to Help." *Economist,* June 1, 1991, pp. 9–10.

Howard, Michael. "The Springtime of Nations." *Foreign Affairs,* 69 (1989/90), 17–32.

Howe, Marvine. "Sex Discrimination Persists, According to a U.N. Study." *New York Times,* June 16, 1991, Section 1, p. 4.

Huntington, Samuel P. "Democracy's Third Wave." *Journal of Democracy,* 2 (Spring 1991a), 12–34.

Huntington, Samuel P. *The Third Wave.* Norman, Okla.: University of Oklahoma Press, 1991b.

Huntington, Samuel P. "The West: Unique, Not Universal." *Foreign Affairs,* 75 (November/December 1996), pp. 28–46.

Ikenberry, G. John. "The Myth of Post–Cold War Chaos." *Foreign Affairs,* 75 (May/June 1996), pp. 79–91.

Isaacs, Harold. "Independence for Vietnam?" In Marvin E. Gettleman, ed., *Vietnam.* New York: Fawcett, 1965.

Jacobson, Jodi L. "Gender Bias: Roadblock to Sustainable Development." *Worldwatch Paper No. 110.* Washington, D.C.: Worldwatch Institute, 1992.

Jacobson, Jodi L. "Women's Reproductive Health: The Silent Emergency." *Worldwatch Paper No. 102.* Washington, D.C.: Worldwatch Institute, 1991.

Kane, Hal. "Leaving Home." In Lester Brown et al., *State of the World 1995.* New York: Norton, 1995.

Keohane, Robert O. "Institutional Theory and the Realist Challenge After the Cold War." In David A. Baldwin, ed., *Neorealism and Neoliberalism: The Contemporary Debate.* New York: Columbia University Press, 1993.

Keohane, Robert O. "Theory of World Politics: Structural Realism and Beyond." In Ada Finifter, ed., *Political Science: The State of the Discipline.* Washington, D.C.: American Political Science Association, 1983.

Keohane, Robert O., and Joseph S. Nye, Jr., *Power and Interdependence.* Boston: Little, Brown, 1977.

Kissinger, Henry A. *White House Years.* Boston: Little, Brown, 1979.

Koenig, Louis W., ed. *The Truman Administration: Its Principles and Practice.* New York: New York University Press, 1956.

Kolko, Gabriel. *The Roots of American Foreign Policy.* Boston: Beacon Press, 1969.

Kolko, Gabriel, and Joyce Kolko. *The Limits of Power.* New York: Harper & Row, 1972.

Kriesberg, Louis, and Ross Klein. "Changes in Public Support for U.S. Military Spending." *Journal of Conflict Resolution,* 24 (March 1980), 79–111.

Lampe, John R. "Policy Forum: Bosnia—After the Troops Leave." *Washington Quarterly,* 19 (Summer 1996), 73–77.

Landay, Jonathan S. "Policy Forum: Bosnia—After the Troops Leave." *Washington Quarterly,* 19 (Summer 1996), 66–73.

Lewis, Paul. "Stoked by Ethnic Fighting, Refugee Numbers Grow." *New York Times,* November 10, 1993, Section A, pp. 1,7.

Los Angeles Times, December 17, 1989, Section Q, p. 1.

Lowenthal, Abraham F. *The Dominican Intervention.* Cambridge, Mass.: Harvard University Press, 1972.

Magdoff, Harry. *The Age of Imperialism.* New York: Monthly Review Press, 1969.

Manchester, William. *American Caesar.* Boston: Little, Brown, 1978.

Mansbach, Richard W., Yale H. Ferguson, and Donald E. Lampert. *The Web of World Politics.* Englewood Cliffs, N.J.: Prentice-Hall, 1976.

McColm, R. Bruce. "The Comparative Survey of Freedom: 1991." *Freedom Review,* 22, No. 1 (1991), 5–6, 12.

Morgenthau, Hans. *Politics Among Nations.* 4th ed. New York: Knopf, 1967.

Mutua, Makau wa. "African Renaissance." *New York Times,* May 11, 1991, Section 1, p. 13.

Nathan, James A. "The Missile Crisis: His Finest Hour Now." *World Politics,* 27 (January 1975), 256–281.

Nelan, Bruce W. "Europe Slams the Door." *Time,* July 19, 1993a, pp. 11, 38–40.

Nelan, Bruce W. "Not Quite So Welcome Anymore." *Time,* Special Issue, Fall 1993, pp. 10–15.

Passel, Jeffrey S., and Michael Fix. "Myths About Immigrants." *Foreign Policy,* No. 95 (Summer 1994), pp. 151–160.

Ray, James Lee. *Democracy and International Conflict.* Columbia, S.C.: University of South Carolina Press, 1995.

Remmer, Karen. "Democracy and Economic Crisis: The Latin American Experience." *World Politics,* 42 (April 1990), 315–335.

"Review of U.N. and U.S. Action to Restore Peace." *Department of State Bulletin,* 23 (July 10, 1950).

Russett, Bruce. *Grasping the Democratic Peace.* Princeton, N.J.: Princeton University Press, 1993.

Schlesinger, Jr., Arthur. "Origins of the Cold War." *Foreign Affairs,* 46 (October 1967), 22–51.

Small, Melvin, and J. David Singer. *Resort to Arms.* Beverly Hills, Calif.: Sage Publications, 1982.

Starr, Harvey. "Democratic Dominoes: Diffusion Approaches to the Spread of Democracy in the International System." *Journal of Conflict Resolution,* 35 (June 1991), 356–381.

Stern, Geoffrey. "Soviet Foreign Policy in Theory and Practice." In F. S. Northedge, ed., *The Foreign Policies of the Powers.* New York: Free Press, 1974.

Stoessinger, John G. *Why Nations Go to War.* 6th ed. New York: St. Martin's Press, 1993.

Stone, I. F. *The Hidden History of the Korean War.* New York: Monthly Review Press, 1952.

Sylvester, Christine. *Feminist Theory and International Relations in a Postmodern Era.* New York: Cambridge University Press, 1994.

Tickner, J. Ann. *Gender in International Relations.* New York: Columbia University Press, 1992.

United Nations, *Permanent Missions to the United Nations.* New York, 1996.

"UN Warns of Global Migration." Associated Press, circa July 7, 1993. Published in the *Tampa Tribune,* Nation/World, p. 6.

Waltz, Kenneth. *The Theory of International Politics.* New York: Random House, 1979.

Whiting, Allen. *China Crosses the Yalu.* New York: Macmillan, 1960.

Whitworth, Sandra. *Feminism and International Relations.* New York: St. Martin's Press, 1994.

PART II

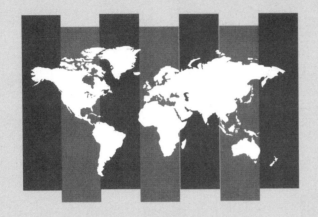

Inside States:
The Impact of
Individuals, Groups,
and Organizations

CHAPTER 3

The Public, Ethnicity, and Special Interests

Let us turn now from the overview of the history of global politics (and the study of global politics) to consider factors that influenced the course of that history and are likely to affect the future of the global political system. Chapters 1 and 2 concentrated on *what* has happened. History is not abandoned at this point, but the emphasis shifts to the question of *why* international political events, policies, and interactions turn out as they do. In this chapter, we begin analyzing the impact that people and groups inside states have on foreign policies and international relations. We focus first on ordinary citizens and on the effects of their opinions and activities on the foreign policies of states. Then we turn to an analysis of various kinds of subnational groups that are concerned with foreign policy issues or become more directly involved in international politics in their own right. Such groups are usually formed on the basis of a common economic interest or ethnic background, and there are signs that their influence is growing.

PUBLIC OPINION
AND INTERNATIONAL POLITICS

Most people in the United States do not know or care very much about international politics. That is the conclusion reached in a number of thoughtful essays and some empirical research on the subject (Almond, 1950; Almond and Verba, 1963; Scammon and Wattenberg, 1957, p. 299). Examples abound. "[I]t has been easy to portray the American public as one knowing little about major political issues and not eager to learn more" (Nincic, 1992, p. 27). Surveys show that in 1979 only about 34 percent of Americans knew which two countries were involved in the Strategic Arms Limitations Talks (SALT) (Russett, 1990,

p. 89). The war in Vietnam was one of the most intensely debated foreign policy issues in United States history. Fifty-eight thousand American soldiers lost their lives. The war generated more domestic unrest than the United States had seen since the Civil War. And yet in 1985, less than two-thirds of the American public knew that the United States had supported South Vietnam against North Vietnam in that war (Nincic, 1992, p. 28). A study by the National Geographic Society in 1988 reported that many Americans could not find the United States, much less England, Greece, Hungary, or Poland on a world map, and that fully half did not know that France, China, and India have nuclear weapons (Beck, 1988, p. 11).[1] In short, it is widely agreed that "the vast majority of citizens hold pictures of the world that are at best sketchy, blurred, and without detail, or at worst so impoverished as to beggar description" (Robinson, 1967, p. 1).

In any society, individuals are most likely to be concerned about problems that affect them directly and over which they feel they have some control. Problems on the scale of international politics often seem to fail on both counts. Wars, economic crises, and coups in one part of the world can have a dramatic impact on the lives of individuals in other parts of the world. The disintegration of the Soviet Union, for example, can lead to reductions in the defense budget and the closing of military bases all over the country. But the connection between events in certain countries and their impact on individuals in other countries is seldom so clear. And even if the effect of international events is great, individuals in the countries affected do not have enough knowledge to be able to see the link between such events and their local impact. Add to this the fact that even when the link is clear, most individuals feel they have no control over the event or its consequences, and it is not hard to see why most people, even in countries whose citizens are on average relatively wealthy and highly educated, do not know or care very much about international politics. For example, Thomas Risse-Kappen (1991, p. 481) concludes that in France, Germany, and Japan as well as in the United States, only about "20–30 percent of the public indicate serious concern about foreign affairs."[2] This relatively small number of people who pay attention to and are relatively knowledgeable about foreign policy issues and international politics is sometimes referred to as the **attentive public.**

Since only a rather small proportion of the public know or care very much about most foreign policy issues, it would be logical to conclude

---

[1] National Public Radio reported in July of 1993 that only about 50 percent of Americans had ever heard about NAFTA, the North American Free Trade Agreement.

[2] In support of this assertion Risse-Kappen cites Smith (1985) and Hastings and Hastings (1982–1983, 1983–1984). See also Gabriel Almond and Sidney Verba (1963).

that most people rarely do very much to let their opinions be known or attempt to persuade others to accept their point of view. That logical conclusion is supported by concrete evidence. In the United States, for example, the Vietnam War provoked an unusual amount of interest for a foreign policy issue. Yet a survey of a representative sample of Americans in 1967 found that although most people expressed a concern about the war, most had done nothing to reflect their concern. Only 13 percent reported that they had made any attempt at all to persuade others to change their views on the war. Only 3 percent had bothered to write letters to newspapers or political officials, and only 1 percent had taken part in marches or demonstrations.[3]

The next logical conclusion would be that public opinion does not have much impact on foreign policy. Logic and some evidence seem to support each other in this regard, but the difficulty in assessing the impact of public opinion should be stressed. Broadly speaking, what makers of foreign policy do often seems correlated with what the public prefers, in dictatorships as well as democracies. Diplomats and other foreign policy officials are fond of saying that "public opinion demanded" a concession or a hardline stand with respect to a foreign policy issue. But does the public influence decisions, or do government officials manipulate public opinion to support their point of view and then announce decisions they had settled on in advance? "Can anyone thoroughly separate the chicken from the egg? . . . Clearly public opinion and policymaking interact, sometimes with one leading and sometimes the other. . . ." (Russett, 1990, p. 109).

It is probably safe to say that in general public opinion has a greater impact in democratic states than in autocracies. It would be a mistake, however, to conclude that public opinion can be ignored entirely in autocratic states. Public opinion on the war in Afghanistan, for example, apparently affected Soviet foreign policy with respect to that war (and may ultimately even have played a role in bringing down the whole regime.) In all states, foreign policymakers must play a **two-level game,** minimizing adverse consequences of some international developments but taking advantage of opportunities that other such events may bring, while at the same time appealing to the general public (and influential domestic interest groups), and on occasion appeasing their domestic political antagonists. "Neither of these two games can be ignored by central decision-makers, so long as their countries remain interdependent, yet sovereign" (Putnam, 1988, p. 434).

Probably a majority of scholars, though, believe that elites (people in leadership positions within political, economic, or military organiza-

---

[3] Sidney Verba and Richard A. Brody, 1970, pp. 325–332; cited in K. J. Holsti, 1995, p. 261.

tions) influence the public more, especially with regard to foreign policy issues, than vice versa, and that in any case, elites that deal with foreign policy issues usually do not feel very constrained by public opinion. Some analysts go so far as to claim that "no major foreign policy decision in the United States has ever been made in response to spontaneous public demand" (Barnet, 1971, p. 243). In many countries, even democratic ones, "there are many cases in which crucial foreign policy decisions have been taken in the absence of mass public consensus" (Risse-Kappen, 1991, p. 481).[4]

This claim might seem to contradict the experience of many readers, who have noticed how closely politicians watch public opinion polls. Even presidents seem to have reacted to public opinion concerning foreign policy issues rather dramatically in recent times. President Johnson was apparently persuaded not to seek reelection in 1968 by public opposition to his Vietnam War policy. President Carter, faced with rapidly declining popularity as the 1980 election drew near, approved an attempt to rescue the U.S. hostages in Iran, which failed miserably. In 1993, in an apparent response to public concern about increasing immigration, President Clinton continued energetic steps to prevent Haitian refugees from escaping from their homeland into the United States, even though he had condemned his predecessor, George Bush, for adopting such a policy.

But one can get an exaggerated impression of the impact of public opinion on foreign policy by concentrating on such events. President Johnson, for example, might have decided not to run for reelection in 1968 because of public opinion against his war policy, but it is less clear that public opinion changed that policy. The war continued (for U.S. troops) for five more years. President Franklin Roosevelt, in the years before the Second World War, was faced with overwhelmingly isolationist attitudes among the general public. Even so, he worked quietly behind the scenes to prepare the United States for war and never swayed from his conviction that the United States would have to resist actively the aggressive policies of Germany and Japan at some point. President Johnson made a concession to public opinion by campaigning as a "dove" in favor of peace in the election of 1964, but we now know that he planned to escalate the Vietnam War as soon as the election was over. President Carter knew that public opinion polls showed that turning over the Panama Canal to Panama was a tremendously unpopular idea. He negotiated the treaty anyway, apparently figuring that an educa-

---

[4] Risse-Kappan (1991, p. 481) goes on to cite West German decisions to rearm and join NATO in the early 1950s and French decisions to build an independent nuclear force in the 1950s and leave NATO's military institutions in the mid-1960s.

President Jimmy Carter is the focus of Iranian demonstrators' wrath during the hostage crisis of 1979, an event that damaged his bid for re-election in 1980. SOURCE: AP/Wide World Photos.

tional campaign would persuade most of the public (and the U.S. Senate) to support its ratification. He was right.

This impression that decision makers tend to treat public opinion as a problem to be dealt with rather than a guide to policy has been confirmed in recent research based on interviews with officials in the National Security Council and the State Department in the United States. The results of the interviews showed quite clearly that "when public opposition does emerge, the reaction of most officials is . . . not to change the policy in question, but to try to 'educate' the public, thereby bringing public opinion in line with the policy" (Powlick, 1991, p. 636).

There are some signs, in addition to the ignorance displayed by the public in surveys about foreign policy issues, that this attitude concerning public opinion on foreign policy matters is justified. In other words, it is possible that if public opinion does have an impact on policy, that impact often is not beneficial. One of the best-known relationships between public opinion and foreign policy in the United States involves the **rally-round-the-flag effect,** which increases the president's popularity whenever he elects to use force with respect to some foreign policy issue (Mueller, 1973). In fact, some evidence indicates that U.S. presidents are aware of this phenomenon and initiate forceful policies in order to reap domestic political benefits. U.S. presidents may be particularly likely to use force in response to foreign policy crises if, for example, the economy or their own popularity is declining (James and Oneal, 1991, p. 328).

Fortunately for those of us who would like to believe that democracy has a mostly beneficial impact on foreign policy, the evidence that democratic pressures make national leaders more bellicose does not all point in the same direction. In the first place, the rally-round-the-flag effect is "far from automatic . . . . One can easily identify international crises . . . in which no significant positive rally took place" (Brody, 1991, p. 77). One analysis of 102 cases in the United States when the public might have been expected to rally around the president reveals that in fact the average change in the president's approval rating after those cases was 0 percent (Lian and Oneal, 1993, p. 277).[5] In addition, it turns out that democratic states over the last two hundred years "have tended to get into relatively more wars early in the election cycle and fewer wars late in the cycle." In other words, when the democratic pressure

---

[5] This is not the only evidence casting doubt on the "rally-round-the-flag effect." Having reviewed additional evidence about the unreliability of this effect, Patrick James and John Oneal (1991, p. 328) argue that "if presidents do employ America's armed forces to arrest declining popularity or influence elections, a program of education for U.S. leaders seems badly needed, because the rally effect is neither certain nor strong."

of elections is most intense, democratic states are less likely to get involved in international wars (Gaubatz, 1991, p. 212).

Democratic governments may also be better able than undemocratic states to signal their resolve to adversaries in international negotiations, especially over crises. Potentially, democratic states stand to suffer greater **"audience costs"** following unsuccessful international policies or setbacks. That is, democratic governments can lose support, and even lose political power altogether, in the wake of unpopular foreign policy setbacks. Knowing that democratic states face this risk, their opponents may be more likely to find their bargaining positions credible, and therefore to believe that they (the democratic states) will not back away from them under pressure. Thus, these greater audience costs may help democratic states stay out of crisis situations that escalate all the way to war (Fearon, 1994; Eyerman and Hart, 1996).

In fact, paradoxically, the greater vulnerability of democratic governments to audience costs, to retaliation from and negative evaluations by public opinion, may increase generally the ability of democratic governments to bargain or negotiate effectively in international settings. In playing the two-level game referred to earlier, "the stronger a state is in terms of autonomy from domestic pressures, the weaker its relative bargaining position internationally. For example, diplomats representing an entrenched dictatorship are less able than representatives of a democracy to claim credibly that domestic pressures preclude some disadvantageous deal" (Putnam, 1988, p. 449). In other words, negotiators from democratic states can say to their counterparts from more autocratic regimes, "I would like to be able to accept the deal you propose, but my hands are tied; if we accept that deal, we are likely to lose the next election." Having their "hands tied" in this manner can give them bargaining leverage unavailable to negotiators representing governments less vulnerable to the influence of public opinion.

Is Public Opinion Moody or Wise?

A common opinion among specialists in the field is that public opinion on foreign policy is subject to wildly fluctuating moods and cannot be counted on for consistent support of foreign policy commitments (Almond, 1950; Holsti, 1992, p. 439). But the available evidence does not consistently support such a negative view of public opinions regarding foreign policy. There certainly are fluctuations in public opinion about foreign policy issues, but they are not "unpredictable or irrational shifts." Opinion shifts from 1935 to 1985 regarding issues such as isolationism, the Cold War, the Korean War, the United Nations, Vietnam, and détente, for example, were arguably "understandable in terms of changing circumstances and changing information. Moreover, . . .

most of them [were] reasonable, or sensible, in that they reflect in a logical fashion the impact of new information" (Shapiro and Page, 1988, pp. 243–244.)[6]

Public opinion seems to have reacted in interesting and arguably "rational" ways to the policies of U.S. presidents vis-à-vis the Soviet Union during the Carter and Reagan administrations. The public tended to express, at any given moment, concern for whichever kind of policy it felt was in danger of being slighted. President Carter, perceived as dovish, received greater support in public opinion polls when he followed assertive policies with respect to the Soviet Union. President Reagan, on the other hand, received the greatest support for his policies vis-à-vis the Soviets when, contrary to perceptions that he was "hawkish," or aggressive, he was more conciliatory. This is arguably rationality, even wisdom on a rather high level, exerting a moderating impact on behavior toward the principle antagonist of the United States (Nincic, 1988).

In a similar vein, the public in the United States seems capable of differentiating between uses of force by the United States for different kinds of purposes in a discriminating way. In general, public opinion responds more favorably to force when it is used to resist aggression than when it is applied to impose internal political change on another state. Improvements in the public approval ratings of presidents "following military action to impose foreign policy restraint [that is, to resist aggression] are nearly 4 percent greater . . . than when internal political change is the principal objective" (Oneal, Lian, and Joyner, 1996, p. 273; see also Jentleson, 1992).

Ignorant Individuals and a Wise Public?

We have, then, a puzzling paradox. When questioned individually, the public seems ignorant about foreign policy and international politics. But when the positions taken by the public are examined in the aggregate, opinions as well as attitude changes seem rational. How is it possible that people who individually have such inadequate knowledge about foreign policy issues can as a group take positions and behave in an apparently informed manner with respect to those issues?

Classical economic theories are based on assumptions that consumers and business firms are rational, and that they react to market incentives in an informed and logical fashion. Studies of consumers and firms, though, consistently find that these assumptions are unrealistic,

---

[6] Shapiro and Page (1988, p. 244) conclude that they "feel justified in speaking of a 'rational' public."

that individual consumers are usually not very well informed, and that business firms process information and make decisions in a manner far different from the way classical economic assumptions predict (March and Simon, 1958). Yet even though the average consumer is not very well informed or energetic when it comes to purchases, and despite the fact that individual firms do not make decisions in a very rational way, in the aggregate consumers and firms behave as if they were quite well informed and rational. That is, markets usually operate in a fairly efficient manner, as they should according to theories based on assumptions about individual consumers and firms. Market economies, for example, are not typically plagued either by massive surpluses caused by firms overproducing unwanted goods or by serious shortages of desirable goods. The firms produce goods and services in amounts and kinds, for the most part, that consumers purchase in ways that reward efficient firms and penalize inefficient ones.

Similarly, perhaps individual citizens do not know very much (or care very much) about foreign policy issues. So, on the surface they seem badly situated to make intelligent choices regarding those issues. Still, it is possible that collectively, when they respond to public opinion polls or vote, for example, they behave as if they were quite well informed and logical. That is, the positions they take and support are generally reasonable.[7]

There are reasons to hope that public opinion in most countries of the world is becoming better informed, and perhaps more influential, in relation to foreign policies. "The expansion of analytic skills is . . . worldwide in scope. Not only for citizens in democratic and industrialized societies, but also for Afghan tribesmen and Argentine gauchos, for peasants in India and protesters in Chile, for guerrillas in Peru and students in the Philippines, for blacks in South Africa and Palestinians in Israel, the interdependence of global life and the consequences of collective actions are daily experiences" (Rosenau, 1990, p. 373). One reason for this change is that higher educational levels are increasing almost everywhere. "Enrollments in higher education have been increasing since 1970 in every part of the world. . . . The same has been true since 1960 in primary and secondary education as well, and for both males and females" (Rosenau, 1990, p. 354). Another reason has to do with the worldwide spread of television. Even in such desperately poor countries as India and China, over half of the population now has access to television. "Access to television has become sufficiently global in

---

[7] "Many of the familiar deficiencies of individuals' opinions—weak information bases, lack of structure, instability over time, and the like . . . are overcome in the aggregation process, so that collective opinion is highly stable, well structured, and responsive to the best available information" (Shapiro and Page, 1988, p. 213).

scope that it must be regarded as a change of [fundamental] proportions" (Rosenau, 1990, p. 339, 343).

This global information explosion is almost certainly buttressed in its impact on public opinion by the fact that people in every country tend to take their cues from "opinion leaders," the small portion of the public that is well informed about foreign affairs, in part because of that explosion (Hughes, 1978, pp. 23–24). Jane Doe may not know much about the latest international trade agreement, but she knows that her friend Mary Somebody does, and Jane will form her opinion about it by consulting with Mary, perhaps without actually learning very much about the issue except for Mary's opinion about it. Multiplied many times over, this process may help resolve the paradox between ill-informed individuals and an apparently wise general public. Interesting evidence indicating that such a process takes place suggests that the "rally-round-the-flag" effect in the United States applies only when opinion leaders do not oppose the president over a given crisis. "Opposition leaders in some crisis situations lose their incentive to criticize presidential performance, and when this happens, the public rallies. In aggregate terms, a lack of critical opinion leadership can outweigh even relatively unambiguous evidence of policy failure and hence pave the way for positive evaluations of presidential performance" (Brody, 1991, p. 77).

Even though the general public in most countries of the world does seem to be moving in the direction of becoming better informed about foreign policy issues, there are apparently important differences, even among democratic states, in the ability of public opinion to have an impact on foreign policy. Variations in the domestic political structures of states, even if they are all "democratic," may account for these differences. The United States, France, Japan, and Germany, for example, all responded quite differently to the dramatic changes in Soviet foreign (and domestic) policies that occurred during the 1980s. "The degree to which political institutions are centralized and the degree to which the state dominates the policy networks seem to be the determining factors" (Risse-Kappen, 1991, p. 511). The United States appears to have the least centralized political institutions; the impact of public opinion there is correspondingly more important. In France, the domestic political structure seems to have the greatest dampening impact on the influence of public opinion on foreign policies. In Germany and Japan, the influence of public opinion on foreign policies falls somewhere in between the extremes of the United States and France (Risse-Kappen, 1991; see also Richard Eichenberg, 1989).

In spite of these apparent cross-national differences in the impact of public opinion on foreign policies and international politics, the seeming ability of the public in most democratic states generally to arrive at prudent conclusions on foreign policy issues can help resolve a dilemma concerning a democratic theory of the making of foreign policy. "Open covenants openly arrived at" was one of President Woodrow Wilson's principles, adopted in the belief that secret deals between professional diplomats and makers of foreign policy were a part of traditional international politics that led to disasters such as the First World War. The trouble with that idea, according to anti-Wilsonians, is that diplomats are unable to exercise their talents for compromise if the public is a participant in the negotiating process. When the public looks on, diplomats are subject to political pressures that require them to take extreme positions from which it becomes virtually impossible to retreat as negotiations continue. If the uninformed and moody public is kept out of the process, the wisdom and talents of professional diplomats can be given full play, and the result will be a better foreign policy and decreased probability of violent conflict.

But is it true that foreign policy is best left in the hands of experts? It is certainly possible to argue to the contrary, and to claim that the experts who have had a largely free hand in making foreign policy as long as the modern state system has been in existence have made their share of mistakes. Even so, no matter how fervently one believes in democracy, it is difficult to argue that the public ought to have an important input into foreign policy decisions, in light of the evidence that most citizens seem to know so little about foreign policy issues. It is less difficult, perhaps, if one keeps in mind the distinction between the knowledge that separate individuals may have about issues and the possible (if paradoxical) validity of the positions to which the public in the aggregate will adhere. The public's positions on issues may be formed as if individuals are well informed, even though in fact they are not, in part because of the effect of the relatively well-informed opinion makers (that is, the attentive public) on the attitudes of average citizens.

SUBNATIONAL GROUPS
AND INTERNATIONAL POLITICS

Perhaps more important than the influence of public opinion in general is that wielded everywhere by interest groups in particular as they exert a concentrated effort to have an impact on foreign policy. Are their efforts successful? What are generally the most powerful interest groups in a society? How can one tell?

Political scientists have had only limited success in answering such questions for either democratic societies or authoritarian ones. In the

1950s, many U.S. political scientists were enthusiastic about group theory and tried to develop ideas about how the various groups in a democratic society exert influence and which groups are most successful (Truman, 1951). But group theory met with limited success (Garson, 1974, p. 1505). One major reason for this lack of success involves the nature of the influence process and the concept of influence.

Certainly there are interest groups in every society that attempt to influence foreign policy, and many of their efforts are visible. Interest groups pay for advertisements in the media, support their lobbying personnel, and contribute to the campaigns of friendly politicians. Other activities of interest groups are less visible. Lobbyists talk to members of Congress at private lunches, secretly threaten to withdraw financial support from uncooperative senators, offer financial support for subversive CIA activities against unfriendly foreign governments, and so on. The impact they have is difficult to determine.

But it is almost as difficult to determine the effectiveness of the more open and visible activities of interest groups. If *influence* means the ability to affect behavior, how does one tell if an interest group is influential? The fact that a group favors a policy that is later adopted is insufficient evidence of the impact of its efforts. The policy might have been adopted anyway. Or the political decision makers may have persuaded the lobbying groups to favor the adopted policy, not vice versa. Finally, some powerful third group may have influenced both the lobbying group in question and the political decision makers to favor a given policy. Influence is difficult to trace. It is so difficult, in fact, that some political scientists have suggested that the concept is too vaguely defined to be useful and that the temptation to rely on it so heavily should be resisted (March, 1966, pp. 68–70).

Unfortunately, perhaps, the theoretical development that would persuade political scientists to do so has not occurred, and the question of which groups in a society are most influential still attracts great interest. The answer by group theorists of the 1950s emphasized the pluralistic nature of the U.S. political system. They seemed satisfied that the outcome of pressure group competition in the system was beneficial. The happy conclusion was that the stronger organized groups would be prevented from taking undue advantage of their strength because of overlapping memberships; that is, some or most of the members of strong groups would also belong to weaker groups and thus would be inclined to protect them. The group theorists of the 1950s were not worried about the fate of unorganized interests, arguing that they constituted "potential interest groups" that could mobilize and become actual organized groups if their interests were seriously threatened (Truman, 1951, pp. 34–35).

Critics of such an optimistic conclusion pointed out that in fact the pressure-group system in the United States and elsewhere operates with an upper-class bias, since wealthy, educated people are more likely to participate in any political process and pressure groups, for example, heavily overrepresent business interests (Schattschneider, 1960, pp. 31–32). A more general criticism, which can be applied to competing groups in either democratic or authoritarian societies, holds that smaller special interest groups enjoy certain crucial advantages. Large groups in pursuit of a goal, such as influencing foreign policy, must deal with the serious problem that no individual member has a logical reason for contributing to the group effort. Because the group is large, the absence of one individual's effort is not likely to make much difference. And large groups are often not in a position to deny the benefit of their accomplishments to any of their members, even those who have not contributed to the group's success. If all members are likely to benefit from a large group's success no matter how little they contribute to that success, and if each individual effort is not likely to make much difference one way or the other to the probability of success, there is not much incentive for members of such groups to contribute. Members of small groups are in a very different situation. Each one represents a significant portion of the whole, and the absence of his or her efforts may have a significant effect on the probability of the group's success. Because the group is small, if one member of the group refuses to contribute to the group effort, he or she is easily identifiable and may be subject to penalties imposed by the rest of the group (Olson, 1968, pp. 33–36).[8]

Consider a concrete example. Imagine that the U.S. government is about to decide whether to raise the tariff on the import of foreign steel. Foreign steel manufacturers have the benefit of cheaper labor, and they can produce steel for less and offer it for a lower price than U.S. manufacturers can afford to do. Naturally, U.S. steel manufacturers do not want this kind of competition, and they lobby for an increase in tariffs on foreign steel. U.S. consumers, on the other hand, like lower-

---

[8] Readers familiar with these arguments by Mancur Olson will recall that they apply, strictly speaking, only to groups in pursuit of public goods. A public good is any good that, if consumed by one person in a group, cannot be feasibly withheld from others in the group. In the discussion in the following paragraphs regarding tariffs, steel is not a public good as ordinarily defined, but I believe that the lower price of steel and lower tariff barriers are public goods. If the tariff is lowered, for example, the benefit cannot be feasibly withheld from any member of the group of steel consumers. In short, Olson's arguments apply, perhaps with less formal precision, to groups in pursuit of a wide variety of goods not ordinarily thought of as public.

priced steel products (such as automobiles), and they form a potential group opposed to the increase in tariffs on foreign steel. Which group is more likely to influence the government's decision?

Every consumer of steel in the country has an interest in keeping the price of steel low, which might lead one to conclude that consumers will be able to defeat the much smaller number of steel producers. But of course no single steel consumer can contribute very much to the group effort. Whether or not Congress defeats tariff increases or the president decides against higher tariffs on foreign steel is going to depend very little on the activities of one consumer. Every consumer knows this and cannot be blamed for concluding that writing a letter to his or her member of Congress or contributing to a consumers' advocate group that is lobbying against higher tariffs really is not going to make much difference one way or the other. The clincher is that whether or not a particular steel consumer contributes to the effort to defeat higher tariffs, he or she will benefit if the effort is successful. Steel consumers who do contribute to a successful effort to keep the tariff low cannot induce the **free riders** to help in that effort because they cannot use the incentive of telling them, "We'll only let you take advantage of lower prices if you join us." In contrast, the steel manufacturers are few in number and can see that their actions may indeed make a difference to the outcome of the struggle. Probably more important, the steel producers and their associated labor unions will be vitally concerned with the tariff on foreign steel, whereas the vast majority of steel consumers will be only vaguely aware, or totally unaware, of it.

It can be argued that in any free-market system where **"distributional coalitions"** such as the steel firms and the labor unions in this example are allowed to operate in an untrammeled fashion long enough, they will win these battles so often that they will cause slow growth and stagnation for the entire economy (Olson, 1982). Special-interest groups, though, do not always win.

In fact, it is perhaps surprising how often they lose. In the United States, such losses can be attributed partly to the fact that "Congress [gave] up the authority to set individual tariff rates in 1934 when it delegated to the executive the authority to negotiate reciprocal tariff reduction" (Lenway 1985, p. 34).[9] And historically, the U.S. president is

---

[9] "The passage of the Reciprocal Trade Act in 1934 marked a turning point in American foreign-trade policy. For the first time, the leading role in tariff-setting passed from Congress to the Executive" (Bauer, Pool, and Dexter, 1968, p. 11). But more recently "Congress has been actively reinserting itself into the process of making trade policy (notably in the 1988 Trade Act) . . ." (Coneybeare, 1991, p. 81).

the prime advocate of free trade in the U.S. political process. "The group with the greatest interest in opposing increased trade protection consists of all consumers" (Lenway, 1985, p. 26). So in effect, the president represents that group and discourages Congress from engaging in rampant logrolling, in which each member of Congress would trade his or her vote in support of a tariff protecting industries in other congressional districts in return for votes from other members of Congress in favor of interests in his or her district. Finally, protectionism is held at bay in the U.S. political system by bad memories of what happened when the Smoot-Hawley Act, implementing record high tariffs, was passed in 1930. There is little doubt that the predominant impression among Americans familiar with the history of that era is that the effects of the Smoot-Hawley Act were disastrous and that the Second World War might even have been caused to an important extent by the subsequent economic dislocations in Europe caused by high tariffs in the United States.

Questions and dilemmas raised by international trade issues are at least as much moral and ethical as economic. Is it fair for the U.S. government, in effect, to require millions of American citizens to pay more for certain products in order to save the jobs of a few thousand of their fellow citizens? Philosophical speculation on such questions understandably fails to elicit much sympathy from automobile workers in Detroit or steelworkers in Pittsburgh who have lost jobs to foreign competition.[10] And even though protectionist measures might take from the relatively poor (the workers in developing countries) and give to the relatively wealthy (the workers and managers in uncompetitive U.S. industries), is it ethical for U.S. government officials to allow such considerations to sway their judgment? They may feel personally that it is wrong to penalize poor workers in Third World countries for the sake of saving jobs in the United States. But government officials are not acting in a personal capacity; they are acting as agents of the people who elected them. In that role, they are responsible primarily for the welfare of their own constituents. (If they are concerned about the welfare of Third World workers, they could make personal sacrifices on their behalf on their own time.) They might rationalize antiprotectionist steps as being in the interests of large numbers of U.S. consumers. But is it really asking too much of consumers to pay, say, $5 or $10 more a year for the shoes they buy in order to save the jobs of U.S. workers, who would otherwise face the major disruption and tragedy of long-term

---

[10] I admit that my skepticism about protectionist measures would evaporate in the face of a flood of high-quality, inexpensive, imported college professors.

unemployment? These issues are discussed further in Chapter 7, and related questions regarding the launching of the North American Free Trade Area (NAFTA) are explored in Chapter 10.

THE MILITARY-INDUSTRIAL COMPLEX

One pressure group in a position to exert a significant influence on foreign policy in many countries is the group involved in producing and using a nation's military hardware. The **military-industrial complex** achieved particular notoriety in the United States during the Vietnam War, although the term itself was introduced into the U.S. political lexicon several years earlier by President Eisenhower. And the idea (as opposed to the phrase) that munitions makers successfully plot to bring about large wars so that they can make a huge profit selling arms to the war makers goes back much further, both in the United States and elsewhere. In 1934, some sixteen years after the First World War ended, there was a flurry of interest in the United States in the substantial profits made by weapons manufacturers and banks through sales to the Allies in that war. For months a Senate committee, headed by Gerald P. Nye of North Dakota, held widely publicized hearings marked by revelations of spectacular profits, and it seems clear that many Americans were convinced by the revelations that they had been maneuvered into the First World War for the sake of corporate profits. In Europe, the famous Krupp family has been held accountable for the slaughter of generations of soldiers in a series of European wars (Manchester, 1968).

The accusations made against the U.S. military-industrial complex during the Vietnam War were not restricted to assertions that it had plotted to bring about the war. Rather, the organization and structure of the U.S. military and its relationship to industries that supply weapons were probed for inherent biases in favor of larger defense budgets. Purchases by the military, for example, are often arranged by generals on the one hand and retired generals working for weapons manufacturers on the other. Such arrangements are especially cozy from the viewpoint of the military-industrial complex, because the cost of any deals that are made, as well as cost overruns that may occur if the weapons turn out to be more expensive than originally estimated, are passed on to U.S. taxpayers. Taxpayers are unlikely to complain, though, because many of them benefit from a large defense budget; for example, when large defense contracts are awarded to industries in their districts or when military bases are established near their places of business. Members of Congress in districts blessed with such defense budget largesse are naturally reluctant to trim the budget. Finally, universities that receive large research contracts out of the budget are another part of the complex that pushes for increasingly large defense budgets.[11]

But to say that military-industrial interests play an important role in foreign policy formation is different from saying that they dominate the process. By 1979, the defense budget in the United States was ten times larger than it had been in 1949; but welfare spending in 1979 was twenty-five times that for the year 1949 (Johnson, 1983, p. 639). A significantly larger portion of the budget was spent on social programs even after the Reagan administration made a determined effort to increase the proportion assigned to the Defense Department. And even though Reagan's efforts to increase defense budgets were successful, on average the Pentagon's share of the budget was lower as a percentage of the GNP during his years in office than it was during the Kennedy and Johnson years or during the Nixon and Ford years (Cushman, 1988, p. 1).[12]

The end of the Cold War has provided an interesting challenge to the military-industrial complex in the United States, as well as an intriguing opportunity to evaluate its strength and influence. The demise of the Soviet Union has denied the U.S. military-industrial complex its primary rationale for large defense budgets. The strongest version of the theory stressing the impact of the military-industrial complex would suggest that the Soviet Union's disappearance should make no substantial difference in the ability of those interests to generate continuing large increases in defense budgets. But the data on defense budgets shown in Figures 3.1 and 3.2 do not support such a theory. Whether we focus on American defense budgets in terms of constant dollars or as a proportion of the federal budget, we see that the end of the Cold War (roughly around 1989) appears to have had a definite impact on military expenditures in the United States. One can argue, in the light of such data, that the complex has been able to slow down the erosion in defense budgets more than a purely rational response to the disappearance of the Soviet Union would require. And it is certainly true that even quite liberal members of the U.S. Congress, who were traditionally more skeptical of defense expenditures during the Cold War, have objected to the shutting down of military bases in *their* districts. In addition,

---

[11]This powerful coalition of the armed forces, Congress, and influential groups in the private sector, particularly private industry, is often referred to as the "iron triangle." See Adams (1988, pp. 70–78).

[12] Admittedly, the Vietnam War accounts to some extent for the lower proportion of the GNP devoted to defense in the Reagan years; but even some peacetime budgets during the Eisenhower and Kennedy administrations (1955 and 1962, for example) were proportionately higher than the Reagan budgets.

Figure 3.1 U.S. Defense Budget, 1979–1999

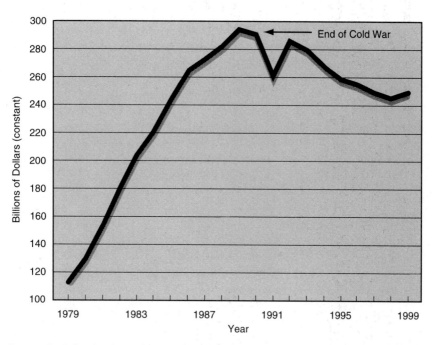

SOURCE: Data for this figure from *Historical Tables: Budget of the United States Government* (Washington, D.C.: Office of Management and Budget, 1996). Figures for 1996 to 1999 are estimates.

debates over military base closings have revealed that many in Congress are interested in preserving defense expenditures to preserve jobs, even if the expenditures are not necessary for national security. But in the absence of a threat from the Soviet Union, the military-industrial complex in the United States has proved unable to generate support for continually *increasing* defense budgets. This decline in post–Cold War defense budgets is consistent with a systematic analysis of military spending in the United States during the Cold War, which reported that "the greatest influence on change in U.S. military spending is change in Soviet military spending" (Hartley and Russett, 1992, p. 910).

The second-tier major powers (Russia, China, Great Britain, France, and so on) also have military-industrial establishments that exert influence on the foreign policies of their respective countries. The military in Russia has been humiliated by many developments in recent years, including its inability to quell the rebellion in Chechnya. There is some danger that elements in the military, and their supporters, will produce a leader in the coming years bent on restoring the glory of Russia's Cold

Figure 3.2   U.S. Defense Budget, 1979–1999 as a Proportion of Federal Budget

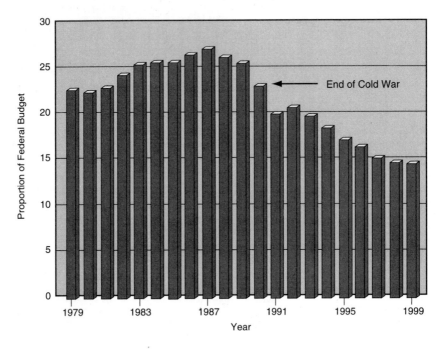

SOURCE: Data for this figure from *Historical Tables: Budget of the United States Government* (Washington, D.C.: Office of Management and Budget, 1996). Figures for 1996 to 1999 are estimates.

War years (not to mention some of the budget it shared with the industrial establishment). The military in China also seems intent on increasing its strength and, consequently, Chinese influence in the world.

It will be interesting, also, to see what role the military establishments will play in the policies of newly emergent Germany and Japan in the coming years. The memories of the Second World War in those countries cause many German and Japanese citizens to be suspicious about allowing their military forces to play any important role in peace-keeping ventures sponsored by the United Nations, for example.

In developing countries, the military-industrial complex loses most of its industrial flavor because these nations are less industrialized and because their armies, navies, and air forces are not supplied by domestic firms. Rather, they get most of their weapons and equipment from one or more of the major powers (Brazil, though, and recently South Africa are two of the world's more important exporters of military weaponry). This dependency on imports weakens the symbiotic ties between the military and industrial elements in most developing countries.

It obviously does not, however, weaken the influence of the military on the foreign policies of less developed or newly industrializing countries. States that fit into these categories differ greatly, and making generalizations about them is dangerous. But the prevalence of military influence and military governments in much of the developing world, at least until the recent global wave of democratization, has been clear. Even in the newly democratic governments in some developing countries, the military has often seemed to be in charge, exerting a controlling influence behind a facade of democracy (in Guatemala and the Philippines, for example). And the military actively resists or subverts democratizing impulses in places like Peru and Nigeria. The military establishments of a great number of developing countries have a crucial impact not only on foreign policy but on all policy.

Circumstances that foster the influence of the military in developing countries can be roughly divided into those involving weaknesses in the domestic structures of the respective societies and those involving penetration from outside. Most countries in Latin America, Africa, and Asia do not have a strong tradition of constitutional rule. There are no accepted procedures for seeking and assuming positions of political control. As a result, the various social groups interested in gaining positions of political power use techniques of confrontation rather than formal competition based on rules.

> Each group employs means that reflect its peculiar nature and capabilities. Wealthy people bribe; students riot; workers strike; mobs demonstrate; and the military coup. . . . The techniques of military intervention are simply more dramatic and effective than others because, as Hobbes put it, "When nothing else is turned up, clubs are trumps" (Huntington, 1968, p. 196).

Even in an international political vacuum, it seems likely that the frequency of military coups and governments dominated by the military in developing countries would be high. But these countries do not exist in a vacuum, and the international political system provides several incentives and reinforcements for military elements to assume political power. The United States, for example, has historically provided a steady supply of weaponry to a variety of military dictatorships. Great Britain and France join in the competition to make sophisticated military hardware available to developing countries. The Soviet Union was quite willing during the Cold War to supply military governments having even a vague anti-American or radical hue with great quantities of military equipment. Now Russia, desperate for "hard currency," is anxious to sell weapons to a wide variety of clients in exchange for dollars to purchase desperately needed imports. One result of the easy availability of such military equipment during the Cold War was that armies, navies, and air forces of virtually every country in the developing world were aware that they could stage a coup and be certain of substantial support from at least one major power. They knew they would be able to obtain, probably on easy credit terms, enough equipment to intimidate the most fervent radical or reactionary domestic political opponents.

But such support is no longer guaranteed in the post–Cold War world, as the leaders of a quasi-coup in Guatemala in 1993 discovered when the civilian who was the ostensible leader of the coup was forced to step down in the face of international pressure (*United States Institute of Peace Journal*, 1993). One analyst has pointed out that "when President Jorge Serrano of Guatemala suspended constitutional rule in 1993, the OAS . . . condemn[ed] the action . . . and raise[d] the specter of economic and political sanctions. In the face of that threat, Serrano resigned and constitutional order was restored" (Talbott, 1996, p. 53.) Another observer argues that in Brazil "over time, democratically elected politicians have successfully contested the power of the military over a broad range of issues and narrowed its sphere of influence" (Hunter, 1995, p. 427).[13] In contrast, the government of Saddam Hussein in Iraq is an extreme example of the kind of regime that can be created in part by collaboration between governments and weapons manufacturers eagerly seeking customers in the less democratic developing countries.

ETHNICITY AND INTERNATIONAL POLITICS

Since the end of the Cold War, ethnicity and clashes among ethnic groups have almost become the functional equivalent of nuclear weapons in their potential to be the scourge of the earth.[14]

---

[13] A number of developments led Strobe Talbott (1996, p. 53), a deputy secretary of state in the Clinton administration, to conclude, "In Latin America, the trend that began in the 1980s when Argentina, Brazil, and Chile made the transition from military dictatorship to civilian, parliamentary rule has proved to be not only durable but self-reinforcing." Wendy Hunter (1997, p. 173), though focusing on Brazil, concludes also in relation to Argentina and Chile that "if democracy remains a minimally viable system of governance, the competitive dynamic it unleashes can be expected to drive the military to retreat further before an emerging and advancing civil and political society."

[14] "Animosity among ethnic groups is beginning to rival the spread of nuclear weapons as the most serious threat to peace that the world faces" (Maynes, 1993, p. 5).

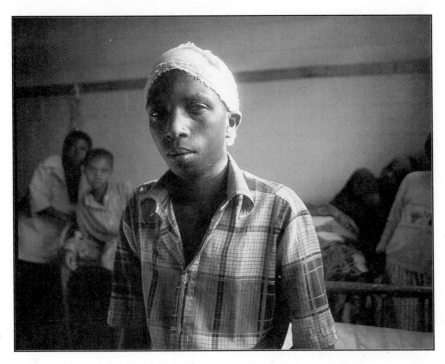

These refugees have fled from areas of ethnic conflict in Rwanda, one of many countries experiencing such conflict in the 1990s. SOURCE: Liz Gilbert/Sygma.

Ethnic strife threatens the integrity and even the existence of a set of countries that girdles the globe. Ethnic conflicts certainly appeared to be involved in the process that led to the dissolution of the Soviet Union. French separatists in Quebec, some fear, could set off a chain reaction that might lead to the dissolution of Canada. The largest democratic state in the world, India, is increasingly besieged by conflict focusing on ethnic grievances.[15] Probably the ethnic conflict grabbing the biggest, ugliest headlines in the 1990s occurred in the former Yugoslavia.

What Is Ethnicity?

An obvious prerequisite to a useful discussion of ethnicity and ethnic conflict in international politics is a clear definition of the term *ethnic*

---

[15] "In recent years . . . India's prospects for continued democratic stability have been threatened by Sikh demands in the Punjab; the unresolved problem of Kashmir; and, even more seriously, by the rise of militant Hindu nationalism" (Welsh, 1993, p. 55).

POLICY CHOICES

Dealing with Ethnic Grievances

ISSUE: There are many ethnic groups in the world that wish to have a nation-state of their own, but this will involve the dismemberment of currently existing states.

Option #1: The United States and the United Nations can treat all these problems as matters of domestic concern only.

Advantages: (a) The United States and the United Nations can conserve their resources to deal with truly *international* problems. (b) The United Nations will avoid getting tied up in conflicts within the organization regarding which internal disputes to deal with, and which to disregard. (c) The United States and the United Nations will avoid the risks of making situations worse by intervening.

Disadvantages: (a) Ethnic problems may invite unilateral interventions from single states in the various regions, creating international problems that might have been easier to deal with at an earlier stage. (b) Since most ethnic conflicts are increasingly domestic rather than international, the United Nations risks becoming irrelevant to the globe's most serious conflicts. (c) Hundreds of thousands of people may suffer

group. With ethnic conflict so prominent in the news on a daily basis, it might seem that everybody must have a pretty clear idea what the term *ethnic* means. Appearances are deceiving. For example, in the early 1990s the former Yugoslavia, as noted above, was the site of probably the most publicized "ethnic" conflict in the world. And yet one writer argued in a 1993 issue of the influential quarterly *Foreign Affairs* that "Yugoslavia's 'ethnic war' is waged among three communities [the Muslims, the Croatians, and the Serbians] possessing no distinct physical characteristics or separate anthropological or 'racial' origins. . . . The notion of an exclusive, and exclusionary ethnic existence for each of the Yugoslav peoples is an invention" (Pfaff, 1993, p. 101). Similarly, it was claimed that "in Rwanda . . . the differences between the Hutu and the Tutsi were far from absolute. Many intermarriages had occurred" (Nye, 1993, p. 17).

It is commonly assumed that for an ethnic group to qualify as such, it must have some distinguishing physical or "racial" characteristic. But "'ethnicity' is a controversial concept that has sparked intense debate among social scientists" (Frye, 1992, p. 602). The controversy has driven many analysts to a definitional strategy suggesting that "if any group defines itself as an ethnic group, that is good enough for me." One oppression at the hands of governments that are insensitive to the needs or aspirations of minority ethnic groups.

Option #2: The United States and the United Nations could energetically defend the principle of national self-determination, which suggests that all "peoples" deserve to have their own nation-state if they so desire.

Advantages: (a) The United Nations will become a major player in attempts to resolve the most serious violent conflicts in the global system today. (b) Hundreds of thousands of people could be rescued from insensitive, perhaps even racist, oppression. (c) Interventions on behalf of oppressed peoples might undermine autocratic governments, leading to their replacement by democratic governments.

Disadvantages: (a) Operations on behalf of oppressed minorities could become expensive for both the United States and the United Nations. (b) Activism of this sort by the United States and the United Nations might encourage additional minorities to aspire to establish their own states, increasing instability on a global scale. (c) Schisms and disagreements about which minorities are truly oppressed and deserving of external support may weaken the ability of the United Nations to deal with truly international problems.

formal definition of *ethnicity*, for example, asserts that it is a "*subjective* [emphasis added] sense of shared identity based on objective cultural or regional criteria" (Frye, 1992, p. 602). Another writer takes this strategy to an even simpler extreme by defining an ethnic group as a "group of people who define themselves as distinct from other groups because of cultural differences" (Ryan, 1990, p. xiii).

One problem arising from this sort of definition is the vagueness of the term *cultural*. What does **culture** mean? It can refer to a "whole way of life." Or it can refer more specifically to arts and other creative efforts (Williams, 1989, p. 4). A recent comprehensive review of ethnic minorities defines communal groups (that is, ethnic groups) as "groups whose core members share a distinctive and enduring collective identity based on cultural traits and lifeways that matter to them and to others with whom they interact" (Gurr, 1993, p. 3). This definition too, leaves open the question of the meaning of *culture* (not to mention *lifeways*), but in the project from which the definition comes (the *Minorities at Risk* project headed by Ted Robert Gurr), five relatively specific cultural traits are relied upon to identify ethnic groups. They are (1) language or dialect, (2) social customs, (3) religious beliefs, (4) physical appearance, and (5) region of residence (Gurr, 1990, p. 9). For the purpose of this discussion, we will define an ethnic group as one that perceives itself to be culturally distinct in terms of its language, customs, religious beliefs, physical appearance, and/or region of residence.[16]

These bases of distinction tend to go together. According to the comprehensive review in *Minorities at Risk*, for example, only about 10 percent of minorities in Third World countries are distinct in terms of only *one* of these cultural characteristics (Gurr, 1990, p. 9). Most ethnic groups that perceive themselves as such not only have a different language but also have at least one other distinctive cultural trait having to do with their customs, religious beliefs, physical appearance, or the place where they live. As we have seen earlier, it can be argued that the civil war in the former Yugoslavia did not constitute ethnic conflict, because the Croats, the Muslims in Bosnia, and the Serbs are not "racially" distinct. But because these groups are distinct in terms of their religious beliefs and their region of residence, then by our definition they are distinct ethnic groups, and they can be said to have engaged in ethnic conflict.

The Scope of Ethnic Conflict in the Global System

Because defining an ethnic group is difficult, there are widely disparate estimates of how many such groups there are in the world. One source asserts there are 862 ethnic groups within the nation-states of the world (Aziz Said, 1977, p. 4). Another report by a pair of political scientists estimates that there are 575 ethnic groups with aspirations (some already achieved) to become nation-states (Neilsson and Jones, 1988). A geographer has identified five thousand "nations," or "distinct communities in the contemporary world that could claim to be national peoples" (Gurr, 1990, pp. 9–10). *The World Directory of Minorities* provides information on 170 communal groups (cited in Gurr, 1993, p. 5). Ted Robert Gurr's *Minorities at Risk* project (1993), focusing on "nonstate communal groups that were politically salient during the post–World War II era," has identified 233 such groups.

It is clear from all these data that there are an awful lot of ethnic groups in the world. It is equally safe to conclude that the politics, domestic and international, of virtually every state in the world are affected in important ways by the activities of these ethnic groups. Gurr (1993, p. 10) declares that three-fourths of the 127 largest countries in the world have at least one politicized minority. Walker Connor (1973) argued twenty years ago that all but fourteen of modern states have at

---

[16] Other writers add such factors as "dress, food, music, crafts, and architecture, as well as laws, customs, and institutions" (Smith, 1993, p. 29).

least one significant minority. More recently, Joseph Nye (1996, p. 19) points out that "[l]ess than 10 percent of the 170 states in the world are ethnically homogeneous. Only half have one ethnic group that accounts for as much as 75 percent of the population." Quite often, ethnic groups are spread out beyond the confines of one state. Such situations can create pressures to extend the political power of the homeland to include the ethnic compatriots currently outside the boundaries of the country in which they live. Such pressures are commonly referred to in discussions of international politics as **"irredentist"** pressures. "Irredentist movements usually lay claim to the territory of an entity—almost invariably an independent state—in which their in-group is concentrated, perhaps even forming some local majorities. The original term *terra irredenta* means territory to be redeemed . . . The territory to be regained sometimes is regarded as a part of a cultural setting (or historic state) or an integral part of one homeland" (Carment and James, 1995, p. 84).

Of the 233 communal groups identified by Gurr's *Minorities at Risk* project, about 65 percent are the victims of economic discrimination, and about 75 percent are the targets of political discrimination (Gurr, 1993, p. 44). Of the 179 minority groups in the Third World identified in that survey, more than two-thirds have ethnic compatriots in two or more adjacent countries (Gurr, 1990, pp. 4–5). That ethnic minorities are often subjected to discrimination and that current state boundaries seldom coincide with the physical distribution of ethnic groups have made ethnic conflict a virtual epidemic in today's global political system. "Wherever one looks in the world there seems to be an unresolved ethnic conflict underway" (Ryan, 1990, p. xi). David Lake and Donald Rothchild (1996, p. 41) note that "since the end of the Cold War, a wave of ethnic conflict has swept across parts of Eastern Europe, the former Soviet Union, and Africa. Localities, states, and sometimes whole regions have been engulfed in convulsive fits of ethnic insecurity, violence, and genocide." The human and political costs of ethnic conflict have already reached substantial proportions and threaten to get worse. There were some eighty guerrilla and civil wars fought by rebelling ethnic groups from 1945 to 1980, such as the Karen and Kachin in Burma, the Nagas and the Tripuras in India, the Eritreans in Ethiopia, the Palestinians in Israel, the Kurds in Iraq, and the Basques in Spain (Gurr, 1993, p. 318). Because of this ethnic conflict, there have been "rights denied, immiseration, exodus of refugees, mass murder, democracy subverted, development deferred . . . regional wars" (Gurr, 1990, p. 2). The list of ethnic problems in the world seems nearly endless. Michael Brown (1993, p. 3) points out:

> The war in Bosnia-Herzegovina has received the most attention in the West because of the intense coverage it has received from the Western

media, but equally if not more horrific conflicts are underway in Afghanistan, Angola, Armenia, Azerbaijan, Burma, Georgia, India, Indonesia, Liberia, Sri Lanka, Sudan, and Tajikistan. Other troublespots abound—Bangladesh, Belgium, Bhutan, Burundi, Estonia, Ethiopia, Guatemala, Iraq, Latvia, Lebanon, Mali, Moldova, Niger, Northern Ireland, Pakistan, the Philippines, Romania, Rwanda, South Africa, Spain, and Turkey, for example. . . .

Brown just mentions Rwanda in passing, as one troublespot among many. He probably did not expect that Rwanda was soon to become "the site of the worst genocide since the Holocaust" (Nye, 1996, p. 17).

Why Is Ethnicity So Important Now?

Ethnic conflict is not new, as a moment's reflection on the legendary battle between David and Goliath or the Roman custom of throwing Christians to the lions will reveal. In more recent times, the Turkish government is suspected of murdering about 1.5 million Armenians, mostly during the First World War (Rummel, 1991a, p. 18). The Nazis in Germany killed 6 million Jews and perhaps as many as 14 million people of other ethnic groups, such as Slavs, Serbs, Czechs, Poles, and Ukranians (Rummel, 1991b). There were mass murders of members of ethnic groups in East Bengal in 1971, in Kampuchea in 1977, and in Uganda in 1978.

But it is true that violence focused on or fostered by ethnic conflict did increase in the 1980s. In fact, "every form of ethnopolitical conflict has increased sharply since the 1950s. . . . [B]etween 1950 and 1990, violent protest and rebellion both quadrupled" (Gurr, 1993, p. 316). And since 1990, the end of the Cold War and the end of communism in the Soviet Union and Eastern Europe have seemingly brought to the fore long-festering ethnic conflicts in such places as Armenia, Azerbaijan, Georgia, Moldova, and Tajikstan, not to mention the dissolution along ethnic lines of Yugoslavia and Czechoslovakia, as well as antiethnic violence in Germany, ominous statements by Hungarian government officials about the need to protect Hungarian ethnic compatriots in neighboring countries, and so on.

Keeping in mind that ethnic conflict has occurred for centuries, it is still appropriate to ask: "Why the apparent explosion of ethnic passions and ethnic conflict and violence now, in the last five or ten years, and especially since the end of the Cold War?" It might be admitted first that the academic field of international politics (as well as, perhaps, the contemporary global political system) is ill equipped to deal with, or to explain persuasively, this outburst of ethnic passion, since it has a history of ignoring ethnic groups and their relationship to international politics. As one current specialist in ethnic conflict observes, "The post-war world has been dominated by the ideological battle between Western liberalism and Soviet style Marxism," and "neither of these systems of belief have shown much concern for ethnicity" (Ryan, 1990, p. xix). "Liberals" in the classic Western tradition have tended to see the emphasis on collective rights by emotional ethnic groups as a dangerous threat to the individual human rights that they hold dear. Radical and Marxist scholars, on the other hand, have tended to view ethnic groups and their ethnically based political passions as annoying diversions on the road to communism. In short, as the prominent analyst of ethnicity Walker Connor argued a couple of decades ago, international politics as an academic field has had a regrettable (from his point of view) tendency to treat ethnicity as an "ephemeral nuisance" (Connor, 1972; cited in Ryan, 1990, p. xxix).

Perhaps partly because they have been considered not only annoying but of marginal importance, ethnicity and ethnic conflict also seem to have been confusing to students of international politics as well. In recent decades, it has commonly been hypothesized that "ethnic conflict generally tends toward violence because the structure of the international system—a bipolar system—prohibited conflict between the major powers but not among its clients" (Carment, 1993, p. 146). In other words, during the Cold War it often appeared that antagonism between the superpowers made ethnic conflicts worse. In Angola, for example, the United States and other Western powers tended to support the Ovimbundu people in the southern part of the country against the Soviet-supported Mbundu-led coalition that controlled the government. The result was a civil war that dragged on for years. In Indonesia troops invaded East Timor in 1975 after East Timor declared its independence, and reportedly killed 200,000 people. Reports of brutality by the Indonesian government against the East Timorese people were continual after that invasion, but "western governments have turned a blind eye to Indonesian policies because they value their relations with Indonesia, because they want a strong and stable ally, and because they fear communist influence in East Timor" (Ryan, 1990, p. 12). This is another example, it seems, where the Cold War conflict made ethnic conflict worse.

But the end of the Cold War has hardly seemed to be a cure-all for the world's epidemic of ethnic strife. On the contrary, it and the end of communism have obviously brought to the surface a host of violent conflicts in Eastern Europe and the former Soviet Union. And the end of global competition between the superpowers has not brought to an end many conflicts that previously seemed to be primarily a function of that competition. We can now see that even without superpower encouragement, ethnic groups in Angola, the Sudan, Afghanistan, Burundi, Burma, and so on are perfectly capable of slaughtering each other in great numbers.

The debate over whether the Cold War encouraged or dampened ethnic passions and conflict is reminiscent of an even more fundamental issue regarding the relationship between economic modernization and ethnicity. Traditional Western scholarship has viewed ethnicity as a phenomenon destined to be overcome by broader, stronger modernizing forces. "Twentieth century approaches to the study of ethnicity in politics can be traced to the writings of Marx and Durkheim, both of whom evaluated ethnic identities as part of a larger set of phenomena subject to transformation by the forces of economic modernization" (Newman, 1991, p. 453). For Marx, as we have noted, attachment to ethnic groups was an annoying obstacle that would surely and ultimately give way to more powerful forces moving the nations of the world to socialism. For the sociologist Emile Durkheim, and then a whole generation of modernization theorists, especially in the United States, "nation-building" efforts were destined to erode old-fashioned loyalties to smaller, outdated, even quaint ethnic groups. "A major assumption of western social science in the post-war decades was that ethnic conflict would disappear as nations modernize and minority groups were assimilated. Industrialization would lead to increased contact and community between different groups. Urbanization would take place. Gradually this would result in . . . acculturation, which would result in a transfer of loyalty from the ethnic group to the nation-state" (Ryan, 1990, p. xix). In other words, the nation-states of the world were to become "melting pots" in which anachronistic divisions between ethnic groups would dissolve and "everybody" would adopt the more modern attitude of loyalty to one's country.

History has not been kind to this theory. In a manner reminiscent of the way predominant opinion seems to have shifted from the notion that the Cold War made ethnic conflict worse to the obviously contradictory theory that the end of the Cold War has inflamed ethnic passions and conflict, there has emerged something of a consensus that rather than ameliorating ethnic conflict, economic modernizing forces actually increase its likelihood. "Although many scholars endorsed . . . [the] melting pot modernization approach, the weight of . . . evidence eventually overwhelmed these theoretical arguments . . ." (Newman, 1991, p. 454). Now it is more commonly argued that modernizing and centralizing governments provoke a backlash from ethnic groups that fear losing their identity in the move toward a more integrated state, or that economic modernization increases contact between ethnic groups that increasingly perceive themselves in competition with each other. Walker Connor, for example, argues that "economic modernization does not undermine ethnic divisions but invigorates them by bringing together previously isolated ethnic groups that suddenly find themselves competing for the same economic niches" (Newman, 1991, p.

455). Alvin Toffler asserts that economic processes in the most recent decades, with their emphasis on computers, decentralization, and flexibility, also encourage ethnic passions. In the computer information age, economic producers are able to offer ever more specialized, personalized products for ever more narrowly defined consumer groups—in grocery stores, hobby shops, automobile dealer showrooms, or bookstores. "Under the impact of the new production system, resistance to the "melting pot" is rising everywhere (Toffler, 1990, p. 243). Similarly, Joseph Nye argues:

> Technological change has had . . . contradictory effects. It has made the economy global but made politics more parochial . . . With state sovereignty eroded through global interdependence, the political efficacy and legitimacy of many governments [are] less assured. Many groups have had their sense of identity and community challenged by economic dislocation and the collapse of communism. They have become susceptible to the parochial political appeals of political entrepreneurs who hope to seize power in states whose governments have been weakened by the collapse of communism or the ebb and flow of the global economy (Nye, 1996, p. 16).

So, during the Cold War it was commonly argued that the confrontation between the United States and the Soviet Union made ethnic conflicts worse. Now that the Cold War has ended, we are told that its demise has worsened ethnic conflict. At one time, analysts were relatively confident that economic progress and modernization would ameliorate ethnic conflict, but now that global economic integration has reached new heights, it seems that it may instead also increase the intensity of strife between ethnic groups.

Resolving Ethnic Conflicts

Democratic governance is one logical solution to the ethnic conflict. "Minorities in the . . . democracies . . . have two distinctive traits. Their grievances usually are expressed in protest, rarely in rebellion, and the most common response by government . . . is to accommodate their interests rather than forcibly subordinate or incorporate them" (Gurr, 1993, p. 139). In states where governmental power is exercised autocratically, struggles for control of the government are likely to be more desperate, and violent. If the struggles pit ethnic groups against each other, massive violence between them is a logical outcome. Although it is true that the Civil War in the United States was one of the bloodiest domestic conflicts in history, in general, democratic "societies bleed off conflict in divergent directions, preventing that fatal congruence of cleavages and oppositions that leads to intense struggles over societal powers and consequent extreme violence" (Rummel, 1976, p. 370).

But it is difficult to impossible to initiate democratic reforms in a country already torn by ethnic conflict. In fact, many analysts are convinced that transitions to democracy are likely to increase ethnic strife, even if relatively entrenched, stable democracy may ultimately prove to be an important solution to it. Carment and James (1995, p. 104) provide systematic evidence that "high political constraint [by which they mean democratic controls on the use of political power] reduces threat perception and belligerent behavior" by states involved in conflict over ethnic issues. But they argue that this finding must be taken with a "grain of salt," and it is clear that they believe that politicians in democratic countries might use ethnic grievances and strife for their own purposes in ways that could increase conflict.

Even if ethnic problems in a given country are free of international, irredentist complications, however, "moving from an authoritarian environment to one that is more open creates a fertile climate for hatred and prejudice" (de Nevers, 1993, p. 75). In several Middle Eastern countries today, for example, it seems that Islamic fundamentalists might use democratic means (as in Algeria) to achieve power with the intent to terminate democracy once that goal is achieved. Under those conditions, it is difficult to see how democratic reforms will help resolve ethnic conflicts. (See the map on page 113.)

The United Nations, as will be discussed in more detail in Chapter 11, is involved in efforts to deal with ethnic conflicts in Yugoslavia, Somalia, Cyprus, Lebanon, Kashmir, India, and Rwanda. Efforts by the international community to deal with ethnic strife in Rwanda have been particularly controversial, with some analysts arguing that those efforts have actually provided a base of operations for those who committed genocide, thus prolonging the conflict for years.

An attempt to anticipate the future of ethnic conflicts throughout the world needs to take into account, unfortunately, the extent to which ethnic conflicts in Europe have been "resolved" in roughly the Yugoslavian fashion, namely, with "ethnic cleansing," forced migrations, and displaced peoples. "Europe's nationality problem was 'solved' by wars and population transfers over the span of centuries" (Jalali and Lipset, 1993, p. 60). Peace settlements after the First World War redrew boundaries in such a way as to decrease the percentage of ethnic peoples without a state or self-government from about 26 percent in 1910 to about 7 percent in 1930. As a result of the Second World War, 20 million people settled in new homelands. Often they were relocated with little attention to their own interests or wishes. For example, "3 million Germans [were] forced to abandon lands their families had occupied for centuries, banished with nothing but tattered clothes and bandaged feet into a harsh winter. The expulsion of Sudeten Germans from their

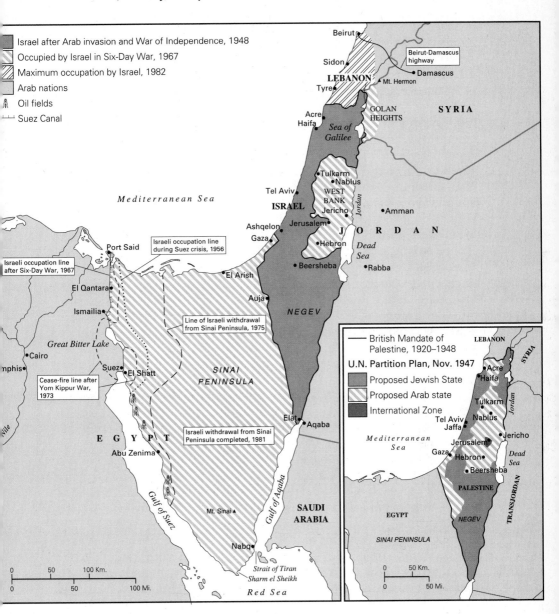

Conflict in the Middle East Israel's problems with intifada on the West Bank and the Gaza Strip were products of its decades-long struggle with its Arab neighbors.

villages in Czechoslovakia still resonates 50 years later as one of World War II's most contentious incidents" (Drozdiak, 1996, p. 1). As a result of such episodes of brutality and relocation, the share of Europe's total population belonging to ethnic minorities without autonomy or self-government was reduced to about 3 percent (Jalali and Lipset, 1993, p. 60).[17]

The implications of this history of relationships among ethnic groups in Europe for much of Asia, the Middle East, and Africa are sobering, if not downright depressing. Nationalism as an ideological movement emerged in Europe as a result of the French revolution in the late eighteenth century. It took nearly two centuries of massive relocations and wars for the peoples of Europe to sort themselves out and redraw boundaries in such a way that the distributions of ethnic groups and national boundaries were made largely congruent. And even so, the United Kingdom has yet to resolve the situation in Northern Ireland; Spain faces continuing conflict with the Basques and Catalans; and France still has problems with the Bretons and the Corsicans. Must Africa, Asia, and the Middle East go through these relocations and wars to establish a match between the physical distribution of peoples and legitimate national boundaries?[18] Or to put this partially rhetorical question in more specific but equally gloomy terms, are "Arab-Israeli Wars," complete with refugees and relocations, destined to be duplicated throughout the rest of the Middle East, in Africa, and in Asia?

Anyone who hopes for a more peaceful and stable global political system in the twenty-first century must hope that this is not the case. Even centuries of wars and relocations in Europe have not resolved all the ethnic problems there, and Stalin's forced relocations of millions in the Soviet Union certainly did not resolve all of those ethnic conflicts. It is, in fact, nearly futile to hope that peaceful relationships among the ethnic groups of the world can be established by relocating people and redrawing national boundaries.

Africa, for example, is faced with probably the greatest number of ethnic conflicts of all the continents. These problems are often traced to Africa's colonial heritage. According to Joseph Nye (1996, p. 19), "Africa . . . is a continent of a thousand ethnic and linguistic groups squeezed into some 50-odd states, many of them with borders determined by colonial powers in the last century with little regard to traditional ethnic boundaries."

But consider the map on page 115 showing the geographical distribution of ethnic groups in Africa. The colonial powers did undoubtedly

---

[17] Jalali and Lipset get these figures from Krejic and Velimski (1981).

[18] Compared to Africa, the Middle East, and Asia, Latin America has been relatively free of ethnic conflict, partly because those nation-states have been independent since the early 1800s. See Gurr (1993, p. 26). Nevertheless, peasant rebellions in Chiapis in Mexico and by the Sendero Luminoso in Peru certainly have ethnic underpinnings.

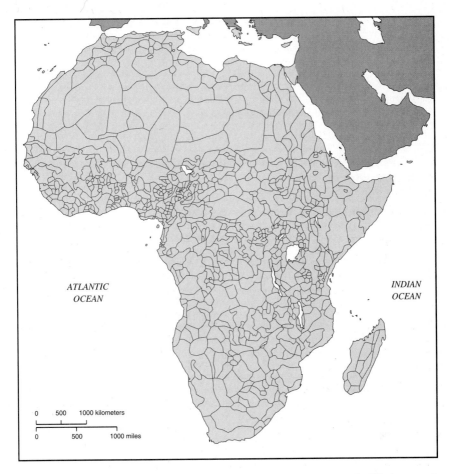

Ethnic Groups of Africa SOURCE: Martin Ira Glassner and Harm J. de Blij, *Systematic Political Geography,* 4th ed. (New York: John Wiley and Sons, 1989), 532. Copyright © 1989 by John Wiley & Sons, Inc. Reprinted by permission of John Wiley & Sons, Inc.

draw national boundaries in Africa that arbitrarily cut across and/or combined disparate ethnic groups. But the number and distribution of ethnic groups in Africa is such that even had they attempted to be more sensitive in that regard, they would have found it nearly impossible to satisfy all the national aspirations of the various ethnic groups. There are too many of them, and they are not organized in nice, neat, nation-size geographical packages. Obviously there are many areas in Africa where ethnic groups are intermingled in the same territory. Ethnic peace will never come to Africa (or anywhere else in the world) if it depends on every ethnic group satisfying its aspirations to national autonomy and self-determination. In short, no amount of national boundary redrawing is going to resolve all, or even most, of the ethnic conflicts in the world. Such redrawings of boundaries historically create as many problems as they resolve. The former Soviet Republic of Georgia, for example, has broken away from Russia, to be confronted itself by a rebellion in its own region of Abkhazia. The Eritreans have successfully established independence from Ethiopia, but "the Eritrean nationalists themselves are an amalgam of Muslims and Christians who, if they gain autonomy, are likely to fracture along . . . ethnic lines" (Gurr, 1993, p. 38). In the former Yugoslavia, the Macedonians have broken away from Serbia, only to face sullen, irredentist pressures from the 20 percent of its population that is Albanian, not to mention its even smaller Serbian population. There is no end in sight to this kind of process.

It is incumbent upon those of us who live in the major industrialized countries, secure in our national identities within nation-states in existence since 1776, or much longer, not to be condescending toward ethnic groups with frustrated desires for national autonomy and self-determination. It is too easy for us to say (or feel): "Why can't those people (in Rwanda, Lebanon, Georgia, Burundi, India, or Northern Ireland) just give up their delusions of national grandeur and learn to live together?" Even so, the conclusion of Ted Gurr, the author of one of the more comprehensive surveys of ethnic conflicts in the world, seems reasonable. He observes that a strategy of reconstructing the state system so that state boundaries correspond more closely to the social and cultural boundaries among ethnic communities would "create as many problems as it resolved." According to Gurr, "A more constructive and open-ended answer is to pursue the . . . coexistence of ethnic groups and plural states. . . . [Ethnic] groups should have the protected rights to individual and collective existence and to cultural self-expression without fear of political repression. The counterpart of such rights is the obligation not to impose their own cultural standards or political agenda on other peoples" (Gurr, 1993, pp. 323–324).

SUMMARY

The general public probably has a limited impact on the foreign policies of most states because individuals do not typically know or care very much about international politics. Yet there is evidence, for example, that the general public in the United States in the aggregate does respond in a knowledgeable fashion to foreign policy issues. This phenomenon may occur because large numbers of uninformed citizens take their cues from better-informed friends and opinion leaders, allowing their aggregated opinions to be "rational" and, perhaps, increasing the potential of public opinion to have an impact on foreign policies.

Subgroups within every society have more intense opinions about certain foreign policy issues than does the general public, and they may have a correspondingly greater impact on policies regarding those issues. For example, industrial firms and labor unions in the United States adversely affected by foreign imports may persuade Congress to pass high tariffs to protect them from those imports, even though such tariffs impose higher costs on millions of consumers.

The military-industrial complex in the United States has obviously been successful in attempts to capture large portions of the federal budget in the United States. But the end of the Cold War has deprived the military-industrial complex of its primary rationale for ever-larger defense budgets, and in fact defense budgets have been shrinking—important evidence regarding the limits of its influence. The United States and several other major powers supply military weapons to military governments, or governments heavily influenced by the military, in several developing countries. There has been an increase in the number of democratic governments in the developing world in recent decades, and some encouraging evidence indicates that even relatively new and fragile democratic regimes have had some success in reducing the grip of the military on political power in their countries. Still, the easy availability of weapons makes it more likely that governments dominated by the military in some developing countries, such as Iraq, will come to or retain power.

Finally, ethnic groups in almost every country of the world have a profound impact on international politics. Although ethnic strife has a long history, it has increased steadily since the Second World War. It used to be argued that the Cold War exacerbated ethnic conflicts in many countries, and it also used to be asserted that economic and political modernization would eventually dissolve divisions between ethnic groups. Now it is more commonly argued that the end of the Cold War has brought ethnic conflicts to the surface and that modernization or increasingly close integration of the world's economy has the effect of encouraging ethnic conflict. The continent of Europe has gone through centuries of ethnic relocations, forced and otherwise, and massive international wars, which have made the boundaries of the countries there more evenly matched with the geographic distribution of ethnic groups. But even Europe is not free of ethnic conflicts, and Africa, the Middle East, and Asia contain large numbers of ethnic groups with unmet and probably unsatisfiable aspirations for national autonomy. There are too many ethnic groups, distributed in too haphazard a fashion, to allow the resolution of the world's ethnic conflicts by relocation and boundary redrawing. If peace and stability are to be established in the global political system, ethnic groups will have to learn how to live together in at least some of the existing political, national entities within which their individual and collective rights are recognized and protected.

KEY TERMS

attentive public

two-level game

rally-round-the-flag effect

audience costs

free riders

distributional coalitions

military-industrial complex

ethnic group

culture

irredentist

SOURCES

Adams, Gordon. "The Iron Triangle: Inside the Defense Policy Process." In Charles W. Kegley, Jr., and Eugene Wittkopf, eds., *The Domestic Sources of American Foreign Policy: Insights and Evidence.* New York: St. Martin's Press, 1988.

Almond, Gabriel. *The American People and Foreign Policy.* New York: Harcourt Brace Jovanovich, 1950.

Almond, Gabriel, and Sidney Verba. *The Civic Culture.* Princeton, N.J.: Princeton University Press, 1963.

Barnet, Richard J. *The Roots of War.* Baltimore: Penguin Books, 1971.

Bauer, Raymond A., Ithiel de Sola Pool, and Lewis Anthony Dexter. *American Business and Public Policy.* New York: Atherton Press, 1968.

Beck, Joan. "Americans Are Saps at Maps and Not Too Hot at Anything Else." *New York Times,* circa August 1988. Published in the *Tampa Tribune,* August 5, 1988, Section A, p. 11.

Brody, Richard A. *Assessing the President: The Media, Elite Opinion, and Public Support.* Stanford, Calif.: Stanford University Press, 1991.

Carment, David. "The International Dimensions of Ethnic Conflict: Concepts, Indicators, and Theory." *Journal of Peace Research,* 30 (May 1993), 137–150.

Carment, David, and Patrick James. "Internal Constraints and Interstate Ethnic Conflict." *Journal of Conflict Resolution,* 39 (March 1995), 82–109.

Coneybeare, John A. "Voting for Protection: An Electoral Model of Tariff Policy." *International Organization,* 45 (Winter 1991), 57–81.

Connor, Walker. "Nation-Building or Nation-Destroying?" *World Politics,* 24 (April 1972), 319–355.

Connor, Walker. "The Politics of Ethnonationalism." *Journal of International Affairs,* 27, No. 1 (1973), 1–21.

"Coup Galvanizes Guatemala to Restore Democracy." *United States Institute of Peace Journal,* 6 (October 1993), 4–5.

Cushman, John H. "The Coming Crunch for the Military Budget." *New York Times,* November 27, 1988, Section 4, p. 1.

de Nevers, Renee. "Democratization and Ethnic Conflict." In Michael E. Brown, ed., *Ethnic Conflict and International Security.* Princeton, N.J.: Princeton University Press, 1993.

Drozdiak, William. "50 Years On, Expulsion Rankles for Sudeten Germans." *International Herald Tribune,* December 6, 1996, p. 1.

Eichenberg, Richard. *Public Opinion and National Security in Western Europe.* Ithaca, N.Y.: Cornell University Press, 1989.

Eyerman, Joe, and Robert A. Hart, Jr. "An Empirical Test of the Audience Cost Proposition: Democracy Speaks Louder Than Words." *Journal of Conflict Resolution,* 40 (December 1996), 597–616.

Fearon, James D. "Domestic Political Audiences and the Escalation of International Disputes." *American Political Science Review,* 88 (September 1994), 577–592.

Frye, Timothy M. "Ethnicity, Sovereignty and Transition from Non-Democratic Rule." *Journal of International Affairs,* 45 (Winter 1992), 599–623.

Garson, G. David. "On the Origins of Interest-Group Theory: A Critique of a Process." *American Political Science Review,* 68 (December 1974), 1505–1519.

Gaubatz, Kurt Taylor. "Election Cycles and War." *Journal of Conflict Resolution,* 35 (June 1991), 212–244.

Gilpin, Robert. *The Political Economy of International Relations.* Princeton, N.J.: Princeton University Press, 1987.

Gurr, Ted Robert. *Minorities at Risk.* Washington, D.C.: United States Institute of Peace, 1993.

Gurr, Ted Robert. "Third World Minorities at Risk Since 1945." Background Paper Prepared for the Conference on Conflict Resolution in the Post–Cold War World, U.S. Institute of Peace, October 3–5, 1990.

Hartley, Thomas, and Bruce Russett. "Public Opinion and the Common Defense: Who Governs Military Spending in the United States?" *American Political Science Review,* 86 (December 1992), 905–915.

Hastings and Hastings (eds.). *Index to International Public Opinion, 1982–1983.* New York: Greenwood, 1984.

Hastings and Hastings (eds.). *Index to International Public Opinion, 1983–1984.* New York: Greenwood, 1985.

Holsti, K. J. *International Politics.* 7th ed. Englewood Cliffs, N.J.: Prentice-Hall, 1995.

Holsti, Ole R. "Public Opinion and Foreign Policy: Challenges to the Almond-Lippmann Consensus." *International Studies Quarterly,* 36 (December 1992), 439–466.

Hughes, Barry. *The Domestic Context of American Foreign Policy.* San Francisco: Freeman, 1978.

Hunter, Wendy. *Eroding Military Influence in Brazil.* Chapel Hill, N.C.: University of North Carolina Press, 1997.

Hunter, Wendy. "Politicians Against Soldiers: Contesting the Military in Post-Authoritarian Brazil." *Comparative Politics,* 27 (July 1995), 425–443.

Huntington, Samuel P. *Political Order in Changing Societies*. New Haven, Conn.: Yale University Press, 1968.

Jalali, Rita, and Seymour Martin Lipset. "Racial and Ethnic Conflict: A Global Perspective." In Demetrios Caraley and Cerentha Harris, eds., *New World Politics: Power, Ethnicity and Democracy*. New York: The Academy of Political Science, 1993.

James, Patrick, and John R. Oneal. "The Influence of Domestic and International Politics on the President's Use of Force." *Journal of Conflict Resolution*, 35 (June 1991), 307–332.

Jentleson, Bruce W. "The Pretty Prudent Public: Post Vietnam American Opinion on the Use of Military Force." *International Studies Quarterly*, 36 (March 1992), 49–74.

Johnson, Paul. *Modern Times*. New York: Harper & Row, 1983.

Krejic, Jaroslav, and Vitezslav Velimsky. *Ethnic and Political Nations in Europe*. New York: St. Martin's Press, 1981.

Lenway, Stefanie Ann. *The Politics of U.S. International Trade*. Boston: Pitman, 1985.

Lian, Bradley, and John R. Oneal. "Presidents, the Use of Military Force, and Public Opinion." *Journal of Conflict Resolution*, 37 (June 1993), 277–300.

Manchester, William. *The Arms of Krupp*. Boston: Little, Brown, 1968.

March, James G. "The Power of Power." In David Easton, ed., *Varieties of Political Theory*. Englewood Cliffs, N.J.: Prentice-Hall, 1966.

March, James G., and Herbert A. Simon. *Organizations*. New York: Wiley, 1958.

Maynes, Charles William. "Containing Ethnic Conflict." *Foreign Policy*, No. 90 (Spring 1993), 3–21.

Mueller, John. *War, Presidents, and Public Opinion*. New York: Wiley, 1973.

Newman, Saul. "Does Modernization Breed Ethnic Conflict?" *World Politics*, 43 (April 1991), 451–478.

Nielsson, Gunnar, and Ralph Jones. "From Ethnic Category to Nation: Patterns of Political Modernization." Paper prepared for delivery to the annual convention of the International Studies Association, St. Louis, Mo.: March 1988.

Nincic, Miroslav. *Democracy and Foreign Policy*. New York: Columbia University Press, 1992.

Nincic, Miroslav. "The United States, the Soviet Union, and the Politics of Opposition." *World Politics*, 40 (July 1988), 452–475.

Nye, Joseph. "Conflicts After the Cold War." *The Washington Quarterly*, 19 (Winter 1996), 5–24.

Olson, Mancur. *The Logic of Collective Action*. New York: Schocken Books, 1968.

Olson, Mancur. *The Rise and Decline of Nations*. New Haven, Conn.: Yale University Press, 1982.

Oneal, John R., Brad Lian, and James H. Joyner, Jr. "Are the American People 'Pretty Prudent'? Public Responses to U.S. Uses of Force, 1950–1988." *International Studies Quarterly*, 40 (June 1996), 261–280.

Pfaff, William. "An Invitation to War." *Foreign Affairs*, 72 (Summer 1993), 97–109.

Powlick, Philip J. "The Attitudinal Bases for Responsiveness to Public Opinion Among American Foreign Policy Officials." *Journal of Conflict Resolution*, 35 (December 1991), 611–641.

Putnam, Robert D. "Diplomacy and Domestic Politics: The Logic of Two Level Games." *International Organization*, 42 (Summer 1988), 427–460.

Risse-Kappen, Thomas. "Public Opinion, Domestic Structure, and Foreign Policy in Liberal Democracies." *World Politics*, 43 (July 1991), 479–512.

Robinson, John P. *Public Information About World Affairs*. Ann Arbor, Mich.: Institute for Social Research, 1967.

Rosenau, James N. *Turbulence in World Politics*. Princeton, N.J.: Princeton University Press, 1990.

Rummel, R. J. "The Armenian Genocide." Draft. Department of Political Science, University of Hawaii, 1991a.

Rummel, R. J. "20,946,000 Victims: Nazi Germany." Draft. Department of Political Science, University of Hawaii, 1991b.

Rummel, R. J. *Understanding Conflict and War: The Conflict Helix*. Vol. 2. Beverly Hills, Calif.: Sage, 1976.

Russett, Bruce M. *Controlling the Sword*. Cambridge, Mass.: Harvard University Press, 1990.

Russett, Bruce M. *What Price Vigilance?* New Haven, Conn.: Yale University Press, 1970.

Ryan, Stephen. *Ethnic Conflict and International Relations*. Brookfield, Ver.: Dartmouth Publishing, 1990.

Said, Abdul Aziz. "A Redefinition of National Interest, Ethnic Consciousness, and U.S. Foreign Policy." In Abdul Aziz Said, ed., *Ethnicity and U.S. Foreign Policy*. New York: Praeger, 1977.

Scammon, Richard M., and Ben J. Wattenberg. *The Real Majority*. New York: Berkley, 1970.

Schattschneider, E. E. *The Semisovereign People*. New York: Holt, Rinehart & Winston, 1960.

Shapiro, Robert Y., and Benjamin I. Page. "Foreign Policy and the Rational Public." *Journal of Conflict Resolution*, 32 (June 1988), 211–247.

Smith, Anthony D. "The Ethnic Sources of Nationalism." In Michael E. Brown, ed., *Ethnic Conflict and International Security*. Princeton, N.J.: Princeton University Press, 1993.

Smith, Tom W. "The Polls: America's Most Important Problem, Part I: National and International." *Public Opinion Quarterly*, 49, No. 2 (1985), 264–274.

Talbott, Strobe. "Democracy and the National Interest." *Foreign Affairs*, 75 (November/December 1996), 47–63.

Toffler, Alvin. *Power Shift*. New York: Bantam Books, 1991.

Truman, David. *The Governmental Process*. New York: Knopf, 1951.

Verba, Sidney, and Richard A. Brody. "Participation, Policy Preferences, and the War in Vietnam." *Public Opinion Quarterly*, 34, No. 3 (1970), 325–332.

Welsh, David. " Domestic Politics and Ethnic Conflict." In Michael E. Brown, ed., *Ethnic Conflict and International Security*. Princeton, N.J.: Princeton University Press, 1993.

Williams, Raymond. *Resources of Hope*. London: Verso, 1989.

CHAPTER 4

Making Foreign Policy: Bureaucrats, Diplomats, Leaders, and Logic

One of the main functions of national governments is making policy decisions about how to deal with the international environment. Those decisions are the product of a wide array of factors including the workings of bureaucracies, bargaining strategies, and the influence of individual leaders at the top of national governments, from elected presidents to dictators-for-life. Yet there is good evidence to indicate that despite the multifaceted and potentially confusing process that produces them, foreign policy decisions are (with some obvious exceptions) essentially logical in the long run. That is, the decisions reflect a sensitivity by decision makers to the possible costs and potential benefits of the various options that are available. This chapter focuses on the impact of large bureaucracies, foreign policy professionals known as diplomats, and individual leaders on foreign policy decision making, as well as the evidence that despite some appearances to the contrary, foreign policy decisions are typically rational.

FOREIGN POLICY BUREAUCRACIES

The study of bureaucratic organizations in the last few decades has centered on two major questions: "Should bureaucracies make decisions in a rational manner?" and "Do bureaucracies make decisions in a rational manner?" The answer to the first question might seem obvious; rationality must be an admirable goal to which bureaucracies and executives who administer them should aspire. Who, for example, would deny that executives should step back, on occasion, from daily concerns and deal with issues and problems that have not yet reached the crisis stage? It makes good sense (or so it seems) for an executive confronted with a decision to consider every possible alternative solution to the problem at hand. Having done so, the executive should obviously turn to assessing the probable success of each alternative and the costs involved in implementing each alternative. The final step in this rational process would be selecting the alternative that offers the best combination of a high probability of success and low cost. As one analyst of foreign policy making has put it, "By . . . rationality I mean the process of gathering information, ranking values, considering all possible courses of action, carefully weighing the pros and cons of each of them, and seeking to maximize values" (Hybel, 1993, p. 104).

Standard Operating Procedures and Prearranged Responses

Perhaps, in the best of all possible worlds, executives in large organizations would base their decisions on a rational approach. But many organization theorists, led by Herbert Simon (1957),[1] have argued plausibly that the actual process in which bureaucracies come to decisions is not based on what might be called *comprehensive rationality*. First, whether the goal of the organizations they head is to sell as much breakfast cereal as possible or to formulate foreign policies, executives typically do not have time to step back from daily crises and anticipate problems looming in the future. Crises, ranging from minor to catastrophic, dominate the executive's ordinary day to the point that time for a broad philosophical approach to the goals of the organization is very scarce indeed. And the rational approach to problem solving involves a strategy that is unrealistically thorough. An executive, even with the help of the organization, cannot possibly consider every alternative solution to a problem. There is literally an infinite number of such alternative solutions, and searching for information about them is costly. Also, estimating the probability of success and the costs of implementing each alternative solution of which the executive and the organization are already aware is a process that cannot be pressed to the end prescribed by comprehensive rationality. Even for the most brilliant executive, knowledge is limited, and increasing it costs time and money, both of which are in limited supply for every organization.

Faced with severe limitations in information, time, and resources, executives and large bureaucracies, according to Simon and others, display a tendency to rely on **standard operating procedures** (SOPs) developed in the past, or on a **repertoire of prearranged responses.** SOPs and repertoires, or standard routines for dealing with problems or approaching goals, simplify the crucial problem of coordinating the

---

[1] Another important work in this field is Cyert and March (1963).

different parts of the bureaucracy. The implementation of both has already been analyzed and coordinated. If it becomes obvious that the SOPs and the *repertoire* of prearranged responses will not suffice, bureaucracies do not usually search for all possible alternatives. Instead, they give the most serious consideration to alternatives involving only incremental changes in SOPs and prearranged responses (Lindblom, 1959, p. 81). And the choice is not the one that the executive and his or her subordinates believe is the best possible one, but one that is good enough, or satisfactory. In other words, decision makers do not optimize, or pick the best strategy conceivable; instead, they **"satisfice,"** or settle for a solution they feel is sufficiently satisfactory to get them through the crisis (Simon, 1957, p. 89).

Several foreign policy analysts accept and build upon the essential point of organization theorists that decision making in large organizations is rarely "rational." A **cybernetic** theory of foreign policy decision making, for example, argues that such decision makers are typically both unable and unwilling to engage in the complex steps necessary to achieve "rationality," and that instead they approach problems with an intuitive approach based on past experience and simple analogies (Steinbruner, 1974). Another analyst argues that foreign policy makers respond to stress, and a shortage of time and energy, by relying on simple analogies and even simple-minded "causal explanations" regarding past events that form the basis of these analogies (Hybel, 1993). A **"noncompensatory" theory** of foreign policy decision making asserts that decision makers do not engage in the careful weighing of various alternatives according to their likely costs and benefits. In a "rational" process, decision makers might calculate that a possible shortcoming associated with one alternative can be *compensated* for by potential offsetting advantages involving that same alternative. But foreign policy makers are typically inclined instead to focus on one criterion, such as the extent to which various choices are likely to have an impact on their political fate at home (Mintz, 1993). Similarly, another model of foreign policy making is based on the assumption that the extent to which policymakers are rational depends on the circumstances surrounding a decision. "Rationality" is most likely if stress is neither too high nor too low. Otherwise, and probably most of the time, decision makers approach problems in a manner too simple to be described as "rational." They may, for example, make decisions according to a **"maximin principle,"** which

> suggests that decision makers single out an alternative whose worst outcome is preferred to the worst outcome stemming from any other alternative. . . . The implication of the maximin rule is that the weighting of the consequences associated with the various outcomes is minimized

or avoided altogether. Decision makers resort in such cases to a conservative worst-case analysis and select the "least of all evils" rather than the optimal or satisficing policy option (Maoz, 1990, p. 205).

"Rationality" and the 1914 Crisis

Bureaucratic reliance on prearranged responses played an apparently important role in the process that led to the First World War. Even a small dose of rational capability to deviate from prearranged procedures might well have altered the outcome of that process. But the Russians, to take a critical example, were set in their ways, even more than the average military bureaucracy (Tuchman, 1962, p. 61).

By 1911, pursuant to the alliance formed between the two countries in 1894, Russia had joined with France in a plan to attack Germany simultaneously in case of war. The Austro-Serbian struggle sucked Germany in, so the Russians put in motion their prearranged response for the attack against Germany. As noted in Chapter 1, Kaiser Wilhelm put in a request to Czar Nicholas to delay or at least partially reduce the Russian mobilization process. Nicholas attempted to do so. He issued an order for partial mobilization, but his generals refused to implement it. "The Russian General Staff . . . argued forcefully that a partial mobilization was impossible for technical military reasons relating to the mobilization plans" (Levy, 1986, p. 201).[2] They were afraid that any delay would give their enemies a chance to get an insurmountable lead on the Russians in the mobilization process. But the Russian military bureaucracy was also responding in the way any incrementalist would expect. The Russian military had laid out its mobilization plan many years before the Austro-Serbian crisis in 1914. Once the plan was already being implemented, the Russian generals unanimously declined to deviate from the plan (Stoessinger, 1993, p. 14).

The German military responded to the 1914 crisis with the same inflexibility. When German troops were already mounting an attack against Belgium and France, Kaiser Wilhelm thought he saw a chance to avoid a two-front war, if only the German army could be turned around and a last-minute change put into effect that would have involved an attack against Russia instead of France. The German chief of staff, Moltke, said that such a thing could not be done. Historian Barbara Tuchman (1962, pp. 74–75) describes the process that the kaiser wanted to modify in the hour of crisis:

---

[2] Levy (1986, p. 201) goes on to explain that "the institution of a general mobilization while a partial mobilization was under way would have delayed for months a systematic general mobilization against Germany. This would leave Russia dangerously exposed."

Once the button was pushed, the whole vast machinery for calling up, equipping, and transporting two million men began turning automatically. Reservists went to their designated depots, were issued uniforms, equipment, and arms, formed into companies and companies into battalions, were joined by cavalry, cyclists, artillery, medical units, cook wagons, blacksmith wagons, even postal wagons, moved according to prepared railway timetables to concentration points near the frontier where they would be formed into divisions, divisions into corps, and corps into armies ready to advance and fight. One army corps alone—out of the total 40 in the German forces—required 170 railway cars for officers, 965 for infantry, 2960 for cavalry, 1915 for artillery and supply wagons, 6010 in all, grouped in 140 trains and an equal number again for their supplies. From the moment the order was given, everything was to move at fixed times according to a schedule precise down to the number of train axles that would pass over a given bridge within a given time.

Is it any wonder that Moltke was reluctant to try to rearrange these procedures at the last moment?

The reluctance by the Russians and the Germans to alter their prearranged responses in this moment of crisis also corresponds with theories of foreign policy making emphasizing factors other than SOPs and prearranged responses. Undoubtedly, under the pressure of the moment, there was a tendency to simplify matters in the manner stipulated by the cybernetic theory of decision making. Then, too, it is quite clear that many decision makers involved were relying on a simple historical analogy involving the Franco-Prussian War, in which rapid mobilization seemed to be a key to a quick victory by the Prussians. The maximin principle also played a role in these decisions. The decision makers involved seemed not to be aiming at the best possible solution to their problems. They seemed more intent on avoiding the worst possible disaster, namely, suffering a devastating attack while too busy trying to adjust their prearranged responses to changing circumstances to be able to deal with it.

"Rationality" and the Cuban Missile Crisis

Many writers have pointed to the impact that bureaucratic rigidity and other forms of "irrationality" had on the process that led to the First World War, but it is easy to gain the impression from these writings that the rigidity or irrationality was unusual, a function of the peculiarities of the time or of the personalities involved. This impression is, of course, mistaken. The reasons that bureaucracies adhere to SOPs and prearranged responses did not disappear with the end of the First World War. It is predictable that large foreign policy bureaucracies will use SOPs, and the tendency has influenced several crises since 1914.

For example, SOPs and prearranged responses played an important role in the development of the Cuban missile crisis in 1962. The Soviets sent the missiles to Cuba in utmost secrecy, using various deception devices to mislead any observer. Yet when the missiles arrived in Cuba, no attempt was made to camouflage the sites, and, even more incredible, the surface-to-air missile (SAM), medium-range ballistic missile (MRBM), and intermediate-range ballistic missile (IRBM) sites constructed in Cuba were built to look exactly like the SAM, MRBM, and IRBM sites in the Soviet Union (Allison, 1971, p. 107).[3] Also, the Soviet military personnel arrived in Cuba wearing slacks and sport shirts to hide their identity, but they left the Cuban docks formed in ranks of four and piled into truck convoys. Furthermore, they decorated their barracks with standard military insignia (Allison, 1971, p. 109). All these indications, but especially the construction of the missile sites in Soviet style, made it rather easy for the United States, by way of U-2 flights, to figure out what was happening.

What accounts for this seemingly irrational behavior? Why the great secrecy and deception on the one hand and the blatant lack of secrecy on the other? The most plausible answer involves the bureaucratic tendency to adhere to SOPs. The delivery of the missiles to Cuba and their movement from the docks to the sites were the responsibilities of the GRU (Soviet military intelligence) and the KGB (the Communist Party intelligence organization). "Security is their standard operating procedure" (Allison, 1971, p. 110). So the missiles were hidden successfully until they reached their sites. What happened then is one of the many questions analyzed at two conferences (one held in Cambridge, Massachusetts, in 1987 and the other in Moscow in 1989) on the Cuban missile crisis that brought together many of those who participated in the decision-making processes during the crisis in both the U.S. and the Soviet governments. According to the organizers of these conferences, "It appears that the reason the Soviets failed to camouflage the missiles is that the Soviet standard operating procedures for constructing nuclear missile sites did not include the use of camouflage. All previous installations had been on Soviet territory; the installation crews in Cuba simply overlooked the importance of disguising their activities on foreign soil under the watchful eyes of the Americans" (Allyn, Blight, and Welch, 1989/90, p. 153). As for the shirt-and-slack-clad soldiers arriving at the Cuban docks, it is reasonable to guess that delivering them there was also the responsibility of organizations devoted to secrecy. But once they had arrived at their Cuban barracks, they adhered to procedures as if they were still in the Soviet Union.

---

[3] This discussion of the missile crisis relies heavily on Allison's work.

Shown above is one of the sites where Soviets placed nuclear missiles in Cuba in 1962. Because the missile sites were constructed according to the same standard operating procedures used to erect sites within the Soviet Union, the American government soon realized that Soviet missiles had been delivered to Cuba. SOURCE: John F. Kennedy Library.

The U.S. bureaucracies involved in the crisis were not immune to the tendency to adhere to SOPs or prearranged responses. The list of options considered by President Kennedy and his advisers was affected greatly by the repertoire of prearranged responses that the military had developed in the event of a crisis calling for an attack on Cuba. For example, one option considered by U.S. decision makers was a surgical air strike that would eliminate the Soviet missiles already in place. The U.S. Air Force insisted that this kind of strike would result in extensive collateral damage and probably fairly large numbers of Soviet casualties and would not necessarily knock out all the Soviet missiles.

Both these arguments may have been untrue from a rational point of view. The air force was not caught off guard by this opportunity to attack Cuba. Action against Castro by the United States had been anticipated, and a prearranged response had been carefully worked out. The trouble was that, given the context of the missile crisis and the desire for a surgical air strike, the response called for a strike of intolerable dimensions. "The 'air strike' option served up by the Air Force called for extensive bombardment of all storage depots, airports, and the artillery batteries opposite the naval base at Guantanamo Bay, as well as all missile sites" (Allison, 1971, p. 110). In short, when asked about the feasibility of a surgical air strike, the air force had modified its prearranged response, but only incrementally. It added the missile sites to the list of targets to be bombed. It subtracted nothing. To do so, the U.S. joint chiefs of staff insisted, would pose an unacceptable risk.

SOPs also affected the imposition of a quarantine by the United States designed to prevent missile-bearing Soviet ships from getting to Cuba. President Kennedy and his advisers decided on the quarantine, and the U.S. Navy set its SOPs into motion. The complexity of the task should not be underestimated. The quarantine was designed to monitor almost one million square miles of ocean. The navy assigned 180 ships to the task. Then, virtually at the last moment, the British ambassador suggested to Kennedy that precious time might be gained if the quarantine were modified. Originally, it was designed to intercept Soviet ships eight hundred miles from Cuba. If the quarantine procedures could be changed so that the Soviet ships would not be intercepted until they got to within, say, five hundred miles of Cuba, this delay would give the Soviets a substantial amount of extra time in which, it was hoped, they could change their minds. Kennedy agreed that this was a good idea and immediately ordered the navy to move the line of interception closer to Cuba.

The British ambassador's suggestion was unquestionably rational, and if bureaucracies behaved rationally, Kennedy's order would have been carried out without complaint. But the navy complained loudly: procedures could not be modified at the last minute in such a major way without some colossal foul-up, which, under the circumstances of the missile crisis, would have repercussions of horrifying dimensions. But Kennedy and his secretary of defense, Robert McNamara, were insistent, and the navy finally gave in.

Or did it? The navy did assure Kennedy that the line of interception had been pulled back, but an examination of the evidence on how the sighting and boarding of the ships was timed "confirms other suspicions. . . . Existing accounts to the contrary, the blockade was *not* moved as the President had ordered" (Allison, 1971, p. 130).[4] In short, even when confronted with the possibility that much of the world might be

---

[4] The account of this episode involving the quarantine procedures can be found on pp. 127–132. However, the validity of Allison's account has been challenged by, among others, Caldwell (1978, p. 628): "There are several intuitive reasons for believing that the Navy originally set the blockade at 800 miles and that this was moved in to 500 miles as a result of the presidential order."

devastated by a nuclear holocaust, the navy, according to some evidence, refused to modify its SOPs substantially.[5]

If Kennedy had issued the orders for the air strike despite the air force's warnings, or if the navy had intercepted Soviet ships eight hundred miles from Cuba despite Kennedy's order, and if either event had proved instrumental in the outbreak of a third world war, historians (if any were left) would probably have recognized a striking parallel between the First World War and the third. In fact, in a manner anticipated by theorists of foreign policy making who emphasize the tendency of decision makers to rely on simple analogies, President Kennedy himself pondered the potential for the Cuban missile crisis to result in catastrophe in a manner reminiscent of the crisis in 1914. "Having recently read Barbara Tuchman's book *The Guns of August* [about World War I], he mused about the miscalculations of the Germans, the Russians, the Austrians, the French, and the British, the confusion within each government that allowed the lot to tumble into war" (Allison, 1971, p. 218).

In 1914, the generals did not modify their prearranged responses to narrow the scope of the developing crisis. And in 1962, the U.S. Air Force and U.S. Navy did not modify their SOPs to limit the damage of an air strike or give the Soviets more time to consider alternatives. The fact that the Cuban missile crisis did not result in a third world war should obscure neither the similarity of the crises in 1914 and 1962 nor the effect that the persistent adherence of large bureaucracies to SOPs and prearranged responses can have on international politics.

"Rationality" and the Persian Gulf War

Obviously it is not necessary to go as far back in history as the First World War or even the Cuban missile crisis to find examples of foreign policy decision-making processes, especially during times of crisis, that relied on much less than totally "rational" strategies or procedures. Many analysts view the Persian Gulf War, which began with Iraq's attack on Kuwait in August 1990 and culminated in a retaliatory response by a coalition of states led by the United States in early 1991, as rife with "irrational" actions and policies on both sides. For example, American policymakers were surprised by Iraq's attack, even though

---

[5] At one point, McNamara pressed Chief of Naval Operations George Anderson for details on the navy's procedures for boarding Soviet ships. Anderson replied by picking up the *Manual of Naval Regulations* and waving it in McNamara's face, telling him that if he wanted to know what was to be done, he should simply refer to the *Manual*. McNamara is reported to have replied, "I don't give a damn what John Paul Jones would have done. I want to know what you are going to do, now" (quoted in Allison, 1971, p. 131).

"Saddam Hussein did not attempt to achieve surprise, and US officials had more than sufficient evidence to conclude that an invasion of Kuwait was probable" (Hybel, 1993, p. 33). Not only did the United States fail to respond in a "rational" way with an attempt to deter this impending attack; in retrospect the U.S. response seems to have encouraged Saddam Hussein to implement his plan. In April 1990, in response to a request by Hussein relayed by the Saudis to the United States, the United States assured Iraq that Israel would not attack Iraq as long as Iraq did not attack Israel (Hybel, 1993, p. 35).[6] By July 23, 1990, Iraq had 30,000 troops poised on the Kuwaiti border. U.S. State Department spokesperson Margaret D. Tutweiler chose that day to declare that the United States had "no defense treaties with Kuwait, no special defense or security commitments to Kuwait." Then a couple of days later U.S. Ambassador April Glaspie met with Saddam Hussein and (at least according to an Iraqi transcript of the meeting), assured him that the United States had "no opinion on the Arab-Arab conflicts, like your border disagreement with Kuwait" (Stoessinger, 1993, p. 192).[7]

Having thus (albeit unwittingly) encouraged Hussein to launch his attack, the United States, as one might suppose both from the crises that led to the First World War and the Cuban missile crisis respectively and from general bureaucratic tendencies, responded by implementing a prearranged response for a crisis in this part of the world. President Bush's advisers presented him with "Operation Plan 90-1002," a plan originally drafted to repel an attack by Iran or the Soviet Union and now marginally restructured in order to address the problem of defending Saudi Arabia or liberating Kuwait. This plan was somewhat reminiscent of the prearranged plans devised by the American military to launch a full-scale invasion of Cuba, which were put on the table for discussion during the Cuban missile crisis in response to policymakers' desires for a possible "surgical" strike against the missiles in Cuba. As in that situation, the presence of this prearranged response may have had an arguably "irrational" impact on the decision-making process. Secretary of State James Baker, at least, is known to have felt at the time that the

---

[6] The possible importance of these assurances was emphasized by the Saudi ambassador to the United States, Prince Bandar bin Sultan, shortly after Iraq's attack on Kuwait. "Saddam," according to Bandar, "had sought and received American and Israeli assurances he would not be attacked. He had protected his western flank with Israel, freeing him to do what he wanted on the east with Kuwait" (Woodward, 1991, p. 239; cited by Hybel, 1993, p. 113).

[7] Glaspie later insisted in a hearing before the U.S. Senate Foreign Relations Committee that she had warned Saddam that the United States would insist that the crisis with Kuwait be resolved in a nonviolent manner, and that this warning had been deleted from the Iraqi record of the meeting (Stoessinger, 1993, p. 192).

American response to the crisis had not been decided upon "rationally"; instead, he felt that "the level of force had been decided . . . by Operation Plan 90-1002" (Hybel, 1993, pp. 62–78).

Then, too, President Bush relied heavily on simple historical analogies in order to make his decision about what to do after Iraq had occupied Kuwait. In a simplified manner that the cybernetic theory of decision making would predict, George Bush based his decision on lessons from the "1938 Munich debacle" and on the assumption that Hussein and the attack he had launched on Kuwait were reminiscent of Hitler and his surprise attacks in the 1930s (Hybel, 1993, pp. 8–9). President Bush and his advisers also relied on analogies involving the Vietnam War in this strategic planning. "President Bush demanded of the military that they avoid at all costs another Vietnam" (Freedman and Karsh, 1991, p. 16). Basing policy on this particular analogy produced at least a couple of contrasting effects on American responses to the crisis. It led to the use of overwhelming force against Iraq, in an attempt to avoid American casualties. But it also made the United States cautious once that overwhelming force had successfully removed Iraqi troops from Kuwait. Bush and his advisers resisted the temptation (whether "rationally" or wisely or not is debated to this day) to invade Iraq and remove the Hussein regime. "Restricting the objectives to the liberation of Kuwait did not involve the risk of a Vietnam-type quagmire. . . . It is of note that when the United States began to get sucked into the postwar civil war in Iraq, it was this fear of a quagmire that was most often mentioned" (Freedman and Karsh, 1991, p. 17).

President Bush also, according to one analyst, utilized a "noncompensatory" process of evaluating the alternatives available to him after Iraq had occupied Kuwait. The president apparently had made up his mind to attack Iraq by December 1990. "There was no comprehensive evaluation of the alternatives as would be required by a compensatory process. . . . 'There was little or no process where alternatives were systematically weighed and argued'" (Woodward, 1991, p. 320; cited by Mintz, 1993, p. 607). Instead, President Bush eliminated the options of unilateral withdrawal, or containment (that is, simply keeping troops in the area to protect Saudi Arabia and other states in the region) "using the noncompensatory strategy of elimination" (Mintz, 1993, p. 610).

It might seem strange to question the rationality of the responses and policies adopted by the United States in the Persian Gulf War in light of its clear success in removing Iraqi troops from Kuwait at such a relatively low cost in American lives.[8] But critics of models based on

---

[8] "On the eve of the ground war President Bush was warned to expect some 5000 casualties. In the event, U.S. battle deaths were under 150" (Freedman and Karsh, 1991, p. 37).

the assumption that foreign policies are typically based on rationality will argue that "this case, more than many others, establishes that success does not prove rationality. The momentous decision of 17 January 1991 [to launch the war against Iraq] was not the outcome of a rational process . . ." (Hybel, 1993, p. 79). Of course, defenders of "rational choice" models of foreign policy making will, as we shall see below, argue conversely that foreign policy failures do not necessarily justify the conclusion that the processes that produced them are "irrational."

Nevertheless, there are good reasons to conclude that Saddam Hussein's decisions in this crisis were also a good deal less than rational. There are indications, first of all, that Saddam's invasion of Kuwait was a product of economic desperation. Iraq's long war with Iran had left it $70 billion in debt (Stoessinger, 1993, p. 189). Since Iraq had also suffered the loss of half a million soldiers in that war (Singer, 1991, p. 63), one might conclude that another war so soon (the Iran-Iraq war had lasted from 1980 to 1988) would have been the last thing a rational decision maker would seek out.[9] But in retrospect some analysts are convinced that "the invasion [was] a desperate attempt to shore up [Hussein's] regime in the face of the dire economic straits created by the Iran-Iraq war" (Freedman and Karsh, 1991, p. 10).

Having brought on economic sanctions with his invasion (which of course only worsened the economic problems he was ostensibly attempting to solve), Hussein managed to convince himself that his strategy would ultimately work by relying on simple and, as it turned out, misleading historical analogies. Influenced both by American reactions to casualties in Vietnam and the U.S. retreat from Lebanon after the loss of fewer than three hundred Marines to a terrorist attack in 1983, Saddam told the U.S. ambassador to Iraq in April 1990 (less than four months before the attack on Kuwait), "Yours is a society which cannot accept 10,000 battle dead" (Freedman and Karsh, 1991, p. 15). Perhaps that was not such an "irrational" misperception. We will never know for sure. What we do know is that Hussein's confidence that he would be able to inflict something like 10,000 casualties on American forces was apparently based on an analogical thinking relating the Iran-Iraq war to his upcoming battle with the United States. After all, his troops had inflicted 750,000 deaths on Iranian soldiers during the

---

[9] And that is what American foreign policy makers tended to believe. "U.S. intelligence . . . had concluded that although Saddam Hussein wanted to become the Gulf region's dominant figure, the costs absorbed by his country during its war against Iran would restrain him from using force in the immediate future. . . . [U.S. officials] were convinced that it would be 'irrational' for Saddam to initiate a new war after having paid such a high price during the Iran-Iraq war" (Hybel, 1993, pp. 30, 51).

POLICY CHOICES

Dealing with International Aggression

ISSUE: Saddam Hussein has invaded and occupied Kuwait (August 1990), and the United States (as well as the United Nations) must decide on an appropriate response.

Option #1: The United States and the United Nations can impose economic sanctions on Iraq and wait for several months, perhaps even a year, for the sanctions to force Saddam Hussein to evacuate Kuwait.

Advantages: (a) Military options are always unpredictable in their outcome to some extent; a military attack could result in complications and problems that will be avoided with this step. (b) It will be easier to create a consensus for this step in the U.N. Security Council and the U.S. Congress, avoiding a divisive dispute that could preoccupy both bodies. (c) The United States has had strained relationships with many Arab states because of its support for Israel; consequently, while those Arab states are likely to be more tolerant of economic sanctions, a military attack might further strain those relationships.

Disadvantages: (a) Economic sanctions might not work. Pressures created by the sanctions may cause the unity of the coalition to break down and the resulting leaks may allow Iraq access to vital supplies and financial resources before it is forced to evacuate Kuwait. (b) The price of oil is likely to remain high as long as Iraqi troops remain in Kuwait, posing a potential threat to oil wells in Saudi Arabia or Bahrain. Economic sanctions will take a while to work, and the added cost for oil will impose a penalty of billions of dollars on all who must import it. (c) The sanctions will enable

1980s (Singer, 1991, p. 63). But a substantial part of Iran's army consisted of ill-equipped teenagers. Iraq not only had superior firepower; its air force had given it complete control of the air during that war. In short, "Saddam's failure to distinguish between the coalition forces confronting him and the poorly equipped and ill-trained Iranian army led him to the mistaken belief that Iraq's defensive posture would suffice to inflict unacceptable pain on the enemy" when and if the coalition forces attacked his troops occupying Kuwait (Freedman and Karsh, 1991, p. 36). The Iraqi army found itself unable to mount anything like effective resistance to the devastating attack by coalition forces. But neither the

Saddam Hussein to blame all economic problems on those states that impose the sanctions, resulting in an even more entrenched, immovable Hussein regime.

Option #2: The United States and the United Nations can organize a massive coalition and attack Iraqi troops in Kuwait from the air, and then on the ground.

Advantages: (a) If such an attack is postponed indefinitely, hundreds of thousands of troops will have to be stationed in the desert through a long hot, anxiety-ridden summer. (b) If Saddam Hussein invades Kuwait, and meets no firm, military resistance, other potential aggressors may be inclined to accept the risks of launching such an attack; a firm military response may help deter future aggression. (c) A successful military operation will resolve the situation more quickly than sanctions and result in a significantly lower price for oil in a much shorter time.

Disadvantages: (a) Some military analysts anticipate that the Americans and the allied forces could suffer large numbers of casualties in an attack on Iraqi forces in Kuwait, who have had months to dig in and prepare. That level of casualties might make it politically impossible to continue the military operation until Iraqi troops are dislodged from Kuwait. (b) An attack led by the United States might energize anti-American or Islamic fundamentalist elements in several important Arab states, resulting in the overthrow of important, more moderate regimes that are tolerant of the United States (such as Egypt). (c) Such an attack on Iraq might be viewed by Arab states and citizens as blatant favoritism for Israel, which has long been in defiance of U.N. resolutions to remove its troops from territory taken over in the war of 1967, and possibly jeopardize U.S.-Arab relations for years to come.

Note: In retrospect, the attack seems to have been a success. But that could have been the result of rampant dumb luck, rather than a wise policy choice.

United States nor the Iraqis, arguably, dealt with this crisis in anything like a "rational" manner.

Are Foreign Policies Rational?

Still, people who emphasize the tendency of organizations to adhere to SOPs, prearranged responses, and simplified decision-making tactics such as simple historical analogies may thereby exaggerate that inclination. Knowledge of organizational procedures, for example, may allow a better understanding of the events to which they pertain, but in most cases procedures do not necessarily have a decisive effect on the shape of events. In virtually all the examples just discussed, other factors probably played a more decisive role than SOPs, prearranged procedures, cybernetic reasoning, simple historical analogies, and so on.[10]

Consider first the crisis leading to the First World War. The Russian generals were reluctant to call off general mobilization not only because of an attachment to their SOPs but also because they calculated that, given Russia's geographic expanse and relative military inefficiency, any delay in mobilization might put Russia at a considerable disadvantage in the opening weeks of a general war. In addition, as one contemporary historical analysis concludes, "the Russian generals . . . did press for early mobilization. But this was only because they thought that war was unavoidable for political reasons, a view that the civilian government also shared" (Trachtenberg, 1990/91, p. 148). And the German generals did not refuse to call off their attack on France purely out of some nonrational attachment to prearranged procedures. Those procedures were based primarily on the reasonable calculation that France could mobilize more quickly than Russia and thus must be dealt with first. The German military planners also expected France to launch a determined offensive thrust and so leave itself open to a deadly counteroffensive. The plans of the armies in the respective countries in August 1914 "not only reflected the belief that states are vulnerable and conquest is easy; they actually caused the states adopting them to *be* vulnerable" (Snyder, 1984, p. 114). And events at the beginning of the First World War were to prove that the calculations of the Germans regarding the vulnerability of the French were *almost* correct. The Germans came close to repeating their quick victory in the Franco-Prussian War in the nineteenth century.[11] In short,

> the idea that the First World War came about because statesmen were overwhelmed by military imperatives and thus "lost control" of the situation . . . was [not] the product of careful and disinterested historical analysis. . . . The remarkable thing about the claims that events moved "out of control" in 1914 is how little basis in fact they actually have (Trachtenberg, 1990/91, pp. 148, 150).

---

[10] The logic of some of the following arguments is the same as that offered by Levy (1986, p. 137) when he says that "if political decisionmakers adhere to . . . original plan[s] for [strategic] reasons, then the explanation for the rigid adherence to . . . original plan[s] lies with military necessity, rather than the nature of the routines themselves."

[11] "As it happened, the [German] offensive came close to proving itself again as decisive as in Bismarck's wars. If the offensive momentum once lost could never be regained, it was almost never lost in the first place" (Quester, 1977, p. 83).

In the Cuban missile crisis, organizational procedures and bureaucratic politics may well have accounted for some interesting anomalies, such as the Soviet failure to camouflage the missile sites in Cuba or the delay in the American U-2 flights. But it would be a mistake to attempt to understand the Cuban missile crisis solely, or even primarily, in terms of organizational procedures and bureaucratic politics. For example, "the Soviet Union had never before stationed strategic nuclear weapons outside its own territorial borders" (Allison, 1971, p. 40). Obviously, if one approaches the crisis convinced that bureaucracies are characterized by strict adherence to SOPs, one will find it difficult to understand why the Soviets took the step that precipitated the crisis in the first place; furthermore, one will have no idea when to expect such drastic departures from SOPs. And the U.S. decision on a quarantine rather than a surgical air strike may have been dictated to some extent by the air force's reluctance to modify its prearranged plans for an attack on Cuba. But the crucial calculation that such a strike might not destroy all the missiles in Cuba and might result in Soviet deaths could well have emerged (and, indeed, might have been more likely to emerge) even in the absence of the air force's prearranged plans.

Finally, it may well be that during the Persian Gulf crisis George Bush relied on "cybernetic" processes and simple historical analogies to conclude that he must respond militarily to Iraq's annexation of Kuwait. And Saddam Hussein likewise may have been misled by conclusions based on analogies with the Vietnam War, the U.S. experience in Lebanon, and the Iran-Iraq War. But a lot of other people were consulted before Bush made his decision, and the considerable support that the president received for his decisions was probably based on a more complex array of considerations than, for example, equating Hussein with Hitler. Hussein did commit a pretty clear violation of international law, setting a precedent with easily conceivable damaging consequences. His control of Kuwait and threat to Saudi Arabia added substantially to the price of oil all over the world, creating hardships for millions. Perhaps, if given more time, the economic sanctions might have worked. But on the other hand, Saddam Hussein is *still* in power after *years* of sanctions, and even after suffering the devastating defeat in Kuwait. And in retrospect, Hussein may have been excessively optimistic about the resistance he could mount to an attack by the coalition he faced. He obviously drastically overestimated the amount of suffering he could impose on that coalition. But he did not necessarily have to be "irrational" to do this. The evening before the ground attack against Iraq began, President Bush himself "was warned to expect some 5000 casualties" (Freedman and Karsh, 1991, p. 37).

THE "RATIONALITY" OF DECISION MAKING

Another reason for limiting the weight one gives to "irrational" forces (such as SOPs and bureaucratic politics) in explaining how foreign policy decisions are made is that such decisions, especially in times of crisis, later appear to have been "rational" when analyzed systematically. For example, in *The War Trap*, Bruce Bueno de Mesquita (1981) analyzes decisions made by states to initiate international wars (and other less serious military conflicts) from 1816 to 1974. He assumes that these decisions were made in a "rational" way—that is, that decision makers calculated expected gains and losses from their actions and avoided actions that would bring net losses. This assumption is admittedly debatable. It will seem unrealistic to those who focus on the impact of SOPs, bureaucratic infighting, cybernetic processes, and simplified historical analogies on decision making. Also, wars are often thought of as the epitome of irrationality, so the assumption that decision makers on the brink of war are rational will strike many people as a crucial initial step in exactly the wrong direction.

Such skepticism may be based partially on a misunderstanding of the term *rational* as used by theorists such as Bueno de Mesquita. So called **"rational choice"** theorists typically have an extremely simple and straightforward notion of what it means to be rational. For them actors are being rational if, when confronted with "two alternatives which give rise to outcomes . . . [they] choose the one which yields the . . . preferred outcome" (Luce and Raiffa, 1957).

It is quite clear that many critics of rational choice models have much more ambitious notions of rationality in mind when they argue that rational choice models are unrealistic. This in turn means that at least sometimes they criticize explanations based on assumptions that decision makers are rational for ignoring many factors that they (the rational choice explanations) do consider. "Can a . . . rational actor have preferences rooted in an incomplete, imperfect, or even erroneous information? Yes," according to one defender of rational choice models. "Can an individual whose vision is clouded by the pressures of time and stress in a crisis still be considered rational? . . . Yes" (Zagare, 1990, p. 242).

> In this perspective, rationality implies neither education nor refinement nor common sense nor reasonableness. . . . [Rational choice theorists] therefore do not hesitate to attribute rationality even to rats or to "seriously disturbed and/or very stupid people with no education and who had been institutionalized for long periods of time"[12] (Weede, 1996, p. 5).

---

[12] Weede is quoting here from McKenzie and Tullock (1978).

In this context, therefore, *rational* obviously does not mean "normal," and certainly not "wise" or "totally objective." Bueno de Mesquita (1981, p. 31) points out that, as he uses the concept, "it is entirely conceivable that people like Hitler or Goering [were] completely rational though aberrant and abhorrent. . . . Being rational simply implies that the decision maker uses a maximizing strategy in calculating how best to achieve his goals." In such theories, the goals of the decision maker are basically treated as given. The assumption is that the decision maker will select options that he or she perceives as likely to lead to the achievement of those goals.

Bueno de Mesquita presents his theory in the form of calculations that national leaders make when considering the initiation of a war against another state. The theory posits that leaders calculate their expected utility for initiating a war, that is, they estimate the probability of a victory weighted by the potential payoff of a victory. In making these calculations, the crucial factors they take into account are the military-industrial capability that their own state possesses (compared with that of their opponents), the probability that additional states will enter into the fray on either side, and the military-industrial capabilities of those additional states. Decision makers also pay close attention, according to Bueno de Mesquita's theory, to the structure of formal alliances among all the states involved in the dispute, for example, to help them estimate the probability that additional states will enter into the conflict, and on which side. According to this theory, unless the net result they derive from all these calculations is that they can win, and that the payoff from that win is great enough to offset the risk that they might lose, policymakers will not initiate a war.

In fact, it is very unlikely that national leaders approach decisions to initiate wars precisely in the manner described by Bueno de Mesquita. His theory is based on a simplification of the decision-making process that, if valid, incorporates the most fundamental factors that affect that process. The theory asserts *not* that decision makers actually sit down and make the calculations precisely as described by the theory, but rather that decision makers will behave *as if* they had made such calculations. Historically, actual decisions to initiate wars have doubtless been quite different from one another in many ways and have been affected by many factors not taken into account by Bueno de Mesquita. Yet if his theory is based on factors so central to decision making that it captures the essence of that process, then the predictions made by the theory will be accurate.

How does this theory stand up under scrutiny? In the most general terms, a look at all pairs of states for each year from 1816 to 1974 reveals that war initiations were thirty-six times more likely when the expected utility for the initiator was positive than when it was not (Bueno de Mesquita, 1984, p. 354). It might also be relevant to note that one analyst concludes from his review of wars since 1400 that "it is impossible to identify a single case in which it can be said that a war started accidentally in which it was not, at the time the war broke out, the deliberate intention of at least one party that war should take place. . . . A decision to make war . . . when it occurs, is deliberate and intentional. . . ." (Luard, 1986, p. 232).

This theory may to some extent have been modified in ways that might make it more acceptable to some of its critics. While the original version specified only the necessary conditions for a war to be initiated, a more recent modification specifies both the necessary and sufficient conditions for eight different outcomes of conflict among states—for example, that the status quo will be preserved, that the target state will acquiesce to the initiator's demand, that the dispute will be resolved by negotiation, or that war will be initiated by one of the states in the dispute (Bueno de Mesquita and Lalman, 1992). One of the main adjustments this more recent theory makes is that it takes into account the impact of domestic politics. That is, decision makers are assumed not only to be focused on the "national interest" in the manner of more traditional theories of international politics (i.e., "realist" theories) but also to be concerned, in fact *primarily* concerned, about their own personal interest, most important, to stay in power. One of the more interesting implications of this modified theory, especially in light of the discussion in Chapter 6 about the historical absence of war between democratic states, is that whether or not states involved in disputes are democratic is crucial to an understanding of conflict processes between states.

Another version of the same basic theory or model may go even further in responding to critics of a "rational choice" approach to foreign policy and international politics. It has been refined into a tool that can be used to forecast policy decisions and the results of bargaining, negotiation, and conflict in a wide variety of political settings (Bueno de Mesquita, Newman, and Rabushka, 1985, 1996). In this modified form, the model focuses on competition among groups within and across national boundaries, as opposed to governments in opposing states. Rational choice approaches are often criticized for assuming that states are **unitary rational actors,** that is, that they think, make decisions, and in general behave as if they were rational, individual human beings. "One of the key characteristics of the approach under consideration here, however, is that it rests on a general bargaining model that can treat states as unitary actors, or analyze bargaining among subnational actors, even individual leaders" (Ray and Russett, 1996, p. 452).

Rational choice models are often criticized for what many consider to be excessive simplicity. But this one looks at the interactions involved in bargaining situations in precise detail, from the separate viewpoints of each player in every pair of players involved in the process. In addition, it takes into account psychological factors such as the attitudes of each of the players toward risk, that is, whether they tend to be risk averse, or relatively risk acceptant. Some theories based on rational choice principles are rarely, if ever, tested against data from real situations, to see if their possibly impeccable mathematical derivations apply in practice as well as under often unrealistic assumptions. But this model is virtually always evaluated on the basis of data about the "real world."

Finally, this model is quite abstract and therefore does not take into account the individual idiosyncratic factors of each particular bargaining situation. For example, it is applied to negotiations involving adherents of Islam in the Middle East as well as Catholics in Latin America, without explicitly taking into account the vast cultural differences between the Middle East and Latin America. Implicitly, however, this approach to the analysis of political bargaining, negotiation, or conflict does incorporate insights regarding cultural differences by relying on area specialists and "experts" on individual countries for the basic data on which predictions are made. These traditionally trained academic specialists are asked to specify who the major players are in the situation being analyzed, and then to rate each of those players numerically according to the power or resources they have in this bargaining situation, what their position is on the issue at hand, and how much they care about the issue being negotiated. It is important to understand that these experts are *not* asked to make predictions, and the predictions produced by the model do not represent some kind of average opinion among the experts—in fact, typically only one expert is consulted. Quite frequently, in fact, the forecasts based on this model contradict what the experts feel is going to happen. And more often than not, the model's forecasts turn out to be valid by a substantial margin, even though they are different from what most of the experts would have predicted.[13]

This model has been used with considerable success to forecast political decisions and political interactions in more than sixty countries with respect to more than two thousand political issues. Accurate forecasts have predicted, for example, the rise to power of Yuri Andropov as a successor to Leonid Brezhnev in the Soviet Union, the rise to power of Hashemi Rafsanjani in Iran, the decision by the Chinese government to crack down on prodemocracy advocates in Tiananmen Square in China, and the defeat of Daniel Ortega and the Sandinista government by the coalition led by Violetta Chamorro in the 1990

---

[13] "A number of predictions by [this forecasting model] have contradicted those made by the intelligence community, nearly always represented by the analysts who provided the input data. In every case, the [model's] forecasts proved to be correct" (Feder, 1995).

election in Nicaragua (Bueno de Mesquita, 1993).[14] On the basis of data available in May 1991, the model produced a prediction that a coup would occur shortly in the Soviet Union, and that it would fail (Ray and Russett, 1996). More recently, the model produced an accurate prediction that NAFTA would be passed by the U.S. Congress (Fuchs, Kugler, and Pachon, 1997) and that Boris Yeltsin would win the presidential election in Russia in 1996 (Kugler and Abdollahian, 1997).[15] Bueno de Mesquita, Newman, and Rabushka (1996, p. 98), in advance of both Hong Kong's incorporation into the People's Republic of China in 1997 and the death of Deng Xiaoping (which the authors fearlessly predicted would ultimately come to pass), predicted that although China has promised to preserve Hong Kong's free-market economy for at least fifty years, "political troubles in China will probably force a reexamination of such promises. Indeed, we believe that Hong Kong will fall victim to the political upheaval between central and regional powers [in China]. The slowing of economic progress will not happen without harming Hong Kong." As of this writing, the validity of that prediction is yet to be determined.

And predictions based on this model are not *always* borne out. For example, in September and October 1990, analyses based on the model suggested that the crisis initiated by Iraq's attack on Kuwait in August of that year would be resolved peacefully.[16] The creator of the "noncom-

---

[14] It is only fair to point out that to some extent it is necessary to rely on Bueno de Mesquita's evaluation of the success of his own approach, since many of the forecasts in question are not and were not publicly available before the predicted events occurred. But Stanley Feder has published a recently declassified report for the CIA about the model (Feder 1995), and in 1989 he asserted that this model "has been gaining increased acceptance at the agency and has resulted in accurate predictions in 90 percent of the situations in which it has been utilized." See "Statistics, Analysts Help CIA Make Political Forecasts," *Salt Lake City Tribune*, March 1, 1989. Several additional sources of evidence, together with a list of recently published predictions, are discussed in Ray and Russett (1996) and in Feng and Kugler (1997).

[15] For this author's evaluation of these and several other recent efforts at political forecasting based on Bueno de Mesquita's model, see Ray (1997). The model is also discussed in detail, and applied to several issues arising in recent years in the European Union, in Bueno de Mesquita and Stokman (1994).

[16] "In September and October, the model forecasted peaceful outcomes" (Kugler, Snider, and Longwell, 1994, p. 142). The authors go on to point out, however, that "reconsidering this evaluation with hindsight we note that our judgment was clouded by a personal desire to see a peaceful resolution of the Gulf crisis" (p. 142). They also indicate that forecasts based on the model had suggested that Israel would not attack Iraq during this crisis, and that this forecast received "an important test . . . after Israel was attacked by SCUD missiles on January 17. . . . Most experts initially assumed that Israel would react following a well established pattern of prior Israeli retaliation policy. We now know that Israel chose not to retaliate. . . . Thus, Israel's January actions were precisely anticipated by the analysis of political dynamics in September and October" (Kugler, Snider, and Longwell, 1995, p. 138).

pensatory" model of decision making discussed earlier, taking note of this mistake, argues that it indicates a weakness in analyses and forecasts based on the assumption of rationality (Mintz, 1993).

Nor is Bueno de Mesquita's theory in its more general form beyond criticism. It has generated lively disputes ever since it first appeared in 1981 (Majeski and Sylvan, 1984; Wagner, 1984; Luterbacher, 1984; Moul, 1987, Nicholson, 1987; Simowitz and Price, 1990). But the ability of analysts relying on the expected utility approach to demonstrate that in past crises states have typically acted as if they based their actions on rational calculations, as well as to make accurate predictions about political decisions and the results of interactions between groups within states, suggests that there is indeed a consistent element of rationality in most policymaking processes, especially if one keeps in mind the modest definition of "rationality" upon which models of this kind are typically based.

DIPLOMATS AND BARGAINING

Diplomats—that is, those people officially engaged in government-to-government negotiations or bargaining—are often misunderstood and unappreciated. In the popular conception, the essence of the diplomatic profession is deceit ("An ambassador is an honest man sent to lie abroad for the commonwealth," Sir Henry Wotton observed in 1604) and professional diplomats are almost universally suspected of having lost touch with their home countries and the values of their citizens. They typically spend so much time out of the country that they only naturally become more sympathetic to the concerns of the "foreigners" with whom they live than does the average citizen who rarely leaves the country; and that sympathy can easily be mistaken for diminished loyalty.

Also, to the average person, diplomats seem to play a lot of silly games when they negotiate. At the truce negotiations during the Korean War, for example, diplomats spent considerable time and energy discussing the relative height of flags placed on the negotiating table. At the Paris peace talks aimed at ending the Vietnam War, diplomats wrangled for weeks (while soldiers and citizens died) over the shape of the bargaining table. Why do diplomats engage in such seemingly senseless behavior?

An important part of the answer involves a fundamental attitude that diplomats, as well as national leaders, seem to have concerning bargaining and negotiating with their counterparts. Although this concern is not made explicit in every case, diplomats involved in international bargaining are almost always less concerned about the issue immediately at hand than about the impact of the settlement on resolving future issues. Let us consider first the implicit bargaining that goes on between nations (and their leaders) over crucial issues of peace and war.

It is highly probable, for example, that in 1939 Britain and France chose to take a hard line against Germany when it invaded Poland not because the leaders in those countries were primarily concerned about Poland per se but rather because they were worried about how the settlement between Poland and Germany would affect the resolution of future European territorial issues. Because they had already backed down in the face of several of Hitler's aggressive actions (for example, against Austria and Czechoslovakia), the British and the French felt that they could not allow Hitler to resolve his conflict with Poland with such ease that he would conclude that any future conflict could be settled just as easily and victoriously. Similarly, although Kennedy and his advisers were quite concerned about the missiles the Soviets had placed in Cuba in 1962, the missiles themselves were not their greatest concern. Rather, their main worry was that if they allowed the Soviets to get away with sneaking missiles into Cuba, it would be impossible to predict the Soviets' next scheme, and the ability of the United States to deter such schemes would be called into serious question.[17] At the time of the Vietnam War, Vietnam was not that valuable to the United States either economically or strategically. But U.S. policymakers at the time made clear, with their talk of Munich and the domino theory, that they were very concerned about how an unsatisfactory outcome of the Vietnam War might affect future conflicts. Subversives all over the world, it was believed, might be so encouraged by a North Vietnamese victory that similar wars of national liberation would break out in several other parts of the world.

After the American hostages were seized in Iran, President Carter was not concerned mainly with getting them back. If that had been his top priority, he presumably could have secured their release by returning the shah to Iran or by giving in to other Iranian demands. Carter's primary concern was that if he gave up too much too soon to get the hostages back, the idea that the United States could be coerced into significant concessions by simply seizing U.S. diplomats would become widespread in the years to come.

And even in the case of Iraq's attack on Kuwait in 1990, despite the intrinsic value of all the Kuwaiti oil, it was not only the fate of Kuwait that was on the minds of the leaders of the United States and the other members of the anti-Iraq coalition when they mounted the massive effort to resist that attack. The precedent was also bothersome. This is

---

[17] "All were deeply concerned to avoid setting a precedent whereby the Soviets believed they might deceive the United States and then escape unpunished when caught in the lie. . . . If the United States failed to stand up to Khrushchev in such a blatant case of deception, what gamble would he try next?" (Blight, Nye, and Welch, 1987).

not to say that only principles and precedents were at stake or that oil was irrelevant. On the contrary, one important reason for resisting Iraq's takeover of Kuwait was to prevent the Iraqi regime from concluding that it might also seize the oilfields of Saudi Arabia, Bahrain, and Qatar with equal ease. There was also the broader concern, evoked in President Bush's comparisons of Saddam Hussein with Hitler and his references to a new world order, that if Iraq's invasion were allowed to go unchallenged, states all over the world would be more tempted to resolve their disputes with military force, especially in cases such as Iraq's dispute with Kuwait, where one state had such a clear military advantage.

Nations and their diplomatic representatives are especially concerned about the impact of settling present issues on future issues because precedents and the status quo have an almost sacred place in international relations.

> Whoever has a thing, it is his unless another can show cause why not. Whatever the existing position, that is right until someone can show better. If a state which demands or makes changes cannot show this, it is suspect as a force for chaos. . . . The *status quo* has a prima facie justification against the revisionist in all eyes, usually even his own (Northedge and Donelan, 1971, p. 77).

Diplomats engaged in bargaining are always concerned that a concession on the present issue will imply that concessions on similar or related issues in the future will be expected and will be very difficult to refuse.

In short, because the status quo is so important, and because the settlement of the present issue can establish a precedent for the settlement of future issues (that is, alter the status quo), diplomats are anxious to avoid giving the impression that they make concessions easily. The shape of the bargaining table may not itself be important, but concessions quickly granted on that issue may create expectations of quick concessions on other issues that will be difficult to overcome. And if the diplomat creates the impression that he or she is a little crazy for being so stubborn about the shape of the bargaining table, that may not be all bad. As one well-known scholar of bargaining in international politics points out, "If a man knocks at a door and says that he will stab himself on the porch unless given $10, he is more likely to get the $10 if his eyes are bloodshot" (Schelling, 1960, p. 22). In other words, the man is more likely to get the money if he somehow conveys the impression that he is actually crazy enough (because his eyes are bloodshot) to stab himself if refused. Similarly, if a diplomat can convey the impression that he or she is really a tough nut to crack even on such a seemingly minor issue as the shape of the bargaining table, that reputation may stand him or her in good stead during negotiations over the more important issues.

Of course, taking a hard line can sometimes lead to unfortunate outcomes. The United States, for example, refused for years to back down in its battle with North Vietnam over the fate of South Vietnam and yet failed to achieve its objective despite that prolonged effort. One might assume that states would learn from such experiences that a more conciliatory bargaining strategy is called for. But systematic analysis of eighteen serious international disputes that occurred between 1905 and 1962 reveals that diplomats and other makers of foreign policy may not draw such conclusions from previous foreign policy failures. "Prudence suggests that a state that has suffered a recent defeat— whether through war or by being forced to submit in an escalating crisis—should act with greater caution in the next encounter with the same adversary." But what the analysis of these eighteen disputes shows instead is that "policymakers view crisis bargaining as a test of a state's power and resolve, so that unsuccessful outcomes are seen as resulting from a failure to demonstrate sufficient resolve." So when states lose one conflict, "the lesson tends to be to use more coercive bargaining the next time" (Leng, 1983, pp. 415–416).

The logic or theory behind such a coercive strategy is that "effective . . . bargaining [is] dependent on exploiting the other side's fear of war through the use of credible threats and punishments, that is, on demonstrating a willingness to accept the risk of war to achieve state objectives" (Leng, 1993, p. 191). This is an important component of the "realist" theory discussed in Chapter 2. This outlook on international politics leads to what might be called a **"bullying" strategy** of bargaining, because it relies heavily on force and threats of force, as opposed to compromises and "carrots," or rewards, for desired behavior. A bullying strategy relies almost exclusively on severe threats and punishments until and unless the bargainer's demands are accepted.

But diplomatic bargaining is not a simple game in which one succeeds by adopting extreme positions or acting tough all of the time. Data on forty international crises that occurred between 1816 and 1980 indicate that a bullying strategy was used only about 35 percent of the time. Almost as often, the participants in those crises instead utilized a more flexible and conciliatory **"reciprocating" strategy,** in which one side imitates or duplicates the kind of diplomatic moves made by the other party regarding a dispute or crisis. Bargainers who engage in a reciprocating strategy respond to coercive or bullying moves involving force or the threat of force with threatening or violent moves of their own. But unlike "bullies" who rely on threats or force regardless of what the other side does, reciprocating strategists respond in a cooperative or conciliatory way to compromising moves and signals from the other side (Leng, 1993, p. 200).

"Realists" would expect that bullying strategies work better than reciprocating strategies, while some social scientists who analyze bar-

One important site of international diplomatic bargaining is the Security Council of the United Nations. Here the U.S. Ambassador to the U.N., Madeleine Albright, votes for a measure opposed by the ambassador from the United Kingdom (on her right), but supported by the ambassador from Venezuela (on her left). Source: AP/Wide World Photos.

gaining believe that the "realistic" assumption is unduly pessimistic. Such strategies are insufficiently sensitive, in this antirealist view, to the danger that hardline bargaining can lead to an escalation of coercive moves that will precipitate wars that neither side wants. In the analysis of forty crises mentioned earlier, "bullying" strategies led to war in almost two-thirds of the crises in which they were used, while reciprocating strategies achieved either a diplomatic victory or a compromise nearly two-thirds of the time. Does this mean that reciprocating strategies are always preferable? That depends partly on the priority that decision makers involved in international negotiations and crisis situations give to avoiding international war. Clearly, avoiding war is not always the highest priority for policymakers. Sometimes, for example, they may consider it even more important in confrontational situations to achieve victory or avoid defeat., And some evidence suggests that states are more likely to gain a victory by adopting a bullying strategy (Leng, 1993, p. 200).[18]

Also, any state determined to change the status quo may need to resort to coercive or bullying strategies. When President Bush and his coalition partners wanted to persuade Saddam Hussein to give up

SOURCE: Gable/Cartoonists & Writers Syndicate.

control over Kuwait in 1990–91, it is doubtful that a reciprocating strategy would have worked. "Finding themselves in a . . . position against an adversary intent on defending its *fait accompli*, the United States and its allies could achieve their objectives only through a coercive strategy" (Leng, 1993, p. 220).[19]

In short, although diplomats may take extreme positions that make them look a little silly, sometimes such positions are effective bargaining tools that reflect an understanding of the importance of precedents in international politics. Similarly, the decentralized character of the global political system, where every state must ultimately protect its

---

[18] However, since "statesmen have been more likely to choose belligerent influence strategies when . . . they have been relatively optimistic regarding the consequences of war" (Leng, 1993, p. 201), and since that optimism has probably been based on an advantage in military-industrial capabilities, it might have been superior military strength that accounted for the success of the bullying strategy rather than the strategy itself.

[19] Leng comes to this conclusion even though he is quite critical of the way in which Bush carried out this strategy, arguing that "President Bush's approach to bargaining can be criticized for its lack of flexibility and unnecessary bellicosity . . . by publicly committing himself to reject any face-saving way out for Iraq, Bush may have thrown away the only feasible possibility of achieving [his] stated objectives without war" (Leng, 1993, p. 221). Interestingly, Kugler, Snider, and Longwell (1994, p. 141), relying on the forecasting model discussed above, come to a similar conclusion: "The Bush Administration could have minimized conflict within its coalition, and, concurrently maximized potential gains by coordinating efforts with Saudi Arabia and Kuwait. . . . In sum, the U.S. Gulf policy was sub-optimal in the sense that a negotiated outcome not much different from that achieved by war was at hand."

own interests, often tempts decision makers to adopt coercive bargaining strategies. But just as often, states will bargain in a more conciliatory or reciprocating fashion, meeting coercive moves with coercive responses and cooperative signals with cooperation. Coercive strategies may help states gain diplomatic victories (and avoid humiliating defeats), especially if the states employing them seek a change in the status quo, but history also suggests that they carry a higher risk of war than do reciprocating strategies. Those more conciliatory strategies have produced substantially more peaceful outcomes in international disputes.

GREAT-MAN THEORIES OF HISTORY

Chapter 3 and this chapter have focused on the effects of public opinion on foreign policies, narrowed the focus to the role of specific interest groups within the general public in making foreign policy, and continued the narrowing process with a discussion of the impact of government bureaucracies and diplomats on international politics. This process, carried to its logical extreme, arrives at a consideration of individual leaders in the conduct of foreign policy in particular and world politics in general.

Great-man theories of history that emphasize the impact of individual leaders on historical events have an intuitive appeal. Explanations of important events in terms of abstract factors such as public opinion, bipolarity, and even the military-industrial complex seem lifeless and relatively difficult to understand. In contrast, explanations that emphasize the role that great leaders play in determining the outcome of important events are generally more interesting, if only because they reduce events to a human scale that is easier to understand and identify with. History as a discipline has a bias in the direction of great-man theories in that it seeks out the unusual, the dramatic, and the memorable (Quester, 1974, p. 249). Tidbits about the impact of a leader's relationship with parents or lovers on momentous decisions enliven any historical account and make the writer and the reader feel informed about the events being studied. In addition, historical accounts that emphasize the bravery and the wisdom of individual leaders make pleasant and inspiring reading, whereas those that stress the stupidity and wickedness of national leaders provide us the pleasure of indulging in righteous indignation.

But these theories of history rely so heavily on unique factors in explaining the world's affairs that they may obscure similarities among different and important events. If events really are determined to an important extent by idiosyncratic features of the personalities of the leaders involved, then they are essentially unpredictable. The factors that determine which particular individuals will be national leaders at various times are obviously so numerous and random that making specific predictions about the process that brings particular individuals to the top is impossible. If it is impossible to predict which specific individual will emerge as the national leader, then it will obviously be just as impossible to predict a country's foreign policies, since according to a great-man theory, these policies will be a function of the peculiar personality traits of the individual leader.

An approach contrary to great-man theories emphasizes the strength of the constraints under which individual leaders operate. The contours of this approach emerge in more detail in the following pages. For now, it is enough to stress that explanations of behavior and events in the international political system that rely on visible, concrete factors— such as the structure of the international system or the structure of the states involved—are more promising from a scientific viewpoint than are great-man theories. If it is true that even leaders with very different idiosyncratic personality traits react in similar ways to concrete, visible characteristics of the international system, such as the distribution of power among the most important states or the type of political regime (democratic versus dictatorial, for example) in which they operate, then behavior and events within the international system are more predictable. (See Figure 4.1.)

Consider an extreme, but instructive, example. In this century, the individual national leader whose particular personality characteristics seem to have had the greatest impact on the course of recent world politics was Adolf Hitler. His unique political genius enabled him to rise from lowly prisoner to dictatorial leader of Germany in less than ten years. He built Germany into a formidable military force and used that force in ways he had personally planned well ahead of time, as described in the pages of *Mein Kampf*.

In the context of this discussion, it is particularly interesting to note that Hitler fought and was wounded in action in the First World War. He could easily have been killed. If he had been, according to the great-man theory of history, events in the 1930s would have been dramatically different. There would have been no Hitler in Germany, and Germany's foreign policies might have been so different that the Second World War could have been avoided. In short, the course of world politics might have been changed crucially and in an obviously unpredictable manner by the removal of one individual from the international system.[20]

---

[20] A recent version of this argument is made by John Mueller (1989, p. 65). "Hitler, in short, was neither symptom nor figurehead. He invented Naziism, he made it work, and he caused World War II."

Figure 4.1   The Funnel of Causality

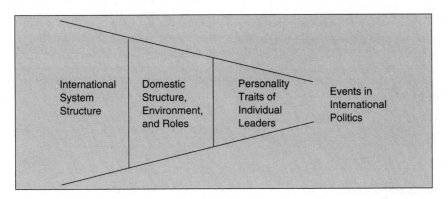

One can attempt to predict international events if the theory is valid that country leaders with diverse personalities will react similarly to concrete aspects of the global system.

SOURCE: Angus Campbell et al., *The American Voter* (New York: Wiley, 1960); James N. Rosenau, "Pre-theories and Theories of Foreign Policy," in R. Barry Farrel, ed., *Approaches to Comparative and International Politics* (Evanston, Ill.: Northwestern University Press, 1966); Charles W. Kegley, Jr., and Eugene R. Wittkopf, *American Foreign Policy* (New York: St. Martin's Press, 1979).

From a scientific viewpoint, it must be hoped that the world's political system does not operate in this fashion.[21] If momentous events such as the Second World War really did depend to a crucial extent on such random trifling matters as where exactly in Hitler's body a shell fragment hit, then theories that attempt to explain world politics in terms of larger, more visible structural characteristics of the international system, or of the states involved, would be doomed to consistent failure by the tremendous impact of relatively trivial, randomly operating factors. An alternative explanation of events such as the Second World War that did not rely on random factors would point out that if a shell fragment had killed Hitler in the First World War, Germany would still have lost. Germany would still have been blamed officially for the war by the victorious powers and would have been charged the same substantial reparations. Hitler's death would not have saved Germany from the traumatic experience of the inflation of the early 1920s or the Depression of the early 1930s.

---

[21] By this I do not mean that scientifically inclined scholars of world politics are glad that Hitler was not killed in the First World War, but rather that scientists must assume that events are not determined primarily by randomly operating factors.

Having experienced all these devastating blows, Germany, or any important state, would, it seems likely, have produced and supported a Nazi-type leader, even if Hitler had died in the First World War. Finally, having such a leader, Germany's foreign policies in the late 1930s might well not have been dramatically different even if it had been led by someone else.

In short, the Second World War was predictable in the sense that it was brought about by concrete, visible factors—notably Germany's defeat in 1918, inflation, and the worldwide Depression and its impact on Germany—in a way that would have remained unaltered had a random shell fragment taken a slightly different path. Such an argument might be criticized for being invulnerable to contrary evidence. One can say that if a state loses a world war and is officially blamed for causing it, as well as being subjected to reparations, inflation, and depression, it will produce an Adolf Hitler or someone like him. The prediction is invulnerable to criticism because such a chain of events is highly unlikely to recur.

But that chain of events is not totally unlike others. Other nations have experienced depressions, for example, and there seems to be a fairly predictable tendency for radical political forces (for example, fascism) to thrive under bad economic conditions. (Consider, for example, the meteoric, if short-lived, success of Vladimir Zhirinovsky in economically devastated Russia in the early 1990s.) Even if there is no such pattern, the fact that there is a relationship between economic adversity and the strength of radical political parties allows the assertion that Germany was likely to produce a leader like Hitler to be subjected to at least a partial test.

Yet Hitler was not just any extremist; he was unusually talented, in a demonic way, and he was extraordinarily evil. The suggestion that Germany might have produced another Hitler if the original had been killed (of course, we do not know he really was the original; perhaps somebody even worse was killed in the First World War) may strike some people as ludicrous. And in truth, it may be unlikely. But that does not mean that Germany's foreign policy or the international political system of the 1930s would have been drastically different without Hitler. Whoever had been Germany's leader in the 1930s would have had to deal with the same problems. And Hitler was certainly not the only German who had ideas that led to aggressive German policies. For example, as early as 1922, one reason the Germans signed the treaty with the Soviet Union at Rapallo was that it allowed them to avoid the provisions of the Versailles peace treaty against rearmament. They were able to rearm on Soviet territory, which was beyond the scope of monitoring by the peace treaty. And this treaty was signed well before Hitler had any influence on the German government. Even if Hitler had not lived, Japan and Italy would have carried out their aggressive policies of the 1930s, thus demonstrating to any German leader the probable success of an aggressive policy on the part of Germany. Given the structure of the international system and Germany's domestic structure, Germany might well have followed policies quite similar to Hitler's even if the personality of Germany's leader had been quite different from Hitler's.

> Policy-makers occupy roles in the same sense that being a father of a child constitutes occupancy of a role. Such positions embrace certain responsibilities that have to be performed and expectations that have to be met if their occupants are to remain in them. Whatever prior experiences an official may have had, and regardless of the outlook and talents he may have previously developed, he has to make some adjustments which render his attributes and behavior compatible with the formal and informal requirements of his policy-making responsibilities (Rosenau, 1968, p. 23).

Many people object to this kind of argument on philosophical grounds. If human behavior is predictably a function of environment, then there is no free will. Human beings cannot be blamed for their behavior, nor can they be given any credit. Particularly in the realm of world politics, where leaders are typically blamed for wars and given credit for unusual wisdom and courage following victories, accepting the crucial role of the political environment in explaining human behavior involves a radical departure from tradition. But in any realm, many people are reluctant to accept a deterministic view of the world: it robs human beings of dignity.

The question of free will versus determinism is, of course, an ancient philosophical one, and it is important to understand that for the present, at least, this question cannot be settled on empirical grounds. Still, any analysis of human behavior almost inevitably entails an assumption about whether that behavior is free or determined. The assumption in this book is that it is both. Human behavior is obviously determined to some degree by environment, but not totally so. The goal of any social science is to discover the limits to the impact of the environment (or heredity) on behavior. Pursuit of that goal does not imply a belief that the environment (or heredity) is totally determining.

Finally, it should be clear that the issue of free will versus determinism is related to but different from the question concerning the impact of individual leaders' idiosyncratic personality traits on world politics. One can believe that those personality traits have a tremendous impact and still have a deterministic philosophy. A leader, for example, might in this view be entirely unable to escape the influence of a domineering parent and also have a substantial effect on world politics. Belief in the importance of the environment provided by the international and domestic political systems in which a leader operates, as against the importance of the environment created by a particular leader's private life, is not necessarily more deterministic than a philosophy of history stressing the importance of idiosyncratic personality traits. And this belief may be wrong. To the extent that it is, attempts to analyze world politics in a way that deemphasizes national leaders' individual personalities will be misleading. To the extent that this belief is correct, it will facilitate the development of a science of world politics.[22]

Still, studying individual leaders can be valuable. First, individual leaders may be examined as examples of individuals in general rather than in terms of their unique or idiosyncratic personality characteristics. As individuals, leaders share psychological traits and mechanisms with people in general that can have an important impact on international politics. For example, all individuals, national leaders included, have perceptual screens, "belief systems" (Holsti, 1962), or "operational codes" (Leites, 1951) with which they interpret information. There is no escaping such mechanisms; the world is so complicated and so full of information that everyone must be selective, choosing to concentrate on certain bits of information and ignoring others. Franklin Roosevelt had at his disposal information that could have led him to anticipate the Japanese attack on Pearl Harbor in 1941. Stalin was warned repeatedly before June 1941 that the Germans were about to attack the Soviet Union. Truman had lots of information from which he might have concluded that the Chinese *would* intervene in the Korean War if MacArthur led his troops into North Korea. But all three leaders were the victims of perceptual screens that led them to discount or ignore the evidence concerning possible attack from an enemy. One might attribute this screening to idiosyncratic personality problems of these individual leaders, but a more useful approach would be to analyze the impact of perceptual screens and operational codes on individuals and leaders in general and to apply the insights such studies show to the particular leaders involved in specific situations, such as those experienced by Roosevelt, Stalin, and Truman. Such explanations are more useful because they can be applied more widely and can help us understand more events in different places. In contrast, explanations stressing the impact of some peculiar personality trait of Roosevelt, Stalin, or Truman are obviously more limited in application. They might help us understand the events involving Stalin or Truman, but when confronted with other leaders in other places, we would have to begin a search for peculiar personality traits that might have had an effect on their decisions or on events in which they were involved.

---

[22] The impact of personality characteristics of leaders on world politics is not impossible to deal with scientifically. See, for example, Hermann (1978), Etheridge (1978), and Shepard (1988).

SUMMARY

In this chapter we have analyzed the impact of governmental bureaucracies and decision-making organizations, diplomats, and individual leaders on foreign policies and international politics. Bureaucratic organizations tend to adhere to SOPs in a way that can have an important impact on the way foreign policy organizations behave in times of crisis, and policies produced by governments are often the product to some extent of political infighting among different parts of the bureaucratic apparatus. But analyses of foreign policies and interactions among states, as well as political events within countries that rely on an expected utility approach, suggest that there is an important element of rationality in those policies and interactions. Diplomats often seem to engage in behavior that seems silly, on the surface, and they are often tempted to engage in coercive bargaining strategies. However, strategies that sometimes seem silly make sense as bargaining tools, and coercive bargaining strategies quite clearly carry a greater risk of international war, which can be avoided with more conciliatory reciprocating bargaining strategies. "Great-man" theories of international politics emphasize the impact of individual leaders' personalities in a way that can obscure general patterns. Those patterns will be more readily discerned if one emphasizes instead the potential impact on policies and interactions among states of the structure of the international system, as well as aspects of the domestic political systems within which individual foreign policy leaders operate.

KEY TERMS

standard operating procedures (SOPs)
repertoire of prearranged responses
satisfice
cybernetic theory
noncompensatory theory
maximin principle

rational
rational choice
unitary rational actors
"bullying" strategy
"reciprocating" strategy
"great-man" theories

SOURCES

Allison, Graham T. *Essence of Decision.* Boston: Little, Brown, 1971.

Allyn, Bruce J., James G. Blight, and David A. Welch. "Essence of Revision: Moscow, Havana, and the Cuban Missile Crisis." *International Security,* 14 (Winter 1989/90), 136–172.

Anderson, Paul, and Timothy J. McKeown. "Changing Aspirations, Limited Attention, and War." *World Politics,* 40 (October 1987), 1–29.

Blight, James G., Joseph S. Nye, Jr., and David A. Welch. "The Cuban Missile Crisis Revisited." *Foreign Affairs*, 66 (Fall 1987), 170–188.

Bueno de Mesquita, Bruce. *The War Trap*. New Haven, Conn.: Yale University Press, 1981.

Bueno de Mesquita, Bruce. "A Critique of 'A Critique of The War Trap.'" *Journal of Conflict Resolution*, 28 (June 1984), 341–360.

Bueno de Mesquita, Bruce. "The Game of Conflict Interactions: A Research Program." In Joseph Berger and Morris Zelditch, eds., *Theoretical Research Programs: Studies in the Growth of Theories of Group Process*. Stanford, Calif.: Stanford University Press, 1993.

Bueno de Mesquita, Bruce, and David Lalman. *War and Reason*. New Haven, Conn.: Yale University Press, 1992.

Bueno de Mesquita, Bruce, David Newman, and Alvin Rabushka. *Forecasting Political Events*. New Haven, Conn.: Yale University Press, 1985.

Bueno de Mesquita, Bruce, David Newman, and Alvin Rabushka. *Red Flag over Kong*. Chatham, N.J.: Chatham House, 1996.

Bueno de Mesquita, Bruce, and Frans Stokman (eds.). *European Community Decision Making*. New Haven, Conn.: Yale University Press, 1994.

Caldwell, Dan. "A Research Note on the Quarantine of Cuba, October 1962." *International Studies Quarterly*, 22 (December 1978), 625–634.

Campbell, Angus, Philip E. Converse, Warren E. Miller, and Donald E. Stokes. *The American Voter*. New York: Wiley, 1960.

Cyert, Richard M., and James G. March. *A Behavioral Theory of the Firm*. Englewood Cliffs, N.J.: Prentice-Hall, 1963.

Etheridge, Lloyd S. "Personality Effects on American Foreign Policy, 1898–1968." *American Political Science Review*, 72 (June 1978), 434–451.

Feder, Stanley. "Factions and Policon: New Ways to Analyze Politics." In H. Bradford Westerfield, ed., *Studies in Intelligence Inside CIA's Private World*. New Haven, Conn.: Yale University Press, 1995.

Freedman, Lawrence, and Efraim Karsh. "How Kuwait Was Won: Strategy in the Gulf War." *International Security*, 16 (Fall 1991), 5–41.

Fuchs, Doris, Jacek Kugler, and Harry Pachon. "Mexico: NAFTA, Elections and the Future of Political and Economic Reforms." Special Issue of *International Interactions*, edited by Jacek Kugler and Yi Feng. (1997).

George, Alexander, and Juliette George. *Woodrow Wilson and Colonel House*. New York: Dover Publications, 1964.

Halperin, Morton H. "Why Bureaucrats Play Games." *Foreign Policy*, No. 2 (Spring 1971), 70–90.

Hermann, Margaret G. "Effects of Personal Characteristics of Political Leaders on Foreign Policy." In Maurice East, Stephen A. Salmore, and Charles F. Hermann, eds., *Why Nations Act*. Beverly Hills, Calif.: Sage Publications, 1978.

Hybel, Alex Roberto. *Power over Rationality*. Albany, N.Y.: State University of New York Press, 1993.

Holsti, Ole R. "The Belief System and National Images: A Case Study." *Journal of Conflict Resolution*, 6 (September 1962), 244–252.

Kegley, Charles W., Jr., and Eugene R. Wittkopf. *American Foreign Policy*. New York: St. Martin's Press, 1979.

Kissinger, Henry A. "Domestic Sources of Foreign Policy." In Robert L. Pfaltzgraff, ed., *Politics and the International System.* Philadelphia: Lippincott, 1972.

Kugler, Jacek, Lewis Snider, and William Longwell. "From Desert Shield to Desert Storm." *Conflict Management and Peace Science,* 13 (Spring 1994), 101–113.

Kugler, Jacek, and Mark Abdollahian. "Power Transition in Russia." Special Issue of *International Interactions,* edited by Jacek Kugler and Yi Feng (1997).

Leites, Nathan. *The Operational Code of the Politburo.* New York: McGraw-Hill, 1951.

Leng, Russell J. *Interstate Crisis Behavior, 1816–1980: Realism Versus Reciprocity.* Cambridge, U.K.: Cambridge University Press, 1993.

Leng, Russell J. "When Will They Ever Learn? Coercive Bargaining in Recurrent Crises." *Journal of Conflict Resolution,* 27 (September 1983), 379–419.

Levy, Jack S. "Organizational Routines and the Causes of War." *International Studies Quarterly,* 30 (June 1986), 137, 193–222.

Lindblom, Charles. "The Science of 'Muddling Through.'" *Public Administration Review,* 19 (Spring 1959), 79–88.

Luard, Evan. *War in International Society: A Study in International Sociology.* New Haven, Conn.: Yale University Press, 1986.

Luce, Duncan R., and Howard Raiffa. *Games and Decisions: Introduction and Critical Survey.* New York: Wiley, 1957.

Luterbacher, Urs. "Last Words About War?" *Journal of Conflict Resolution,* 28 (March 1984), 165–182.

McKenzie, Richard B., and Gordon Tullock. *The New World of Economics.* 2nd ed. Homewood, Ill.: Irwin, 1978.

Majeski, Stephen, and David Sylvan. "Simple Choices and Complex Calculations: A Critique of the War Trap." *Journal of Conflict Resolution,* 28 (June 1984), 316–340.

Maoz, Zeev. *National Choices and International Processes.* Cambridge, U.K.: Cambridge University Press, 1990.

Mazlich, Bruce. *Kissinger: The European Mind in American Policy.* New York: Basic Books, 1976.

Mintz, Alex. "The Decision to Attack Iraq: A Noncompensatory Theory of Decision Making." *Journal of Conflict Resolution,* 37 (December 1993), 595–618.

Moul, William B. "A Catch to the War Trap." *International Interactions,* 13, No. 2 (1987), 171–176.

Mueller, John. *Retreat from Doomsday: The Obsolescence of Major War.* New York: Basic Books, 1989.

Nicholson, Michael. "The Conceptual Bases of the War Trap." *Journal of Conflict Resolution,* 31 (June 1987), 346–369.

Northedge, F. S., and M. D. Donelan. *International Disputes: The Political Aspects.* New York: St. Martin's Press, 1971.

Quester, George H. *The Continuing Problem of International Politics.* Hinsdale, Ill.: Dryden Press, 1974.

Quester, George H. *Offense and Defense in the International System.* New York: Wiley, 1977.

Ray, James Lee. "A Post-Mortem on the Predictions: Criteria, Complaints and Compliments." Special Issue of *International Interactions,* edited by Jacek Kugler and Yi Feng (1997).

Ray, James Lee, and Bruce Russett. "The Future as Arbiter of Theoretical Controversies: Predictions, Explanations and the End of the Cold War." *British Journal of Political Science,* 26 (1996), 441–470.

Rosenau, James N. "Pre-theories and Theories of Foreign Policy." In R. Barry Farrel, ed., *Approaches to Comparative and International Politics.* Evanston, Ill.: Northwestern University Press, 1966.

Rosenau, James N. "Private Preferences and Political Responsibilities." In J. David Singer, ed., *Quantitative International Politics.* New York: Free Press, 1968.

Schelling, Thomas C. *The Strategy of Conflict.* Cambridge, Mass.: Harvard University Press, 1960.

Shepard, Graham H. "Personality Effects on American Foreign Policy, 1969–84: A Second Test of Interpersonal Generalization Theory." *International Studies Quarterly,* 32 (March 1988), 91–123.

Simon, Herbert. *Administrative Behavior.* 2nd ed. New York: Free Press, 1957.

Simon, Herbert. *Models of Man.* New York: Wiley, 1957.

Simowitz, Roslyn, and Barry L. Price. "The Expected Utility Theory of Conflict: Measuring Theoretical Progress." *American Political Science Review,* 84 (June 1990), 439–460.

Singer, J. David. "Peace in the Global System: Displacement, Interregnum, or Transformation?" In Charles W. Kegley, Jr., ed., *The Long Postwar Peace.* New York: HarperCollins, 1991.

Snyder, Jack. "Civil-Military Relations and the Cult of the Offensive, 1914 and 1984." *International Security,* 9 (Summer 1984), 108–146.

"Statistics, Analysts, Help CIA Make Political Forecasts." *Salt Lake City Tribune,* March 1, 1989.

Steinbruner, John D. *The Cybernetic Theory of Decision.* Princeton, N.J.: Princeton University Press, 1974.

Stoessinger, John G. *Why Nations Go to War.* 6th ed. New York: St. Martin's Press, 1993.

Trachtenberg, Marc. "The Meaning of Mobilization in 1914." *International Security,* 15 (Winter 1990/91), 120–150.

Tuchman, Barbara. *The Guns of August.* New York: Macmillan, 1962.

Wagner, R. Harrison. "War and Expected Utility Theory." *World Politics,* 36 (April 1984), 407–423.

Weede, Erich. *Economic Development, Social Order, and World Politics.* Boulder, Colo.: Lynne Rienner, 1996.

Woodward, Bob. *The Commanders.* New York: Simon & Schuster, 1991.

Zagare, Frank. "Rationality and Deterrence." *World Politics,* 42/2 (January 1990), 238–260.

PART III

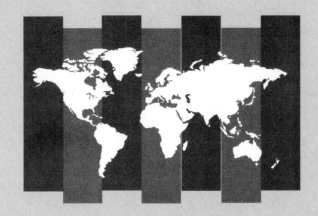

States,
The Primary Actors

CHAPTER 5

States, Nations, and Power

For at least three hundred years, sovereign **states** have been the most important political organizations in the global system. They are **sovereign** because they claim a monopoly on legal violence within their boundaries and freedom from interference by forces outside their boundaries. Their preeminence has not gone unchallenged, and there are good reasons to believe that these particular organizations may not allow humankind to deal with problems that become more serious as the twenty-first century approaches. Even so, states are still a very important kind of political entity and are likely to remain significant even if other types of organizations become more influential. An understanding of global politics necessarily involves a grasp of the history and essential characteristics of states.

"NATIONS" AND "STATES"

The terms **"nations"** and "states" are commonly treated as interchangeable in discussions of international relations. The name of the subfield itself, inter*national* relations, is an example of this practice; the subfield actually focuses on *states* most of the time. Passionate loyalty to one's state is typically referred to as "nationalism." Then, too, "state" tends to be synonymous with "government," and when analysts refer to the kind of loyalty that can arouse people to risk their lives in defense of their state, they do not usually mean state in the sense of government. Patriotic people have a strong emotional attachment to something less transient than the politicians or bureaucrats who happen to be in power at a particular moment. They are willing to fight to protect their nation, inspired by nationalism.

Strictly speaking, then, *nation* and *state* are not exactly interchangeable terms, and the distinction between them shows signs of becoming particularly important in the modern era. "In its pristine meaning, a nation is a group of people whose members believe they are ancestrally related. It is the largest group to share such a myth of common descent. . . ." In short, at the core of nationalism in this sense of the word is a "sense of shared blood" (Connor, 1992, p. 48). A state, on the other hand, is a kind of political organization, or a government that exercises supreme authority over a defined territory (Lerche and Said, 1979, p. 120; Plano, Greenberg, Olton, and Riggs, 1973, p. 360). In addition, "there has been a historical tension between state sovereignty, which stresses the link between sovereign authority and a defined territory, and national sovereignty, which emphasizes a link between sovereign authority and a defined population" (Barkin and Cronin, 1994, p. 108). This tension has been particularly obvious after fundamental upheavals in the international system, from the Napoleonic Wars in the early nineteenth century to the First World War, the Second World War, and most recently the end of the Cold War.

THE HISTORICAL ORIGINS OF THE MODERN STATE

Modern European states were born in violence. They arose from the devastation of the Thirty Years' War in Germany, which lasted from 1618 to 1648. "About two-thirds of the total population had disappeared; the misery of those that survived was piteous in the extreme. Five-sixths of the villages in the empire had been destroyed" (Hayes, 1921, p. 231). The **Peace of Westphalia,** signed in 1648, is widely recognized as the dividing line between a medieval Europe dominated by small, localized political units under the comprehensive authority of the Holy Roman Empire and/or the pope and a modern Europe where states became recognized as sovereign. In a sense, the Peace of Westphalia marked the separation of church and state on the level of world politics. The Holy Roman Empire and the pope continued to exist, but their political power had been all but destroyed.

The Peace of Westphalia did not, of course, immediately transform Europe from a large collection of small, local entities under one universal authority into a small number of parallel sovereign states. But the idea of states as hard-shelled, impenetrable units did develop in a

Martin Luther inspired the Reformation in Europe. The Reformation disrupted the unity of medieval Europe and played a role in creating a new system in Europe based on nation-states, which was brought into being by the Peace of Westphalia in 1648. SOURCE: German painting, 15th–16th century by Lucas Granach the Elder (workshop of) Martin Luther, 1546. Courtesy of the Fogg Art Museum/Harvard University Art Museums; Gift of Meta and Paul J. Sachs.

relatively short time after 1648. Shortly before 1648 scholars of international law such as Grotius still thought in terms of just and unjust wars and considered it perfectly appropriate for one state to intervene in the affairs of another in order to protect the citizens from oppression. But some fifty years later, Pufendorf, another student of international law, writing with the benefit of the experience of the Thirty Years' War and the Peace of Westphalia, concluded that such interference by one state in the affairs of another was a violation of sovereignty (Herz, 1959, pp. 50–51).[1]

Religious Divisions, Economic Transformations, and Technological Developments

The process culminating in the Peace of Westphalia and the birth of the modern state was set in motion by three revolutionary developments, one in the realm of the spiritual, and the other two in the areas of economic relationships, transactions over long distances and broad areas, and military technology. The spiritual unity of Europe had been rent by the Reformation. It was torn again when Calvinism added its anti-Catholic voice to Lutheranism. France, in an effort to weaken the hold of the Hapsburg royal family over the numerous principalities of the Holy Roman Empire, stirred up these religious divisions. Perhaps the divisions would have led to the violent horrors of the Thirty Years' War without the aid of France; in any case, those horrors made it obvious that the Christian community of medieval Europe was a fragile edifice indeed and was in need of replacement. The replacement that came out of the Peace of Westphalia was the sovereign state. The unrestrained violence of the religious wars might be avoided if each ruler recognized the exclusive rights of others over their domestic realms. In the post-Westphalia period, the idea resulted in the extension of the concept of sovereignty beyond the dimensions described by Jean Bodin, the French legal scholar credited with making the first systematic presentation of the concept, in his *Six Books on the State*, published in 1586. Bodin's work was a defense of the divine right of the French king to rule in an absolute manner, but Bodin's concept of sovereignty did not imply a right to rule arbitrarily or above the law. Nor did it originally imply that a state fell under no superior obligations in its relations with other states (Brierly, 1963, p. 11). But because of the urge to avoid catastrophes such as the Thirty Years' War, the concept of sovereignty came to imply that the state had an absolute power over its subjects and an absolute right to be free from interference by other states in the exercise of that power (Morse, 1976, pp. 33–34).

---

[1] Jack Levy (1983, p. 22) acknowledges that the conventional opinion of political scientists is that the modern state system originated in 1648 but argues, interestingly, that the "French invasion of Italy at the end of 1494 and the Treaty of Venice in March 1495 mark the coalescence of the major European states into a truly interdependent system of behavior."

It is possible that if the divisions in Christendom in the fourteenth and fifteenth centuries had not been accompanied by changes in economic forces and in military technology, the Thirty Years' War and the Peace of Westphalia might have established impenetrable sovereign units that were nevertheless similar in size to the numerous small units that went into that war. But first and possibly most fundamentally, economic changes powerfully reinforced the strength of central political authorities in what were soon to become recognizably modern states. Feudal authorities tended to restrict trade and commerce, making it almost impossible to conduct economic transactions across longer distances, or indeed anywhere outside the jurisdiction of typically quite small feudal political units. As merchants and entrepreneurs who wanted to conduct economic transactions became wealthier and more influential, they increasingly came to value political systems and leaders who could exert their authority over larger areas, and enforce commitments to similar entities elsewhere. During this transitional era, nation-states came into competition with city-states, such as those in Italy, and city-leagues, such as the Hanseatic League in what ultimately became Germany. However, the city-states and the city-leagues were not really "sovereign"; they could not enforce their authority effectively over large territories, nor could they enforce commitments between themselves in as effective a manner as territorial-based, sovereign states proved themselves able to do.

> Sovereign territorial states, city-leagues, and city-states all tried to tap into the new sources of economic wealth, particularly long-distance trade. . . . Sovereign rulers were better at centralizing jurisdiction and authority. . . . Sovereign territoriality proved to have long-term advantages in that it created more certitude in the domestic economic environment (Spruyt, 1994, pp. 527–536).

Typically, the kinds of economic factors that contributed to the emergence of sovereign, territorial states in Europe are overlooked by those who focus on the impact of dramatic changes in military technology.[2] But it seems likely that those changes reinforced evolutionary developments evoked by the economic forces of the time. Around A.D. 1200 stone castles represented the ultimate in military defense, and they were scattered all over western Europe. The rulers of those castles were often legally within the domain of superiors such as

---

[2] "We do well to ask how the above account squares with the prevalent view that changes in warfare lay at the heart of state formation" (Spruyt, 1994, p. 550).

the holy Roman emperor or the king of France. But the fact that the castles or the fortified cities were militarily self-sufficient gave them independence, and emperors and kings were rulers of the local barons in name only. (This gave the barons the power to disrupt and discourage the increasingly important long-distance economic transactions discussed above.)

Military technology came to exert a strong force against this state of affairs. "The sudden maturation in 1450 A.D. of the cannon, after a long infancy, as the destroyer of castles made a further and large change in the art of war in favor of the centralized state . . . and in favor of the monarch over the feudal barons" (Bean, 1973, p. 208). The appearance of gunpowder on the battlefields accelerated the process of eliminating smaller political units in favor of larger units, such as states. Between 1400 and 1600, large numbers of the smaller entities lost their independence; the Thirty Years' War brought this process to a climax. After the Peace of Westphalia, fortified cities and castles increasingly gave way to fortresses lining the borders of states, at least partly because the cities and castles could no longer defend themselves against attackers equipped with the new military technology.

But how did the increasingly powerful monarchs at the head of territorial states acquire the ability to use this new military technology effectively? "Changes in warfare favored larger and more expensive armies, which necessitated more taxation and rational government" (Spruyt, 1994, p. 550). Sovereign states proved themselves more capable than city-states or city-leagues of providing this increased taxing power and rational government (Rasler and Thompson, 1985). So the evolution and increasing importance of both economic transactions over large areas and innovations in military technology combined to allow territorial, sovereign states to prevail, first in Europe, and eventually over the entire globe.

At roughly the same time that Europe came to be dominated by states, processes were set in motion that led Europe to dominate the world (and eventually helped set the stage for the emergence of sovereign states even in the remotest areas of the globe). States such as Spain, Portugal, Great Britain, and the Netherlands sent explorers to stake claims in the Western Hemisphere and establish greater contact with East Asia. After the explorers, and sometimes with them, came traders and colonizers, who began exploiting the economic resources of the New World and developing international trade with Asia.

According to a theoretical approach known as **world-system analysis** and also, intriguingly enough, according to more conservative and neoclassical economic analysis, the fact that Europe was divided into independent nation-states rather than united in an empire was crucial to its economic success.[3] "In the early Middle Ages there can be no doubt that China was a more advanced society than western Europe economically, technologically, and scientifically" (Weede, 1996, p. 51). But empires, such as those in Asia, were overcentralized, rigid, and relatively unproductive in economic terms. As a result, in this view, East Asia came to be dominated by Europe, which was more flexible.

In Africa, Latin America, and North America, the Europeans mined gold, grew sugar, and acquired slaves, incorporating these geographic areas into the modern world system. According to advocates of the world-system approach (but not according to neoclassical economic theories), this integration into the global economic system dominated by Europe was disastrous for the long-run future of the "peripheral" areas outside Europe. They became trapped in a role in the international division of labor that was fraught with difficulties. Non-European areas supplied primary products and commodities to Europe, which in turn furnished them with textiles and other manufactured goods produced by Europe's relatively more sophisticated technology. As a result, Europe became increasingly advanced in economic terms, and the peripheral areas lagged far behind, becoming more and more dominated by Europe economically as well as politically (Wallerstein, 1974, 1980).

That the world's economic system did develop an international division of labor cannot be disputed, nor can it be denied that Europe assumed a predominant position in that system for centuries. Whether or not the rest of the world suffered from these developments is less certain. The Europeans, of course, saw themselves as spreading civilization throughout the world. If they benefited more from the emergence of the "modern world system," this was, from their viewpoint, only natural, because they had started down the road to economic development earlier than other countries, the very regions they were now assisting in the effort to catch up. This process included instances of brutal exploitation, and the development of the slave trade is an example of European economic tactics no one defends today. Still, as British economist Joan Robinson (1962, p. 45) puts it, "the misery of being exploited by capitalists is nothing compared to the misery of not being exploited at all." Incorporation into the Euro-centered international economic system created lots of problems, but people who remained isolated from that system did not live in a pristine paradise either.

---

[3] "Conflict among states constituted a forerunner to and a functional equivalent of constitutional limitations of governmental authority. . . . The greater degree of freedom in Europe and the greater degree to which European producers and traders could make their own decisions (and reap most of the benefits therefrom) resulted largely from interstate competition in Europe and led to miraculous economic growth" (Weede, 1996, p. 44).

Whether poor states today should concentrate on breaking the ties to the industrialized world that have been built up over the centuries or on becoming more closely integrated with that world is a controversial question that is discussed in Chapter 8.

The Eighteenth Century

In the eighteenth century, the large important European states were ruled by centralized monarchies, and wars between the states were usually conflicts between royal dynasties. Typically, one royal family would object to an increase in the power of another royal family. These conflicts and the resulting wars would typically be resolved on the **balance-of-power principle.** This principle implied that it was dangerous for all states to allow any one state to become too powerful. Just what was too powerful was in constant dispute, of course, but in practice the balance-of-power principle usually served to preserve the existing distribution of power among the Great Powers, which became more clearly defined as the eighteenth century progressed. Any change in the status quo that worked to the detriment of a given Great Power made that state (or royal family) feel entitled to some compensation (Schuman, 1958, pp. 70–71).[4]

The eighteenth century saw a series of balance-of-power wars, with the British and French being the major protagonists. The wars between kings were fought by soldiers of various nationalities employed for the purpose, and the diplomats who negotiated the peace settlements were virtually indifferent to nationalistic divisions (Rosecrance, 1963, p. 20).

The same cosmopolitanism applied in the diplomatic corps of European states. Denmark used German diplomats, Russia employed Englishmen and Frenchmen, and Spain recruited diplomatic talent from Italy and Holland. Indeed, cosmopolitanism extended to heads of states. Britain had a German king, and the Spanish king was a grandson of Louis XIV of France.

The Impact of the French Revolution

The French Revolution, for better or worse, put an end to a national cosmopolitanism in Europe. The original aims of the revolution were liberty, equality, and brotherhood for the French people. The aims implied the end of aristocratic rule in France, but more important, they implied that the state belonged to the people. Kings could no longer say, *"L'état, c'est moi"* ("I am the state"). The acts of the government came

---

[4] The theory of the balance of power is discussed in more detail in Chapter 14.

Napoleon, pictured above at the height of his power in 1812, revolutionized international politics by his heavy reliance on conscription to create armies infused with the spirit of nationalism. SOURCE: Painting by Jacques-Louis David, *Napoleon in His Study,* Samuel H. Kress Collection, © 1994 Board of Trustees, National Gallery of Art, Washington.

to be viewed as acts of the citizenry, and the revolutionary French constitution of 1793 was ratified by a large popular majority. As popular will linked itself with the actions of its political representatives, tremendous support for the government arose. As a consequence, the government came to be regarded as the head of a national society of

French people—not, as in the case of the "ancien régime," the ruler of a mere "geographical expression" (Rosecrance, 1963, p. 34).

If the French Revolution had been self-contained, its impact on international politics might have been less dramatic. But the revolution became expansionist. To be sure, this shift was to some extent a reaction to perceived threats from the outside. But the French became convinced that their ideals were too good and too important to be confined in application to one state, and with Napoleon's leadership they set out to spread those ideas throughout Europe.[5] To do this, Napoleon used the *levée en masse,* or conscription.[6] Soldiers were no longer mercenaries, but patriots who fought in defense of or for the glory of the state. Eventually, the other states of Europe found they could not resist or defeat an army of patriots without copying its methods and its nationalism. France's enemies became nationalistic in self-defense. Even so, it took the combined forces of Napoleon's enemies almost two decades to defeat him finally at Waterloo in 1815.

In the aftermath of the Napoleonic Wars, the continental European states were anxious to quell the flame of nationalism, or at least liberal nationalism. "The peace settlements concluded at the first Peace of Paris (1814) and the Treaty of Vienna (1815) [after the Napoleonic Wars] clearly reflected the value of the state over the nation" (Barkin and Cronin, 1994, p. 117). A Bourbon king was restored to the throne of France. Somewhat ironically, France itself became the instrument used by the continental European powers to crush liberalism in Spain in 1823. But the efforts of conservatism to defend the principle of legitimacy against the onslaught of liberal nationalism were, in the long run, doomed to failure. Although none of the conflicts was great enough to seriously disrupt the system set up at the end of the Napoleonic era, wars of national liberation became commonplace after Napoleon was finally banished from the European mainland. The Greeks fought for liberation from the Turks. The Poles rose up against the Russians. The Hungarians and the Italians rebelled against the Austrians.[7] An ocean

---

[5] "So convinced were the French of the blessings of the new nationalism for themselves that they could not conceive how it could fail to bless all other peoples" (Hayes, 1920, p. 45).

[6] "Napoleon's use of a conscript army, rather than a professional aristocratic military, [was] something that was unheard of in even the most autocratic states" (Barkin and Cronin, 1994, p. 116).

[7] "Rebellions, mostly nationalist in character, occurred regularly within the German principalities, the Netherlands, the Italian states, Greece, Poland, France, Spain, and ultimately within the Austrian Empire. . . ." Almost all of these rebellions were "put down by collectively sanctioned force" (Barkin and Cronin, 1994, p. 119).

away, the Latin American states obtained their freedom from Spain. And so it went until Serbian nationalistic aspirations led to the First World War and thus helped to destroy the European system established a hundred years earlier by the major powers at the Congress of Vienna in 1815. Between the world wars, many colonies of European states began to show signs of restlessness; after the Second World War, peacefully or otherwise, colonies turned into states in great profusion. The Vietnamese, the Algerians, the Angolans, the Hungarians, the Israelis, and the Palestinians, to name a few, have all engaged in violent conflict in the post–Second World War era, inflamed to some degree by the spirit of nationalism that was born in the era of the French Revolution and Napoleon. In short, although many in the less developed countries may resent past European domination and the handicaps imposed on them as peripheral areas were integrated into the modern world system, in one way, at least, peoples in the rest of the world have engaged in the sincerest form of flattery with respect to Europe. They have adhered enthusiastically to the European concept of nationalism and have clearly desired to imitate Europe by developing modern states.

Nations, States, and Nationalism

The idea mentioned earlier that a nation by definition refers to ethnic or racial ties is not inevitable, immutable, or logically necessary. It has developed and evolved over time. The idea of the nation as it came out of the American and French Revolutions bore considerably more resemblance to that of the state. (This is another reason that the two words tend to be used interchangeably today.) In the era of those revolutions, the "institutional and territorial concept of the . . . nation [was] defined by the work and the frontiers of the state." *Nation*, in this sense of the word, "stressed the equality of all citizens rather than the need to discriminate between [people] on the basis of culture or language." It was only later that theorists of nationalism "insisted that a nation rests on cultural, ethnic, and linguistic uniformity and distinctiveness, and can be defined only in cultural, ethnic and linguistic terms" (Hinsley, 1973, pp. 43–46).

In a sense, the Cold War contest between the United States and the Soviet Union (or between democracy and autocracy, or capitalism and socialism) has been replaced by a conflict between two ideas regarding nationalism. One of these ideas regards nationalism as properly focused on existing "nation-states," political entities recognized by most other states in the global political system with a seat in the United Nations, and so on. The other idea insists that nationalism applies more importantly and more passionately to a people sharing not only residence in the same state in common but having a common culture, language, and even bloodline, or ancestry. As discussed in Chapter 3, such ethnic loyalties have already helped to tear apart the Soviet Union and Yugoslavia, and they are tearing at the seams of such widely dispersed federations and even unitary states as India, Sri Lanka, South Africa, the Sudan, and Canada. In addition, the international community seems more tolerant of these assaults on the sovereignty of existing states, and even willing to assist them in situations like that in the former Yugoslavia or the former Soviet Union. "The end of the cold war has seen a reaction against realpolitik and against noninterference in the domestic affairs of other states . . ." (Barkin and Cronin, 1994, p. 125). It almost begins to seem that the period after the Second World War known as "decolonization," in which colonies "belonging" to major colonial powers broke away and became states on their own, will continue, but now resulting in the dissolution of existing states, instead of the separation of colonies from their imperial masters.

As also discussed in Chapter 3, ethnic groups are so widely and unevenly dispersed around the globe that they cannot possibly all be contained in neat little geographic boundaries within nation-states of their own. And it does seem that "the sense of kinship which lies at the heart of national consciousness also accounts for the ugly manifestations of inhumanity that often erupt in the relations among national groups" (Connor, 1992, p. 54). Such manifestations of inhumanity in the former Yugoslavia, in Azerbaijan, or in India, for example, seem especially pointless and frustrating to many outside observers when the ethnic differences on which they are based rest on shaky ground historically. "It is clear that the myth of common descent which defines the nation will seldom accord with factual history" (Connor, 1992, p. 49).

But such outside observers should remember how difficult it is for people with loyalties to nation-states with a secure, long-term existence to empathize with people denied what they see as a legitimate right to express and institutionalize their own unfulfilled national identities. "It is fashionable for Western observers," one noted scholar of nationalism points out, "securely ensconced in their own national identities forged in toil and blood several centuries ago, to pour scorn on the rhetorical excesses . . . of nationalist intellectuals in nineteenth century Europe or twentieth century Africa and Asia" (Smith, 1986, p. 2). In any case, it seems clear even in an age when some argue that the nation-state has become an outmoded form of organization (as we shall discuss in Chapter 13 regarding transnational, or nonnational entities, for example) that the global political system is in for a prolonged period of strife and instability stemming from the frustrated nationalistic passions of ethnic groups ambitious to establish nation-states of their own.

POWER

If states have traditionally been considered the most important kind of political organization in the global system, the **power** of states has been treated as the most important concept in the study of world politics. But what *is* power? Although it is central to the study of world politics,[8] the concept has been defined in a confusing variety of ways. Perhaps the two most important types of definitions of power distinguish between what a state *possesses* and what a state is able *to do.* One important definition is provided by Hans Morgenthau (1967, p. 26) in his classic text, *Politics Among Nations*: "When we speak of power, we mean man's control over the minds and actions of other men." But it is quite clear that many analysts also think of power as being embodied in resources that a state possesses, such as the size of its population, its geographical size, or the size of its gross national product (GNP).[9]

Most of the confusion about power as a concept in the study of international politics arises from the complex relationship between a state's control over resources on the one hand and its ability to affect the behavior of others—or to control outcomes in international disputes, conflicts, and wars—on the other. Some confusion might be avoided if we (1) reserved the word *power* to refer to the resources that give a state the potential to control outcomes and (2) referred to the actual ability of states to control outcomes as *influence.*[10] But the confusion surrounding the concept of power in the analysis of international politics cannot be resolved with a couple of simple definitional distinctions. If State A is more powerful than State B in the sense that it possesses more resources, then we expect State A also to prevail in conflicts, at least most of the time. Exceptions to that rule are surprising, regardless of whether we define power as control over resources *and* control over outcomes or whether we reserve the term *influence* for the latter type of control. But exceptions do exist. For example, the United States, with its vast nuclear arsenal and much larger military force, took on North Vietnam in a conflict over the fate of South Vietnam, and North Vietnam won. The Soviet Union invaded Afghanistan in 1979 and pulled its troops out in 1989, leaving behind a chaotic situation that

---

[8] In fact, it can be argued that "the concept of power is perhaps the most fundamental in the whole of political science" (Lasswell and Kaplan, 1950, p. 75).

[9] "Power is the means by which international actors deal with one another. It implies *possession*" (Jones and Rosen, 1982, p. 229).

[10] One noted French analyst of international politics, Raymond Aron (1964; cited in Wrong, 1979), pointed out that French speakers are less likely to become confused in this way because they use the word *puissance* to indicate potential or capacity, and *pouvoir* to refer to the actual ability to control outcomes.

persists to this day. In short, although the Soviets did not exactly lose the war in Afghanistan, the government the Soviets were protecting did not last long after their departure. It seems fair to conclude that the tremendous advantage in resources that the Soviets had over Afghanistan did not make it easy for them to prevail. They fought for ten years and left behind a shaky government that ultimately fell to Islamic elements of the type that they (the Soviets) had been determined to keep out of power.

A common response to this kind of **paradox of unrealized power** (in which far more powerful states lose in conflicts with apparently much weaker states) is that the ostensibly more powerful states somehow failed to translate their powerful resources into actual power.

The United States did not win the Vietnam War, according to this type of explanation, because it did not want to win badly enough, or at least not as much as the North Vietnamese did. Similarly, the former Soviet Union got bogged down in Afghanistan for so long and with such uncertain results because it did not devote sufficient effort to the task. "'He had the cards but played them poorly' is the theme of such explanations" (Baldwin, 1979, pp. 161–194).[11]

Explanations of this type are dangerous because they cannot be disproved. It might seem that explanations that cannot be disproved are the best possible kind. But a moment's thought will lead to a different conclusion. If there is no conceivable evidence that can disprove an explanation, then it cannot help us understand the world. "Because it explains everything," as the saying goes, "it really explains nothing." You might devise a theory, for example, that in conflicts between two states, the state with the bigger army will always win. A critic could point out that although the United States had a much bigger army than North Vietnam, it lost the war against that country. You could save your theory by saying that the state with the bigger army will always win unless it doesn't really want to, and that is what happened in Vietnam. But you could then save your theory with that tactic in every imaginable case. "To take [this type of theory] to an absurd but illuminating extreme, one can imagine a power analyst saying 'I just don't understand how a country with so many two-headed goats, so much smog, and so many asses' jawbones could have lost World War III. It must have been due to a lack of . . . commitment on the part of the leaders'" (Baldwin, 1979, p. 164). Because this type of argument is totally invulnerable to evidence, it does not really matter how silly the particular contents are. It still cannot be disproved.

---

[11] This discussion of power borrows freely from David Baldwin's article but deviates from his arguments in ways of which he would almost certainly disapprove.

Dealing with the Paradox of Unrealized Power

There are better ways to deal with the paradox of unrealized power, ways that can help us to understand international politics better. The solution to the paradox suggested here is based primarily on the **KISS** (**"Keep It Simple, Stupid"**) **principle.**[12] Social scientists adhere to this principle for two main reasons. First, all scientists share a suspicion that the world works in basically simple ways. When two theories explain the same thing equally well, and one is more parsimonious than the other (in the sense that it incorporates fewer factors or stipulates simpler relationships among those factors), scientists repeatedly find that the simpler one turns out to be more valid. The other reason social scientists adhere to the KISS principle is that brainpower, for individuals and for all researchers collectively, is limited. It makes sense, then, to devote only as much brainpower to understanding different problems as is necessary. Simpler explanations leave more brainpower to tackle additional problems, and thus deserve a certain bias in their favor.

God's Preference for Larger Battalions

The best strategy for dealing with the paradox of unrealized power begins with the realization that such "upsets" in international conflicts, especially if they escalate to war, are unusual.[13] The Roman historian Tacitus, as well as Comte de Bussy, Frederick the Great, Napoleon, and Voltaire (among others) have all been credited with aphorisms to the effect that "God is always on the side of the larger battalions."[14] In other words, when two states engage in conflict, the leaders and generals of both may pray for success, but usually the state with the greater military force has a better chance of having its prayers answered, thus, allegedly, revealing God's preferences in such matters.

If, for example, we look at the thirty wars between two states that occurred between 1816 and 1965, we find that the state with the larger armed force won all but nine of those conflicts (Cannizzo, 1980). A review of interstate wars involving major powers over the last five

---

[12] Philosophers of science refer to it as the "principle of parsimony." Carl Hempel (1966, p. 41), for example, explains that, according to this principle, "if two hypotheses accord with the same data, and do not differ in other respects relevant to their confirmation, the simpler one will count as more acceptable."

[13] The following discussion is based in large part on Ray and Vural (1986).

[14] Frank Leahy, a former football coach at Notre Dame, once noted that "prayers work better when the players are big."

hundred years shows that major powers usually win wars they fight against minor powers and, further, that in more recent centuries major powers have become involved more often in wars with minor-power opponents only. Not surprisingly, the percentage of victories major powers achieved in those more recent wars has increased (Wang and Ray, 1994).

Chapter 4 explored a theory devised by Bruce Bueno de Mesquita explaining why states initiate wars and other interstate conflicts. That theory is based to an important extent on an index of military power, and the results of tests of that theory indicate that such power is a key to success in a large proportion of those conflicts (Bueno de Mesquita, 1981). "Most interstate wars [are] won by the stronger nation or coalition. . . . [E]xamples of conflicts in which militarily inferior nations emerged as victors . . . are exceptional rather than typical cases" (Maoz, 1983, p. 220).

Still, the theory based on God's bias in favor of large battalions is much less than perfect, as is demonstrated by the examples of the United States versus North Vietnam and the Soviet Union versus Afghanistan. And, as noted above, nine states with smaller military forces have won two-state wars between 1816 and 1965. But it is possible to modify that explanation only slightly, keeping it simple and yet allowing it to deal with the paradox of unrealized power in many cases. If the state with the larger battalions does not win, it can be argued, the state with the smaller battalions must have received help from powerful friends. Thus the larger battalions do win, in a sense, even if they are not all directly engaged in the conflict.

Based on the idea that God is always on the side of the larger battalions, this type of power analysis would therefore predict that the United States would win a war against North Vietnam. When that prediction turns out to be wrong, it will be necessary to alter the theory. But according to the KISS principle, the theory should be modified as little as possible and in a simple manner. If smaller battalions win, according to the modified theory, they must have gotten help from powerful friends. In the case of Vietnam, of course, the existence of that help is quite easy to establish. Both Russia and China gave material as well as moral support to the regime in North Vietnam. Hawks in the United States called for bombing North Vietnam back into the Stone Age or turning it into a parking lot (somewhat contradictory suggestions), and if the contest had been clearly confined to the United States and North Vietnam, there is not much doubt that the United States had the capability to do both. U.S. policymakers rejected those suggestions, and even more moderate ones, at least partly because the moral support offered to the North Vietnamese regime by the Soviets and the Chinese (propaganda in radio broadcasts, speeches in the United Nations, and so

U.S. Marines landing at Da Nang, Vietnam in 1965. The United States failed to win the war against North Vietnam even though it had much larger and better-equipped military forces. SOURCE: AP/Wide World Photos.

on) led them to fear Soviet or Chinese retaliation if they moved too vigorously against North Vietnam. Having accepted that limitation as a "rule of the game," the United States then found that the material support supplied to North Vietnam by powerful friends (especially the Soviets) made it very difficult (if not, perhaps, entirely impossible) to win the war against North Vietnam.

Similarly, when the Soviets invaded Afghanistan, an analysis based on the idea that God is always on the side of the larger battalions would have predicted an easy, quick Soviet victory. Since that did not occur, our theory must be altered, and the KISS principle would lead us to suspect that the Afghan rebels must have been getting help from powerful friends. The existence of such help for the rebels is more difficult to document than in the Vietnam War, and one should be prepared to give up the idea if no evidence of help surfaces. But in this case, considerable evidence has come to light suggesting that the CIA cooperated with such countries as Egypt, Saudi Arabia, Pakistan, and China in efforts to funnel military equipment to the Afghan rebels. In fact, the United States devoted billions of dollars to supporting the rebels during the decade-long war. Accordingly, the theory that God is always on the side of the larger battalions unless the smaller battalions get help from powerful friends apparently holds true in the case of the Soviet Union versus the rebels in Afghanistan.[15]

That theory also receives interesting support from the results of the Persian Gulf War in 1991. Before that war began, some people expressed fears that the United States might get bogged down in another Vietnam-type situation in the Middle East. There were good reasons for such fears. The location of the conflict, for example—far away from the United States and right next to (as well as inside) Iraq—created difficulties for the United States for reasons soon to be discussed.

But crucial differences between the challenge the United States faced in Vietnam and that posed by Iraq made it very unlikely that the United States would get into difficulties resembling those that developed in its war against North Vietnam. North Vietnam relied on guerrilla warfare in its own territory; by simply staying in the field for years, its troops outlasted the invaders. Iraq attempted to use conventional means to hold territory where its troops were unwelcome. The most fundamental difference, certainly from the point of view of the theoretical ideas discussed here, was that while North Vietnam had powerful allies, Iraq had none. On the contrary, while China abstained on the key votes regarding the resolutions committing the United Nations to the removal of Iraqi forces from Kuwait, every other major power in the world supported those resolutions and the military effort against Iraq. Since Iraq got no support from powerful friends, and the United States was not only much more powerful but also received help from its powerful friends, it was quite predictable that Iraq would be defeated, and quite easily.

Prudent readers will suspect that such an assertion can be made with confidence only in retrospect. But one model for predicting the outcomes of international wars (published in 1983) relies to an important extent on a comparison of the composite military-industrial capabilities (discussed in some detail in Chapter 6) of the opposing parties, taking into account the likely involvement of third parties in a conflict very much according to the notions of power discussed here. Application of the formulas in that model to the relevant data concerning the United States and Iraq produces a forecast of eighty-eight fatalities for the United States in the Persian Gulf War, an extremely low number but

---

[15] Schweizer (1996) provides detailed evidence regarding the extensive support provided by the Reagan administration to anti-Soviet rebels in Afghanistan, as well as the more wide-ranging campaign waged by that administration to undermine the Soviet Union (by supporting Solidarity in Poland, for example). The main source of the evidence he cites is his own confidential interviews with key figures in the Reagan administration.

not very different from the remarkably few actual American casualties in the war (Bueno de Mesquita, 1983).[16]

In addition, an analysis of all interstate wars in the years from 1816 to 1975 shows that the initiators of those wars were much more likely to win if their targets did not get help from third parties and, further, that "initiators . . . are likely to attack target states they know they can defeat if these targets are not joined by coalition partners" (Gartner and Siverson, 1996, p. 4).[17]

Further Modifications?

A theory based entirely on a comparison between the military-industrial capabilities of the two main belligerents, as well as those of their friends, may not completely explain the outcome of the Gulf War, what happened in Afghanistan, or the difficulty the United States experienced in Vietnam. Whether an explanation is good enough in such cases is a judgment about which reasonable people can certainly disagree. One must somehow decide whether the help supplied by powerful friends to the smaller battalions is sufficient, given the difference in power resources available to the contestants, to account for the outcome of the conflict. Was the help received by North Vietnam from the Soviets and the Chinese, for example, sufficient to offset entirely the tremendous superiority in power resources available to the United States over Vietnam? How about the help supplied by powerful friends to the Afghan rebels? Was the superiority of the battalions sent into battle by the United States and its allies sufficient to explain the collapse of the Iraqi army (which was, after all, rather substantial) once the ground assault began? Ultimately, if the analysis of power suggested here is to be entirely convincing, the resources of the larger battalions as well as those of the smaller battalions and their powerful friends will have to be measured; only then will it be possible to make the kind of comparisons necessary to determine whether our modified theory allows accurate predictions.[18]

---

[16] Neither the data regarding the United States and Iraq nor the specific calculations based on these data were publicly available before the war occurred, so this was not a verified, "real time" prediction, as were some of the forecasts made by Bueno de Mesquita and various others discussed in Chapter 4.

[17] Related research indicates that "nations with unreliable allies are more likely to surrender if attacked than are nations with reliable allies" (Smith, 1996, p. 16).

[18] Important steps in that direction can be found in Organski and Kugler (1980), as well as in Kugler and Domke (1986), who demonstrate that apparently paradoxical outcomes can be explained if one takes into account the help that winners received in the form of foreign aid or the proportion of the total army of the winning side contributed by allies.

The Loss-of-Strength Gradient

Even if we take into account help from powerful friends, some international conflicts have surprising winners. The winning side in some conflicts appears to have a lot less power on its side, as indicated by military resources, and so our theory will have led us, wrongly, to expect the other side to win. This error is unfortunate, theoretically speaking (even if the "good guys" win all such wars), because we must modify our theory again and make it more complicated. But the KISS principle does not suggest that we should stick with theories that are *too* simple to cope with a complex world. What it does suggest is that, in addition to help from third parties, another fundamental factor that ought to be taken into account in any attempt to predict the outcome of an international conflict is its location. The main reason location is crucial is that it is difficult to exercise power over long distances. "The further from home any nation has to operate, the longer will be its lines of communication, and the less strength it can put in the field." The concept that summarizes this idea is often referred to as the **loss-of-strength gradient** (Boulding, 1963, p. 231).

The loss-of-strength gradient could obviously help to explain the outcome of the war between the United States and North Vietnam. South Vietnam was thousands of miles from the United States, and it bordered North Vietnam. If North Vietnam had tried to support a rebel government in the southern part of the United States, the outcome of the struggle would probably have been quite different. It is also interesting to note that Bueno de Mesquita provides general evidence indicating that the location of a conflict does affect its outcome. He makes his predictions regarding the initiation and the outcomes of interstate conflicts on the basis of calculations that take the loss-of-strength gradient into account, and those predictions are correct most of the time (Bueno de Mesquita, 1981, pp. 153–154). In contrast, Afghanistan borders on the Soviet Union, and the Soviets still had a tremendously difficult time dealing with Afghani rebels. Thus, if help from friends by itself is not sufficient to explain these difficulties, the loss-of-strength gradient cannot help us understand the Soviets' difficulties in Afghanistan.

The Impact of Resolve

What other factors, then, should we consider in cases such as the Soviet Union's war in Afghanistan, where neither help from friends nor the geographical location of the struggle seems sufficient to account for the outcome? One possible candidate that we have already mentioned several times is the will to win, or **resolve.** Recall the warning, and it is a useful one, that since the will to win is invisible, one can always argue that the losing side had less of it, thus creating even for silly theories an easy escape from criticism. But if this invisible will to win left visible traces, then silly arguments and their advocates might not escape exposure so easily, and perhaps not at all. Claims that the unexpected loser of a conflict had less will to win than the surprise victor could be verified or discredited, and explanations based on resolve could stand or fall on their merits.

It is tempting to pursue this idea regarding the impact of resolve on conflict outcomes because it is so plausible. In the case of the war between the United States and North Vietnam, for example, many other factors played a role in determining the outcome. Yet it surely seems logically and intuitively obvious, even if difficult to establish in terms of measurable indicators, that the Vietnamese did have a greater will to win and that this is one important reason they did win. Even though the United States did make a determined effort, devoting billions of dollars, tens of thousands of lives, and eight long years to the cause, it still seems clear that North Vietnam's resolve was greater. The stakes of the conflict were much greater for North Vietnam. The United States became involved in the war in defense of relatively abstract principles or distant goals involving the domino theory, the importance of upholding commitments, and making the world safer for capitalism. (We will avoid here the controversy regarding which of these factors was most important.) From the North Vietnamese viewpoint, the purpose of the war was immediate, clear, and important: to rid their land of foreign invaders and to unify the country—in short, to liberate it.

The United States did have a much larger military force than North Vietnam. But it also had a large number of other foreign policy issues competing for resources, attention, and effort, such as the confrontation with the Soviet Union, the defense of Western Europe, the protection of Israel, and preservation of the stalemate in Korea. For North Vietnam, the war against the regime in the South and its U.S. supporters was close to being its only foreign policy concern, certainly the only really pressing matter to which it devoted substantial resources and persistent attention.

In sum, the North Vietnamese will to win was greater than that of the United States, which had to devote power to the pursuit of other goals. And one need not rely entirely on logical or intuitive arguments to establish this point. The greater North Vietnamese will to win was reflected, for example, in the fact that the maximum number of U.S. troops in Vietnam at the peak of the war was less than 0.25 percent of the U.S. population (Mack, 1975, p. 197). North Vietnam mobilized a much larger proportion of its smaller population; the number of North Vietnamese soldiers killed (about 500,000, or 2.5 percent of the population) was probably equal to the number of Americans deployed. The Vietnamese, then, showed a considerably greater "willingness to suffer" (Rosen, 1972), which is essentially equivalent to the will to win (Mueller, 1980). Also, remember that the United States did not really lose the war against North Vietnam but rather ceased to participate actively without winning, and that its South Vietnamese allies did not lose the war until many months after the U.S. withdrawal. Then it becomes clear that the important role of the will to win in explaining the North Vietnamese victory could be established even with rather crude indicators.

Similar arguments can be made regarding the Soviets in Afghanistan. Some estimates indicate that 1 million Afghani soldiers lost their lives in that war, out of a population of some 15 million. Soviet casualties numbered about 55,000 (up to 1988), out of a much larger population of 280 million people (Singer, 1991, p. 73). Like the United States, the Soviet Union, while it was fighting its war in Afghanistan, had a whole range of other issues with which it was concerned. The rebels in Afghanistan, in contrast, were determinedly single-minded in their goal of ousting the Soviets from their country. Almost certainly, the rebels had a greater will to win the conflict in their own country than did the Soviet army.

Then, too, it seems likely that the Iraqi soldiers who attempted during the Persian Gulf War to hold their positions in Kuwait against the U.S.-led coalition were devoted to their task with nothing remotely resembling the zeal with which Vietnamese soldiers fought against the American forces during the Vietnam War. The Vietnamese soldiers were fighting for the liberation and unification of their nation. The Iraqi soldiers were fighting to hold on to territory just recently annexed by means of an invasion. Saddam Hussein tried to argue that Kuwait had been part of Iraq historically, but it seems unlikely that that argument was very persuasive, even for Iraqi soldiers. Perhaps that is one reason, in addition to the much bigger battalions it faced, that the Iraqi army was expelled from Kuwait with relative ease.

It can be demonstrated that the will to win, although itself not directly observable, does leave visible, measurable traces. One analysis of several examples of the paradox of unrealized power shows, for example, that one could not have correctly predicted the winner of the Arab-Israeli wars, the Vietnam War, the war between China and India in 1962, or the Korean War by comparing the power of the contestants in terms of concrete military resources available to them. However, if one takes into account the level of "tax effort" made by the competing states, reflected in the ratio of taxes successfully extracted to the amount that theoretically could have been extracted given the level of wealth in the economy in each of the states, then it is possible (when

The ground war against Iraq in March 1991 turned out not to be as difficult as expected, in part because troops like those shown surrendering to UN forces were not committed to the cause for which they were expected to risk their lives. SOURCE: AP/Wide World Photos.

this information is combined with that about help from third parties) to predict the winners of these contests correctly (Organski and Kugler, 1980, pp. 78–79). This type of analysis turns out to be valid because the tax effort made by a state reflects, apparently with some accuracy, the will of the political system to pursue its purposes, for example, to prevail in international conflict.

Another analysis of a representative sample of 164 serious disputes between states that occurred in the period 1816 to 1976 finds that predictions about the winners of those disputes based on the military resources available to the disputants simply are not accurate. "Power is unrelated to dispute outcomes" (Maoz, 1983, p. 222). It is important to realize that this analysis focuses on a set of serious disputes, *most* of which did not escalate to war. As we have seen earlier, concrete military resources have an important impact on the outcomes of international wars. But even for interstate wars, the "balance of resolve" may be more closely related to the outcomes than is the "balance of power." That is, states with a greater will to win, or resolve, are more likely to win than states that enjoy an advantage only in terms of concrete military resources, such as larger defense budgets.

But this pattern should be interpreted only with the impact of **selection effects** in mind. "The historical cases we use to evaluate theories—typically become 'cases' by virtue of prior choices made by individuals" (Fearon, forthcoming; cited by Gartner and Siverson, 1996). Smaller, weaker states almost certainly choose carefully when they decide to become involved in serious disputes with larger, more powerful counterparts. In other words, a smaller state probably avoids such disputes unless it feels that for some reason it has a good chance of emerging the winner. In contrast, a bigger, more powerful state may more consistently prevail quietly, before conflicts of interest become more visible in the form of overt disputes. Such selection effects might create the false impression that resolve is more important than it really is; still, the "will to win" is a factor that needs to be kept in mind, probably, to account for the outcome of some substantial portion of disputes between states.

More Is Not Always Better: The Infungibility of Power

If some dispute outcomes continue to seem mysterious after the balance of power and the geographic location of the conflict have been taken into account and after contributions to that balance by the allies of the original disputants have been considered, some evidence indicates that the balance of resolve ought to be included in explanations of conflict outcomes. If we confront cases that cannot be accounted for even with this rather complex theory, we might need to consider the fact that there are many types of power resources and that resources effective against certain targets for some specific purposes are useless in different situations. Political power is not **fungible** in the way that economic power is. That is, one type of political power resource cannot easily be replaced by another type, while all economic resources can be changed into money and one type replaced with another with relative ease. In other words, when it comes to power resources, more is not always better. "The theme of such explanations is not 'he had the cards but played them poorly,' but rather, 'he had a great bridge hand but happened to be playing poker'" (Baldwin, 1979, p. 166).

In the case of the United States versus North Vietnam, this particular kind of addition to our theory would help us see that the United States had many power resources that were not relevant to the contest. Its vast nuclear arsenal, for example, did not help in the political struggle to win the hearts and minds of the people in South Vietnam. Its clearly superior ability to wage conventional war was not relevant to the contest with Vietcong guerrillas. Despite important differences in the two struggles, the Soviets may have discovered in Afghanistan that their nuclear weapons and their conventional war-fighting capabilities were equally irrelevant there.

In short, when analyzing conflicts between states in international politics, it is sometimes necessary to admit that not all the power resources available to the side with the larger battalions will be effective. When the United States engaged in a conflict with the state of Iran over the fate of the hostages in Teheran, its nuclear weapons really did not help in getting Iran to give up the hostages. Dependable helicopters might have been more important. In fact, resources that are an advantage in some situations may actually detract from power in others. For example, if a state develops nuclear missiles capable of destroying an adversary in a first strike, those missiles may detract from its power to deter an adversary from beginning a nuclear war. The opponent might be made so nervous by its vulnerability to a devastating first strike that it will be tempted to launch one of its own (Schelling, 1960, pp. 205–254).[19]

No resource, then, not even the tremendous destructive potential of nuclear weapons, gives a state power over everybody with respect to every political issue. Different kinds of resources lead to power over different groups of people, with respect to specific types of issues. This point can be summarized with reference to the **scope** and **domain** of different power resources. The scope refers to the specific issues over which certain resources allow a state (or any holder of those resources) to exert influence. The domain refers to the set of people over whom a given resource allows its possessor to exert influence. "There is general agreement in the . . . power literature that a minimum specification of a power relation must include both scope and domain" (Baldwin, 1980, p. 497). God may usually be on the side of larger battalions, but sometimes larger battalions lose if the resources they possess are not relevant to the scope (the issues) or the domain (the set of people) involved in a particular conflict.

SUMMARY

States have been the most important political entities in the global system for at least three hundred years. Nations are cultural entities made up of peoples who consider themselves ancestrally related. Al-

---

[19] Maoz (1989, p. 239) makes essentially the same point when he argues that "excessive control over resources may sometimes cause the loss of control over outcomes."

though "nations" and "states" are terms often used as synonyms, the latter term refers more specifically to governments that exert supreme authority over specifically defined territory. States came to dominate the international system in a process—marked in the seventeenth and eighteenth centuries by religious divisions and the evolution of long-distance economic transactions as well as related technological developments—which provided central governments with greater power. The French Revolution in the late eighteenth and early nineteenth centuries introduced nationalistically inspired armies to international politics. In the present era, nations without independent states of their own have already dissolved the former Soviet Union and the former Yugoslavia, for example, and they threaten to disrupt additional existing states throughout the world.

Power has historically been a very important concept in the study of international politics. Despite that importance, it has been defined in a confusing variety of ways. Two of the most important definitions suggest that power is control over resources on the one hand and over outcomes on the other. Most of the confusion about power as a concept in the study of international politics arises from the complex relationship between a state's control over resources and its control over outcomes in international disputes, conflicts, and wars.

For example, sometimes states with abundant military resources lose in conflicts with states that have far fewer resources. Such cases give rise to the paradox of unrealized power—that is, situations in which apparently more powerful states fail to prevail. Such paradoxical events should not be allowed to obscure the fact that in disputes that escalate to war, the state with the larger military force is likely to win. When this does not happen, it is important to modify as little as possible the simple theory that God is always on the side of larger battalions. The goal should be to develop a theory that is as simple as possible and that works as well as possible, because simple theories historically seem to be more valid and have the additional virtue of allowing the conservation of brainpower. One simple modification of the theory stressing the importance of larger battalions takes into account the contributions to the balance of power made by allies of the states involved in disputes. Considerable evidence also indicates that the will to win, or the balance of resolve, as well as the skill with which resources are used or domestic political problems and considerations are dealt with, can help us to explain the outcomes of disputes in which large battalions do not win. Finally, if additional modifications seem necessary, one should take into account that many types of power resources effective against certain targets for some specific purpose are relatively useless in different situations.

KEY TERMS

states
sovereign
nations
Peace of Westphalia
world-system analysis
balance-of-power principle
power
paradox of unrealized power

KISS ("Keep It Simple, Stupid")
   principle
loss-of-strength gradient
resolve
selection effects
fungible
scope
domain

SOURCES

Baldwin, David. "Interdependence and Power: A Conceptual Analysis." *International Organization,* 34 (Autumn 1980), 471–506.

Baldwin, David. "Power Analysis and World Politics." *World Politics,* 31 (January 1979), 161–194.

Barkin, J. Samuel, and Bruce Cronin. "The State and the Nation: Changing Norms and the Rules of Sovereignty in International Relations." *International Organization* (Winter 1994), 107–130.

Bean, Richard. "War and the Birth of States." *Journal of Economic History,* 33 (March 1973), 203–221.

Boulding, Kenneth. *Conflict and Defense.* New York: Harper & Row, 1963.

Brierly, James L. *The Law of Nations.* 6th ed. New York: Oxford University Press, 1963.

Bueno de Mesquita, Bruce. "The Costs of War: A Rational Expectations Approach." *American Political Science Review,* 77 (June 1983), 347–357.

Bueno de Mesquita, Bruce, and David Lalman. *War and Reason.* New Haven, Conn.: Yale University Press, 1992.

Bueno de Mesquita, Bruce. *The War Trap.* New Haven, Conn.: Yale University Press, 1981.

Cannizzo, Cynthia A. "The Costs of Combat: Death, Duration, and Defeat." In J. David Singer, ed. *The Correlates of War II: Testing Some Realpolitik Models.* New York: Free Press, 1980.

Connor, Walker. "The Nation and Its Myth." *International Journal of Comparative Sociology,* 33 (1992): 48–57.

Fearon, James. "Selection Effects and Deterrence." In Kenneth Oye, ed., *Deterrence Debate.* Ann Arbor, Mich.: University of Michigan Press, 1997.

Gartner, Scott Sigmund, and Randolph M. Siverson. "War Expansion and War Outcome." *Journal of Conflict Resolution,* 40 (March 1996), 4–15.

Hayes, Carlton J. H. *Essays on Nationalism.* New York: Macmillan, 1920.

Hayes, Carlton J. H. *A Political and Social History of Modern Europe.* New York: Macmillan, 1921.

Hempel, Carl. *Philosophy of Natural Science.* Englewood Cliffs, N.J.: Prentice-Hall, 1966.

Herz, John. *International Politics in the Atomic Age.* New York: Columbia University Press, 1959.

Hinsley, F. H. *Nationalism and the International System.* London: Hodder & Stoughton, 1973.

Jones, Walter S., and Steven J. Rosen. *The Logic of International Relations.* 4th ed. Boston: Little, Brown, 1982.

Kugler, Jacek, and William Domke. "Comparing the Strength of Nations." *Comparative Political Studies,* 19 (April 1986), 39–70.

Lasswell, Harold D., and Abraham Kaplan. *Power and Society.* New Haven, Conn.: Yale University Press, 1950.

Lerche, Charles O., Jr., and Abdul A. Said. *Concepts of International Politics in Global Perspective.* 3rd ed. Englewood Cliffs, N.J.: Prentice-Hall, 1979.

Levy, Jack S. *War and the Modern Great Power System, 1495–1975.* Lexington: University Press of Kentucky, 1983.

Mack, Andrew. "Why Big Nations Lose Small Wars: The Politics of Asymmetric Conflict." *World Politics,* 27 (January 1975), 175–200.

Maoz, Zeev. *Paths to Conflict.* Boulder, Colo.: Westview Press, 1982.

Maoz, Zeev. "Power, Capabilities, and Paradoxical Conflict Outcomes." *World Politics,* 41 (January 1989), 239–266.

Maoz, Zeev. "Resolve, Capabilities, and the Outcomes of Interstate Disputes, 1816–1976." *Journal of Conflict Resolution,* 27 (June 1983), 195–229.

Mastanduno, Michael, David A. Lake, and G. John Ikenberry. "Toward a Realist Theory of State Action." *International Studies Quarterly,* 33 (December 1989), 457–474.

McKeown, Timothy J. "The Foreign Policy of a Declining Power." *International Organization,* 45 (Spring 1991), 257–279.

Morgenthau, Hans J. *Politics Among Nations.* 4th ed. New York: Knopf, 1967.

Morse, Edward. *Modernization in the Transformation of International Relations.* New York: Free Press, 1976.

Mueller, John E. "The Search for the 'Breaking Point' in Vietnam: The Statistics of a Deadly Quarrel." *International Studies Quarterly,* 24 (December 1980), 497–519.

Organski, A. F. K., and Jacek Kugler. *The War Ledger.* Chicago: University of Chicago Press, 1980.

Plano, Jack C., Milton Greenberg, Roy Olton, and Robert E. Riggs. *Political Science Dictionary.* Hinsdale, Ill.: Dryden Press, 1973.

Rasler, Karen, and William Thompson. "War Making and State Making: Governmental Expenditures, Tax Revenue, and Global War." *American Political Science Review,* 79 (June 1985), 491–507.

Ray, James Lee, and Ayse Vural. "Power Disparities and Paradoxical Conflict Outcomes." *International Interactions,* 12, No. 4 (1986), 315–342.

Robinson, Joan. *Economic Philosophy.* Chicago: Aldine, 1962.

Rosecrance, Richard. *Action and Reaction in World Politics.* Boston: Little, Brown, 1963.

Rosen, Steven. "War Power and the Willingness to Suffer." In Bruce M. Russett, ed., *Peace, War, and Numbers.* Beverly Hills, Calif.: Sage Publications, 1972.

Schelling, Thomas C. *The Strategy of Conflict.* Cambridge, Mass.: Harvard University Press, 1960.

Schuman, Frederick L. *International Politics: An Introduction to the Western State System.* 6th ed. New York: McGraw-Hill, 1958.

Schweizer, Peter. *Victory: The Reagan Administration's Secret Strategy That Hastened the Collapse of the Soviet Union.* New York: Grove/Atlantic Inc., 1996.

Singer, J. David. "Peace in the Global System: Displacement, Interregnum, or Transformation." In Charles W. Kegley, Jr., ed., *The Long Postwar Peace.* New York: HarperCollins, 1991.

Smith, Alistair. "To Intervene or Not to Intervene: A Biased Decision." *Journal of Conflict Resolution,* 40 (March 1996), 16–40.

Smith, Anthony D. *The Ethnic Origins of Nations.* New York: Basil Blackwell, 1986.

Spruyt, Hendrik. "Institutional Selection in International Relations: State Anarchy as Order." *International Organization,* 48 (Autumn 1994), 527–558.

Wallerstein, Immanuel. *The Modern World-System.* 2 vols. New York: Academic Press, 1974, 1980.

Wang, Kevin, and James Lee Ray. "Beginners and Winners: The Fate of Initiators of Interstate Wars Involving Great Powers Since 1495." *International Studies Quarterly,* 38 (March 1994), 139–154.

Weede, Erich. *Economic Development, Social Order, and World Politics.* Boulder, Colo.: Lynne Rienner, 1996.

Wrong, Dennis H. *Power: Its Forms, Bases, and Uses.* New York: Harper & Row, 1979.

CHAPTER 6

Comparing States and Foreign Policies

This chapter discusses the problems involved in measuring **power,** or in determining which state has the "larger battalions." After describing a quantitative index of power, it evaluates the results of the application of this index to a set of important states from 1900 to 1995. It then describes foreign policy analysis based on **systematic comparisons** of whole categories of states, comparisons that focus on such attributes of states as their power resources and their political regimes, to cite two important examples. The chapter concludes with a discussion of what can be learned about foreign policies from the results of such comparisons.

MEASURING POWER

Despite widespread agreement that power is difficult to measure, both students and leaders of states continue to try. They usually focus on power resources that enhance a state's ability to apply brute force or its ability to kill people and destroy things. This approach can be misleading, for several reasons. First, as discussed in Chapter 5, different power resources are neither easily interchangeable nor always relevant to certain conflicts or situations in which attempts to influence behavior are made. Second, a focus on military force as power can obscure the fact that, as a rule, relations between nations are peaceful, and brute force, or even the threat of brute force, is not really that common. "Realists" and many other traditional scholars of international politics have taught us to think that international politics is dominated by violence, that each state must look out for itself in a system that is essentially lawless. But, in fact, "the expectation of and disposition to violence between states is limited to a very few bilateral relations" (Rummel, 1979, pp. 45–46).[1] There are currently almost twenty thousand pairs of states in the international system. Most of these pairs have little contact with one another, and violence or threats of violence are quite rare between pairs that do interact.

Therefore, when one state attempts to influence another (that is, to exert power), quite often its military power resources are irrelevant, or nearly so. "International relations . . . is dominated by bargaining power: international trade, treaties, agreements, tourist and student movements, migration, technical aid, capital flows, exchange rates, and so on" (Rummel, 1979, p. 4).

Still, it is argued here that the traditional focus on power as the ability to exert brute force is not entirely misleading. Occasions when force is actually used or explicitly threatened are numerically quite small, but the importance of brute force in international politics always lurks beneath the surface of more peaceful transactions. A state may get its way (exert power) by promising economic aid, but the promise may well be more effective if the potential recipient knows that it could become the victim of force if it refuses the aid. Also, force is not used or threatened very often in international politics, but the occasions when it is used or threatened are often more important than those much more numerous occasions when nonmilitary power resources come into play. Indeed, a state's very existence can be at stake on those rare occasions when its ability to exert brute force is actually tested.

For that reason, foreign policy makers are usually conscious, to some extent, of the possibility of war and of the relative ability of the larger states in the system to wage war. The international system has experienced catastrophic world wars twice in this century. It might happen again. Even if the probability is small (and we must certainly hope it is), the possible consequences of being badly prepared for war are so disastrous that the possibility must be continually considered. In short, military power resources are of crucial importance, and the traditional focus on those resources developed for good reasons. "Power is in the last instance the ability to wage successful war" (Spykman, 1944, p. 60).

The Ingredients of Military Power

One ingredient of power that has always been important, and will continue to be so, is a large population. No state with a very small population can be extremely powerful militarily. This correlation does not mean that there is a perfect relationship between military power

---

[1] Similarly, Goertz and Diehl (1992, p. 151) point out that "certain pairs of states—enduring rivalries—account for a large portion of international conflict and war."

Industrial capacity, exemplified above by powerful engines for Douglas transport planes utilized during the Second World War for transporting supplies, gliders, and paratroopers, has provided an important basis for military power in the modern age. SOURCE: UPI/Corbis-Bettmann.

and the size of a state's population. The examples of China and India make clear the possibility of having too much of what is generally a good thing. Even so, one of the most obvious criteria for distinguishing powerful from weaker nations is population size. And both China and India may yet succeed in taking advantage of their large populations as a source of influence in the international system.

A second factor that determines a state's military power is its industrial capacity. It is safe to say that since the death of Napoleon, the most powerful nation on earth has been the nation with the greatest industrial capacity. Great Britain dominated the world throughout most of the nineteenth century, not only because it had the world's largest navy but also because it had industrialized earlier and faster than any other country on earth. The rise of U.S. industrial might and U.S. status as the most powerful state in the world in the twentieth century are not coincidental.

The two world wars have accentuated the role of industrial capacity in determining a state's power, and the introduction of nuclear weapons into modern military arsenals has continued the trend. Developing and maintaining delivery systems and a large number of nuclear weapons are technologically and economically demanding tasks for any state. A large and sophisticated industrial plant is necessary if a state is to marshal a sufficient quality and quantity of technological abilities and generate enough wealth to bear the cost of nuclear weapons and modern delivery systems.

A third crucial determinant of a state's military power is the size and quality of its military establishment. The nation with the largest army, navy, and air force, though, is not necessarily the world's most powerful state. It may, for example, find that its ability to destroy things and kill people is overshadowed by another state in the long run (for example, in a long war) because the other state will in time be able to assemble and equip a larger military force. Perhaps even more important, the total supply of available people is becoming progressively less important as military technology becomes more sophisticated and capable of greater destructive power. An army equipped with tactical nuclear weapons will probably be more than a match for a much larger force that is not so equipped. In a sense, war has become more automated, and the importance of sheer numbers of bodies in the military has diminished accordingly.

If a state has a large population, a productive industrial sector, and a large and sophisticated military force, it is virtually certain to be quite powerful. Other elements go into making a state powerful, but those just mentioned are probably the three most important. Of the additional factors, possessing large quantities of **natural resources** might be next. Modern wars and modern economies require large amounts of oil, coal, iron, and other raw materials. If a state has these within its boundaries, its power is enhanced. But this factor may be less crucial than the previous ones. In several instances, states have achieved substantial power without the good fortune of having a large quantity of natural resources within their boundaries. Both Great Britain and Japan are islands lacking in large supplies of most natural resources, but they both became Great Powers. And Germany has not been blessed with abundant natural resources. All these states had to acquire access to substantial supplies of natural resources to become very powerful, which proved possible even though the resources had to be obtained from outside their national boundaries. The fact that the United States has, and the former Soviet Union had, great supplies of natural resources within their boundaries gave them an advantage and may be an important reason why both emerged, during the Cold War era, as the most powerful states in the international system. But the history of this century indicates that access to large quantities of natural resources is sufficient for a state to be powerful; possession is not necessary.

Geography and Geopolitics

Many important writers in the history of international politics have argued that **geographic factors** can have a crucial impact on a state's power. The eighteenth-century French political philosopher Montesquieu, for example, believed that climate was important. "Great heat enervates the strength and courage of man, and . . . in cold climates they have a certain vigor of body and mind, which renders them patient and intrepid, and qualifies them for arduous enterprises" (quoted in Aron, 1966, p. 183). U.S. geographer Ellsworth Huntington (1945) pointed out that most of the world's great civilizations developed, not by coincidence, in temperate zones where the average temperature ranged from 65 to 70 degrees Fahrenheit. Although a correlation between climate and "vigor" of peoples does seem to exist, the predominant opinion today is that the causal connection is weak. One prominent international relations theorist asserts, for example, that "today, no one believes that the courage or cowardice of peoples is a function of climate" (Aron, 1966, p. 184).

Of greater impact on theories of international politics have been the writings of several proponents of **geopolitics.** Alfred Thayer Mahan (1897), a U.S. naval officer, noted the coincidence between the rise of Great Britain to preeminence in the world and the development of its navy, and he argued that naval capabilities were the key to national power. Sir Halford Mackinder, a British geographer, responded that Mahan had let Britain's temporary predominance lead him to overemphasize the importance of sea power. Actually, according to Mackinder, history reveals a constant battle between sea power and land power, and whereas technological developments favored naval power in the nineteenth century, the advent of railroads and the internal combustion engine meant that land power would assume the dominant position in the twentieth century (Dougherty and Pfaltzgraff, 1990, pp. 61–64).

An appreciation of the importance of land power led Mackinder to analyze the globe as a kind of chessboard on which the game of international politics is played. Three-fourths of that chessboard, Mackinder noted, is water. Three contiguous continents—Asia, Europe, and Africa—constitute two-thirds of the available land. Mackinder referred to this land mass as the **World Island.** The other one-third of the land on the globe is made up of the smaller islands of North America, South America, and Australia.

The key to dominating this chessboard, according to Mackinder, was the **heartland,** roughly the middle of the World Island occupied by the former Soviet Union and Eastern Europe. Mackinder thought the World Island contained such a large proportion of the world's resources that whoever controlled it would, in effect, occupy an impenetrable fortress from which to rule the world.

Mackinder's ideas appealed to a German geographer, Karl Haushofer, who became Hitler's favorite geopolitician. Haushofer may have been partly responsible for Hitler's obsession with *Lebensraum* ("living space") to the east and his unswerving determination to conquer Russia and the heartland. In any case, "Haushofer's influence was considerable in military circles and became the basis for many of Hitler's conceptions of Nazi expansion" (Dougherty and Pfaltzgraff, 1990, p. 65).

Nicholas Spykman, a U.S. scholar of international politics writing in the early 1940s, criticized Mackinder's ideas and modified the major thrust of geopolitical thinking. He argued that Mackinder was right to emphasize that the balance of power in the World Island was crucial to the security of the "offshore" states. But Spykman also believed that Mackinder had overemphasized the importance of Eastern Europe and the heartland. The key to controlling the World Island, Spykman asserted, is the **rimland,** the area around the outside of the heartland (roughly, western Europe, the Middle East, and southern and eastern Asia). Spykman (1944, p. 43) summarized his view with the slogan, "Who controls the rimland rules Eurasia; who rules Eurasia controls the destinies of the world."

One of the most impressive aspects of Spykman's geopolitical analysis involves the accuracy of his predictions about the shape of international politics after the Second World War. Although the German-Japanese alliance posed the immediate threat to the balance of power on the World Island, Spykman predicted that after the war Russia and China would present a similar threat. And just as the United States had come to the aid of the offshore island of Britain in the First and Second World Wars, he also predicted that after the second war the United States would find itself committed to protect its current enemy, the offshore island of Japan. The protective policy toward Japan would have the same goal as that toward Great Britain—that is, preventing domination of the World Island (Spykman, 1942, p. 472). It is easy to see why some analysts conclude that Spykman's rimland hypothesis was "a central theoretical foundation of George F. Kennan's famous postwar proposal for a 'policy of containment' of the Soviet Union" (Dougherty and Pfaltzgraff, 1990, p. 63), which served as the basis of U.S. foreign policy after the Second World War.

Geography and geopolitical ideas may well have served as important bases for assessing the power of nations in the past. But is it not true that contemporary technological developments have made geopolitical thinking obsolete? Surely air power and ballistic missiles with nuclear weapons have made the distinctions and relationships among the heart-land, the rimland, and the World Island meaningless.

Or perhaps not. It is possible that the new relationship between the United States and the republics of the former Soviet Union, especially Russia, will reduce the significance (as well as the size) of their vast nuclear arsenals in world politics. Further,both traditional geopolitical issues and conventional military means (combined with small nuclear forces developed by recent additions to the nuclear club) could replace the significance of ideology and nuclear technology in the international politics of the Cold War era. If it is not true that future wars will be fought with large arsenals of nuclear weapons and will last only a few minutes, but instead may be more prolonged contests between mostly conventional military forces, then geopolitical ideas may be of renewed importance.

A Simple Index of Power

No index of power can take into account all the factors that allow a state to exercise influence in the international system. But even a simple index based on a few of the important, tangible elements that make a state powerful can reveal key characteristics about the structure of that system. The point is illustrated here by constructing an index based on three concrete factors discussed earlier. The index measures a state's power in terms of demographic, industrial, and military dimensions. A state's **total population** is the indicator that reflects the demographic component of power. Three indicators of industrial capacity are in-cluded: (1) **urban population,** (2) **steel production,** and (3) **fuel consump-tion.** Finally, the number of **military personnel** supported by a state and the size of its **military expenditures** are the indicators of the military dimension of power.

The index presented here gives equal weight to each indicator for the whole period under discussion. This is an admittedly arbitrary decision whose main virtue is simplicity, a virtue not to be taken lightly in the context of a preliminary discussion of operational measures of power such as this one. For purposes more ambitious than this discussion, a more complex or refined measure might be justified. The implications of some possible modifications are considered later in this discussion.

The index is applied to the **major powers** in the international system since 1900. At the beginning of the century, according to a fairly firm consensus among scholars of diplomatic history, the following states were major powers: Austria-Hungary, France, Great Britain, Italy, Japan, Germany, Russia, and the United States. Austria-Hungary's status as a Great Power was permanently destroyed by the year 1918; Russia and Germany, having also lost that status in the First World War, nevertheless regained it in 1922 and 1925, respectively. The Second World War eliminated the Axis powers (Germany, Italy, and Japan) from major-power status, as well as temporarily removing France's major-power status from 1940 to 1944. China first appears on the list of major powers in 1950. At what point Germany and Japan again deserved to be counted as major powers is a controversial question. A consensus may be emerging that they were entitled to be classified as such by 1990. In order to trace their ascent to that status during the contemporary era, Japan and Germany are included in Table 6.1 starting in 1980.

The index is applied to the major powers every fifth year, starting in 1900, with some exceptions around the years of the two world wars. Each state is given an index score that reflects the proportion of each of the power factors it possessed at each observation point. For example, in 1900 the United States accounted for 16 percent of the total population of all the major-power states at the time, 22 percent of their urban population, 39 percent of their steel production, and 38 percent of their fuel consumption. Finally, in 1900, 3 percent of the military personnel in major powers were located in the United States, and U.S. military expenditures amounted to 13 percent of the total military expenditures made by major powers in that year. The single power index score assigned to the United States in that year is simply the average of these six figures, or 22 ([16 + 22 + 39 + 38 + 3 + 13]/6 = 22).

This index of power has obvious limitations (as do the results of its application in Table 6.1). It focuses on military power and ignores the geopolitical factors discussed earlier. It does not take into account who is trying to influence whom to do what and so may well distort the relative power of different states in specific situations. This limitation is especially relevant because the index also does not take into account alliance ties or any intangible elements of power, such as skill, will, or purpose.

Still, the index quite clearly portrays important changes in the structure of the international system from 1900 to 1995. Notice, for example, the increase in the power of Germany before the First World War. Germany surpassed Great Britain in 1905, and by 1913 had become the most powerful country in Europe. Germany's unseating of the longtime greatest power in Europe (Great Britain) and rapid rise to the top of the power structure in that continent might well have been one of the unsettling elements that caused the system to collapse in 1914. Notice, too, the extent to which the United States benefited, in terms of its power advantage over the other major powers, as a result of the First World War. The substantial increase in the power of Germany before the Second World War is reminiscent of that before the First World War. Germany's defeat of France, as well as its own defeat by the Soviet Union, is foreshadowed in the figures for 1938. Also, if one calculates

Table 6.1   Distribution of Power Among Major Powers, 1900–1992

1900		1905	
State	Index Score	State	Index Score
United States	22	United States	25
Great Britain	21	Russia	23
Germany	16	Germany	15
Russia	16	Great Britain	14
France	10	France	8
Austria-Hungary	6	Japan	6
Japan	4	Austria-Hungary	6
Italy	4	Italy	4

1910		1913	
State	Index Score	State	Index Score
United States	26	United States	26
Russia	18	Germany	18
Germany	17	Russia	17
Great Britain	14	Great Britain	14
France	9	France	9
Austria-Hungary	6	Austria-Hungary	6
Japan	5	Japan	5
Italy	4	Italy	5

1920		1925	
State	Index Score	State	Index Score
United States	45	United States	34
Great Britain	22	Soviet Union	18
France	14	Great Britain	14
Japan	9	Germany	11
Italy	9	France	10
		Japan	8
		Italy	6

Continued on page 198

Table 6.1 Continued

1930		1935	
State	Index Score	State	Index Score
United States	31	Soviet Union	27
Soviet Union	23	United States	22
Great Britain	12	Germany	15
Germany	11	Great Britain	10
France	10	Italy	9
Japan	8	Japan	8
Italy	6	France	8

1938		1946	
State	Index Score	State	Index Score
Soviet Union	25	United States	52
United States	23	Soviet Union	25
Germany	20	Great Britain	18
Great Britain	10	France	6
Japan	9		
France	7		
Italy	5		

1950		1955	
State	Index Score	State	Index Score
United States	38	United States	39
Soviet Union	27	Soviet Union	28
China	22	China	20
Great Britain	9	Great Britain	8
France	5	France	5

Table 6.1 Continued

1960		1965	
State	Index Score	State	Index Score
United States	33	United States	34
Soviet Union	27	Soviet Union	29
China	27	China	25
Great Britain	7	Great Britain	7
France	6	France	5

1970		1975	
State	Index Score	State	Index Score
United States	33	Soviet Union	34
Soviet Union	30	United States	29
China	27	China	28
Great Britain	6	Great Britain	5
France	5	France	4

1980		1985	
State	Index Score	State	Index Score
Soviet Union	28	Soviet Union	31
China	25	China	26
United States	23	United States	23
Japan	10	Japan	9
West Germany	6	West Germany	5
Great Britain	4	France	3
France	4	Great Britain	3

Continued on page 200

Table 6.1 Continued

1990		1995	
State	Index Score	State	Index Score
Soviet Union	29	United States	29
United States	25	China	29
China	21	Russia	13
Japan	9	Japan	11
Germany	7	Germany	7
France	4	Great Britain	5
Great Britain	4	France	5

SOURCE: All of the figures in this table up to and including those for 1990 are taken from the analogous table in the 6th edition of *Global Politics*, and most are based on data supplied by the Correlates of War project at the University of Michigan. The data for 1990 and 1995 were compiled by myself. (Sums for years that deviate from 100 are accounted for by rounding errors.)

the combined power of the Axis coalition relative to that of the Allies, it is clear that the Axis faced a nearly impossible task. U.S. supremacy in the international system is reflected quite clearly in the figures for the years immediately following the Second World War, and the emerging tripolarity in later years is also quite apparent. Finally, the data reflect Japan's appearance as a major actor on the world stage in the 1980s.

Did the Soviet Union really become the most powerful state in the world in 1975, and did it continue in that position until 1990, or right up to the point of its disintegration? Can China really be almost equal to the United States in power, as the most recent data available (for 1995) indicate? There are several good reasons to doubt these implications of the index, because it is biased against the United States in several respects in addition to those already mentioned. Total population, military expenditures, and steel production may all be given too much weight. The index also probably does not give sufficient weight to the productive capacity of the economies of the major powers. That capacity indicates the ability of a state to produce both an abundance of military hardware should a long war like the Second World War recur and weapons based on advanced technology, such as missiles, computers, and (perhaps) laser beams of sufficient quality and in sufficient quantity to deter, or perhaps even fight, a nuclear war. For those reasons, A. F. K. Organski and Jacek Kugler (1980, pp. 33–34), for example, use the **Gross National Product (GNP)** as their basic measure of power.

A focus on the GNP, or the very similar **Gross Domestic Product (GDP)**,[2] as a measure of power is especially interesting these days because that index reflects several dramatic changes, both in the "real world" and in the way important international financial institutions compare the economic outputs of different countries. The "real world" changes involve the disappearance of the Soviet Union and dramatic growth in the economic productivity of China in recent years. Also, in 1993 both the International Monetary Fund (IMF) and the World Bank concluded that GNPs should be compared in terms of purchasing power parities rather than international exchange rates. In other words, when converting other countries' currencies into dollars for the purpose of estimating the size of their economic products, the IMF and the World Bank now assess what those currencies can actually buy within the countries in question rather than the amount paid for those currencies in dollars in international markets.

Table 6.2 presents the GDPs for 1995 of the major powers calculated according to purchasing power parities. One result of China's rapid growth, together with the new way of measuring economic output, is

---

[2] The GDP differs from the GNP in that it includes all goods and services produced within a given country by all people residing there, both citizens and noncitizens. GNP reflects the total product of a country's nationals (citizens), whether or not they reside in that country. These differences tend to be offsetting to some extent for most countries; therefore, the figures are quite similar for most countries.

Table 6.2 Gross Domestic Products (1995 Estimates) of Major Powers, Compared in Terms of Purchasing Power Parities (in trillions of dollars)

State	Gross Domestic Product
United States	$7.25
China	$3.50
Japan	$2.70
Germany	$1.45
France	$1.17
Great Britain	$1.14
Russia	$0.80

SOURCE: Central Intelligence Agency, *The World Factbook 1996,* http://www.odci.gov/cia/publications/nsolo/factbook/us/htm, 1996.

that China's GDP is possibly larger than that of Japan; and in light of its current rapid growth rate (and Japan's recent recession), China is likely soon to have, if it does not already, the second largest economy in the world. Still, although China and the United States are about equally powerful according to the original index based on total population, urban population, military expenditures, military personnel, iron/steel production, and energy consumption, an index based on GDPs indicates that China is only about 50 percent as powerful as the United States.

The index used in Table 6.1 does not take into account the fact that, as noted in Chapter 5, powerful friends can have a crucial impact on any situation in which one state tries to influence another state, be it a world war or a vote in the U.N. General Assembly. The United States has powerful friends in the North Atlantic Treaty Organization (NATO), has been closely allied with Japan for decades now, and has been (at least until the unrest in China in 1989) on quite good terms with the People's Republic of China. In contrast, the Soviet Union, even though its relations with the People's Republic of China improved substantially in 1989, was virtually without really powerful friends in its last years of existence. It lost all of its most important allies with the official death of the Warsaw Pact in Eastern Europe in 1991. If one considers that the very integrity of the Soviet Union was (as is obvious in retrospect) threatened by internal political strife, then one must conclude that this index (because it does not directly consider the extent to which a country might be torn apart by internal political problems) grossly overstates the power of the Soviet Union just before it disappeared from the scene altogether. The index based on GDPs, though, may err in the opposite direction. No doubt the economy in Russia is in terrible shape, as is naturally reflected in data regarding its GDP. Militarily, and politically, Russia has probably not fallen as far and as fast as Table 6.2 indicates.

No index of power will capture all the subtle aspects and dimensions of the concept of power as it is used in the study of international politics. The scores in Table 6.1 are a crude indicator of power, even though they are based on "one of the most widely used and important data sets within the . . . international politics research community" (Park and Ward, 1988, p. 191). With variations and refinements, it has been used with considerable success in a large number of research efforts. In short, this index has served as an important baseline for many efforts to measure power, but no index can serve all purposes equally well. It is very important for analysts to use data "applicable to individual theories, rather than search for a universal, all-purpose scale of power relationships" (Merritt and Zinnes, 1989, p. 27).

China's rapidly growing economy has attracted the attention of foreign investors (like the credit card company featured in an advertisement above at the airport in Chengdu), as well as those who monitor China's "power." SOURCE: Jim Levitt/Impact Visuals.

CATEGORIZING STATES AND THEIR FOREIGN POLICIES

The power of a state is one attribute that clearly has an impact on its foreign policies, but surely there must be others. How do we decide what those others might be?

Currently there are almost two hundred independent states in the international system. Each state has unique characteristics and so, to an extent, unique foreign policies. Still, all the states of the world are not *entirely* different from one another, and it seems likely that the similarities shared by different groups of states may have an important impact on their foreign policies and their behavior in the global system. Concentrating on the unique characteristics of states and their unique historical experiences obscures similarities among states and foreign policies and makes the study of global politics even more bewildering than it already is.

Categorizing States

If the preceding statement is true, the compelling question becomes, "What differences among states make a difference with regard to their foreign policy behavior?" As a first step toward answering this question, a large number of national attributes can be eliminated. It seems unlikely, for example, that the percentage of red-haired people living in a state, a predominance of maple trees, or the ratio of ugly to beautiful people has a significant impact on a state's foreign policy. Eliminating such qualities, though, still leaves a large number of state characteristics that seem, logically and intuitively, to be related to foreign policy. The type of government, the level of education of the population, the number and kinds of political parties, the wisdom of political leaders and their cultural background, the size and domestic influence of the military establishment, the geographic location, the extent of freedom of the press, the sophistication of the scientific and technological establishments, the amount of internal unrest, and the mental and physical health of the population are merely some of the factors that might plausibly be related to a state's foreign policy behavior. How do we choose the factors that are most important?

First, not all conceivably relevant factors can be considered. If it turns out that *all* factors are about equally important, no matter what categories are defined, states will differ according to criteria other than those used to define a category, and thus the foreign policy behavior of states within the same category would be so diverse as to defy any attempt to discover similarities. This could be the case. But it is preferable to assume that some factors can be ignored and that others are much more important. If this assumption is useful, we shall find that states that are similar with respect to these more important factors also show important similarities in their foreign policy behavior.

The next step is to decide which factors, or national attributes, have the greatest impact on a state's foreign policy. This task can be approached in two basic ways. The first depends on logic, intuition, and common sense and might be labeled the *theoretical approach* to the problem. The other, *empirical approach*, concentrates on available data about states and involves manipulating the data so as to maximize distinctions between categories of states. Interestingly, the theoretical and empirical approach analyses show a substantial convergence.

James Rosenau (1966) not only discusses the difficulties of deciding which factors have the greatest impact on foreign policies but also stresses the necessity of doing so if any progress is to be made in the scientific study of such policies.[3] Rosenau then presents a "pre-theory," a major feature of which is a set of categories into which he suggests states should be sorted for the purpose of analyzing their foreign policies. He does not discuss his choice of categories in any depth, but it is clear that he has based his choices on a combination of his knowledge of traditional studies of foreign policy and an intuitive analysis of the contemporary international system. The first fundamental distinction that Rosenau emphasizes is that between large and small states. He then stresses the importance of the distinction between developed and underdeveloped societies and the difference between open and closed societies. These three distinctions serve to sort states into eight different categories, as displayed in Table 6.3 on page 206. The clear implication of Rosenau's "pre-theory" is that, of all the possible distinctions among states, these eight categories are the most fundamental and important for the purpose of studying foreign policy behavior.

Since that article appeared, evidence has accumulated indicating that Rosenau may have been right. For example, one empirical analysis of 236 variables pertaining to eighty-two independent nations revealed that the three factors most useful for defining categories of states that are as similar as possible to one another while at the same time as distinct as possible from nations in different categories are **size, wealth, and type of political system** (Sawyer, 1967). This approach compares remarkably well with the intuitively derived set of factors proposed by Rosenau. At least two other such analyses indicate that states differ from one another most fundamentally in terms of size, wealth, and type of political system (Russett, 1967; Rummel, 1969).

Categorizing Foreign Policy Behavior

Impressive as this accumulation of evidence may be, the discovery that states fall most clearly into categories defined according to size, stage of economic development, and type of political system does not necessarily imply that these national attributes have the greatest impact on foreign policies. That conclusion must await a comparison of the foreign policy behavior of the states that fall into the different categories. And first we must decide just what kinds of behavior we are going to look at. The difficulty of this task should not be overlooked. As one critic of the field of comparative foreign policy has put it, "Getting a clear fix on what the actors do is darn hard work—first, there are lots of

---

[3] According to Charles Hermann and Gregory Peacock (1987, p. 23), "It is beyond question that Rosenau's pre-theory essay resulted in the self-conscious emergence of CFP [Comparative Study of Foreign Policy] as an area of inquiry."

Table 6.3 Rosenau's Typology of States

	Large Country				Small Country			
State of the economy	Developed		Underdeveloped		Developed		Underdeveloped	
State of the polity	Open	Closed	Open	Closed	Open	Closed	Open	Closed
Example	U.S.	U.S.S.R.	India	Red China	Holland	Czecho-slovakia	Kenya	Ghana

Source: James N. Rosenau, "Pre-theories and Theories of Foreign Policy," in R. Barry Farrel, ed., *Approaches to Comparative and International Politics*, p. 48. Copyright © 1966 by Northwestern University Press. Reprinted by permission of the publisher.

possible 'actors' and, second, putting it bluntly, actors do one hell of a lot of things" (Morgan, 1975, p. 166).

This problem is similar to the problem leading to the categorization of states. The aim is to generalize. To avoid devising a different explanation for each state, states are categorized in ways that allow the application of one kind of explanation to several states. Similarly, to avoid constructing a unique explanation for every example of a foreign policy behavior, these behaviors are categorized in such a way that behaviors within a single category have similar causes. If this approach is successful, then factors that account for classes of foreign policy behavior can be isolated.

Let us begin by specifying that "foreign policy consists of those discrete official actions of the authoritative decisionmaker of a nation's government, or their agents, which are intended by the decisionmakers to influence the behavior of international actors external to their own polity" (Hermann, 1972, p. 72). The important question becomes, "How can foreign policies be categorized in such a way that policy actions within the same category have similar causes?" As was the case with categorizing states, several criteria make little sense and can be discarded immediately. Discrete official actions could be sorted into two categories: (1) those promulgated on Monday, Wednesday, and Friday and (2) those taken on the other four days of the week. Or foreign policy actions could be divided into those taking place in months containing the letter *r* and those occurring during other times of the year. Neither strategy seems very promising, though, because it is unlikely that policy actions categorized together in this way would have anything important in the way of common origins. But what if foreign policy behaviors were divided into those that are cooperative and those that are antagonistic or hostile? This division would make more sense, and several scholars have suggested that such a categorization of foreign policy is helpful for understanding international politics (Wolfers, 1961; Aron, 1966). Another frequent suggestion implies that the most fundamental and important distinction between foreign policy actions is that between actions aimed at preserving the status quo and those directed at changing it.

Relationships Between National Attributes and Foreign Policies

Will Rosenau's typology of states be useful for the study of foreign policies? If it is, the foreign policies of large, powerful states will be found to be dramatically different from those of smaller, weaker states; the policies of developed states will differ substantially from those of underdeveloped states; and states with open political systems will have policies that contrast sharply with those of states controlled by closed political systems. There is evidence that size, wealth, and type of political system do indeed correlate more strongly with several kinds of foreign policy behaviors, as well as voting behavior in the United Nations, than alternative national attributes such as governmental stability, population density, and urbanism (Moore, 1974, pp. 254–255). Steven Holloway (1990) finds that wealth and type of political system have an important impact on voting in the U.N. General Assembly. Similarly, Soo Yeon Kim and Bruce Russett (1996) report that North-South issues tend to predominate in post–Cold War voting in the U.N. General Assembly (the North-South split tends to reflect conflicts between bigger, more powerful states and smaller states on the one hand and between richer and poorer states on the other). They also note that the type of political system (democratic versus autocratic) tends also to be one of the most important national attributes in terms of its impact on that voting. Additional evidence suggests that large states, for example, are much more active participants in the international system (McClelland and Hoggard, 1969). There also seems to be a clear pattern of larger states issuing more protests and accusations and engaging in troop movements and taking up arms more often. More developed states tend to sever relations less often and engage in a somewhat smaller proportion of conflictive acts than less developed states do (Sullivan, 1976, pp. 110–113). There is also evidence supporting assertions to the effect that "large developed states are . . . likely to be more militaristic in their foreign policy" and that disputes among major powers are more likely historically (since 1816) to escalate all the way to war than those among Third World states (Gochman and Maoz, 1984).[4]

Some of these findings are worth noting, but this kind of research provokes more interest when it is directed toward questions that have served as the bases for long-standing controversies. For example, one hypothesis that has a long history among theorists of international relations points to a possible relationship between the amount of **internal unrest** in a country and the amount of foreign conflict in which it becomes involved. The idea is that societies with a lot of internal unrest, such as riots, strikes, coups, and the like, are societies in which the tenure of the ruling elite is likely to be insecure. This insecurity may tempt the elite to distract the attention of restless citizens by initiating quarrels, perhaps even wars, with other countries. The elite hopes this

---

[4] Since the Second World War, though, major powers have virtually never fought each other directly, although the U.S.-dominated United Nations forces did clash with the People's Republic of China in the Korean War.

ploy will take the minds of the people off their domestic grievances and focus their antagonism against foreign enemies.

Two analyses of conflict data, one pertaining to the years 1955 to 1957 and a follow-up effort focusing on data from 1958 to 1960, have found that nations with a lot of internal unrest and domestic conflict are *not* more likely to become involved in **foreign conflict** than states that do not suffer from this kind of unrest (Rummel, 1963, 1964; Tanter, 1966). Given the plausibility and persistence of the idea that there is a relationship between domestic and foreign conflict, this finding is rather surprising. One researcher concluded that it might be the result of lumping together all kinds of states into the same analysis. He decided to see whether different kinds of states might exhibit different types of relationships between domestic and foreign conflict. He categorized the same nations included in the earlier analyses according to the type of political system they had, using the following three categories: (1) personalist systems, primarily one-person dictatorial governments; (2) centrist systems, primarily socialist or Communist governments; and (3) polyarchic systems, primarily industrial democracies such as the United States, West Germany, and Sweden. Focusing on different types of political regimes in this manner reveals that states with personalist regimes, for example, do tend to have more foreign conflict if they are experiencing domestic conflict (Wilkenfeld, 1968, p. 57).

More recent research efforts, which continue to focus on the idea that there will be a link between domestic conflict and foreign conflict under certain specified conditions, have provided evidence that states are unlikely to initiate a war unless they have positive expected utility for doing so. If a state's leaders involved in one of a hundred cases since 1948 calculated that the probability of victory and the payoff from the war were sufficiently large to make the expected utility from a war positive, then the data indicate that internal conflict has tended to lead to an increase in external conflict (James, 1988, p. 114). Research in a similar vein finds that the United States, for example, has been more likely to adopt aggressive or militaristic policies at times when the U.S. economy is not performing well (Ostrom and Job, 1986; Russett, 1990; James and Oneal, 1991), and that U.S. presidents have been more likely to be assertive or forceful in their foreign policies in the wake of a loss of support from their own political party (Morgan and Bickers, 1992).

Another one of the more persistent hypotheses in the literature on international relations since the First World War involves the idea that **democratic states** adopt foreign policies that differ from the policies of **dictatorial states.** Because of that persistent idea, reiterated by Rosenau in his pre-theory, there have been several analyses of the differences between states with open and closed political systems. Several early research efforts (East and Gregg, 1967; Salmore and Hermann, 1970; Zinnes and Wilkenfeld, 1971; East and Hermann, 1974) led one review of work in that era to conclude that "open systems engage in less overall conflict . . . than do closed systems, both in the long and short run" (Sullivan, 1976, p. 136).

Scholarly interest in the question of whether or not democratic states are less likely than autocratic states to become involved in international wars has flourished recently. Several articles report that this is not the case (Small and Singer, 1976; Chan, 1984; Weede, 1984). The concentrated interest in recent years in relationships among democratic states (to be discussed below) has been marked by repeated assertions to the effect that though democratic states may be unusually peaceful in their relationships with one another, they are *in general* just as war-prone, or conflict-prone, as other states. Recently, though, this assertion has at least become controversial, with several analysts reporting that by some measures, at least, democratic states are in fact less conflict- or war-prone than states in general, and not just in their relationships with one another (Rummel, 1995; Siverson, 1995; Benoit, 1996; Rousseau, Gelpi, Reiter, and Huth, 1996; Huth, 1996; Gleditsch and Hegre, 1997).

A clearer (but not perfect) consensus has emerged regarding the idea that democratic states are less likely to become involved in wars against *each other*. R. J. Rummel (1975–1981) makes a spirited defense of this argument in his five-volume study of international conflict and war. Related ideas about the "peace-loving" nature of democratic republics have, in fact, a very long history, going back at least to Immanuel Kant in 1795. Perhaps the best evidence in support of Kant's (and Rummel's) argument that democratic states will not war against each other is, on the surface at least, convincing and simple. "Even though liberal states have become involved in numerous wars with nonliberal states, constitutionally secure states have yet to engage in war with each other" (Doyle, 1983a, p. 213). One evaluation of the proposition that democratic states do not fight international wars against each other concludes that "the evidence is conclusive that . . . there is one aspect of the military behavior of democratic states . . . that is clearly distinguished from that of non-democratic states: . . . democratic states do not fight each other" (Levy, 1988, p. 66).

It is true, of course, that the validity of this proposition is heavily dependent on the definitions of "democracy" and "war" that one adopts. It is easy to discredit the idea by adopting very broad definitions; it would be equally easy to make the proposition invulnerable to contrary evidence, but also empirically meaningless, by adopting a definition of *democracy* that is so strict as to eliminate virtually every state that has ever existed. But in this writer's view, at least, "if democracy is defined as a type of political system in which the identities of the leaders of the executive branch and the members of the national legislature are selected in elections involving at least two independent political parties, in which at least half the adult population is eligible to vote, and in which the possibility that the governing party will lose has been established by historical precedent, then . . . none of those [controversial] cases is appropriately categorized as an international war between democratic states" (Ray, 1995a, pp. 124–125).

The absence of wars between democratic states is interesting, but it is not conclusive enough to prove that democratic states are unusually peaceful in their relationships with one another. Some critics argue that although democracy may correlate with peace, this is largely because peaceful conditions produce democratic states, rather than the other way around (Thompson, 1996).[5] Other critics focus on the number of opportunities that all states have had to fight wars against each other. In recent years, there have been about 190 states in the global political system. This means that there are roughly 17,995 pairs of states in the system (190 times 189 divided by 2). In earlier years, when the number of states was lower (about 50), the number of pairs of states was of course also lower. But it was still quite large. And the number of democratic states has (until quite recently, at least) been relatively small, so that the proportion of pairs made up of democratic states has always been quite small. In short, this means that the fact that democratic states have not fought each other in war may not be as remarkable as it seems at first, because the mathematical probability that they would do so is not very large. The lack of wars between democratic states may in fact be no more remarkable than the absence of wars over the same period between two states whose names both begin with the letter *Z*. This has been one of the more prominent criticisms of the evidence produced in favor of the **democratic peace proposition** (Spiro, 1994).

Still, the proposition about peaceful relations among democratic states may be worth pursuing. Democratic states have been among the most important and powerful nations in the world in the twentieth century, and the fact that they have not fought each other could be significant, because important powerful states, all other things being equal, are especially prone to war (Bremer, 1980). Also, the number of democratic states in the world has grown significantly in recent years. "Historians may see 1991 as the year when the idea of liberal democracy gained global domination for the first time in history. . . . [In 1991] for the first time . . . liberal democracies, even in fragile or embryonic form, far outnumbered any other political system" (McColm, 1991, p. 5). By

---

[5] Thompson (1996, Abstract) concludes that "further research on whether peace antecedes democracy or the other way around appears warranted."

1997, a similar annual review concluded that "nearly 42 percent of the countries of the world provide their citizens with a high degree of political and economic freedom and safeguard basic civil liberties. . . . The expansion of democracy is continuing. There are today 118 electoral democracies, the highest total in history . . ." (Karatnycky, 1997, pp. 5, 8). In short, for at least the last couple of decades, the statistical chances for two democratic states to get involved in wars with each other have not been trivial.

The reason that such an event has not occurred may be that modern democratic states are relatively wealthy, that they trade a lot with each other, that they have been unified by common interests created by the threat of a common enemy (the Communist states; see Farber and Gowa, 1995), or that all democratic states have been under the influence of "U.S. hegemony." But European states, for example, have been among the wealthiest and most trade oriented in the world for most of this century, and that did not, before they turned uniformly democratic, prevent them from continually fighting wars against one another. In general, a review of wars in the past century and a half reveals that "of the ten bloodiest interstate wars, every one of them grew out of conflicts between countries that either directly adjoined one another, or were involved actively in trade with one another" (Gaddis, 1986, p. 112). In terms of those criteria, Europe should still be a war-prone continent, but for some reason it clearly is not. In addition, some recent research indicates that under certain conditions international trade can exacerbate, rather than reduce, conflict (Barbieri, 1996). Whereas alternative, somewhat contradictory evidence suggests that trade has a pacifying impact but does not have a confusing effect on the relationship between democracy and peace (that is, trade does not make it appear that democracy causes peace when in fact it does not; see Oneal, Oneal, Maoz, and Russett, 1996).

If having a common enemy is a key to peace, why did the opposition of capitalist states, with their many anti-Communist alliances (NATO, CENTO [Central Treaty Organization], SEATO [Southeast Asia Treaty Organization], and several bilateral alliances) not prevent wars (and other lower-level military conflicts) among socialist states, such as those between the Soviet Union and Hungary; Czechoslovakia, China, and Afghanistan; China and Vietnam; and Vietnam and Cambodia? Meanwhile, relationships among states on the democratic side of the Cold War were not always entirely tranquil either. El Salvador fought a war against Honduras in 1969, Turkey and Greece became involved in a war over Cyprus in 1974, and Great Britain fought with Argentina over the Falkland (or Malvinas) Islands in 1982. It is no accident, from the point of view of democratic peace theorists, that all of these wars on the

non-Communist side of the Cold War involved at least one undemocratic state; and clearly common viewpoints on the Cold War were no
guarantee of peaceful relationships (Ray, 1997).

In recent years, there has been an impressive accumulation of evidence supporting the idea that democratic states avoid wars with each
other because they are democratic. Statistical analyses of data on regime
types and the incidence of wars between states, from 1816 to the
modern era, suggest that this situation is unlikely either to have occurred just by chance or to be spurious, that is, brought about by some
third factor[6] (Maoz and Abdolali, 1989; Maoz and Russett, 1992, 1993;
Bremer, 1992; Russett, 1993; Oneal, Oneal, Maoz, and Russett, 1996;
Oneal and Ray, 1997). In addition, sweeping historical studies of "republics," for example, in ancient Greece, among Italian city-states, and
among the cantons of historical Switzerland (Weart, 1994); ethno-
graphic and anthropological studies of territorially based societies (Ember, Ember, and Russett, 1992); and experiments in social psychological
laboratories (Mintz and Geva, 1993) all support the democratic peace
proposition.

In support of this empirical evidence that democratic states are
unlikely to fight international wars against each other, analysts have
focused on two or three possible theoretical explanations. One is a
normative explanation emphasizing that decision makers in democracies have cultural expectations about how conflicts can be resolved in
a peaceful manner, based on compromise instead of violence, which
will carry over from their domestic political experiences into international politics, particularly when they are involved in conflicts with
other democratic states (Russett, 1993). A second type of explanation
focuses on structural constraints that make it difficult or unlikely for
decision makers in democracies to fight wars against each other (Bueno
de Mesquita and Lalman, 1992). One of these argues that when democratic governments bargain with each other, they both observe the
democratic institutions in their counterparts and infer that opposition
to government policies will exist. The constraints that this opposition
puts on both governments when two democratic states become involved in a conflict with each other make them much more likely to

---

[6] For example, wealth might make states both democratic and peaceful, which would
mean that the correlation between democracy and peace would appear to be causal, even
though it was actually only statistical. But there are statistical techniques for dealing with
such confusing possibilities, showing that the relationship between democracy and peace
is not spurious. Similar analyses reveal that it is also not alliance ties, like those evoked
by the Cold War, that account entirely for peaceful relationships among democratic states
(see Bremer, 1992; Maoz and Russett, 1993).

settle disputes by negotiation rather than through warfare (Bueno de Mesquita and Lalman, 1992).[7]

An extension of this structural explanation focuses in a similar way on the desire of all political leaders to stay in power, and on the size of the coalitions they may need to satisfy in order to do so. Autocratic leaders depend on relatively small coalitions of supporters, and so in the wake of a lost war can maintain the loyalty of such coalitions with payoffs, bribes, political favors, and political corruption or repression. Democratic leaders, on the other hand, depend on such relatively large coalitions for support that if they suffer defeat in a war, they are unable to mollify their coalitions in a similar manner (Bueno de Mesquita and Siverson, 1996). Democratic states, it turns out, are particularly formidable opponents in interstate wars (Lake, 1992). The prowess of democratic states in wars is especially intriguing in light of arguments and findings involving the impact of international wars on the tenure of political regimes. One recent analysis reveals, for example, that "regimes that initiate wars and do not prevail are at the highest risk of being replaced" (Bueno de Mesquita, Siverson, and Woller, 1992, p. 643). Related research suggests that democratic regimes are particularly prone to replacement after the onset of an international war and that losing the war increases that probability even more (Bueno de Mesquita and Siverson, 1993). In short, perhaps "democracies avoid wars against each other in part because they anticipate that democratic governments will be particularly difficult to defeat, and that they imperil the tenure of their regimes by getting involved in wars against other democratic regimes" (Ray, 1995a, p. 41).

Perhaps the most profound implication of evidence of the lack of wars between democratic states is that a world full of democratic states would be substantially less prone to war. That implication is particularly interesting in this era, when there seems to be a worldwide trend toward democratization. "The increasing number of liberal states announces the possibility of global peace this side of the grave or world conquest" (Doyle, 1987, p. 191). Figure 6.1 shows the average level of democracy in all the states in the world from 1825 to 1985.[8] The graph roughly reproduces in terms of an operational measure what one prominent political scientist refers to as the "three waves" of democratization

---

[7] Related to this argument about the impact of regime type on bargaining between states are findings that democratic states are particularly likely to allow mediators to intervene in disputes between them, and that such mediation is more likely to succeed in disputes between democratic states than it is when the disputes involve at least one state that is not democratic (Dixon, 1993, 1994).

[8]The data on which Figure 6.1 is based are in Polity II, a data set that includes annual scores for most of the regimes in the world, described in Gurr, Jaggers, and Moore (1989).

Figure 6.1   Average Democracy Score, International System, 1825–1985

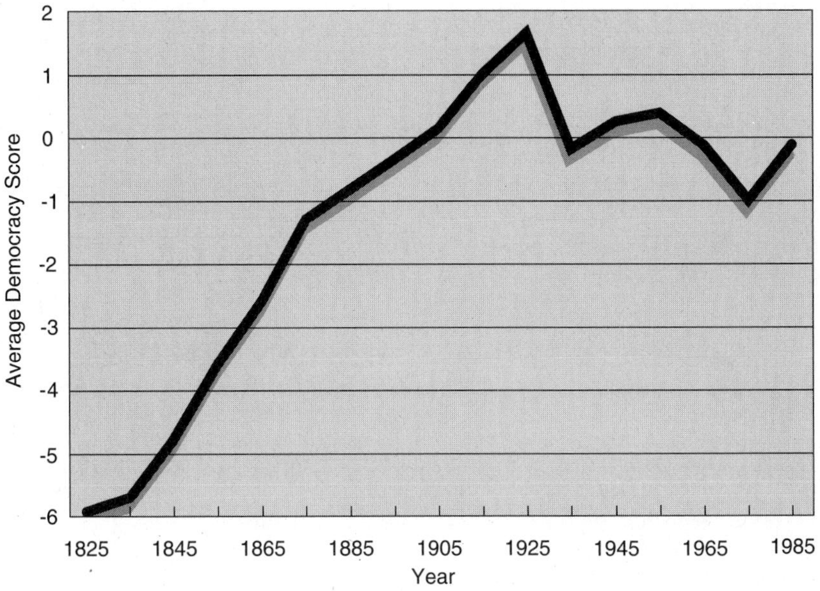

SOURCE: Reprinted by permission of Sage Publications Ltd. from James Lee Ray (1995), "Global Trends, State-Specific Factors and Regime Transitions, 1825–1993" *Journal of Peace Research,* Vol. 32(1), pp. 49–63. Copyright © 1995.

that have occurred in the modern international system (Huntington, 1991). Comparable data covering the years 1960 to 1994 show that the **third wave,** starting in the early 1970s, continues into the 1990s.

It is clear, though, that the global trend toward democracy is tenuous.

> In rough and admittedly marginally exaggerated terms, the former Soviet Union, China, and India have total populations of 300 million, 1.2 billion, and 1 billion respectively. Together, their 2.5 billion people constitute almost half the population of the world. With a continuation of autocracy and/or serious setbacks for democracy certainly possible in all three places (not to mention in a whole series of new, fragile democracies in Asia, Africa and Latin America), confidence in the continuation of the global "march of democracy" has to be tentative at best (Ray, 1995c, p. 346).

In the view of Freedom House, "the polarization of the world into democratic/free and dictatorial/unfree camps is occurring at a rapid pace" (Karatnycky, 1994, pp. 6–7). And some political scientists have found evidence to suggest that "the very constitutional restraint, shared

Figure 6.2   Global Trends in Democracy and Autocracy, 1960–1994

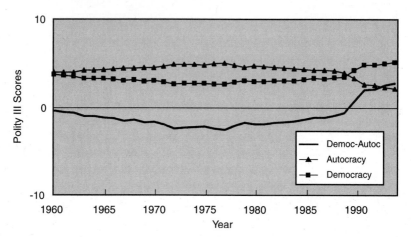

SOURCE: Reprinted by permission of Sage Publications Ltd. from Keith Jaggers and Ted Robert Gurr (1995), "Tracking Democracy's Third Wave with Polity III Data," *Journal of Peace Research*, Vol. 32(4), p. 476. Copyright © 1995.

commercial interests, and international respect for individual rights that promote peace among liberal states can exacerbate conflicts in relations between liberal and nonliberal societies" (Doyle, 1983b, pp. 324–325). Democratic states may tend, at least partly because they are democratic, to adopt intolerant, aggressive, or at least assertive policies toward their powerful, nondemocratic counterparts. In addition, there is some evidence to indicate that although stable, democratic states do indeed have peaceful relationships with each other, newly democratizing states can be particularly war-prone (Mansfield and Snyder, 1995). Fortunately, additional evidence indicates that this conflict-producing impact of democratization is most likely to occur only if a state going through such a transition happens to be surrounded by autocratic states (Oneal and Russett, 1997; Oneal and Ray, 1997).

In any case, the differing characteristics of domestic political regimes do seem to account for important variations in relationships among the states having those different regime types. No international conflict between states has ever escalated into war unless at least one state involved was not democratic. Relationships between democratic and nondemocratic states are perhaps especially likely to be tense. Democratic states may also be particularly likely, because they are democratic, to intervene in the domestic political affairs of weak, nondemocratic states. In short, a wide array of international relationships can be analyzed within what might be called a Kantian framework, or even a paradigm (Kuhn, 1962). In addition, it is at least not unreasonable to hope that "if all major powers were to become democracies, then big wars could be consigned to humankind's barbarian past" (Weede, 1996, pp. 155–156).

Caveats

All scientific knowledge is tentative, and the knowledge developed about foreign policy behavior is more tentative than most. What we have discussed in this chapter are correlations among variables. It is by now trite to say so, but we must remember that correlation does not necessarily imply causation. Still, the absence of war among democratic states is particularly striking. And the evidence regarding the differences between relationships among democratic states and relationships among other categories of states (democratic with nondemocratic, nondemocratic with nondemocratic) can certainly be viewed as "policy relevant." Specifically, it could be construed as empirical support for a consistently stated goal of U.S. foreign policy in the Third World—that is, to encourage democracy. Radical, and even liberal, critics of U.S. foreign policy often question the sincerity of U.S. foreign policy makers who declare that they favor democracy in Third World countries, partly because the United States so often supports nondemocratic forces and partly because of the role the U.S. government has played in destabilizing democratic governments, for example, that of Salvador Allende in Chile in the early 1970s and Nicaragua's in the 1980s (Forsythe, 1992). Also, the research regarding the impact of democratic regimes on international relationships has so far had little or nothing to say about what are (or are not) appropriate and effective ways to encourage the emergence of such regimes in other countries.

That does not mean that research on comparisons of foreign policy can never enhance its degree of policy relevance. Basic research often turns out to have practical applications that are not immediately obvious. Policymakers may eventually see that they have a better chance to make wise decisions to resolve particular problems if they are aware of scientific generalizations about the class of problems to which the case of immediate concern belongs.

In other words, foreign policy makers are often faced with situations that are roughly analogous to those faced by managers of major league baseball teams. No scientific knowledge about baseball will necessarily lead them to the correct choice of a pinch hitter in a particular game, but if they are aware that, in general, left-handed hitters do better than right-handed hitters against right-handed pitchers, they are more likely to make a larger proportion of wise choices. Similarly, while it is unlikely that foreign policy makers will want to base any particular decision entirely on scientific findings, it is possible that being familiar with such findings might lead them to make a larger proportion of wise choices in the long run.

POLICY CHOICES

Support the Spread of Democracy, or Support Pro-American Regimes?

ISSUE: Substantial evidence indicates that democratic states have peaceful relationships with each other, but in regions such as the Middle East, democratic elections threaten to empower political elements that are antagonistic to the United States.

Option #1: The United States can stand aside or even encourage democratic elections that bring to power anti-American elements in the hope that relationships can be improved in the long run.

Advantages: (a) The United States might reap important long-term benefits from a principled consistent policy favoring democracy instead of an expedient, obviously inconsistent policy that supports democratic elements only at times and in places where those elements are pro-American. (b) Democratic governments in various regions like the Middle East might have better, more stable relationships with each other than autocratic governments even if they are temporarily more anti-American than their autocratic predecessors. (c) A failure to support democratic elections, which inevitably appears to be a stance in favor of the current autocratic government, antagonizes important elements within the opposition who are likely to be in power some day, given the global trend against the continuation of undemocratic governments.

Disadvantages: (a) Stable, autocratic regimes may be preferable to some developing countries where the people may be too poor or uneducated to sustain a democratic government. (b) If democratic regimes come to power with obvious U.S. support, the United States will be blamed for any problems or shortcomings that come to light after those democratic regimes assume power. (c) For the

SUMMARY

Power is a difficult concept to define, much less to measure. Nevertheless there are numerical indicators of power that can provide some insight into the distribution of power and influence in the international system. One such indicator, based on a state's total population, urban population, iron and steel production, fuel consumption, military personnel, and military expenditures, is applied here to the major powers in the international system since 1900. The scores based on these data are problematic in various ways, but they still provide a foreseeable future, the United States is likely to need stable, good relationships with at least some autocratic governments, all of which will become suspicious and even antagonistic if the United States plays an overly active role in encouraging democratic reforms that terminate their regimes.

Option #2: The United States can consistently support autocratic pro-American regimes that actively prevent elections threatening to bring anti-American elements to power.

Advantages: (a) It is difficult or impossible to consistently manage or influence the evolution of domestic politics in other states; it makes more sense to devote time and energy to creating stable relationships with whatever government happens to be in power in a given state. (b) When a state is ready for democratic governance, an autocratic regime will dissolve without outside interference or intervention. Until that time comes, the United States might as well preserve friendly relationships with the government that is actually in power. (c) Democratic governments are more unpredictable. Even if the original, new democratic government is not anti-American, new anti-American elements may soon come to power. The national interest of the United States is better served by a policy of support for stable, consistent, pro-American autocratic regimes.

Disadvantages: (a) All the pro-democratic rhetoric by American policymakers appears to be hypocritical, cynical propaganda when the American government supports autocratic regimes in return for short-term political benefits. (b) Autocratic governments that oppress their own people for years, during which the United States openly supports them, are consistently replaced by regimes that are understandably and vigorously anti-American, such as the Sandinista regime that ousted Anastazio Somoza in Nicaragua and the Islamic fundamentalist regime still in power in Iran. (c) Public opinion in the United States does not understand or support, in the long run, a policy in favor of autocratic governments.

reasonable picture of changes in the distribution of power over the last century. Such scores might usefully be supplemented with additional data on states' GDPs.

Different kinds of states have different kinds of foreign policies, according to many theorists of world politics. Perhaps the most fundamental distinctions among states involve their size or power, their wealth, and their domestic political systems. Democratic states have not generally fought, and perhaps are not likely to fight, international wars against each other. Perhaps, however, it is peace that produces democracy (instead of the other way around), and newly democratizing states may thus be especially war-prone. Still, several intriguing patterns in international politics and the foreign policies of states seem clearly related to characteristics of the political regimes of those states.

KEY TERMS

power
systematic comparisons
natural resources
geographic factors
geopolitics
World Island
heartland
rimland
total population
urban population
steel production
fuel consumption
military personnel

military expenditures
major powers
Gross National Product (GNP)
Gross Domestic Product (GDP)
size
wealth
type of political system
internal unrest
foreign conflict
democratic states
dictatorial states
democratic peace proposition
third wave

SOURCES

Aron, Raymond. *Peace and War.* New York: Praeger, 1966.

Barbieri, Katherine. "Economic Interdependence: A Path to Peace or a Source of Interstate Conflict?" *Journal of Peace Research,* 33 (February 1996), 29–50.

Benoit, Kenneth. "Democracies Really Are More Pacific (in General): Reexamining Regime Type and War Involvement." *Journal of Conflict Resolution,* 40 (December 1996), 636–656.

Bremer, Stuart A. "Dangerous Dyads: Conditions Affecting the Likelihood of Interstate War, 1816–1965." *Journal of Conflict Resolution,* 36 (June 1992), 309–341.

Bremer, Stuart A. "National Capabilities and War Proneness." In J. David Singer, ed., *Correlates of War II: Testing Some Realpolitik Models.* New York: Free Press, 1980.

Bueno de Mesquita, Bruce, and David Lalman. *War and Reason.* New Haven, Conn.: Yale University Press, 1992.

Bueno de Mesquita, Bruce, and Randolph M. Siverson. "Explaining Democratic War Behavior." Manuscript, 1996.

Bueno de Mesquita, Bruce, and Randolph M. Siverson. "War and the Survival of Political Leaders: A Comparative Analysis." Prepared for the Annual Meeting of the American Political Science Association, Washington, D.C.: September 1–4, 1993.

Bueno de Mesquita, Bruce, Randolph M. Siverson, and Gary Woller. "War and the Fate of Regimes: A Comparative Analysis." *American Political Science Review,* 86 (September 1992), 638–646.

Chan, Steve. "Mirror, Mirror on the Wall . . . Are the Freer Countries More Pacific?" *Journal of Conflict Resolution*, 28 (December 1984), 617–649.

Dixon, William. "Democracy and the Management of International Conflict." *Journal of Conflict Resolution*, 37 (March 1993), 42–68.

Dixon, William. "Democracy and the Peaceful Settlement of International Conflict." *American Political Science Review*, 88 (March 1994), 14–32.

Dougherty, James F., and Robert L. Pfaltzgraff, Jr. *Contending Theories of International Relations*. 3rd. ed. New York: Harper & Row, 1990.

Doyle, Michael W. "Kant, Liberal Legacies, and Foreign Affairs." *Philosophy and Public Affairs*, 12 (Summer 1983a), 205–235.

Doyle, Michael W. "Kant, Liberal Legacies, and Foreign Affairs, Part 2." *Philosophy and Public Affairs*, 12 (Fall 1983b), 323–353.

Doyle, Michael W. "Liberal Institutions and International Ethics." In Kenneth Kipnis and Diana T. Meyers, eds., *Political Realism and International Morality*. Boulder, Colo.: Westview Press, 1987.

East, Maurice A., and Philip M. Gregg. "Factors Influencing Cooperation and Conflict in the International System." *International Studies Quarterly*, 11 (September 1967), 244–269.

East, Maurice A., and Charles F. Hermann. "Do Nation-Types Account for Foreign Policy Behavior?" In James N. Rosenau, ed., *Comparing Foreign Policies*. New York: Wiley, 1974.

Ember, Carol R., Melvin Ember, and Bruce Russett. "Peace Between Participatory Polities." *World Politics*, 44 (July 1992), 573–599.

Farber, Henry S., and Joanne Gowa. "Polities and Peace," *International Security*, 20 (Fall 1995), 123–146.

Forsythe, David P. "Democracy, War, and Covert Action." *Journal of Peace Research*, 29 (November 1992), 385–396.

Gaddis, John Lewis. "The Long Peace: Elements of Stability in the Postwar International System." *International Security*, 10 (Spring 1986), 99–142.

Gleditsch, Nils Petter, and Havard Hegre. "Peace and Democracy: Three Levels of Analysis." *Journal of Conflict Resolution*, 41 (April 1997).

Gochman, Charles S., and Zeev Maoz. "Militarized Interstate Disputes, 1816–1976: Procedures, Patterns, and Insights." *Journal of Conflict Resolution*, 28 (December 1984), 585–616.

Goertz, Gary, and Paul F. Diehl. "The Empirical Importance of Enduring Rivalries." *International Interactions*, 18 (No. 2), 151–163.

Gurr, Ted Robert, Keith Jaggers, and Will H. Moore. *Polity II Codebook*. Department of Political Science, University of Colorado, mimeo, 1989.

Hermann, Charles. "Policy Classification: A Key to the Study of Foreign Policy." In James N. Rosenau, Vincent Davis, and Maurice East, eds., *The Analysis of International Politics*. New York: Free Press, 1972.

Hermann, Charles, and Gregory Peacock. "The Evolution and Future of Theoretical Research in the Comparative Study of Foreign Policy." In Charles F. Hermann, Charles W. Kegley, Jr., and James N. Rosenau, eds., *New Directions in the Study of Foreign Policy*. Boston: Allen & Unwin, 1987.

Holloway, Steven. "Forty Years of United Nations General Assembly Voting." *Canadian Journal of Political Science*, 23 (June 1990), 279–296.

Huntington, Ellsworth. *Mainsprings of Civilization*. New York: Wiley, 1945.

Huntington, Samuel. *The Third Wave.* Norman, Okla.: University of Oklahoma Press, 1991.

Huth, Paul. *Standing Your Ground: Territorial Disputes and International Conflict.* Ann Arbor, Mich.: University of Michigan Press, 1996.

Jaggers, Keith, and Ted Robert Gurr. "Tracking Democracy's Third Wave with Polity III Data." *Journal of Peace Research,* 32 (November 1995), 469–482.

James, Patrick. *Crisis and War.* Montreal: McGill-Queen's University Press, 1988.

James, Patrick, and John R. Oneal. "The Influence of Domestic and International Politics on the President's Use of Force." *Journal of Conflict Resolution,* 35 (June 1991), 307–332.

Kant, Immanuel. "Perpetual Peace." In Peter Gay, ed., *The Enlightenment.* New York: Simon & Schuster, 1974.

Karatnycky, Adrian. "Freedom in Retreat." *Freedom Review,* 25 (February 1994), 4–9.

Karatnycky, Adrian. "Freedom on the March." *Freedom Review,* 28 (January–February 1997), 5–30.

Kim, Soo Yeon, and Bruce Russett. "The New Politics of Voting Alignments in the United Nations General Assembly." *International Organization,* 50 (Autumn 1996), 629–652.

Kuhn, Thomas S. *The Structure of Scientific Revolutions.* Chicago: University of Chicago Press, 1962.

Lake, David. "Powerful Pacifists: Democratic States and War." *American Political Science Review,* 86 (March 1992), 24–37.

Levy, Jack S. "Domestic Politics and War." *Journal of Interdisciplinary History,* 18 (Spring 1988), 66, 653–673.

Mahan, Alfred Thayer. *The Influence of Seapower upon History, 1660–1783.* Boston: Little, Brown, 1897.

Maoz, Zeev, and Nasrin Abdolali. "Regime Types and International Conflict, 1816–1976." *Journal of Conflict Resolution,* 33 (March 1989), pp. 3–36.

Maoz, Zeev, and Bruce Russett. "Alliances, Contiguity, Wealth, and Political Instability: Is the Lack of Conflict Among Democracies a Statistical Artifact?" *International Interactions,* 17 (No. 3, 1992), 245–268.

Maoz, Zeev, and Bruce Russett. "Normative and Structural Causes of Democratic Peace, 1946–1986." *American Political Science Review,* 87 (September 1993), 624–638.

Mansfield, Edward, and Jack Snyder. "Democratization and War," *Foreign Affairs,* 74 (May/June 1995), 79–97.

McClelland, Charles, and Gary Hoggard. "Conflict Patterns in the Interaction Among Nations." In James N. Rosenau, ed., *International Politics and Foreign Policy.* Rev. ed. New York: Free Press, 1969.

McColm, R. Bruce. "The Comparative Survey of Freedom: 1991." *Freedom Review,* 22, No. 1 (1991), 5, 6, 12.

Merritt, Richard L., and Dina A. Zinnes. "Alternative Indexes of National Power." In Richard J. Stoll and Michael D. Ward, eds., *Power in World Politics.* Boulder, Colo.: Rienner, 1989.

Mintz, Alex, and Nehemia Geva. "Why Don't Democracies Fight Each Other? An Experimental Assessment of the 'Political Incentive' Explanation." *Journal of Conflict Resolution,* 37 (September 1993), 484–503.

Moore, David. "National Attributes and Nation Typologies: A Look at the Rosenau Genotypes." In James N. Rosenau, ed., *Comparing Foreign Policies.* New York: Wiley, 1974.

Morgan, Patrick M. *Theories and Approaches to International Politics.* 2nd ed. Palo Alto, Calif.: Page-Ficklin, 1975.

Morgan, T. Clifton, and Kenneth H. Bickers. "Domestic Discontent and the External Use of Force." *Journal of Conflict Resolution,* 36 (March 1992), 25–52.

Morgan, T. Clifton, and Valerie Schwebach. "Take Two Democracies and Call Me in the Morning: A Prescription for Peace?" *International Interactions,* 17 (No. 4, 1992), 305–320.

Oneal, John R., Frances H. Oneal, Zeev Maoz, and Bruce Russett. "The Liberal Peace: Interdependence, Democracy, and International Conflict, 1950–1985." *Journal of Peace Research,* 33 (February 1996), 11–28.

Oneal, John R., and James Lee Ray. "New Tests of Democratic Peace," *Political Research Quarterly* (1997).

Oneal, John R., and Bruce Russett. "The Classical Liberals Were Right: Democracy, Interdependence, and Conflict 1950–1985." *International Studies Quarterly,* 41 (June 1997), 267–294.

Organski, A. F. K., and Jacek Kugler. *The War Ledger.* Chicago: University of Chicago Press, 1980.

Ostrom, Charles W., Jr., and Brian L. Job. "The President and the Political Use of Force." *American Political Science Review,* 80 (June 1986), 541–566.

Park, Kun Y., and Michael D. Ward. "A Research Note on the Correlates of War National Capability Data: Some Revised Procedures Applied to the 1950–1980 Era." *International Interactions,* 14, No. 3 (1988), 191–200.

Ray, James Lee. *Democracy and International Conflict.* Columbia, S.C.: University of South Carolina Press, 1995a.

Ray, James Lee. "The Democratic Path to Peace," *Journal of Democracy,* 8 (April 1997), 49–64.

Ray, James Lee. "Friends as Foes: International Conflict and Wars Between Formal Allies." In Charles S. Gochman and Alan Ned Sabrosky, eds., *Prisoners of War.* Lexington, Mass.: Lexington Books, 1990.

Ray, James Lee. "Global Trends, State-Specific Factors and Regime Transitions, 1825–1993." *Journal of Peace Research,* 32 (February 1995b), 49–64.

Ray, James Lee. "Promise or Peril? Neorealism, Neoliberalism and the Future of International Politics." In Charles W. Kegley, Jr., ed., *Controversies in International Relations Theory: Realism and the Neoliberal Challenge.* New York: St. Martins Press, 1995c.

Ray, James Lee. "Understanding Rummel." *Journal of Conflict Resolution,* 26 (March 1982), 161–187.

Rosenau, James N. "Pre-theories and Theories of Foreign Policy." In R. Barry Farrel, ed., *Approaches to Comparative and International Politics.* Evanston, Ill.: Northwestern University Press, 1966.

Rousseau, David L., Christopher Gelpi, Dan Reiter, and Paul K. Huth. "Assessing the Dyadic Nature of the Democratic Peace, 1918–1988." *American Political Science Review,* 90 (September 1996), 512–532.

Rummel, R. J. "Democracies ARE Less Warlike than Other Regimes." *European Journal of International Relations,* 1 (December 1995), 457–479.

Rummel, R. J. "Dimensions of Conflict Behavior Within and Between Nations." *General Systems Yearbook,* 8 (1963), 1–50.

Rummel, R. J. "Indicators of Cross-National and International Patterns." *American Political Science Review,* 63 (March 1969), 127–147.

Rummel, R. J. "Testing Some Possible Predictors of Conflict Behavior Within and Between Nations." *Peace Research Society (International) Papers,* 1 (1964), 79–111.

Rummel, R. J. *Understanding Conflict and War.* 5 vols. Beverly Hills, Calif.: Sage Publications, 1975–1981.

Russett, Bruce. "Economic Decline, Electoral Pressure, and the Initiation of Interstate Conflict." In Charles S. Gochman and Alan Ned Sabrosky, eds., *Prisoners of War.* Lexington, Mass.: Lexington Books, 1990.

Russett, Bruce. *Grasping the Democratic Peace.* Princeton, N.J.: Princeton University Press, 1993.

Russett, Bruce. *International Regions and the International System.* Chicago: Rand McNally, 1967.

Salmore, Stephen A., and Charles F. Hermann. "The Effect of Size, Development and Accountability on Foreign Policy." *Peace Science Society Papers,* 14 (1970), 16–30.

Sawyer, Jack. "Dimensions of Nations: Size, Wealth, and Politics." *American Journal of Sociology,* 73 (September 1967), 145–172.

Siverson, Randolph M. "Democracies and War Participation: In Defense of the Institutional Constraints Argument." *European Journal of International Relations,* 1 (December 1995), 481–489.

Small, Melvin, and J. David Singer. "The War-Proneness of Democratic Regimes, 1816–1965." *Jerusalem Journal of International Relations,* 1 (Summer 1976), 50–69.

Spiro, David E. "The Insignificance of Liberal Peace." *International Security,* 19 (Fall 1994), 50–86.

Spykman, Nicholas J. *America's Strategy in World Politics.* New York: Harcourt, Brace, 1942.

Spykman, Nicholas J. *The Geography of Peace.* New York: Harcourt, Brace, 1944.

Sullivan, Michael. *International Relations: Theories and Evidence.* Englewood Cliffs, N.J.: Prentice-Hall, 1976.

Tanter, Raymond. "Dimensions of Conflict Behavior Within and Between Nations, 1958–1960." *Journal of Conflict Resolution,* 10 (March 1966), 41–64.

Thompson, William R. "Democracy and Peace: Putting the Cart Before the Horse?" *International Organization,* 50 (Winter 1996), 141–174.

Ward, Michael Don (ed.). "New Research in Geopolitics." Special issue of *International Interactions,* 17, No. 1 (1991).

Weart, Spencer. "The History of Peace Among Republics." *Journal of Peace Research,* 31 (August 1994), 299–316.

Weede, Erich. "Democracy and War Involvement." *Journal of Conflict Resolution,* 28 (December 1984), 649–664.

Weede, Erich. *Economic Development, Social Order, and World Politics.* Boulder, Colo.: Lynne Rienner, 1996.

Wilkenfeld, Jonathan. "Domestic and Foreign Conflict Behavior of Nations." *Journal of Peace Research*, 5, No. 1 (1968), 56–69.

Wolfers, Arnold. "The Pole of Power and the Pole of Indifference." In James N. Rosenau, ed., *International Politics and Foreign Policy.* New York: Free Press, 1961.

Zinnes, Dina, and Jonathan Wilkenfeld. "An Analysis of Foreign Conflict Behavior of Nations." In Wolfram E. Hanreider, ed., *Comparative Foreign Policy: Theoretical Essays.* New York: McKay, 1971.

PART IV

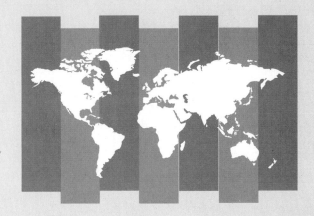

Interactions of States

CHAPTER 7

Interdependence Among Rich States: West-West Relationships

Having looked inside states for determinants of their foreign policies, (in Chapters 3 and 4) and analyzed entire states as social entities (Chapters 5 and 6), we now begin to look at interactions among different kinds of states. This chapter analyzes relationships among the wealthier, more industrialized countries of the **West,** sometimes referred to (rather ethnocentrically) as the **First World.** Chapter 8 focuses on the relationships between these states and the poorer, developing states, mostly in the Southern Hemisphere and therefore often referred to as the **South** (as opposed to the richer states in "the North"). The term **Second World** has traditionally been used to refer to the Communist states. During the Cold War, therefore, less developed countries as a group were often referred to as **Third World** states, but as the Cold War recedes and there are now distinctly fewer Communist states, that term sounds increasingly anachronistic. (Some writers argue that the formerly Communist states of Eastern Europe should now be categorized with those states in "the South,"[1] but others expect Eastern Europe ultimately to become more integrated with Western Europe and so join the First World.) Chapter 9 is devoted to a discussion of the relationship between the Western industrialized states (a category that with bad geographical but plausible economic and political logic usually includes Japan) and the **East,** which was dominated by the Soviet Union but may come to be identified more with the Communist People's Republic of China. Chapter 9 then analyzes the history of the nuclear confrontation between the United States and the Soviet Union, and it goes on to explore the *possibility* that the relationship between the United States

---

[1] See, for example, Saul Landau (1990). For a valuable discussion of the utility of comparisons of Eastern Europe with the developing world, see Nelson (1993).

and Russia has been permanently transformed. It concludes with a discussion of the possible implications of the rapid rise in power and influence in the last decade or so of the People's Republic of China and its relationship with the United States and the rest of the Western industrialized world.

As noted in Chapter 2, until the 1970s most people considered the topics discussed in this chapter to be too technical and apolitical to be of much interest to students of international political relations. The rules by which the rich industrialized states (and the rest of the non-Communist world) conducted international commerce with each other were devised in four or five years after the Second World War, and several factors worked to make those rules uncontroversial, as well as apparently uninteresting. One of these factors was a steady, positive rate of economic growth in almost all the industrialized countries. Another important factor was the unquestioned U.S. domination of the world's economic transactions. As long as these factors persisted and the United States supported the structure of the economic system in the non-Communist world, economic relationships among rich countries seemed rather divorced from politics, which centered on meeting the Communist threat. But when the system ran into serious problems, and American economic preeminence began to fade, all those technical problems suddenly seemed very political. They had always *been* political, of course; what had been missing was overt political conflict over economic arrangements in the non-Communist world. This chapter examines the structure of economic relationships among the rich industrialized countries of the world and the process by which those relationships have become an increasingly prominent political issue in recent years.

THE BRETTON WOODS SYSTEM

In the five years after the Second World War, the United States led the way in an international effort to create what became known as the **Bretton Woods system.** The name comes from a meeting that was held at Bretton Woods, New Hampshire, in 1944; it was attended by forty-four countries, all of which were anxious to devise some economic rules and regulations that would help the world avoid the kinds of international economic catastrophes of the 1930s that had seemed to play such a key role in the process culminating in the Second World War. At that meeting in Bretton Woods and at a meeting in Geneva, Switzerland, three years later, the rules of the international economic game in the non-Communist world were hammered out. Those rules, and the system, rested on three main pillars, as shown in Figure 7.1.

Figure 7.1 The Bretton Woods System

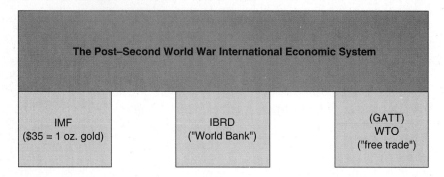

Founded in New Hampshire in 1944, the Bretton Woods system strove to manage the international money system, rebuild war-torn countries, and regulate international trade.

The International Monetary Fund

The first of the three pillars of the Bretton Woods system concerned international monetary management, and the organization created to help states cope with problems in this area was the **International Monetary Fund (IMF).** By 1947, the United States and the IMF had set up a system based on the U.S. dollar, backed by gold. The price of gold was set at U.S. $35 per ounce, and that was the standard by which all other currencies in the world were to be measured. In other words, the official value of the Japanese yen, for example, would be stated in terms of its relationship to a dollar or an ounce of gold. The countries that joined the IMF system agreed to keep their exchange rates (the value of their currencies) in relation to dollars and gold, fixed within a narrow range. The IMF monitored those exchange rates and stood ready to help any country whose currency threatened to fall lower in real value than its official exchange rate indicated.

Such a threat might originate, for example, from a consistently uneven balance of trade. Let us imagine that Italy goes through a period of years when it imports much more from the United States than it exports to the United States. At the end of every year, Italy, in effect, has to settle accounts with the United States to make up the difference in the value of what it imports and exports. According to the rules of the system set up by the IMF and the United States after the Second World War, Italy must pay up in either U.S. dollars or gold—the two being interchangeable (until 1971) because the United States has promised to support its dollars with gold. If, in order to do this, the Italian government almost entirely depletes its supply of dollars or gold (its so-called reserve currencies), international confidence in the Italian lira will deteriorate. The official value of a lira will not be the same as its real value. The *real* value (determined by what people will actually give up in exchange for lire) will be lower than the *official* value, and everybody involved in economic transactions based on lire will start to demand more of them in exchange for U.S. dollars (or anything else of value) than the official exchange rate stipulates. It is crises such as these that the IMF was designed to meet.

In this scenario, to prevent the real value of the lira from falling significantly lower than the official value, the Italian government must "support" it. That means it must be willing to buy lire at the official price. As long as the Italian government is willing and able to buy lire at the official price, the real value and the official value will stay reasonably close. Everybody involved in transactions based on the lira will realize that the real value and the official value are essentially identical because the Italian government, at least, will pay the official price for its own currency. Therefore, everybody will pay the official price for lire, secure in the knowledge that they can in turn sell those lire to the Italian government at that price. In time, having built up confidence in the value of the lira, the Italian government will not have to buy such great quantities. The crisis will be over.

Until the crisis passes, the Italian government must obtain dollars or gold with which it can buy lire. Because Italy is a member of the IMF and contributes to the fund, it can borrow dollars or gold from the fund to support its currency, thus keeping the official value and the real value in line and adhering to a fixed exchange rate.

From 1947 to 1971, this type of arrangement helped the rich industrialized countries to avoid most serious monetary crises and to keep the different national currencies at **fixed exchange rates.** When the values of currencies were threatened for some reason, the member states would borrow from the IMF to support them, and the fixed official exchange rates would be maintained. People engaged in international commerce could be confident of the relative value of different currencies, and international trade and commerce were thus simplified and encouraged. The confidence engendered by fixed exchange rates was one factor that contributed to the growth in trade and in the economies of the industrialized countries after the Second World War.

The World Bank

The second pillar of the post–Second World War economic system was the **International Bank for Reconstruction and Development (IBRD),** or the **World Bank.** This organization was originally designed (as the

"Reconstruction" in its name suggests) to provide capital for the re-building of those countries devastated by the war. It was also supposed to aid economic development for **less developed countries (LDCs),** and at Bretton Woods the LDCs tried to ensure that developmental aid for them would have at least as high a priority as economic assis-tance to those countries devastated by the war. Those efforts were unsuccessful. The United States felt that postwar reconstruction de-served a higher priority and that economic development should be spurred primarily by domestic efforts. Outside assistance might be necessary, but the capital should come from private rather than govern-ment sources. So in theory, the documents on which the World Bank was founded gave equal weight to reconstruction and development. But those documents also urged a special regard for the problems of those countries devastated by the Second World War; "the developed coun-tries that dominated the World Bank unanimously agreed that European postwar reconstruction would be the first priority for the Bank" (Spero and Hart, 1997, p. 168).

The emphasis in World Bank activities began to change, however, as early as the 1950s. By that time, the countries devastated by the Second World War had been reconstructed. Then an increasing number of former colonies and LDCs achieved independence, entered the United Nations, and began to lobby effectively for economic aid from the developed countries. Also, although under Stalin the Soviets had tended to ignore the poor countries of the world, by 1956—under the leadership of Nikita Khrushchev—the Soviets began actively to support develop-ment efforts and wars of national liberation in LDCs, thus making the South one of the primary theaters of the Cold War. The attitude of the United States and other developed countries about public aid to devel-oping countries changed in response to these developments, and those changes were reflected in the activities of the World Bank. In 1956, the World Bank created the International Finance Corporation (IFC) to encourage private investment in underdeveloped countries. And in 1960, the United States took the lead in creating the International Development Association (IDA) "as a separate institution closely inte-grated with the World Bank" (Spero and Hart, 1997, p. 170). The IDA makes loans at low interest rates to Third World countries, to be used for development projects. In short, although the World Bank originally was concerned with relationships among the more industrialized coun-tries of the world, it has over the years become primarily an aid-giving institution focusing on LDCs. It has come to serve as a forum for discussion among the richer countries about treatment of LDCs rather than an organization that is directly involved in relationships among the developed countries.

The World Trade Organization
(The General Agreement on Tariffs and Trade)

The third pillar of the Bretton Woods system was the **General Agreement on Tariffs and Trade (GATT).** The original plan after the war called for the creation of an institution to be known as the International Trade Organization (ITO), but opposition in the U.S. Congress killed that idea. In the beginning, the GATT was merely a trading agreement among twenty-three nations, meant to be in force only until the ITO came into being. "When the ITO failed to materialize, the GATT was transformed from a temporary agreement into a[n] . . . institutional framework in which governments pursued multilateral regulations and discussed trade policy" (Finlayson and Zacher, 1981, p. 562).

The primary function of the GATT is to encourage an increase in international trade and reduce barriers to that trade, whether in the form of tariffs, quotas, or other impediments such as regulations regarding labor standards or environmental protection (see Figure 7.2). One important means of fulfilling its main function is to encourage nations to abide by the **most-favored-nation principle.** This principle involves a commitment not to discriminate. If State A decides to give a break to State B (say, to lower its tariffs on shoes coming from State B), it must, according to the GATT, give the same break to all the other states from which it imports shoes.[2] In other words, State A is obliged to offer the same favorable terms on shoes to all states that it offers to the most favored nation among its trading partners.[3] The GATT encourages countries to abide by the most-favored-nation principle in order to remove barriers to trade (especially tariffs); that goal in turn is inspired by the notion that nations ought to specialize in the production of those goods they can produce most efficiently. If each nation specializes in those economic tasks in which it enjoys a **comparative advantage**—that is, if it specializes in the export of those products it can produce at the lowest *relative* cost (relative, that is, to anything else it might produce,

---

[2] That is, all the other nations belonging to the GATT, or the World Trade Organization.

[3] The phrase is clearly confusing, creating the impression that the status involves some special privilege, rather than treatment equivalent to that offered to many other states. In 1996 the U.S. Senate "voted unanimously to change the name of the controversial trade status bestowed annually by the U.S. on countries with which it has normal trade relations. The new name? 'Normal trade relations'" (*Wall Street Journal*, September 12, 1996, p. A16.). However, the House of Representatives refused even to consider or vote on this resolution, apparently because some members who object to the extension of most-favored-nation status to China want to perpetuate the confusing impression that it involves some special privilege, rather than a widely extended normal courtesy.

Figure 7.2 Changes in Tariff Rates in the Era of GATT (World Trade Organization)

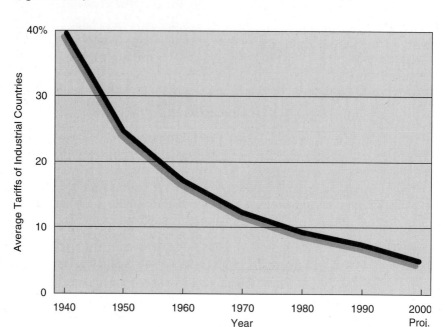

There have been eight rounds of GATT negotiations, including the one just completed. The first round was held in 1947.

SOURCE: Data from the Centre for International Economics; office of the U.S. Trade Representative.

even if it can produce nothing or everything at a lower *absolute cost*)— according to advocates of **free trade,** all states will then be better off.[4] The most (of everything) that *can* be produced *will* be produced, and then naturally there will be more of everything to go around. If, in contrast, nations adopt high tariffs to protect jobs in industries or other economic activities in which they do *not* enjoy a comparative advan-

---

[4] According to the principle of comparative advantage, even an imaginary country that can produce everything at an absolute cost lower than any other country in the world would be better off specializing in the production and export of those goods it produces most efficiently—that is, at the lowest *relative* cost. Also, a nation that can produce nothing at the lowest absolute cost should concentrate on those tasks it performs best, and even other countries that could produce those goods more cheaply should import those goods from that nation, so that the generally more efficient or productive nations can concentrate their energies on what they do best, even if it does lots of things better than everybody else.

tage, less of everything will be produced, there will be less to go around, and all states will be less well off than they could be.

In fact, the GATT has allowed many exceptions to the most-favored-nation principle and has not come close to creating a system where free trade reigns supreme. Still, until recently at least, it has almost certainly helped reduce barriers to international trade and thus has encouraged its growth. In short, "there can be little doubt that the GATT has had an important role in the evolution of postwar international trade relations" (Finlayson and Zacher, 1981, p. 602). And on January 1, 1995, the GATT evolved into the **World Trade Organization (WTO),** as one result of the **Uruguay Round** of international trade negotiations that began in 1986. "WTO is more powerful that GATT, incorporating trade in goods, services, and ideas and has more binding authority. . . . Replacing the GATT, which was never more than a provisional set of rules with a small secretariat in Geneva, the World Trade Organization (WTO) will be the umbrella organization covering the old GATT and all the new agreements reached in the Uruguay Round" (The McLeod Group, 1994, p. A14). It is generally conceded that the WTO is more powerful than GATT and covers broader areas of international trade (such as services, "intellectual properties," and "trade-related investment measures"); in fact, approving its creation raised fears that it may threaten national sovereignty in some countries, such as the United States.

How the System Worked

In economic terms, this system based on the IMF (supporting a dollar standard), the World Bank, and the GATT (fostering free trade) certainly worked well for the non-Communist industrialized countries. It did not, though, work precisely in the way it was intended to work, because the United States allowed certain distortions in the system to operate against its own best short-run economic interests and in favor of Western Europe and Japan. For example, one exception to the most-favored-nation principle in the GATT rules allowed nations forming a customs union to discriminate against the outside world. The most important of these was the European Community (EC), or Common Market, now known as the European Union (EU) (see Chapter 10), which was encouraged by the United States even though it adopted tariff barriers against U.S. products and did some harm to U.S. trading interests. Japan was allowed to use a variety of protectionist measures in 1960s even though it became a member of the GATT trade was accepted where the United States did not have advantage and discrimination was tolerated where U. have an advantage" (Krasner, 1979, pp. 496–497). Al States purposely incurred balance-of-payments deficits ern Europe and Japan in the 1950s and early 1960s to provide a flow of dollars for the other industrialized countries.

Why was the United States so generous to the Western Europeans and Japanese in the 1950s and 1960s? It is safe to say that more than altruism was involved. Perhaps the most important reason was political. The United States felt threatened by the Soviet Union in the first couple of decades after the war and also believed that economically prostrate (and politically valuable) countries in Western Europe and Japan were vulnerable to Communist subversion. The United States did what it could to foster its allies' rapid economic growth and thereby substantially decrease their vulnerability to such subversion, as well as increase their value as allies against the Soviet threat.

There were long-run economic advantages, too, in the type of policies adopted by the United States in the years immediately following the war. An impoverished Western Europe and Japan would not provide lucrative markets for U.S. exports. But U.S. generosity would create economic leverage for the United States in Western Europe and Japan, which would be advantageous to the United States once the other industrialized countries were back on their economic feet. To sum up, after the Second World War, the United States was by far the most important entity within the non-Communist world's economic system. As such, it had the most urgent need to see that the system worked well. Because it could not work well unless Western Europe and Japan recovered economically from the ravages of war, the United States provided important support for that recovery.

These U.S. efforts were quite successful. Western Europe and Japan staged remarkable recoveries from the devastation of the Second World War, and the preponderant position of the United States in the non-Communist industrialized world was modified in important ways. By 1960, the United States had already allowed so many dollars to leave the country that for the first time the value of dollars overseas became greater than the value of U.S. gold reserves. The flow of dollars out of the country continued throughout the 1960s and was accelerated during the Vietnam War. In 1952, the United States held 68 percent of all international monetary reserves; by 1977 that share had fallen to 6 percent. A similar deterioration occurred in the United States' position in international trade. In 1947, the United States accounted for 32 percent of world exports. In 1974, it accounted for only 11 percent of world exports. (In the meantime, the EC had become the largest trading entity in the world.) By 1971, the flow of cash out of the United States was so great, and imports into the United States so far exceeded U.S. exports in value, that a balance-of-payments crisis and a balance-of-trade crisis occurred simultaneously.

NIXON'S SURPRISE

Under the rules of the Bretton Woods system in operation at that time, the United States could not devalue its currency because the U.S. dollar, tied to the price of gold, constituted the standard by which all the other currencies were measured and on which their values were based. Since the dollar served as the anchor of the system, it could not be tampered with. In August 1971, President Nixon decided to change the rules of the system dramatically.[5] He announced that the U.S. dollar would no longer be convertible to gold. Ever since the creation of the Bretton Woods system in the 1940s, the United States had promised to exchange dollars for gold at the rate of $35 an ounce whenever holders of dollars wished to make such an exchange. But by 1968, U.S. holdings of gold were so low that the United States was quite reluctant to give up gold for dollars; thus it did its best to discourage such transactions. In 1971, President Nixon abandoned even the official promise to back up dollars with gold. He also imposed a 10 percent surcharge on imports into the United States.

Two fundamental aspects of the Bretton Woods system were thus substantially altered in 1971. First, when the United States pulled the props out from underneath the international monetary standard, which asserted that U.S. $35 equals an ounce of gold, all the currencies of the world were deprived of a fixed standard by which their value could be ascertained. Fixed (and therefore stable) exchange rates came to an end, because the standard according to which they were fixed was abolished. From 1971 to the present, **floating exchange rates** have replaced fixed exchange rates (see Figure 7.3).[6] This shift means that the relative value

---

[5] Several analysts stress the fact that this step represented an unwillingness by the Nixon administration to accept any further sacrifices for the sake of the international monetary system. Joanne Gowa (1983, p. 181), for example, argues that "the Bretton Woods regime broke down [on August 15, 1971] because of the hierarchy of priorities that prevailed within its most important state, a hierarchy that ranked the health and ultimately the survival of the regime well below the maintenance of state autonomy in the conduct of domestic economic and foreign policy." C. Fred Bergsten (1972, p. 204) argues that Nixon's move was "a straightforward attempt to export U.S. unemployment to other countries." Similarly, David P. Calleo (1982, p. 3) asserts that for Nixon "the demands of domestic prosperity and foreign economic obligations seemed in direct opposition. . . . Rather than continue the recession to save the dollar, Nixon let the dollar depreciate to save his Administration."

[6] Actually, there was an agreement in December 1971 to reestablish a more flexible system of fixed exchange rates, an agreement that President Nixon hailed at the time as "the greatest monetary agreement in the history of the world." But this "greatest monetary agreement," as Spero and Hart (1997, pp. 21–22) note, "lasted little over a year."

Figure 7.3   Fluctuations in Exchange Rates, Six Industrialized Countries, 1970–1994

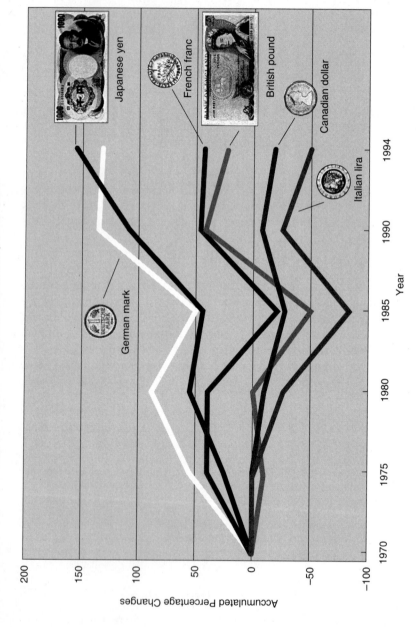

The values of national currencies in relationship to the U.S. dollar have fluctuated substantially since fixed exchange rates were eliminated in 1971.

SOURCE: Data compiled by the author from tables in the *New York Times*, circa July 1 in the selected years from 1970 to 1994.

of the different currencies is established by market forces, and the value of one currency in exchange for another is determined by what people (and central banks) are willing to pay on any given day.

The other aspect of the Bretton Woods system that was affected by President Nixon's announcement in August 1971 was the U.S. commitment to support the system itself. Until 1971 the United States had been willing to base its monetary and trade policies at least in part on considerations of what was good for the world economy as a whole. (Again, as noted earlier in this chapter, this does not mean that U.S. policymakers were astoundingly altruistic.) By 1971, the economic problems of the United States, both domestic and international, had become so serious that the U.S. government "demanded the right to manage its own currency in the pursuit of national objectives, just like any other country" (Ruggie, 1981, p. 147).[7]

THE ECONOMIC TURMOIL OF THE 1970s

The impact of Nixon's announcement in 1971 would have been profound under any circumstances. But the world economy was just beginning to recover and accommodate itself to that shock when it was hit in 1973 with a 400 percent increase in the price of oil. The members of the **Organization of Petroleum Exporting Countries (OPEC)** set the price of oil in terms of U.S. dollars and are generally paid in dollars. With the price of oil dramatically increased, a torrent of dollars left the industrialized countries, including the United States, and went to Saudi Arabia and the other leading oil producers. It can be said of any kind of money that the more of it is around and available, the less valuable it is. When the price of oil increased, the number of dollars in circulation also increased, and that is one reason that throughout most of the 1970s, the value of the dollar fell relative to gold and other foreign currencies. This fall was also probably an important factor contributing to the double-digit inflation that hit the United States and several other industrialized countries in that decade.

It was during the 1970s, too, that analysts of relationships among industrialized countries began to focus on their **interdependence** (Keohane and Nye, 1977). What were once seen as purely domestic problems in the industrialized countries came to be seen as problems with an important impact on other industrialized countries. Inflation in the United States fuels inflation elsewhere. Japanese decisions about sup-

---

[7] Ruggie (1981, p. 147) goes on to point out that "this right, although entirely legitimate, is fundamentally incompatible with the U.S. practice of deciding for the world economy as a whole the most central of issues."

porting the yen or about how many cars to export have an obvious impact on the economies of the United States and Western Europe. In general, the economies of the industrialized countries have become more clearly intertwined, and each national economy has become more sensitive and vulnerable to developments in other economies. This interdependence has brought with it economic benefits (U.S. consumers, for example, have been given the opportunity to buy more fuel-efficient cars), but it has also led decision makers to feel that they are losing control of their national economies. Such feelings give rise to **protectionist pressures** (that is, pressure to erect high tariff barriers or quotas to keep foreign imports out) and temptations to adopt other policies that might bring short-run benefits to individual countries. But taking such actions can then lead to countermeasures and long-term consequences that would be detrimental to the entire non-Communist industrialized world.

THE DECLINE OF AMERICAN HEGEMONY?

In the early 1980s, economic growth in most industrialized countries was too slow, inflation and unemployment were too high, and the price and supply of oil (and other energy resources) were too uncertain. Some analysts traced those problems to the relative decline of the United States as an economic power. "Part of the world's economic problems today," explained one well-known economist (Kindleberger, 1981, p. 248), "is that the United States has resigned (or has been discharged) as leader of the world economy, and there is no candidate willing and acceptable to take its place." A widely accepted explanation for the economic problems of the United States stressed the decline in productivity (output of economic goods and services per hour of effort) in various important sectors of the American economy. The Japanese had learned to produce automobiles more efficiently than U.S. automakers, and U.S. steelmakers also had been outclassed by several foreign competitors. American productivity had increased, on the average, 3 percent a year before 1965, but from the middle of 1977 to 1981, productivity had been decreasing 1 percent a year (Thurow, 1981, p. 119). And in the middle of the Reagan era, U.S. productivity was lagging not only relative to its own past record but also in comparison with its chief competitors—Germany, Japan, France, and Britain.

Productivity might seem to be a rather esoteric concept, of real interest only to technicians, but persuasive historical evidence indicates that a productivity decline in a country such as the United States can have profound implications for that nation's role in the global political system. In fact, one prominent analyst of the history of the world's economic and political system argues that a relative decline in productivity is one of the first signs that a predominant state in the "world system" is losing its grip (Wallerstein, 1980).

Ronald Reagan came to office in 1981 determined to deal with the productivity problem. There is evidence that he achieved that goal. By 1985, U.S. businesses were investing heavily in plants and equipment. In that year, such investments were higher, as a share of gross national product, than in any other year in the post–Second World War period (*Economic Report of the President*, 1986, p. 4). Those investments had shown important signs of paying off by the following year (1986), when the United States led the industrialized world in improving manufacturing efficiency (Wallis, 1988, p. 3).[8]

Pessimistic Prognostications

Yet even as George Bush was being swept into the White House in 1988 by six years of continuous growth, low inflation, low unemployment, and (less publicized) resurgent manufacturing productivity, speculation about the economic (and, consequently, political) decline of the United States continued unabated. The most publicized example of this speculation and pessimistic prognostication (from the United States' viewpoint) was historian Paul Kennedy's book *The Rise and Fall of the Great Powers* (1987).[9] What Kennedy's book suggested about the United States was that it was on the verge or in the process of suffering a fate similar to that of many Great Powers since 1500. According to Kennedy, Spain in the 1600s, Britain in the 1900s, and Hitler's Germany in the 1940s all had a similar problem: they became overcommitted militarily. Keeping their commitments involved military expenditures so great that the economies of their states, and so their political power bases, became fatally undermined. In Kennedy's view, "The United States runs the risk, so familiar to historians of the rise and fall of previous Great Powers, of what might roughly be called **'imperial overstretch'**: that is to say, decision-makers in Washington must face the awkward and enduring fact that the sum total of the United States' global interests and obligations is nowadays far larger than the country's power to defend them simultaneously."

---

[8] The president's Council of Economic Advisers also pointed out that same year that "manufacturing has experienced particularly strong economic growth" (*Economic Report of the President*, 1988, p. 20).

[9] "The most significant book on international affairs published in the late 1980s was Paul Kennedy's *The Rise and Fall of the Great Powers*," Kurth, 1993, p. 156).

Kennedy's arguments reinforced skepticism about the "capitalist world system" and its leader, the United States, that originated in the era of "stagflation" (slow growth with high inflation) of the 1970s. Several writers then proclaimed the end of U.S. hegemony and explained the economic problems of the entire industrialized world as a result of that decline. The reasoning, summarized in **hegemonic stability theory,** was based on an analogy with the Great Depression, during which national economies allegedly continued to contract because no leading nation had the economic strength and willingness to direct and enforce global economic cooperation (Kindleberger, 1973). This theme was echoed in books with such suggestive titles as *Eagle Entangled* (Oye, Rothchild, and Lieber, 1979) and *After Hegemony* (Keohane, 1984).

The Rise and Fall of the Great Powers also expressed many themes found in George Modelski's historical analysis of the international system. Modelski argues that the global system since 1500 has gone through several leadership cycles. In these cycles, one world leader has provided the basis for world order until it was challenged and replaced, usually in a process involving a global war. Since 1500, the **world leaders** have been, in turn, Portugal, the Netherlands, Great Britain, and the United States. The processes bringing these leading world powers to the fore, and the timing of those processes, are presented in Table 7.1 below.

As the table shows, leading world powers tend to reign for about one hundred years. Toward the end of their cycle, they are challenged, usually by a state with considerable military power. Typically, the challenger is defeated, but the world power is replaced anyway, by a nation with a superior economic base. (The major exception to these ideas involves Great Britain, which after an initial century of world

Table 7.1   A Summary of the World Leadership Cycle

The World Leader	The Challenger	The Successor
Portugal, 1494–1579	Spain	Netherlands
Netherlands, 1580–1689	France	Great Britain
Great Britain, 1689–1792	France	Great Britain
Great Britain, 1792–1914	Germany	United States
United States, 1914–?	Soviet Union	?

SOURCE: Based on George Modelski and Patrick M. Morgan, "Understanding Global War," *Journal of Conflict Resolution*, 29 (September 1985), pp. 391–419.

leadership, from 1688 to 1792, maintained itself as the world leader after a challenge by France.)

There is an obvious inference to be drawn from this schematic history, although Modelski himself has refrained from making it.[10] Like Portugal, the Netherlands, and Great Britain before it, the United States faces (or, at least, has faced until recently) a primarily military challenge from the Soviet Union. Waiting in the wings, ready and seemingly able to take over world leadership on the basis of its primarily economic strength, following the precedents of the Netherlands, Great Britain, and the United States in that regard, is Japan.

As recently as 1990, one adherent of Modelski's approach observed that the performance of the American economy "is reminiscent of the British record one hundred years earlier," and also claimed that there are enough differences between the problems Great Britain faced and the current situation of the United States that "some middle position between [an] optimistic prediction of the American revival and . . . speculations on the prospects for a Pax Nipponica [that is, the rise of Japan to the status of world hegemony]. . . seems the safest wager" (Thompson, 1990, p. 232). It is a useful step toward the achievement of modesty regarding our ability to predict future developments in the evolution of the global political (and economic) system to acknowledge that since 1990 the Soviet military challenge to the United States has disappeared altogether (with the demise of the Soviet Union); now the most formidable challenge to the United States seems to emanate from neither the Soviet Union nor Japan, but from China.

THE SOURCES OF AMERICAN
(AND WESTERN WORLD) ANXIETY

The potential threat to the United States from China is discussed in Chapter 9. That threat may well become more serious in a decade or two or three. As the twenty-first century approaches, though, the threat that looms largest (at least in some minds) in the United States and most other relatively wealthy industrialized countries seems to be the pervasive effects of **globalization.** Japan, Europe, and the United States all seem today to have serious and disconcerting economic (and related political) problems traceable to the increasingly intense impact of global economic forces. These forces appear (to some, at least) to be

---

[10] In fact, he comes close to rejecting it explicitly when he argues that the period since 1973 "cannot be defined as that of a loss of position . . . for the United States" and projects that the United States will remain the world leader for decades (Modelski, 1981, p. 80).

responsible for creating massive **economic insecurity** and **greater economic inequality** in the United States as well as in other relatively wealthy industrialized countries, not to mention the entire world. "Global integration," according to former U.S. Labor Secretary Robert Reich, "means the relatively unskilled are competing with millions of people willing to work at a fraction of their wages" (Greenhouse, 1993, p. 3). There were, for example, 18 million fewer jobs for manufacturing workers in the United States in the middle 1990s than there were in 1965, even though manufacturing output in the United States rose 38 percent (Glassman, 1993, p. 1). A cover story from *Business Week* (not exactly a hotbed of leftist criticism of the United States) in the middle 1990s declared that "the well-paying blue-collar jobs that gave U.S. workers rising living standards for most of this century are vanishing. Today, you can all but forget about joining the middle class unless you go to college" (Bernstein, 1994, p. 78).

The growing number of relatively uneducated, unskilled people in the United States who cannot find productive employment may be connected to the growing problem of high crime rates and violence in America. Men who cannot find legal employment with good pay resort to crime, creating a shortage of eligible mates for women, who must rely on low-paying jobs or government subsidies to survive. This problem has become international in its scope and impact. In 1993, the deputy secretary of foreign affairs from Singapore noted that "since 1960 the U.S. population has increased 41 percent while violent crime has risen 560 percent, single-mother births by 419 percent, divorce rates by 300 percent and the percentage of children living in single-parent homes by 300 percent." These problems create doubts in the minds of foreign observers, perhaps, about the viability of democracy and the individual freedoms on which it is based. The deputy secretary of foreign affairs in Singapore concluded, at any rate, that "freedom can cause problems," and that Americans need to be more humble about the virtues of democracy, instead of "confidently preach[ing] the virtues of unfettered individual freedom, blithely ignoring the visible social consequences" (Mahbubani, 1993, p. 14).

Doubts about the viability of democracy and the wisdom of subjecting one's domestic economy to the effects of globalization are reinforced by the fate of middle-class workers in the United States. It is not only the relatively underprivileged in the United States who seem to be suffering from insecurity in the wake of increased integration of the American economy with the global economic system. In 1996, front-page stories in the *New York Times* appeared under large headlines such as "ON THE BATTLEFIELD OF BUSINESS, MILLIONS OF CASUALTIES." Such stories noted that 43 million jobs have been erased in the United States since 1979, and that although far more jobs than that were

Table 7.2   Large Layoffs in the 1990s, United States

Company	Jobs Cut	Share of Work Force
AT&T	123,000	30%
I.B.M.	122,000	35
General Motors	99,400	29
Boeing	61,000	37
Sears, Roebuck	50,000	15
Digital Equipment	29,800	26
Lockheed Martin	29,100	17
BellSouth	21,200	23
McDonnell Douglas	21,000	20
Pacific Telesis	19,000	19
Delta Airlines	18,800	26
GTE	18,400	14
Nynex	17,400	33
Eastman Kodak	16,800	13
Baxter International	16,000	28

Based on layoff announcements reported in major newspapers. Percentage figures refer to the company's total work force at the time of the announcement (the earliest if more than one).

SOURCE: From *The New York Times,* March 3, 1996, p. A4. Copyright © 1996 by The New York Times Company. Reprinted by permission.

created during that time, "increasingly the jobs that are disappearing are those of higher-paid white collar workers, many at large corporations, women as well as men, many at the peak of their careers." (Table 7.2 illustrates some of the large layoffs in the middle 1990s.) The same story notes that workers with at least some college education make up the majority of people whose jobs are being eliminated (Uchitelle and Kleinfield, 1996, p. 1). Similar stories report interviews with alumni of Bucknell University, for example, who "have lost their belief in the future and their faith in the rules of hard work rewarded. In the new economy of layoffs, limitation and job insecurity, their expansive confidence has eroded" (Johnson, 1996, p. 1). Middle-class residents of Dayton, Ohio, in the wake of large layoffs by National Cash Register

SOURCE: ARLO & JANIS reprinted by permission of Newspaper Enterprise Association, Inc.

there, feel that "everything, seemingly, is in upheaval. . . . America is deep in mid-passage between two economic eras: the old era of making things and job security, and the new one of service and technology, takeovers, layoffs and job insecurity. And the entire cloth of society, which most people in Dayton once wore so comfortably, feels as if it is out of style and could just wear out" (Rimer, 1996, p. 1).

Well-known economic analyst Jane Bryant Quinn (1996, p. C1) noted in the mid-1990s that the U.S. economy had generated 20 million jobs between 1983 and 1993, but "employers offered more high-wage jobs (technicians, professionals) and low-wage jobs (generally hourly workers), with fewer jobs in the middle." With relatively unskilled workers getting lower pay, and middle-class workers losing their jobs altogether, it is easy to conclude that the rich in the United States must be getting richer while the poor are getting poorer. And, indeed, it is often observed as the twenty-first century approaches that economic inequality is on the rise in the United States. According to Jane Bryant Quinn (1996, p. C1), for example, "without question, it's a great time to be rich. Between 1977 and 1992, America's most prosperous fifth gained in real income after tax . . . the richest 1 percent raked in a 91-percent gain. The middle, however, just held its own while the poorest fifth grew 17 percent poorer still." And *Business Week* (Bernstein, 1994, p. 78) notes that "since the late 1970s, an explosion of income inequality has occurred. . . . Families in the mostly college-educated top quarter . . . have prospered. . . . Families in the bottom quarter . . . are stranded in low-wage limbo. This has led to the widest **rich-poor gap** since the Census Bureau began keeping track in 1947. Top-fifth families now rake in 44.6% of U.S. income, vs. 4.4% for the bottom fifth." (See Figure 7.4 about the growing gap.)[11]

---

[11] This story goes on to note that "as recently as 1980, the top got 41.6%, the bottom 5.1%" (Bernstein, 1994, pp. 78–79).

Figure 7.4   A Growing Gap Between Rich and Poor Families

Income Level	Average Family Income As Share of National Income		Average Family Income in Thousands of 1992 Dollars		
	1980	1992	1980	1992	% Change
TOP 25%	48.2%	51.3%	$78,844	$91,368	UP 15.9%
SECOND 25%	26.9	26.3	44,041	46,471	UP 5.5%
THIRD 25%	17.3	16.0	28,249	28,434	UP 0.7%
BOTTOM 25%	7.6	6.5	12,359	11,530	DOWN 6.8%

DATA: Census Bureau

SOURCE: Reprinted from the August 15, 1994 issue of *Business Week* by special permission. Copyright © 1994 by the McGraw-Hill Companies.

That these problems of unemployment, or job insecurity, and economic inequality in the United States have something to do with increasing integration of the globe's national economies seems more likely in light of the evidence that other industrialized economies, while becoming more integrated, are also experiencing similar problems regarding a scarcity of jobs with good pay and increasing inequality. "While concerns over unemployment are mounting in Japan, the same fears have reached a near fever pitch in Western Europe, where one in nine workers is currently without a job. Every Western European nation is experiencing worsening unemployment" (Rifkin, 1995, p. 199). And in 1996, the *New York Times* noted that "following reports that gaps between rich and poor in the United States are wider than they have been in half a century, a U.N. survey . . . finds the phenomenon is worldwide, with the wealthiest and poorest people living in increasingly separate worlds" (Crossette, 1996, p. 1). This inequality seems to be increasing both within countries (*Business Week*, August 10, 1992, p. 16) and across the entire globe. "An emerging global elite, mostly urban-based and interconnected in a variety of ways, is amassing great wealth and power, while more than half of humanity is left out" (Crossette, 1996, p. 1). In addition, "the incomes of the richest 20 percent of the world's people are approximately 140 times those of the poorest 20 percent. . . . The world now has more than 350 billionaires whose combined net worth equals the annual income of the poorest 45 percent of the world's population" (Korten, 1996, p. 16).

Why is this increase in inequality occurring? The implication of this discussion so far, supported by numerous analysts, is that globalization is a key factor. Over the last fifty years, one such analyst points out, "international trade has expanded by roughly 12 times and foreign direct investment has been expanding at two or three times the rate of trade expansion." Not by coincidence, or so it seems, "The earth has more poor people today than ever before. There is an accelerating gap between the rich and the poor" (Korten, 1996, p. 15).

And indeed this explanation seems based at least in part on persuasive logic. What is occurring is not exactly a result of "free trade," or the free movement of capital, because rich as well as poor countries have adopted a variety of tariffs, import and investment controls, and quotas in an attempt to curb the effects of globalization. Still, as the world's economy becomes more closely integrated, every country in the world feels increasingly intense market-based pressures to allocate its resources to those economic pursuits at which it is best, or most productive, so that whatever it produces can be sold in the global marketplace. As the number of newly industrialized countries in the developing world increases and the trend toward world economic integration continues, it is inevitable (perhaps) that what richer countries like the United States, Japan, and those in Western Europe do best involves technologically complex and knowledge-based economic activities that create jobs primarily for well-trained and highly educated people. In addition, it would seem logical to conclude that as advanced technologies allow ever greater efficiency, making it possible for fewer people to carry out more and more of the tasks involved in the production of goods and services, the resulting rewards and economic benefits will become ever more concentrated in the hands of this shrinking elite of technocrats and entrepreneurs.

But there is not universal agreement that it is globalization that is making inequality worse. Some analysts put more emphasis on **technological changes,** most notably **computers** and other **information technologies.** Economist Peter Drucker, for example, observes that "in the 1990s only an insignificant percentage of manufacturing goods imported into the United States are produced abroad because of low labor costs. While total imports in 1990 accounted for about 12 percent of the U.S. gross personal income, imports from countries with significantly lower wage costs accounted for less than three percent . . ." (Drucker, 1994, p. 64). Drucker's point is that technological innovations such as the computer are creating a knowledge-based economy, which is more fundamental to the fate of blue-collar workers and other less well educated groups than is globalization per se.

On the other hand, still other analysts argue that globalization and technological innovations are basically two sides of the same coin, and that they work together to produce drastic changes in national economies that benefit primarily a small elite, to the devastating detriment of the majority. Jeremy Rifkin (1995, p. 21), for example, points out that "faced with increasing competition from abroad and greater competition within each industry at home, companies searched for new ways to cut costs and improve market share and profits. They turned to the new computer and information technologies in the hopes of increasing productivity in lean times." As we shall see below, Rifkin believes that companies have attained this goal only too well.

One possible response to these problems is to implement government-sponsored **training programs** to retrain the people most hurt by these economic dislocations. "The most important economic development of our lifetime has been the rise of a new system for creating wealth, based no longer on muscle but on mind" (Toffler, 1990, pp. 8–9). Obviously, then (or so it would seem), government-sponsored programs are needed to help people to equip their minds to deal with the economic transformation caused by globalization and technological developments.

Unfortunately, such training programs do not appear to help much. One American public policy specialist argues that "the most flagrant examples of wasteful government spending are federal and state job-training programs, hampered as they are by duplication, waste, and conflicting regulations" (Lawson, 1996, p. 9.)[12] More generally, the *Economist* reports that state-run training programs in both the United States and Europe have disappointing records.

> In a growing body of research, economists have compared groups who enter government training schemes with similar groups who do not. In almost every case, these studies have found that the schemes have failed to improve either the earnings or the employment prospects of their clients (*Economist*, April 6, 1996, p. 19).[13]

In any case, if Jeremy Rifkin is correct, such training programs are a pitifully inadequate response to a fundamentally revolutionary problem that faces the United States, other wealthy industrialized countries, and indeed the entire world in this age of globalization and new technologies. Rifkin observes that "global unemployment has now reached the

---

[12] This story goes on to note that "the General Accounting Office estimates that the federal government oversees some 154 separate job-training programs, administered by more than a dozen different agencies" (Lawson, 1996, p. 9.)

[13] This story goes on to report that "in the United States, the Department of Labour runs $5 billion-worth of elaborate training schemes directed at the disadvantaged. How much do they help their clientele? 'Zero is not a bad number,' concludes James Heckman of the University of Chicago, who directed a government-financed study of the Job Training Partnership Act, America's largest such programme."

SOURCE: Rob Rogers reprinted by permission of United Features Syndicate, Inc.

highest level since the great depression of the 1930s. . . . Already, millions of workers have been permanently eliminated from the economic process, and whole job categories have shrunk, been restructured, or disappeared" (Rifkin, 1995, p. xv). Rifkin has no doubt about the source of these problems. Current economic changes are of such a character that "the only new sector emerging is the **knowledge sector,** made up of a small elite of entrepreneurs, scientists, technicians, computer programmers, professional educators and consultants" (Rifkin, 1995, p. xvii). According to Rifkin, "now, for the first time, human labor is being systematically eliminated from the production process. . . . Intelligent machines are replacing human beings in countless tasks, forcing millions of blue and white collar workers into unemployment lines, or worse still, breadlines" (Rifkin, 1995, p. 3). Rifkin concludes in his book, ominously entitled *The End of Work,* that "massive unemployment of a kind never before experienced seems all but inevitable in the coming decades," and that "chances are that the growing gap between the haves and the have-nots will lead to social and political upheaval on a global scale" (1995, pp. 5, 13).

Doubts About the Sources of Anxiety

Perhaps in light of this evidence of the baneful effects of globalization, the world's nations, including the United States, would be well advised to disengage from the globalization process, erect protectionist barriers, and put strict controls and limits on foreign investment. But there are some powerful counterarguments. "An unambiguous lesson of the last 40 years is that increased participation in the world economy has become the key to domestic growth and prosperity. Since 1950 there has been a close correlation between a country's domestic economic performance and its participation in the world's economy" (Drucker, 1994, p. 104). And as the world's economy has become more closely integrated, its performance has been quite impressive. In fact, "it has been growing faster for the past 40 years than at any time since modern economies and the discipline of economics emerged in the eighteenth century" (Drucker, 1994, p. 99).

But surely this growth has been concentrated in wealthy countries, and is it not true that the rich are getting richer and the poor are getting poorer on a global scale? Relationships between rich and poor countries are discussed in more detail in Chapters 8 and 12. Here it should be noted that there are certainly some signs that what might be called monetary wealth, such as annual incomes, are in the process of becoming more concentrated in the hands of the wealthiest. But in terms of arguably more important, broader indicators of "wealth" —access to food, shelter, and health care, for example— the picture is certainly less clear, and perhaps even downright encouraging, as discussed in more detail below. For the moment, suffice it to say that since the 1960s, although globalization has accelerated up to its current rather frantic pace, the proportion of people in the world who are hungry on a continuing basis has declined substantially. "A smaller percentage of the world's people are hungry today than was the case a few decades ago. . . . Fewer than one in five people goes hungry today compared to one in three in 1969" (Robinson and Sweet, 1997, p. 59).

As for the situation in the wealthier countries, at least some of the most recent evidence, particularly in regard to the United States, gives cause for less than total pessimism about the effects of globalization. The United States has by far the largest economy in the world. It has in recent times been fully exposed to the forces of globalization, and has in fact officially embraced those forces.[14] In 1995, the value of U.S. exports as a proportion of the nation's GNP was higher than Japan's

---

[14] "Today, the U.S. has an international economy, increasingly dependent upon imports, exports, and foreign investment" (Stokes, 1997, p. 78).

(Stokes, 1997, p. 78). In addition, "foreign investment in the U.S. and American investment abroad have also grown dramatically in recent years. Since 1989, the total value of U.S. investment abroad has grown by more than 50%, and foreign investment in the U.S. has increased by nearly a third" (Stokes, 1997, p. 78).

And how has the U.S. economy fared during this period of increasingly intense exposure to the forces of globalization? In the first place, some of the problems caused by globalization may have been exaggerated by some reports in the media. For example, although **downsizing,** that is, massive layoffs of employees by large corporations (see Table 7.2), has certainly had a devastating effect on a large number of Americans in recent years, "in retrospect, the specter of downsizing proved far less threatening than suggested by our near hysteria. Recent government reports indicate that downsizing was only marginally worse at its peak and marginally more persistent during the 1990s than in past economic cycles" (Rattner, 1996, p. A17). Similarly, job insecurity in the 1990s may not after all have been so much greater than in times past. "Workers today are spending as many years at the same job as they always did, data from the federal government, private surveys and benefits consultants now suggest. . . . Job tenure—the number of years on the same job—is the same or even higher than it was 20 or 30 years ago" (Crenshaw, 1995, p. 22).

In addition, nobody denies that the American economy is producing a lot of jobs. At the beginning of 1997, *Time* magazine reported that "superhot job spots are far more than exceptions to the still unrelenting rule of frequent downsizing. They reflect a tireless expansion and fundamental shifts in the workplace that have created more than 11 million new jobs since 1991, slashed unemployment to 5.3 percent, and turned the country into the world's hottest job machine" (Greenwald, 1997, p. 55). Many of these jobs can be traced directly to increased exports by American firms.[15] And many, even most of these, are good jobs. "The economy's historic shift toward better jobs continue[s]. Almost 60 percent of the new service jobs [created] during . . . 1994–96 were professional or managerial positions, almost double the proportion in the last two economic recoveries" (Rattner, 1996, p. A17). American workers, in addition, continue to be more productive than their counterparts in other wealthy industrialized countries. A 1996

---

[15] "Export-related jobs accounted for 23% of private industry new-job growth between 1990 and 1994. And in the last half-decade, jobs supported by exports have risen four times faster than overall private-industry job creation. As a result, 12 million Americans now owe their jobs to exports, out of a civilian labor force of 67 million people" (Stokes, 1997, p. 78).

report reveals, for example, that "Japanese workers were only 53 percent as productive as Americans, while Germans . . . were 90 percent as productive" (Walter, 1996, p. A15). In short, as the *New York Times* reported in 1997 in a story headlined "The Rehabilitation of Morning in America," "The world's juggernaut economy has turned out to be America's, not Japan's or Germany's" (Uchitelle, 1997, Section 4, p. 1).

But surely this recently sterling performance of the U.S. economy is a typical, globalization-produced phenomenon that benefits mostly a small upper crust of swashbuckling entrepreneurs and knowledge-oriented techno-nerds? Maybe not. In 1996, "in a reversal of what has been a long-term trend toward greater income inequality, the Census Bureau report said that the poor, the working class and the middle class increased their share of the nation's aggregate income, while the percent of total household income earned by the top 20 percent declined slightly. . . ." (Holmes, 1996a, p. 3). Similarly, the *1997 Economic Report of the President in the United States* points to "promising statistics" suggesting that income inequality, for the first time in twenty years, is finally reversing (Uchitelle, 1997, Section 4, p. 1). Finally, some recent data indicate that not only is income inequality in the United States decreasing, but so, too, is inequality in the broader category of "wealth," which is "the stock of assets that people own at a given time: stocks, bonds, homes, and other real estate, or business."[16] A 1997 study concludes that "the share of wealth held by the richest 1 percent of households rose from 31.5 percent in 1983 to 36.2 percent in 1989, and then fell to 30.4 percent in 1992. Thus, over the full cycle, inequality decreased slightly . . ." (Weicher, 1997, pp. 15, 25).

But are these apparent benefits of globalization (and/or technological changes) not restricted to the upper and middle classes? Are not the lower classes and underprivileged in the United States left behind in misery, especially in contrast to the poor in Europe, where governments generally support social safety nets and job security more energetically? Maybe not. The proportion of people in the United States living in poverty declined in both 1994 and 1995 (Holmes, 1996a, p. 3).

But how about the poorest of the poor in the United States, who tend to be concentrated among the African-American population? Peter Drucker, overall not a pessimist about the effects of globalization, argues that current trends have "aggravated America's oldest and least tractable problem: the position of blacks. . . . Since the Second World War more and more blacks have moved into blue-collar unionized mass-production industry—that is, into jobs paying middle-class and

---

[16] "Income is the money people receive over a period of time" (Weicher, 1997, p. 15).

upper-middle-class wages while requiring neither education nor skill. These are precisely the jobs, however, that are disappearing."[17]

And Jeremy Rifkin is particularly eloquent about the consequences of recent technological developments and globalization on African Americans. In a chapter titled "Technology and the African-American Experience," Rifkin (1995, p. 80) laments that "today, millions of African-Americans find themselves hopelessly trapped in a permanent under-class. Unskilled and unneeded, the commodity value of their labor has been rendered virtually useless by automated technologies that have come to displace them in the new high-tech global economy."

But by 1995, persuasive data indicated that the quality of life for blacks in the United States is improving substantially (see Figure 7.4). The black teenage birthrate fell by 9 percent in 1995 and dropped 17 percent between 1991 and 1995. "Blacks are the only group whose inflation-adjusted median income exceeds what it was in 1989. . . ." In 1995, life expectancy for black men rose to its highest level since 1984. By 1995, the proportion of young black adults who had completed high school matched that of whites for the first time. "Verbal scores on Scholastic Assessment Tests and performance on other national tests have been rising faster for black students than for whites . . ." (Holmes, 1996b, pp. A1, A13). And overall, the 1995 data indicate that "for the first time since 1959, when the Census Bureau started keeping such statistics—and probably the first time in history—the number of blacks under the poverty rate dipped below 30 percent" (Holmes, 1996a, p. 3).

Finally, recent data indicate that the poorer classes in the United States are not just doing better than they did before. Cross-nationally, the American economy is apparently not doing too badly by its less fortunate citizens. One study, for example, indicates that "America's poverty rate . . . [ranks] below those of all other West European countries, including Sweden . . . and Germany . . ." (*Economist*, November 5, 1994, p. 20).

Even a careful reading of all these statistics, however, might lead a reader to the frustrating conclusion that there are "lies, damned lies, and statistics," to coin a phrase. The data are apparently contradictory and confusing, at least on some points. It seems reasonable to conclude, therefore, that the "lies, damned lies, and statistics" view is a step closer to wisdom than a confident belief that globalization (and recent technological changes) are wreaking unalloyed havoc on the United States and

---

[17] Drucker (1994, p. 62) does point out that "in the fifty years since the Second World War the economic position of African-Americans in America has improved faster than that of any other group in American social history—or in the social history of any country. Three fifths of America's blacks rose into middle-class incomes; before the Second World War the figure was one twentieth."

Figure 7.5   Quality of Life Is Up for Many Blacks, Data Say

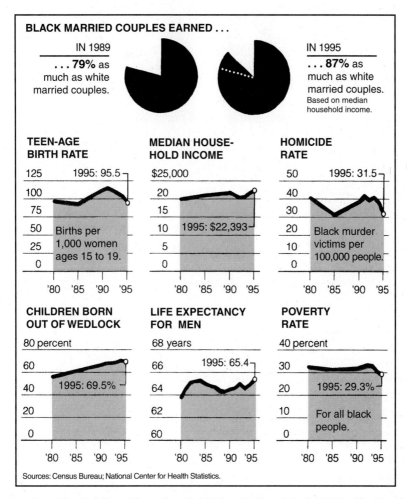

BLACK MARRIED COUPLES EARNED . . .

IN 1989
. . . 79% as much as white married couples.

IN 1995
. . . 87% as much as white married couples.
Based on median household income.

TEEN-AGE BIRTH RATE

125   1995: 95.5
100
75
50   Births per
25   1,000 women
0   ages 15 to 19.

'80 '85 '90 '95

MEDIAN HOUSE-HOLD INCOME

$25,000
20
15
10   1995: $22,393
5
0

'80 '85 '90 '95

HOMICIDE RATE

50   1995: 31.5
40
30
20   Black murder
10   victims per
0   100,000 people.

'80 '85 '90 '95

CHILDREN BORN OUT OF WEDLOCK

80 percent
60
40   1995: 69.5%
20
0

'80 '85 '90 '95

LIFE EXPECTANCY FOR MEN

68 years
66   1995: 65.4
64
62
60

'80 '85 '90 '95

POVERTY RATE

40 percent
30
20   1995: 29.3%
10   For all black
0   people.

'80 '85 '90 '95

Sources: Census Bureau; National Center for Health Statistics.

the entire world population. The data might even be interpreted as a basis for some optimism regarding the overall effects of recent technological developments, as well as globalization. Admittedly, most of these data are quite recent and may reflect only a short upward blip in the more fundamental downward trends upon which many analysts of globalization have focused in recent years. Still, it is difficult to reconcile recent data on job creation, job security, economic inequality, and poverty rates in the United States with the idea that the overall impact of globalization is indubitably harmful.

SUMMARY

The international economic system set up in the non-Communist industrialized world after the Second World War was based on three principal organizations: the IMF, the World Bank, and the GATT. That system, based to an important extent on fixed exchange rates and free trade, worked well for the industrialized countries until the 1970s. In 1971, the United States "closed the gold window," putting an end to the system in which gold and dollars were perfectly convertible at the rate of U.S. $35 per ounce of gold. The first OPEC increase in the price of oil in 1973 was another shock to the international system and helped produce a combination of high inflation and slow growth throughout the rest of the 1970s.

When OPEC increased the price of oil again in 1979, the second oil shock helped throw the industrialized world into a recession. In 1982, it brought the United States the deepest recession it had experienced since World War II. Immediately thereafter, the United States entered into the longest period of peacetime growth in its history. This growth was accompanied by low inflation and low unemployment.

But most recently, the impact of globalization, that is, the increasing integration of the world's national economies, seems to have brought greater economic insecurity and increasing economic inequality to the entire global economy. Several sources indicate that wealth and income are becoming more concentrated among a decreasing number of people in the world, and that wealth and income are also becoming more unequally distributed within most wealthy, industrialized countries.

However, in the world as a whole, during this period of increasing global economic integration, the proportion of people in the world who are consistently hungry, for example, has decreased substantially since the 1960s. In addition, quite recent data from the United States suggest that publicity about large layoffs by large corporations and increasing inequality may have created a misleadingly negative picture about the most recent trends in the American economy and the overall impact of globalization. Job insecurity in the United States has actually not been very much greater in recent years than in previous decades. Starting in 1995, the data actually show decreases in the inequality of income distribution, as well as in the inequality of the distribution of wealth. Recent data also reveal substantial improvements in the economic well-being of African Americans and indicate that poverty rates in the United States compare favorably with those in all of Western Europe. Since all these data have become available at a time when the American economy is clearly becoming more integrated with global economic processes, they must create some doubt about the wisdom of national policy options involving a retreat or withdrawal from those global economic processes.

KEY TERMS

West
First World
South
Second World
Third World
East
Bretton Woods system
International Monetary Fund (IMF)
fixed exchange rates
International Bank for Reconstruction and Developed (IBRD)
World Bank
less developed countries (LDCs)
General Agreement on Tariffs and Trade (GATT)
most-favored-nation principle
comparative advantage
free trade
World Trade Organization (WTO)
Uruguay Round

floating exchange rates
Organization of Petroleum Exporting Countries (OPEC)
interdependence
protectionist pressures
productivity
The Rise and Fall of the Great Powers
imperial overstretch
hegemonic stability theory
world leaders
globalization
economic insecurity
greater economic inequality
rich-poor gap
technological changes
computers
information technologies
training programs
knowledge sector
downsizing

SOURCES

Bernstein, Aaron. "Inequality: How the Gap Between Rich and Poor Hurts the Economy." *Business Week*, August 15, 1994, pp. 78–83.

Crenshaw, Albert B. "So Much for the Myth of the Mobile Work Force." *The Washington Post National Weekly Edition*, January 28, 1995, p. 22.

Budget of the United States Government: Analytical Prospectives. Washington, D.C.: U.S. Government Printing Office, 1994.

Crossette, Barbara. "Income Disparity Grows." *New York Times*, July 15, 1996. Published in the *Tampa Tribune*, July 15, 1996, Nation/World, p. 3.

Drucker, Peter F. "The Age of Social Transformation." *The Atlantic Monthly*, November, 1994, pp. 53–80.

Drucker, Peter F. "Trade Lessons from the World Economy." *Foreign Affairs*, 73 (January/February 1994), 99–108.

Finlayson, Jack A., and Mark W. Zacher. "The GATT and the Regulation of Trade Barriers: Regime Dynamics and Functions." *International Organization*, 35 (Autumn 1981), 561–602.

"For Richer, For Poorer." *Economist*, November 5, 1994, pp. 19–21.

Glassman, James K. "Jobs in America." *Washington Post*, circa October 17, 1993. Published in the *Tallahassee Democrat*, October 17, 1993, Section F, p. 1.

Gowa, Joanne. *Closing the Gold Window*. Ithaca, N.Y.: Cornell University Press, 1983.

Greenhouse, Steven. "Clinton Seeks to Narrow a Growing Wage Gap." *New York Times*, December 13, 1993, Section C, pp. 1, 3.

Greenwald, John. "Where the Jobs Are." *Time*, January 20, 1997, pp. 55–61.

Holmes, Steven A. "Income Up and Number of Poor Down." *International Herald Tribune*, September 28–29, 1996a, p. 3.

Holmes, Steven A. "Quality of Life Is Up for Many Blacks, Data Say." *New York Times*, November 18, 1996, pp. A1, A13.

"Jobless Rate Soars for 24 Wealthy Nations." *Tampa Tribune*, July 21, 1993, Nation/World, p. 4 (an Associated Press Report).

Johnson, Kirk. "In the Class of 70, Wounded Winners." *New York Times*, March 7, 1996, pp. 1, 12–14.

Kennedy, Paul. *The Rise and Fall of Great Powers*. New York: Random House, 1987.

Keohane, Robert O. *After Hegemony*. Princeton, N.J.: Princeton University Press, 1984.

Keohane, Robert O., and Joseph S. Nye. *Power and Interdependence*. Boston: Little, Brown, 1977.

Kindleberger, Charles F. "Dominance and Leadership in the International Economy." *International Studies Quarterly*, 25 (June 1981), 242–254.

Kindleberger, Charles F. *The World in Depression, 1929–1939*. Berkeley: University of California Press, 1973.

Korten, David C. "The Limits of the Earth." *The Nation*, July 15/22, 1996, pp. 14–18.

Krasner, Stephen D. "The Tokyo Round: Particularistic Interests and Prospects for Stability in the Global Trading System." *International Studies Quarterly*, 23 (December 1979), 491–531.

Kurth, James. "The Decline and Fall of Almost Everything." *Foreign Affairs*, 72 (Spring 1993), 156–162.

Lawson, Lisa H. "Government's Training Targets Yesterday's Jobs." Knight Ridder Financial News. Published in the *Tampa Tribune*, July 26, 1997, Nation/World, p. 9.

Mahbubani, Kishore. "The Dangers of Decadence: What the Rest Can Teach the West." *Foreign Affairs*, 72 (September/October 1993), 10–14.

The McLeod Group, "WTO: The New Age of Trade." An advertisement appearing in the *New York Times*, April 15, 1994, p. A14.

Modelski, George. "Long Cycles, Kondratieffs, and Alternating Innovations: Implications for U.S. Foreign Policy." In Charles W. Kegley, Jr., and Pat McGowan, eds., *The Political Economy of Foreign Policy Behavior*. Beverly Hills, Calif.: Sage Publications, 1981.

"'Most Favored Nation' Bows to a More Favored Phrase." *Wall Street Journal*, September 12, 1996, p. A16.

Oye, Kenneth A., Donald Rothchild, and Robert Lieber (eds.). *Eagle Entangled*. New York: Longman, 1979.

Quinn, Jane Bryant, "Wage Inequality Hurt Bush's Re-Election Bid, and Could Hurt Clinton's." *Tallahassee Democrat*, April 14, 1996, p. C1.

Rasler, Karen, and William R. Thompson. "Global Wars, Public Debts, and the Long Cycle." *World Politics*, 35 (July 1983), 489–516.

Rattner, Steven. "Downsizing the Downsizing Crisis." *New York Times*, October 16, 1996, p. A17.

Rifkin, Jeremy. *The End of Work*. New York: G. P. Putnam's Sons, 1995.

Rimer, Sara. "A Hometown Feels Less like Home," *New York Times*, March 6, 1996, pp. 1, 8–10.

Ruggie, John. "The Politics of Money." *Foreign Policy*, 43 (Summer 1981), 139–154.

Spero, Joan, and Jeffrey A. Hart. *The Politics of International Economic Relations*. 5th ed. New York: St. Martin's Press, 1997.

Robinson, Gail, and William Sweet. "Environmental Threats to Stability: The Role of Population Growth." In Nancy Hoepli-Phalon, ed., *Great Decisions '97*. New York: Foreign Policy Association, 1997.

Stokes, Bruce. "Globalization: Workplace Winners and Losers." In Nancy Hoepli-Phalon, ed., *Great Decisions '97*. New York: Foreign Policy Association, 1997.

Thompson, William R. "Long Waves, Technological Innovation, and Relative Decline." *International Organization*, 44 (Spring 1990), 201–234.

Thurow, Lester. "The Moral Equivalent of Defeat." *Foreign Policy*, 42 (Spring 1981), 114–124.

Toffler, Alvin. *Powershift*. New York: Bantam Books, 1990.

Uchitelle, Louis. "The Rehabilitation of Morning in America." *New York Times*, February 23, 1997, Section 4, p. 1.

Uchitelle, Louis, and N. R. Kleinfeld. "On the Battlefield of Business, Millions of Casualties." *New York Times*, March 3, 1996, pp. 1, 14–17.

"The Wage Gap Is Widening in Other Countries, Too." *Business Week*, August 10, 1992, p. 16.

Wallerstein, Immanuel. "Friends as Foes." *Foreign Policy*, 40 (Fall 1980), 119–131.

Wallis, Allen. "The United States in the World Economy." *Current Policy No. 1076*. Washington, D.C.: U.S. Department of State, Bureau of Public Affairs, May 10, 1988.

Weicher, John C. "Increasing Inequality of Wealth?" *The Public Interest*, No. 126 (Winter 1997), 15–25.

CHAPTER 8

Rich States and Poor States: North-South Relationships

This chapter discusses relations between rich states and poor states in the global political system. **Imperialism** is discussed first. Why did the European states (and, to some extent, Russia, Japan, and the United States) engage in imperialistic behavior in the late nineteenth and early twentieth centuries? What accounts for the neoimperialistic behavior of the United States (and the Soviet Union) in more recent decades?

After analyzing some of the more popular answers to those questions, we switch the focus to the attempts by **less developed countries (LDCs),** or the South of the global system, to develop economically in the post–Second World War era. **Dependency theory** and **world-system analysis,** both theories about relationships between rich, developed states and poor, underdeveloped states, posit that those relationships tend to have a deleterious impact on the poor states. They have proved to be popular explanations of problems that developing countries have faced in their quest for economic well-being and political independence. However, in recent years the *prescriptions* or solutions offered by at least some versions of dependency theory or world-system analysis have become less influential, even if some of their *descriptions* of the problems faced by poor countries retain much of their credibility. One reason for this decline has been the success of the four **Asian Tigers**—Singapore, Hong Kong, South Korea, and Taiwan, followed more recently by other East Asian imitators such as Indonesia, Thailand, and Malaysia—countries that seem to violate the essential tenet of dependency theory and world-system analysis advising autonomy and decreased ties to the industrialized countries. Another reason involves attacks on dependency theory by classical Marxists and by changing ideas about socialism in what might be described as the "core" of the socialist world, namely the Soviet Union (as well as China). The Soviet Union has disappeared altogether, and its main successor state, Russia, has now given up its socialist orientation. China is still officially a socialist country, but it has adopted many market-oriented policies, and it has also opened up its economy to contacts with the outside world in a way that is contrary to the ideas of dependency theorists or world-system analysts.

The key topics of this chapter, therefore, are relationships between the richer and poorer areas of the globe as seen by theories of imperialism, the content and current fate of dependency theory and world-system analysis, and the potential relevance of the recent economic performance of several countries in East Asia to that of other developing countries. After comparing the success of the East Asian **newly industrialized countries (NICs)** with the obvious failures of "socialism" in such developing countries as North Korea, Vietnam, Mozambique, and Cuba, the chapter goes on to discuss the implications of that comparison for decisions about development strategies. It concludes with a consideration of the debate regarding alleged **urban bias** in many developing countries (and development strategies) and of an apparently emerging consensus about the important **role of women** in the process of **economic and political development** in the poorer countries of the world.

IMPERIALISM

Probably the most widely believed explanation of imperialism is that developed by **V. I. Lenin** in his famous book *Imperialism: The Highest Stage of Capitalism* (1917, 1939). Lenin, by his own admission, relied heavily on the earlier writings of English economist **John Hobson.** According to Hobson, capitalism labored under a great difficulty as long as it was confined to its home base. Great wealth was concentrated in the hands of a few, while the vast majority of workers were very poor. Because the workers were poor, capitalist economic systems suffered from underconsumption; consumers could not buy what the capitalists could produce. Thus, capitalists needed outlets to provide investment opportunities for their surplus capital. Opportunities were created by imperialism. Colonies were acquired to provide the capitalists with the opportunities for profitable investment that were not present at home because of underconsumption (Hobson, 1902).

The Relationship Between Capitalism and Imperialism

This explanation made sense to many people at the time it appeared, partly because a contemporary phenomenon cried out for explanation. Starting in about 1870, virtually every large state in the world indulged in an imperialistic binge. Britain, France, and Germany were active in Africa and Asia. Japan defeated China in 1895 and Russia in 1905, acquiring territory in both cases. Russia expanded overland to the east. The United States took on Spain in 1898 and acquired the Philippines, Puerto Rico, and Cuba. Why was this happening? Hobson thought he had the answer.

And so, to some extent, did Lenin. Writing during the First World War, he argued that free competition in capitalist societies ultimately results in the establishment of monopolies, as losers in the competition are eliminated. Once monopolies emerge, according to Lenin, they extend their tentacles worldwide to acquire "sources of raw materials, for the export of capital, for spheres of influence" (Lenin, 1917, 1939, p. 124).

Lenin's Revision of Marxism

Lenin, unlike Hobson, was also concerned with the task of modifying Marxist theory to account for a couple of disturbing (to a Marxist, that is) contemporary phenomena. (Hobson was not concerned with saving Marxism because he was not a Marxist.) Marx had argued that workers in capitalist countries would become progressively more impoverished until they reached the point of rising up and overthrowing their capitalist masters. Ultimately, proletarian solidarity would overwhelm national boundaries, and states—with their boundaries and their wars—would wither away.

In the decades before the First World War, things had not been developing in the manner a Marxist might expect. The workers in the capitalist states were not becoming progressively more impoverished. By modern standards, to be sure, working conditions and wages were atrocious, but there was a nearly universal trend toward improvement in both. Even so, as the First World War approached, most socialists apparently believed that the common interests of the working classes in the opposing capitalist states would prevail in case of armed conflict, and that the workers would join hands across national boundaries in combined opposition to the capitalists who wished to lead them into war against each other. Instead, in the hour of crisis in August 1914, the workers and their leaders in the socialist parties proved steadfastly patriotic. Lenin was among those socialists who found this difficult to accept:

> [He] would not at first believe that Social Democrats had decided to support the war effort of the German government. . . . When informed of the event, he could explain it only as a plot of the capitalist press. It had,

Lenin, who developed a widely influential theory of imperialism, addresses a crowd in Moscow's Red Square, May 1919. SOURCE: AP/Wide World Photos.

with obvious intent, wrongly reported the stand of the German socialists (Waltz, 1954, p. 137).

This explanation, Lenin soon discovered, was wrong. He ingeniously devised another, which survives in the minds of many adherents to this day. At least some workers, Lenin said, were not becoming impoverished and were actually loyal to the bourgeois class because they were being bought off. And these bribes were financed by imperialism:

> The receipt of high monopoly profits by the capitalists . . . makes it economically possible for them to corrupt certain sections of the working class, and for a time a fairly considerable minority [of that working class], and win them to the side of the bourgeoisie of a given industry or nation against all the others (Lenin, 1917, 1939, p. 126).

In other words, **capitalism** must exploit to survive, but the **exploitation** does not necessarily impoverish all workers in a capitalist society because modern capitalists have colonies to exploit, and this makes it possible to coopt members of the working class at home. These bribes ruin working-class solidarity and postpone the revolution based on the solidarity Marx had predicted. With some variations, Lenin's theory of war and the relationship between capitalism and imperialism regained popularity in the Western world in the wake of the war waged in Vietnam by the United States (Magdoff, 1969; Kolko, 1969).

The Leninist Theory and the Evidence

How persuasive are these arguments, as they apply either to pre–First World War imperialism or to U.S. foreign policy after the Second World War? In both eras, it must be admitted, some evidence supports a Leninist interpretation of the history of global politics. During the earlier era, the major capitalist states did export huge amounts of capital overseas, and they became dependent on foreign investments in the sense that the resulting profits were substantial. In the later era, the United States also dramatically increased the level of its foreign investments, and it now relies on foreign sources for many important raw materials. And if the United States has not acted in an imperialistic manner in the sense of establishing formal control over new colonies or attacking its capitalist rivals, it has engaged in an updated form of **neoimperialism.** In addition to obvious activities such as the Vietnam War, the United States has consistently and energetically supported the status quo, often a reactionary status quo, in many developing countries. In Syria, Iran, Guatemala, and Chile, to name only a few of the better-known cases, the Central Intelligence Agency (CIA) helped subvert governments that were not deemed sufficiently friendly to the U.S. government or American economic interests. Elsewhere, reactionary governments have been sustained by foreign aid, military aid, and private sources of financial support. According to some critics of U.S. foreign policy, the plain pattern of support for the status quo throughout the developing world is motivated primarily by a desire to make the world safe for capitalism.

Critics of Lenin's ideas, as they apply to either era being discussed, have relied mainly on an argument that demonstrates a weakness in the link between the foreign economic activities and political imperialistic policies of capitalist states. It is true that in the late nineteenth century the great capitalist powers did invest heavily overseas and did grab a substantial number of new colonies. But the two activities were not necessarily causally connected, and in fact very little foreign investment in that era went to the newly acquired colonies. By 1913, for example, less than half of the foreign investment originating in Great Britain went to its empire; the British had more money invested in the United States than in any colony or other foreign country, and most of the capital invested in the empire was not located in the new colonies added in the previous decades. Most French capital, as Lenin knew (1917, 1939, p. 64), was invested in Russia and other European countries. In 1914, Germany had invested some 25 billion marks abroad, but only 3 percent of that went to Asia or Africa, and only a small part of that was invested in German colonies. The United States never had significant colonial holdings in the formal sense, and what was sent to its colonies in the way of foreign investment was inconsequential. Briefly, in no case did a capitalist state rely heavily on its newly acquired colonies as outlets for foreign investment during the era that Lenin analyzed (Langer, 1935; Fieldhouse, 1972; Blaug, 1972).

Similar arguments can be made with regard to the modern relationship between the United States and LDCs, which it allegedly treats in a neoimperialistic manner. U.S. economic reliance on LDCs, at least in terms of foreign investment and international trade, is simply not very substantial. In 1991, for example, earnings on foreign investment in LDCs accounted for only 40 percent of total U.S. earnings on foreign investments and for "an infinitesimal part of its total GNP [gross national product]" (Spero and Hart, 1997, p. 157). Similarly, the minor importance to the United States of trade with countries of the South is demonstrated by the fact that in 1993, U.S. exports to developing countries represented only about 3.1 percent of the U.S. GNP (Spero and Hart, 1997, p. 158). It does not seem likely, at least according to critics of neo-Leninist interpretations of U.S. foreign policy, that such relatively insignificant U.S. economic interests in the Third World can account for the shape of U.S. foreign policy vis-à-vis those nations.

What about raw materials? The United States produces most of the minerals used by its industry, but the Department of State has noted that industry "depends on foreign suppliers to meet some or all of its needs for more than 20 of the 80 strategic and critical [nonfuel] minerals included in national defense stockpiles" (U.S. Department of State, 1985, p. 61). Many of those minerals are located in LDCs, and the United States does import large quantities of oil from some developing countries. Could this need be the explanation for neoimperialistic policies? Perhaps, but there is room for doubt. Consider first the relationship between the United States and suppliers of the most critical natural resource, oil, in the 1970s. Despite some efforts to stem the tide, the United States became increasingly reliant on Middle Eastern oil throughout most of the 1970s. Yet the United States did not abandon Israel, attack any Middle Eastern country, or (as far as we know) destabilize or arrange the overthrow of any Middle Eastern government. In fact, the experience of the 1970s would suggest that increased U.S. reliance on LDCs for raw materials does not strengthen the neoimperialist tendencies of the former but rather improves the bargaining power and relative economic standing of the latter.[1]

A Defense of Leninism

Defenders of Leninism as it applies to the earlier era of imperialism have had to acknowledge that the newly acquired colonies of the late nineteenth and early twentieth centuries did not serve as crucially important outlets for foreign investment or exports, or as particularly valuable sources of raw materials.[2] It can be argued that the colonies were nevertheless acquired for economic reasons, because the imperialists thought the colonies were going to *become* important economically. There is plenty of evidence in the form of statements by leading politicians in the earlier imperialist era to support this assertion.[3] Proponents of a Leninist critique of U.S. foreign policy vis-à-vis LDCs argue that comparisons of earnings on foreign investments in developing countries with the total U.S. GNP are misleading. The total GNP reflects several facets of economic activity that are not very important, such as various kinds of services (as opposed to goods), perfume production, and earnings by major league baseball teams. One neo-Marxist critic of U.S. foreign policy asserts that the small percentages cited to demonstrate U.S. independence from LDCs focus misleadingly on annual flows of foreign investment abroad and do not take into account the accumulated levels of capital equipment abroad to which the annual flows contribute (Magdoff, 1969, pp. 9–16). Another argument points out that even though foreign economic activity may not constitute an overwhelming portion of the total U.S. economy, the activity is crucial to a few corporations, and these corporations are typically the largest and most influential, capable of pushing U.S. foreign policy in a neoimperialist direction.

---

[1] "Northern dependence on Southern raw materials is also limited. Raw materials in general are not as significant as Marxist theory suggests . . ." (Spero and Hart, 1997, p. 158).

[2] Some colonies did supply raw materials, but not necessarily to the mother country. "The great industrial countries got but a fraction of their raw materials from the colonies, and the colonies themselves continued to sell their products in the best market" (Langer, 1935, p. 106).

[3] Joseph Chamberlain, for example, a leading British proponent of imperialism, said in 1888 that "if tomorrow it were possible . . . to reduce by a stroke of the pen the British Empire to the dimensions of the United Kingdom, half at least of our population would be starved" (Langer, 1951, p. 77).

An Alternative Thesis

An alternative explanation of pre–First World War imperialism and post–Second World War U.S. foreign policy offered by critics of Leninist ideas emphasizes the role of **national security considerations** in the activities of capitalist states. In this view, Britain obtained new colonies in self-defense because Germany and France were doing the same, and all the great imperial powers of that era were sure that these colonies would be strategically valuable in any future conflict (Quester, 1977, p. 88). Similarly, the real reason for U.S. resistance to a Communist regime in South Vietnam and to anti-American governments throughout the developing world (such as in Nicaragua) was not economic but strategic. U.S. policymakers genuinely feared the strategic consequences of hostile political control of countries in Asia, Africa, and Latin America, and any economic losses that radical regimes in these areas might cause Americans were clearly of secondary importance to these policymakers.

The controversy, then, boils down to a question of motives. Why do policymakers in capitalist states behave the way they do? Are they motivated primarily by the economic interests of capitalists or by national security? Since motives are invisible, this is a difficult question. It is easy to find statements by policymakers implying that their primary motives are economic, but it is even easier to find statements indicating that decision makers are motivated entirely by national security considerations. And, of course, it is possible that both motives play a role in some decisions or that each plays the principal role in different decisions.

Some leverage for resolving this debate may be created by the fact that Leninist theorists insist that it is capitalism as an economic system that leads to imperialism. One apparent weakness in this argument stems from the fact that imperialism existed long before the appearance of capitalism. Since Lenin (1917, 1939, pp. 81–82) was aware of this problem, however, he emphasized the unique aspects of capitalist imperialism. Imperialism did exist before capitalism, but imperialism in the capitalist era is somehow different, and its causal origins are special.

A skeptic might reasonably ask why anyone should believe that something that has been occurring for centuries (such as imperialism) should acquire new, different causes in the late nineteenth and early twentieth centuries. Still, logically speaking, that possibility cannot be ruled out, and Leninists could be right when they argue that if capitalism is destroyed, imperialism will disappear. But several important test cases are available now that are not very encouraging. Capitalism was destroyed in Russia in 1917. After that, the Communist government of the former Soviet Union was quite imperialistic in its relations with the non-Russian people of that country; signed a treaty with Nazi Germany, one aim of which was to dismember Poland; and treated its Eastern European neighbors in an imperialistic manner after the Second World War. Soviet troops invaded Hungary in 1956 and Czechoslovakia in 1968 when those states threatened to step out of line, and the Soviets must surely accept some responsibility for the crackdown in Poland beginning in late 1981.

Events in Southeast Asia in recent years are obviously relevant to this discussion. The Soviet Union sent troops into Afghanistan in 1979. Communist regimes took over in Vietnam and Cambodia (Kampuchea), and these countries were adopted as client states by the regimes in the Soviet Union and China, respectively. Vietnam proceeded to attack and occupy Kampuchea, and China attacked Vietnam in retaliation. As Paul Sweezy (1979, p. 23), a Marxist, noted in reaction to such events involving the socialist societies of the world, "They go to war not only in self-defense, but to impose their will on other countries—even ones that are also assumed to be socialist." In light of such rampant conflict (and imperialism) among socialist states, Sweezy (1979, p. 23) concluded in 1979 that "it is not an exaggeration to say that by now the anomalies have become so massive and egregious that the result has been a deep crisis in Marxian theory." In retrospect, it is natural to wonder whether the revolutionary changes in Eastern Europe and the obvious weakening of the socialist faith in the Soviet Union and several LDCs countries in recent years were not at least in part caused by this deep crisis in Marxian theory.

Defenders of the Marxist-Leninist thesis that the destruction of capitalism (and the advent of worldwide socialism) would bring imperialism to an end typically responded to criticism in one of two ways. They acknowledged that socialist states were guilty of imperialistic behavior but insisted that this was because (1) they were surrounded by hostile capitalist states, or (2) none of the so-called socialist states was really socialist. A truly socialist state would not be imperialistic.

While it was not difficult to believe that Soviet behavior in Eastern Europe (before 1989) was motivated by fear of capitalist states, it was much harder to accept that threats from capitalist states accounted for the Soviet occupation of Mongolia, the tensions between the Soviets and the Chinese, the Vietnamese occupation of Kampuchea, and the Chinese attack on Vietnam. In all these cases, the Communist states were clearly responding to threats from each other.

ECONOMIC DEVELOPMENT

The main concern of Lenin and other theorists of imperialism was to explain why rich (or capitalist) states behave the way they do toward poor states. With the birth of dozens of new states in the years after the

Second World War, interest was sparked on the other side of the imperialistic coin, so to speak. From the point of view of these new states,
understanding why states behave imperialistically is only part of the
problem. The other part focuses on the question of how best to deal with
the international environment—dominated to an important extent by
richer, larger states—to achieve economic well-being and political independence. So far, at least, theories purporting to answer these questions
have been much more numerous than examples of success in attaining
these goals. The experience of LDCs in the five decades since the Second
World War has discredited one theory after another concerning the most
effective ways to speed development.

In the 1950s, the United States dominated the world economically,
and Americans likewise tended to dominate the discussion about economic development in academic circles as well as in international
forums. Even Americans, of course, had a variety of ideas about how the
emerging new countries could best achieve economic growth, but a few
basic themes and assumptions were widely shared. One of these was
that Britain, the United States, and the other Western industrialized
countries served as a historical model that the new countries should try
to emulate in their efforts to develop politically and economically. This
meant, in the orthodox view, that the new countries should adopt
free-enterprise systems based on individual initiative and democratic
political systems. In general, development theories in the 1950s stressed
the importance of internal changes in the new states as crucial to their
economic development. The people would have to be educated and
socialized to give up their old-fashioned ideas. Urbanization was considered desirable for its impact on the education and socialization
process, and industrialization, with its attendant concentration of people in the cities and capital-intensive activities, was presumed to be the
primary goal of developing countries. All these processes would be
accelerated by a maximum amount of contact between rich countries
and poor countries in the form of international trade, foreign investment, and foreign aid.

Things turned out differently. Until very recently, a **democracy** in the
American and Western European sense of the word was very rare in the
Third World. There are so many convincing explanations for this dearth
that it is difficult to decide which one is most important. One explanation is rather condescending: the people of poor countries were not ready
for democracy because they were insufficiently educated or not mature
enough to run their own governments. If this idea were espoused only
by Western intellectuals, it might have aroused more indignation in the
LDCs than it actually did. But political leaders in LDCs themselves
often made similar assertions (and still do) when defending their own
autocratic regimes. In addition, democracy was often associated with
the old colonial powers, and that served to discredit it in many poor

countries. Perhaps most important, the Soviet Union seemed to many in the 1950s, 1960s, and on into the 1970s to demonstrate the necessity for authoritarian leadership if rapid economic development were to be accomplished in the twentieth century. This view was supported by many American scholars of political development (Huntington, 1968, pp. 137–138). The notion that strong (that is, authoritarian) governments were necessary if developing countries were to be able to deal with the rigors of the political and economic development process in the twentieth century also received an important boost from the appearance in the 1950s and 1960s of dependency theory.

THE DEVELOPMENT
OF DEPENDENCY THEORY

Dependency theorists differ from orthodox analysts in the industrialized Western states most fundamentally on two points. First, as noted earlier, orthodox analysts of economic and political development who considered the problems of newly independent nations after the Second World War tended to assume that the path to economic and political success for those countries was essentially the same path followed by rich, industrialized countries in the North. The rich countries had started down that path earlier, so naturally they were more advanced than newly independent countries. The way for the latecomers to catch up was to emulate the early birds. They had been democratic, so LDCs should strive to be so too. So-called heavy industries had been leading sectors of their economies decades earlier, so LDCs should focus their efforts on such industries. And since these industries had developed under capitalist, market-oriented systems, that must be the type of system best suited to the needs of the LDCs. If, in short, LDCs would adopt development strategies as similar as possible to those tried-and-true strategies devised by Great Britain, the United States, and the other rich countries, before too long they would progress down the same trail those countries had blazed earlier, reach a **takeoff stage,** and enjoy the fruits of modern prosperity.

The world looks quite different from the viewpoint of dependency theorists. True, industrialized countries started down *a* path to wealth before the Third World countries. But dependency theorists believe that LDCs must follow a different path just *because* richer countries got that head start. Countries that are industrializing now moved into a kind of economic power vacuum when they began the development process. LDCs must now compete in a system dominated economically, politically, and militarily by states that have already become relatively rich and powerful. This different situation, according to dependency theorists, calls for strategies quite different from those used in earlier days by states such as Great Britain and the United States. Dependency theorists believe that adopting a strategy similar to that relied upon by the currently rich countries would perpetuate a process that orthodox economists and historians in the North tend to overlook when they analyze the historical experience of wealthy industrialized states. That process transfers wealth from poorer regions and countries to wealthier countries. Such a redistribution of wealth, in the view of most dependency theorists, is a more or less natural consequence of capitalism. Orthodox economists and historians in the developed states must acknowledge that colonialism and imperialism existed, but they understate the extent to which economic progress in the rich Northern countries was based on exploitation of the currently underdeveloped regions. In short, dependency theorists assert that rich countries got rich, to an important extent, by making poor countries poor. And here again, of course, is a factor pointing in the direction of development strategies quite different from those used in earlier epochs. Current LDCs have no relatively defenseless, untouched areas available for exploitation—the key to success for capitalist states.

The second fundamental disagreement between orthodox scholars from developed countries and dependency theorists (in addition to the one regarding the relevance of development strategies used by First World countries for currently poor countries) involves starkly different estimates of the relative impact of external and internal factors on the process of development. The former asserted after the Second World War that the changes necessary to bring economic progress to LDCs were largely *internal* to those countries, and most orthodox analysts still believe this to be true. In short, internal domestic political and economic changes are the key to political and economic progress. Dependency theorists do not deny that internal changes are necessary, but from their point of view First World analysts seriously underestimate the extent to which the problems of LDCs are caused by factors *external* to those countries, such as the impact of the international economic and political environment.

These basic ideas have been developed into two main strands of radical thought and critiques regarding the international economic system and relationships between poor states and rich states. The first (dependency theory) was developed by Latin American economists such as Dos Santos (1970) and Cardoso and Faletto (1978), as well as Western European analysts such as Frank (1968) and Galtung (1971). It has tended to focus on the impact of trading relationships between rich countries and poorer countries. The second, known as world-system analysis, (Wallerstein, 1974, 1979, 1988), although certainly not ignoring international trade, has tended to emphasize the impact of **multinational corporations** and **foreign investment** on the relationships between the richer and poorer regions of the global economic system. Much of the empirically oriented research it spawned is summarized in Bornschier, Chase-Dunn, and Rubinson (1978) and Bornschier and Chase-Dunn (1985).

The Impact of International Trade

Why, according to dependency theorists, does international trade tend to have a deleterious impact on poor countries? Their main argument is that many poor countries depend heavily on the export of one or two raw materials or commodities; that is, they suffer from **commodity concentration.** According to the theory, they developed this reliance in the historical process of becoming integrated into the capitalist world system. As long as they depend on international trade (as most LDCs do for a very large proportion of their GNP), and especially if they are also heavily dependent on one key trading partner (that is, suffer from **partner concentration**), they will never break out of this role to which they have been relegated in the world's division of labor. The problem is exacerbated by the rich countries' refusal to abide by the free trade doctrine when it does not suit their purposes. They erect high tariff barriers or adopt quotas to protect their own domestic economic interests against competition from cheap labor or cheap commodities in the poor countries.

Dependency theorists also argue that the **terms of trade** involving the primary products on which developing countries depend have deteriorated steadily. That is, the amount of a given raw material they must export to get a manufactured product in return keeps growing. For example, the amount of rice that Myanmar must export to obtain a refrigerator from some industrialized country keeps getting larger as the years go by. Also, the prices of raw materials and commodities fluctuate in a notorious fashion. Occasionally, the prices of exports from developing countries, such as copper, coffee, or sugar, have been very high, and the producers have experienced temporary windfalls. But in the next year, the prices of those same products have dropped precipitously, and the developing countries that export them have therefore suffered grievous balance-of-trade deficits and other painful dislocations in their highly vulnerable economies.

The Impact of Foreign Aid

From the viewpoint of dependency theorists, foreign aid supports elites in dependent countries whose interests are tied more closely to the elites of the richer capitalist countries than to their own countries. The elites often use that aid to suppress people who would like to achieve a degree of national autonomy. Furthermore, aid builds up debts that poor countries have a great deal of difficulty repaying. They must structure their economies in such a way as to earn foreign exchange rather than to feed the people in their own country. In recent years, foreign aid levels have dropped, but private banks have to some extent stepped in where governments have backed out. Now many developing countries (Mexico and Brazil, for example) have built up crushing debts to private banks, and those debts have the same deleterious effects as debts to governments for foreign aid.

Foreign aid, dependency theorists also complain, is usually "tied." That is, it can only be spent on products or services provided by the donor country. In this way, it serves primarily as a crudely disguised subsidy to the corporations and firms that provide these products and services to the countries receiving foreign aid.

Also, particularly now that poor countries have built up international debts, to qualify for more aid or loans they must follow recommendations for restructuring their economies laid down by international organizations such as the International Monetary Fund (IMF) or the International Bank for Reconstruction and Development (IBRD). The reform efforts advocated by the IMF in particular call for the governments of developing countries to abolish import controls, devalue their exchange rates, curb government expenditures (often on social services or food subsidies for the poor), control wage increases, and welcome foreign investment (Todaro, 1985, pp. 556–557).

> [T]he IMF and IBRD impose stringent conditions on their borrowers; conditions, stress the radical analysts, that open the door for their penetration by the trade and investment of rich states. . . . Less developed countries not willing to conform to IMF and IBRD suggestions find themselves denied not only loans from these institutions but also credit through private channels or bilateral aid programs (Walters and Blake, 1992, p. 161).

Thus, from the point of view of dependency theorists, foreign aid is a form of neocolonial political control only slightly more subtle than old-fashioned colonialism. Foreign aid is, in short, a form of "imperialism" (Hayter, 1971, 1985; Payer, 1974, 1982).

The Impact of Multinational Corporations

One reason developing countries turned to bank loans in the late 1970s involved their suspicions about foreign investments by multinational corporations (MNCs). MNCs provoke some of this suspicion because they are so large. In fact, many of them, by some measures, are larger economic units than developing countries themselves. As noted in Chapter 13 in the discussion of these corporations as important examples of transnational organizations, if the GNPs of countries are compared with the gross annual sales of MNCs, several of the largest economic units in the world are not states, but corporations.

According to dependency theorists, as well as world-system analysts, foreign investment in developing countries by MNCs does much more harm than good. For example, MNCs take more money out of countries in the form of remitted profits than they put into them. They create some jobs, but due to the use of capital-intensive technology, their net impact on employment in a country is actually negative, because they drive out of business local entrepreneurs who rely on labor-intensive technology more appropriate for poor countries with large surpluses of available labor. The economic benefits MNCs do bring tend to be concentrated in areas and among people who are already relatively well off, and so they exacerbate the already unequal distribution of wealth in developing countries. If MNCs have such bad effects, one might reasonably wonder, why do so many developing countries welcome them with open arms? (In fact, there are few, if any, countries in the world today that do not actively seek foreign investment, including socialist countries like China, Vietnam, and Cuba.) The answer, according to both dependency theorists and world-system analysts, is that MNCs coopt the leadership and elites of poor countries, bribing them, in effect, to accept foreign investment that benefits those leaders and a small elite but is detrimental to the country as a whole.

MNCs and their defenders, of course, do provide counterarguments to all these criticisms. These criticisms, as well as the counterarguments, are examined in more detail in Chapter 13.

DEPENDENCY THEORY AND NATIONAL DEVELOPMENT STRATEGIES

The ideas of dependency theorists have been put to the test most clearly in those countries where socialist revolutions of varying intensity have occurred. Probably the socialist country with the greatest accomplishments in the developing world is Cuba, where until recently, at least, the physical quality of life, in terms of indicators such as life expectancy, infant mortality, and literacy, was very respectable, especially by Third World standards. But whether Cuba could have achieved these successes without generous subsidies from the Soviet Union was open to doubt. The answer to that question was always of more than merely academic interest, because if subsidies from the Soviet Union were not to be forthcoming for other socialist experiments, and if Cuba's accomplishments were highly dependent on those subsidies, the relevance of Cuba's experience for other developing countries, and the potential for those other countries to duplicate Cuba's successes, would be correspondingly uncertain.

The extent to which the apparent successes of Cuba's socialist policies depended on Soviet subsidies has been easier to assess in recent years, since the Soviet Union has disbanded and the subsidies have mostly terminated. It is now quite clear that Cuba had become very dependent on trade and aid with the Soviet Union and its allies in Eastern Europe. Denied that trade and aid, the Cuban economy suffered disastrous setbacks. "[T]he Cuban economy . . . declined approximately 4 percent in 1990, fell another 25 percent in 1991, and dropped an additional 15 percent in 1992. . . ." In "the last four years . . . its national income fell nearly 50 percent" (Zimbalist, 1993, pp. 151–152). More recently, the Cuban economy has improved, but this improvement has been achieved by some important modifications in Castro's policies. "He now has no alternative but to reintegrate Cuba into an international community he never anticipated" (Smith, 1996, p. 100).[4]

So Castro may survive well past the end of the Cold War.[5] But Cuba's economic fate is unlikely to inspire emulation of its socialist ideals. And none of the other countries following socialist policies, such as Nicaragua, Ethiopia, Tanzania, Angola, Vietnam, or North Korea, has attained such shining economic success as to provoke widespread admiration and emulation elsewhere in the Third World.[6] Admittedly, many of these socialist societies have had apparently legitimate excuses for their economic problems, such as U.S.-backed subversive warfare in the case of the former Sandinista regime in Nicaragua, harassment by South

---

[4] Smith (1996, pp. 100–101) goes on to point out that tourism has now replaced sugar as Cuba's principal hard currency earner, and that "foreign investment has been key to Cuba's economic turnaround. This influx of capital has been given a new impetus by a foreign investment law enacted in mid-1995 that makes it possible for foreign investors to own Cuban enterprises outright . . . in virtually every area of the economy."

[5] "Castro continues to enjoy considerable popular support (whether or not a majority), and the army and security forces are behind him" (Smith, 1996, p. 100).

[6] At the time of writing, North Korea may be the only country in the world to adhere to "traditional" socialist policies. "For a long time, many people remained skeptical about claims that North Korea really was on the brink of starvation. But, in the face of growing evidence, a consensus is emerging that North Korea is indeed on the verge of a major disaster. . . . Rations have been reduced to starvation levels over a long period of time and [international aid] agencies have given warning that millions are now at risk of malnutrition and death" (Economist, April 19, 1997, p. 40).

Africa in the cases of Mozambique and Angola, and massive war damage in Vietnam. Even so, the developing world has apparently been affected by the demise of socialism in the Soviet Union, China, and Eastern Europe; one-party socialist states in such far-flung places as Nicaragua, Angola, Benin, Mozambique, Ethiopia, and Vietnam have either abandoned socialism or adopted market-oriented economic reforms even while maintaining one-party rule.

THE "ECONOMIC MIRACLE" OF EAST ASIA

Much to the chagrin of most dependency theorists, the countries whose economic performances have attracted attention and emulation in recent decades are located in East Asia. The earliest success stories came to be referred to as the "Asian Tigers." Singapore, South Korea, Taiwan, and Hong Kong have been "by most measures the outstanding development success stories in the past 40 years" (Foreign Policy Association, 1986, p. 58).[7] And these states have not just achieved a rapid rate of growth in the aggregate size of their respective economies. Even large increases in the GNP can leave much of the population no better off, or even relatively worse off than before compared with only a few beneficiaries of such increases. The Asian Tigers "have apparently been able to overcome strong cross-national patterns suggesting that 'good things do not tend to happen together.' . . . [T]he East Asians' record of 'growth with equity' sharply distinguishes them from other developing countries that have also undergone rapid growth" (Chan and Clark, 1990, pp. 4–5).

All this has been troublesome for dependency theorists because the Asian Tigers follow development policies quite different from those advocated by dependency theory. All four have striven to become more closely integrated into the world's economic system and have achieved success by stressing a high volume of exports to the industrialized states. "Dependency analysis, even in its revised . . . formulation, had not predicted and could not explain this record of economic growth and industrial diversification" (Hawes and Liu, 1993, p. 630). For these reasons, "by the end of the 1970s the World Bank had singled out the four Asian NICs as models to be studied by the second rung of develop-

---

[7] More recently, according to the U.N.'s *Human Development Report*, "The experience of the fast-growing Asian economies—Hong Kong, the Republic of Korea, Singapore and Taiwan . . . shows how sustained long term growth can expand employment (by 2–6% a year), reduce unemployment (down to less than 2.5%) and raise productivity and wages. This in turn reduced inequality and poverty" (United Nations Development Programme, 1996, p. 5).

ing countries" (Broad and Cavanaugh, 1988, p. 81). It is quite clear that the encouragement of the World Bank, as well as independent evaluations by observers in LDCs, provoked widespread emulation. "East Asia . . . [stands] today as a paradigmatic success story . . . held up as the standard cure for nearly any country seeking to make the difficult transition from economic stagnation to prosperity" (Sharma, 1995, p. 22).

The Asian Tigers have also embarrassed dependency theorists by taking the lead in transforming the relationship between LDCs and the industrialized countries in the area of international trade. Dependency theory suggests, at least in some of its forms, that LDCs are trapped into a role in the international trading system in which they export mostly primary products and commodities. But in fact, "while manufactures amounted to merely 5 percent of all Southern exports to the North in 1955 and only 15.2 percent in 1980, they had jumped to 53.5 percent by 1989" (Weede, 1996, p. 67).[8] And this trend was not wholly due to the Asian Tigers. In fact, nations accounting for about two-thirds of the population of the developing world have successfully severed dependence on their single largest traditional primary export. Diversification of exports for developing countries has progressed to the point at which "manufactures are rapidly claiming an ever larger share of exports in most developing countries, and already have a share in exports almost equal to primary products in countries representing the majority of population in the developing world" (Riedel, 1984, pp. 61–62). In short, the four Asian Tigers have demonstrated convincingly that it is not true that "the system" permanently relegates developing countries to the role of exporting only primary products. Their success in escaping that kind of role has been duplicated elsewhere well enough to argue that it is quite relevant to the rest of the developing world.

In 1988, though, two analysts of global trends in economic development suggested that the Asian Tigers "were the product of a radically different world economy. . . . It is time to ask whether any more developing countries can really hope to become the South Korea of the late 1980s or the Hong Kong of the early 1990s" (Broad and Cavanaugh, 1988, pp. 98, 10). But in fact several additional East Asian nations do seem to have gone a long way toward duplicating the success of the original Tigers in the last ten years or so. In that most recent decade, for example, the economic growth rate in Malaysia was 8 percent; "growth has been associated with full employment, low inflation and Malaysia's economic transformation from a producer of primary commodities to a

---

[8] In 1987, "for the first time ever, developing countries earned more from exports of manufactures than from agriculture and mining" (*Economist*, October 3, 1987, p. 115).

manufacturer of sophisticated industrial goods. . . . The income of the poorest 40% of the population increased by 9% a year in 1973–93. . . . Growth with equity continues to characterize Malaysia's rapid progress . . ." (United Nations Development Programme, 1996, p. 60).[9] Indonesia has rapidly expanded its exports in recent years, and reduced its incidence of poverty from 29 percent to 17 percent from 1980 to 1990. Life expectancy in Thailand was 63 in 1984 (Sivard, 1987, p. 49) and increased to 69.2 by 1993 (United Nations Development Programme, 1996, p. 135). Most fundamentally and most important, China, itself home to about one-sixth of the population of the globe, has become very export oriented and open to foreign investment. For example, exports to the United States alone now account for "5 percent of China's official measure of GDP compared to less than 1 percent in 1980" (Hale, 1997, p. 47), so that China's positive annual balance of trade with respect to the United States now totals $40 billion (Bernstein and Munro, 1997, p. 26). By 1991, China was the second largest recipient of foreign investment in the world (Weede, 1996, p. 113). During this era of increased openness and export orientation, "some 150–200 million people, equivalent to half the population of Western Europe, have worked their way out of poverty . . . a revolution in wealth-creation on a scale unparalleled in modern history" (*Economist*, February 22, 1997, p. 20).

Most East Asian countries following an outward-looking, export-oriented development strategy during the 1980s enjoyed "per capita income growth of more than 7% . . . a record exceeding anything experienced" (United Nations Development Programme, 1996, p. 11). The future for East Asia may be even brighter. By the year 2020:

> the Chinese economy may be about 40 percent larger than the U.S. economy. Among the "great seven," there will remain only two Western economies: the United States and Germany (as number six, barely ahead of South Korea) but five Asian countries: China, Japan, India, Indonesia, and South Korea. Beyond that, Thailand may be economically larger than France, and Taiwan may outdistance Italy, Russia and Britain (Weede, 1996, p. 114).

---

[9] In addition, "Malaysia reduced its poverty rate incidence from 49% to 14% between 1970 and 1993" (United Nations Development Programme, 1996, p. 60).

The Asian Tigers ▶

The "Tigers" in East Asia (Hong Kong, South Korea, Taiwan, and Singapore) industrialized rapidly in the 1960s and 1970s, following an export-led strategy that other developing countries have tried to emulate.

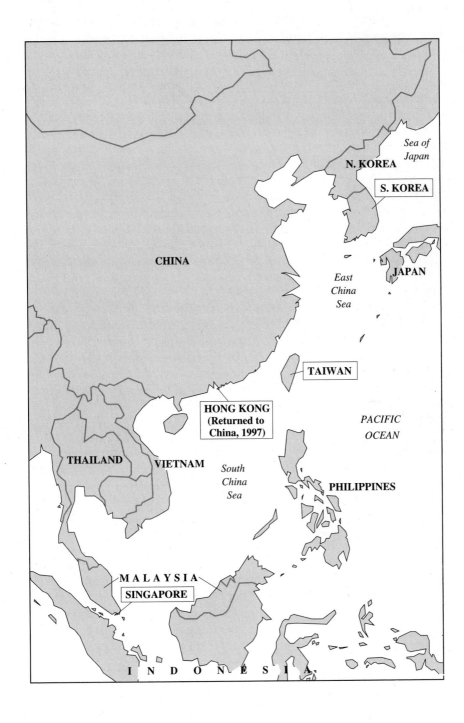

On the other side of the coin, though, several dimensions of the recent experiences of many rapidly developing East Asian states do not discredit dependency theory, but rather validate at least some of its prescriptions. One study of Taiwan's experience points to several aspects of its evolution that support dependency theory. Taiwan has demonstrated, for example, the importance of "the eradication of colonial institutions, effective land reform, government-directed structural transformation, national management, and regulation of foreign multinationals" (Clark, 1987, p. 327). Another analyst notes that "the socioeconomic structure and the patterns of income distribution in South Korea and Taiwan were relatively egalitarian even before the transition to export-led growth, in large part because of the extensive business/commercial re-structuring and comprehensive agrarian reforms that had been undertaken in these countries in the 1940s and 1950s . . ." (Sharma, 1995, p. 23). Dependency theory tends to advocate protective tariffs as a means of isolating developing countries from some of the harmful effects of the international economic environment. "All of the East Asian [countries], with the exception of Hong Kong, used protection to develop infant industries, even after the shift to an export-oriented strategy" (Haggard, 1986, p. 351). In the same vein, other analysts argue that "the authoritarian regime of South Korea . . . achieved spectacular growth rates by practicing command economics. . . . Government incentives, subsidies, and coercion fueled the drive for heavy industry in such areas as iron and steel that market forces would have rendered uncompetitive in the early stages" (Broad, Cavanaugh, and Bello, 1990–91, p. 148).

In general, scholars analyzing the success of the East Asian states have often "emphasized the pattern of extensive state intervention in the market" (Hawes and Liu, 1993, p. 631), and one prominent analyst of the success of East Asian economies concludes that "*most* Anglo-American development economists have a mistaken understanding of Korea and Taiwan as 'low-intervention' countries, especially with reference to trade, and they rely on this mistaken understanding to validate a low-intervention prescription elsewhere" (Wade, 1992, p. 284).

The rapidly developing states of East Asia, then, have neither adhered zealously to principles of free trade and the free market nor entirely avoided some of the policies that dependency theorists might suggest. But they do seem to have violated fundamental tenets of dependency theory regarding self-reliance and breaking away from the world capitalist system. Analysts who point out how far most East Asian states have deviated from neoclassical, laissez-faire economic policies have so successfully made their point that many of those states are now perceived as ideal examples proving the need for governments to intervene energetically in economic processes to accomplish their development goals.

Even more recently, though, arguments have surfaced that East Asian states have reached the end of their periods of growth, thus proving that such interventionist policies will not work in the long run. For example, "in 1996, in particular, there was such a sharp deterioration in the corporate profitability and stock market performance of Thailand and South Korea that many analysts now regard their economies as structurally flawed, not just cyclically depressed" (Hale, 1997, p. 44). And well-known economic analyst Paul Krugman has argued that the Asian miracles are in some sense artificial and will prove to be short-lived, based as they have been on Soviet-like command economy principles (Krugman, 1994).[10]

Then, too, there are those who believe that the transfer of control of Hong Kong to China in 1997 will bring economic hard times to that former British colony, and that China itself is headed for relatively hard times economically. A forecasting effort based on the model discussed in Chapter 4 predicted in 1996 that in China, after Deng Xiaoping's death (which occurred in February 1997) "there is likely to be a sudden and dramatic collapse of support for market reforms. . . . Hong Kong will fall victim to the political upheaval between central and regional powers [in China] . . . (Bueno de Mesquita, Newman, and Rabushka, 1996, pp. 98–97).[11]

So East Asia's economic success[12] is, depending on whom one reads or believes, either a tribute to the wisdom of neoclassical, market-oriented economic policies or the result of energetic intervention by strong state governments. And that success is bound either to lead Asia to dominate the twenty-first century or to prove short-lived. Analysts such as Krugman provide a useful reminder that impressions and opinions on such matters can change in a relatively short time; it was not too long ago that the Soviet Union (in the wake of its success with the sputniks, for example) seemed to be an economic paragon of success destined to dominate the world. But for the moment almost nobody denies that many East Asian countries have achieved rapid economic

---

[10] "At first, it is hard to see anything in common between the Asian success stories and the Soviet Union of three decades ago. . . . And yet there are surprising similarities. The newly industrializing countries of Asia, like the Soviet Union of the 1950s, have achieved rapid growth in large part through an astonishing mobilization of resources" (Krugman, 1994, p. 70).

[11] On the other hand, as another analyst of Hong Kong's transition argues, "All economic indicators suggest that Hong Kong's transition is going relatively well. The stock market is at an all-time high. The real estate market is booming. . . . Recent public opinion surveys find that confidence in the future is close to 80 percent" (Ching, 1997, p. 56).

[12] "During 1960–1993 per capita income in East Asia grew at more than 5% a year—the highest rate in the world" (United Nations Development Programme, 1996, p. 39).

growth, with benefits distributed in a relatively equitable fashion, in a manner that has attracted the attention of academic as well as policy-oriented analysts seeking to overcome obstacles to economic development in poor countries.

DEVELOPING STATES AND THE FUTURE
OF THE INTERNATIONAL
ECONOMIC SYSTEM

Regardless of what kind of policies LDCs might adopt, many economic and political analysts are convinced that they will not work unless the globe's entire economic system is transformed. In the 1970s, this basic idea culminated in the call for a **new international economic order (NIEO).** Dependency theory (and theorists) were influential both in developing ideas that served as the basis for the NIEO and in inspiring unity among the disparate group of countries referred to as the Third World.[13] The origins of this quest can be traced to the early 1960s, when LDCs united behind the idea of a worldwide conference on this problem, resulting in the first U.N. Conference on Trade and Development (UNCTAD) in 1962. At about the same time, a coalition of developing Southern states became known as the **Group of 77,** a name it retains even though it is now much larger. The Group of 77 wanted more foreign aid, especially multilateral aid through both the World Bank and the IMF, rather than bilateral country-to-country aid. They also argued for a new international currency to replace the U.S. dollar, freer access to markets in rich countries, and commodity agreements to stabilize the prices of raw materials and primary products on which they depend. Finally, they pushed for international controls over foreign investment and international management of projects to develop the wealth on the world's seabeds.

"By the close of the 1970s," according to two well-known analysts of international economic affairs, "the South's strategy based on unity, commodity power, and the NIEO had reached a dead end" (Spero and Hart, 1997, p. 230). Just as OPEC's success in the 1970s helped get the NIEO a lot of attention, its demise and disarray in the 1980s contributed to the virtual disappearance of the NIEO from that decade's agenda. By

---

[13] "Most developing countries have explicitly accepted the arguments that attribute their underdevelopment to the working of the international economic system rather than indigenous characteristics of their own societies. . . . The belief system of dependency is a key factor in explaining the exceptional unity maintained by the Third World in its quest for a New International Economic Order" (Krasner, 1981, pp. 143–144).

the 1980s, attempts by producers of other raw materials to duplicate OPEC's success were all thoroughly frustrated. Recession in the early 1980s depressed prices for most commodities, and by the middle of the decade even the continued existence of OPEC, much less its effectiveness, came into question.

Finally, the success of some developing countries, such as the Asian Tigers, within the old system and the new willingness of the most populous Communist country in the world, the People's Republic of China, to open up and become more closely integrated with the world's economic system as currently constituted all combined to take some of the steam out of the Third World campaign on behalf of the NIEO.

The International Debt Problem

Another reason that enthusiasm about the NIEO decreased in the 1980s had to do with the emergence of the international debt problem among Third World countries. Many deeply indebted countries became so enveloped in this problem that they focused on *it* rather than broader issues regarding reform of the international economic system.

One of the roots of the international debt problem that emerged in the 1980s involved OPEC's action in 1973 of quadrupling the price of oil. The importance of oil to each domestic economy in the world and to international economic intercourse is difficult to overstate. The dramatic change in oil prices set in motion flows of capital and economic changes whose ramifications (almost all negative, including those felt by most of the oil exporters that initiated the price increase) are still with us today.

First, naturally enough, the price increase brought billions of dollars to OPEC countries and other oil exporters. They deposited much of that money in large banks in the United States and Europe. Despite the entirely understandable joy created in much of the Third World by OPEC's success, the change in the price of oil put many of those countries in dire economic straits. That problem was dealt with in large measure by transforming a large portion of OPEC profits into Third World debt. "London and New York bankers voluntarily [and for a profit] became risk-bearing intermediaries for transferring the oil money from one group of developing countries—the oil exporters—to another—the non–oil-producing, capital starved, less developed countries . . . of the Third World" (Amuzegar, 1987, p. 141).

In order to understand the tragic nature of what was to follow, it is important to realize first how rational and wise all this seemed in the 1970s. The OPEC price increase had brought the member countries billions of dollars, which they deposited in several of the largest banking institutions in the world. That increase created a crisis for developing countries that needed to pay for their oil imports. What could have been more logical for those countries than to obtain loans from the banks that had recently received huge deposits from the oil exporters? "This recycling of oil wealth was welcomed wholeheartedly by the LDCs that wanted credit for their . . . import needs." It also served the needs of other interested parties. "Industrial governments and aid donors also welcomed an easy way to finance poorer countries' import bills. Moreover, the recycling process compensated Western economies for the deflating effect of higher oil payments" (Amuzegar, 1987, p. 141). In other words, the fact that banks in industrialized countries could use the deposits from oil-exporting countries to provide loans for which they could charge interest to some extent offset the pain inflicted on Western economies by the higher oil prices.

The recycling process worked rather well in the 1970s. The prices of exports from developing countries rose at an average annual rate of 14.7 percent from 1973 to 1980, and the volume of their exports rose 4 percent a year during that time (Krueger, 1987, p. 168). Real per capita gross domestic product (GDP) in developing countries grew at an annual rate of 3.2 percent from 1973 to 1980. This rate was not terrific, but considering that the growth rate in industrialized countries was only 2.1 percent in those years, it did not indicate a terrible crisis (World Bank 1988, p. 2).[14]

That terrible crisis was soon to come, though, triggered by the second OPEC price increase in 1979. "With the second oil price increase, the [industrialized countries] by and large adopted anti-inflationary macroeconomic policy stances. The result was a severe worldwide recession, sharply falling commodity prices, and the highest real interest rates in the postwar era" (Krueger, 1987, p. 169). In other words, when the price of oil increased dramatically for the second time in a decade, the governments of industrialized countries took several painful steps to protect themselves, mostly to avoid uncontrollable inflation. They raised interest rates; their economic growth slowed. By 1982, the U.S. economy had gone into the deepest recession since the Second World War. Recessions in most other developed countries soon followed.

The economic slowdown in the rich countries soon led to depression-type conditions in many LDCs. First, world trade slowed to a crawl, and developing countries found it impossible to export their commodities to the industrialized countries. "1981 had the dubious distinction of being the first year since 1958 to experience an actual decrease in world trade in current dollar terms, a shrinkage of 1 percent" (Broad and

---

[14] Even the highly indebted countries experienced real growth rates of 2.8 percent from 1973 to 1980 (World Bank, 1988, p. 187).

Cavanaugh, 1988, p. 90). The value of world trade continued to fall for the next two years. Along with the *volume* of exports from LDCs, the *value* of those exports fell as well. Food commodity prices dropped 15 percent from 1981 to 1985. The prices of minerals and metals fell 6 percent during that time. The terms of trade for developing countries— that is, the relationship between the prices of the goods they export and the goods they import—turned against them violently in 1986. They had to export 30 percent more that year to receive the same volume of imports as the previous year; the result was a loss of $94 billion to the developing world. Somewhat ironically, one of the commodities whose prices dropped most precipitously was oil. This meant that developing countries such as Mexico and Nigeria, which had benefited spectacu- larly from oil price increases in the 1970s, found themselves in the 1980s suffering in a way that was virtually indistinguishable from their oil-starved peers.

Choices for Developing Countries

By the early 1990s, there were signs that some of the problems of the 1980s were beginning to recede, and opportunities for export-oriented growth revived. In 1991, for example, the *Far Eastern Economic Review* reported that

> for the third year running, economic growth in Malaysia, Thailand, and Indonesia is expected to equal or exceed that of Hong Kong, Singa- pore, South Korea and Taiwan. Asia's newly industrialized countries . . . Malaysia and Thailand are industrializing as fast as South Korea and Taiwan did in the 1970s. . . . Foreign investment has been pouring into Malaysia, Thailand, and Indonesia in the past five years (Holloway, 1991, p. 51).

As discussed in more detail in Chapter 9, China's economy has been booming in the 1990s, and China has welcomed foreign investment and emphasized exports. The *New York Times* reported in 1993 that

> almost 40 years after the emergence of the so-called Dependency School in Latin America—the theorists who argued that developing coun- tries need to protect their resources from being ravaged by multinational corporations, the argument has been turned around. . . . Now . . . hopes are being pinned on the prospect of interdependence with the United States and other advanced industrial nations, through diversified and efficient economies that can compete in free trade (Nash 1993, Section 4, p. 6).

In short, by the middle of the 1990s, market-oriented and **export- oriented strategies** seemed to have evoked something of a consensus among academics and policymakers in the richer industrialized countries as well as politicians in power in the poorer countries of the world. But the consensus was far from perfect, and in Latin America in particular there have been signs of a growing impatience with the market-oriented reforms that have swept through the region in the last ten or fifteen years. In 1996, public opinion polls in seventeen Latin American countries revealed that over 70 percent of respondents were unhappy about recent current economic trends in those countries. The major problem is unemployment, even in countries where economic growth has been rapid.[15]

> Unemployment . . . is the single most compelling economic issue in the region at the close of the millennium. Five countries have official [un]employment rates above 15 percent, led most significantly by Argentina's 17 percent. In nine countries, unemployment has risen since 1991. . . . Despite moderate economic growth and recovery since 1989, unemployment has risen almost steadily (Schreiberg, 1997, p. 168).

This analyst concludes that "the primary road out of Latin America's poverty pit is a major overhaul of its appallingly poor school systems" (Schreiberg, 1997, p. 171). The East Asian countries that have enjoyed rapid growth with relatively egalitarian distribution of the benefits have all invested heavily in public education,[16] that is, educational programs supported energetically by the central government, which do not rely on market forces to achieve educational goals.

In addition, critics of market and export-oriented strategies can point to such places as Kerala, a state in India with 30 million people (making it about as populous as Canada, for example), for potentially valuable lessons about the development process. In 1957, voters in Kerala elected the first Communist majority to the state legislature. Since then, Kerala's voters have elected "three solidly leftist governments," including a leftist democratic front that came to power in the early 1990s, which contained as two of its main parties the Communist Party of India-Marxist and the Communist Party of India (Franke and Chasin, 1991, pp. 4–5).[17]

It is one of India's poorest states, and yet its population has the highest life expectancy and literacy rate in India, as well as the lowest infant mortality rate and birthrate (Broad, Cavanaugh, and Bello, 1990–1991, p. 144). "Male life expectancy (69 years) is 10 years higher than

---

[15] "Argentina's economy grew at an average pace of 7 per cent a year from 1991 to 1994—while the number of jobs increased by only 1 per cent" (Schreiberg, 1997, p. 169).

[16] "East Asian countries have heavily invested in critical public goods such as primary education" (Hale, 1997, p. 45).

[17] Franke and Chasin conclude that the "lessons from Kerala" suggest that "progressives—including communists—can play a major and positive development role."

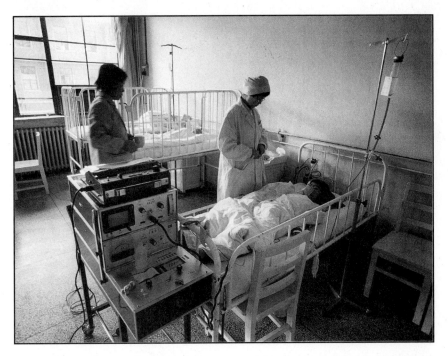

The People's Republic of China is one of the poorest countries in the world, but a life expectancy of 70 years in China suggests that its health care system works quite well in spite of relatively modest per capita expenditures on medical care. SOURCE: Jean-Pierre Lafont/Sygma.

the Indian average and equal to Hungary's. Female life expectancy (74) is 15 years higher than the Indian average and higher even than Russia's" (United Nations Development Programme, 1996, p. 81; see also Sen, 1993).

It might also be relevant to point out in this context that life expectancy in the People's Republic of China, although one of the poorest countries in the world, is 70 years. In some respects, health care in China is better than in the United States. For example, life expectancy at birth in Shanghai, China's largest city, is now 75.5 years, compared to a life expectancy in New York City, the largest city in the United States, of 73 years for whites and 70 years for nonwhites. And while China has adopted many market-oriented policies in recent years, its health care system is a government-based system established in the Maoist era (Kristoff, 1991, Section A, pp. 1, 6).

In short, problems in many Latin American states, as well as successes in places such as Kerala in India and the People's Republic of China, seem to point to the conclusion that "socialism" might have been prematurely buried under a kind of public relations onslaught by the forces in favor of market-oriented capitalism and export-led development in the late 1980s on into the 1990s. But the point of this discussion is that the terms *socialism* and *capitalism* are not free of ambiguities. In their purest forms, those terms denote extreme ends of a continuum, and most countries fall somewhere in the middle of that continuum. An interpretation of the problems of socialist states like the former Soviet Union, Poland, North Korea, Mozambique, and Cuba in the late 1980s as an unalloyed victory for "capitalism" may be unjustified. In the first place, it is important to recognize that "the concept of 'market' is . . . broader than that of 'capitalism'" (Gilpin, 1987, p. 16). The essence of a market is the central role of prices arrived at in bargaining between buyers and sellers, while the essence of capitalism is the private ownership of the means of production and the existence of free labor. Theoretically, at least, socialist states could establish market systems. The most populous country in the world, China, seems to be trying to put this theory into practice.

Since virtually all the countries of the world have mixed economies, with the government playing an active role in the economy even if market forces also play an important role, some students of political economy have concluded that "capitalism is too ambiguous a label to be used as an analytical category" (Gilpin, 1987, p. 16). But while it is important to acknowledge that it is difficult to establish precisely the point at which capitalism ends and socialism begins (or vice versa), the distinction between capitalism and socialism is not necessarily meaningless. The problems leading to the demise of the former Soviet Union may well suggest with some force that it is a mistake for governments to expropriate virtually all the means of production; that is, it is possible to go too far in the socialist direction. And as we have seen, the experiences of the recently economically successful countries in East Asia do not indicate that governments in developing countries should give private entrepreneurs or market forces an entirely free rein. Rather, they seem to demonstrate that governments might be well advised to take an active role in the economy, but in a manner that is compatible with and supportive of at least some market forces.[18] In short, it seems fairly safe to conclude from an analysis of developing countries over the last few decades that neither a socialist revolution nor pure laissez-faire capitalism is likely to solve all of their problems.

---

[18] "East Asian states performed functions that went far beyond the norms of prescribed neutral policy. The market-oriented policies were accompanied by discretionary state intervention that complemented and directed rather than negated market forces . . . the East Asian states through discrete and targeted interventions created an environment supportive of competitive market forces" (Sharma, 1995, p. 23).

In Support of Peasants and Women

Such an analysis of the recent history of developing countries might also support the conclusion that two groups especially deserving of government support in the development process are peasants and women. An argument in favor of a bias toward the rural sectors of developing economies would begin with the observation that "most would-be NICs remain predominantly agricultural societies; hence the starting point of internal-demand-led development must be in farming" (Broad and Cavanaugh, 1988, p. 99). Numerous precedents support this viewpoint, starting with the first colony to emerge as an independent nation, the United States. Much of China's economic success in the past ten or fifteen years was based largely on reforms in its agricultural system. Japan, Taiwan, and South Korea all engaged in energetic agrarian reform programs at early crucial stages of their postwar economic development.

One noted specialist in economic development has stated that typically in developing societies, "the 60 to 80 percent of people dependent on agriculture are still allocated barely 20 percent of public resources. . . . So long as the elite's interests, background, and sympathies remain predominantly urban . . . the city will get the resources" (Lipton, 1984, p. 93). In a similar vein, another economist has noted that "the population of the capital city . . . will tend to have more influence on public policy than their rural and provincial cousins because of the inadequacies of the transportation system. Popular demonstrations, strikes, and riots in the capital are a special threat to governments" (Olson, 1982, p. 170). Under the threat of those demonstrations, strikes, and riots (and influenced by the fact that they live with these people, some of whom may be friends), government elites have often adopted policies that discourage agricultural production. They keep food prices low, for example. "The size of this urban bias, or the burden imposed on agriculture, can be very large" (Weede, 1996, p. 74).[19] They also keep local currencies overvalued, so that urban elites can purchase foreign goods at lower prices, while rural interests have a more difficult time exporting agricultural products. High tariffs protect import-substituting industries in the cities, making the people in the countryside pay higher prices for the manufactured products they buy from the cities.

All this may be changing. The idea that policies distorted in favor of the urban sector hurt the country as a whole—perhaps solidified by the

---

[19] Weede (1996, p. 74) cites research indicating that the prices of agricultural goods in Latin America would be 42 percent higher in the absence of government intervention based on this urban bias, for example.

examples of agriculture providing a basis for economic improvement in such diverse places as the United States, Australia, Japan, China, and South Korea—shows signs of catching on. In addition, several African countries took steps to correct this urban bias in the 1980s and 1990s (Brooke, 1988; Becker, Hamer, and Morrison, 1994).

But at least one study of these steps to correct urban bias in Africa indicates that those steps may have gone too far, and that the resources of the cities in Africa have to be harnessed to efforts to develop these countries (Becker, Hamer, and Morrison, 1994). Then, too, there is the fact that developing countries are becoming more urbanized at a rather frantic pace as the new millennium approaches. From 1950 to 1995, the number of cities in the developed world with a population over a million doubled. But in the developing world, the number of cities with a population of a million or more increased from 34 to 213, a sixfold increase. In addition, "an unholy synergy created in the developing world when explosive population growth, industrialization, and capital scarcity meet means dangers on an unprecedented scale" (Linden, 1996, p. 56). The population of cities worldwide may increase from 300 million in 1950 to 6 billion in the year 2050, and over half the world's population will be living in cities by the year 2025 (Linden, 1996, pp. 53, 65). It may well be wise to end policies that discriminate against rural populations and depress food production, but it is certainly not the time to replace an urban bias in developing countries with a rural bias overlooking the importance of cities.

Another sector of the economy in most developing countries that can benefit from paradoxical (to those committed to "pure" capitalism or socialism, at any rate) governmental or political efforts to shape market forces involves the country's female population. As discussed in more detail in Chapter 12, women are subjected to some forms of economic and political discrimination by the men who dominate the economic and political systems of virtually every country of the world. But in the poorer countries, gender bias is arguably a more serious problem. In other words, "gender bias is a worldwide phenomenon, but it is especially pernicious in the Third World, where most of women's activity takes place in the non-wage economy for the purpose of household consumption" (Jacobson, 1992, p. 6). Because women make up about half the population of every country in the world, this problem has come to be seen by many specialists in economic development as a major obstacle to economic progress in poor countries. "Gender bias is . . . a primary cause of poverty, because in its various forms it prevents hundreds of millions of women from obtaining the education, training, health services, child care, and legal status needed to *escape* from poverty" (Jacobson, 1992, p. 7).

One dramatic example of the importance of bringing women into the economic mainstream of a country pertains to one of the poorest countries of the world, Bangladesh, where average annual per capita income is about $208 (Moore, 1992, p. 13A). In 1983, the **Grameen Bank** ("village" bank) was founded by **Muhammad Yunus,** a professor of economics. Yunus's original idea was to provide *very* small loans to people in general, but his ideas were not originally received with enthusiasm by economists or bankers. " 'Where is the collateral?' the bankers asked. 'These people can't even read' " (Mathews, 1993, p. 7A).

Yunus ultimately had to take out the first loans himself. Those loans were put to good use and repaid, but still local bankers would not provide the capital to fund more such loans on a continuing basis. So he had to get the support of the government to enable poor people to obtain these loans so that they could become, in effect, entrepreneurs. (Does that make this a "socialistic" or a "capitalistic" policy?) Today, the Grameen Bank has more than a thousand branches, whose 11,000 employees have lent about $1 billion to 2 million borrowers, mostly illiterate women (Doll, 1997, p. 7). It lends over $30 million dollars a month, and 97 percent of those loans are repaid, despite the fact that the bank charges a hefty 20 percent interest rate (Mathews, 1993, p. 7A).[20]

Originally, loans from the Grameen Bank were divided about equally between men and women. But Yunus soon discovered that "in the families in which the women received the loans, the children were better cared for, the houses were better maintained." He also found that while women spent the money on their families, men often squandered it on luxuries or drugs. Women also repaid the loans more dependably (Moore, 1992, p. 13A). The result is that today nearly all the borrowers are women. "When a bank focuses on women," according to Yunus, "the impact on society is greater. Men are more likely to use additional income to make their own lives more comfortable. . . . Poor women who have a little extra income use it to bring back their children who have been living with and working with other families. When the children come back, their mothers see that they receive an education" (Doll, 1997, p. 10). And approximately 65 percent of those who get loans averaging about $100 have achieved significant economic improvements in their lives. About half have risen above the poverty line (Mathews, 1993, p. 7A).

---

[20] In December 1993, the World Bank donated 2 million dollars to the Grameen Bank in recognition of its successes ("Bangladesh Bank Helps Poor Women," *Tampa Tribune,* December 2, 1993, Nation/World, p. 6).

Muhammad Yunus, shown above, the founder of the Grameen Bank in Bangladesh, created a program based on small loans that has highlighted the key role of women in the economic development process. SOURCE: © Tim Campbell, in cooperation with Vanderbilt University Magazine.

What is most important about the Grameen Bank is the generally applicable nature of its lessons and successes. "Scattered around the world are thousands, perhaps tens of thousands of success stories like Yunus's program was 10 years ago" (Mathews, 1993, p. 7A). The importance of focusing development efforts on women has become commonly accepted wisdom. The *Human Development Report* published by the United Nations Development Programmme in 1996, for example, declared that "several studies suggest that income is more likely to be spent on human development when women control the cash" (United Nations Development Programme, 1996, p. 69). The report goes on to cite studies showing that increases in women's income improve the nutritional status of families seven times as much as do equivalent increases in the incomes of men. "In Cote d'Ivoire, it has been calculated that if women had as much control over cash income as men, the share of food in the household would go up by 9%, while that of cigarettes would fall by 55% and that of alcohol by 99%" (United Nations Development Programme, 1996, p. 69). In short, evidence is rapidly accumulating in support of the proposition that political ("socialistic"?) efforts to allow women to benefit from market ("capitalistic"?) forces are key to alleviating poverty in the developing world.

Democracy and Economic Development

As noted in Chapter 2 (and elsewhere), a global trend toward democracy throughout most of the 1970s and the 1980s appeared to have suffered at least a temporary reversal by the mid-1990s. Still, there are many more democratic states in the world now than twenty years ago, and many of the more recently converted states are in the developing world. In fact, "between two-thirds and three-quarters of the people in developing countries live under relatively pluralistic and democratic regimes" (United Nations Development Programme, 1996, p. 20). In addition, Freedom House in its 1997 annual review of political trends in the world asserted that democracy "made important strides around the world in 1996 as the number of free countries grew from 76 to 79, the largest number since the Survey was launched in 1972" (Karatnycky, 1997, p. 5). In light of the evidence that democratic states do have foreign policies and interrelationships different from those of undemocratic states, the survival of the relatively new democracies in the developing world (and in the post-Communist world) is of considerable theoretical as well as political importance.

It seems quite clear that newer democracies in particular are vulnerable to periods of economic crisis. In Africa, for example, several dictatorships fell after the demise of the Soviet Union and the end of the Communist regimes in Eastern Europe in the early 1990s. But by 1993, one journalist noted that "democracy in Africa, a candle of hope that flickered briefly, is melting." His explanation of the demise of hopes for democracy in Africa is straightforward. "[C]atastrophic economic conditions were not on the side of democracy. . . . People have suffered a drastic fall in living standards. This has undermined the tolerance and patience necessary for democracy" (Dowden, 1993, pp. 16–17).

It seems apparent that the dire economic problems of the Soviet Union toward the end of the 1980s, plus the fact that all of the seventeen countries in the world with a per capita GNP over $10,000 and a life expectancy of seventy-five years or over (in 1988) were democratic, convinced a lot of people in the Third World that democracy was a necessary condition for economic success (World Bank, 1990, p. 179). And there is an impressive theoretical as well as empirical case to be made for the argument that political democracy does provide a promising basis for economic development.

Theoretically, it can be argued, for example, that autocratic leaders will ultimately be seduced by an irresistible urge to enrich themselves at great cost to the societies they rule. Autocrats, in other words, have an incentive to "extract the maximum attainable social surplus for the society to achieve . . . personal objectives" (Olson, 1993, p. 571). On the other side of the coin, according to this argument, "the conditions that are needed to have individual rights needed for maximum economic development are the same conditions that are needed to have a *lasting* democracy" (Olson, 1993, p. 572). That is why only stable democracies have reached the highest levels of economic development and have maintained those levels across generations. In contrast, "though experience shows that relatively poor countries can grow extraordinarily rapidly when they have a strong dictator who happens to have unusually good economic policies, such growth lasts only for the ruling span of one or two dictators" (Olson, 1993, p. 572).

Empirically, one recent careful analysis of the relationship between democracy and economic growth, as well as broader indices of the physical quality of life in 104 developing countries in the 1980s, concludes that democracy and economic performance mutually reinforce each other. "Improvements in economic well-being will facilitate the transition to democracy and full provision of political rights will enable nations to promote economic prosperity" (Pougerami, 1992, p. 375). Other analysts report that the correlation between democracy and economic growth is more a result of the impact of growth on democracy, rather than of democracy on growth (Burkhart and Lewis-Beck, 1994; Londegran and Poole, 1996).[21] Still another research report argues that "the level of economic development does not affect the probability of transitions to democracy but . . . affluence does make democratic regimes more stable" (Przeworski and Limongi, 1997, p. iii). But these analysts do not support an argument rather regularly made by analysts of an earlier era that "political participation must be held down . . . in order to promote economic development" (Huntington and Dominguez, 1975, p. 60; cited by Przeworski and Limongi, 1997). On the contrary, they argue, "democracy, while not apparently a direct cause of economic development, certainly does it no harm" (Burkhart and Lewis-Beck, 1994, p. 907).

It is also interesting to note, in light of repeated recent famines in Africa, for example (as well as the disastrous famine that apparently occurred in Mao Zedong's China during the Great Leap Forward of the

---

[21] Burkhart and Lewis-Beck (1994, p. 903), for example, report specifically that "economic development 'causes' democracy, but democracy does not 'cause' economic development."

late 1950s) that "no democratic country with a relatively free press has ever experienced a major famine. . . . This generalization applies to poor democracies as well as to rich ones" (Sen, 1993, p. 43).[22]

There are, then, both persuasive theoretical arguments and empirical evidence in favor of the proposition that democracy is good for economic development. But in the short run the crucial, well-publicized exceptions to any putative rule regarding the relationship between regime type and economic success may have more impact on the contemporary global political system. A former member of the Chinese Communist Party suggests, for example, that the Chinese leadership repressed the prodemocracy movement at Tiananmen Square in 1989 on the grounds that the four Asian Tigers had all adhered to authoritarian tactics until after they had achieved a relatively high level of economic development (Binyan, 1989, p. 22). Since then, even Francis Fukuyama, author of the article "The End of History," which argues that democracy has won an irreversible victory in a global ideological battle, has observed that "'soft authoritarianism' of countries like Singapore is the one potential competitor to Western liberal democracy, and its strength and legitimacy is growing daily" (Branegan, 1993, p. 36). Singapore is a tiny country of 3.1 million people, and although it is not of great significance on the global political scale by itself, its influence as an example to emulate may be far greater than its small population would indicate. "Singapore . . . has . . . found an ardent fan in mainland China (pop. 1.16 billion), where officials are studying the city-state for ideas on how they can throw off Marxist economics but keep dictatorial political control" (Branegan, 1993, p. 36). A 1992 *New York Times* story entitled "China Sees Singapore as Model for Progress" quoted China's leader Deng Xiaoping as saying that "Singapore's social order is rather good. Its leaders exercise strict management. We should learn from their experience, and we should do a better job than they do" (Kristoff, 1993, p. 4).

This is not to say that Singapore by itself can evoke a worldwide trend toward autocracy. But each of the original influential Asian Tigers clung to autocratic methods until recently, *after* they had achieved quite high levels of development. And another relatively small country currently

---

[22] Sen goes on to point out that the Great Leap Forward in China caused between 23 and 30 million deaths, concluding that "the lack of political opposition and a free press allowed the disastrous policies" (Sen, 1993, p. 44; see also Rummel, 1991, pp. 248–249). The *Human Development Report 1996* argues that "if there are no elections, no opposition parties, no forums for public criticism, those who rule do not have to worry about the political consequences of failing to prevent a famine. That Botswana and Zimbabwe have been successful in preventing famine, and Ethiopia and Sudan have not, is testimony to the importance of political participation and democracy in helping people meet their basic needs" (United Nations Development Programme, 1996, p. 58).

Lee Kuan Yew, long-time leader of Singapore, is an articulate and influential spokesperson for "soft authoritarianism." SOURCE: Reuters/Bettmann Newsphotos.

enjoying considerable economic prosperity, Chile, shows signs of having a similar political impact beyond its boundaries. Chile was ruled by the dictator Augusto Pinochet from 1973 to 1990. Life expectancy in Chile before Pinochet was 63.6. After Pinochet, life expectancy rose to 71.8 (Codevilla, 1993, p. 129). In 1995, the *Wall Street Journal* reported from Santiago, Chile, that "from the construction cranes dotting the skyline to the modernist paintings decorating the subway, this capital has a thriving air that seems more characteristic of a Scandinavian country than a Latin American one." And in discussing how Chile has achieved its widely noted economic successes in recent decades, this report goes on to note that "of course, Chilean economic reformers had an advantage in dealing with dissent: They worked for a military dictatorship that could suppress opposition to policies that inflicted short-term pain" (Moffett, 1995, p. 1).

Chile, like at least some of the Asian Tigers, seems now to be moving toward democracy. But it began this movement after almost two decades of harsh authoritarian rule under Pinochet. Pinochet's regime was certainly one inspiration for Alberto Fujimori's antidemocratic coup in Peru in 1992, and Peru is showing some signs of economic recovery. Pinochet and Fujimori probably helped to inspire a coup (ultimately unsuccessful) in Venezuela in 1992.

Still, in 1997 one noted analyst of Latin American politics pointed out that "since 1976 in the Spanish-American countries and Brazil, no civilian constitutional president elected in free and fair elections has been overthrown by the armed forces" (Dominguez, 1997, p. 100).[23] The poverty of Africa seems a particularly unpropitious setting for the development of democracy, but even in Africa, since 1990 twenty-seven countries have held multiparty presidential elections, twenty-one of them for the first time. In addition, since 1980, opposition parties have been legalized in thirty-one African countries (United Nations Development Programme, 1996, p. 42). "In recent years," one East Asian parliamentarian and journalist notes, "there has arisen a class of theories that reject democracy on the ground that it is somehow incompatible with some of the characteristics of 'Asians' and 'Asian' societies." But this same Asia observer concludes that "though they were intriguing when first put forth, [these theories] have not been able to stand up to critical analysis" (Ng, 1997, p. 12). And though the hugely important nation of China is apparently influenced by the "soft authoritarianism" of Singapore, there is in fact a battle of sorts going on between Singapore and the more democratic Taiwan for the role of a "model" to mainland China. "As different as they are, these two island nations have one important thing in common. Both offer a vision of the future for 1.2 billion Chinese on the mainland. . . . Their competition for the mainland's soul makes for the most interesting rivalry in Southeast Asia" (Shenon, 1995, Section 4, p. 1).[24] In short, "recent (even post–Cold War) democratic success stories in such diverse places as Nicaragua, Malawi,

---

[23] And this in a region which "could once have been described as the land of the unfree and the home of the coup" (Dominguez, 1997, p. 100).

[24] "Taiwan is a continual annoyance for authoritarian governments in Asia, for it tends to put the lie to the idea that Asians are different from all other people; that, even after they have achieved prosperity and security, they prefer a government that restricts the rights of the individual whenever they conflict with the rights of the larger society" (Shenon, 1995, Section 4, p. 4).

Botswana, South Africa, Sierra Leone, Mongolia, Haiti and even Russia indicate that democracy is not a cultural flower destined to bloom only in northwestern Europe and North America" (Ray, 1997, p. 61).

SUMMARY

In the decades before the First World War, most major powers of the world were imperialistic; they established new colonies in Latin America, Africa, and Asia by military force. The most influential theory explaining this new imperialism, developed by Lenin, traced it to the capitalistic economic systems of those major powers. Because concentrated wealth made it impossible for capitalists to prosper at home, according to Lenin they needed new markets abroad, new fields of investment, and secure access to the raw materials in other countries. Hence, they caused their governments to engage in imperialism. However, most of the imperialistic powers of the earlier age never relied very much on their new colonies as sources of raw materials, markets for exports, or fields of investment. Neither has the United States relied very crucially on developing countries as export markets or fields of investment for most of the post–Second World War period. Both the imperialism of the pre–First World War period and some admittedly neoimperialistic policies of the United States after the Second World War may have been inspired to some important extent by national security concerns at least as much as economic incentives. In any case, the Leninist idea that imperialism will be eliminated by the worldwide emergence of socialism has been largely discredited by relationships among socialist states after the Second World War, and by the demise of both the Soviet Union and the Communist regimes of Eastern Europe.

Since the Second World War, both dependency theory and world-system analysis have attempted to explain poverty in developing countries. They blame that poverty primarily on domination of the global economic system by rich, powerful capitalist states, which they claim makes it necessary for LDCs to adhere to policies of economic development radically different from those based on democracy and capitalism historically followed by most of the currently rich countries. But the economic and political failure of many socialist Third World countries contrasts sharply with the success of Hong Kong, Singapore, Taiwan, and South Korea—followed more recently by other East Asian states such as Indonesia, Malaysia, and Thailand. These successes have discredited most prescriptions by dependency theorists. Strategies emphasizing exports and market forces clearly predominate in most developing countries today. However, governments in most LDCs, including most of the East Asian Tigers, engage in energetic interventions in their economies, and such "socialistic" tendencies have produced successful results in places like the Indian state of Kerala and China. Government policies to modify market forces in favor of rural sectors and women also show signs of producing important economic benefits, although the rapid rate of urbanization in LDCs today makes it especially important to include large cities in development plans. Democracy may be quite compatible with, and even necessary for, economic development in the long run. But in the short run, the economic successes of the (until recently) autocratic governments of the four Asian Tigers, Chile, and China (especially compared with the economic disasters in nascent democracies in the former Soviet republics and eastern Europe) may imperil the continued existence of many of the new democratic regimes that have emerged recently in developing countries, as well as a global trend toward democracy. Still, after a setback earlier in the 1990s, at present there are hopeful signs of the continuation of such a trend in Latin America, Africa, and Asia.

KEY TERMS

imperialism
less developed countries (LDCs)
dependency theory
world-system analysis
Asian Tigers
newly industrialized countries (NICs)
urban bias
role of women
economic and political development
V. I. Lenin
John Hobson
capitalism
exploitation
neoimperialism

national security considerations
democracy
takeoff stage
multinational corporations
foreign investment
commodity concentration
partner concentration
terms of trade
new international economic order
  (NIEO)
Group of 77
export-oriented strategies
Grameen Bank
Muhammad Yunus

SOURCES

Amuzegar, Jahangir. "Dealing with Debt." *Foreign Policy*, No. 68 (Fall 1987), pp. 140–158.

"Bangladesh Bank Helps Poor Women." *Tampa Tribune*, December 2, 1993, Nation/World, p. 6 (an Associated Press Report).

Barnet, Richard J. *Real Security*. New York: Simon & Schuster, 1981.

Becker, Charles M., Andrew M. Hamer, and Andrew R. Morrison. *Beyond Urban Bias in Africa*. Portsmouth, N.H.: Heinemann, 1994.

Bernstein, Richard, and Ross H. Munro. "The Coming Conflict with America." *Foreign Affairs*, 76 (March/April 1997), 18–32.

Binyan, Liu. "Deng's Pyrrhic Victory." *New Republic*, (October 1989), 21–24.

Blaug, Mark. "Economic Imperialism Revisited." In Kenneth Boulding and Tapan Mukerjee, eds., *Economic Imperialism*. Ann Arbor: University of Michigan Press, 1972.

Bornschier, Volker, and Christopher Chase-Dunn. *Transnational Corporations and Underdevelopment*. New York: Praeger, 1985.

Bornschier, Volker, Christopher Chase-Dunn, and Richard Rubinson. "Cross-National Evidence of the Effects of Foreign Investment and Aid on Economic Growth and Inequality." *American Journal of Sociology*, 84 (November 1978), 651–683.

Branegan, Jay. "Is Singapore a Model for the West?" *Time*, January 18, 1993, pp. 36–37.

Broad, Robin, and John Cavanaugh. "No More NICs." *Foreign Policy*, No. 72 (Fall 1988), 81–104.

Broad, Robin, John Cavanaugh, and Walden Bello. "Development: The Market Is Not Enough." *Foreign Policy*, No. 81 (Winter 1990–91), 144–162.

Brooke, James. "Africa's Push to Become Self-Sufficient." *New York Times*, August 21, 1988, Section 4, p. 7.

Burkhart, Ross E., and Michael S. Lewis-Beck, "Comparative Democracy: The Economic Development Thesis," *American Political Science Review*, 88 (December 1994), 903–910.

Cardoso, Fernando Henrique, and Enzo Faletto. *Dependency and Development in Latin America*. Berkeley and Los Angeles: University of California Press, 1978.

Chan, Steve, and Cal Clark. "Can Good Things Go Together? A Virtuous Cycle in East Asia." *International Studies Notes*, 15 (Winter 1990), 4–9.

Clark, Cal. "The Taiwan Exception: Implications for Contending Political Economy Paradigms." *International Studies Quarterly*, 31 (September 1987), 327.

Codevilla, Angelo. "Is Pinochet the Model?" *Foreign Affairs*, 72 (November/December 1993), 127–141.

Doll, Gaynelle. "Unconventional Wisdom." *Vanderbilt Magazine*, 79 (Winter 1997), 6–11.

Dominguez, Jorge I. "Latin America's Crisis of Representation." *Foreign Affairs*, 76 (January/February 1997), 100–113.

Dos Santos, Theotonio. "The Structure of Dependence." *American Economic Review*, 60 (May 1970), 231–236.

Dowden, Richard. "A Continent Slipping into Darkness." *World Press Review*, January 1993, pp. 16–17.

"Economic and Financial Indicators." *Economist*, October 3, 1987, p. 115.

"Educating Girls a Boon to Nations." *Tampa Tribune*, September 7, 1993, Nation/World, p. 4 (an Associated Press Report).

Fieldhouse, D. K. "Imperialism: An Historiographical Revision." In Kenneth Boulding and Tapan Mukerjee, eds., *Economic Imperialism*. Ann Arbor: University of Michigan Press, 1972.

Frank, Andre G. *Development and Underdevelopment in Latin America.* New York: Monthly Review Press, 1968.

Franke, Richard W., and Barbara H. Chasin. "Kerala State, India: Radical Reform as Development." *Monthly Review,* 42 (January 1991), 1–23.

Galtung, Johan. "A Structural Theory of Imperialism." *Journal of Peace Research,* 8, 1971, 81–117.

Gilpin, Robert. *The Political Economy of International Relations.* Princeton, N.J.: Princeton University Press, 1987.

Haggard, Stephen. "The Newly Industrializing Countries in the International System." *World Politics,* 38 (January 1986), 343–370.

Hale, David. "Is Asia's High Growth Era Over?" *The National Interest,* No. 47 (Spring 1997), 44–57.

Hawes, Gary, and Hong Liu. "Explaining the Dynamics of the Southeast Asian Political Economy." *World Politics,* 45 (July 1993), 629–660.

Hayter, Teresa. *Aid as Imperialism.* Baltimore, Md.: Penguin, 1971.

Hayter, Teresa. *Aid: Rhetoric and Reality.* London: Pluto Press, 1985.

Hobson, John. *Imperialism: A Study.* London: Allen & Unwin, 1902.

Holloway, Nigel. *Far Eastern Economic Review,* 1991. Cited in *World Press Review,* May 1991, p. 51.

Huntington, Samuel. *Political Order in Changing Societies.* New Haven, Conn.: Yale University Press, 1968.

Huntington, Samuel, and Jorge I. Dominguez. "Political Development." In F. I. Greenstein and N. W. Polsby, eds. *Handbook of Political Science,* Vol. 3. Reading, Mass.: Addison-Wesley, 1975.

International Monetary Fund. *World Economic Outlook, October 1993.* Washington, D.C.: IMF, 1993.

Karatnycky, Adrian. "Freedom on the March," *Freedom Review,* 28 (January–February 1997), 5–29.

Jacobson, Jodi L. *Gender Bias: Roadblock to Sustainable Development* (Worldwatch Paper 110). Washington, D.C.: Worldwatch Institute, 1992.

Kolko, Gabriel. *The Roots of American Foreign Policy.* Boston: Beacon Press, 1969.

Krasner, Stephen D. "Transforming International Regimes." *International Studies Quarterly,* 25 (March 1981), 119–148.

Kristoff, Nicholas D. "China Sees Singapore as a Model for Progress." *New York Times,* August 9, 1993, Section 4, p. 4.

Kristoff, Nicholas D. "Chinese Grow Healthier from Cradle to Gra⌐ " *New York Times,* April 14, 1991, Section A, pp. 1, 6.

Krueger, Anne O. "Origins of the Developing Countries' Debt 1982." *Journal of Development Economics,* 27 (October 198⌐

Krugman, Paul. "The Myth of Asia's Miracle." *Foreign Aff* ber/December 1994), 62–78.

Langer, William. "A Critique of Imperialism." *Foreign* 1935), 102–119.

Langer, William. *The Diplomacy of Imperialism.* 2r 1951.

Lenin, V. I. *Imperialism: The Highest Stage of Ca⌐* tional Publishers, 1939 (first published in 19⌐

Londregan, John B., and Keith T. Poole. "Does High Income Promote Democracy?" *World Politics*, 49 (October 1996), 1–30.

Linden, Eugene. "The Exploding Cities of the Developing World." *Foreign Affairs*, 75 (January/February 1996), 52–65.

Lipton, Michael. "Urban Bias and Inequality." In Mitchell A. Seligson, ed., *The Gap Between Rich and Poor*. Boulder, Colo.: Westview Press, 1984.

Magdoff, Harry. *The Age of Imperialism*. New York: Monthly Review Press, 1969.

Mathews, Jessica. "Out of Bangladesh Emerges a Model Bank to Fight Poverty." *Washington Post*, circa December 27, 1993. Published in the *Tallahassee Democrat*, December 27, 1993, p. 7A.

Moffett, Matt. "Mexico Might Learn from Fall of the Peso in Chile Last Decade." *Wall Street Journal*, January 16, 1995, pp. A1, A6.

Moore, Molly. "Banks Lending to Women Changes Lives of Poverty." *Washington Post*, circa August 23, 1992. Published in the *Tallahassee Democrat*, August 23, 1992, p. 13A.

Nash, Nathaniel C. "Chile's Engine Revs Up with Free Trade's Fuel." *New York Times*, December 26, 1993, Section 4, p. 6.

Ng, Margaret. "Why Asia Needs Democracy." *Journal of Democracy*, 8 (April 1997), 10–23.

"North Korea: A Terrible Truth." *Economist*, April 19, 1997, p. 40.

Olson, Mancur. "Dictatorship, Democracy, and Development." *American Political Science Review*, 87 (September 1993), 567–576.

Olson, Mancur. *The Rise and Decline of Nations*. New Haven, Conn.: Yale University Press, 1982.

Payer, Cheryl. *The Debt Trap: The IMF and the Third World*. New York: Monthly Review Press, 1974.

Payer, Cheryl. *The World Bank: A Critical Analysis*. New York: Monthly Review Press, 1982.

Pougerami, Abbas. "Authoritarian Versus Nonauthoritarian Approaches to Economic Development: Update and Additional Evidence." *Public Choice*, 74 (1992), 365–377.

Przeworski, Adam, and Fernando Limongi. "Modernization: Theories and Facts." *World Politics*, 49 (January 1997), 155–183.

Quester, George. *Offense and Defense in the International System*. New York: Wiley, 1977.

Ray, James Lee. "The Democratic Path to Peace." *Journal of Democracy*, 8 (April 1997), 49–64.

Riedel, James. "Trade as the Engine of Growth in Developing Countries, Revisited." *Economic Journal*, 94 (March 1984), 56–73.

Rummel, R. J. *China's Bloody Century*. New Brunswick, N.J.: Transaction Publishers, 1991.

Schreiberg, David. "Dateline Latin America: The Growing Fury." *Foreign Policy*, No. 106 (Spring 1997), 161–176.

Sen, Amartya. "The Economics of Life and Death." *Scientific American* (May 1993), pp. 40–47.

___, Shalendra. "Neo-Classical Political Economy and the Lessons from ___." *International Studies Notes*, 20 (Spring 1995), 22–27.

Shenon, Philip. "Either Filthy and Free or Clean and Mean." *New York Times*, February 5, 1995, Section 4, pp. 1, 4.

Sivard, Ruth Leger. *World Military and Social Expenditures, 1987–1988*. Washington, D.C.: World Priorities, 1987.

Smith, Wayne S. "Cuba's Long Reform." *Foreign Affairs*, 75 (March/April 1996), 99–112.

Sweezy, Paul. "A Crisis in Marxian Theory." *Monthly Review*, 31 (June 1979), 20–24.

"Third World Development: Old Problems, New Strategies." *Great Decisions '86*. New York: Foreign Policy Association, 1986.

Todaro, Michael P. *Economic Development in the Third World*. 3rd ed. New York: Longman, 1985.

United Nations Development Programme. *Human Development Report 1996*. New York: Oxford University Press, 1996.

U.S. Department of State. *Atlas of United States Foreign Relations*. Washington, D.C.: Bureau of Public Affairs, 1985.

Wade, Robert. "East Asia's Economic Success." *World Politics*, 44 (January 1992), 270–320.

Wallerstein, Immanuel. *The Capitalist World-Economy*. Cambridge, U.K.: Cambridge University Press, 1979.

Wallerstein, Immanuel. *The Modern World System I*. New York: Academic Press, 1974.

Wallerstein, Immanuel. *The Modern World System III*. New York and San Diego: Academic Press, 1988.

Walters, Robert S., and David H. Blake. *The Politics of Global Economic Relations*. Englewood Cliffs, N.J.: Prentice-Hall, 1992.

Waltz, Kenneth N. *Man, the State, and War*. New York: Columbia University Press, 1954.

Weede, Erich. *Economic Development, Social Order, and World Politics*. Boulder, Colo.: Lynne Rienner, 1996.

World Bank. *World Development Report 1990*. New York: Oxford University Press, 1990.

Zimbalist, Andrew. "Dateline Cuba: Hanging on in Havana." *Foreign Policy*, No. 92 (Fall 1993), 151–167.

CHAPTER 9

East-West Relationships: The Emerging Post–Cold War Era

In March 1985, Soviet President Konstantin Chernenko died, to be replaced by **Mikhail Gorbachev.** On December 25, 1991, Gorbachev resigned as president of the Soviet Union. On the same day, the Soviet flag was lowered over the Kremlin, to be replaced by the flag of Russia. The Soviet Union was dead. Control of its nuclear arsenal passed to the Russian president, Boris Yeltsin.

Some Russians dream of reviving the Soviet Union, but probably the **Cold War** is over. The Cold War was never *really* a war, and so it never officially began or ended. Perhaps the fall of the Berlin Wall in November 1989 will be remembered as the symbolic end of the Cold War.

The Cold War unofficially started after the Second World War at some time in the late 1940s. It is clear that the nuclear era of international politics began when the United States dropped two atomic bombs on Japan in 1945, and the nuclear confrontation between the United States and the Soviet Union commenced in 1949 when the Soviets tested their first nuclear bomb. Between 1949 and the fall of the Berlin Wall in 1989, there occurred the most intense, dangerous, geographically wide-ranging, expensive, but still peaceful confrontation between any two countries in the history of the world. Though the Cold War never produced direct military combat between the United States and the Soviet Union, the end of the Cold War has served as a kind of functional equivalent to "World War III," involving a process with curious similarities to the impact of the two previous world wars.

Like World Wars I and II, a consequence of the event (that is, the end of the Cold War) was that a major empire was dismembered, important political boundaries in Europe were reorganized, and several nations were politically transformed. And just as the ancient institution of monarchy met its effective demise in Europe in World War I and as the newer but more dangerous and seemingly virile ideologies of nazism and fascism were destroyed by World War II, so a major political philosophy, communism, over which a great deal of ink and blood had been spilled, was discredited and apparently expunged in World War III (Mueller, 1992, p. 66).

This chapter analyzes first the historical Cold War relationship between the United States and the Soviet Union. It focuses next on the question of why the Cold War ended and what its termination might tell us about competing approaches to understanding international politics. The chapter goes on to discuss the implication of the end of the Cold War for relationships between the United States and other industrialized countries, on the one hand, and the now independent republics of the former Soviet Union, on the other. Finally, it examines the possible impact of the end of the Cold War on the future of the global political system and on the key role China is likely to play in that future.

THE COLD WAR CONFRONTATION BETWEEN THE UNITED STATES AND THE SOVIET UNION

During most of the Cold War era, the United States and the Soviet Union possessed about 95 percent of the world's nuclear warheads. As a result, each superpower had enough firepower to obliterate the other's citizens several times over. Were there *any* good reasons for the Americans and the Soviets to keep stockpiling fantastically destructive weapons for decades, or did the process continue for as long as it did because both sides succumbed to madness, the greed of their respective military-industrial complexes, or incredibly foolish pride?

Thinking the Unthinkable

Since millions of people would have died in any **nuclear war,** it might seem logical to conclude that such a conflict was always unthinkable and virtually certain not to occur. But the nuclear confrontation between the United States and the Soviet Union would have been much less serious and intractable than it was for decades if the probability of nuclear war were virtually zero. In fact, under certain conditions, it might have been rational for one or both sides to initiate a nuclear war, because there was always the possibility that the superpowers would

Figure 9.1 The Prisoners' Dilemma

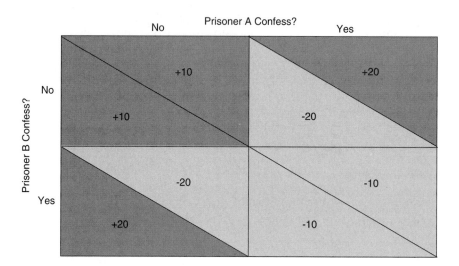

The game theory matrix shows the payoff to each prisoner for confessing or not confessing a crime to the sheriff.

find themselves in what has become known in **game theory** as the **"prisoners' dilemma."**[1]

The structure of such a game is presented in Figure 9.1 above. It is important to understand this structure not only for the insight it can provide into the nuclear confrontation between the United States and the Soviet Union but because states in the decentralized international system quite often face dilemmas of this kind when they attempt to cooperate with each other. Cooperation may often entail valuable payoffs for both sides; during the Cold War cooperation was necessary to avoid nuclear war and to ensure the very survival of both sides. But even if the payoff is overwhelmingly important, there is no guarantee that the necessary cooperation will occur.

The prisoners' dilemma game gets its name from a story that is devised in order to describe its structure. Two suspects are imprisoned by a sheriff with a problem. The sheriff admits that there is not enough evidence to convict either suspect if they both refuse to confess. In that outcome of the game, depicted in the upper left-hand cell of the matrix

---

[1] Game theory is "a body of thought dealing with rational decision strategies in situations of conflict and competition, where each participant or player seeks to maximize gains and minimize losses" (Plano, Greenberg, Olton, and Riggs, 1973, p. 68).

in Figure 9.1, each player wins 10 points. But the sheriff also informs the prisoners that if one of them does confess, the confessor will go free and receive a large reward (that is, receive the 20 points indicated in the upper half of the upper right-hand cell, or the lower half of the lower left-hand cell of the matrix), whereas the other will be hanged (the outcome represented by the –20 points in the lower half of the upper right-hand cell or the upper half of the lower left-hand cell of the matrix). If, finally, both suspects confess on the same day, they will each receive long prison sentences, as is indicated by the –10 points in the upper and lower halves of the lower right-hand cell of the matrix.

Each prisoner has two possible strategies: to confess or not to confess. Which is the rational strategy from their individual points of view? Social scientists have debated the definition of **rationality** at some length, but in the context of games like this, game theorists point out a couple of important ways in which self-interested calculations lead the suspects to confess. If each suspect decides *not* to confess, the maximum possible loss that each faces (if the other chooses to confess) would be death. But if each prisoner decides to confess, the worst that can happen (if the other chooses the same strategy) is that he or she will get a long prison sentence. Because both players can minimize their maximum possible losses by confessing, arguably that is the rational strategy for both of them.

Alternatively, each player might try to maximize his or her winnings rather than to minimize losses. In that case, each suspect is again likely to calculate that confession is the better strategy. If the other prisoner confesses, he or she will suffer a loss of 10, rather than 20 points (death). If the other prisoner does not confess, he or she will win 20, rather than only 10, points. In other words, each player can calculate that confession will maximize his or her payoff, whatever the other player decides to do. So despite the fact that the prisoners collectively would be better off if they did not confess, whether they concentrate on minimizing their maximum possible losses or on maximizing their winnings, both suspects will opt for the strategy that (since they both select it) will lead to many years of prison.

Could the United States and the Soviet Union have found themselves confronted with a similar dilemma during the tense years of their nuclear confrontation? It is conceivable, as Figure 9.2 suggests. In the situation depicted there, both sides are clearly better off if neither starts a nuclear war, as the +10 points in both halves of the upper right-hand cell indicate. But if either or both sides can launch a first strike destroying their opponent's ability to retaliate, the temptation to do so might become overwhelming. (Such a situation is depicted by +20 points and the –20 points in the upper right-hand and lower left-hand cells.) If the decision makers on both sides want to win as much as possible, regard-

Figure 9.2   Potential Nuclear Dilemma Between the Superpowers

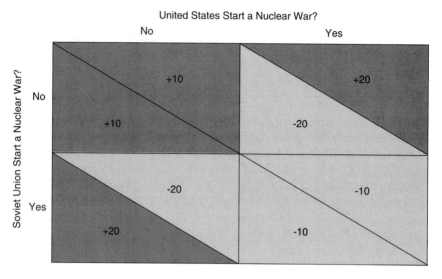

Applied to the nuclear confrontation between the United States and the Soviet Union, the logic of game theory suggests that both countries could find themselves in a situation where it would be "rational" to launch a nuclear attack.

less of what the opponent does, they will both decide to attack. Even if we optimistically assume that nuclear weapons have a sobering effect on both sides, leading them to think more conservatively about minimizing their possible losses (rather than winning as much as possible), they might still both decide to send their missiles hurtling toward each other. If they both attack simultaneously, they might both destroy some of each other's missiles on the ground, thus cutting their own losses to, say, 50 million lives. If they do *not* minimize their possible losses (that is, if both launch a nuclear attack), they risk losing virtually everything: each would lose at least 100 million people and all ability to resist domination by its opponent in the postwar world. Confronted with such a situation, leaders on both sides might reason as follows: "Our side, of course, would not dream of committing such a horrifying and repugnant act as launching a first strike. We are too honorable and humanitarian to do such a thing. But I am not so sure about the Soviets [Americans]. Being Communists [capitalists], they are inherently imperialistic. And they know that if they strike first, they will win. Worse, they know that we know that they will win if they strike first. Because they know that we know that they will win if they strike first, they might well conclude that we will strike first, if only to avoid catastrophe. Considering this, they are sure to attack. Thus, we must launch a nuclear attack. We may lose 50 million people, but if we do not strike now, we might lose 100 million. So by striking now, we are saving ourselves from possible domination in the postwar world and the lives of at least 50 million people!"

The Prisoners' Dilemma and the Real World

Fortunately, the real-world nuclear confrontation between the United States and the Soviet Union was always fundamentally different from the structure of the prisoners' dilemma game in at least one crucial respect. In the game, the ability of the first strike to eliminate all of the enemy's weapons and thereby allow the initiator of a nuclear war to escape retaliation is certain. In the real-world nuclear confrontation, a first strike that deprived the other side of any significant ability to retaliate always seemed highly unlikely. In other words, the leaders of the former Soviet Union and the United States were usually quite confident that if they were the victim of a first strike, their **second strike capacity** would enable them to deliver a devastating counterattack.

Technology and Stability

But the Cold War nuclear confrontation was often quite tense, because **technological developments** always posed a danger that a nuclear war might become winnable (or, in other words, that a "prisoners' dilemma" might arise). As early as 1960, Henry Kissinger pointed out that "every country lives with the nightmare that even if it puts forth its best efforts its survival may be jeopardized by a technological breakthrough on the part of its opponent" (Kissinger, 1960; cited in Majeski, 1986, p. 175). And such nightmares were magnified during the Cold War by the fact that each side was making determined efforts to achieve such break-throughs, whether by developing more accurate **intercontinental ballistic missiles (ICBMs)**, or **submarine-launched ballistic missiles (SLBMs)**, or ballistic missile defense systems like President Ronald Reagan's **Strategic Defense Initiative (SDI).**

Innovations of that type were inspired in part by the fact that successful **deterrence** was not ensured merely because a first strike would not *in fact* be successful. A deterrence strategy was effective *only if* the leaders of the other side could not even *imagine* that a first strike might be successful. To be more precise, during the Cold War the leaders of the United States and the Soviet Union had to contend continuously with the possibility that deterrence might break down and a nuclear war might break out if the decision makers on either side became convinced that the other side *imagined* that its enemies *be-*

lieved that a first strike might be successful. As long as these **reciprocal fears of surprise attack**[2] existed, there was always the possibility that a nuclear war might occur, not only because of an accident or insanity but also because one side or the other (or most dangerously, both sides) would find itself in a position where nuclear war seemed, by some calculations, a logical option.

ARMS RACES AND THE END OF THE COLD WAR

Under those conditions, it is not so surprising that the United States and the Soviet Union had very large defense budgets and accumulated weapons at a very rapid rate for four decades after the Second World War. From the point of view of the decision makers on both sides, they were only protecting themselves. But from the point of view of many outside observers, the arms race between the United States and the Soviet Union was very dangerous. It would ultimately, many felt, lead to the nuclear holocaust that both sides were ostensibly trying to avoid. Even as recently as 1979, Hans Morgenthau (whose prominent role in the development of the field of international politics is discussed in Chapter 2) declared that "the world is moving ineluctably toward a third world war—a strategic nuclear war. I do not believe that anything can be done to prevent it" (Mueller, 1995, p. 323).[3]

The arms race between the Soviet Union and the United States was clearly dangerous, not to mention incredibly wasteful in purely economic terms. But it does seem to have come to an end without disaster. This is not an historically unprecedented outcome for arms races. Consider the list of arms races presented in Table 9.1. Notice that only five of the thirteen arms races listed there ended in war and that four of those five were associated with the Second World War. With respect to these four latter cases, one can reasonably argue that "the military factor which was most important in bringing [the Second World War] about was the failure of Britain, France, and the Soviet Union to engage in the arms race with sufficient vigor, their insufficient response to the rearmament of Germany" (Bull, 1971, p. 352).

---

[2] "Fear that the other may be about to strike in the mistaken belief that we are about to strike gives us a motive for striking, and so justifies the other's motive . . . .'He thinks we think he thinks we think . . . he thinks we think he'll attack; so he thinks we shall; so he will; so we must'" (Schelling, 1970, p. 207).

[3] Mueller (1995, pp. 191–193) cites similar assertions by such well-known analysts and observers as Arnold Toynbee, Albert Einstein, Herman Kahn, C. P. Snow, and Jonathan Schell.

Table 9.1 Huntington's List of Arms Races in the Nineteenth and Twentieth Centuries

Participants	Duration	Outcome
1. France vs. England	1840–1866	Peace
2. France vs. Germany	1874–1894	Peace
3. England vs. France and Russia	1884–1904	Peace
4. Argentina vs. Chile	1890–1902	Peace
5. England vs. Germany	1898–1912	Peace
6. France vs. Germany	1911–1914	War
7. England vs. United States	1916–1930	Peace
8. Japan vs. United States	1916–1922	Peace
9. France vs. Germany	1934–1939	War
10. U.S.S.R. vs. Germany	1934–1941	War
11. Germany vs. England	1934–1939	War
12. United States vs. Japan	1934–1941	War
13. U.S.S.R. vs. United States	1946–1989?	Peace

Source: Samuel P. Huntington, "Arms Races: Prerequisites and Results," in Robert J. Art and Kenneth N. Waltz, eds., *The Use of Force* (Boston: Little, Brown, 1971), p. 367. Reprinted by permission of John F. Kennedy School of Government, Harvard University.

Some even more thoroughly systematic analyses of arms races in general have not found that they make wars much more likely. One study of arms races between 1816 and 1980 reports that "military buildups . . . have little direct effect on the likelihood [of] war. Only approximately 20 percent of arms races . . . were . . . followed by war" (Diehl, 1985, p. 342).[4] A more recent study, though, reports that states involved in serious disputes and an arms race at the same time are substantially more likely to end up in a war against each other than are states involved in disputes when no arms race is under way (Sample, 1997).

This evidence does not necessarily justify the conclusion that arms races are dangerous. Perhaps states conducting arms races are less likely to get involved in serious disputes in the first place, so that if one

---

[4] Diehl goes on to point out that this 20 percent figure is not significantly different from the results of conflicts he examined that were *not* preceded by arms races.

compared states in arms races with states not in arms races (rather than comparing states in serious disputes simultaneously in arms races with other states in serious disputes, but not in arms races), the rapidly arming states would be seen to be less likely to become involved in war. Admittedly, on the other hand, it is certainly possible that arms races increase tensions and thus cause wars that otherwise would not have occurred. But it is perhaps equally plausible that states become involved in arms races because they accurately perceive their disputes with other states as being sufficiently serious to lead to war, and that the subsequent wars are more the result of those existing dangers than the result of the arms accumulations themselves. In short, it is clear that "arms races have been a preliminary to war. . . . But just as clearly, many wars have not been preceded by such mutual arms buildups, and many arms races never end in war" (Cashman, 1993, p. 182).[5]

And now what certainly seemed potentially the most dangerous arms race in the history of the world has come to an apparent conclusion with the peaceful dissolution of the Soviet Union. It can even be argued that the arms race, or the American decision to participate in it with such determination, made an important contribution to that outcome. "An emerging conventional wisdom seems to hold that the end of the Cold War represents a victory for Western strategies of 'peace through strength. . . .' Standing tough against the Soviets seems to have paid off" (Risse-Kappen, 1991, p. 162). Even more specifically, a "new conventional wisdom" suggests that "the Reagan administration's military buildup delivered the knock-out punch to a system that was internally bankrupt and on the ropes" (Deudney and Ikenberry, 1992, p. 124). One admiring analysis of the foreign policy of the Reagan administration asserts:

> Moscow spent tens of billions of dollars it could ill afford responding to SDI, according to Roald Z. Sagdayev, who headed the Soviet Space Research Institute in the 1980s. "This program became priority No. 1 after Mr. Reagan's announcement of the 'Star Wars' in 1983." He believes the spending weakened the Soviet Union and may have contributed to its demise (Schweizer, 1994, p. 197).[6]

It can clearly be argued that **policies of** hardline **peace through strength** pursued before and during the Reagan administration played a

---

[5] One of the main sources of evidence to support this statement is Morrow (1989, p. 502): "Disputes preceded by arms races do escalate to war more often than other disputes, but they do not overwhelmingly escalate to war."

[6] As the title implies, Jay Winik's (1996) *On the Brink: The Dramatic, Behind-the-Scenes Saga of the Reagan Era and the Men and Women Who Won the Cold War* carries a similar message.

key role in the demise of the Soviet Union and the end of the Cold War. In what is now the post-Soviet era, it is easy to forget that as recently as the 1970s, the Soviet Union was generally perceived to be on the road to much bigger and better things. In 1981, one well-known analyst of the Soviet Union observed that "the Brezhnev era [Leonid Brezhnev ruled the Soviet Union from 1964 to 1982] will probably go down in history as the most successful period of Soviet international and domestic development. Internationally it was a period when the Soviet Union fulfilled its major postwar dream: to achieve strategic parity with the United States and become a truly global power" (Bialer, 1980–81, p. 999).

But then Ronald Reagan was elected president of the United States in 1980, and he pushed through Congress the largest peacetime increases in the defense budget in the history of the country. He authorized an invasion of Grenada to put down a left-wing coup in 1983. Against vocal opposition, and large demonstrations in the streets of many Western European cities, he persuaded the NATO allies to stick by their 1979 decision to deploy 572 new intermediate-range missiles in Western Europe. President Reagan also funneled substantial military aid to rebels in Afghanistan, who were fighting Soviet troops there, and he formulated the **Reagan Doctrine,** which called for covert support for rebels against regimes supported by the Soviet Union in places like Nicaragua, Angola, Cambodia, and Ethiopia. Perhaps most significantly, as noted above, in March 1983, Ronald Reagan launched SDI, an elaborate plan to develop defense systems against ballistic missiles. Supporters of this decision (and of SDI) "talk as though SDI brought down the Soviet regime all by itself" (Sestanovich, 1993, p. 28).[7]

Responses by the Critics of Hardline Policies

Theoretical and political critics of hardline policies like those adopted by the Reagan administration in its early years are reluctant to accept this interpretation of the 1980s as leading up to the dramatic events of the late 1980s and early 1990s. Some analysts argue, for example, that it was not the aggressive policies of the early 1980s that led to the

---

[7] According to Peter Schweizer, the Reagan administration also conspired with the Saudis to bring down the world price for oil, which had a devastating impact on the economy of the Soviet Union. "Oil was the Kremlin's most significant export earner, in some instances accounting for more than half of Soviet hard currency. . . . [In] August 1985, a stake was driven silently through the heart of the Soviet economy. The Saudis opened the spigot and flooded the world market with oil. . . . In November 1985, crude oil sold at $30 a barrel; barely five months later it stood at $12. For Moscow, over $10 billion in valuable hard currency evaporated overnight . . ." (Schweizer, 1995, pp. 140, 242–243).

eventual demise of the Soviet Union and the end of the Cold War as much as President Richard Nixon's relatively conciliatory policies leading to détente between the Soviet Union and the United States in the 1970s. According to this view, one of the results of détente was the **Helsinki Accords,** signed in 1975. The main purpose of the accords, from the Soviet point of view, was to obtain official recognition of the post–World War II European borders.[8] The Soviets hoped the agreement would legitimate the political regimes of the states in Eastern Europe, which they considered so crucial to their own security.

Ironically, though, it seems that the Helsinki Accords ultimately helped subvert the Communist regimes in both Eastern Europe and the Soviet Union. In exchange for recognizing the post–Second World War borders in Europe, the United States and the Western European participants at the Helsinki Conference extracted from the Soviets official commitments to uphold human rights, as well as an agreement to submit to a series of periodic reviews of how well those commitments were being adhered to. At the time, there was a lot of cynicism about this aspect of the Helsinki Act, more formally known as the **European Agreement on Security and Cooperation.** The famous Russian author and critic of the Soviet Union, Alexander Solzhenitsyn complained that the meeting in Helsinki amounted to the "funeral of Eastern Europe" (Sestanovich, 1993, p. 5), implying that the West had foolishly agreed to the permanent existence of the Soviet Union's empire in Eastern Europe in exchange for meaningless promises by the Soviets regarding human rights. And in fact, the Soviet promises were almost certainly not sincere. But "Soviet gains from the accompanying international recognition of its client states in Eastern Europe did not, as the Brezhnev regime expected, strengthen domestic legitimacy of the Soviet regime. Rather . . . the legitimacy of Soviet political practices [came] under systematic assault by internal dissidents and by powerful networks of human rights watchdog organizations such as Amnesty International and Helsinki Watch [which] . . . subverted the legitimacy of authoritarian and totalitarian regimes" (Deudney and Ikenberry, 1991/92, p. 105). It is, in short, not a ridiculous exaggeration to assert that ultimately those regimes were embarrassed to death.[9]

Another argument against the view that aggressive, hardline policies precipitated the end of the Cold War asserts instead that it was the conciliatory gestures and policy innovations of Reagan's second term that deserve the credit. Reagan was always seemingly uncomfortable

---

[8] "The Russian purpose [in the Helsinki Conference] was to secure general endorsement of the post Hitlerian frontiers in Europe which no peace conference had ever ratified . . ." (Calvocoressi, 1991, p. 63).

[9] Sestanovich (1993, p. 32); Calvocoressi (1991, pp. 63–64); Gaddis (1992/93, pp. 25–26).

relying on nuclear weapons for the defense of the country. One of the reasons for his commitment to SDI was that he hoped it would make nuclear weapons obsolete. "Reagan's strong anti-nuclear views expressed at the November 1985 Geneva summit were decisive in convincing Gorbachev that it was possible to work with the West in halting the nuclear arms race" (Deudney and Ikenberry, 1992, p. 127). When the president followed up at the October 1986 Reykjavik summit with a proposal to Gorbachev to do away with nuclear weapons entirely, "Reagan's . . . anti-nuclearism provided the crucial signal to Gorbachev that bold initiatives would be reciprocated rather than exploited" (Deudney and Ikenbery, 1992, p. 127).

Eventually, Reagan and Gorbachev came to an agreement to sign the **Treaty on Intermediate-Range Nuclear Forces (INF)**, the first disarmament treaty actually to eliminate some nuclear weapons. Often, the hardline policy of insisting on the deployment of intermediate-range missiles in Western European countries despite massive demonstrations against them in several Western European cities is credited with providing this breakthrough. But it can certainly be argued that it was rather Reagan's antinuclearism and the generally conciliatory policies of his later years in office that produced this significant step toward the end of the Cold War (Deudney and Ikenberry, 1992, p. 128).

Internal Factors, External Factors, and the Demise of the Soviet Union

All of the competing ideas just discussed share a common assumption: that forces outside the Soviet Union were crucial to its evolution and demise, and the resulting end of the Cold War. Contrasting ideas insist that external forces played only a minor role, and that actually it was factors internal to the Soviet Union that brought about its (and the Cold War's) demise. Some writers, for example, stress the influence of Mikhail Gorbachev, obviously expounding a version of the great-man theory discussed in Chapter 4 (Rush, 1993). But probably the single most prevalent notion regarding the dissolution of the Soviet Union stresses the impact of its inefficient domestic economic system. "The core legitimacy of . . . Soviet rule was provided by the Marxist thesis that public ownership of the means of production, and the unified direction of production toward public objectives, would make a socialist economy more efficient than a capitalist one, with its anarchic pursuit of private gain" (Kontorovich, 1993, p. 36). So because the Soviet economy performed so badly, the legitimacy of the Soviet regime collapsed.

Why, then, did the Soviet economy seem to do so badly, especially in the 1980s? Several analysts who stress Soviet domestic issues argue that the real causes of the continuously declining growth rate of the Soviet Union, of the poor quality of its products, and of its many other deficiencies are to be found in central planning by direct controls. The Soviet economy was an economy run by bureaucrats without information provided by real market prices, without the incentives to be efficient enforced by market competition, and without much incentive to develop and introduce new technology (Holzman, 1992, p. 16).

Intriguingly, an apparently contradictory argument is that it was not economic woes that brought down the Soviet Union, but rather economic modernization and development. In spite of all the Soviet Union's economic problems during the Communist era, it was also dramatically transformed in several possibly crucial ways. In the 1920s, only about 20 percent of the Soviet population lived in urban areas. By 1960, that figure had increased to 50 percent (Fukuyama, 1993, p. 17). "At the end of World War II, half of the Russian people were peasants. Now only 12.5% are peasants" (Pye, 1990, p. 10). The Soviet populace also became much better educated in the four or five decades before the Soviet Union disintegrated. At the end of the 1950s only 9 percent of the workers and 2 percent of the peasants in the country had more than an elementary education. By the middle of the 1980s, over 80 percent of the manual workers had more than an elementary education. Perhaps even more important for the political evolution of the Soviet Union, a huge highly educated class emerged. During Gorbachev's time, 15 million Soviet citizens held college degrees. About 40 percent of the urban population (which was, as we have seen, substantial) consisted of "intelligentsia," or technically trained "specialists" (Pye, 1990, p. 10). In fact, the professional class in the Soviet Union, in its last years, was arguably "numerically, the largest in the world" (Bialer, 1988, p. 407). This large number of urbanized, educated people in the Soviet Union arguably became too sophisticated and influential to be ruled by a condescending, arbitrary, and overbearing government bureaucracy. They ultimately demanded a say in running the country, and their demands, according to at least some observers, were the main force that led to the subversion and disintegration of the Soviet Union.

So what was it that led to the end of the Soviet Union and the Cold War? Economic stagnation and failure, or economic modernization and development? Somewhat paradoxically, it may well be that both economic success and economic failure played key roles in determining the fate of the Soviet Union. The Soviet system did bring the country through a rapid industrializing process from the 1920s up to about the 1970s, even if it was brutal and inefficient in many ways. In the process, obviously, a large proportion of Soviet citizens became highly educated. Those were the Soviet successes. But in retrospect, one can see that by the 1980s, the failures became more important, primarily because the nature of the challenge faced by the Soviet system changed. It had achieved industrialization. What it needed to do in the 1980s was adapt to the technological forces transforming modern economies. The most advanced economies in today's global system do not rely primarily on industrialization for their dynamism. The industrial age is being super-seded by the **information age,** in which *"knowledge* [emphasis added] . . . turns out to be not only the source of the highest-quality power, but also the most important ingredient of . . . wealth" (Toffler, 1991, p. 17). And the demise of the Soviet Union seems to suggest rather powerfully that "truly modern technological societies cannot flourish except in an atmosphere permitting a certain degree of freedom" (Fukuyama, 1993, pp. 15–16). In other words, if an economic system in the contemporary era is going to compete successfully with other systems relying on such technological innovations as copying machines, fax machines, and (most important) computers, it must have a large talented class of people adept in the use of all those recent and rapidly evolving technolo-gies. And that class of people simply cannot function effectively within the confines of autocratic political control. Mikhail Gorbachev, and many other Soviet citizens, came to realize this and decided that the system in the Soviet Union needed to be radically transformed.

> Just as Gutenberg's invention of the movable type in the mid-15th century led to the diffusion of knowledge and loosened the Catholic Church's grip on knowledge and communication in Western Europe . . . so the appearance of the computer and new communications media in the mid-20th century smashed Marxism's control of the mind in the coun-tries it ruled or held captive (Toffler, 1991, p. 405).

But this explanation regarding the disappearance of the Soviet Union relies entirely on forces and factors internal to the country. Just as the successes of the Soviet economic system explain the disintegration of the Soviet Union only when combined with an emphasis on its ultimate failures, internal factors provide the best explanation for the demise of the Soviet Union only when external factors are also taken into ac-count. The internal problems in the Soviet Union probably would not have created real pressure for change if they had not left the Soviet Union looking so bad in comparison with its major competitors in the global economic and political system. Ultimately, the Soviet system collapsed, and the Cold War ended, because the Soviet Union's internal problems rendered it obviously incapable of remaining one of the wealthiest and most powerful states in the world. "It seems doubtful," according to one analyst sympathetic to this type of explanation, "that the military pressure imposed by the United States and its allies will be certified as the exclusive or even the primary determinant of the transformation of the Soviet Union and its alliance system. The rise of the global economy had a great deal to do with it" (Steinbruner, 1996, p. 174).

Why Didn't We See It Coming?

It is easy to come up with plausible explanations of the demise of the Soviet Union and the end of the Cold War after the fact. There were not very many analysts of international politics, though, who predicted either event in advance.[10] In fact, one well-known specialist on the Cold War has argued that "none of our major theories of world politics came close to anticipating the end of the cold war" (Gaddis, 1992, p. A44).[11] This is, according to the same analyst, damning evidence against the academic field of international politics. He concludes that the failure of international relations analysts to predict the end of the Cold War proves that theories on which those analysts relied are "bankrupt" (Gaddis, 1992, p. A44).

But to conclude that the theories in field of international politics are bankrupt because few analysts specifically predicted the end of the Cold War is, perhaps, too harsh, or at least insufficiently discriminating. For example, the theoretical approach discussed in Chapter 6, stressing the peaceful nature of relationships between democratic states, quite clearly implies that if the autocratic protagonist in a cold-war type conflict moves toward democracy, antagonism should decrease.[12] "Substantial movement in the direction of democracy in the Soviet Union (and ultimately Russia) did take place between 1986 and 1991" (Ray and

---

[10] U.S. Senator Daniel Patrick Moynihan predicted in 1980 that "the Soviet Union is a seriously troubled, even sick society. . . . The defining event of the decade might well be the break-up of the Soviet Empire." He also predicted, though, in 1975, that "liberal democracy on the American model increasingly tends to the condition of monarchy in the 19th century: a holdover form of government, one which persists in isolated or peculiar places here and there . . . but which has simply no relevance to the future" (see Mueller, 1995, p. 192).

[11] This argument is developed in more detail in John Lewis Gaddis (1992/93).

[12] The following argument is based on the assumption that predictions should be defined as contingent statements, while "prophecies" should be thought of as assertions about the future unrelated to conditions or contingencies. "World War III will begin on October 6, 1998" would be an example of a prophecy as opposed to a prediction.

[13] Polity III, for example, provides data on virtually all regimes in the world on an annual basis, and it shows the Soviet Union (and Russia) with a score of 0 in 1986, 5 in 1989, and 7 in 1991 (on a democracy scale from 0 to 10), while the Freedom House annual report providing somewhat similar data shows the Soviet Union with the lowest democracy score possible in 1986 (a 7, on a scale going from 7 for the least democratic to 1 for the most democratic) to a score of 3 by 1990. (See Jaggers and Gurr, 1995; Gastil, 1989; and McColm, 1992.)

Russett, 1996, p. 460).[13] In addition, one analyst, writing in 1980, did specifically suggest that the **democratic peace proposition** might be relevant to attempts to predict the future of the Cold War, and that "stable peace could be possible . . . if the government of the Soviet Union were to evolve into something more democratic than the current 'state socialism' " (Russett, 1982; cited in Ray and Russett, 1996).

BEYOND THE COLD WAR

The end of the Cold War has released the world from the risk of the devastating holocaust that would have resulted from a nuclear war between the United States and the Soviet Union, a fact that occasionally seems to get lost in the nostalgia sometimes expressed for the simpler days of the Cold War in the post–Cold War world. It is also possible that the United States and the republics of the former Soviet Union will ultimately not only stop being deadly enemies but will emerge as quite similar states with genuinely friendly relations.

The United States and Russia: From the Cold War to Convergence?

In 1960, economist Walt Rostow argued that political systems based on Marxism were likely to arise only in states going through the early stages of industrialization. Rostow predicted that as the economies of the Communist states developed, their leaders would find Marxist-Leninist ideology progressively less appropriate to their needs. In fact, he felt that their economic development would eventually reach a stage when that ideology would disappear altogether. "Communism," he concluded, "is likely to wither in the age of high mass consumption" (Rostow, 1960, pp. 133–162).

In contrast, another economist, John Kenneth Galbraith, also writing in the 1960s, called attention to factors that he felt would cause the United States to become more like the Soviet Union. Basically, Galbraith's view was that economies dominated by large industrial firms are bound to become more similar over time, even if they operate in social systems with divergent ideologies. "The enemies of the market," according to Galbraith, "are . . . not socialists. It is advanced technology and the specialization of men and process that this requires and the resulting commitment of time and capital. These make the market work badly when the need is for greatly enhanced reliability—when planning is essential." Galbraith felt that these **convergent tendencies** would surface in industrial societies "however different their popular or

The destruction of the Berlin Wall symbolized the beginning of an era in which Western industrialized countries are likely to have more cooperative relationships with the formerly Communist countries; the two groups of countries may also adopt increasingly similar political and economic systems. SOURCE: AP/Wide World Photos.

ideological billing," and that the impact of these tendencies would be beneficial for the relationship between them. "In time, and perhaps in less time than may be imagined, [they] will dispose of the notion of inevitable conflict based on irreconcilable difference" (Galbraith, 1967, pp. 44, 396, 398).

Both the end of the Cold War and the way in which it ended have been interpreted in some circles as a repudiation of **convergence theory,** that is, the idea that the Soviet Union and the United States are likely to become increasingly similar to each other over time. Zbigniew Brzezinksi, for example, (President Carter's national security adviser from 1977 to 1981), has declared that "instead of the once acclaimed theory of 'convergence,' of the two competing systems [the Soviet Union and the United States], the reality is that of one-sided conversion" (Brzezinski, 1992, pp. 33–34). Historian Arthur Schlesinger has argued even more vigorously that "after seventy years of trial, communism turned out—by the confession of its own leaders—to be an economic, political, and moral disaster. Democracy won the political argument between East and West. The market won the economic argument" (Schlesinger, 1992, p. 53).

It must be acknowledged that convergence theory did not forecast the disintegration of the Soviet Union, and that disintegration can justifiably be considered an indication of the theory's shortcomings. But if Russia and perhaps several other of the more important republics of the former Soviet Union, such as the Ukraine, do ultimately emerge as states much more like the United States, economically and politically, than the Soviet Union ever was, convergence theory could still be vindicated on a fundamental level.

The hope and belief that this may occur does not necessarily flow from a conviction that the United States is the political ideal toward which all states look for guidance. The notion of convergence, as it applies to the Soviet Union vis-à-vis the United States (and also to the former individual Soviet republics vis-à-vis the United States), suggests movement by all the countries involved toward some middle ground. Recent dramatic movement by the former Soviet Union, and now by Russia and some other republics in the direction of political and economic processes more like those in the United States, as well as statements like Brzezinski's regarding "one-sided conversion" and Schlesinger's that "the market won the economic argument," obscure the extent to which the United States (and all other Western industrialized societies) have been moving in the direction of "socialism" for many decades.

Since the 1930s, though, it has become increasingly difficult to argue that the economy of the United States is based on a purely "private enterprise" system. Large industrial firms are not really operated by their owners, the stockholders. Those in charge of day-to-day decisions are hired managers (Burnham, 1960), and these managers must deal with federal government regulators and planners at every turn.

The federal government, for example, mandates that all large firms engaged in interstate commerce pay a minimum wage. Through civil rights laws, the federal government has an important impact on hiring, promotion, and firing policies. Environmental protection laws and consumer protection regulators give federal administrators additional tools to control ostensibly "free" enterprises. The federal government orders automakers in Detroit, for example, to put safety belts and catalytic converters in cars, and to design their automobiles to meet guidelines for gasoline consumption.

In addition, for every full-time employee they hire, large industrial firms in the United States must contribute to federal government funds for unemployment compensation, workers' compensation, and Social Security. If a large and important corporation, such as the Chrysler Corporation or a major savings and loan institution, is threatened with bankruptcy, the federal government will bail it out.

There was much political rhetoric in the 1980s in the United States about the virtues of the free market, along with promises to get the government "off people's backs." But the cutbacks during the Reagan and Bush administrations had only a minimal impact on most of the programs developed under Lyndon Johnson's "Great Society" and "War on Poverty." The Social Security budget (and Social Security taxes), not to mention the Medicare and the Medicaid programs, increased dramatically under the Reagan administration. President Reagan came into office promising to abolish the U.S. Department of Energy and the U.S. Department of Education. He did not actually abolish any cabinet-level department; instead he created a new one, for veterans' affairs. In 1986, after the "Reagan Revolution" had been fully implemented, public expenditures on health and education were higher in the free-enterprise-oriented United States than they were in the socialistic Soviet Union, not only in absolute amounts (which is not surprising, perhaps, since the U.S. GNP was at least twice the Soviet GNP at that point) but also in terms of the *proportion* of the two countries' respective GNPs devoted to those purposes (Sivard, 1989, p. 47).

In short, convergence theory is not based on the ethnocentric notion that the United States is the political norm toward which states everywhere are leaning. On the contrary, it suggests that the political and economic systems of *all* the most dominant and important states in the world will, over time, become more similar to *one another*. This change will occur not only because autocratic countries like the republics of the former Soviet Union and the states of Eastern Europe will become more democratic but also because capitalistic countries like the United States will (and have for decades already) become more socialistic. This notion (and it may well be that it is not sufficiently elaborate or specific to deserve the label "theory") does not necessarily suggest that all the countries of the world are fated to follow an economic and political trail of development blazed by the United States. Rather, it suggests that despite their great cultural and historical differences, most people in most countries of the world have similar needs for adequate food, shelter, and health care. Most governments of the world strive to meet those needs, for altruistic reasons and/or to keep themselves in power and/or to make their states more advanced, more powerful, and more influential. These governments, with essentially similar goals, therefore observe one another closely to see which methods, processes, and policies achieve those goals most successfully. The most successful methods, processes, and policies will attract the most emulation, and the political and economic structures, especially in those states where the greatest proportion of people have enough food, decent housing, and health care, will become increasingly similar.

That, at least, is the "theory," and the end of the Cold War (so far, at least) constitutes substantial evidence in its favor. However, there are also substantial grounds for pessimism regarding problems associated with the end of the Cold War. Let us review some of the most pressing of these.

Nuclear Weapons and the Future

From 1945 until 1993, the United States deployed about 70,000 nuclear warheads, while the Soviet Union made about 55,000. Currently, although their stockpiles of such weapons are much reduced, the United States in 1995 still deployed around 8,000 warheads, while the Russians still had around 7,235 such nuclear weapons (Sublette, 1996, pp. 1–2; Stockholm International Peace Research Institute, 1996, p. 634). Fortunately, "Russia has signed reciprocal agreements with the United States, the United Kingdom and China stating that they will not target their missiles at each other while they are on normal alert status" (Lepingwell, 1995, p. 68).[14]

Although it is certainly fortunate that the two vast arsenals of the United States and the Soviet Union are no longer deployed in a tightly organized fashion, ready to initiate what would surely have been the most lethal war in history, the disintegration of the Soviet Union did create new dangers. "The collapse of the Soviet Union left Soviet strategic forces scattered across the newly independent states. Missile

---

[14] Lepingwell goes on to note, though, that "the missiles could be retargetted quickly in a crisis" (Lepingwell, 1995, p. 68).

and bomber bases were distributed across Russia, Ukraine, Belarus, and Kazakhstan . . ." (Lepingwell, 1995, p. 65). The good news is that "Belarus, Kazakhstan, and Ukraine have transferred to Russia all the strategic and tactical nuclear warheads they inherited following the collapse of the Soviet Union" (Spector, McDonough, Webb, and Koblentz, 1997, p. 1). The bad news is that continued reform in Russia toward democracy is not assured. It is not at all inconceivable that ultranationalist, Communist, or fascist leaders could take over in Russia and return control of massive nuclear power to intensely antagonistic hands. It is also frighteningly possible that the painful and bloody disintegration of Yugoslavia might be duplicated in the former Soviet Union.

As the discussion of ethnic groups in Chapter 3 showed, the boundaries of the republics of the former Soviet Union do not divide the major ethnic groups there into neat geographic categories. "Indeed, not a single non-Russian nation in the [former] Soviet Union is without a significant intermingling of Russian or some other ethnic minority" (Brzezinski, 1989/90, p. 8). A gloomy but not unrealistic prediction would be that some ultranationalist leader reminiscent of Slobodan Milosevic (such as Vladimir Zhirinovsky) will come to power in Russia and try to establish a "Greater Russia" in the former Soviet Union along the lines of the Greater Serbia to which Milosevic aspired (and perhaps still does) in the former Yugoslavia. (See the map on page 325.)

That makes it especially fortunate that in January 1993 President Bush and President Yeltsin signed the Strategic Arms Reduction Talks, or **START II Treaty,** which bans all land-based **multiple independently targetable reentry vehicles (MIRVs)** and commits both parties to make phased reductions in their strategic nuclear forces, bringing to a culmination a drastic post–Cold War reduction in nuclear weapons on both sides, depicted in Figure 9.3.

After a rather prolonged debate, the U.S. Senate ratified START II in January 1996. As of this writing, the Russian Duma has still not ratified the treaty. If START II is ratified, both the United States and Russia will have reduced the number of warheads they deploy by about two-thirds since 1990.

Whether or not the Russian Duma ratifies START II is of immediate and substantial importance. But even more important in the long run to the future of U.S.-Russian relations (and of their still formidable nuclear arsenals) is the fate of democratic reform both in Russia and in the other former republics of the Soviet Union. From 1991 to 1995, Russia's GDP fell by 35 percent (*World Press Review*, February 1997, p. 23). Understandably, then, "in the new Russia, freedom has led to disappointment. . . . The poverty rate is soaring. Life expectancy for men is plunging. The murder rate is twice as high as it is in the United States and many times

The Former Soviet Union

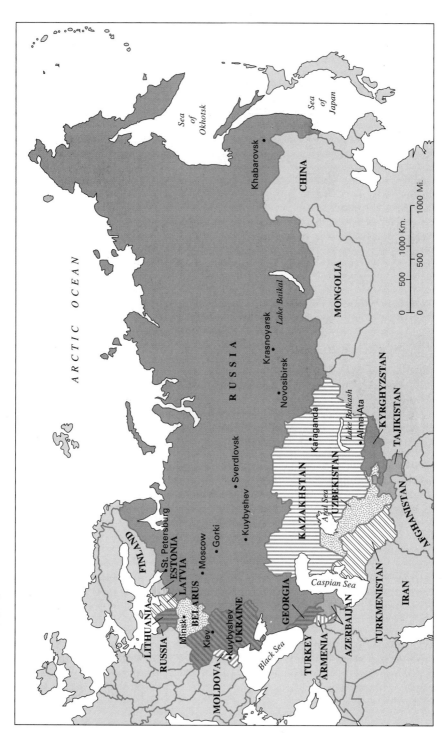

In the wake of the failed coup by hardliners in the Soviet
Union in August 1991, Boris Yeltsin here waves the new
Russian flag in front of the Russian Parliament building.
Yeltsin is still the leader of Russia. The ultimate fate of
reforms there is uncertain. SOURCE: Epix/Sygma.

higher than in European capitals to the west" (Remnick, 1997, pp. 35,
37). The Russians have no democratic traditions and history, and perhaps they never will.

But Russia did have a reasonably democratic election in 1996, won
by Boris Yeltsin. Gregory Yavlinsky (1997, p. 3), a member of the
Russian Duma (as well as a candidate for president of Russia in 1996),
asserts that "Russia's 1996 presidential election represents a tremendous success in the country's historical development. . . . We did hold

Figure 9.3   Reductions in U.S. and Soviet/Russian Strategic Nuclear Forces Mandated by START II

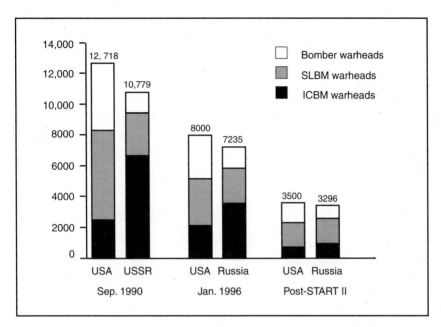

orderly presidential balloting, the first election of any kind for a head of state since 1613."[15] There are substantial bases for optimism about the future of democracy in Russia. It "is an increasingly urban nation, with a literacy rate of 99 percent. Nearly 80 percent of the Russian economy is in private hands. Inflation . . . dropped from a runaway 2,500 percent in 1992 to 130 percent in 1995" (Remnick, 1997, p. 48). At least some knowledgeable observers feel that "democratic values are beginning to take root in postcommunist Russia" (Shevtsova and Bruckner, 1997, p. 25).

In a possibly (but not necessarily) related transformation, Russia's "citizens show every indication of refusing to return to the maximal-ism of communism or the xenophobia of hardline nationalism" (Rem-

---

[15] Yavlinsky (1997, p. 3) goes on to explain that "Yeltsin's election in 1991 does not count, since he was chosen head of the Russian Republic of the old Soviet Union, and not of an independent Russian Federation, which did not yet exist."

nick, 1997, p. 48). One indication of this is the cautious manner in which post–Cold War Russia has dealt with many of its foreign policy problems. Many expected that Russia might, after 1991, pursue with troublesome zeal such revisionist goals as recovering Crimea from the Ukraine, absorbing Russian territories from northern Kazakhstan or eastern Ukraine, and acquiring some sort of protectorate authority over Russian minorities in Estonia. But *"every single one of these issues is less charged, and less urgent than it was five years ago"* (Sestanovich, 1996, p. 12; emphasis in the original). Neither the future of domestic politics in Russia nor the future course of its foreign policies is easy to predict, and disasters (from the democratic or the Western point of view) are easy to envision. But those disasters are not inevitable.

The Threat of Proliferation of Weapons of Mass Destruction

Even if Russia and the other republics of the former Soviet Union develop into peace-loving democratic states, the world will not be safe from the threat of nuclear weapons. Nations other than the United States or Russia (or Great Britain, France, and China, which have each had nuclear weapons for decades now) might acquire nuclear weapons, and perhaps the threat that these new owners of nuclear weapons will actually use them may be greater than that which existed during the Cold War. This danger is typically referred to as the threat posed by **nuclear proliferation,** or the spread of nuclear weapons beyond the five major powers that developed nuclear weapons during the 1940s, 1950s, and 1960s. "International concern about nuclear proliferation has rapidly increased since the end of the Cold War. A recent survey found that Americans believe that the nuclear danger facing them is actually worse now than during the Cold War itself" (Karl, 1996/97, p. 87). One reason for this is that former Soviet republics such as Ukraine, Belarus, and Kazakhstan possess weapons-grade nuclear materials, and little capacity for controlling their distribution; in addition, "desperate economic conditions in these countries provide considerable incentive for individuals, laboratories or factories to profit by exporting nuclear materials and technology" (Deutsch, 1992, p. 129). In short, "weapons grade uranium and plutonium are still beyond the reach of most proliferants and terrorists, but the disintegration of the Soviet Union made accessing these materials and sophisticated nuclear know-how far easier than in the past" (Sopko, 1996/97, p. 10).

The Dangers (and the Benefits?) of Nuclear Proliferation

Even during the Cold War, the Soviet Union and the United States cooperated in an effort to prevent other states from acquiring nuclear weapons. They helped draft a treaty on the nonproliferation of such weapons in the late 1960s that went into effect in 1970. The hope that the **Nuclear Nonproliferation Treaty (NPT)** would restrict the nuclear club to a membership of five (that is, China, France, Great Britain, the Soviet Union, and the United States) was crushed in May 1974 when India exploded a "peaceful" nuclear device. Since that time, though, no nation has made its acquisition of weapons obvious with a test or an announcement. "An observer who suggested in 1990 that, by the end of 1995, 183 states would be parties to the NPT, and that the treaty would be made permanent without formal opposition would have been accused of gross over-optimism. Yet that situation now exists" (Stockholm International Peace Research Institute, 1996, p. 587). And there have been several more specific, possibly significant successes in the antinuclear proliferation effort in recent years. In the early 1990s, South Africa dismantled an arsenal of six nuclear weapons and signed the NPT in 1991. Belarus, Kazakhstan, and Ukraine have not only, as already noted, transferred to Russia all the strategic and nuclear warheads they inherited as a result of the collapse of the Soviet Union; they have also joined the NPT and opened their nuclear facilities to inspection by the **International Atomic Energy Agency (IAEA).** Argentina and Brazil have brought into force a nuclear-free zone in that part of the world through the Treaty of Tlatelolco, and have also accepted IAEA inspections. Algeria agreed to join the NPT in 1995. And North Korea "agreed to freeze and ultimately dismantle its nuclear weapon program under the October 1994 U.S.-North Korean Framework Agreement" (Spector, McDonough, Webb, and Koblentz, 1997, p. 2).[16]

But several states have apparently taken various steps toward acquiring the ability to produce nuclear weapons. Israel almost certainly has around a hundred; and India is estimated to have more than sixty, which in part explains why Pakistan, an enemy of India in three wars since 1948, probably has around fifteen to twenty-five nuclear weapons (Spector, McDonough, Webb, and Koblentz, 1997, p. 1). Since the Persian Gulf War in 1991, "the world knows that even though Iraq signed the NPT it managed to mount a massive covert program to acquire nuclear and other weapons of mass destruction. . . . The Iraqi program involved

---

[16] Spector et al. (1997, p. 2) go on to note, though, that before that agreement had been formalized, North Korea may have "separated enough weapon-grade material for a nuclear device."

more than 10,000 qualified technical people who remain in place as a competent cadre" (Deutsch, 1992, pp. 120, 126). Iran and Libya are all believed by various specialists in the field of proliferation to be taking steps toward the acquisition of nuclear weapons capability (Carney, Hornik, Peterzell, and Shannon, 1993; Deutsch, 1992; Spector et al., 1997).

Could the spread of nuclear weapons be good news? It has been argued for some time now that nuclear proliferation in the Middle East has the potential to bring stability to that volatile region (Rosen, 1977; Feldman, 1981a, 1981b). Additional well-known figures in the field have asserted in more general terms that "proliferation may serve the global desire for peace" (Bueno de Mesquita and Riker, 1982, p. 299), and that "the spread of nuclear weapons is something that we have worried too much about and tried too hard to stop . . . the measured spread of nuclear weapons is more to be welcomed than feared" (Waltz, 1982, pp. 29–30). The end of the Cold War has evoked an argument to the effect that stability in Europe would be enhanced if Germany acquired nuclear weapons (Mearsheimer, 1990, pp. 6–7). The same author has argued that the cause of peace would be served if the Ukraine developed nuclear weapons (as a deterrent against Russia; Mearsheimer, 1993). Other analysts argue that India and Pakistan have been particularly likely to use their nuclear weapons against each other,[17] and yet, despite ongoing tensions over Kashmir, India and Pakistan have not fought any kind of war since 1971 (when India became embroiled in the civil war that resulted in the dissolution of Pakistan and the creation of Bangladesh), and have of course never engaged in nuclear conflict. Another proliferation "optimist" argues that "the leaders of medium and small powers alike tend to be extremely cautious with regard to the nuclear weapons they possess . . . the proof being that, to date, in *every* region where these weapons have been introduced, large-scale interstate warfare has disappeared" (van Creveld, 1993, p. 124; emphasis in the original).

One main objection to optimism about the impact of nuclear proliferation in the developing countries involves the vulnerable nature of nascent nuclear forces. One of the possible virtues of the large nuclear forces in the hands of the Soviet Union and the United States was that they made both states relatively safe from the destabilizing impact of technological breakthroughs (Intriligator and Brito, 1984, p. 63). Even without such breakthroughs, emerging nuclear forces in the developing world will be vulnerable to preemptive strikes, and so they will tempt

---

[17] "Because of a surfeit of powerful and interlocking factors that are at work in pushing India and Pakistan toward military conflict, one would intuitively expect that the subcontinent is a 'least likely' case for peaceful proliferation outcomes" (Karl, 1996/97, p. 102).

such strikes. "Even if both sides prefer not to preempt, each may fear that the other side will; consequently, both may decide to launch at the first (perhaps fake) indication of an attack" (Fetter, 1991, p. 29). In other words, "prisoners' dilemmas" are likely to arise.

A technologically advanced state like Germany might be able to avoid, or minimize, this problem. But there are certainly reasons for skepticism that a Germany with nuclear weapons would be good for the stability of Europe. One writer argues that "a . . . Germany going nuclear is guaranteed to provoke the worst nightmares amongst its neighbors" (Risse-Kappen, 1990/91, p. 219). Others insist that Germany shows no signs of a desire to acquire nuclear weapons, and that its neighbors will not "tolerate a nuclear Reich" (Hoffmann, 1990, p. 192).

Nuclear proliferation "optimists" do point out, in response to the argument that new nuclear arsenals in developing countries will be particularly vulnerable to preemptive strikes (and therefore, perhaps, particularly likely to evoke such strikes) that "unless counter-force attacks [that is, attacks against other weapons, such as nuclear missiles] are executed with improbable accuracy and effectiveness—all the more improbable in view of the rudimentary intelligence capabilities possessed by new proliferators—they are impossible using the sparse arsenals that emerging nuclear states are likely to deploy against each other" (Karl, 1996/97, p. 105). In fact, considering the initial implausibility of the argument that the spread of such awful weapons as nuclear bombs would be a good thing, it might well be fair to acknowledge that proliferation "optimists" make a convincing case. As even one prominent proliferation "pessimist" admits, "Nuclear weapons may well have made *deliberate* nuclear war less likely" (Sagan, 1994, p. 516).

But on the other hand, even some prominent "optimists" are inclined to admit that "pessimists are correct to point out that the exigencies of crisis can transform the character of nuclear operations, increasing the possibilities of accidents" (Karl, 1996/97, p. 113). A recent, careful, logical, and formal mathematical analysis of the proliferation problem concludes that "even if the risk of a deliberate nuclear war is reduced as a result of deterrence, the risk of a nuclear war due to accidents, irrationality, or political instability is likely to be the dominant effect of proliferation" (Brito and Intriligator, 1996, p. 212).

In the end, perhaps it is most important to point out that the costs of guessing wrong on this issue are not equal in both directions. If nuclear proliferation is discouraged when actually it is beneficial, the cost is the loss of a boost to stability and a somewhat larger probability of conventional wars. If proliferation is encouraged when it is actually dangerous (even if it makes war a less *rational* option), then tolerating or encouraging proliferation would be experimentation in the absence of any solid evidence on which to base estimates of the results.

Beyond Nuclear Weapons:
Ballistic Missiles, Chemical Weapons, and
Biological Weapons

Even if nuclear weapons can be kept under control, the post–Cold War world promises to be a dangerous place because of the rapid spread of ballistic missiles and the potential diffusion of chemical and biological weapons. Some twenty-five countries, most in the developing world, have acquired or attempted to acquire ballistic missiles. Nine of them are in the Middle East, but India and Pakistan, North and South Korea, Brazil and Argentina, Taiwan, and South Africa either have or have tried to get ballistic missiles (Fetter, 1991, p. 5).

The horrors of nuclear weapons are relatively well publicized. Chemical weapons are less familiar. They produced some 100,000 fatalities and over 1 million casualties in the First World War, but they were not used in the Second World War, probably because both sides had them, and thus deterred each other from using them. This potential deterrent capability provides an obvious incentive for acquiring them today.

Chemical weapons such as phosgene (a choking agent) or nerve agents (which induce nausea, coma, convulsion, and death) are estimated to be capable, if attached to ballistic missiles, of killing forty to seven hundred times as many people as missiles equipped with conventional weapons (Fetter, 1991, p. 11).

Biological weapons are even more lethal. Ballistic missiles might be equipped with "bombs," for example, that could spread anthrax bacteria. Anthrax can kill within a matter of days. Vaccines must be administered before infection to be effective. Antibiotic treatments are of uncertain effectiveness. In short, anthrax delivered by ballistic missiles could be as lethal as at least small nuclear weapons (Fetter, 1991, p. 23).

But, "especially with a chemical or biological device, a crude dispersal system may be enough to kill thousands and cripple a major metropolitan area" (Sopko, 1996/97, p. 8). Terrorism on a large scale has been rare in the United States, but the bombing of the World Trade Center in New York City in 1993 and of the Alfred P. Murrah federal building in Oklahoma City in 1995 may have marked the beginning of a new era. Six people were killed and a thousand injured in the World Trade Center bombing. One hundred and sixty-eight people died and five hundred were wounded in Oklahoma City. The incident in New York City could have been much worse had the chemical weapon been delivered not in a common truck but in some technologically sophisticated ballistic missile. "The bombing of [the] World Trade Center . . . was meant to topple the city's tallest tower onto its twin, amid a cloud of cyanide gas. Had the attack gone as planned, tens of thousands of Americans would have died" (Mylroie, 1995/96, p. 3). A dozen Islamic fundamentalists, each of whom had come to the United States from Middle Eastern countries, were ultimately tried and convicted for this attack.

In March 1995, Aum Shinrikyo, a Japanese Buddhist sect, attempted to murder tens of thousands of people by placing eleven sarin-filled bags wrapped in newspapers on five subway trains. Twelve people were killed and more than five thousand hospitalized. And in 1993, a U.S. federal agency estimated that "a crop duster carrying a mere 100 kilograms of anthrax spores could deliver a fatal dose to up to 3 million residents of the Washington D.C. metropolitan area" (Sopko, 1996/97, pp. 8, 12).

Why would nations want to acquire chemical or biological weapons? They are much more lethal than conventional weapons, they have nearly the military effectiveness of small nuclear weapons, but they are cheaper and easier to acquire than nuclear weapons. They are "a poor man's nuclear weapon."

The incidents just mentioned, in New York City, Oklahoma City, and Tokyo, suggest "a trend toward nonstate actors becoming proliferation threats" (Sopko, 1996/97, p. 6). Still, as the director of the U.S. Arms Control and Disarmament Agency has noted, "At least 20 countries—many hostile to us—have or seek chemical weapons" (Holum, 1997, p. 3). Although the threat from nonstate organizations (to which more attention is devoted in Chapter 13) is quite ominous, the more orthodox international threat posed by states armed with chemical or biological weapons is not to be dismissed lightly. In January 1993, a **Chemical Weapons Convention (CWC),** which aims for the destruction of all chemical weapons by the year 2003, was opened for signing; and by early 1997, 160 nations had signed it. For some time the United States was *not* among those countries. However, shortly before the deadline in April 1997, at which time the convention would have gone into effect whether or not the United States had agreed to it, the U.S. Senate did agree to ratify it. According to the U.S. Director of Arms Control and Disarmament Agency (ACDA), the CWC will "give us more information about these threats—not least by short notice inspections of suspect sites, public or private—and will make the information actionable, because even possession of chemical weapons will be illegal, whereas it is entirely permissible [otherwise]" (Holum, 1997, p. 3). There is also a **Biological Weapons Convention (BWC)** dating from 1972. Most countries have signed it, but "it is virtually toothless in terms of ensuring compliance" (Holum, 1997, p. 3). It is clear that though the end of the Cold War has eliminated the threat of a truly massive nuclear war, at least for the time being, it has not delivered the world from the menace posed by nuclear weapons, ballistic missiles, and chemical or biological weapons. For the foreseeable future, a growing list of both state and nonstate organizations will continue to threaten their enemies with a deadly combination of nuclear, chemical, and biological weapons of mass destruction.

NEW THREATS IN THE POST–COLD WAR WORLD: FUNDAMENTALIST ISLAM AND CHINA?

This chapter began with the observation that the Cold War and its ending have had an impact reminiscent of that produced by the two world wars of this century. An empire has fallen apart, many nations have been politically transformed, and a major ideology has apparently been discredited. This analogy may have ominous implications for the post–Cold War world. After the First World War, the coalition that emerged victorious soon fell apart. The United States refused to join the League of Nations. Britain and France fell to quarreling about the treatment of Germany. And ultimately, of course, within a brief twenty years the Second World War occurred.

After the Second World War, too, the victorious coalition could not be maintained very long. The two most important members of that coalition, the United States and the Soviet Union, confronted each other in the Cold War.

The Cold War never became a hot war, but it was nevertheless a tense, conflict-ridden confrontation. In the wake of the Cold War, the major powers are free of serious conflicts with each other to a degree that is unusual, if not unprecedented. The extent to which they cooperated with each other against Iraq in the Persian Gulf War (even though China merely abstained on the crucial votes in the U.N.'s Security Council) may be the most significant indication of that high level of unity. But the fate of the winning coalitions that emerged from the First and Second World Wars must make us wonder about the stability of the coalition that has emerged from the Cold War.

Islam: The Green Peril?

Although the possible replacement of Boris Yeltsin by an antidemocratic, anti-Western, ultranationalist, or even fascist leader in Russia may constitute the more likely route to a dangerous confrontation reminiscent of the Cold War, some analysts believe that there is an entirely new threat on the horizon. In this view, Islam is a threat reminiscent of the Red Menace of the Cold War era; "**the Green Peril**— green being the color of Islam—is a cancer spreading around the globe"

(Hadar, 1993, pp. 27–28). In 1996, a *New York Times* story pointed out that "the end of the cold war has sparked a kind of intellectual contest to identify the biggest and most credible new enemy. . . . One threat has resonated in the public mind: Islamic holy war." The story goes on to point out that in 1995 the secretary general of the North Atlantic Treaty Organization (NATO) declared that "Islamic fundamentalism is at least as dangerous as Communism was," and that the Speaker of the House of Representatives, Newt Gingrich, helped to persuade Congress to approve $20 million in covert aid to moderate the behavior of the Islamic fundamentalist regime in Iran by warning about "totalitarian Islam" (Sciolino, 1996, pp. 1, 6). And Samuel Huntington, in developing his well-known thesis about "The Clash of Civilizations" in contemporary global politics, argues that "conflict along the fault line between Western and Islamic civilizations has been going on for 1,300 years. . . . This centuries-old military interaction between [the] West and Islam is unlikely to decline. It could become more virulent" (Huntington, 1993, pp. 31–32).

The threat of fundamentalist Islam is certainly not entirely fanciful. There are about 900 million Muslims in some forty-four Islamic countries, extending from Senegal on the west coast of Africa to Indonesia in the Far East (Esposito, 1991, p. 3). (See the map on page 337.) In addition, there are certainly important strains of thought within Islam that are opposed to democracy and to human rights as perceived by most democratic countries.[18] It is also true that "powerful Islamic movements have sprung up to emulate Ayatollah Ruhollah Khomeini's victory in Iran as they challenge Western allies in Algeria, Egypt, Kuwait, Bahrain, Pakistan" (Sciolino, 1996, p. 1). Iran, the site of a successful revolutionary Islamic government, is commonly seen as the leader of this Islamic threat. Teheran's goals, allegedly, are to establish anti-Western regimes from North Africa east to the Persian Gulf, and on into Central Asia. Iran, in this view, aims to control the oil-rich Persian Gulf area, destroy Israel, and begin to expand the influence of militant Islam into the Horn of Africa, southern Europe, the Balkans, and the Indian subcontinent (Hadar, 1993, p. 29). And the bombing of the World Trade Center exemplified this threat in an all-too-concrete form for Americans. When Sheik Omar Abdel Rahman was sentenced to life imprisonment for his part in the conspiracy aimed at killing thousands of people in the World Trade Center, "he portrayed his prosecution as part of a new cold war against Islam" (Sciolino, 1996, p. 1).

---

[18] "Those who believe in universal human rights (and women's rights in particular), democratic government, political tolerance, and pluralism and in peace between the Arabs and Israelis cannot be complacent about the growing strength of militant Islamic movements in most Middle Eastern countries" (Miller, 1993, p. 45).

Islamic fundamentalists, like these pictured above in a mosque in Algeria, have become an important political force in most Middle Eastern countries. SOURCE: Pascal Parrot/Sygma.

But the **Iranian revolution** at the heart of Islamic fundamentalism, and the inspiration for its expansionist goals, has come upon hard times. During the seventeen years since the fundamentalists came to power, the population of Iran has doubled to about 64 million people, while its oil income has decreased by two-thirds. As a result, "the vast majority of Iranians are much worse off after 17 years of theocratic rule than they were during the shah's era. . . . The revolution is imploding" (Wright, 1996, pp. 161–163). And although there are, as noted above, about 900 million Muslims in the world, they are not all militant by any means, and they are spread out among dozens of countries across a wide geographic area. In addition, Islamic fundamentalism is not an ideology with global aspirations. "Unlike communism, Islamic fundamentalism confines its aspirations to one portion of the world—the Muslim world. . . . Communism sought . . . world domination. Islamic fundamentalism does not and never will" (Karabell, 1996/97, p. 80). In short, militant Islam is probably too dispersed and too geographically limited in its aims to constitute in and of itself a serious threat to the United States,

Islamic Populations of the World

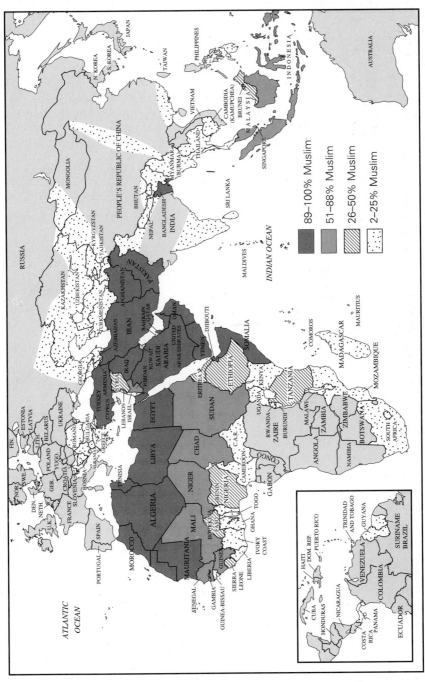

SOURCE: Based on John L. Esposito, *Islam: The Straight Path* (Expanded Edition). New York: Oxford University Press, 1991, p. 2.

Western Europe, Japan, and the rest of the democratic countries of the world.

Radical Islam might, however, coalesce with other antidemocratic, and anti-Western forces of truly impressive proportions. China might form the core of this antidemocratic coalition. And there are already some signs that this coalition is beginning to emerge. Saudi Arabia has purchased ballistic missiles with a range of 3,500 kilometers from China. China and North Korea have supplied nuclear technology, with possibly weapon-relevant implications to such countries as Iran, Libya, and Algeria, as well as Pakistan. As Samuel Huntington (1993, p. 47), has pointed out, "A Confucian-Islamic military connection has thus come into being, designed to promote acquisition by its members of the weapons and weapons technologies needed to counter the military power of the West."

China and the Future of International Politics

It is interesting to note, in consideration of the future impact of China in the international political system, the **power transition theory** of A. F. K. Organski, namely, that "a large power discrepancy between the dominant nation and the rest of the nations below it ensures the security of the leader and the stability of the [international] order as a whole" (Organski, 1968, p. 365). Conversely, Organski (1968, p. 370) feels that "war is most likely when the power of the dissatisfied challenger and its allies begins to approximate the power of those who support the status quo."[19] Writing in 1968, Organski concluded that the Soviet Union was unlikely to surpass the United States in the coming decades. But, he then declared,

> China is another story. . . . The question is not whether China will become the most powerful nation on earth, but rather how long it will take her to achieve this status. . . . [T]he United States will retain world leadership for at least the remainder of the twentieth century, perhaps even for a longer time, but the position will eventually pass to China (Organski, 1968, p. 486).

---

[19] Although Organski limits the scope of his theory to the modern industrial age, Woosang Kim (1992, pp. 153–172) reports that data covering the years from 1648 to 1815 also suggest that "when the challenging great power . . . catches up with the dominant power, great power war is most likely." The basic idea that power shifts of this type are a cause of war has a long history, going back to Thucydides (republished in 1954) and V. I. Lenin (1917, reprinted in 1939).

Figure 9.4 China's Rapidly Growing Economy

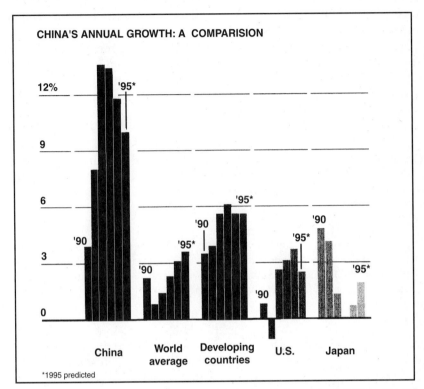

CHINA'S ANNUAL GROWTH: A COMPARISION

SOURCE: From *The New York Times,* February 18, 1996, p. 26. Copyright © 1996 by The New York Times Company. Reprinted by permission.

Keeping this prediction in mind, one might note with interest and perhaps a little trepidation some recent calculations that China's economy is already the second largest in the world in terms of its GDP (see Table 6.2 on page 201). And China, with about 1.2 billion people, has by far the largest population of any state in the world. It is also almost universally agreed that China's economy is growing extraordinarily rapidly (see Figure 9.4).

No wonder, then, that in March 1996 the cover story of *World Press Review* focused on "China: Awakening to a New Age" and that this cover story was followed by another in June 1997 entitled "Can't We Just Get Along: Global Fears of a New Cold War." (The story focused on the burgeoning threat from China and the possibility of a new "axis" forming between China and Russia.) In the same vein, a cover story in the *New York Times Magazine* in 1996 announced that "The Twentieth

Century Starts Here: China Booms. The World Holds Its Breath" (Buruma, Faison, and Zakaria, 1996), and the featured article in the March/April 1997 issue of the influential quarterly *Foreign Affairs* focused on "The China Threat" (Bernstein and Munro, 1997; Robert S. Ross, 1997). China's economic potential is not confined to its current boundaries. It officially took control of Hong Kong in July 1997. It might ultimately unite with the "Republic of China" on Taiwan. And Chinese emigrants, many already economically quite successful, are spread in great numbers throughout much of Asia.

As discussed in Chapter 6, the size of a nation's economy is widely conceded to be a key indicator of its political power and influence. But China is not content (as, for instance, Japan has been) to rely entirely on economic success to bolster its power. It is investing in its military might.

> China's real annual defense budget amounts to a minimum of $87 billion per year, roughly one-third that of the United States and 75 percent more than Japan's. Moreover, the figure was 11.3 percent higher in 1996 than in 1995, and 14.6 percent higher in 1995 than in 1994. . . . China is now engaged in one of the most extensive and rapid military buildups in the world (Bernstein and Munro, 1997, p. 25).

In short, it is easy to conjure up an ominous scenario. According to at least one theoretical notion, the global political system is destabilized when the dominant nation is challenged by a growing, dissatisfied power. "The major wars of recent history have all been wars involving the biggest power in the world and its allies against a challenger . . . who had recently risen to power thanks to industrialization. One could almost say that the rise of such a challenger guarantees a major war" (Organski, 1968, p. 361).[20] A recent update of this power transition theory points out first that the theory's credibility is enhanced because it can account for the peaceful outcome of the Cold War, since "the Soviets did not overtake the United States during their stage of transitional growth in power." This same analyst also presents data indicating that "recent Chinese growth rates are very impressive, and suggest that a potential transition to parity between the People's Republic and the United States within the next few decades is possible" (Lemke, 1997, pp. 28, 30) (see Figure 9.5).

In short, at some point in the twenty-first century, China (and its allies) might be in a position to pose a serious challenge to the United States (and its allies).

China's economy is still relatively underdeveloped. It has a long way to go before it becomes a truly modern, technologically advanced soci-

---

[20] See also Organski and Kugler (1980).

Figure 9.5   Trends in U.S. and People's Republic of China GDPs (Trillions of Purchasing Power Parity Dollars, 1980–2010

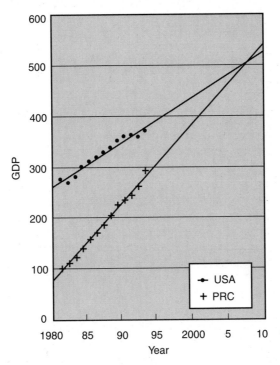

SOURCE: Reprinted by permission of Sage Publications Ltd. from Douglas Lemke (1997), "The Continuation of History," *Journal of Peace Research,* Vol. 31 (1), p. 31. Copyright © 1997.

ety. But even if China's economy does keep growing, and it does eventually become powerful enough to challenge the United States, there is reason to hope that this need not necessarily be destabilizing for the global political system, especially if China were to become a democratic state in the meantime. Historically, uneven rates of growth and power shifts between the most powerful states in the system often appear to have been associated with major wars between dominant states and their challengers. But some evidence suggests that "democratic states have not gone to war against one another, [even] though they have experienced power shifts" (Schweller, 1992, p. 268). In fact, "only nondemocratic regimes wage preventive wars against rising opponents" (Schweller, 1992, p. 238). Power transition theory also suggests that only "dissatisfied" rising challengers will come into conflict with leading or hegemonic states. Presumably, from the point of view of power transition theory, if China were to become democratic in the near future, it would become more satisfied with the current structure of the international system, and so unlikely to become involved in serious, militarized conflict with the United States. However, available evidence also shows that although it is true that democratic leading states have not launched preventive wars against even undemocratic challengers, undemocratic challengers have often initiated a war against democratic leaders (Schweller, 1992, p. 257).

The Political Evolution of China

So the implications of a significant increase in the power of China in the next century depend crucially on its internal political evolution. At the time of writing, the Chinese government is firmly committed to **neoauthoritarianism,** the rationale for which depends to an important extent on the experiences of the Asian Tigers—Hong Kong, Singapore, South Korea, and Taiwan—in Southeast Asia. From the point of view of advocates of neoauthoritarianism, all four of those states achieved economic success under authoritarian governments. It was only *after* they achieved a relatively high level of economic development that South Korea and Taiwan, for example, began to move in the direction of democracy.

Current comparisons between the former Soviet Union and the People's Republic of China seem rather strongly to bolster this rationale for neoauthoritarianism. According to common perceptions, at any rate, Gorbachev in the Soviet Union and his successors first implemented political reform and only later tried to implement economic reforms. In China, political reforms are being postponed, and economic reforms have been given priority. The key point is that this strategy of economic reform first and political reform later (maybe) seems to be working very well, especially in contrast with what is happening in Russia and the other republics of the former Soviet Union.

Still, analysts of China's political future are divided in their opinions, both in their feelings about what is likely to happen and in their ideas about what the United States might do to influence that future. Some feel that China may well be headed for turmoil and perhaps even political disintegration, especially in the wake of the death of Deng Xiaoping in early 1997. In 1995, two years before Deng's death, one specialist predicted:

> China today faces a series of pressures stemming from population growth and the declining ability of agriculture and state-owned industries to expand employment. These pressures will soon bring economic and political conflicts to a boil. . . . We can expect a terminal crisis in China within the next 10 to 15 years (Goldstone, 1995, pp. 35, 43).

But in the same year another analyst predicted with some confidence that "China stands a reasonable chance of completing the inevitable economic and political transitions to modernity with peace and stability" (Huang, 1995, p. 56).

Bruce Bueno de Mesquita, the developer of the political forecasting model discussed in Chapter 4, and others have consulted several expert analysts in order to use that model to consider the evidence regarding China's future political evolution. Given the data produced by the observers Bueno de Mesquita et al. consulted, the model produces a fairly gloomy prediction about China's political fate after Deng dies. (This forecast was generated in 1996, before Deng's death.)

> Our model shows that [after Deng's death] economic reform will continue for the time being; however, there is likely to be a sudden and dramatic collapse of support for market reforms . . . the country becomes divided and . . . uncertainty will likely deal a serious blow to growth. . . . There will be political upheaval between central and regional powers (Bueno de Mesquita, Newman, and Rabushka, 1996, pp. 97–98).

In contrast, when analyst Henry Rowen addresses (1996, p. 61) the question of when China will become a democracy, his answer is a straightforward "around the year 2015," which, the reader might note, is right around the time that at least one projection (in Figure 9.5) suggests that the China will begin to approach the United States in terms of "power" as indicated by GDP. In the meantime, in the absence of war between democratic states, perhaps one should at least temper some of the pessimism that has surfaced in the wake of the end of the Cold War with the realization that "for the first time in history a small number of great democracies—the United States, Japan, Germany, France, Britain, and Italy . . . have most of the world's power" (Singer and Wildavsky, 1993, p. 4).[21]

SUMMARY

The Cold War confrontation between the United States and the Soviet Union was the most dangerous, pervasive but still peaceful international rivalry in world history. Throughout the Cold War, both sides continued to stockpile nuclear weapons well beyond the point where each had enough firepower to kill the other's citizens several times over.

---

[21] In the opinion of these authors, this means that the United States "will achieve [its] essential foreign policy goals—the long term protection of American freedom and peace—without doing anything, as long as most powerful nations continue to be democracies" (Singer and Wildavsky, 1993, p. 197).

These stockpiles of weapons, though, did protect both sides from the threat of a disarming first strike, which might have deprived them of their ability to retaliate. Fears about such a first strike were heightened on both sides by the fact that both the Americans and the Soviets invested so much in research and development, creating the danger that some technological breakthrough might make a successful first strike possible.

But the incredibly dangerous and expensive arms race between the United States and the Soviet Union has come to an end, without the global catastrophe that many argued it would ultimately bring. That is not an unprecedented outcome. Most arms races have not ended up in international war. In fact, determined American efforts to keep up or stay ahead of the Soviet Union in the arms race, particularly during the Reagan administration, are arguably responsible for bringing the Cold War to a successful conclusion from the American point of view.

Critics of this point of view assert that it was conciliatory policies that brought the Soviet Union down, rather than uncompromising opposition. Détente during the 1970s, for example, made possible the signing of the Helsinki Accords, which not only legitimized post–Second World War boundaries (something the Soviets wanted) but also set up a formal process of reviewing the human rights records of the Soviet Union and other Eastern European regimes. That played an important role, some argue, in delegitimizing all of those regimes. Other critics believe that it was the conciliatory policies of the later years of the Reagan administration rather than the hardline policies of its earlier period that helped make the transformation and the demise of the Soviet Union possible.

In contrast to those ideas, which stress the impact of external forces on the fate of the Soviet Union, another set of arguments emphasizes the effect of internal factors. The most common argument is that the Soviet Union's inefficient economic system brought it down. Another, seemingly contradictory, notion holds that dictatorship in the Soviet Union was ultimately subverted by advancing economic development, increased urbanization, and the ever higher educational levels attained by so many in Soviet society.

The most convincing theories about the fall of the Soviet Union take into account combinations of these factors. Economic development and increased education did make an increasing share of the Soviet population unwilling to accept the dictatorship of the Soviet Union, but economic failures by the 1980s in a new information, computer-oriented era also hastened its end. . But neither of these factors, perhaps, would have led to the demise of the Soviet Union and the end of the Cold War had it not been so obvious how poorly the country was faring compared to its more democratic and market-oriented counterparts in the international system.

It can be argued that the failure of most theories to predict the end of the Cold War indicates the poor quality of all theories in the field of international politics. It is true that "realist" theories stressing concrete, power-related factors and neglecting the role of ideas in international politics cannot explain the end of the Cold War even in retrospect. But theories that point out the peaceful nature of relationships between democratic states would forecast that if the autocratic contender in the Cold War becomes more democratic, antagonism between its major opponents should dissolve.

The end of the Cold War may herald the beginning of an era in which the former republics of the Soviet Union (and its former Communist allies in Eastern Europe) increasingly resemble Western, democratic industrialized states. This will occur not only because the former Communist states become more democratic and market oriented but also because the Western industrialized democracies will continue, according to convergence theory, to engage in the socialistic practices they have been adopting for decades.

The end of the Cold War has not liberated the world entirely from the dangers of nuclear weapons. Some theorists argue that, just as nuclear weapons created the basis for peace between the United States and the Soviet Union through more than forty conflict-ridden years, they can also stabilize tense relationships in the developing world, or in Europe (if Germany were to acquire nuclear weapons). Nuclear proliferation may have made intentional wars less likely, but at the same time may have increased the probability of accidents and unintentional escalation to nuclear conflict.

Many countries appear to be attempting to acquire ballistic missiles and alternative weapons of mass destruction, such as biological and chemical weapons. Biological and chemical weapons are cheaper and easier to acquire than nuclear weapons. Some progress in dealing with the dangers of these weapons has been made through the CWC and the BWC.

Even if the reform efforts of the former republics of the Soviet Union all succeed, the currently predominant coalition of democratic states in the international system may face threats in the future from fundamentalist Islam and/or from the People's Republic of China. China's economy is growing rapidly, and according to some recently revised methods of accounting, is already about half as large as that of the United States. Power transition theory, for example, suggests that the international system can fall into devastating conflicts like the two world wars of the twentieth century if the leading state in the system (like the United

States) is challenged by a rapidly rising power like China. But a close review of such transitions in the past suggests that they will remain peaceful if both the leading state and the challenger are democratic. So the future of post–Cold War international politics in the twenty-first century may depend crucially on the domestic political evolution of China and on whether or not it becomes a democratic state. Expert opinion on the probability that this will happen is divided.

KEY TERMS

Mikhail Gorbachev
Cold War
nuclear war
game theory
prisoners' dilemma
rationality
second strike capacity
technological developments
intercontinental ballistic missiles
 (ICBMs)
submarine-launched ballistic
 missiles (SLBMs)
Strategic Defense Initiative (SDI)
deterrence
reciprocal fears of surprise attack
peace through strength policies
Reagan Doctrine
Helsinki Accords
European Agreement on Security
 and Cooperation
Treaty on Intermediate-Range
 Nuclear Forces (INF)

information age
democratic peace proposition
convergent tendencies
convergence theory
START II Treaty
multiple independently targetable
 reentry vehicles (MIRVs)
nuclear proliferation
Nuclear Nonproliferation Treaty
 (NPT)
International Atomic Energy Agency
 (IAEA)
Chemical Weapons Convention
 (CWC)
Biological Weapons Convention
 (BWC)
The Green Peril
Iranian Revolution
power transition theory
neoauthoritarianism

SOURCES

"Bad, Worse, Worst." *World Press Review*, February 1997, p. 23.

Bernstein, Richard, and Ross H. Munro. "China I: The Coming Conflict with America," *Foreign Affairs*, 76 (March/April 1997), 18–32.

Bialer, Seweryn. "Gorbachev's Program of Change: Sources, Significance, Prospects." *Political Science Quarterly*, 103 (Fall 1988), 403–460.

Bialer, Seweryn. "The Harsh Decade: Soviet Policies in the 1980s." *Foreign Affairs*, 59 (Spring 1981), 799–1020.

Brito, Dagobert L., and Michael D. Intriligator. "Proliferation and the Probability of War." *Journal of Conflict Resolution*, 40 (March 1996), 206–214.

Brzezinski, Zbigniew. "The Cold War and Its Aftermath." *Foreign Affairs,* 71 (Fall 1992), 31–49.

Brzezinski, Zbigniew. "Post-Communist Nationalism." *Foreign Affairs,* 68 (Winter 1989–1990), 1–25.

Bueno de Mesquita, Bruce, David Newman, and Alvin Rabushka. *Red Flag over Hong Kong.* New Haven, Conn.: Yale University Press, 1996.

Bueno de Mesquita, Bruce, and William Riker. "An Assessment of the Merits of Selective Nuclear Proliferation." *Journal of Conflict Resolution,* 26 (June 1982), 287–306.

Bull, Hedley. "The Objectives of Arms Control." In Robert J. Art and Kenneth N. Waltz, eds. *The Use of Force.* Boston: Little, Brown, 1971.

Burnham, James. *The Managerial Revolution.* Bloomington, Ind.: Indiana University Press, 1960.

Buruma, Ian, Seth Faison, and Fareed Zakaria. "The 21st Century Starts Here. China Booms. The World Holds Its Breath." *New York Times Magazine,* February 18, 1996, pp. 28–44.

"Can't We Just Get Along: Global Fears of a New Cold War." *World Press Review,* June 1997, 6–11.

Cashman, Greg. *What Causes War?* San Francisco, Calif.: Jossey-Bass, 1993.

Carney, James, Richard Hornik, Jay Peterzell, and Elaine Shannon. "Fighting Off Doomsday." *Time,* June 21, 1993, pp. 37–38.

"China: Awakening to a New Age." *The World Press Review,* March 1996, pp. 8–11.

Creveld, Martin van. *Nuclear Proliferation and the Future of Conflict.* New York: Free Press, 1993.

Deudney, Daniel, and G. John Ikenberry. "The International Sources of Soviet Change." *International Security,* 16 (Winter 1991/92), 74–118.

Deudney, Daniel, and G. John Ikenberry. "Who Won the Cold War?" *Foreign Policy,* No. 87 (Summer 1992), 123–138.

Deutsch, John M. "The New Nuclear Threat." *Foreign Affairs,* 71 (Fall 1992), 120–137.

Diehl, Paul. "Arms Races to War: Testing Some Empirical Linkages." *Sociological Quarterly,* 26 (September 1985), 331–349.

Esposito, John L. *Islam: The Straight Path.* New York: Oxford University Press, 1991.

Feldman, Shai. "A Nuclear Middle East." *Survival,* 23 (May–June 1981a), 107–116.

Feldman, Shai. "Peacemaking in the Middle East: The Next Step." *Foreign Affairs,* 59 (Spring 1981b), 756–780.

Fetter, Steve. "Ballistic Missiles and Weapons of Mass Destruction." *International Security,* 16 (Summer 1991), 5–42.

Fukuyama, Francis. "The Modernizing Imperative." *The National Interest,* No. 31 (Spring 1993), 10–18.

Gaddis, John Lewis. "The Cold War, the Long Peace, and the Future." *Diplomatic History,* 16 (Spring 1992), 234–246.

Gaddis, John Lewis. "The Cold War's End Dramatizes the Failure of Political Theory." *The Chronicle of Higher Education,* July 22, 1992, p. A44.

Gaddis, John Lewis. "International Relations Theory and the End of the Cold War." *International Security*, 17 (Winter 1992/93), 5–58.

Galbraith, John Kenneth. *The New Industrial State*. New York: Signet Books, 1967.

Goldstone, Jack A. "The Coming Chinese Collapse." *Foreign Policy*, No. 99 (Summer 1995), 35–52.

Hadar, Leon T. "What Green Peril?" *Foreign Affairs*, 72 (Spring 1993), 27–42.

Hoffmann, Stanley. "Correspondence: Back to the Future, Part III: International Relations Theory and Post–Cold War Europe." *International Security*, 15 (Fall 1990), 191–192.

Holum, John, "On the Need for Arms Control." http://www.usis-israel.org.il/publish/press/arms/archive/1997/january/ac10128.htm, 1997.

Holzman, Franklyn. "Inefficient Soviet Economy Halted Cold War." *New York Times* (Letter to the Editor), November 22, 1992, Section A, p. 16.

Huang, Yasheng. "Why China Will Not Collapse." *Foreign Policy*, No. 99 (Summer 1995), 54–68.

Huntington, Samuel P. "The Clash of Civilizations?" *Foreign Affairs*, 72 (Summer 1993), 22–49.

Intriligator, Michael D., and Dagobert L. Brito. "Can Arms Races Lead to the Outbreak of War?" *Journal of Conflict Resolution*, 28 (March 1984), 63–84.

Jaggers, Keith, and Ted Robert Gurr. "Tracking Democracy's Third Wave with the Polity III Data." *Journal of Peace Research*, 32 (November 1995), 469–482.

Karl, David J. "Proliferation Pessimism and Emerging Nuclear Powers." *International Security*, 21 (Winter 1996/97), 87–119.

Karabell, Zachary. "Fundamental Misconceptions: Islamic Foreign Policy." *Foreign Policy*, No. 105 (Winter 1996/97), 77–90.

Kim, Woosang. "Power Transition and Great Power War from Westphalia to Waterloo." *World Politics*, 45 (October 1992), 153–172.

Kontorovich, Vladimir. "The Economic Fallacy," *The National Interest*, No. 31 (Spring 1993), 35–45.

Lenin, V. I. *Imperialism.* New York: International Publishers, 1917, reprinted in 1939.

Lepingwell, John W. R. "START II and the Politics of Arms Control in Russia." *International Security*, 20 (Fall 1995), 63–91.

Majeski, Stephen J. "Technological Innovation and Cooperation in Arms Races." *International Studies Quarterly*, 30 (January 1986), 175–191.

Mearsheimer, John J. "Back to the Future: Instability in Europe After the Cold War." *International Security*, 15 (Summer 1990), 5–56.

Mearsheimer, John. J. "The Case for a Ukrainian Nuclear Deterrent." *Foreign Affairs*, 72 (Summer 1993), 50–66.

Miller, Judith. "The Challenge of Radical Islam." *Foreign Affairs*, 72 (Spring 1993), 43–56.

Morrow, James D. "A Twist of Truth: A Reexamination of the Effects of Arms Races on the Occurrence of War." *Journal of Conflict Resolution*, 33 (September 1989), 500–529.

Mueller, John. "Quiet Cataclysm: Some Afterthoughts about World War III." *Diplomatic History*, 16 (Winter 1992), 66–75.

Mueller, John. *Quiet Cataclysm*. New York: HarperCollins, 1995.

Mylroie, Laurie. "The World Trade Center Bomb," *The National Interest*, No. 42 (Winter 1995/96), 3–15.

Organski, A. F. K. *World Politics*. 2nd ed. New York: Knopf, 1968.

Organski, A. F. K., and Jacek Kugler. *The War Ledger*. Chicago: University of Chicago Press, 1980.

Plano, Jack C., Milton Greenberg, Roy Olton, and Robert E. Riggs. *Political Science Dictionary*. Hinsdale, Ill.: Dryden Press, 1973.

Pye, Lucian. "Political Science and the Crisis of Authoritarianism." *American Political Science Review*, 84 (March 1990), 3–19.

Ray, James Lee, and Bruce Russett. "The Future as Arbiter of Theoretical Controversies: Predictions, Explanations and the End of the Cold War." *British Journal of Political Science*, 26 (October 1996), 441–470.

Remnick, David. "Can Russia Change?" *Foreign Affairs*, 76 (January/February 1997), 35–49.

Risse-Kappan, Thomas. "Correspondence: Back to the Future, Part III: Realism and the Realities of European Security." *International Security*, 15 (Winter 1990/91), 218–219.

Risse-Kappen, Thomas. "Did 'Peace Through Strength' End the Cold War?" *International Security*, 16 (Summer 1991), 162–188.

Rosen, Steven J. "A Stable System of Mutual Nuclear Deterrence in the Arab-Israeli Conflict." *American Political Science Review*, 71 (December 1977), 1367–1383.

Ross, Robert S. "China II: Beijing as a Conservative Power." *Foreign Affairs*, 76 (March/April 1997), 33–44.

Rostow, W. W. *The Stages of Economic Growth*. London: Cambridge University Press, 1960.

Rowen, Henry S. "The Short March: China's Road to Democracy." *The National Interest*, No. 45 (Fall 1996), 61–70.

Rush, Myron. "Fortune and Fate." *The National Interest*, No. 31 (Spring 1993), 19–25.

Russett, Bruce. "Causes of Peace." In Caroline M. Stephenson, ed., *Alternative Methods for International Security*. Washington, D.C.: University Press of America, 1982.

Sagan, Scott D. *The Limits of Safety: Organizations, Accidents, and Nuclear Weapons*. Princeton, N.J.: Princeton University Press, 1994.

Sample, Susan. "Arms Races and Dispute Escalation: Resolving the Debate?" *Journal of Peace Research*, 34 (February 1997), 7–22.

Schelling, Thomas. *The Strategy of Conflict*. Cambridge, Mass.: Harvard University Press, 1970.

Schlesinger, Jr., Arthur. "Some Lessons from the Cold War." *Diplomatic History*, 16 (Winter 1992), 47–53.

Schweizer, Peter. *Victory: The Reagan Administration's Secret Strategy That Hastened the Collapse of the Soviet Union*. New York: Atlantic Monthly Press, 1994.

Schweller, Randall L. "Domestic Structure and Preventive War: Are Democracies More Pacific?" *World Politics*, 44 (January 1992), 235–270.

Sciolino, Elaine. "The Red Menace Is Gone. But Here's Islam." *New York Times*, January 21, 1996, Section 4, pp. 1,6.

Sestanovich, Stephen. "Did the West Undo the East?" *The National Interest*, No. 31 (Spring 1993), 5, 26–34.

Sestanovich, Stephen. "Geotherapy: Russia's Neuroses, and Ours." *National Interest*, No. 45 (Fall 1996), 3–13.

Shevtsona, Lilia, and Scott A. Bruckner. "Where Is Russia Headed? Toward Stability or Crisis?" *Journal of Democracy*, 8 (January 1997), 12–26.

Singer, Max, and Aaron Wildavsky. *The "Real" World Order: Zones of Peace, Zones of Turmoil*. Chatham, N.J.: Chatham House Publishers, 1993.

Sivard, Ruth Leger. *World Military and Social Expenditures 1989*, 13th ed. Washington, D.C.: World Priorities, 1989.

Sopko, John F. "The Changing Proliferation Threat." *Foreign Policy*, No. 105 (Winter 1996/97), 3–20.

Spector, Leonard S., Mark G. McDonough, Gregory P. Webb, and Gregory D. Koblentz. *Tracking Nuclear Proliferation*: Book Abstract, http://ceip.org/pubstr96.htm, May 9, 1997, pp. 1–2.

Steinbruner, John. "Cold War Comics." *Foreign Policy*, No. 104 (Fall 1996), 169–177.

Stockholm International Peace Research Institute, *SIPRI Yearbook 1996*. New York: Oxford University Press, 1996.

Sublette, Carey. "Nuclear Weapons Frequently Asked Questions." http://www.onestep.com/milnet/nukeweap/NFAQ12.HTM, Version 2, August 23, 1996.

Thucydides, *The Peloponnesian War*. Baltimore, Md.: Penguin Classics, 1954.

Toffler, Alvin. *Powershift*. New York: Bantam Books, 1991.

Toffler, Alvin. *The Third Wave*. New York: Bantam Books, 1980.

Waltz, Kenneth N. "The Spread of Nuclear Weapons: More May Be Better." *Adelphi Papers*, No. 171. London: International Institute of Strategic Studies, 1982.

Winik, Jay. *On the Brink: The Dramatic, Behind-the-Scenes Saga of the Reagan Era and the Men and Women Who Won the Cold War*. New York: Simon & Schuster, 1996.

Wright, Robin. "Dateline Tehran: A Revolution Implodes." *Foreign Policy*, No. 103 (Summer 1996), 161–174.

Yavlinsky, Gregory. "Where Is Russia Headed?: An Uncertain Prognosis." *Journal of Democracy*, 8 (January 1997), 4–26.

PART V

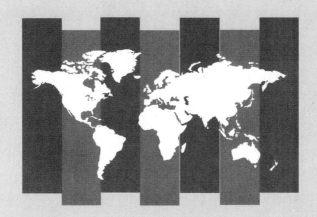

International Organizations and Transnational Actors

CHAPTER 10

Coalitions, Alliances, and Economic Communities

The previous chapters looked at the impact of internal factors on states' foreign policies and at relationships among various categories of states (rich with other rich, rich versus poor, and East versus West). This chapter begins to analyze the interactions of states within informal groups and organizations, such as **political coalitions,** and within more formally established groups like **alliances** and **economic integration organizations.** Alliances are organized around political and military issues, whereas economic integration organizations, of course, focus primarily on economic issues. Each organization has its own peculiar characteristics, and the chapter discusses the specific experiences of some of the more important ones, such as the **North Atlantic Treaty Organization (NATO)** and the **European Union (EU).** But it also stresses the similarities and patterns that can be discerned from analyzing and comparing the historical records of alliances and integration organizations in the last two centuries or so.

INTERNATIONAL ALLIANCES

Coalitions seem to be an inevitable result of interaction among sovereign political units. "Wherever in recorded history a system of multiple sovereignty has existed, some of the sovereign units involved in conflicts with others have entered into alliances" (Wolfers, 1968, p. 269). Alliances were part of interstate relations in ancient India and China, in Greece during the era of city-states, and in Renaissance Italy. They have been a constant feature of the political landscape since the rise of the modern nation-state in the mid-seventeenth century.

Why are coalitions such a prominent part of international relations? The most common answer given by policymakers is that they are a necessary defense against aggression. Often, or perhaps most of the time, defense is the actual motive for the formation of alliances. But some alliances are formed for more aggressive purposes. The pact between Nazi Germany and the Soviet Union in 1939, which resulted in the immediate dismemberment of Poland, is probably the most prominent twentieth-century example of an alliance that was formed precisely for the purpose of carrying out aggression as opposed to deterring it.

Balance-of-Power Theory Versus Game Theory

Whether for defensive or offensive purposes, alliances are usually formed to give members an advantage in interstate conflicts. But under what conditions states are most likely to form alliances, who will ally with whom, what kinds of alliances are most effective and cohesive, and what effects alliances have on the stability of the international system are issues about which there is still substantial disagreement. The most traditional set of answers is supplied by the **balance-of-power theory,** discussed in more detail in Chapter 14. According to the theory, nations form alliances when any state in their midst becomes so powerful that it threatens to establish hegemony, or domination of the system. Through the mechanism of alliances, the balance is preserved, and if war is not avoided, at least the powerful, aggressive state is denied victory. Most balance-of-power theorists would argue that alliances so used are beneficial, indeed necessary, for the stability of the international system.

A contrasting view of alliance formation in the international system is based on **game theory** and small-group laboratory experiments. Within this tradition, William Riker has developed an idea he calls the **size principle:** in social situations meeting certain assumptions, "participants create coalitions just as large as they believe will ensure winning and no larger" (Riker, 1962, pp. 32–33). In effect, Riker predicts that the pattern of alliances in the international system will result from two contradictory intentions held by states: (1) to join a winning coalition and (2) to win as much as possible for themselves. Obviously, the first aim will lead each state to prefer larger alliances because they can ensure victory. The second leads each state to prefer smaller alliances because they can provide the biggest share of whatever there is to win. The result of such contradictory aims, according to Riker and others, will be alliances that are just as large as they must be to win but no larger.

Thus, whereas balance-of-power theorists predict that states will form alliances to prevent the appearance of a winner, Riker predicts the opposite (Zinnes, 1970, p. 359). His theory predicts that winning alliances will appear and that they will be **minimum winning coalitions.**

Historical Evidence

The most convincing evidence in favor of the size principle comes from the relatively rare occasions when **grand coalitions** have appeared in the international system. Grand coalitions can be defined as coalitions of almost everybody against almost nobody. A clear implication of the size principle is that such coalitions will soon fall apart. There is no way for such coalitions to win anything, because there is nobody left from whom to win. An advocate of the size principle would predict that such coalitions will break up so that member states can win something from each other. And that is exactly what has happened.

After the Napoleonic Wars at the beginning of the nineteenth century, for example, Great Britain, Austria, Prussia, and Russia constituted a grand coalition because France was defeated as the only other Great Power in the world. The coalition began to show signs of disunity as early as the Congress of Vienna, at which the postwar arrangements were determined, in 1815. Austria and Britain secretly allied with the French against the Russians and the Prussians. According to Riker (1962, p. 69), "Hence followed this astonishing result: Austria and England, both of whom had been fighting France for nearly a generation, brought a reconstituted French government back into world politics and allied with it against their own former allies in the very moment of victory."[1]

The process was still visible, but not quite as clear-cut, after the First World War. Because of the revolution in Russia and Germany's defeat, the United States, Great Britain, and France constituted another grand coalition (Zinnes, 1970, p. 359).[2] This coalition also began to break up almost immediately after its enemy was defeated. The United States refused to join the League of Nations. Great Britain and France began to disagree about how the defeated Germany should be treated. France, in general, wanted to be much tougher on Germany than did the British. This antagonism reached something of a climax when France invaded

---

[1] As we shall see in Chapter 14, this breaking up of grand coalitions can also be interpreted as evidence in favor of balance-of-power theory, even though Riker's size principle differs from balance-of-power theory in other respects.

[2] Japan and Italy also might be included in this coalition. Both adhered to the pattern of rapidly becoming unhappy with the grand coalition—Japan largely because the League refused to adopt the principle of racial equality, and Italy because its territorial demands were not met.

Germany to collect reparations and the British angrily accused the French of aggression.

The most spectacular dissolution of a grand coalition took place after the Second World War. During the war, the United States, the Soviet Union, and Great Britain (with some help from France) constituted what was fairly close to a minimum winning coalition. But after the war, with Italy defeated and Japan and Germany nearly prostrate, the Big Three became a grand coalition. Controversy continues among U.S. historians about the origins of the Cold War (see Chapter 2). The orthodox Western view, briefly, is that the Cold War was the result of Soviet aggression and hostility: Stalin was paranoid and took several steps, particularly in Eastern Europe, that gave the Americans no choice but hostile retaliation. The revisionist view is that the Americans, motivated by their own economic interests in Eastern Europe (and those of their Western European allies) and led by President Truman, whose anticommunism bordered on the hysterical (especially when contrasted with the attitudes of President Roosevelt), made an unjustifiable attempt to prevent the Soviets from consolidating their position in Eastern Europe. To adherents of the size principle, this controversy is largely "sound and fury, signifying nothing." The Cold War, they argue, occurred as a more or less inevitable result of the breakup of the grand coalition. The fact that the only state in the world strong enough to threaten the United States was the Soviet Union, and vice versa, also played a role. Ideological differences may have exacerbated the split to a degree. The respective personalities of Stalin and Truman were almost certainly trivial compared with other factors. Citing the size principle as it applies to grand coalitions, Riker (1962, p. 7) explains: "Having defeated the Axis, the winners had nothing to win from unless they split up and tried to win from each other."[3]

The size principle may have direct but unhappy implications for contemporary international politics. As discussed in Chapter 9, the Cold War and its demise can be viewed rather plausibly as the functional equivalent of the First and Second World Wars and their conclusions (Mueller, 1992). As in the First and Second World Wars, the

---

[3] All three of the examples are discussed on pages 69–71 of *The Theory*. Steven Brams (1975, p. 244) points out that this evidence in favor of the size principle as it applies to international politics is "historical in nature and not particularly susceptible to quantification and rigorous empirical testing. Nonetheless, it has the virtue of being systematic: Riker did not ransack history for isolated examples that support the size principle but rather considered all instances of relevant cases within the spatially and temporally defined limits he set. To the extent that these cases . . . are representative of zero-sum situations generally, they allow him to draw more general conclusions than would be adduced from anecdotal evidence alone."

culmination of the Cold War has produced something like a grand coalition of almost everybody against almost nobody. Relationships among almost all of the major powers are quite normal and even friendly, although the rather militantly undemocratic China remains somewhat aloof from this grand coalition. Will this grand coalition go the way of previous such coalitions, breaking up into quite antagonistic smaller coalitions? Certainly the size principle would suggest this outcome.

On the other hand, if Russia and China were to emerge as democratic states, the democratic peace proposition (discussed in Chapter 6) and its adherents would dictate a fundamental transformation of international politics (Rummel, 1979; Russett, 1993; Singer and Wildavsky, 1993). In its strongest form, the theory on which the democratic peace proposition is based leads to the prediction that dangerous antagonisms among *democratic* major powers, with their accompanying competitive alliances, arms races, and even international wars (at least among the democratic states, as long as they remained democratic) will not reappear.

The Importance of Pivotal Power

Another concept from game theory that may give some insight into alliance formation in the international system is **pivotal power.** The kind of situation in which "the tiny are mighty" occurs regularly in multiparty parliaments. Two large parties may constitute by far the greater share of a potential ruling coalition, but if they need a small third party to put them over the top, they may well be willing to give that party political rewards out of proportion to the resources it will contribute to the coalition. "Coalition theory . . . posits that pivot parties . . . will obtain payoffs greater than their share of resource contribution" (Groennings, 1970, p. 74).

Similarly in international politics, in any coalition game, the greater the necessity of including a player in a coalition to make it a winning one, the greater that player's pivotal power. States with very small resource bases may exert a disproportionate influence on international alliance formation if they find themselves enjoying a generous portion of pivotal power. France after the Napoleonic Wars found itself in just such a situation. It had disrupted and antagonized much of Europe over the previous fifteen to twenty years. Even so, before Napoleon was finally disposed of, France had the other states in the system competing for its allegiance, and it was generally restored to a position of influence and prestige with amazing speed. An explanation for this transformation that relies on the "great-man theory" (see Chapter 4) heaps praise on the French foreign minister of the time, Charles de Talleyrand.[4] According to this theory, Talleyrand was so adroit, clever, and diplomatically engaging that despite the atrocious behavior of the French nation, he managed to get the major powers of Europe to treat France with respect in the very moment of defeat. A game theory approach to the success of France after Napoleon would analyze the situation quite differently, pointing out that despite France's recent defeat and correspondingly meager resource base, the structure of the international system was such that France enjoyed a healthy measure of pivotal power. The coalitions of Britain and Austria on the one hand and Russia and Prussia on the other needed to include France in their coalition to make it a winning one.

Germany was in a similar situation after the Second World War. Having suffered through two world wars, several leaders in the victorious states concluded that Germany deserved to be banished forever as a major nation-state. Yet in a few short years, West Germany had received generous foreign aid, and the Americans even insisted that it be rearmed. Given Hitler's abominable behavior, how did this shift happen? Was West German Chancellor Konrad Adenauer's genius or powerful personality responsible for this remarkable acceptance of West Germany after the Second World War? Certainly, game theorists would be no more impressed by Adenauer's genius than by Talleyrand's allegedly clever diplomacy. Rather, they would point out the similarity between the position of West Germany after the Second World War and that of France after the Napoleonic Wars. West Germany, in this case largely because of the developing Cold War conflict between the Soviet Union and the United States, found itself blessed with pivotal power, despite the devastation its resource base had suffered in the war. The United States came to see quickly that it might need to gain the support of West Germany to ensure that the Western coalition was a winning one.

Less developed countries throughout most of the Cold War enjoyed similar good luck. Despite very small resource bases, they were perceived by the Soviet Union and the United States as having considerable pivotal power. The result was that these small nations influenced the policies of the two superpowers more than one might have thought possible on the basis of their small size. This influence was reflected importantly in the foreign aid programs both superpowers launched, partly in an attempt to win friends among the developing countries. In

---

[4] See, for example, Nicolson (1961), Cooper (1964), and Brinton (1963). Not all historically minded analyses agree. See Kissinger (1964, p. 148).

this respect the end of the Cold War was disadvantageous to the developing countries. Neither the United States nor the Soviet successor state of Russia has as much incentive to contribute to foreign aid programs as both did when they were competing so intensely with each other during the Cold War. Perhaps this is one reason, at least, that in recent years the U.S. foreign aid budget as a percentage of U.S. Gross Domestic Product (GDP) has dropped to its lowest point in history, and that U.S. foreign assistance programs are currently at their lowest level, in real dollar terms, in fifty years (U.S. Agency for International Development, 1996, p. 9).

The Utility of Formal Theories

The applicability of formal game theory to international politics should not be exaggerated. Conclusions derived from game theory are based on assumptions that are often highly unrealistic. For example, Riker's size principle is based on the assumptions that the players are *rational,* that they have access to all relevant information, and that the game being played is **zero sum.**[5] A game is zero sum if the amount that one player wins equals exactly what the other player loses—in other words, the winnings of one player added to the losses of the other produce a sum of zero. No cooperation is possible, because there is no solution to a game that allows all players to win something. States, and their decision makers, act rationally at times, but they never have access to all the relevant information, and conflict situations in international politics are virtually never zero sum. Even in total war, the game is usually *variable sum,* meaning that, depending on the strategies adopted by the players, the winnings and the losses need not necessarily add up to zero (as in zero-sum games). If, for example, all the players cooperate to avoid the use of poison gas during an international war, or to treat prisoners humanely, they may all win.

Because the assumptions on which formal theories are based are rarely met, predictions based on them may turn out to be inaccurate. There are several reasons why coalitions in world politics are often much larger than minimum winning ones. For example, states are unlikely to want to take the risks involved in forming such coalitions. In a parliament, just forming a coalition big enough to win ensures victory. In world politics, once the coalition is formed, it may well have

---

[5] Rationality is defined roughly as preferring winning to losing (see Chapter 4). Riker also assumes that side payments are permitted. Game theorists are not restricted to these assumptions. Not all games, for example, are based on the assumption of perfect information.

to defeat an opposing coalition in a war. Also, any attempt to form a minimum winning coalition may be foiled by the difficulty of measuring power. What was thought to be just enough to win may turn out to be insufficient. Even if that problem does not occur, a minimum winning coalition may have to fight long and hard to win the war, whereas a much larger coalition might win easily.

It might be expected, then, that larger coalitions would be quite common and that these coalitions might not collapse as quickly as calculations based on the size principle would suggest. And a systematic review of the historical record shows that larger international alliances do not, as a matter of fact, show any tendency to break up faster than small alliances do (Bueno de Mesquita and Singer, 1973, p. 266).

Such a lack of fit between reality and the predictions of formal theories should not, though, lead us to discard the theories as useless. They may point out patterns that would not have been apparent otherwise. And the fact that they are based on unrealistic assumptions is a quality shared with respectable theories in the most advanced sciences.[6] According to Newtonian physics, for example, objects that fall to earth should accelerate at the rate of thirty-two feet per second per second. It is probably true that in any given year, over 90 percent of the objects that fall to earth are either raindrops, snowflakes, or leaves. Although raindrops come closer than snowflakes and leaves, it is still safe to say that not one of these objects, as it falls to earth, accelerates at the rate of thirty-two feet per second per second. Given the substantial inaccuracy of Newtonian predictions as they apply to reality, it might seem reasonable to conclude that Newton was a numbskull. That conclusion would, of course, be a mistake. Newton was a scientist who, when theorizing, relied on simplifying assumptions.

In short, the criticism that game theory is too "simple" to capture the complexity of international politics is "misguided. . . . Simplicity actually enhances the power of the theory for grasping complexity" (Snidal, 1985, p. 44).

Who Will Ally with Whom?

One perspective on alliances that is strikingly different from formal game theory is based on the idea that alliances are formed between states that share a common ideology, common economic and political

---

[6] As Duncan Snidal (1985, p. 28) points out: "The purpose of any theory—including game theory—is not [to] reproduce reality, but to increase our understanding of fundamental processes by simplifying it."

systems, or similar cultural characteristics. The contrast between this kind of theory and formal theories arises because the latter tend to treat all states as identical, with each responding to system structure or some set of incentives in a rational manner. This may be another way in which such formal theories do not supply an accurate picture of reality, because states may tend to prefer alliance partners with whom they share common national attributes. Recent evidence on this tendency is mixed. One analysis (Siverson and Emmons, 1991) suggests that democracies have been more likely to ally with one another than with other kinds of states throughout most of the twentieth century. But a reevaluation (Simon and Gartzke, 1996) of this issue argues that this tendency for democratic regimes to ally with one another was obvious only during the Cold War era. And it may be that democratic states are more likely than autocratic states to ally with one another only if autocratic states are all lumped together rather indiscriminately for the purpose of the comparison. At least one study suggests that autocratic states, if they are separated into "firmly autocratic" and "mixed autocratic" categories, have been consistently more likely than democratic states to ally with one another from 1816 onward (Thompson and Tucker, 1997).[7]

Although it may be true that states similar in terms of ideology, political system, or culture are more likely to ally with one another than dissimilar states are, there are plenty of exceptions to the rule. One important origin of such exceptions stems from another principle of coalition formation that can be summarized in the statement "My enemy's enemy is my friend." Republican France, for example, allied with czarist Russia in 1894 because they had a common enemy, Germany. Republican France allied with the Communist Soviet Union in 1935 for the same reason. Two of the clearest examples of ideological similarities being overridden by the principle "My enemy's enemy is my friend" in post–Second World War international politics arose from the conflict between Pakistan and India. The two newly independent nations fought over Kashmir in 1947. In the ensuing decade, they developed sharply contrasting political systems. India was democratic, while Pakistan was ruled by a military dictatorship. The dictatorship, though, was staunchly anti-Communist and aligned itself with the Western world in not one but two alliances: the **Central Treaty Organization**

---

[7] Thompson and Tucker (1997) base their categorizations of regimes on data provided by Gurr, Jaggers, and Moore (1989). In this data set, countries are assigned scores from –10 (most autocratic) to +10 (most democratic). Countries in the middle of this range, displaying a mixture of democratic and autocratic characteristics, are referred to by Gurr, Jaggers, and Moore, as well as by Thompson and Tucker, as *anocratic* regimes.

(CENTO) and the **Southeast Asia Treaty Organization (SEATO).** Despite membership in these two strongly anti-Communist alliances, Pakistan soon found itself with a strong Communist ally. Pakistan's enemy, India, became involved in a border dispute with China, which erupted into a war in 1962. China thus emerged as the enemy of Pakistan's enemy, and by the mid-1960s, Pakistan had membership in two Western military alliances and simultaneously maintained friendship with the People's Republic of China.

This conflict produced further coalitions of strange bedfellows. While Pakistan developed into a military dictatorship strongly allied with the forces of Western democracy, democratic India remained resolutely neutral in the Cold War conflict. But in 1971, as the civil war between West and East Pakistan became more serious and India decided it must intervene, Indian Prime Minister Indira Gandhi (still a democratic leader at the time) abandoned India's long-standing policy of nonalignment and signed a treaty of friendship with the Soviet Union. Why? Because by that time the Soviet Union was an enemy of India's enemy, China. In short, nations may form alliances more with an eye to the national security benefits they can expect from the alliance than out of emotions generated by political or philosophical sympathies, especially when those two considerations point in opposite directions (Lalman and Newman, 1991, p. 251).

Alliances and War

At least equal in interest to the question of who will ally with whom are questions concerning the effects of alliances on incidences of international war. Alliances have usually been intended to help a state avoid war or to help it win a war already in progress. Whether or not alliances serve the first purpose well is a matter of some dispute in the literature of international relations. It may be true that a state threatened with aggression can deter the potential aggressor by acquiring one or more formal allies. But these alliances also may convince the potential aggressor that it is the victim of a strategy of encirclement, which in turn can lead to several undesirable reactions. For example, the aggressor target of the alliances may go out and seek its own alliance partners. Before the initial alliance was formed, the potential aggressor may have had trouble finding such partners because the important states in the area were not aware of the lines of cleavage in the system. But an alliance or two could conceivably polarize the situation to the point where the potential aggressor will find it easy to form a counteralliance. Also, alliances can clarify the situation in such a way as to allow a potential aggressor to calculate just how much help will be needed to launch a successful war.[8] At worst, the polarized situation can result in the very thing that the original alliance was designed to avoid—an enemy attack. The attack might be carried out either because the original alliance made the enemy afraid or because the enemy's confidence was bolstered by the alliance it created in response to the original coalition.

This analysis is all highly speculative, of course, and it seems fairly clear that in the past, such speculation has been influenced heavily by the role that alliances played in the previous big war. Take, for example, the Franco-Prussian War of 1870. France lost that war badly partly due to its lack of allies. In the months leading up to the war, French leaders believed that Austria-Hungary, or perhaps Italy, might come to their aid if France became involved in a conflict with Prussia (Howard, 1961, pp. 46–48). But when the time came, France found itself alone. Both Austria and Italy left the French to their sad fate.

World leaders could have concluded, as a result of the experience of France in 1870, that wisdom with respect to alliances lies in ensuring that one's potential alliance partners sign on the dotted line so that they are clearly committed when a crisis occurs. (France had relied on vague assurances of assistance before the Franco-Prussian War.) And that is the lesson that many decision makers in leading European states seem to have learned.

As a result of the dramatic Prussian victory over France, "statesmen grew more fearful of isolation, and they made greater efforts than in the pre-1870 era to establish and maintain alliances in peacetime" (Thies, 1991, p. 348). The rate at which the European Great Powers formed alliances in the period from 1875 to 1910 was significantly higher than the rate from 1814 to 1874 (McGowan and Rood, 1975, p. 866). By 1914, the European state system was virtually honeycombed with formal alliances. These alliances seem in retrospect to have been an important part of the problem that led to a major conflagration because of an intrinsically unimportant spat between Austria and Serbia. Alliance ties sucked Germany into the conflict. After Russia became involved, alliances then entangled France and Britain. Thus, alliances came out of the First World War with a rather tarnished reputation.

That tainted reputation did not deter France from forming many alliances in the interwar years, but it may have deterred French leaders from relying on alliances or from cultivating them to the point where

---

[8] "Bilateral alliances both reveal any added support that a state may have, and the amount of support that a potential belligerent may need. . . . The reduction of uncertainty brought about by such information may be all that is needed to facilitate an aggressor's desire to attack another state" (Bueno de Mesquita, 1981, p. 151).

they might have been useful. France had alliances with several Balkan states and with the Soviet Union but relied on the Maginot Line in a manner that contradicted these alliance commitments. The French, as noted previously, never did solidify the Soviet alliance, and they abandoned their Balkan allies at the moment of crisis.

Great Britain avoided alliances in Eastern Europe altogether after the First World War, and both Britain and France made only half-hearted and disastrously ineffective attempts to form an alliance with the Soviet Union. The United States did form an alliance of sorts with its Latin American neighbors in the 1930s but refused to become involved in any arrangement that was more directly connected with the developing European (or Asian) conflict and more likely to deter aggression. "In the late 1930s . . . policymakers and strategists who had lived through the trench warfare stalemates of 1914–18 believed that conquest was difficult and slow. Consequently they thought that they could safely stand aside at the outset of a conflict, waiting to intervene only if and when the initial belligerents showed signs of having exhausted themselves" (Christensen and Snyder, 1990, p. 148). So policymakers deliberately avoided commitments to enter into wars immediately in the form of alliance treaties. Again, in retrospect the avoidance of alliance bonds seemed disastrous. If only effective alliances with the targets he attacked before his move against Poland had been formed against Hitler, he might not have had the nerve to begin the Second World War.

In short, right or wrong, alliances came out of the Second World War with their reputation for deterring aggression restored, at least in the eyes of U.S. policymakers. The United States, in the years following the Second World War, formed the most extensive set of formal alliances in the history of the world—the **Rio Pact** in Latin America, CENTO in the Middle East, SEATO in Asia, and a treaty between Australia, New Zealand, and the United States (**ANZUS**) in the South Pacific—to implement its policy of containment. Several bilateral pacts were added later. The keystone of the U.S. system of alliances was, of course, the North Atlantic Treaty Organization (NATO), centered on Western Europe. Having already signed an alliance with Communist China, the Soviets soon organized the **Warsaw Pact** to counterbalance NATO (and in response to the rearming of West Germany), thus solidifying the **bipolarization** of the international system. This proliferation of alliances after the Second World War was inspired, like the rapid rate of alliance formation after the quick Prussian victory over France in 1870, by perceptions regarding the scope and pace of warfare. "Just as the Prussian [victory] over . . . France encouraged statesmen to scramble to line up allies in advance of the next war, the tremendous destructive-

These are the first NATO troops arriving at the Sarajevo airport to set up a command center in Bosnia in 1995. Under current conditions, some think NATO ought to be expanded, and others believe it ought to be disbanded. Source: Jon Jones/Sygma.

ness of the Second World War encouraged states that had formerly sought safety in neutrality . . . to lobby for admission to NATO in an attempt to avoid becoming a battlefield in a future war" (Thies, 1991, p. 349).

The structure of the alliance network that emerged after the Second World War changed considerably over the next few decades and was transformed quite dramatically in 1991. The Sino-Soviet alliance ceased to exist in 1961. For several complicated reasons involving Middle Eastern politics at the time, the United States never did join CENTO, and that organization died. SEATO was disbanded in 1975. In the confrontation between the United States and the Soviet Union, NATO and the Warsaw Pact were by far the most important alliances for each of the superpowers.

When the Warsaw Pact was disbanded in 1991, its demise naturally called into question the continuing necessity and purpose of its major rival, NATO. Defenders of NATO today insist that it deserves credit for preserving peace in Europe since 1945 and that it would be a mistake to disband it even though the Warsaw Pact is dead. And in fact, NATO's most enthusiastic supporters believe that it is crucial to expand its membership to take in several Central and Eastern European states like Poland, Hungary, the Czech Republic, and perhaps Slovakia, not so much as a defense against a possible Russian attack, but rather to solidify these new democracies in Eastern Europe. According to one proponent of NATO's inclusion of new states in East-Central Europe, "An expansion of NATO today . . . must have as its primary purpose the internal transformations of new member states" (Odom, 1995, p. 45). Another proponent argues similarly: "Democracies are essentially peaceful in their external behavior, in particular vis-à-vis other democracies. NATO's explicit goal of protecting its member countries against totalitarian threats from inside as well as outside serves to maintain the peaceful character of . . . relations among member states" (Kaiser, 1996, p. 130).

But a disturbing counterargument suggests that such a step would imperil democracy in Russia. A former speechwriter for Mikhail Gorbachev, for example, warns that a NATO expansion unaccompanied by accommodations to Russian objections might lead to the transformation of Russia into a "loose cannon" in world politics (Pushkov, 1997, p. 62). And an American opponent of NATO expansion

> sees the creation of an even larger European bloc from which Russia is excluded as a lasting wound in the tender Russian psyche, which could in time cause that nation's political culture to be dominated by feelings of humiliation. Making the analogy to the German humiliation at Versailles, he speaks of the unwitting creation of a "Weimar Russia" (Apple, Jr., 1997, p. 4).[9]

Solidifying democracy in East-Central Europe at the cost of bringing dictatorship to Russia would almost certainly not be a good bargain. One escape from this dilemma might be to argue that in the wake of the demise of the Soviet Union, NATO has lost its purpose and ought to be disbanded or replaced altogether. Or perhaps, moving entirely in the other direction, NATO ought to be expanded to include not only East-Central European states but Russia itself (Bell, 1990). This might seem a neat solution to the dilemma in question, if it were not for a consistent research finding that pairs of allied states are more likely than pairs of

---

[9] Similarly, Karl-Heinz Kamp (1995, p. 126) argues that "it is important to take special precautions to avoid a Russian perception of Western encirclement, since it would inevitably weaken democratic forces in Moscow in favor of nationalists around the country."

unallied states to fight wars against each other (Bueno de Mesquita, 1981; Ray, 1990; Maoz and Russett, 1992; Bremer, 1992).[10]

Doubts about expanding NATO or relying on alliances to achieve stability and peace in Europe could also be reinforced by the possibility that such an expansion might provoke the very attacks it would be intended to avoid. "The greater a nation's expectation that its allies will support it, the more likely it is to undertake actions that can lead to war" (Smith, 1996, p. 33). It is more likely, perhaps, that extending NATO into East-Central Europe might provoke attacks because alliance ties between countries in that region and the current members of NATO would turn out to be unreliable. An historical review of alliances reveals that alliance commitments have been honored on only about 27 percent of the occasions on which they have been tested in actual conflicts (Sabrosky, 1980; cited by Morrow, 1994). Of course it is likely that unreliable alliance ties are precisely the ones likely to be tested, whereas reliable alliances may well produce their intended deterrent effect most of the time. "It is unreliable alliances that . . . [attract] attacks. Only a small proportion of alliances need to be unreliable to generate the empirical observation that alliances are on average unreliable" (Smith, 1995, p. 418).

Would the United States and the rest of NATO respond as promised to attacks on their new allies in East-Central Europe? Even more to the point, perhaps, would potential attackers *believe* that NATO would defend its newest members? There is certainly room for doubt. "After seeing how reluctant George Bush and Bill Clinton were to send American troops to Bosnia, and how quick Mr. Clinton was to pull back from Somalia and Haiti when the going got nasty, it is not easy to visualize a future American president sending American soldiers to central Europe to sort things out there" (Apple, 1997, p. 1).[11] Additional research indicating that the possession of nuclear weapons does not seem to add much to the ability of their possessors effectively to deter potential

---

[10] Probably this positive correlation between alliance membership and war proneness for pairs of states is in part a statistical artifact (that is, a spurious correlation) brought about by the fact that states in geographical proximity are more likely both to join in alliances together *and* to fight wars against each other, even though the alliance ties do not *cause* the states to fight those wars (Bremer, 1992, p. 334). Still, that correlation forcefully suggests that alliance ties (for example, among Western Europe, East-Central Europe, and Russia) would fall far short of a guarantee of peace.

[11] "Suppose that Ukraine attacked the Slovaks just after they had joined NATO: would Americans really be ready to die for Bratislava? Would the alliance be prepared to use nuclear weapons to defend Romania from the Russians?" (*Economist*, June 1, 1996, p. 21).

attacks against "protégés" must add to concerns about the wisdom of extending NATO membership to a significant number of states in Central Europe (Huth and Russett, 1984, 1988; Huth, 1988).[12]

The hope that bringing East-Central European countries into NATO might help solidify their newly democratic regimes seems based in part on the experience of Germany. Making West Germany a member of NATO in the 1950s does seem in retrospect to have solidified its transition from Nazism to democracy. But there is no systematic evidence that membership in such an alliance will consistently consolidate a nation's democracy, and quite a bit of impressionistic evidence indicates that alignment with the United States, for example, is certainly no guarantee of stable democracy. During the 1960s, even though most countries in the region were members of the Rio Pact, "sixteen military coups took place in the Latin American countries" (Levinson and de Onis, 1970, p. 77).

There are, though, encouraging indications that the United States and its NATO allies might just be able to have their cake and eat it, too, in the sense of being able to extend NATO membership, slowly, to various countries in East-Central Europe while at the same time mollifying Russia by including it in various other formal arrangements to stabilize the region. NATO's **Partnership for Peace,** for example, "comprises all Central and East European states as well as the former Soviet republics, including Russia; it carries out joint military planning and exercises and has developed other means to adapt the national military forces and equipment of interested partner states to NATO standards" (Ruggie, 1997, p. 117). And in mid-1997, NATO and Russia signed a security agreement that entails some commitment by NATO not to deploy nuclear weapons or military forces in the new member states.[13] This agreement has to be approved by NATO's sixteen member nations,

---

[12] Fearon (1994, p. 266) argues credibly that nuclear weapons only appear to have an ineffective extended deterrent effect, because states only challenge other states with nuclear weapons over issues that are perceived to be relatively unimportant to their possessors. But Fearon acknowledges that "challengers will threaten nuclear powers over issues on which a concerted response by the defender is initially quite uncertain," which is precisely the kind of situation that might arise in East-Central Europe after states in that region joined NATO.

[13] The commitment is vague. Soon after the agreement was signed, Boris Yeltsin declared that it ensured that NATO would not station nuclear weapons or military forces in the territory of any new member states, but "NATO officials said it contains no pledge about nuclear forces and merely reaffirms NATO's statement that it has 'no intention, no reason, and no plan' to deploy nuclear weapons there" (Associated Press, May 15, 1997, p. 4).

SOURCE: Campbell/Cartoonists & Writers Syndicate.

but for the moment it seems to have calmed Russian fears.[14] At least Boris Yeltsin has declared that "we will accept the situation much more calmly than before. If we were anxious before this document . . . after it is signed our anxieties will go away" (Associated Press, May 15, 1997, p. 4).

So NATO membership will probably be offered to Poland, Hungary, and the Czech Republic in 1997, although Turkey has threatened to veto such an invitation unless it (Turkey) is invited to join the European Union. Such countries as Romania, Slovenia, and Slovakia may be added before too long. Lithuania, Estonia, and Latvia are eager to be included. It remains to be seen whether NATO can be expanded to this extent without provoking a Russian backlash, and perhaps one day, retaliation.

---

[14] "Moscow is to be included in NATO decisions—given the right to suggest, to kibitz, to bring pressure on the others to operate by consensus. There will be no Russian veto, but it could be time-consuming to bring the Russians around and costly to vote them down, on operational matters and on questions like ultimate membership for Baltic nations" (Apple, 1997, p. 4).

ECONOMIC INTEGRATION IN
WESTERN EUROPE

Alliances are coalitions of states that have primarily military or national security goals. Since the Second World War, numerous coalitions have been formed by states whose goals are more economic in nature. Of course, political and economic goals are often intertwined. This has been especially true of such organizations in Europe.

Shortly after the Second World War, the threat of Soviet domination led Winston Churchill to call for a "United States of Europe." In the succeeding years, there were several attempts to bring European countries closer together. Responding in part to Churchill's suggestion, in 1949 thirteen Western European nations, plus Iceland and Turkey, formed the Council of Europe, made up of an assembly appointed by national parliaments and a committee of national ministers (Calvocoressi, 1991, p. 198).

Federalism Versus Neofunctionalism

The impetus toward international organization in Europe received two important boosts in 1948. First, the Soviets backed a successful coup in Czechoslovakia. Second, they blockaded West Berlin, making it necessary for the United States to supply the city from the air. One immediate response to the perceived Soviet threat was the creation of NATO. By 1950, there were two separate but related European unification movements to facilitate dealing with the Soviets and at the same time to ensure against any future trouble with a rejuvenated Germany.

One movement was based on what became known as the **federalist philosophy of integration.** The heart of this philosophy is summarized neatly in the slogan "The worst way to cross a chasm is in little steps." In other words, any attempt to unify several nation-states into a federal union must be wholehearted, not incremental. The incipient federal government must be given substantial political power from the beginning. René Pleven, French premier in 1950, suggested the creation of an all-European army. The Americans originally opposed this plan but were persuaded to support it by the summer of 1951 (Acheson, 1969). This was a federalist idea par excellence, going to the heart of the sovereignty of the separate European states—the control of their armies. It was hoped that this plan would allow the Europeans both to thwart any aggressive designs the Soviets might have and to rearm the Germans without giving them control of weapons or troops. Spurred on, perhaps, by the beginning of the Korean War and the fear that North

Korea's attack was a diversionary tactic devised by the Soviets to gain a free hand in Europe, five out of the six states involved in the plan to create the integrated European army (the **European Defense Community**) approved it. But in 1954, the French parliament voted to postpone further discussion of the idea, and it faded away.

The **neofunctionalist philosophy of integration** fared better. The original functionalists argued that integration of independent states could best be achieved by first creating a central organization with authority over technical economic tasks (Mitrany, 1943). Neofunctionalists, led by **Jean Monnet** of France, often referred to as the founder of the **European Community (EC),** argued that an integration organization should seek out activities that are specifically defined but also politically important. Neofunctionalists also stressed the development of **supranational political institutions,** with power superior to that of the governments of the member nations, whereas functionalists were satisfied with more loosely knit organizations. According to neofunctionalists, the strength of an integration organization that selects its initial activities wisely will grow with time. Monnet, for example, used the goal of integrating the coal and steel markets as a rationale for promoting the integration of social security and transportation policies. He argued that this was the only way to counteract distortions in coal and steel prices (Jacobson, 1979, p. 72). As the member states saw the economic benefits resulting from the activities of the central organization, neofunctionalists believed, they would be willing to give that organization broader authority. One technical task would **spill over** into other tasks until the integrating forces were virtually overwhelming. The neofunctionalist organization would end up running everything, and at this stage the process of giving it political power would be little more than a formality to which the formerly independent member states would have no objections (Haas, 1958).

These ideas were put into practice by way of the **Schuman plan** (named for Robert Schuman, the French foreign minister), proposed in 1950. Devised by Jean Monnet, the plan called for the creation of a common market in Europe for the coal and steel industries. In 1951, France, West Germany, Italy, Belgium, the Netherlands, and Luxembourg signed the **Treaty of Paris,** launching the **European Coal and Steel Community (ECSC).**

By almost any standard, the ECSC was an immediate success. The benefits its members derived were sufficiently obvious that by 1955, negotiations were under way for a more comprehensive approach to European integration. These negotiations culminated in the **Treaty of Rome,** signed by the same six states in 1957, which created two new organizations, the **European Economic Community (EEC)** and the **European Atomic Energy Community (Euratom).** These two organizations, together with the ECSC, formed the nucleus of what became known (starting in 1967) as the European Community (EC). When the **Treaty of Maastricht** (discussed below) came into effect in late 1993, the organization officially adopted its current name, the European Union (EU).

The European Union

The Treaty of Rome outlined the structure of institutions for the EEC (and now the EU) in a manner reminiscent of the Treaty of Paris. The EU has, in effect, executive, legislative, and judicial institutions. The **European Court of Justice,** for example, fulfills a role that is somewhat like that of the U.S. Supreme Court in the United States. The court consists of fifteen judges who serve six-year terms. The primary function of the court is to settle disputes concerning the provisions of the treaties that established the organization, as well as laws passed with respect to the treaties.

Although the court is clearly one of the more obscure institutions in the EU, it has acquired supranational powers of some significance. In ordinary courts of international law, only states can be heard. Individuals are not allowed to take legal complaints to such courts, and states traditionally have insisted that this custom be adhered to rigorously. But individuals in the EU can be heard before the European Court of Justice, and there have been cases in which the supreme court of a member state has deferred to the judgment of this court.

The European Court of Justice also can hear cases brought by member states, other institutions of the EU, and corporations affected by treaty provisions. For example, if France imposes tariffs on inexpensive Italian wines, complaints against the tariffs by the Italian government or the affected Italian companies may be taken to the court, which will decide if the tariffs are legal according to the Treaty of Rome. The court hears a number of such cases every year and appears to be developing the potential, at least, to become a supranational judicial institution. "Its rulings are binding for all Courts of the Member States, which have to set aside national law if it does conflict with European law" (Siebelink and Schelfhout, 1997).[15]

The executive functions of the EU are shared by the **Commission,** the **Council of Ministers,** and the **European Council.** Originally, the ECSC, the EEC, and Euratom had separate commissions and councils, but in 1967 they were unified into a single body. The European Council was added to the formal EU structure in 1974. The Commission is the

---

[15] "The Court also has the possibility to impose fines on Member States that don't comply with its ruling" (Siebelink and Schelfhout, 1997).

The European Union   Originating with six member countries, the EU now has 15 members.

supranational part of this executive "branch" within the institutional structure. It is made up of commissioners appointed by each of the national governments, but they are to act independently in the interests of the EU as a whole. There are currently twenty Commission members, two from each of the larger states (Germany, France, Italy, Great Britain, and Spain) and one from each remaining member state. The twenty commissioners prepare the first draft of the council's budget every year and propose policies to the Council of Ministers, which the Commission then guides through the **European Parliament.**

The Council of Ministers includes the foreign ministers, the agricultural ministers, and other ministers from each member country. It reviews and approves decisions made by the Commission. Over the years, major decisions have increasingly been passed on to the European

Council, made up of the heads of all member governments. The European Council meets twice a year. The heads of the separate governments represent the individual interests of the member nations, and it is clear that the council must approve virtually every measure of substantial importance. If the EU does some day become truly supranational, one of the most obvious institutional changes that will be required would involve giving the Commission greater independence from the European Council and the Council of Ministers.

Both the Commission and the Council of Ministers have in recent years been involved in potentially very important steps toward supranationality. In 1985, the Commission drafted a White Paper titled "Implementing the Internal Market." It called for three hundred measures to remove physical, technical, and fiscal barriers to true economic integration. By December 1985, the heads of the member governments had approved the Single European Act (based on the White Paper), calling for the establishment of a single European market by 1992 (referred to as Project 1992). The act also called for important changes in voting procedures in the Council of Ministers. By 1987, the Single European Act went into effect, providing for majority voting rather than unanimous voting on certain issues.[16] Previously, every state had, in effect, veto power over any proposal, since a unanimous vote was required to pass it.

The European Parliament is in formal terms the legislative body of the EU, although actually at this stage in the development of the EU most of the legislative functions are still carried out formally by the executive bodies of the Commission and the Council of Ministers. (This should not seem so strange to Americans. In the United States the president, although formally charged only with *executing* the laws, also plays a key role, and sometimes the predominant role, in *making* the laws, that is, performing a legislative function.) The European Parliament is probably the least powerful of the major institutions making up the EU, but at the same time, it is one of the most intriguing. It took a possibly important step forward in 1979, when its members began to be directly elected to the body. (Previously, they had been selected by the parliaments of the member nations.) It currently has 626 members, and they organize themselves along ideological rather than national lines. As a rule, therefore, the Christian Democratic delegates from the various member states sit, caucus, and vote together (currently as the

---

[16] The 87 votes in the Council of Ministers are distributed as follows: 10 votes (France, Germany, Italy, Great Britain); 8 votes (Spain); 5 votes (Belgium, Greece, the Netherlands, Portugal); 4 votes (Austria and Sweden); 3 votes (Denmark, Finland, Ireland); 2 votes (Luxembourg).

"European People's Party") rather than acting in concert with the other delegates from their respective countries.

"Until the Single European Act came into force in 1987, . . . the budget was the only piece of Community decision-making in which the European Parliament had the say" (Nicoll, 1987–88, p. 27). Since then, the European Parliament has gained control over about one-third of the budget, the part that does not involve the Common Agricultural Policy (a very large part of the budget, as we shall see) or foreign aid. Also since 1987, "the Parliament has had the right to amend or reject legislation approved by the Council, which can overrule the Parliament only by a unanimous vote" (Lutz and McCaffrey, 1988, p. 6). And the Maastricht Treaty gives the parliament the right to veto decisions made by the Council of Ministers (Kaplan, 1994, p. 54). That treaty also makes it possible for the parliament to approve the president of the Commission as well as the Commission as a whole, and to make the Commission as a whole resign if a two-thirds majority so votes. The parliament was most recently elected in 1994; since then the body has assumed for itself the right to question all individual candidates for the Commission, in the same manner that the U.S. Senate holds hearings before confirming candidates for cabinet-level posts (Siebelink and Schelfhout, 1997).

As the only directly elected body within the EU, the parliament can be expected, perhaps, to play an increasingly important role in the organization, if the EU continues on its current ambitious course.

Ultimately, the European Parliament might even pass laws that would take effect within the member states and form the basis of a kind of European government. One might even envision a "prime minister" of Europe arising out of its ranks in the manner that such leaders arise in parliamentary forms of government (such as Great Britain's). And in fact, the European Parliament does elect a "president" or a chair. But in the last ten years the president of the Commission seems to have overshadowed the president (or chair) of the parliament, so that the latter seems to be assuming a role more like that of majority leader in the U.S. Senate, or Speaker of the House of Representatives. The president of the Commission is selected by the European Council and then approved by the European Parliament.[17]

---

[17] "This is formally a consultative vote, though it is hard to imagine a candidate proceeding any further should Parliament's vote be negative" (Siebelink and Schelfhout, 1997). Jacques Delors, president of the Commission from 1985 to 1994, is probably responsible for transforming the position into something more analogous to that of president of the United States. The current president of the Commission, whose term runs to the year 2000, is Jacques Santer.

The Process of Integration

How well have the institutions of the EU worked? Answering that question involves first discussing the question, "What exactly are they trying to accomplish?" The ultimate goals of the community are political, but the intermediate steps are economic. The first step in the economic integration process is the creation of a **free trade area** in which tariffs among the member states are eliminated. This is supposed to increase trade among member states, but free trade areas can be easily infiltrated. A state outside the organization could simply export goods into the member state with the lowest tariffs. Once that was done, the goods could be exported from the infiltrated member state to the other members of the organization and escape the tariffs of the other states as if they had come from within the free trade area. An obvious solution to this problem involves the adoption of a common tariff by the states in the organization, to be applied to all imports coming from the outside. If this is accomplished, the organization reaches the status of a **customs union.**

The next step up the ladder of economic integration is to establish a **common market.** In addition to abolishing intraorganization tariffs and creating a common external tariff, a common market allows the components of production—that is, capital and labor—to move freely across national boundaries. Entrepreneurs from one member state can invest without restriction in any other member state, and workers can freely migrate to any state in the organization to find work. If the member states cooperate to the extent that they jointly plan monetary, fiscal, and social policies, they form an **economic union.** If they turn the planning of these policies over to a unified, supranational body (such as the EU Commission), **total economic integration** is accomplished. According to neofunctionalist ideas, once economic integration reaches this advanced stage, the central integrating organization will be running virtually everything anyway, so there will be no strong objection to advances toward **political integration** and the emergence of a new statelike entity (Balassa, 1961, p. 2).

The Future of the European Community

On January 1, 1993, the European Single Market went into effect, thus officially creating the economic union toward which the organization had been striving since 1957. On November 1, 1993, the agreements contained in the Maastricht Treaty became official, one of which changed the name of the organization to the European Union. The Maastricht Treaty is an ambitious document. "Maastricht established

The Maastricht Treaty was passed over strong objections by citizens in several member states in the European Union. Pictured here are French farmers on a long drive protesting the Treaty. SOURCE: Reuters/Bettmann Newsphotos.

three pillars for what is now styled the European Union: a **common currency,** a **common foreign and security policy,** and a **common justice and internal policy**" (Soros, 1996, p. 8). If all three of these goals were to be accomplished, say, within the next five or ten years, the EU would have become something much closer to a statelike entity.

There is currently disagreement within the EU (and among sympathetic as well as skeptical outside observers) as to whether achieving these goals is likely or desirable. Establishing a common currency would certainly simplify commercial transactions within the EU, and perhaps in the long run would be an economic boon to most member countries.[18] But in the meantime, the struggle to achieve the goal is creating a lot of pain in most of the member states. The Maastricht Treaty asserts that the member countries must achieve a number of ambitious economic goals if they are going to qualify for the **European Monetary Union (EMU),** which at this writing is scheduled to go into effect in January 1999. In early 1998, the member states will be evalu-

---

[18] "Europe needs a common currency. A common market cannot survive in the long run without one" (Soros, 1996, p. 9).

ated to see if they qualify for membership in the EMU. Potential candidates are supposed to have avoided devaluing their currency in at least the previous two years. Their long-term interest rates must be within 2 percentage points of the three lowest interest rates within the EU member countries. Their inflation rates must be no more than 1.5 percentage points higher than the three lowest rates within the member countries. And finally, they must meet the two criteria that have caused the most pain: (1) To qualify for membership in the EMU, member countries must achieve a ratio of national debt to GDP of less than 60 percent, and (2) national budget deficits must be less than 3 percent of GDP.

To achieve these last two goals in relation to the size of the national debt and the size of national budget deficit, most countries in the EU have engaged in a series of austerity measures, usually involving decreases or limitations in government spending, at a time when "Europe has 18 million unemployed and no one knows what to do with them" (Dornbusch, 1996, p. 110). Currently, unemployment in the EU is 10.8 percent, more than twice the rate in the United States. "If life should deal one of its little knocks, most Europeans expect governments to break their fall with generous unemployment payments, health coverage, housing alliances, [and] child care" (Associated Press, May 18, 1997, p. 7A). But many governments are finding that they cannot afford such programs, at least not at the generous levels to which Europeans have become accustomed. Unemployment has hit a record 12.8 percent in France. It is 21.6 percent in Spain. At this writing, economic conditions even in Germany—where unemployment, for example, is 11.2 percent—are sufficiently distressing that even that economic powerhouse within the EU "may have trouble meeting the fiscal standards for participating in the European Union's single currency in 1999" (Associated Press, May 18, 1997, p. 7a).

Such problems lead some observers to believe that the austerity and budget cuts needed to meet the **criteria for membership in the EMU** are ill timed, and likely to lead to a backlash as the citizens within the EU come to blame it for causing hard times, and then making them even harder. In this view, the "EMU has gone from being an improbable and bad idea to a bad idea that is about to come true" (Dornbusch, 1996, p. 112).[19] If it does, what is currently known as the European Monetary Institute will become the **European Central Bank,** which will become

---

[19] In contrast, supporters argue that "the nightmare scenario—that Europe's central bankers will bear down ruthlessly hard on inflation while the Maastricht criteria bear down hard on demand management, driving the entire European economy into permanent recession—is implausible" (Sutherland, 1997, p. 11).

an institution roughly analogous to the U.S. Federal Reserve, with authority over a new European currency, the **euro.**

If the euro (and the European Central Bank) should come into existence, then two fundamental political goals established in the Maastricht treaty will remain. "The Maastricht Treaty . . . created . . . a specific intergovernmental pillar for the **Common Foreign and Security Policy (CFSP).** It created concepts of action—joint and common—which member states would undertake. . . . It provided for a CFSP budget. . . . The CFSP was born in optimism" (Howe, 1996, p. 23). Perhaps the most dramatic of the implications of the third pillar of Maastricht, that is, the common justice and internal policy, would involve doing away entirely with border controls among the member states. At the moment, in fact, "a substantial majority [within the EU] wants to . . . abolish frontier controls" (*Economist*, May 17, 1997, p. 18).

The goal of creating a common foreign policy for the EU highlights the organization's relationship to NATO. If the EU is to have a common foreign and security policy, it will need some authority over the deployment of its members' military forces. One of the many complications facing the coordination of activities between NATO and the EU is that the memberships do not overlap entirely. The United States is not in the EU, of course, but neither are NATO members Canada, Iceland, Norway, and Turkey. And now, thanks to the recent fourth enlargement of the EU in 1995 (all four enlargements are described in Table 10.1), the newest additions Austria, Finland, and Sweden are members of the EU, but not of NATO.

Table 10.1   The Four Enlargements of the European Union

1957 (Original members)	1986 (Third enlargement)	
Belgium	Portugal	
Germany (East Germany was added in 1991)	Spain	
France	**1995 (Fourth enlargement)**	
Luxembourg	Austria	
Netherlands	Finland	
	Sweden	
1973 (First enlargement)		
Denmark	**(Some potential new members)**	
Ireland		
Great Britain	Bulgaria	Romania
	Czech Republic	Slovakia
1981 (Second enlargement)	Hungary	Slovenia
Greece	Poland	

This potential problem might move toward resolution through further enlargement of either the EU or NATO. The Maastricht Treaty created an **Intergovernmental Conference** to deal (in part) with the question of revising the treaty in such a way as to accommodate new members. It is widely believed that extending EU membership is preferable to adding new members in Central Europe to NATO. One analyst argues that "the United States favors Eastern European nations joining the EU as a fast way to integrate them into the Western community of nations without provoking the kind of hostile reaction from Russia that would follow any expansion of [NATO]" (Sieff, 1996, p. 20). Another argues that "opening up EU markets to the exports of Central and East European countries would do more to support their economic and political transitions than any act or utterance by NATO" (Ruggie, 1997, p. 118).

But there are economic as well as political obstacles to such an expansion of the EU. Most East-Central European countries have a substantial agricultural sector.[20] Agricultural subsidies (allocated through the EU's **Common Agricultural Policy**) already account for about half of the EU's annual budget. It is estimated that adding the East-Central European nations will add as much as $15 billion to the burden of agricultural subsidies (Ulbrich, 1996, p. 20). In addition, "European leaders insist that before Turkey can be considered for membership, it must improve its human rights record, end its war against Kurdish rebels and resolve its disputes with Greece. Many Turks consider these to be hypocritical arguments behind which Europeans hide their prejudice against Muslims" (Kinzer, 1996, p. 3). In response to their anger about this perceived prejudice, Turkey has threatened to veto any expansion of NATO unless it is allowed into the EU. Even if this problem can be overcome, any enlargement of the EU will make it even more difficult to govern, not to mention hammer out something like a common foreign policy for the entire organization. Even among its current members, some news accounts insist that "attempts to strengthen common foreign and security policy . . . look like failing. Most members are simply not ready to surrender sovereignty on foreign policy" (*Economist*, May 17, 1997, p. 18).

The EU now seems to be at a crossroads. It will either, it appears, take dramatic steps toward increased economic and political integration—adopting a common currency, abolishing border controls, and establishing a common foreign policy—or it will retreat from these goals and become something like an ordinary trading bloc. There are serious

---

[20] "Studies indicate that when the . . . Central and Eastern European countries enter the EU, the gross domestic product of the EU will increase only by 3 percent but its agricultural area will balloon by more than one-third" (Ulbrich, 1996, p. 20).

doubts about whether the EU can achieve any of the extremely ambitious goals it has set for itself. But the organization does have a rather impressive track record of disproving the predictions of skeptics and pessimists.

ECONOMIC INTEGRATION AMONG DEVELOPING NATIONS

The thrust toward international integration has a different emphasis among less developed countries (LDCs). In Western Europe, the primary motive, at least in the beginning, was probably the avoidance of war. In the developing world, the primary motive for integration is quite clearly economic. The hope is that by integrating the markets of several countries, their collective economic systems will benefit from **economies of scale.** In many cases each developing country cannot by itself provide a market big enough to justify setting up expensive factories that produce heavy machinery. But if the markets of several small countries are combined, a firm with access to the enlarged market may be able to survive and help the members of the organization develop economically.

Political leaders in LDCs also hope that economic integration will allow them to deal better with what they see as unfair competition from industrialized countries. The United States has often warned LDCs, especially in Latin America, about the dangers of setting up high tariff walls to protect infant industries. In the U.S. view, such tariffs protect inefficiency and thus lower overall productivity, which hurts everyone involved. Most LDCs have been reluctant to accept this philosophy of free trade. They argue that if every country specializes in the production of the goods it produces most efficiently, the result will be the continued unsatisfactory international division of labor. The industrialized countries will go on producing the vast majority of processed manufactured goods, while the LDCs will be condemned to second-class status, that is, to producing agricultural products and raw materials. To avoid this fate, most LDCs feel that they must adopt protective tariffs, even if this means, temporarily at least, that they will have to pay higher prices for goods manufactured by their own infant (and thus inefficient) industries. Advocates of integration among LDCs believe that erecting a tariff wall around a market larger than most single developing nations can provide will shorten the period of infancy and allow industries in developing countries to reach a level of efficiency competitive with other industries more rapidly than they would otherwise be able to do.

Obstacles to Integration Among LDCs

In theory, the argument for economic integration sounds convincing. In practice, the results of integration efforts among LDCs have been mixed at best, with no organization in the developing world even approaching the level of institutional development of the EU. One reason may be that neofunctionalism does not work as well in less industrialized countries. The economies are less complex, making **spillover** from one technical economic task to another less likely to occur. Even when spillover does occur, the typical integrating organization in the developing world lacks the necessary administrative and bureaucratic talent to take advantage of the situation. (In contrast, "Eurocrats" have been in abundant supply to take advantage of any opportunity to expand the role of the EU.)

These factors are important impediments to the integration of LDCs, but there is little doubt that the most serious obstacle arises from the creation of problems inside the integrating organization similar to those in the outside world that the LDCs in such organizations are trying to escape. One important motive for integration in the developing world is the hope that free trade areas or customs unions will give industries in these countries a chance to survive in competition with corporations in developed countries. But when developing countries get together in an integrating organization, they create the same kind of market pressures and advantages for relatively developed states inside these organizations that exist in the outside world. For example, industries attracted by the commercial opportunities inside a new customs union tend to gravitate toward the most economically advanced state in the organization, because that state will probably have a larger supply of workers used to the rigors of industrial labor. In addition, the infrastructure (roads, ports, and so on) will be better equipped to handle the demands of modern business, and the consumers in that country will have more money to buy goods produced by the new firm. This does not necessarily mean that inside a customs union, where free trade and a free market prevail, the rich get richer and the poor get poorer. But it probably does mean that the rich will experience a disproportionate share of some benefits brought about by the integration process (Axline, 1977). In turn, even if every state in the organization is better off than it was before integration, the gap between the richer and poorer states may grow. And the growing gap has produced tensions inside economic communities that threaten almost constantly to tear them apart.

There have been differences in the histories of the different organizations, of course. But organizations such as the **East Africa Community** (Kenya, Uganda, and Tanzania), the **Latin American Free Trade Area** (consisting of most South American states plus Mexico, and disbanded in 1980), the **Andean Common Market** (Bolivia, Chile, Colombia, Ecuador, Peru, and Venezuela), the **Economic Community of West African States,** and the **Association of Southeast Asian Nations (ASEAN)** have all experienced difficulties and tensions created by a perceived unequal distribution of the benefits of integration (Rosenthal, 1985; Okolo, 1985; Emmerson, 1987).

A New Approach: The North American Free Trade Agreement

Mexico has taken a new approach to economic integration by opting for a decrease in trade barriers between itself and its large, rich neighbors to the north, the United States and Canada. The 1994 launching of the **North American Free Trade Agreement (NAFTA)** constituted an especially interesting experiment from the point of view of international integration theories, because the disparity in average income between Mexico and the United States is greater than that between any other pair of bordering states in the world. In 1991, the GDP per capita in Mexico was about $7,010, whereas in the United States it was about $24,680 (United Nations Development Programme, 1996, p. 135). According to both critics and supporters of free trade and economic integration, this disparity should make the impact of both free trade and economic integration particularly pronounced and beneficial (or disastrous) depending on one's point of view.

The major point of NAFTA was to eliminate within ten years all restrictions on trade in manufactured products and cross-national investment, and to remove all tariffs and quotas on agricultural goods within fifteen years. According to its supporters, the agreement would bring benefits to all three economies involved. According to classic free trade theory, Mexico, the United States, and Canada would allocate their productive energies to those activities at which they are most efficient. More would be produced, and better-paying jobs would ultimately be created in all three countries. But according to its critics, especially in the United States, hundreds of thousands of U.S. jobs would be lost as industries there relocated to Mexico to take advantage of the low wages. Mexican critics, on the other hand, worried about having Americans dominate their economy. Others worried that increased integration with Canada and the United States would worsen economic inequalities in Mexico and that increased economic clout in the hands of the Mexican rich would slow or eliminate political reform of Mexico's essentially one-party political system (Casteneda, 1993).

On the very day that NAFTA officially went into effect (January 1, 1994), the Mexican government was faced with an armed rebellion in

Ross Perot was one of the most visible leaders of opposition to the North American Free Trade Agreement. SOURCE: AP/Wide World Photos.

the southern state of Chiapis. And the rebels in the Zapatista National Liberation Army in Chiapis were motivated at least in part by opposition to NAFTA. One of their leaders denounced NAFTA as a "death sentence" for Mexico's Indians (*Economist,* January 8, 1994, p. 41). What was defended in some important U.S. circles as a step crucial to the survival of a friendly government in Mexico had apparently provoked a rebellion creating serious doubts about its stability, and possibly even its survival.

Toward the end of 1994, Mexico adjusted its exchange rate, and the value of its currency fell precipitously. Economic conditions in Mexico, for the middle-class as well as the poor, have since rapidly deteriorated. To some analysts, this is proof that the Mexican government mishandled its economic policies leading up to the advent of NAFTA. One such analyst, for example, argues that Mexico's recent economic fate proves that "a country should not wait for a run on its currency and for its foreign reserves to dry up before it adjusts its exchange rate" (Naim,

1995, p. 114).[21] For other analysts, Mexico's problems since the initiation of NAFTA are proof that "neoliberal policies [that is, policies advocating free trade and reliance on market mechanisms] have failed to provide the much-promised path of stable and shared economic growth for Mexico" (Grinspun and Cameron, 1996, p. 163). Undeniably, unemployment and poverty in Mexico are serious problems, and they have almost certainly gotten worse in the NAFTA era. At this writing, the country's macroeconomic performance shows some improvement; inflation is decreasing, and its exports increased by 20 percent in 1996 (*Latin Trade*, 1997, p. 9a). And its supporters in the United States could point out that "in the first year after NAFTA's passage, three way trade among the NAFTA nations [the United States, Mexico, and Canada] soared 17 percent, growing over $50 billion. U.S. merchandise exports to Canada and Mexico grew more than twice as fast as U.S. exports to the rest of the world" (Stern and Paretzky, 1996, p. 214). Just how influential NAFTA turns out to be in the Western Hemisphere, and possibly the rest of the developing world, will depend largely on how well the Mexican government deals with the current unrest and what the impact of NAFTA on Mexico's economy appears to be in the long run.

Chile has already expressed its desire to join NAFTA. Economic integration, both among Latin American states and with their richer neighbors to the North, is currently a hot topic in Central and South America. Six Central American presidents signed an accord in 1993 aimed at creating a trade bloc involving Guatemala, Nicaragua, Honduras, El Salvador, Costa Rica, and Panama. In 1991, Argentina, Brazil, Paraguay, and Uruguay formed the South American Free Trade Area, known as **Mercosur**. From 1991 to 1994, Mercosur's members cut their tariffs sharply, to the point where most goods traded among its members are now tariff free. "The clearest single measure of Mercosur's progress is the growth in trade that it has prompted. From $4 billion in 1990, trade among its for members tripled to $14.5 billion by 1995" (*Economist*, October 12, 1996, p. 5). By U.N. measures, there have been some thirty-one agreements since 1990 to liberalize trade in Latin America and the Caribbean (*Economist*, October 12, 1996, p. 4). And at a meeting in Miami in December 1994, the region's presidents "agreed to forge a **free trade area of the Americas** within a decade" (*Economist*, May 3,

---

[21] Naim goes on to explain that "the political cycle should not be allowed to overwhelm prudent monetary policy. In 1994, which was a difficult election year for the ruling Partido Revolucionario Institutional (PRI), the decisions of the 'independent' Mexican central bank were not sufficiently independent of political calculations. During that year, monetary expansion of more than 20 percent and lax credit policies added to the economic instability created by the decline in foreign investment" (Naim, 1995, p. 115).

"Well, I guess the secret's out about the company move . . ."

SOURCE: From the *Wall Street Journal.* Permission, Cartoon Features Syndicate.

1997, p. 35). At one point, it seemed that this process might involve the addition of Chile, followed by other Latin American countries, to NAFTA. However, it now looks more likely that Mercosur will serve as the core of any movement in that direction, with Brazil in the lead. "Brazil has, in fact, become the leader in regional integration as a result of a combination of weak U.S. leadership and a dramatic boom in its own economy and the trade pact it belongs to—Mercosur" (Bamrud, 1997, p. 3A.). It is probably a sign of things to come that Chile and Bolivia have now been added to Mercosur as associate members.

So economic integration as part of a development strategy is an idea that clearly persists in Latin America. Similar ideas, sometimes supported by Japan, have their advocates in Asia and involve such organizations as ASEAN.[22] African and Middle Eastern countries also periodically move in the direction of closer economic ties to one an-

---

[22] The original members of Indonesia, Malaysia, Philippines, Singapore, and Thailand added Brunei to their membership in 1984, and Vietnam in 1995. "Preparations to admit Cambodia, Laos and Myanmar . . . into ASEAN have been intensified following the decision of the First ASEAN Informal Summit on 30 November 1996 in Jakarta that [those] countries be admitted as ASEAN members 'simultaneously'" (*ASEAN Update,* 1997).

other, and (particularly in the case of Africa) to industrialized European countries. Despite a long list of setbacks for economic integration efforts in the developing world, integration continues to appear as an idea whose time has come, again.

SUMMARY

Coalitions of states emerge with regularity whenever and wherever independent sets of political entities interact. Alliances, or formally organized coalitions of states dealing with matters of national security, have often played a vital role in international politics. Game theory has produced the size principle, which predicts that coalitions will emerge that are just big enough to win, but no larger. One implication of this principle is that grand coalitions, that is, coalitions of almost everybody against almost nobody, will fall apart. Grand coalitions emerged in the global international system after the Napoleonic Wars in the early nineteenth century, and after the First and Second World Wars in the twentieth century. On all three occasions they fell apart quite quickly. The end of the Cold War has had effects reminiscent of the end of the world wars of this century. For example, the major powers now form an incipient grand coalition that acted with impressive unity in the Persian Gulf War against Iraq. But the history of grand coalitions suggests that this one, too, will be short-lived.

Whether or not alliances serve the purpose of deterring aggression and creating peace is a question on which predominant analysts seem to differ, depending on the outcome of the latest big war. France, bereft of allies, was quickly defeated in the Franco-Prussian War of 1870. The major states of Europe seemed to conclude as a result that to avoid a similar disaster, it behooved them to form many alliances in the decades leading up to the First World War. After that war, though, it seemed as though those very alliances had played a key role in turning a small conflict between Austria-Hungary and Serbia into a major conflagration involving virtually all of the world's larger and more powerful states. So in the decades leading up to the Second World War, no strong effective alliances capable of deterring aggression by Hitler were formed. In the wake of the Second World War, U.S. policymakers assumed that the dearth of such alliances had precipitated the war and, consequently, viewed international alliances as crucial to deter future aggression. So the United States created the most extensive system of international alliances in the history of the world in the decades after the Second World War, mostly for the purpose of dealing with the perceived threat from the Soviet Union, which formed its own alliances.

The demise of the Soviet Union casts doubt on the utility of alliances created to deal with possible Soviet aggression, such as NATO. NATO might be disbanded now that the Cold War is over, but some analysts feel that it should instead be expanded to include countries that used to belong to the Warsaw Pact alliance with the Soviet Union, such as Poland, Hungary, and the Czech Republic. NATO might even be expanded to include Russia itself. But whether or not alliances are a reliable antidote to war, even among states belonging to the *same* alliance, is a question on which the historical evidence is dubious at best. Those who advocate the expansion of NATO often do so not for traditional reasons involving geopolitical calculations but because they feel that NATO membership might help solidify democracy in East-Central European states, and perhaps in Russia. One dilemma resulting from this strategy, though, is that including East-Central European states in NATO might provoke the rise of ultranationalist fears in Russia and thus bring antidemocratic forces into power there.

Economic integration organizations are coalitions of states whose primary purpose, unlike that of international alliances, is economic rather than political. The most successful of these is the EU, which has made significant strides toward the creation of a more unified, federal type of political entity since its founding in 1957. Some of the most significant steps have occurred recently: the Single European Act went into effect in 1987, and the Maastricht Treaty was implemented in 1993. The Single European Act officially removed many of the remaining economic barriers to integration, and the Maastricht Treaty called for all members of the EU to use a common currency and to move toward coordination of defense and foreign policies, as well as legal processes within their countries. The struggle to establish the common currency, the EMU, has involved stringent austerity measures and budget reductions at a time when unemployment is a serious problem in virtually all the member states. Movement toward a common defense and foreign policy has been slow, and complicated by the desire to add new members in Central and Eastern Europe. Still, there is apparently serious talk about removing border controls among the member states, and it is widely believed that including East-Central Europe in the EU constitutes a more effective strategy for integration, and one that will be less objectionable to Russia, than including it in NATO.

Economic integration efforts involving developing countries have persisted ever since the 1960s. Those efforts have foundered repeatedly, primarily because the poorer nations involved in those organizations perceive that they receive a smaller share of the benefits of integration than the richer states. NAFTA aims to integrate two relatively wealthy nations, the United States and Canada, with the developing state of Mexico. However, the advent of NAFTA in 1994 coincided with economic crisis in Mexico, which some see as evidence of economic mismanagement by the Mexican government and others as evidence of NAFTA's undesirable economic impact. Mexico's economic performance in the aggregate has improved in recent years, and trade among NAFTA's members has increased. Additional Latin American states, such as Chile, have expressed an interest in joining NAFTA. But Chile has recently become a member of Mercosur, an economic integration organization in South America led by Brazil, now the apparent leader of economic integration efforts in that region. Additional economic integration organizations are active in Latin America, as well as in Africa, the Middle East, and Asia. In short, economic integration as part of an economic development strategy continues to appeal to many developing countries, despite all the problems such organizations have faced in recent history.

KEY TERMS

political coalitions
alliances
economic integration organizations
North Atlantic Treaty Organization (NATO)
European Union (EU)
balance-of-power theory
game theory
size principle
minimum winning coalitions
grand coalitions
pivotal power
zero sum
Rio Pact
Central Treaty Organization (CENTO)
Southeast Asia Treaty Organization (SEATO)
ANZUS
Warsaw Pact
bipolarization
Partnership for Peace
federalist philosophy of integration
European Defense Community
neofunctionalist philosophy of integration
Jean Monnet
European Community (EC)
supranational political institutions
spillover
Schuman Plan
Treaty of Paris

European Coal and Steel Community (ECSC)
Treaty of Rome
European Economic Community (EEC)
European Atomic Energy Community (EURATOM)
Treaty of Maastricht
European Court of Justice
Commission
Council of Ministers
European Council
European Parliament
free trade area
customs union
common market
economic union
total economic integration
political integration
three pillars
common currency
common foreign and security policy
common justice and internal policy
European Monetary Union (EMU)
criteria for membership in the EMU
European Central Bank
euro
Common Foreign and Security Policy (CFSP)
Intergovernmental Conference
Common Agricultural Policy

economies of scale
East Africa Community
Latin American Free Trade Area
Andean Common Market
Economic Community of West
  African States

Association of Southeast Asian
  Nations (ASEAN)
North American Free Trade
  Agreement (NAFTA)
Mercosur
free trade area of the Americas

SOURCES

Acheson, Dean. *Present at the Creation*. New York: Norton, 1969.

Apple, R. W., Jr. "Europe's New Order: Making a Club, Not War." *New York Times*, May 18, 1997, Section 4, pp. 1, 4.

Axline, W. Andrew. "Underdevelopment, Dependence, and Integration: The Politics of Regionalism in the Third World." *International Organization*, 31 (Winter 1977), 83–105.

Balassa, Bela. *The Theory of Economic Integration*. Homewood, Ill.: Irwin, 1961.

Bamrud, Joachim. "Setting the Agenda: From Miami to Brazil." *Latin Trade*, (June 1997), pp. 3A–8A.

Bell, Coral. "Why Russia Should Join NATO." *The National Interest*, No. 22 (Winter 1990), 37–47.

Brams, Steven J. *Game Theory and Politics*. New York: Free Press, 1975.

Bremer, Stuart A. "Dangerous Dyads: Conditions Affecting the Likelihood of Interstate War, 1816–1965." *Journal of Conflict Resolution*, 36 (June 1992), 309–341.

Brinton, Clarence Crane. *The Lives of Talleyrand*. New York: Norton, 1963.

Bueno de Mesquita, Bruce. *The War Trap*. New Haven, Conn.: Yale University Press, 1981.

Bueno de Mesquita, Bruce, and J. David Singer. "Alliances, Capabilities, and War: A Review and Synthesis." In Cornelius Cotter, ed., *Political Science Annual*, Vol. 4. Indianapolis: Bobbs-Merrill, 1973.

Calvocoressi, Peter. *World Politics Since 1945*. 6th ed. London: Longman, 1991.

Casteneda, Jorge. "Can NAFTA Change Mexico?" *Foreign Affairs*, 72 (September/October 1993), 66–80.

Christensen, Thomas J., and Jack Snyder. "Chain Gangs and Passed Bucks: Predicting Alliance Patterns in Multipolarity." *International Organization*, 44 (Spring 1990), 137–168.

Cooper, Duff. *Talleyrand*. London: Cape, 1964.

Dornbusch, Rudi. "Euro Fantasies." *Foreign Affairs*, 75 (September/October 1996), 110–124.

Emmerson, Donald K. "ASEAN as an International Regime." *Journal of International Affairs*, 41 (Summer–Fall 1987), 1–16.

"Europeans Fear Economic Ills Loom." Associated Press, May 18, 1997. Published in *The Tennessean*, May 18, 1997, p. A7.

Fearon, James D. "Signaling Versus the Balance of Power and Interests." *Journal of Conflict Resolution*, 38 (June 1994), 236–269.

"The Future of NATO: A New Kind of Alliance?" *Economist*, June 1, 1996, pp. 19–21.

Grinspun, Ricardo, and Maxwell A. Cameron. "NAFTA and the Political Economy of Mexico's External Relations." *Latin American Research Review*, 31, No. 3 (1996), 161–188.

Groennings, Sven. "Patterns, Strategies, and Payoffs in Norwegian Coalition Formation." In Sven Groennings, E. W. Kelley, and Michael Leiserson, eds., *The Study of Coalition Behavior.* New York: Holt, Rinehart & Winston, 1970.

Gurr, Ted Robert, Keith Jaggers, and Will Moore. *Polity II Codebook.* Boulder, Colo.: Manuscript.

Haas, Ernst. *The Uniting of Europe.* Stanford, Calif.: Stanford University Press, 1958.

Howard, Michael. *The Franco-Prussian War.* London: Davis, 1961.

Howe, Geoffrey. "Bearing More of the Burden: In Search of a European Foreign and Security Policy." *The World Today*, 52 (January 1996), 23–26.

Huth, Paul. *Extended Deterrence and the Prevention of War.* New Haven, Conn.: Yale University Press, 1988.

Huth, Paul, and Bruce Russett. "Deterrence Failure and Crisis Escalation." *International Studies Quarterly*, 32 (March 1988), 29–46.

Huth, Paul, and Bruce Russett. "What Makes Deterrence Work?" *World Politics*, 36 (July 1984), 496–526.

Jacobson, Harold K. *Networks of Interdependence.* New York: Knopf, 1979.

Kamp, Karl-Heinz. "The Folly of Rapid NATO Expansion." *Foreign Policy*, No. 98 (Spring 1995), 116–131.

Kaplan, Roger. "European Union: Now What?" *Freedom Review*, 25 (February 1994), 53–57.

Kaiser, Karl. "Reforming NATO." *Foreign Policy*, No. 103 (Summer 1996), 128–143.

Kinzer, Stephen. "Turkey Finds European Union Door Slow to Open." *New York Times*, February 23, 1997, Section A, p. 3.

Kissinger, Henry A. *A World Restored.* New York: Grosset & Dunlap, 1964.

Lalman, David, and David Newman. "Alliance Formation and National Security." *International Interactions*, 16 (1991), 239–253.

Latin Trade, June 1997.

Levinson, Jerome, and Juan de Onis. *The Alliance That Lost Its Way.* Chicago: Quadrangle Books, 1970.

Levy, Jack S. "Alliance Formation and War Behavior." *Journal of Conflict Resolution*, 25 (December 1981), 581–613.

Lutz, Colleen, and Diana McCaffrey (eds.). *Western European Regional Brief.* Washington, D.C.: U.S. Department of State, Bureau of Public Affairs, December 1988.

Maoz, Zeev, and Bruce Russett. "Alliance, Contiguity, Wealth, and Political Stability: Is the Lack of Conflict Among Democracies a Statistical Artifact?" *International Interactions*, 17, No. 3 (1992), 245–268.

McGowan, Patrick J., and Robert M. Rood. "Alliance Behavior in Balance of Power Systems: Applying a Poisson Model to Nineteenth Century Europe." *American Political Science Review*, 69 (September 1975), 859–870.

"Miles to Go to Amsterdam." *Economist*, May 17, 1997, pp. 17–18.

Mitrany, David. *A Working Peace System*. London: Royal Institute of International Affairs, 1943.

Most, Benjamin A., Harvey Starr, and Randolph M. Siverson. "The Logic and Study of the Diffusion of International Conflict." In Manus I. Midlarsky, ed., *Handbook of War Studies*. Boston: Unwin Hyman, 1989.

Morrow, James D. "Alliances, Credibility, and Peacetime Costs." *Journal of Conflict Resolution*, 38 (June 1994), 270–297.

Mueller, John. "Quiet Cataclysm: Some Afterthoughts About World War III." *Diplomatic History*, 16 (Winter 1992), 66–75.

Naim, Moises. "Mexico's Larger Story." *Foreign Policy*, No. 99 (Summer 1995), 112–130.

Nicoll, W. "EEC Budgeting Strains and Constraints." *International Affairs*, 64 (Winter 1987–88), 27–42.

Nicolson, Harold. *The Congress of Vienna*. London: Methuen, 1961.

Odom, William E. "NATO's Expansion: Why the Critics Are Wrong." *The National Interest*, No. 39 (Spring 1995), 38–49.

Okolo, Julius Emeka. "Integrative and Cooperative Regionalism: The Economic Community of West African States." *International Organization*, 39 (Winter 1985), 121–153.

"Preparations to Admit Cambodia, Laos, and Myanmar into ASEAN Intensified." *ASEAN Update*, January–April 1997, http: //asean.or.id.general/ publication/au1997.htm.

Pushkov, Alexei K. "Don't Isolate Us: A Russian View of NATO Expansion." *National Interest*, No. 47 (Spring 1997), 58–62.

Ray, James Lee. "Friends as Foes: International Conflict and Wars Between Formal Allies." In Charles S. Gochman and Alan Ned Sabrosky, eds., *Prisoners of War*. Lexington, Mass.: Lexington Books, 1990.

Riker, William. *The Theory of Political Coalitions*. New Haven, Conn.: Yale University Press, 1962.

Rosenthal, Gert. "The Lessons of Economic Integration in Latin America: The Case of Central America." In Altaf Gauhar, ed., *Regional Integration: The Latin American Experience*. London: Third World Foundation, 1985.

Ruggie, John Gerard. "Consolidating the European Pillar: The Key to NATO's Future." *The Washington Quarterly*, 20 (Winter 1997), 109–124.

Rummel, R. J. *Understanding Conflict and War*. Vol. 4: *War, Power, Peace*. Beverly Hills, Calif.: Sage Publications, 1979.

Russett, Bruce. *Grasping the Democratic Peace*. Princeton, N.J.: Princeton University Press, 1993.

"Russia, NATO Hammer Out Security Agreement." Associated Press, May 15, 1997. Published in *The Tennessean*, May 15, 1997, Section A, p. 4.

Sabrosky, Alan. "Interstate Alliances: Their Reliability and the Expansion of War." In J. David Singer, ed., *The Correlates of War II*. New York: Free Press, 1980.

Servan-Schreiber, Jean-Jacques. *The American Challenge*. New York: Atheneum, 1968.

Siebelink, Roland, and Bart Schelfhout. "EU Basics." http://eubasics. allmansland.com, 1997.

Sieff, Martin. "European Union Confronts Crippling Growing Pains." *Washington Times* (National Weekly Edition), August 25, 1996, p. 20.

Simon, Michael W., and Erik Gartzke. "Political System Similarity and the Choice of Allies: Do Democracies Flock Together, or Do Opposites Attract?" *Journal of Conflict Resolution*, 40 (December 1996), 617–635.

Singer, Max, and Aaron Wildavsky. *The Real World Order.* Chatham, N.J.: Chatham House, 1993.

Siverson, Randolph M., and Juliann Emmons. "Birds of a Feather: Democratic Political Systems and Alliance Choices in the Twentieth Century." *Journal of Conflict Resolution*, 35 (June 1991), 285–306.

Siverson, Randolph M., and Harvey Starr. "Opportunity, Willingness, and the Diffusion of War." *American Political Science Review*, 84 (March 1990), 47–67.

Smith, Alastair. "Alliance Formation and War." *International Studies Quarterly*, 39 (December 1995), 405–425.

Smith, Alastair. "To Intervene or Not to Intervene: A Biased Decision." *Journal of Conflict Resolution*, 40 (March 1996), 16–40.

Snidal, Duncan. "The Game Theory of International Politics." *World Politics*, 38 (October 1985), 25–57.

Soros, George. "Can Europe Work? A Plan to Rescue the Union." *Foreign Affairs*, 75 (September/October 1996), 8–14.

Stern, Paula, and Raymond Paretzky. "Engineering Regional Trade Pacts to Keep Trade and U.S. Prosperity on a Fast Track." *Washington Quarterly*, 19 (Winter 1996), 211–222.

"A Survey of Mercosur." *Economist*, October 12, 1996, pp. 1–30.

Sutherland, Peter. "The Case for EMU." *Foreign Affairs*, 76 (January/February 1997), 9–14.

Thies, Wallace J. "Randomness, Contagion, and Heterogeneity in the Formation of Interstate Alliances: A Reconsideration." *International Interactions*, 16 (1991), 335–354.

Thompson, William R., and Robert Tucker. "A Tale of Two Democratic Peace Critiques." *Journal of Conflict Resolution* (June 1997) 428–454.

United Nations Development Programme. *Human Development Report.* New York: Oxford University Press, 1996.

"The United States Looks South." *Economist*, May 3, 1997, pp. 35–36.

U.S. Agency for International Development. *Front Lines*, March 1996.

Wolfers, Arnold. "Alliances." In David Sills, ed., *International Encyclopedia of the Social Sciences.* New York: Macmillan and Free Press, 1968.

The World Factbook 1992. Washington, D.C.: Central Intelligence Agency, 1992.

Ulbrich, Jeffrey. "Analysts Wary of Impact of Huge Polish Farm Sector on EU." *Washington Times* (National Weekly Edition), August 25, 1996, p. 20.

Zinnes, Dina. "Coalition Theories and the Balance of Power." In Sven Groennings, E. W. Kelley, and Michael Leiserson, eds., *The Study of Coalition Behavior.* New York: Holt, Rinehart & Winston, 1970.

CHAPTER 11

Universal International Organizations

Chapter 10 discusses organizations consisting of groups of states that have joined together for mutual advantage. This chapter explores organizations of wider scope, primarily the **United Nations** and related organizations, open to all states, whose ostensible goal is to serve the interests of the entire community of states. That they do not always achieve that goal is no reason to discount entirely their impact on global politics. At times they can play a crucial role.

EARLY PEACE-KEEPING ORGANIZATIONS

The first serious attempt to establish continuing international institutions to deal with threats to peace was made in the aftermath of the Napoleonic Wars at the beginning of the nineteenth century. The Congress of Vienna (1815), a meeting attended only by the major powers, dealt with several unsettled political problems and agreed to periodic consultations that became known as the **Concert of Europe.** This agreement led to a series of international meetings in the next decade that were unprecedented because they occurred during times of peace. But as discussed in the previous chapter, the grand coalition that served as the basis for the concert was prone to disunity. Although the concert did successfully establish the precedent of peacetime consultations, after the first decade of its existence it met only in the aftermath of wars to arrange settlements.

So-called **functional organizations** made significant advances in the nineteenth century. Various river commissions were created for the purpose of regulating international commerce and transport, and organizations such as the International Telecommunications Organization (1875), the Universal Postal Union (1874), and the International

Office of Weights and Measures (1875) were established. These institutions are not directly related to peace keeping, but according to a form of **functionalist theory,** they may ultimately serve that end. If the tasks that these organizations undertake proliferate, they may eventually control such a significant portion of international intercourse that they could serve as a basis for some type of world government. At least, a world of states that had become so closely intertwined in a mesh of functional activities and appreciative of the benefits brought by functional organizations would be unlikely, according to this functionalist theory, to degenerate into international warfare (Mitrany, 1943).

International peace conferences at The Hague in 1899 and 1907 were meant to deal more directly with the threat of war by decreasing armament levels. They failed. Still, they began an important trend toward a democracy of sorts in international diplomacy, because for the first time at such conferences, small states were invited and thus given a voice. Only twenty-six states attended the 1899 conference, but forty-four sent delegations to the 1907 meeting. The latter meeting might be considered the precedent for the establishment of institutions such as the General Assembly of the United Nations.

THE LEAGUE OF NATIONS

The next Hague conference was scheduled for 1915. It was not held, for obvious reasons, but the process leading to the outbreak of the First World War convinced many leaders that some permanent international organization needed to be established. In retrospect, many political leaders and scholars concluded that the First World War had occurred because the decision makers involved had lost control of a situation that none of them wanted to see culminate in a war. If, according to this reasoning, there had been a chance to talk things out, a cooling-off period, none of the conflicts that created the crisis would have proved insoluble. The **League of Nations,** it was hoped, would provide a place where future crises could be talked over and procedures stipulated that would institutionalize a cooling-off period.

During the First World War, private societies advocating the establishment of the League sprang up in Britain, France, Italy, and the United States. President Wilson included the creation of such an organization as one of his famous Fourteen Points. The South African leader Jan Smuts published a pamphlet calling for the creation of the League, and it proved to be influential, perhaps because of good timing (it was published in the month between Wilson's arrival in Europe and the beginning of the peace conference).

In any case, the structure of the League was much like that outlined in Smuts's publication. Its three major organs were an assembly, a council, and a secretariat. The assembly consisted of delegations from all the member states, and its main duties involved the election of new members to the organization, debate and discussion of political and economic questions of international interest, and preparation of the annual budget. The council was dominated by the Great Powers, but it also contained nonpermanent members whose identity and number varied throughout the history of the League. Its most important duty was the resolution of international disputes, and to that end it had the power to advise the member states to institute sanctions against any state committing aggression. The secretariat was an international civil service that handled administrative details for the League and compiled information relevant to the various problems and issues with which the League was confronted.

The League will always be most famous for its failures, but it was not a *total* failure. It set precedents, in the establishment of the Secretariat and in the way the entire organization was structured, that provided valuable lessons for those who later established the United Nations. The League is well remembered for the disputes it did *not* settle, but it did play a role in resolving some conflicts, such as the one between Greece and Bulgaria in 1925.

Although the League's covenant provided for potentially effective economic and military sanctions against aggressors, it allowed each member to decide whether aggression had been committed and, if so, whether sanctions would be applied. These loopholes were not in the covenant as a result of oversight. The founders of the League insisted on them, and it seems unlikely that the absence of loopholes would have made any real difference to the behavior of the League's members. Even if the covenant's articles had mandated sanctions, it is unlikely that many states would have been inclined to apply them.

Much the same kind of argument can be made about the most notorious flaw in the structure of the League—the absence of the United States. This absence was brought about by President Wilson's unwillingness to consult and compromise with the U.S. Senate when the covenant was being drafted, by a bitter personal feud between Wilson and Senator Henry Cabot Lodge, and by widespread isolationist sentiment among a significant number of Americans. In any case, after the demise of the League and the ensuing world war, a powerful myth developed that the refusal of the United States to join the League was a crucial cause of its failure. If the United States had not shunned its duty, according to this myth, the League might have been powerful enough to withstand the aggressive policies of Japan, Italy, and Germany.

This thesis seems dubious, however. The United States' desire in 1931 to avoid provoking Japan after it invaded Manchuria differed very little from Britain's desire to avoid undue provocation of Italy after it invaded Ethiopia in 1935. It is by no means certain whether membership in the League really would have induced the United States to adopt policies other than those it actually pursued in the Manchurian and Ethiopian crises (Niemeyer, 1967, p. 49).

In other words, it does not seem likely that mere formal membership in the League would have changed U.S. foreign policy very much. Given that the major threats to the League occurred when the United States was in the throes of the Depression, it seems more likely that if the United States had been a member, it might have withdrawn from the League rather than energetically pursuing its obligations under the covenant.

THE STRUCTURE OF THE UNITED NATIONS

Myth or not, the idea that the failure of the United States to enter the League was a terrible mistake that played a significant role in bringing about the Second World War became widely accepted in the United States. The best evidence is the energetic manner in which the U.S. government strove for the creation of the League's successor, the United Nations. By October 1943, the governments of the United States, Great Britain, the Soviet Union, and China had declared their firm intention to create an international peace-keeping organization after the war. The intention was reaffirmed at several wartime meetings of the Allied coalition, and the final charter was hammered out at a meeting in San Francisco in the spring of 1945. The charter was completed in June, and by July the U.S. Senate had approved it by a vote of 89 to 2. The contrast with the U.S. reaction to the League some twenty-five years earlier could hardly have been more stark. The distinction was made even sharper by the choice of New York City as the home of the new United Nations.

The structure of the United Nations shares many features with that of the League (see Figure 11.1). The **Security Council,** according to the charter, has the primary responsibility for international peace and security. The five permanent members—China, France, Great Britain, Russia, and the United States—have the power of veto in the Security Council. Ten nonpermanent members also serve on the Security Council. The **Economic and Social Council (ECOSOC)** handles the economic and social programs of the United Nations, serving as a clearinghouse and central administrative body for its associated functional organizations, such as the International Labor Organization (ILO), the Interna-

Figure 11.1 The United Nations System

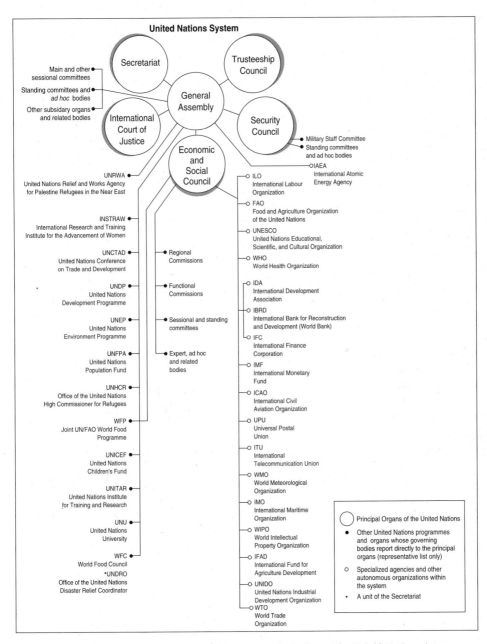

SOURCE: Figure adapted from Robert E. Riggs and Jack C. Plano, *The United Nations: International Organization and World Politics*, Second Edition, by Robert E. Riggs and Jack C. Plano. Copyright © 1994 by Harcourt Brace & Company. Reproduced by permission of the publisher.

tional Monetary Fund (IMF), and the World Health Organization (WHO). The **Trusteeship Council** was set up to monitor the administration of non-self-governing territories transferred from the losers of the world wars and tried to ensure that they were administered in such a way as to speed the independence of such territories. "With the last Trust Territory, Palau, having been granted independence in 1994, the Trusteeship Council is now in abeyance" (UNA in Canada, 1997c).

The **International Court of Justice,** or World Court, composed of fifteen judges elected by the General Assembly and the Security Council, has the twofold function of serving as a tribunal for the final settlement of disputes submitted to it by the parties and acting in an advisory capacity to the General Assembly, the Security Council, and other organs accorded this right of consultation by vote of the General Assembly, on questions of a legal nature that might be referred to it (Goodrich, 1974, pp. 18–19). Decisions made by the court are binding, but no state can be brought before the court without its consent. "Some states have accepted the compulsory jurisdiction of the Court in advance under the Optional Clause of the Statute (Article 36), but because of a myriad of reservations and amendments, the general rule is that only those states that are willing to have their controversies adjudicated by the Court will be parties to cases before it" (Riggs and Plano, 1994, p. 35).

The **General Assembly** is composed of delegations from all the member states, which by 1997 numbered 185 (see Figure 11.2), and has three principal duties. It determines the budget of the organization and (along with the Security Council) selects the **secretary-general,** members of the International Court, and new members of the United Nations. The General Assembly debates any topic within the scope of the charter.

Finally, the **Secretariat,** headed by the secretary-general, serves as an international civil service charged with administering the organization. The secretary-general makes an annual report to the General Assembly and has the right to speak to it at any time, as well as to propose resolutions to the committees of the General Assembly. The secretary-general also has the authority to bring to the attention of the Security Council any matter that in his or her opinion threatens the maintenance of international peace and security.

THE PRINCIPLE OF COLLECTIVE SECURITY

The League of Nations was, and the United Nations is, designed to uphold the concept of **collective security,** which can be defined

Figure 11.2 Membership in the U.N., 1945–1997

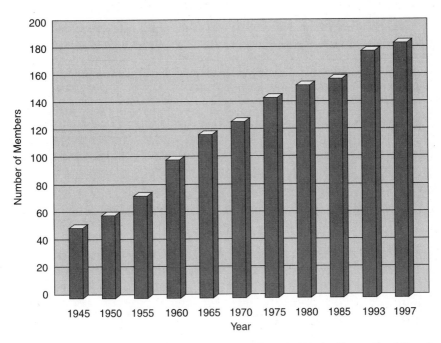

SOURCE: Based on Robert E. Riggs and Jack C. Plano, *The United Nations International Organization and World Politics*, 2nd ed. Belmont, Calif.: 1994, p. 46. Data for 1997 supplied by the author.

briefly as the idea that "aggressive and unlawful use of force by any nation against any nation will be met by the combined force of all other nations" (Claude, 1964, p. 224). In one important way, the structure of the United Nations is better suited to the maintenance of collective security than was the League's. The U.N. Charter

incorporates more elaborate and ambitious provisions for sanctions. Instead of requiring states to impose economic penalties if and when they unilaterally recognize the existence of aggression, and permitting them the exercise of voluntary participation in military sanctions, the Charter brings all enforcement activity under the aegis of the Security Council, conferring on that body the authority to identify the aggressor, to order members to engage in nonmilitary coercion, and itself to put into action the military forces presumably to be placed at its permanent disposal by members of the organization (Claude, 1964, p. 224).

Article 43 of the U.N. Charter specifies how the member nations are to go about creating a military force for the organization:

> All Members of the United Nations . . . undertake to make available to the Security Council, on its call and in accordance with a special agreement or agreements, armed forces, assistance, and facilities, including rights of passage, necessary for the purpose of maintaining international peace and security.

This arrangement, though, is not as airtight as it might appear on the surface. First, the military forces, which according to the charter are to be provided to the Security Council, have never materialized. Second, since every permanent member of the Security Council has the right to veto proposals before the council, it is virtually impossible to implement sanctions against one of the major powers.

Prerequisites for Collective Security

The inability to institute effective sanctions against a major power is only one of the obstacles facing the United Nations in its attempt to establish collective security. There are several logical and theoretical requirements for a successful collective security system.[1] For example, if any nation that uses force aggressively is to be opposed by the combined force of all other nations, there must be some universally agreed **definition of aggression.** Otherwise, it will obviously be impossible for the world community to agree on when the time has come to impose sanctions. There must also be some institution that can make **authoritative decisions about disputes** and designate aggressors. Likewise, there must be some institution or authoritative process for allocating the costs of resisting aggression. The states of the world must be so committed to peace and so loyal to the world community that they will be willing to forsake their own short-range interests by imposing sanctions against states in some remote part of the world that are involved in disputes of no immediate concern to them. Also, if the collective security ideal is to be upheld, the members of a collective security organization must be willing to give up the right to fight to change the status quo and to fight against any state *not* willing to give up that right. **Alliances** are, strictly speaking, logically incompatible with the collective security ideal. That ideal implies a willingness by all

---

[1] These logical and theoretical requirements are taken from discussions by Claude (1964, pp. 223–260), and Mearsheimer (1994/95, p. 32). It might be noted that Mearsheimer in particular is ostensibly and obviously skeptical about the possibility of developing an effective system of collective security, and that Claude, although apparently more sympathetic initially, ultimately emphasizes the difficulties and barriers confronting any effort to implement such a system.

states to oppose *any* state committing aggression, whereas alliances involve precommitments to avoid military action against certain states. Finally, if collective security is to preserve peace, there should be a diffusion of power in the international system so that one or two very powerful states cannot withstand the threat of force by the world community.

Just listing some of the logical requirements for a successful collective security system reveals why the United Nations has had difficulty maintaining such a system. There is no universally accepted definition of *aggression*. International lawyers have been trying to devise one for more than fifty years. Indeed, the General Assembly adopted resolutions in 1969 and 1974 including such a definition (Worldmark Press, 1977, p. 123). But agreement on this definition—or, one suspects, on any other—is virtually impossible to maintain when the time comes to apply it to concrete cases.

In short, "it is sometimes difficult in a crisis to determine who is the troublemaker and who is the victim" (Mearsheimer, 1994/95, p. 31). No international institution has the ability and the authority to specify which states should be the target of collective security sanctions.

The International Court of Justice can hear only those cases willingly brought to it by both sides of the dispute. The Security Council has been hamstrung by the veto any permanent member can impose. The General Assembly is large and unwieldy and, unlike the Security Council, does not have the authority to oblige states to carry out sanctions.

Most U.N. member states' political leaders are quite willing to make verbal commitments to the cause of world peace, but their actions reveal that peace is virtually always second on their list of priorities, if not lower. Leaders are more firmly committed to national security, justice, democracy, national self-determination, or their own credibility. Commitment to the status quo is much less than universal, and several nations are unwilling to give up the right to fight to change it. In fact, it might even be argued that aggression is not always a bad thing. "There are good reasons," for example, one analyst argues, "to applaud the 1979 Vietnamese invasion of Cambodia, since it drove the murderous Pol Pot from power" (Mearsheimer, 1994/95, p. 31). Alliances, and the precommitments they involve, are widespread in the present international system. Furthermore, even long-standing international friendships not formalized by alliances could cause problems for a collective security system.[2] And for most of the post–Second World War period,

---

[2] It is difficult to imagine the United States, for example, using military force against Israel, even if it were branded an aggressor by the international community (Mearsheimer, 1994/95, p. 31).

the United States and the former Soviet Union were so powerful that they could not be intimidated by any implicit or explicit threats made by the United Nations in the name of collective security. When the Soviets invaded Hungary in 1956, Czechoslovakia in 1968, and Afghanistan in 1979 and when the United States invaded the Dominican Republic in 1965, Grenada in 1983, and Panama in 1989, the United Nations could do little to deter the invasions, even if it had been able to come to some kind of nearly universal agreement on the culpability of either superpower.

PEACE KEEPING AS AN ALTERNATIVE TO COLLECTIVE SECURITY

Exclusive concentration on the United Nations' difficulties in establishing a collective security system as envisioned by the writers of its charter might lead to an overly pessimistic conclusion regarding the organization's contribution to peace. The United Nations has at least partially filled the void created by the failure of its efforts to institute collective security with a technique known as **peace keeping.** Although the U.N. Charter says nothing about peace keeping, the technique was used repeatedly to deal with conflicts during the Cold War era that might otherwise have led to dangerous confrontations between the superpowers.

The origins of peace keeping can be traced to the earliest days of the United Nations from 1946 to 1949, when it sent small numbers of military personnel to monitor cease-fires and engage in fact-finding missions in the Balkans, Palestine, Indonesia, India, and Pakistan (Jacobson, 1979, p. 194). But the first major example of a peace-keeping force was created in response to a crisis in the Middle East. When Egyptian leader Gamal Abdel Nasser nationalized the Suez Canal in 1956, Great Britain, France, and Israel (each for its own reasons) joined in an attack on Egypt. Much to the surprise of those three states, the United States *and* the Soviet Union demanded that the attack be terminated immediately. The two superpowers also cooperated in getting the General Assembly to pass resolutions calling for an end to the hostilities. To implement the resolutions (and to avoid the introduction of military forces from one or both of the superpowers), the General Assembly created the U.N. Emergency Force (UNEF). Made up of military forces from ten to twenty-four states at different times in its existence, none of which came from the five permanent members of the Security Council, it was stationed on the Egyptian-Israeli border until 1967. The importance of its contribution to peace in the area may be suggested by the fact that shortly after it was removed, war between Israel and Egypt ensued (Urquhart, 1980, pp. 88–89).[3]

In the years since 1956, the United Nations has used peace-keeping forces in a number of hot spots around the world. "The primary goal of a peace-keeping operation is to halt armed conflict or prevent its recurrence. It achieves this goal by acting as a physical barrier between hostile parties and monitoring their military movements. A secondary purpose of peace keeping is to create a stable environment for negotiations" (Diehl, 1989, pp. 173–174). The United Nations sent a force to Lebanon (the U.N. Observer Group in Lebanon) in 1958, making it easier for the United States to withdraw the marines it had sent into that country to support the pro-Western Lebanese regime of the time. In 1960, the United Nations became rather deeply involved in the civil war that broke out in the Congo after Belgian colonial rule had ended. In this case, U.N. troops became directly involved in the fighting (as they had not in the conflict between Egypt and Israel), and the undertaking became so controversial that the Soviet Union and France refused to pay their share of the expenses for this particular peace-keeping effort.

Despite that setback and the financial and political crisis it created for the United Nations, peace-keeping missions have been organized quite often since the U.N. involvement in the Congo. U.N. troops were sent to Yemen in 1963, to Cyprus in 1964, and again to the Middle East in the wake of the Yom Kippur War in 1973 (troops from UNEF-II, or the second United Nations Emergency Force, were stationed in the Sinai and the Golan Heights) and after the invasion of Lebanon by Israel in 1978 (Bennett, 1980, p. 157).

After the creation of the United Nations Interim Force in Lebanon (UNIFIL), a decade passed before the United Nations mounted another peace-keeping mission (Riggs and Plano, 1994, p. 121). By 1987, there were only five U.N. peace-keeping missions in the world, staffed by fewer than 10,000 troops at a cost of $250 million a year. Even as late as 1992, there were only 11,500 U.N. peace keepers in the world. Then came an explosion of U.N. activity. By 1994, some 80,000 U.N. troops were involved in eighteen peace-keeping missions around the world at a cost of more than $3.3 billion (Lewis, 1997 p. 7). Overall, since 1956, about 750,000 troops have served in some forty-three peace-keeping missions (UNA in Canada, 1997b).

---

[3] Of course, from the Israeli point of view, this incident proved that the U.N. forces are a frail barrier to war. The umbrella was removed, so to speak, just as it began to rain. But it might not have been removed if the Israelis had allowed the U.N. forces to be stationed on their soil.

Peace keeping is a rather tentative and piecemeal approach compared to the grander sweep of collective security. But it may be an especially important function for the United Nations to carry out in the contemporary era. In recent years "most conflicts are within countries rather than between them" (Lewis, 1997, Section 1, p. 4). Until very recently, at least, the United Nations simply has not been equipped to implement collective security. But its reaction to the Iraqi annexation of Kuwait in August 1990 suggests that it may be possible for the organization to move beyond peace keeping and institute a working collective security system. That is essentially what President Bush meant when he responded to that crisis by asserting that "out of these troubled times—a new world order—can emerge" (Bush, 1990, p. 2953). A working collective security system might come into being because it now may be possible for the major powers to cooperate in the establishment of such a system, in which an aggressive move such as Iraq's against Kuwait will be met by the determined resistance of the world community, working through the institutions of the United Nations.

It is also possible, though, that Iraq's attack on Kuwait created an ideal situation for the concept of collective security that is *not* likely to be repeated. "The term 'war' still conjures up an image of massed armies clashing on the battlefield. But this kind of war is now largely a thing of the past. The vast majority of violent disputes today (and quite likely of tomorrow) are . . . civil wars" (Renner, 1993, p. 8). When the United Nations intervenes in civil wars, such as those in the former Yugoslavia and in Somalia, it engages in "peace making" rather than "peace keeping," because in these places there is no peace to be kept. The question of how well the United Nations is suited to the task of "peace making" as opposed to "peace keeping" is explored below.

If it is true that international war is "now largely a thing of the past," that is a milestone in human events that should not go unnoticed. But if more "old-fashioned" wars of the kind precipitated by Iraq's attack on Kuwait should arise, it is fair to wonder how effective the United Nations' reaction will be. "Collective security is likely to be ineffective so long as the aggressor is a permanent member of the Security Council, a client state of a permanent member, or a country able to amass eight votes from the Security Council's 15 members, several of whom will be ruled by venal autocrats." The autocratic leadership of China was persuaded not to veto action against Iraq after its attack on Kuwait, but "China's abstention in the critical council vote authorizing the use of force in the Gulf appears to have been purchased by new World Bank loans, which were approved shortly thereafter."[4] It is not clear that the

---

[4] "In the last five years, more than 90 cases of armed conflict have broken out, practically all of them within states. . . . [T]he U.N. since 1989 has been directly or indirectly involved in more than half of these cases" (Mendez, 1995, p. 22).

United Nations is well placed to deal with such conflicts, nor that it consistently has a beneficial impact when it does. In the summer of 1994, a British journalist noted that American and U.N. intervention in **Somalia** had flooded the market with arms and put the war on hold, but that when the Americans pulled out, "the politics of Somalia reverted to the *status quo ante*, except that the rich and powerful had become richer and better armed" (Jenkins, 1994, p. 13). He also predicted that succumbing to the temptation to send international help to the refugees from the slaughter-filled civil war between the **Hutus** and the **Tutsis** in **Rwanda** would have similarly baneful effects. "Free supplies do not stay free for long. . . . There are already reports of Hutu militias regrouping. They will establish new patterns of leadership, fear, and loyalty. Relief camps motivated by political exile inevitably are umbrellas for revanchism" (Jenkins, 1994, p. 13).

This turned out to be an accurate prediction. Some two years later the *New York Times* published the following account:

> From the start, the Rwandan camps in Zaire have been controlled by the same forces that carried out the genocide in Rwanda and that swear to continue it. . . . The camps, under the flag of the United Nations, became bases for a vicious guerrilla war against Rwanda and local populations in Zaire. . . . Yet for more than two years, the international community has turned a blind eye and poured $1 million a day into supporting them (Gourevitch, 1996, Section A, p. 13).

And another news story published a month later suggests that the problem of the camps was solved only when the aid workers had fled and Tutsi fighters were able successfully to preempt the arrival of more peace keepers. "The Tutsis were afraid that once Westerners arrived, they would impose a cease-fire and freeze the situation with the Hutu militia in control once again of the seething camps. They were afraid of a repeat of 1994: Save the children, save the murderers, save the embers of civil war, prolong forever the exile and suffering of the refugees" (Krauthammer, 1996, p. 13).

In short, at least according to this attempt to interpret the role of the United Nations in the tragedy that unfolded in Rwanda from 1994 to 1996, the efforts of the international community were insufficient to prevent a terrible holocaust. The efforts to respond to the refugees created by the civil war ultimately succeeded mostly in substantially prolonging a painful, brutal status quo based on camps that could not have survived (probably) without the intervention of U.N. and other international agencies, and the problem was not resolved until the U.N and other relief workers were removed from the situation, after which a rather quick solution was achieved.

The high water mark of U.N. peace keeping may have passed. In the years from 1994 to 1996, the number of U.N. peace keepers in the world

Table 11.1 Current U.N. Peace-Keeping Operations

Africa

---

1. Angola—UNAVEM III—United Nations Angola Verification Mission III
2. Liberia—UNOMIL—United Nations Observer Mission in Liberia
3. Western Sahara—MINURSO—United Nations Mission for the Referendum in Western Sahara

Americas

---

4. Haiti—UNSMIH—United Nations Support Mission in Haiti
5. Guatemala—MINUGUA—United Nations Verification Mission in Guatemala

Asia

---

6. India/Pakistan—UNMOGIP—United Nations Military Observer Group in India and Pakistan
7. Tajikistan—UNMOT—United Nations Mission of Observers in Tajikistan

Europe

---

8. Bosnia and Herzegovina—UNMIBH—United Nations Mission in Bosnia and Herzegovina
9. Croatia—UNMOP—United Nations Mission of Observers in Prevlaka
10. Croatia—UNTAES—United Nations Transitional Administration for Eastern Slavonia, Baranja, and Western Sirmium
11. Cyprus—UNFICYP—United Nations Peace-Keeping Force in Cyprus
12. Former Yugoslav Republic of Macedonia—UNPREDEP—United Nations Preventive Deployment Force
13. Georgia—UNOMIG—United Nations Observer Mission in Georgia

Middle East

---

14. Golan Heights—UNDOF—United Nations Disengagement Observer Force
15. Iraq/Kuwait—UNIKOM—United Nations Iraq-Kuwait Observation Mission
16. Lebanon—UNIFIL—United Nations Interim Force in Lebanon
17. Middle East—UNTSO—United Nations Truce Supervision Organization

SOURCE: U.N. Department of Public Information, 1997.

was reduced from 80,000 to 23,000, the annual peace-keeping budget of the U.N. fell from $3.3 billion to $1.3 billion, and the number of peace-keeping operations in force fell modestly from 18 to 17 (see Table 11.1). "The sharp reduction in the size of peacekeeping operations reflects a new mood of caution within the Security Council and the United Nations as to what it can do" (Lewis, 1997, Section 1, p. 4). In addition, at this writing (mid-1997), unpaid bills for peace-keeping operations mounted by the U.N. stand at $1.6 billion. Finally, there is a growing feeling, perhaps, that internal problems within countries might be better dealt with by multinational forces from the region within which that country falls. According to the under secretary in charge of peacekeeping in the United Nations, a consensus has emerged that "peace enforcement and serious peace restoration campaigns will always be the responsibility of a coalition of interested countries using their own forces but with a green light from the Security Council" (Lewis, 1997, Section 1, p. 4). So, in response to chaos in Albania in early 1997, Italian troops led a peace-keeping force of sorts into that country. Later that same year, a coup against a democratically elected government in Sierra Leone led to unrest, and then intervention by troops from Nigeria. The United Nations did not sanction this move by Nigeria, but neither did it condemn it; and the Organization of African Unity approved the intervention (*Economist*, June 7, 1997, p. 44). So the latest indications are, perhaps, that the United Nations will in the future fill a more modest peace-keeping role in places where there is at least a peace of sorts to keep, rather than intervene in places where it is obvious that peace first has to be created. Peace creation, perhaps, will be left to regional, multinational forces, whose activities will be authorized either by the United Nations or by regional organizations.

THE UNITED STATES AND THE UNITED NATIONS

After several Communist and Third World states were added to the General Assembly in the 1950s and 1960s, the United States found it impossible to put together a voting majority with any consistency, and began to become less enamored of the United Nations as a result. Additional deterioration in U.S. influence in the United Nations has been reflected in voting patterns in the Security Council and the General Assembly. During the first two decades of the United Nations' existence, the United States never used its veto in the Security Council, whereas the Soviet Union vetoed proposals brought to that body 103 times. From 1966 to 1975, the United States used its veto power twelve times, and the Soviet Union vetoed eleven propositions. Between 1976 and 1985, the United States felt obliged to veto proposals brought before the Security Council thirty-seven times, while the Soviets vetoed only seven measures. And from 1986 to 1990, the United States exercised its veto power twenty-three times, while the Soviet Union never felt it necessary to veto a single measure. (Curiously, this indicator suggests that the Soviet Union was enjoying an ever-increasing amount of influence in the world, although in fact it was heading for total collapse.)

Voting patterns of this kind are particularly irksome to many Americans, especially members of the U.S. Congress, because of what is perceived as a disparity between what the United States contributes to the United Nations' budget and the influence of those states within the organization that contribute so much less. Because dues are based on the size of a nation's economy, the United States annually pays about 25 percent of the U.N. budget. By the early 1990s, it was paying about 30 percent of the United Nations' peace-keeping bills, although recently the Clinton administration has said it will pay only 25 percent in the future. Still, the United States is the most generous contributor to the U.N. budget by a considerable margin, paying more, for example, than the next two largest contributors (Japan and Germany) combined. Even more irksome, perhaps, from the point of view of U.S. lawmakers, the eight largest contributors to the United Nations provide 73 percent of the budget but have only 4 percent of the votes in the General Assembly. And the remaining 177 countries in the Assembly, which can dominate the proceedings with their votes, contribute only 27 percent of the budget (see Figure 11.3). Yet those countries that contribute only a small

Figure 11.3   Budget Contributions Versus Votes, U.N. General Assembly, 1997

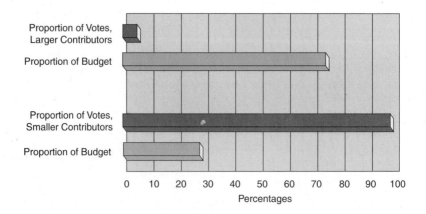

portion determine the budget's size and allocation. In the words of Senator Jesse Helms, chairman of the U.S. Senate Foreign Relations Committee, who is highly critical of the United Nations, its annual budget is "voted on by the General Assembly, where the United States has no veto, and where every nation—whether democratic or dictatorial, no matter how much or how little it contributes to the United Nations—has an equal vote" (Helms, 1996, p. 6).

In response to this situation, the U.S. Congress in 1985 passed the **Kassebaum-Solomon amendment.** "The purpose of the Kassebaum amendment was to give the United States weight on budgetary matters commensurate with its 25 percent contribution" (Krauthammer, 1989, pp. 43–44). This measure cut U.S. appropriations by one-fifth and threw the organization into a financial crisis.

The United Nations remains in financial crisis today; it is currently owed about $2.5 billion, $1.5 billion of which is being withheld by the United States. And Congress is still feuding with the United Nations over budgetary corruption and waste. Senator Helms insists that U.N. bureaucracy should be cut by 50 percent (Helms, 1996, p. 5).[5]

THE FUTURE OF THE UNITED NATIONS

An argument can be made that the United States, as well as the rest of the world, would be better off without the United Nations. One part of that argument would point out the failure of the United Nations to prevent a long string of wars in Korea, Vietnam, the Middle East, and Africa. An even more serious charge is that the United Nations not only fails to resolve conflicts but actually makes them worse.

> The very structure of the U.N. and the pressures of bloc politics draw countries that would otherwise be uninvolved into very divisive disputes. Because votes are tolled up on the big board at the General Assembly and because the world pays attention to such votes, the views of Colombia on Kampuchea become crucial. Colombia must acquire an opinion and then bargain it away to the highest bloc bidder. The result is needless conflict (Krauthammer, 1989, p. 46).

Has the United Nations outlived its usefulness? Despite possible appearances to the contrary, that is not the conclusion toward which this discussion is heading. Despite theoretical obstacles to the goal, it

---

[5] Among the bureaucratic organizations of dubious utility, according to Helms, is the Committee on Peaceful Uses of Outer Space, "which counts among its crowning achievements the passage of a resolution calling upon sovereign nations to report all contacts with extraterrestrial beings directly to the secretary-general" (Helms, 1996, p. 5).

is possible that in the post–Cold War era the United Nations may be able to institute a reasonably effective collective security system. If all or even most of the major powers are democratic, for example, then perhaps, if the democratic peace proposition discussed in Chapter 6 is valid, the post–Cold War collective security system will not have to deal with major powers attacking either each other or, presumably, the increasingly large number of democratic states in the rest of the world. One pair of analysts peering into the post–Cold War era, for example, asserts that "a central pillar of the next world order is that modern democracies do not go to war with one another, do not even seriously imagine the possibility of being at war with one another. . . . Ask yourself if you can imagine war between England, France, Germany, Italy, the United States, or Japan becoming a politically serious possibility" (Singer and Wildavsky, 1993, p. 3).[6]

Then, too, perhaps realist critics of the collective security idea make extreme demands on the concept, insisting that such a system must either be adhered to universally or considered worthless. But partially effective collective security in certain regions of the world might expand and become even more effective over time (Downs and Iida, 1994). At least some pessimistic expectations about the viability of a collective security system in the post–Cold War world seem to have turned out to be unjustifiably skeptical. One prominent realist, for example, has argued that "NATO's January 1994 decision not to expand its membership eastward does not bode well for establishing a collective security system in post–Cold War Europe." He goes on to explain that Russia is "deeply opposed" to such an expansion, and that it is therefore not likely to happen (Mearsheimer, 1994/95, p. 34). But as Chapter 10 showed, the **North Atlantic Treaty Organization (NATO)** and **Russia** have apparently agreed on a **security relationship** that makes NATO expansion eastward likely, at least at the time of writing.[7]

It is true, as critics of the collective security concept point out, that there is no authoritative system for **allocating the burdens of collective**

---

[6] At another point, Singer and Wildavsky (1993, p. 9) observe that since the end of the Cold War "there is every kind of foreboding and hand wringing about growing conflict among the United States, Japan, and a united Europe, and much alarm about renewed German dominance. But no one claims to be able to imagine that the United States will have a war with Japan or Germany or Europe, or that there will be a war between France and Germany, much less between England and France."

[7] A realist such as Mearsheimer might argue that this expansion of NATO is not "meaningful," because the security agreement between NATO and Russia may preclude the placement of weapons or troops in those countries. Also, that realist expectations about NATO's expansion may turn out to be wrong does not necessarily mean that such expansion is a good thing. Technically, at least, the potential new members of NATO are already protected by collective security by virtue of their U.N. membership.

security enforcement. In addition, it would be logical for all states to want to be **free riders** in the pursuit of the public good ("public" in this case meaning the international community) of collective security and to allow other states to take on those burdens (see Chapter 4). In other words, "states will have strong incentives to pass the buck and get other states to pay the heavy price of confronting an aggressor" (Mearsheimer, 1994/95, p. 31). But for some reason, such buck passing or free riding was not a problem in the effort to confront Iraqi aggression against Kuwait in 1990 and 1991.

> The United States was . . . able to secure more than enough contributions (totalling $54.6 billion) to pay for the war. Of the total amount pledged by allies . . . $49 billion was in cash, with the remainder consisting of in-kind contributions of material. The cash amount fully covered the cost of the war, which totaled $31.6 billion. . . . Indeed . . . , the United States might be considered to have made a "profit" of over $17 billion on the war (Campbell, 1993, pp. 83–84).

In addition, it is not as clear as most realists would contend that collective security imposes burdens on states in the form of obliging them to take steps contrary to their own self-interest. Rather, what collective security requires is an ability to consider making some sacrifices in the short run in return for important benefits in the long run. According to the collective security concept, when any state in the system is the victim of aggression, the remaining states need not ask "for whom the bell tolls." Ultimately, in a system where aggression is less systematically resisted, each state is more likely to be victimized itself. On the other hand, in a system where at least a significant portion of powerful states are willing to enforce the principle of collective security, all states may thereby reduce their risk of being victimized. This, at least, is the conclusion reached by two analysts who constructed a **computer simulation** of the global political system for the purpose of estimating the long-term effects of states' adherence to the principles of collective security. According to these analysts

> our results suggest that cooperative behavior directed toward defending other states from aggression benefits not only the system as a whole, but also those individual states that follow such a strategy. . . . States that practice collective security principles are more likely to survive in a realist world than states that operate according to realist principles (Cusack and Stoll, 1994, pp. 33, 56). In short, although realist analysts insist that self-interest will drive states away from adherence to collective security principles, it is possible that an accurate assessment of self-interest would be more likely to have the opposite result.

In addition, although it is true that formal voting power is distributed rather unfairly within the United Nations, it can also plausibly be argued that the United Nations is too dominated by rich and powerful countries like the United States. Observed from the point of view of poorer countries, the United Nations is under the control primarily of "men from rich, industrialized countries. . . ." In the Secretariat, for example, the professional posts are allocated according to the size of a country's financial contributions; as a result, citizens of the United States fill four hundred professional posts, whereas citizens from countries like China and India, with a total population five times that of the United States, are assigned only ninety-five posts. One can predict with some confidence that there will be increasing complaints heard in the halls of the U.N. building in coming years that the United States is using the United Nations in a proprietary way as an instrument to serve its own foreign policy goals. And as profligate as the United Nations may be in its financial dealings, analyzed in context, it is arguably a bargain. The budget for the Secretariat, for example is only about 4 percent of the annual budget for New York City. Some 55,000 people work for the United Nations worldwide, but Disney World employs the same number, and three times as many people work for McDonald's. Peace keeping in 1995, for example, was expensive, but that year's total U.N. peace-keeping budget equaled only about 1.1 percent of the U.S. defense budget (UNA of Canada, 1997a).

And military conflict between—as opposed to within—nation-states *may* have become old-fashioned, but it is still true that "there are approximately sixty-seven interstate border or territorial disputes in the world" (Diehl, 1993, p. 174). U.N. forces may not always be the answer if one of these disputes threatens to escalate, but perhaps a division of labor between the United States and the United Nations is possible that would be acceptable and beneficial to all concerned. "A recent Roper poll . . . [showed that] Americans preferred by a three-to-one margin to send the U.N.'s blue helmets rather than U.S. forces to handle regional conflicts, even if that means that the outcome would not necessarily further unilateral U.S. interests" (Luck, 1992/93, p. 147). This does not mean that the United States can always stay out of such ventures. In fact, many U.N. advocates feel that if the organization is to be effective, the major powers will generally need to take a more active role.

On the other hand, to cope in the coming millennium, the United Nations probably needs to be reorganized to some extent, in a way that plays down the role of at least some major powers. There is a growing feeling that the structure of the Security Council, for example, is anachronistic. The five states that have a **veto** were selected on the basis of the results of the Second World War. An Independent Working Group convened by the Ford Foundation at the request of the U.N. secretary-general concluded that "the Security Council [should] be expanded from its present membership of 15 to a total of approximately 23 Members, of whom not more than five would be new Permanent Members" (Independent Working Group, 1995, p. 16). These five new permanent members would probably include Japan, Germany, and representatives from geographic regions such as Asia, Africa, and Latin America. The working group also recommended that the scope of the veto be restricted, if such an expansion takes place, so that it would be applicable only to peace-keeping and enforcement measures.

In any case, despite all its problems and its current budgetary crisis, it is unlikely that the United Nations will be disbanded. The vast majority of its members from less developed countries (LDCs) find it convenient for a variety of reasons. Many of them cannot afford to establish embassies throughout the world. The United Nations provides a place where they can meet and talk with official representatives of states to which they cannot afford to send ambassadors. This kind of contact is valued, especially at a time when leaders of developing countries generally believe, despite the wide variety of political and economic structures their countries exhibit, that they have many important concerns in common. Also, the United Nations provides a forum and a platform that is probably irreplaceable for most developing nations. If an official from Zaire makes a speech in Zaire, it is likely to go unnoticed in most of the world. But if Zaire's delegate to the United Nations or a visiting dignitary from Zaire delivers a speech in the General Assembly, there is at least a reasonable chance that it will be picked up in the *New York Times* or *Le Monde*. Finally, the structure of the United Nations allows such nations not only to maintain contacts with one another but also to use those contacts to build a coalition that can exert some political clout in the General Assembly as well as in other U.N. institutions and organizations. And if, as mentioned earlier, that coalition creates an imbalance between majority votes in the United Nations and actual political power in the international system, this inequality may not be so bad. In virtually every other forum and arena of interaction in the global system, LDCs suffer a disadvantage in terms of their political and economic power vis-à-vis the industrialized world. Perhaps the United Nations can serve the useful purpose of partially redressing that imbalance. For all these reasons, it seems fairly certain that the United Nations will continue to be supported by most of its members.

The continued existence of the United Nations is probably in the interest not only of LDCs and the United States but also of the entire global political system. It is possible that debates in the General Assembly and the Security Council serve to exacerbate rather than mollify conflict. It is also possible that in the long run the United Nations will not be able to enforce fully the ideals of collective security, despite the success of the world community, using U.N. institutions to a limited extent, in terminating the Iraqi occupation of Kuwait. But at least a couple of lessons gleaned from the historical record of this century indicate that dismantling the United Nations might be a serious mistake. The crisis that culminated in the First World War might conceivably have been resolved if some institutionalized forum for negotiations among the Great Powers, such as that provided by the Council of the League of Nations or the Security Council of the United Nations, had existed. And certainly one cause of the Second World War was the failure of the major powers to support the League of Nations. Both of these assertions are, to be sure, debatable. Even the most vigorous dissenter must agree, though, that they are not entirely implausible. If there is a reasonable chance that an organization such as the United Nations may help the world avoid catastrophes of the magnitude of the world wars, is it not prudent to preserve the organization?

At a time when both positive forces—such as improved communications and transportation—and worldwide problems—such as famine, terrorism, nuclear proliferation, and pollution—are making it increasingly necessary for the world community to function as such, it would surely be a mistake to destroy virtually the only existing symbolic and institutional basis for the community, as flawed as it admittedly is. On a more practical level, intergovernmental organizations such as the IMF and the WHO are expanding the scope of their activities and influence. The same can be said for international nongovernmental organizations such as multinational corporations and professional societies. What other organization is better suited to the progressively more important task of monitoring and coordinating the activities of these international and transnational organizations? The United Nations is not likely to evolve into a world government. It might, though, facilitate the coordination of the world community's efforts to deal with problems that cannot be dealt with effectively by states going their separate ways, especially if the major powers agree that the organization ought to be used for such purposes, as they increasingly seem inclined to do in the post–Cold War era.

SUMMARY

Modern international organizations trace their origins to the nineteenth century, during which the Concert of Europe was established by the Congress of Vienna and several international functional organizations such as the Universal Postal Union and the International Office of Weights and Measures were launched. After the First World War, the League of Nations was set up in the hope that it would prevent such wars from recurring. The League failed to prevent the Second World War, but its temporary existence taught U.S. policymakers, at any rate, that the war happened because of failure to support the League, not because organizations like the League, or the United Nations, are inherently ineffective.

A major purpose of the United Nations is to establish a system of collective security guaranteeing that any victim of aggression in the international system will receive support from the collective weight of the entire international community. There are several logical or theoretical grounds for expecting it to be difficult to create an effective collective security system. *Aggression* is not easy to define, and even if a definition can be agreed upon, its application to concrete cases can be controversial. Precommitments by some nations to other nations in the form of alliances are, strictly speaking, inconsistent with a system of collective security, since the world community must be ready to resist aggression by any state in the world. In addition, all states have a powerful incentive to let other states carry the burden of resisting aggression in any given case.

For all these reasons, over the years the United Nations has invested a lot of time and energy in peace keeping, as opposed to collective security. Peace keeping involves intervening militarily in troublespots of the world to separate antagonistic factions for long enough to allow stable relationships to be restored. Peace-keeping ventures have proliferated in the post–Cold War world—sometimes, as in Rwanda and Somalia, with controversial effects. Peace-keeping activities reached a peak in 1993 and 1994; at the moment, the United Nations seems set on a course of scaling back peace-keeping operations

The United Nations has become unpopular in some U.S. circles because the General Assembly often votes in ways contrary to the wishes of the United States. In addition, it is structured in such a way as to give many states making only minor contributions to the budget substantial influence, while the United States, which pays roughly 25 percent of the annual U.N. budget, does not receive commensurate voting power within the organization.

It is possible in the post–Cold War era that the United Nations might be able to establish at least a partially functioning collective security system. In addition, the United Nations is not very expensive compared with, for example, the annual defense budget of the United States. Finally, the current structure of the United Nations compensates smaller, poorer countries to some extent for their relative inability to be influential outside the organization, and it is useful to them in other ways that probably guarantee it support from the vast majority of its members.

KEY TERMS

United Nations
Concert of Europe
functional organizations
functionalist theory
League of Nations
Security Council
Economic and Social Council
  (ECOSOC)
Trusteeship Council
International Court of Justice
General Assembly
secretary-general
Secretariat
collective security
definition of aggression
authoritative decisions about
  disputes

alliances
peace keeping
Somalia
Hutus
Tutsis
Rwanda
Kassebaum-Solomon amendment
North Atlantic Treaty Organization
  (NATO)
Russia
security relationship
allocating the burdens of collective
  security
free riders
computer simulation
veto

SOURCES

Bennett, A. Leroy. *International Organizations.* 2nd ed. Englewood Cliffs, N.J.: Prentice-Hall, 1980.

Campbell, David. *Politics Without Principle: Sovereignty, Ethics, and the Narratives of the Gulf War.* Boulder, Colo.: Lynne Rienner Publishers, 1993.

Claude, Inis L. *Swords into Plowshares.* 3rd ed. New York: Random House, 1964.

Cusack, Thomas R., and Richard J. Stoll. "Collective Security and State Survival in the Interstate System." *International Studies Quarterly,* 38 (March 1994), 33–59.

Diehl, Paul F. "The Conditions for Success in Peacekeeping Operations." In Paul F. Diehl, ed., *The Politics of International Organizations.* Chicago: Dorsey Press, 1989.

Diehl, Paul F. *International Peacekeeping.* Baltimore, Md.: The Johns Hopkins University Press, 1993.

Downs, George W., and Keisuke Iida. "Assessing the Theoretical Case Against Collective Security." In George W. Downs, ed., *Collective Security Beyond the Cold War.* Ann Arbor, Mich.: University of Michigan Press, 1994.

Goodrich, Leland M. *The United Nations in a Changing World.* New York: Columbia University Press, 1974.

Gourevitch, Philip. "Zaire's Killer Camps." *New York Times,* October 28, 1996, Section A, p. 13.

Helms, Jesse. "Saving the U.N." *Foreign Affairs,* 75 (October 1996), 2–8.

Independent Working Group. *The United Nations in Its Second Half-Century.* http://www.library.yale.edu/un/unhome.htm, 1995.

Jacobson, Harold K. *Networks of Interdependence*. New York: Knopf, 1979.

Jenkins, Simon. "Leave Rwanda Alone." *London Times*, July 10, 1994, Section 1, p. 13.

Krauthammer, Charles. "Let It Sink." In Herbert M. Levine, ed., *World Politics Debated*. 3rd ed. New York: McGraw-Hill, 1989.

Krauthammer, Charles. "Saved by a Failure of Humanitarianism." *Washington Post*, circa November 25, 1996. Reprinted in the *Tampa Tribune*, November 25, 1996, Nation, p. 13.

Lewis, Paul. "How the U.N. Keeps Pace As Fewer Keep Peace." *New York Times*, May 4, 1997, Section 1, p. 4.

Luck, Edward C. "Making Peace." *Foreign Policy*, No. 89 (Winter 1992/93).

Mearsheimer, John J. "The False Promise of International Institutions." *International Security*, 19 (Winter 1994/95), 5–49.

Mendez, Ruben P. "Paying for Peace and Development." *Foreign Policy*, No. 100 (Fall 1995), 19–32.

Mitrany, David. *A Working Peace System*. London: Royal Institute of International Affairs, 1943.

Niemeyer, Gerhart. "The Balance-Sheet of the League Experiment." In David A. Kay, ed., *The United Nations Political System*. New York: Wiley, 1967.

Riggs, Robert E., and Jack C. Plano. *The United Nations: International Organization and World Politics*, 2nd ed. Belmont, Calif.: Wadsworth, 1994.

"Sierra Leone: Nigeria Imperatrix." *Economist*, June 7, 1997, p. 44.

United Nations Department of Public Information, "Current Peace-keeping Operations." http://www.un.org/Depts/DPKO/c_miss.htm, 1997.

UNA in Canada. "Setting the Record Straight: Some Facts About the United Nations." http://www.unac.org/unfaq/record.html, 1997a.

UNA in Canada. "The UN and Peacekeeping." http://www.unac.org/unfaq.peacekee.html, 1997b.

UNA in Canada, "The Workings of the UN." http://www.unac.org/unfaq/workings.html, 1997c.

Urquhart, Brian E. "United Nations Peace-Keeping in the Middle East." *World Today*, 36 (March 1980), 88–93.

Worldmark Press. *The United Nations*. New York: Wiley, 1977.

C H A P T E R   1 2

Ethics, Law, and International Regimes

Chapter 10 discussed organizations comprising limited numbers of states that have joined together for mutual advantage. Chapter 11 analyzed formally established organizations encompassing the entire international system. This chapter focuses on the organization of states in a more broadly defined way. The states in the international system form a community, even though it is not well articulated or formally centralized. Like other communities, the international one is based in part on shared **ethical standards** and **norms** and on **legal principles** intended to induce more orderly and predictable behavior among states as they interact. This chapter explores the role of ethical norms and principles in international politics and discusses some of the more important ethical problems and controversies in today's international system. It concludes with an examination of the role of **international law** and the impact of ethical norms and legal principles that become sufficiently influential to lead to the emergence of **"regimes."**

ETHICS AND THE INTERNATIONAL COMMUNITY

Morality and International Politics

According to a commonly held view, moral principles have nothing to do with international politics, even though they are discussed continually. If defenders of national policies are to be believed, the policies of each and every state in the world conform rigorously to the highest ethical standards and are motivated primarily by the purest altruistic motives.[1] But in the standard skeptical view, **morality** in the context of international politics is like the weather: everybody talks about it, but nobody does anything about it.

Opinions as widespread as this one are not often totally without foundation, and skepticism about the role of moral principles in international politics is supported by considerable evidence and logic. First, historically as well as in modern times, many important actors in international politics have behaved in blatantly immoral ways, apparently free from the influence of ethical considerations.[2] Also, the peoples of the world have very disparate ideas about what constitutes moral behavior. Then, too, the international political system is **anarchic.** There is no central authority, no government, nobody responsible for enforcing laws. "The moral requirements of a state which has somehow to survive in a context of states each of which is potentially a violent criminal and above which there is no political superior with a monopoly of authority to enforce law and order, must be different from that of an individual in an orderly civil society" (Stern, 1973, p. 136).

This fairly typical statement that the moral requirements of states are different from those of individuals looks suspiciously like a euphemistic way of saying that they do not have any moral requirements at all, except to do whatever they must to protect themselves. And this idea, this skepticism about the role of morality in politics, attracts support from widely divergent points on the ideological spectrum. Hans Morgenthau is perhaps best known for this opinion among "realist" U.S. scholars of international politics. He argues, while elaborating on his theory of "realism," that "statesmen think and act in terms of power"; Morgenthau also warns against "equating the foreign policies of a statesman with his philosophic or political sympathies" and asserts that "moral principles cannot be applied to the actions of states" (Morgenthau, 1967, pp. 5–10). Similarly, Marxist writers believe that ethical justifications for political actions are "superstructure" and tools in class warfare (Marx and Engels, 1959, p. 247). Leon Trotsky spoke for many of his Marxist peers when he argued that "the appeal to abstract norms is not a disinterested philosophical mistake but a necessary element in the mechanism of class deception" (Trotsky, 1973, p. 27).

---

[1] "National rhetoric bristles with moral fervor and righteous indignation" (Nelson, 1987, p. 4).

[2] "For some the moral quality of international relations from the Athenians at Melos to the Soviets in Poland is so deplorable that they question whether moral standards in fact apply to the international realm" (Cohen, 1987, p. 15).

Still, a case can be made for the proposition that moral principles should and do play an important role in international politics. Even though violence is common in the international system and there is no centralized authority to enforce moral standards, states do not continuously behave in a disorderly and immoral fashion. In other words, even though there is a constant threat that world politics will degenerate into a war of "all against all," actual warfare is not typical. "The international community possesses a variety of devices for promoting compliance with established norms. These range from such mild sanctions as community disapproval and censure by international organizations to coordinated national policies of economic embargoes of offending states" (Beitz, 1979, pp. 46–47). Most publicity about these sanctions and embargoes focuses on the limitations of their effectiveness. But ethical principles and laws are also violated repeatedly by individuals within domestic political systems, and unless disorder reaches extraordinarily high levels, these numerous violations do not often provoke or justify the conclusion that ethical considerations or laws have no effect on the behavior of individuals within those societies.

Even well-known moral skeptics concede that ethical principles do have an impact on international politics, in a way that would probably surprise some of their more enthusiastic and cynical supporters. In a chapter on international morality, Hans Morgenthau declares that "moral values do not permit certain policies to be considered at all. . . . Certain things are not being done on moral grounds, even though it would be expedient to do them" (Morgenthau, 1967, p. 225). Kenneth W. Thompson, a realist colleague of Morgenthau's who was invited to prepare a posthumous edition of *Politics Among Nations,* asserts in his own writing that even "the most cynical realist cannot afford even in the interest of realism to ignore political ideals. . . . For man is at heart a moral being" (Thompson, 1966, p. 4). Similar sentiments can be found on the left end of the ideological spectrum. Trotsky noted of Lenin that his (Lenin's) "'amoralism' . . . his rejection of supra-class morals, did not hinder him from remaining faithful to one and the same idea throughout his whole life; from devoting his whole being to the cause of the oppressed" (Trotsky, 1973, p. 45).

Moral skepticism, then, in the analysis of domestic as well as international politics, can be and often is taken too far. Nations do pursue goals, such as economic justice, protection of human rights, and the spread of democratic political arrangements. *Some* of the rhetoric by national political leaders who strive for those goals is, to be sure, hypocritical. But "it is only a prejudice that these [goals] are mere masks for self-interest; neither citizens nor governments see such goals that way" (Nelson, 1987, pp. 4–5).

Moral Opinions and Moral Judgments

Even if we grant that international political actors are genuinely influenced by moral standards, it may still be a waste of time to discuss seriously those standards and their application to moral problems. **Moral relativists** insist that "moral judgments are just mere opinion, concerning which there is no point in arguing, as there is no point in arguing about any matters of taste or personal predilection" (Adler, 1985, pp. 109–110). This book rejects extreme moral relativism partly out of reluctance to accept the conclusion implied by such relativism that all foreign policies and international political acts must logically be categorized as amoral, or equally immoral; that, for example, it is impossible to distinguish, morally speaking, between Hitler's attack on Belgium in 1940 and the decision by Belgium's leaders to resist that attack. Also, advocates of moral relativism rely very heavily on distinctions between the ethical judgments of different peoples in various cultures. But these differences do not prove that all such judgments are equally valid. To establish that, "one must . . . prove that all people's basic ethical judgments would differ and conflict even if they were fully enlightened and shared all the same factual beliefs." This proof is virtually impossible to provide, and so moral relativism has not been proved (Frankena, 1973, p. 110). The discussion that follows is based on the assumption that ethical values matter in international politics, that they have an impact on decisions by national leaders and other actors, and that debates about them are not meaningless exchanges of hot air, or "mere opinions."

THE ETHICS OF WAR AND NUCLEAR DETERRENCE

Perhaps the most serious moral dilemmas created by the nuclear confrontation between the United States and the former Soviet Union have been resolved by the collapse of communism in Eastern Europe, the demise of the Soviet Union, and the fundamentally different relationship between the United States and Russia. But as discussed in Chapter 9, reforms in Russia are certainly not irreversible. And several nations in the world have developed or are seeking to acquire nuclear weapons and other weapons of mass destruction, complete with long-range ballistic missiles.

So the world cannot yet stop worrying altogether about weapons of mass destruction and the morality of war in general. And until it can, there is little doubt that nuclear weapons and the doctrine of nuclear deterrence create what is probably the most profound moral dilemma that has ever faced the human species; they also bring into focus with special clarity the more general ethical issues surrounding the use of military force. No matter what the goal to be achieved or the principle defended, the use of nuclear weapons in pursuit of that goal or in defense of that principle entails the possibility that the world will be destroyed. "If it can be shown that a nuclear war is likely to destroy the end(s) for which it is waged, it can have neither political nor moral justification" (Tucker, 1985, p. 32). If no cause can justify the risk of ending life on the planet, then it is important to ask whether it is possible to defend, on moral grounds, a policy of nuclear deterrence that is by definition based on the threat to launch a nuclear attack, which in turn could lead to the demise of the human race. More conventional forms of military force cause less destruction, but they also bring to mind questions about what philosophical analyses of **just wars** refer to as **proportionality,** or the relationship between the evil to be avoided compared with the good to be achieved. In the Persian Gulf War, for example, the U.S.-led coalition did not suffer many casualties, but *perhaps* tens of thousands of Iraqis died, or more. "The Iraqi case . . . serves to remind us that . . . there are . . . some significant moral balances to be struck. . . . The Gulf War was a big one and the harm done has to be measured against the good achieved" (Martin, 1993, p. 8). And at least one prominent scholar of the morality of international wars concludes that the Persian Gulf war was ethical, because Iraq's attack on Kuwait was so unacceptable:

> The boundaries that exist at any moment in time are likely to be arbitrary, poorly drawn, the products of ancient wars. . . . Nevertheless, these lines establish a habitable world. Within that world, men and women . . . are safe from attack; once the lines are crossed, safety is gone (Walzer, 1992, pp. 57–58).

Deontologists Versus Utilitarians

Such a weighing of the costs and benefits may seem a "natural" way of resolving moral dilemmas, but there is an important philosophical tradition that rejects such an approach. **Deontological theories** insist that the morality of an act may be independent of the consequences of that act, that certain acts (or actions based on rules) are inherently good or bad, regardless of their consequences. In this view, actions either conform to valid moral rules—for example, "We ought always to tell the truth," in which case they are moral—or they do not, and so are immoral. "These rules are valid independently of whether or not they promote the good" (Frankena, 1973, p. 17).[3] In other words, according to the deontological point of view, an act is moral if it is based on valid moral principles; it is the rule on which the act is based, rather than the consequences of the act, to which one must look in order to evaluate its morality.

This stance might seem on the surface a stereotypical "head in the clouds" position that only a philosopher could love.[4] But philosophy is full of surprises. Imagine that a fort on the American frontier is surrounded by warriors of an Indian tribe who are convinced, wrongly, that a man inside the fort is responsible for the rape and murder of their chief's wife. They send a message into the fort stating that if the man is not turned over to them, so that he may be executed in some traditionally agonizing manner appropriate to the occasion, they will set fire to the fort, killing everyone inside—men, women, and children. What is the moral decision for the commander of the fort? If the man in question is surrendered, one innocent person will die. If the request to turn him over is denied, the whole community of innocent people seems destined for certain death. Would it be morally right to sacrifice the life of an innocent man to save the lives of many equally innocent people?

Perhaps not. So maybe it is *not* so self-evident that, as **utilitarians** argue, "our actions . . . are to be decided upon by determining which of them produces or may be expected to produce the greatest general balance of good over evil" (Frankena, 1973, p. 34). In the case of nuclear deterrence, deontologists argue that the waters are even muddier than in the above example because the consequences of deterrence are so difficult to discern.

The peaceful end of the Cold War provides a particularly powerful piece of evidence for the utilitarian conclusion that "nuclear deterrence worked." But as indicated in Chapter 9, there are persuasive criticisms even of that plausible conclusion. Such criticisms support the contention of deontologists that calculating the impact of ethical decisions is so difficult that it is a mistake to depend on those calculations for the purpose of making ethical decisions. Even in the *aftermath* of the

---

[3] Frankena (1973, p. 15) also explains that "a deontologist contends that it is possible [for] an action or a rule of action to be the morally right or obligatory one even if it does not promote the greatest possible balance of good over evil for self, society, or universe."

[4] The idea that moral choices should be based on their consequences (the "consequentialist" or utilitarian position), in contrast, is intuitively plausible. Philosophers who disagree with that idea are aware of the problem. For example, in a chapter entitled "The Futility of Consequentialist Arguments," John Finnis, Joseph M. Boyle, Jr., and Germain Grisez (1987, p. 251) acknowledge that "the consequentialist methodology ('Identify and choose the lesser evil') . . . many today consider literally self-evident."

Persian Gulf War, estimates of the number of Iraqi casualties range from several hundred thousand to rather astonishingly smaller numbers. One former military analyst for the Defense Intelligence Agency, for example, argues that "Iraqi civilian casualties are . . . difficult to calculate, but the evidence points to less than 1000 dead" (Heidenreich, 1993, p. 124).[5] Given that ethical decisions about the use of military force in the Persian Gulf crisis had to rely on *forecasts* of the number of deaths to be caused on both sides, the calculations required to base such decisions on utilitarian principles are difficult, to say the least.

ETHICS AND ECONOMIC INEQUALITY IN
THE GLOBAL COMMUNITY

The world may yet be destroyed in a nuclear war, but the end of the Cold War almost certainly diminished the probability of a massive nuclear war. Now, though, **poverty, starvation,** and glaring **inequality in the distribution of the world's wealth** constitute an even more serious problem in some respects. Millions suffer grievously from poverty, and they probably will continue to do so for a long time to come. "Almost a third of the population [in the developing world]—1.3 billion people— lives in poverty. . . . Nearly 800 million people do not get enough food, and about 500 million people are chronically malnourished" (United Nations Development Programme, 1996, p. 20).

Such statistics would be distressing, but marginally more tolerable, if the situation were improving rapidly. But what makes poverty in the developing world, and the gap between rich and poor countries, politically explosive and ethically even more pressing are the indications that the inequalities are growing.

In 1960, the average per capita Gross National Product (GNP) of countries in the developed world (that is, the United States, Canada, most of Europe, Oceania, Israel, and Japan) was U.S. $6,520; in the developing world the figure was U.S. $361, or $6,159 less. By 1988, the average per capita GNP had increased to $13,995 in the world's rich countries and $717 in the poor countries, resulting in a gap of $13,278, an increase of $7,119 over that twenty-eight year period (as measured in

---

[5] David Campbell (1993, pp. 68–69), in contrast, asserts that "what information is available, however, demonstrates that the war resulted in an unprecedented level of death, given its short duration. Greenpeace, which has made the most sustained analysis of casualty figures, estimates that a total of between 177,500 and 243,000 were killed during the air war, the ground war, and the aftermath of the war. Some 70,000 to 115,000 of those people were in the military, while between 72,500 and 93,000 were civilians."

constant 1987 U.S. dollars (Sivard, 1991, p. 50). Another source reveals that "the **gap in per capita income** between the industrial and developing worlds tripled, from $5,700 in 1960 to $15,400 in 1993" (United Nations Development Programme, 1996, p. 2). In addition, "Thirty years ago, the income of the richest fifth of the world's population combined was 30 times greater than that of the poorest fifth. Today, the income gap is more than 60 times greater" (Broad and Cavanaugh, 1995–96, p. 26.) This gap can be reduced to an even more human, and perhaps more comprehensible, level by focusing on the estimated 358 billionaires in the world, who are collectively worth some $762 billion. The poorest 2.5 billion people in the world, or about "45 percent of the world's population—eke out an existence using just under 4 percent of the world's GNP. At the top, 358 individuals own the same percent" (Broad and Cavanaugh, 1995–96, pp. 26–27).

It is even more depressing to realize that there is little prospect that this disparity will decrease in the foreseeable future. Assume that per capita GNP grows at 2 percent per year in the *developed* world and at 5 percent per year in the *developing* world over the ten-year period from 1998 to 2008. This assumption is rather optimistic, implying that

Figure 12.1 Global Income Disparity, 1965–1995, Ratio of Richest to Poorest 20 Percent

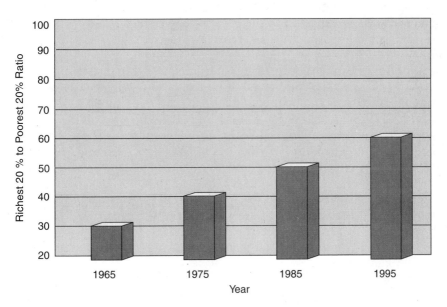

Source: Based on Robin Broad and John Cavanaugh, "Don't Neglect the Impoverished South," *Foreign Policy,* No. 101 (Winter 1995–96), pp. 18–36.

growth rates in the developing world will be two and a half times greater than those in industrialized countries. Even if that rather utopian dream were to come true in the decade from 1998 to 2008, the gap between per capita GNPs would still increase from $13,278 to $15,841, that is, by $2,613.

Part of the solution to this problem is to use different statistics—and this approach is advocated only partially in jest. The differences in the levels of per capita GNPs are so great that given any realistic growth rates in the coming years, the gap between those levels is bound to grow. In other words, the GNPs in industrialized countries are so much larger than those of poor countries that even modest growth rates in the former will add more dollars than will result even from relatively rapid growth rates in the latter.

About the best one can realistically hope for are innovations that would produce 5 percent per capita growth rates in the poor countries and 2 percent growth rates in the rich countries for ten years. Slowing down growth rates in the rich countries to much less than 2 percent would probably retard the growth rates in poor countries and impose hardships on the less advantaged groups in the rich countries as well. Growth rates of significantly more than 5 percent in the poor countries are probably not sustainable. Yet even if we focus on the differences in the absolute levels of per capita GNPs in a thinking experiment where growth rates in rich and poor countries are arguably ideal, the result seems to be deterioration. In short, if even processes as beneficial as we can realistically expect to achieve lead to deterioration and a worsening of the problem in terms of a given indicator, perhaps the indicator is misleading.

A more meaningful impression of the relationship between the rich and the poor of the world is given by the **ratio of the per capita GNP figures** in the rich and poor countries. For example, the ratio of the per capita GNPs in poor and rich countries in 1988 was about 1:19.5. Given an imagined "utopia" for ten years (2 percent growth rates in the rich countries and 5 percent growth rates in the poor countries), that ratio would decrease to 1:15, suggesting, reasonably enough, that extremely favorable processes were improving the situation, not making it worse. Perhaps even more germane, "in 1960, per capita gross domestic product (GDP) in the South stood at 18 percent of the average of Northern nations; by 1990 it had fallen . . . to 17 percent" (Broad and Cavanaugh, 1995–96, p. 22), indicating that inequality did not increase so rampantly during that time period. (In fact, it fell slightly, according to this indicator.)

Per capita income data capture only one aspect of "reality" (as, in other contexts, radical critics of the current world order are quick to point out), and it can be a misleading aspect. They are averages that do not take into account the *distribution* of wealth being produced. The economy of a developing country may grow very rapidly in terms of per capita GNP as a result of wealth increasingly concentrated in the hands of a select few, while most people remain worse off. In contrast, *decreases* in the GNP can mask improvement in living conditions for many people in poor countries. Young people make up the majority of the population of most developing countries. Before recent improvements in health care, many of them died of various diseases or malnutrition. "An increase in the survival rate of the poorest groups usually promotes . . . a fall in per capita income. . . . [T]he average income in the country can fall even if everybody is materially better off" (Bauer, 1984, p. 334). In short, the survival of the young, who typically have no income at all, can depress a country's per capita income, but the decrease does not necessarily indicate a worsening of living conditions as a whole. (Presumably, those children are better off alive than dead.)

Even in terms of income or GNP data, though, the economic picture in the developing world is not uniformly bleak. From 1970 to 1981, if "we look at annual average growth rates of per capita GNP . . . the top fifteen countries in the world were all developing [countries], far outpacing the figures for industrial countries" (Holsti, 1986, p. 361). In the 1990s, the economies of the rich countries have been growing at about 2 or 3 percent a year, while those of the developing countries have been growing at an average rate of about 5 or 6 percent a year. This is because "more countries are industrializing than ever before—and far more quickly than their predecessors ever did. During the industrial revolutions in the 19th century, Britain and America took around 50 years to double real incomes per head. The Asian tigers and China are achieving this within a single decade" (*Economist*, January 8, 1994, p. 16).

In addition, some calculations about the unequal distribution of wealth in the world have been based on a dubious method of converting income figures from various countries into dollar equivalents. Until recently, for example, the International Monetary Fund (IMF) used market exchange rates of currencies to do this. Now, its economists base their calculations on purchasing power parities that take into account what money actually buys in the various countries around the world. We have already seen (in Chapters 6 and 9, for example) that this change has a large impact on estimates of the relative size of the world's economies. A calculation of the distribution of wealth between rich and poor countries using purchasing power parities rather than market exchange rates of currencies reveals that "the share of the world output produced by the rich industrial economies drops to 54% from 73%" (*Economist*, May 15, 1993, p. 15). Overall, "if measured properly, using purchasing-power parities to convert GDPs into dollars, the so-called third world and the former Soviet block already account for almost half of global output" (*Economist,* January 8, 1994, p. 16).

And if we analyze **quality-of-life indicators,** such as **life expectancy** (arguably the most comprehensive statistic available), it is no longer so clear that the developing world is falling farther behind the industrialized countries with each passing year. Data on life expectancy are particularly important in this context, "since life expectancy statistics are calculated by looking at how long *all* the people in a given country live. . . . Although a small number of rich people can have enough money to raise the average income in a country far above what the average person has, nobody can live long enough to raise the average length of life very much" (Singer, 1987, p. 20). In 1950, "citizens of low-income countries . . . had a life expectancy of only 35.2 years" (Seligson, 1984, p. 401), at a time when the average life expectancy in rich countries was about sixty-five.[6] By the early 1970s, life expectancy in the developing world was about fifty-five, while it had reached seventy-one in rich countries (Sivard, 1976, p. 25). Currently, the gap between life expectancy in poor countries and rich countries has diminished to about thirteen years (*Human Development Report 1996,* pp. 149–150). In other words, in the 1950s people in poor countries lived about 55 percent as long as people in rich countries, whereas now they live about 82 percent as long (United Nations Development Programme, 1996, p. 151).

A determinedly pessimistic view of such data would argue that "the overall effect of development efforts . . . [is] that more people now . . . [live] longer in greater misery" (Long and Evans, 1994, p. 44). But a more defensible view (such as the one argued here) is that "death has always been the ultimate threat, and the move from poverty to wealth is first of all a move away from death" (Rosenberg and Birdzell, 1986, p. 3). The improvements in life expectancy data indicate at a minimum that more people are receiving better medical care. Those data, along with data on calorie consumption (United Nations Development Programme, 1996, p. 151), also indicate that more people are getting better access to food.

---

[6] This estimate for life expectancy in rich countries in 1950 is admittedly a rough one. Sivard (1989, p. 25) asserts that "the average infant born today in Western Europe or North America can expect to live to her/his middle 70s, at least 7 years longer than a baby born in 1950," which suggests that life expectancy in the developed world was about 68 in 1950. My calculations for countries currently in the OECD for which data were available in the 1966 *UN Demographic Yearbook* (data were available for all OECD countries except Turkey) show that those countries had an average life expectancy of about 67 in 1950. Unfortunately, Seligson does not indicate where he obtained data on life expectancy in low-income countries in 1950, but because he provides the estimate down to the nearest one-tenth of a year, we can assume that it was an incredibly accurate source.

The United Nations Development Programme has in recent years developed what it calls its **Human Development Index.** "It is a composite index of achievements in basic human capabilities—a long and healthy life, knowledge, and a decent standard of living. Three variables have been chosen to represent those three dimensions—life expectancy, educational attainment and income" (United Nations Development Programme, 1996, pp. 29–30). Figure 12.2 compares the performance of the industrialized world with that of the developing world in terms of this index over the last several decades. It shows a definite trend toward closing the gap between rich countries and poor countries on the composite and reasonably comprehensive indicator of the quality of life. In short, although it is possible that people in general and those in poor countries in particular are "more miserable" than their counterparts two, three, and four decades ago, despite being healthier, better fed, better educated, and better off, it is not likely.

Comprehensive data on standards of living in the world as a whole, or regarding comparisons between rich countries and poor countries over time, provide an important basis for the evaluation of pervasively

Figure 12.2 The Human Development Gap, Rich Versus Poor Countries, 1960–1993

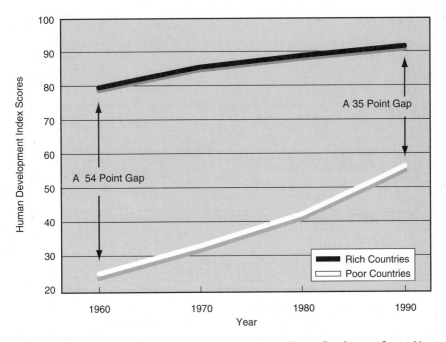

SOURCE: Based on United Nations Development Programme, *Human Development Report.* New York: Oxford University Press, 1996.

pessimistic assertions about catastrophic trends in the distribution of wealth in the world. But most of the data showing recent improvement in living standards in poor countries focus on *averages,* which can mask large discrepancies between countries in various regions. Much of the improvement in life expectancy in developing countries, for example, is simply the result of rather dramatic increases in the index of living standards in China and other Asian countries. "The general picture of the developing world in the latter half of the twentieth century painted by international institutions is one of tremendous progress in improving health and raising incomes; child mortality has been cut in half and incomes have more than doubled. . . . These statistics, however, have been skewed by the tremendous health gains and economic growth of China and the newly industrializing Asian Tigers" (Linden, 1996, p. 55).

While the dramatic improvements in China in particular and many other Asian countries in general should not be overlooked (those countries do contain a very significant proportion of the developing world's population), it is also true that "roughly one billion people—more than at any other time in history—live in households too poor to obtain enough food to provide nourishment for normal work. . . . Another two billion live in conditions [that are] deplorable" (Linden, 1996, pp. 55–56).

Many of these countries and people are concentrated in sub-Saharan Africa. GDP per capita increased at an average annual rate of 5.8 percent in China from 1965 to 1990, but it decreased over the same period in Tanzania, Ethiopia, Somalia, Chad, Zaire, Uganda, Madagascar, Niger, Ghana, Togo, and Zambia. Available calorie supplies increased by over seven hundred calories a day in China from 1965 to 1989, but in Ethiopia, Somalia, Chad, Malawi, Burundi, Zaire, Uganda, Madagascar, Sierra Leone, Kenya, and Togo, calorie supplies were lower in 1989 than they were in 1965 (World Bank, 1992, pp. 218, 272). Food production in sub-Saharan Africa is 20 percent lower now than it was in 1970, when the population was half its current size. The average life expectancy in sub-Saharan Africa is fifty-one years, twelve years lower than in China and India. Of the forty countries that rank lowest on an annual development index published by the United Nations, thirty-one are in Africa (United Nations Development Programme, 1996, pp. 136–137).[7] *In general,* living standards have probably improved in developing coun-

---

[7] But it is also important to realize that even during what is often referred to as the "lost decade" during the 1980s, when per capita GNP fell by nearly 10 percent, "life expectancy increased by five years, from 46 to 51, and infant mortality decreased by a fifth" (United Nations Development Programme, 1996, p. 17). In addition, most recently, "little noticed by the rest of the world, much of sub-Saharan Africa is in the midst of an upturn. Last year its economies grew by 4.4%, faster than for two decades" (*Economist,* June 14, 1997, p. 13.)

tries since the Second World War, perhaps even more rapidly in some respects than they have in rich countries. But there are tragic exceptions to that generalization involving millions of desperate people.

Moral Implications of Trends in Inequality

The moral implications of the controversy about current trends in poverty and economic inequality in the world are clear enough, even though they are not often spelled out explicitly. If poverty is being alleviated as fast as can reasonably be expected, then there is not such a pressing need—logically, politically, or morally—for greater sacrifices on the part of the peoples and countries in the industrialized world. Yet if millions are suffering (a fact not really much in dispute) and the situation is rapidly getting worse, drastic steps, including even painful sacrifices by the rich, might seem clearly called for on pressing moral grounds.

The evidence regarding poverty and inequality is interpreted here to mean that although inequality in terms of per capita GNP or annual per capita income is almost certainly increasing, at least since the Second World War, there has not been a long-term increase in poverty in the less developed countries of the world. In other words, while the differences in per capita GNP figures may well be growing, the broad trend is toward improvement in living standards for people in both rich and poor countries.[8]

The gap in absolute per capita GNP figures is likely to grow over time but to become less important. The difference between people living in poverty and on the edge of starvation (on, say, an income of $1,000 a year) and those who are comfortable (on, say, $16,000 a year) is substantial and glaring. The difference between people earning $20,000 a year and those earning $35,000 is the same $15,000, but the disparity in

---

[8] One counterargument points out that the *absolute* number of poor, starving people in the world is higher now than ever before, even if it is true that the *proportion* of people in the world accurately categorized as such is decreasing; this increase in the absolute numbers of miserable people is therefore proof that global trends in these matters are negative and discouraging. Thus, such statements as "roughly one billion people—*more than at any other time in history*—[emphasis added] live in households too poor to obtain enough food to provide nourishment for normal work" (Linden, 1996, pp. 55–56), cited above, are almost certainly accurate. Although it is argued here that the data on proportions are more important to a resolution of the controversy, the persuasiveness of more pessimistic analysts makes it hard to provide a universally acceptable rationale for that position. It can be pointed out, nevertheless, that although the absolute number of starving people in the world is currently at an all-time high (in large measure because the globe's population is also at an all-time high), so too is the absolute number of people in the world who are *not* poor and starving.

living standards in the second case is clearly less important. Similarly, as per capita GNP and income figures increase in all countries, living standards everywhere will become more similar in *essential* respects, even as differences in terms of absolute per capita GNP figures increase.

In terms of quality-of-life indicators, such as life expectancy or literacy, improvements generally are occurring in most developing countries. And in most cases, those improvements represent a "catching up" with industrialized countries, where, for example, if literacy rates are already 99 percent, no further improvement is possible.

Even so, it is wrong to conclude that the lot of people in developing countries is improving so fast that no actions or sacrifices by people in richer countries are necessary. For example, to repeat, even if economic conditions are currently improving for most poor countries, "conditions in Africa . . . are expected to run contrary to the worldwide decline in poverty" (Long, 1994, p. 14).[9] Encouraging long-term trends in other areas of the world might be speeded up, and certainly should be if millions of lives in the developing world can be saved as a result. If the current desperate economic conditions in many developing countries were caused by the policies and actions of industrialized countries in the past, then the case for drastic action is that much stronger.

Duties of the Rich Toward the Poor

People in poor countries commonly believe that colonialism and imperialism by the industrialized countries laid the basis for contemporary poverty in developing countries. Thus, rich countries are morally obligated to launch vigorous efforts to eliminate that poverty, even if those efforts involve sacrifices by the citizens of those rich countries. Advocates for developing countries would prefer to categorize these efforts as **reparations.**

The most prominent opposing view is that, first, the wealth in the industrialized world was generated most importantly by capital[10] and

---

[9] Long (1994, pp. 14–15) points to a World Bank study asserting that "that continent faces intractable problems such as high population growth, weak basic economic infrastructure; and wars that have devastated Liberia, Angola, Mozambique, Ethiopia, Somalia, and the Sudan. The study projects that over 43 percent of the population south of the Sahara will live in poverty in 2000."

[10] Patrick O'Brien (1982, pp. 3, 18) for example, provides reasonably persuasive data to support his argument that "commerce between core and periphery for three centuries after 1350 proceeded on a small scale, was not a uniquely profitable field of enterprise, and . . . could in no way be classified as decisive for economic growth in Western Europe. . . . [T]he commerce between Western Europe and regions at the periphery of the international economy forms an insignificant part of the explanation for the accelerated rate of economic growth experienced by the core after 1750. . . . For the economic growth of the core, the periphery was peripheral."

innovations originating within the currently rich countries, and that imperialism and colonialism were not crucial to the process. Also, in this view, far from harming most countries in Latin America, Africa, and Asia, contact with colonial imperialists actually brought considerable economic progress to those areas.

It is clear that European colonialists and imperialists did not bring only sweetness and light to Latin America, Africa, and Asia. But what shape would those areas be in today if they had escaped contact with the West? Those few places that were not taken over by Europeans do not seem, on average, to have benefited greatly by that "good luck." For example, "the African states not subject to Western imperialism—Liberia and Ethiopia—are today more backward than those neighbors which [were] colonized" (Dougherty and Pfaltzgraff, 1990, p. 244). Japan is often cited as a shining example of the good things that might have happened to areas had they not been colonized, because Japan was never formally subjected to colonial status. It is certainly a success story in economic terms. But "Britain and other Western powers imposed treaties upon the Japanese that required something approaching free trade with the rest of the world. In particular, a treaty of 1866 restricted the Japanese to a revenue tariff of not more than 5 percent, which lasted until 1899. . . . Trade immediately expanded, and economic growth apparently picked up speed, particularly in the 1880s and 1890s" (Olson, 1982, p. 152). It would seem difficult to trace Japan's economic success to lack of contact with the Western industrialized world.

In general, it also seems difficult to conclude with confidence that current economic problems in developing countries are *primarily* the fault of imperialism and colonialism in previous centuries. Still, there is arguably a strong moral obligation on the part of people in rich countries to assist those starving in poor countries, even if the poverty creating that suffering is not entirely their fault. Traditionally speaking, "it is no part of the morality of states that residents of relatively affluent societies have obligations founded on justice to promote economic development elsewhere" (Beitz, 1979, p. 127). This tradition is based on the idea that states are entirely self-contained communities and that state boundaries limit the range of moral obligations. But the modern era of complex interdependence arguably creates the basis for a nascent community, at least; in such an interdependent world, confining principles of social justice *within* national boundaries constitutes unethical neglect of those in need of assistance.[11] In fact, mere coexistence on the same planet creates a moral obligation among human beings to aid each

---

[11] "When, as now, national boundaries do not set off discrete, self-sufficient societies, we may not regard them as morally decisive features of the earth's social geography" (Beitz, 1979, p. 176).

other in times of stress, and that coexistence obliges rich countries to help poor countries regardless of the origins of their economic problems.

How much should rich countries help poor countries? That turns out to be a complex question from a moral point of view. According to one moral principle, "radical sacrifices" by the rich are in order. "The wealth of a rich individual or a rich nation should be given away until the point where personal or domestic need is as great as that of the people to whom the money or food might be sent" (Hare and Joynt, 1982, p. 165). In other words, the rich are obliged to give until any further sacrifice on their part makes them poorer than those they are assisting.

The logic on which this principle rests is appealing. It suggests that each individual is of equal worth and that resources should be allocated to those most in need. "The owner of the resources is not allowed morally to give his own happiness more weight just because it is his" (Hare and Joynt, 1982, p. 165). But moral codes that require people to be saints may backfire. "We need to have a basic moral code which is not too far beyond the capacities of the ordinary man, for otherwise there will be a general breakdown of compliance with the moral code" (Singer, 1985, p. 255). One can easily imagine that a code requiring people to reduce themselves and their families to penury in order to aid people in other countries they do not even know would inspire cynicism about moral codes in general.

In addition, any strategy for helping poor countries based on calls for large sacrifices by people in rich countries must deal with the fact that individual sacrifices multiplied many times over might, in their aggregate effect, hurt more people in poor countries than they would help. The economies of many poor countries are, for example, quite dependent on trade with rich countries. If the economies of rich countries are booming, consumers there will buy more exports from developing countries. If the economies of rich countries go into recession (as they did in 1982), virtually depression-type conditions are likely to appear in poor countries. So extreme, self-sacrificing generosity by individual consumers in rich countries that results in substantially slower growth rates in those countries could do poor people living in developing countries more indirect harm than direct good.

Perhaps, then, more limited sacrifices by the rich for the sake of the poor would be in order, sacrifices that would conform to the following rule: "A very important natural duty . . . constrains us to further just arrangements not yet established, at least if they can be done without too much cost to ourselves" (Rawls, 1972, p. 115; cited by Beitz, 1985, p. 306). Surely it would be ethical for the rich to give only enough to help the poor but not enough to really hurt themselves. In fact, the poor have too little food, and the rich often eat too much. By giving up some food, the rich could help themselves achieve better health and allow the poor to escape starvation. Let us accept, as a basis for discussion, a moral principle that rich people and rich states are obligated to donate to the poor at least as much as they can easily afford. Given the tremendous surpluses of economic resources available in rich countries, compared with the amounts available in poor countries, even this modest moral obligation, if generally accepted, might well be expected to improve significantly the lives of poor people in poor countries.

Morality and the Impact of Foreign Aid

It is probably unrealistic to expect that this principle can be effectively put into practice on a person-to-person basis. It would be quite inefficient for each individual to make separate arrangements for transferring resources to poor countries. Individual, separate arrangements would cost much more than organized efforts to pool resources before they leave a rich country. In addition, aid arriving in unorganized dribs and drabs is unlikely to have as beneficial an effect as aid arriving in lump sums applicable to larger, more significant projects. "It may be that states, as the primary actors in international politics, are more appropriately situated than individual persons to carry out whatever policies are required to implement global principles" (Beitz, 1979, p. 153).

Unfortunately, though, when states and their governments get involved in the process of transferring resources from people in rich countries to people in poor countries, numerous difficulties arise. Before a rich state can transfer resources to a poor one, it must collect them in the form of taxes. Taxation means extracting money from people who may not want to donate it to poor countries. Some citizens feel that way because they are themselves poor. Given the regressive aspects of tax collection systems even in rich countries such as the United States, where the system is formally progressive, foreign aid may, at least in some cases, involve taking money from poor people in rich countries and giving it to rich people in poor countries.

But even if the taxes are collected mostly from middle-and upper-class people who can afford to donate resources to the poor, what if they do not want to do so? Is it ethical for their elected representatives to take money from them and transfer it to poor countries? It would clearly be ethical if government officials want to donate their own money to indulge their altruistic inclinations, but it is much less clearly altruistic for them to vote to donate their constituents' money.

One resolution of this problem creates alternative ethical dilemmas. Lawmakers can argue that foreign aid is in the national interest. It is not charity. It is given to make friends and influence people in ways favorable to the aid giver. Often, too, the aid must be spent on goods and services produced in the donor country. But this means that, first, the aid goes not to those countries and people who need it most, but to those that are most politically sensitive. The country receiving the largest amount of U.S. foreign aid is Israel—definitely not one of the world's poorer countries. It also means that foreign aid ends up ultimately in the hands of manufacturers and other entrepreneurs in rich countries who sell the products (machinery, steel, and so forth) that aid recipients are forced to buy because of the strings tied to that aid. This is one reason foreign aid is branded as "imperialism" (Hayter, 1971).

Another reason for decrying aid involves the impact it has once it reaches the poor countries. There are a few success stories, but in general the impact of foreign aid in poor countries has often been disappointing. Poverty remains there partly because wealth is not easily transferable on an aggregate basis. If John Doe, an individual, inherits $10 million from his rich uncle, chances are that unless John is incredibly foolish, he will be set for life in economic terms. But wealth for millions of people in a poor country must be based at least in part on economic growth and productivity, not gifts. In short, since foreign aid cannot be sustained in sufficiently large amounts to improve the lives of people in poor countries, it can produce lasting benefits only if used to create self-sustaining economic growth and to increase the **productivity** of poor people in developing countries.

One way to avoid the problems involved in state-to-state foreign aid is to use the services of **nongovernmental organizations (NGOs),** such as **CARE,** or **Save the Children.** Unfortunately, at least in some cases, their efforts tend to be ineffective or even downright destructive, as one observer who has both followed and worked for such organizations reports. According to this observer, these organizations exaggerate numbers of refugees to keep their budgets higher, pay their executives extremely high salaries, and overstate the proportions of their budgets that go directly to recipients in African countries. Somalia is one prominent example:

> For ten years before the famine of 1992, Somalia was the largest recipient of aid in sub-Saharan Africa . . . but most of Somalia's 6 million people never saw a penny. Much of what wasn't filtered out to pay the expenses of the relief agency was lost in the corrupt maze of the Somali government's nepotistic bureaucracy. Only the wiliest and most entrepreneurial of Somalia's people ever saw any tangible benefits from the aid. . . . And when money did drip down to the people it was used in ways designed by a government desperately trying to cling to its diminishing power. And in all these things, Somalia was only a slightly more extreme case of how aid works everywhere. The other recipients of aid in Africa have fared no better than Somalia (Maren, 1997, p. 24).

Foreign aid, like this food arriving in Somalia from the United States, can solve some problems in the short run, but it also creates other problems and is likely to be provided in lesser amounts in the post–Cold War era. SOURCE: Reuters/Bettmann Newsphotos.

The effects of foreign aid are not always and everywhere bad, and this evidence is not an argument for its abolition. Although billions of dollars of aid have been dispensed in recent decades and poverty still prevails in the developing world, some data (such as the life expectancy statistics discussed previously) show improvements in living conditions among the world's poor, at least some of which might be traced to the impact of all that foreign aid.

In times of civil strife combined with disasters like earthquakes, floods, or drought (such as in recent years in Ethiopia, Sudan, and Bangladesh), foreign aid may well achieve important short-term goals and relieve immediate suffering. Such aid can also be interpreted as an encouraging sign that the global community is responding to ethical concerns about human beings in distress. Substantial evidence suggests, though, that the extent to which foreign aid from rich countries can solve the problems of poor countries is severely limited, even if one accepts the argument that rich countries have an ethical obligation to provide such aid. And while "there are those who believe . . . that the world would be better off without the fig leaf that modern humanitarianism increasingly provides [through such NGOs in particular as CARE and Save the Children] . . . it is at least as likely that nothing positive would replace the humanitarian system, however flawed and, in some cases, destructive it can be. The dilemma is real, and there is no clear answer" (Rieff, 1997, p. 137).

THE ETHICS OF INTERVENTION: HUMAN RIGHTS VERSUS STATES' RIGHTS

One way in which many problems of foreign aid might be solved involves bypassing the governments of poor countries. In fact, in principle, a lot of problems in many countries could be solved by outside intervention. Numerous governments continually violate the human rights of their citizens, for example. Some governments stay in power without elections, against the apparent wishes of the majority of people in the country. Other governments simply follow unwise policies, economic or otherwise, that perpetuate needless suffering among their citizens. In a just world, governments that do such things should be subject to the corrective and beneficial influence of people outside the borders of the country being victimized.

But interference in the internal affairs of sovereign states is, in almost every circumstance, against one of the most important principles of international law. The principle of nonintervention "is the most important embodiment of the modern idea that states should be treated as autonomous entities; it is also the main structural principle of a conception of the world, dominant since the mid-seventeenth century" (Beitz, 1979, p. 71). According to most interpretations of international law, states should be left alone. Interference in their internal affairs is not permissible, even for their own good. Outsiders are permitted to intervene only for the sake of protecting a government against outside interference.

Some philosophically oriented analysts of international politics find this right of states to be free of outside interference an intolerable limitation on the range of moral concern. One argument asserts, for example, that only "legitimate states should be free of interference from outsiders" (McMahan, 1987, p. 95). Another posits, in a similar way, that "unjust institutions do not enjoy the same *prima facie* protection against external interference as do just institutions" (Beitz, 1979, p. 121). And on the surface, anyway, there seems no good reason why government leaders should be able to perpetrate all manner of crimes against people under their rule and hide behind the international legal

The billboard in this photo from China says, "Practice birth control to benefit the next generation." China's iron-clad one-child policy has apparently caused a large number of unborn girls to be aborted. SOURCE: AP/Wide World Photos.

principle of nonintervention. In the contemporary era, several analysts have noted that one reason interventions have become more acceptable (especially in the post–Cold War era) "is the increasing acceptance of the protection of individual rights as an international norm" (Mandelbaum, 1996, p. 533).

Almost certainly the most pervasive human rights abuses in the world involve women, who constitute half of the world's population and are subjected to discriminatory policies in virtually all countries. Every year, for example, millions of African girls, and some Asians, are subjected to "female circumcision," or **female genital mutilation.**

Genital mutilation has been inflicted on 80 to 100 million girls and young women. In countries where it is practiced, mostly African, about two million youngsters a year can expect the knife—or the razor or a glass shard, to cut their clitoris or remove it altogether, to have part or all of the labia minora cut off, and part of the labia majora, and the sides of the vulva sewn together with catgut or thorns (Rosenthal, 1996b, Section A, p. 15).

From one point of view, this might be considered a private matter, a culturally based custom of no legitimate interest to outsiders. Or, alternatively, one might argue that "a small number of African and foreign women devote their lives to fighting genital mutilation. But unless they get major help and attention, their struggle may take more generations. No people on earth can give them more help and attention than the president of the United States" (Rosenthal, 1996a, p. 13).[12]

In China, the government's population policy limits families to one or two children. "That makes parents fearful of 'wasting' their quota on a girl" (Kristoff, 1993, p. 4). Ultrasound scanners make it possible to detect the gender of a child before it is born. It is estimated that some 1.7 million unborn girls are identified in this way each year in China and subsequently aborted. In other words, as a result of government policy, something on the order of 12 percent of female fetuses are aborted or otherwise unaccounted for in China every year. Similar patterns can be found in other Asian countries, such as South Korea and India (Kristoff, 1993). Economist Amartya Sen estimates that 100 million women are "missing" in **female deficit** countries, that is, countries whose female populations are smaller than they would be under "normal" circumstances; 44 million and 37 million of these missing women are in China and India, respectively. "The phenomenon of missing women reflects a history of higher mortality for females and a staunch anti-female bias in health care and nutrition in these countries" (Sen, 1993, p. 46).

What should be done about widespread mistreatment and abuse of half the world's population, and by whom? The United Nations is moving toward action in this realm of human rights abuses. It has adopted a **Convention on the Elimination of All Forms of Discrimination Against Women,** which has been ratified by 104 countries. The convention obligates countries to comply with its policies, and to report evidence of compliance to the Committee on the Elimination of Discrimination Against Women (Bunch and Carrillo, 1994, p. 33). The World Health Organization, a functional organization of the United

---

[12] Perhaps the most concrete step advocated by Rosenthal (1996a, p. 13) is to "give more aid to governments actively working against mutilation in their countries, and less, or nothing, to governments that are not."

Nations, has announced its intention to put an end to female circumcision. And in 1993, the United Nations sponsored a World Conference on Human Rights that endorsed an American proposal to create a new U.N. post of high commissioner on human rights (Riding, 1993, p. 2).

Ellen Goodman (1993, p. 15), an American syndicated columnist, argues that "global mistreatment of women is no longer a cultural issue." Unfortunately, perhaps, that conclusion is probably premature. Two African women currently employed in the United States as a lawyer and a college professor, respectively, "take great exception to the recent Western focus on female genital mutilation in Africa." They go on to note that the U.S. State Department now requires African governments to report on the incidence of genital mutilation and that influential lawmakers call for discontinuation of financial aid to governments that do "not address this issue in the manner dictated by the West." "We do not believe," these African women conclude, "that force changes traditional habits and practices. Superior Western attitudes do not enhance dialogue or equal exchange of ideas" (Dawit and Mekuria, 1993, p. 11). The headline for the professors' *New York Times* article is, "The West Just Doesn't Get It." In a similar vein, the director of the East Asian and Pacific bureau of the Ministry of Foreign Affairs of Singapore has argued that "the diversity of cultural traditions, political structures, and levels of development will make it difficult, if not impossible, to define a single distinctive and coherent human rights regime that can encompass the vast region from Japan to Burma, with its Confucianist, Buddhist, Islamic, and Hindu traditions." "Asians," he continues, "do not wish to be considered good Westerners," and he concludes that "the self-congratulatory, simplistic, and sanctimonious tone of much Western commentary at the end of the Cold War and the current triumphalism of Western values grate on East and Southeast Asians" (Kausikan, 1993, pp. 24, 32, 34).

It can certainly be argued with some legitimacy that the "main concern" of this spokesperson from the Ministry of Foreign Affairs in Singapore is to "delegitimate international efforts to address the abuses that particularly characterize his own government and its regional allies: detention without trial and denial of press freedoms" (Neier, 1993, p. 51). But Americans, too, are capable of arguing that international standards of morality are inapplicable to special problems they face. "The U.S., no less than [other] countries . . . claims the right to pick and choose which rights to defend and international laws to uphold" (Stephens, 1993, p. 13). President Clinton, for example, when faced with refugees from Haiti trying to reach Florida, has claimed that international law governing treatment of political refugees does not apply to the United States. The American policy of forcing Haitians to return to Haiti without a hearing to determine their eligibility for political asylum violates an international legal requirement that they be given such a hearing. "Although most nations have banned the death penalty, [Americans] refuse to acknowledge international law on this issue— claiming, in effect, our culture gives us the right to go our own way" (Stephens, 1993, p. 13).

So persistent claims in favor of the right of states to be free of interference from outsiders, buttressed by cultural differences regarding what is moral or ethical, make it difficult to enforce the rights of women in countries where they are obviously and harshly discriminated against. Canada has adopted an interesting approach to dealing with this problem. It has accepted as a political refugee a woman from Saudi Arabia who argued that her opposition to discrimination against women in her homeland put her at risk (*Washington Post*, circa March 3, 1993). One advantage of that approach is that it does not involve direct intervention in the affairs of another sovereign state, certainly not with military force. And it is conceivable that if additional countries adopted Canada's policy, thus increasing the right of exit for women from countries whose female citizens want to leave, this could increase their bargaining power in domestic political processes focusing on women's rights. In distinct contrast, when Fauziya Kasinga left her native Togo in 1994 and immigrated (illegally) to the United States rather than submit to genital mutilation, she awaited hearings for more than a year during which "she endured body searches, shackles, and poor sanitation at a federal detention center" (Rosenthal, 1996a, p. 13).

Women's rights can also be enhanced if those rights, and violence against women, continue to be treated as development issues, as discussed in Chapter 8. And the status of women can be further improved if they are specifically given increased support by the policies of governments and international agencies like the IMF and the World Bank. Finally, international campaigns in the United Nations and affiliated organizations, complemented by the efforts of transnational organizations such as Amnesty International (to be discussed in Chapter 13), to make women's rights a high-priority human rights issue may in the long run improve the political, legal, and economic climate and conditions for the world's female population.

An Emerging Legal Right to Democracy

It is clear that "human rights" is a controversial concept on which to base decisions about which governments are legitimate targets of outside intervention. Would "democracy" perhaps better serve that purpose? Governments elected by their own peoples in fair, competitive elections could be assumed to be legitimate and entitled to run their internal affairs as they see fit. Undemocratic governments could justifiably be subjected to outside intervention. "From the point of view of persons nonvoluntarily subject to a regime, and unable effectively to express or withhold their consent to it, [there is] little moral difference whether the regime is imposed by other members of their own community or by foreign governments" (Beitz, 1979, p. 179).

There does in fact seem to be an emerging international legal right to democratic governance. "Democracy," according to an analysis in the *American Journal of International Law*, "is on the way to becoming a global entitlement, one that increasingly will be promoted and protected by collective international processes." According to this argument, objections to antidemocratic coups in Russia and Haiti in 1991 by leaders from other governments officially registered in such international organizations as the United Nations and the Organization of American States reflect a "new global climate" that has resulted in a "transformation of the democratic entitlement from moral prescription to international legal obligation" (Franck, 1992, pp. 46–47). This new legal norm has the obvious potential to be abused by more powerful countries for their own selfish purposes against weaker countries. But when democratic government threatened to succumb to chaos in Albania in 1997, and when a democratically elected government in Sierra Leone was overthrown by a military coup, regional forces, headed by Italy in the case of Albania and Nigeria in the case of Sierra Leone, intervened in an attempt to restore law and order and democracy. How well these interventions will work is still unclear at the time of writing, and it was at least a little strange to see Nigeria's clearly undemocratic regime aspiring to protect democracy in another country. But there does seem to be a clear trend in the international system toward acceptance of interventions (and limitations on sovereignty) for the sake of protecting democracy.

INTERNATIONAL LAW AND REGIMES

What is ethical and what is legal can be dealt with separately even in discussions of domestic politics. Not all legal behavior is ethical, and illegal behavior (civil disobedience of unjust laws, for example) is not necessarily unethical for individuals within the context of domestic political systems. But legality and morality are even more tenuously related for states in the global community than they are for individuals in domestic politics. Most domestic political systems have regular, accepted procedures for translating ethical values into legal, enforceable rules. Murder is considered unethical in virtually every society, and it is also illegal, meaning that rules against it are enforced, with violators punished according to established procedures.

SOURCE: Riber/Cartoonists & Writers Syndicate.

In the international community, there is typically more diversity of opinion about what is ethical or moral. Even more important, the international community is anarchic; that is, there is no central authority, or government. The business of government is making, applying, and enforcing laws; and because the international political system has no government, it is only natural to conclude that international law either does not really exist or is not really law.

That is a common opinion for several reasons, one of which is that, as pointed out at the beginning of this chapter, states (or their representatives) so often behave in violent and unethical ways. Also, there is no established way to enforce legal rules in the international system. A law in domestic systems is virtually by definition a rule that is enforced, or has force behind it. If there is no enforcement in the global political system, there is no law. Add to this lack of enforcement mechanisms the lack of an authoritative legislative body to formulate laws, and the basis for law in the international system does in fact seem extremely flimsy.

Yet even though there is no enforcer, and no legislative organ for the global community, there is a centralized judicial body, the **International Court of Justice,** or **World Court.** It is the successor to the Permanent Court of International Justice, which was established in 1920. As described in the U.N. Charter, the World Court has fifteen members elected to nine-year terms by the General Assembly and the Security Council. **Article 38 of the Statute of the International Court of Justice** contains a widely accepted statement of the sources of international law. (Since there is no international legislature, international laws have to come from somewhere else.) The statute asserts that international law is based on (1) **international treaties,** (2) **international custom,** (3) the "**general principles of law** recognized by civilized nations," (4) **previous judicial decisions,** and (5) the **writings of recognized legal scholars** or "qualified publicists."

There is little doubt, then, that international law exists, on paper at least. But there is still room for much doubt about its effectiveness. Despite hundreds of treaties, treatises, and rulings by courts, the international legal structure is so filled with loopholes and ambiguities that the ability of international law to constrain state behavior is questionable. Perhaps the most fundamental loophole lies at the heart of international law in the form of the concept of **sovereignty.**

As developed originally by Jean Bodin in *De Republica* (1576), *sovereignty* refers to the supreme lawmaking and law-enforcing authority within a given territory. A state is sovereign in the sense that it is a source of, but not subject to, laws. This notion of sovereignty, which is clear enough within a certain territorial area, becomes problematic when its implications for relations between territorial units are considered: "What in law and logic could be the appropriate relationship between two sovereign states, each incorporating an authority that alleged itself to be supreme, and which recognized no superior?" (Lerche and Said, 1963, p. 101). The answer is that all states must be considered absolutely equal in legal terms.

On this absolute legal equality is based the principle of nonintervention just discussed. No state has the right to interfere in the affairs of any other, since that would imply that the interfering state is somehow superior. Another implication of sovereignty and sovereign equality is that the only rules that are binding on states are ones to which they consent.[13] And even when states give their consent to certain rules they are often "so vague and ambiguous and so qualified by conditions and reservations as to allow the individual nation a very great degree of freedom of action whenever they are called upon to comply with a rule of international law" (Morgenthau and Thompson, 1985, p. 329). Typically, states can be taken into a court of international law (such as the World Court) only if they are willing.[14] And even if they have created law, in effect, by signing a treaty, states are not necessarily bound by that law. One long-standing principle of international law inserts a kind of implicit escape clause into every treaty signed by sovereign nation-states. Referred to as ***clausula rebus sic stantibus,*** this principle stipulates that treaties are binding only "so long as things stand as they are" (Brierly, 1963, p. 335). In other words, if the circumstances as they stood at the time of the signing of the treaty change in some vital way, as determined by one of the signatories to that agreement, the treaty is no longer considered binding. This principle is "capable of being used, and . . . often has been used, merely to excuse the breach of a treaty obligation that a state finds inconvenient to fulfill" (Brierly, 1963, p. 335).

International law, devoid of any centralized enforcement authority and formulated by states in such a way as to preserve their freedom of action, is often cleverly avoided, openly flouted, or simply ignored. When Iranian "students" seized American hostages at the American embassy in Teheran in 1979, the United States took its case to the International Court of Justice. The World Court ruled against the Iranian government but had no effective means to enforce its judgment. The hostages remained trapped in the American embassy for 444 days. The Nicaraguan government repeatedly charged the Reagan administration with violations of international law. The World Court ruled in June 1986, for example, that those complaints were valid. But the United States simply rejected that ruling (and other similar ones), and the court had no apparent effect on the Reagan administration's campaign to depose the Sandinistas.

Perhaps the most famous, or infamous, example of the impotence of international law is the **Kellogg-Briand Pact** of 1928, officially the Treaty Providing for the Renunciation of War as an Instrument of National Policy, or the Pact of Paris. This treaty was an attempt to

---

[13] "The most basic principle of international law is that states cannot be legally bound except with their own consent" (Chayes and Chayes, 1993, p. 179).

[14] "It is axiomatic in international law that no state can be compelled against its will to submit a dispute with another state to an international tribunal" (Morgenthau and Thompson, 1985, p. 329).

outlaw international war. In retrospect, with the Second World War and many other wars having been fought since then, the attempt looks idealistic to a foolish extreme. This spectacular instance of unenforceable aspirations dressed up as an international agreement is important evidence supporting the case against international law and the charge that it is not really law.

But that case and such charges are usually overstated, despite the obvious validity of a claim that the international legal system has serious flaws. International laws are often broken, but so are domestic laws, as the homicide rate in most major U.S. cities demonstrates. The fact that murders occur in every society does not commonly lead to the conclusion that laws against murder have no effect or are not really laws. Granted, domestic laws have force behind them. Some murderers are arrested and jailed, and some are even executed. But the idea that "law works because it is a command backed up by force [is] essentially false" (Fisher, 1973, pp. 140–141). The U.S. government routinely obeys rulings by the U.S. Supreme Court, even though the Supreme Court commands no troops or other means to enforce those rulings. During the Korean War, for example, President Truman ordered the federal government to take over the steel industry so that it would not be shut down by a possible strike. The Supreme Court ordered the return of the steel mills to their private owners. "The Supreme Court had no regiments at its command. . . . Yet the steel mills were returned" (Fisher, 1973, pp. 140–141).

In short, laws, including international ones, are sometimes obeyed even if the fear of punishment is absent. President Truman obeyed the Supreme Court out of respect for the system and with a sense that the system was worth preserving even if it meant losing on the issue at hand. Most people, most of the time, perhaps, obey laws not merely because they fear punishment but because they believe the laws are just.

Or, perhaps, most people obey the majority of laws much of the time because "morality pays." That is, the benefits from moral behavior outweigh the costs, at least in the long run. Take the simple example of the law in most countries requiring motorists to stop at red traffic lights. Even if all the police in a given city were to go on strike, reducing to zero the probability that violators would be arrested, chances are that most people would continue to obey this law. To do otherwise would risk injury or death in a traffic accident. That law, to an important extent, is self-enforcing.

Roughly analogous situations obtain in the realm of international law. For example, there are laws against the mistreatment of personnel representing foreign countries. In fact, diplomatic personnel are in some respects above the law, being granted **diplomatic immunity.** Any government that mistreats diplomats from other countries could, logically speaking, expect its own diplomats to be targets of retaliation. That is clearly one reason the laws regarding the treatment of diplomats have rarely been violated. When the Iranian government held U.S. diplomatic personnel as hostages in 1979 and 1980, its behavior was virtually without precedent.

There are also many consistently observed laws having to do with routine international interactions in the areas of trade, communications, and immigration. These areas are sometimes referred to as "private international law." Disputes in these areas are almost always successfully dealt with through legal channels.

Ethics, Laws, and Regimes

In the area of public international law having to do with government-to-government relations, states and governments may obey laws and adhere to less explicit ethical principles despite the possibility that disobedience would bring immediate and obvious advantages. As the highly nationalistic German historian Heinrich von Trietschke, a fervent advocate of "power politics," argued, "Honest and legal policies are also, ordinarily, the most effective and profitable. They inspire the confidence of other states" (quoted in Aron, 1966, p. 589).

In other words, under some circumstances, morality pays, or at least cooperation pays. In situations structured like the prisoners' dilemma game discussed in Chapter 9, cooperation pays for both players unless one player defects. In laboratory experiments and with historical case studies, Robert Axelrod has shown that such defections can best be avoided if participants pursue a **tit-for-tat strategy.** That is, players can most reliably evoke cooperation if they cooperate on the first move and then do whatever the other player does on subsequent moves. In time, apparently, both players realize that every defection is met by defection and every cooperative move is reciprocated. Over time, it becomes "rational"—that is, it pays—to be consistently cooperative (Axelrod, 1984).

Such consistent cooperation can be the result of merely strategic calculations, but cooperative tendencies among "players" can be strengthened if they are based on norms, rules, or principles. If such norms, rules, and principles become clearly established and recognized by a sufficiently large number of important states in the international system, then a **regime** may emerge. "Regimes," according to one influential definition, are "sets of implicit or explicit principles, norms, rules, and decision-making procedures around which actors' expectations converge in a given area of international relations" (Krasner, 1982, p. 186). Another analyst points out that regimes "may or may not be accompanied by explicit organizational arrangements" (Young, 1980, pp. 332–333). In short, regimes, capable of evoking actors' expectations that foster orderly behavior, can be based on ethical principles, international law, and/or international organizations.

So, for example, there is a regime in the international system regarding the issue of nuclear nonproliferation that is based in part on an explicit treaty, the **Nuclear Nonproliferation Treaty.** This treaty in effect makes proliferation illegal for its signatories, who also cooperate in the effort to prevent the spread of nuclear weapons in ways specifically stated within the treaty. The nonproliferation regime also has an organizational basis in the form of the **International Atomic Energy Agency,** which implements procedures designed to detect the diversion of nuclear materials produced by nuclear power plants for the production of nuclear weapons.

But the norms or principles on which regimes are based are often less explicit, their content rather emerging and becoming clear as a result of states' actual practices and behavior. There is, arguably, a regime in the current international system regarding the mammoth international debts accumulated by developing countries such as Mexico, Brazil, and Turkey. The United States, other industrialized countries cooperating with the IMF, the World Bank, private banks, and governments of Third World countries cooperate in efforts to prevent those debts from destroying the fabric of the international economic structure.

Also, during the Cold War the United States and the Soviet Union developed a regime, or at least a partial regime, for dealing with the nuclear arms race and conflicts that could have escalated into nuclear war. The regime may have been born at the time of the Cuban missile crisis. In subsequent crises, both sides adhered to certain rules of the game in their efforts to prevent such escalation (Nye, 1987).

The Impact of Ethics, Laws, and Regimes

The concept of regimes has provoked intense interest among international relations scholars, especially those who focus on the impact of international institutions, laws, and organizations. It also has provoked energetic criticism. One critic argues that the "concept of regime" has led to "intellectual chaos" (Rochester, 1986, p. 798). Another believes that "scholars have fallen into using the term 'regime' so disparately . . . that it ranges from an umbrella for all international relations to little more than a synonym for international organization" (Stein, 1982, p. 299).

Recently, analysts sympathetic to the idea of regimes have emphasized the importance and benefits of international institutions and have developed a theoretical position that has come to be known as **neoliberal institutionalism.** Robert Keohane (1993, p. 53), for example, has argued that "avoiding military conflict in Europe after the Cold War depends greatly on whether the next decade is characterized by a continuous pattern of institutionalized cooperation." Realists and neorealists, such as John Mearsheimer (1994/95), counter that "institutions are basically a reflection of the distribution of power in the world[;] . . . institutions have minimal influence on state behavior." In response, Keohane and Martin (1995, p. 40) point out that "five years ago Professor Mearsheimer forecast the imminent decline of NATO." "How are we to account for the willingness of major states to invest resources in expanding international institutions, if such institutions are lacking in significance?" Robert McCalla (1996, Abstract) argues that "to understand NATO's persistence after the cold war, we must turn to international institutionalist theories to explain why, contrary to neorealist expectations, NATO remains the key international security institution for its members." It is also relevant in this context that "the same kind of statistical analysis that has established a relation between democracy and peace . . . has recently found an additional, independent relationship between peace and dense networks of intergovernmental organization membership" (Russett, 1996).[15]

Some recent critics of regimes, norms, and treaties—along with attendant organizations created by those treaties—have made a useful point:

> It is not appropriate to counter skepticism about the success of treaties that require steep cuts in nontariff barriers, arms, or air pollution but that contain no enforcement provision with statistics about the average rate of compliance with international agreements that require states to depart only slightly from what they would have done in the absence of an agreement (Downs, Rocke, and Barsoom, 1996, p. 397).

Still, for all of its possible excess optimism and some ambiguity, regime analysis, especially with its recent emphasis on the importance of international institutions, has served as a useful antidote to "hyperrealism"—that is, the idea that international relations consist primarily and most essentially of a war of all against all, in which conflict and violence are the major, if not the only, really important features.

> The realist argument that national actions are governed entirely by calculation of interests . . . is essentially a denial of the operation of normative obligation [that is, obligation inspired by norms rather than enforced by coercion] in international affairs. This position has held the field for some time in mainstream international relations. . . . But it is increasingly being challenged by a growing body of empirical study and academic analysis (Chayes and Chayes, 1993, pp. 185–186).

---

[15] Russett refers here to a paper by Russett and Oneal (1996).

In fact, most states most of the time engage in more cooperative than conflictual behavior. Wars and international crises are the major news stories, but the vast majority of states are not involved in wars and crises on any given day. Instead, they engage in trade, tourism, and student exchanges; they sign cultural agreements; and they participate peacefully together in international sports events, conferences, and normal diplomatic intercourse. Given the anarchical nature of the international system, this cooperation is at least somewhat paradoxical. Regime analysis may provide us with insight into this paradox.

In fact, some forms of regime analysis may not sufficiently emphasize the propensity of states to engage in public-spirited behavior for the good of the global community, even at possible cost to themselves.[16] Individuals usually behave in essentially egocentric, self-interested ways, but there are intriguing, anomalous exceptions to this rule. For example, "why people bother to vote" represents a "long-standing puzzle" for analysts of voting behavior. It is also difficult to understand why Americans, for example, make contributions to the United Fund or public radio and television stations, why they risk their lives in time of war, and why they "do not always cheat when no one is looking" (Margolis, 1982, pp. ix, 4). One of the best-known advocates of social analysis based on the assumption that human beings are "rational" acknowledges, "I have come to believe that social norms provide an important kind of motivation for action that is irreducible to rationality or indeed to any other form of optimizing mechanism" (Elster, 1989, p. 15; cited in Chayes and Chayes, 1993, p. 186).[17] If individuals are capable of sacrificing even their lives for ethical reasons, it does not seem so far-fetched to imagine that individual leaders may at least on occasion promote ethical considerations ahead of, though not necessarily against, the state's national interest when making government decisions. For example, "probably the 'purest'—most moral, least self-interested foreign policy action ever taken on behalf of 'human rights' was the British navy's suppression of the **slave trade** in the nineteenth century" (Kristol, 1986–87, p. 10).[18] **Slavery** was for thousands of years considered an immutable aspect of human nature. But because of the opposition of the British, ultimately joined by many others, norms against slavery became so strong that it virtually disappeared altogether.

The traditional, quite prevalent counterargument is that slavery disappeared only when and because it became unprofitable (Williams, 1944). In this view, slavery's disappearance had nothing to do with

---

[16] The following argument is based largely on Ray (1989).

[17] For similar arguments, see Kratochwil (1989) and Schauer (1991).

[18] For historical arguments supporting this view, see Davis (1984), Drescher (1977), and Eltis (1987).

moral progress and is therefore no indication that ethical principles influence the behavior of governments as well as individuals. Morality, according to one modern student of philosophy, requires "people to act in ways that do not promote their individual self-interest. . . . Living wholly by the principle of enlightened self-love just is not a kind of *morality*" (Beitz, 1979, p. 27). If regimes are based on an entirely self-interested adherence to norms, their existence (disputable as even that turns out to be) does not constitute very good evidence of the potential impact of ethical principles.

But if slavery's (and the slave trade's) disappearance was a result of truly ethical behavior, then here is at least one important example of altruistic government behavior analogous to that found among individuals, such as voting, contributing to charities, and risking death for the sake of their country. And if moral progress or cultural change is capable of eliminating a social practice of such long standing as slavery, perhaps such progress also can eliminate another seemingly indestructible custom in the global political system—namely, international war.

"The major powers have not fought each other since 1945. Such a lengthy period of peace among the most powerful states is unprecedented" (Jervis, 1988, p. 80). As discussed in Chapter 6, democratic states have been unlikely to fight international wars against each other. The use of military force to collect international debts (Luard, 1986, pp. 330, 336) or establish colonies (Axelrod, 1986, p. 1110), so prevalent in the nineteenth and early twentieth centuries, has virtually disappeared, arguably because such uses of military force are no longer ethically acceptable.[19] Even in "a total war, states struggling for survival altered or transcended the expected use of particular forms of military power [such as chemical warfare, during the Second World War], in part because of intentionally constructed international prohibitions on those types of warfare" (Legro, 1997, p. 57). One recent study of war concludes that after five thousand years, cultural and material changes may be combining to inhibit international war. "War," according to this prominent military historian, "seems to me, after a lifetime of reading about the subject, mingling with men of war, visiting the sites of war and observing its effects, may well be ceasing to commend itself to human beings as a desirable or productive, let alone rational, means of reconciling their discontents" (Keegan, 1993, pp. 58–59).

---

[19] Janice E. Thomson (1990) argues that certain norms that have developed have led to the virtual disappearance of the once common practice of recruiting foreigners to serve in national armies. Ethan A. Nadelmann (1990) traces the impact of moral and emotional factors on piracy, slavery, counterfeiting, drug trafficking, aircraft hijacking, and the killing of endangered animal species.

Perhaps, in short, the world wars of this century, combined with the historical tendency of states to ignore international law and ethical principles, have led theorists of international politics to discount too heavily the impact of law and ethics on foreign policies and international politics. In 1989, while Soviet troops were still in Afghanistan, President Mikhail Gorbachev declared that the Soviet intervention in that country was a "sin" (*World Press Review*, April 29, 1989, p. 25). This may have been the first time a major political leader has ever so categorized a military operation of his or her own government, especially while it was still in progress. It may be a straw in the wind—along with more important indications, such as the recent absence of war between major powers or between democratic states, and the end of formal colonialism—showing that we are entering an era in which the importance of ethical and legal prohibitions against the use of military force for settling disputes and resolving conflicts among nations will become increasingly apparent. "Despite confusion and uncertainty, it seems just possible to glimpse the emerging outline of a world without war" (Keegan, 1993, p. 58).

SUMMARY

It is commonly asserted that ethics and moral principles are irrelevant to international politics. But even realists and other moral skeptics do not adhere to such a categorical position. Moral relativism leads to the conclusion that it is impossible, for example, to distinguish ethically between an invasion of Belgium by Germany in the Second World War and the decision by Belgian leaders to defend themselves against that attack. Relativists also argue that debates over ethical issues are based on mere opinions about essentially arbitrary principles. This chapter rejects moral relativism and argues that ethical issues can be analyzed in a way that clarifies moral dilemmas and leads to a more intelligent evaluation of ethical issues and choices.

Nuclear weapons create profound moral dilemmas because their use in defense of ethical principles or other values could destroy the world, or at least kill millions of people instantly. Deontological analysis of such dilemmas insists that ethical choices must be based on sound moral principles rather than on calculations regarding the empirical impact of those choices. In defense of this position, it must be admitted that it is, at best, very difficult to estimate the impact of, for example, nuclear deterrence policies or a decision to resist the Iraqi annexation of Kuwait.

Inequality in the distribution of wealth throughout the world creates an obligation for rich countries to help poor countries relieve the economic misery of so many of their citizens, who are constantly close to starvation. That obligation persists even if it is not completely clear that economic inequalities in the global system are worsening at a rapid rate. The gap in the average GNP per capita between rich countries and poor countries is increasing, but in terms of such indicators as life expectancy or the U.N. Human Development Index, the difference is almost certainly decreasing. Still, millions of people in poor countries are suffering, and in many countries their plight worsens with each passing year. Unfortunately, relying on foreign aid to deal with those problems creates difficult moral dilemmas and practical issues. The involvement of governments in foreign aid processes means that re-sources are often wasted or misdirected, even though on balance such aid from rich countries to poor countries can be justified. NGOs in-volved in the distribution of international charity act in their own interests, resulting in wasteful behavior and even destructive effects on the people who are supposed to benefit from that charity.

According to basic principles of international law, states should be free of interference in their internal affairs. However, the corrupt and oppressive policies of some governments against their own citizens create continuing temptations for more democratic states to ignore or circumvent legal prohibitions against intervening in the domestic af-fairs of other sovereign states. The most pervasive human rights issue in the world at present involves discrimination against the female population. Some argue that an emerging norm countenances interna-tional intervention on behalf of democracy when dictatorships threaten to emerge, or when existing dictatorships suppress democratic aspira-tions.

Continual violations of international law commonly lead to the conclusion that it is so weak and ineffectual that it does not really exist. But high crime rates within states do not lead to the conclusion that domestic law does not exist. In fact, most states obey most international laws most of the time. In part, this occurs because morality pays; that is, states can benefit from a reputation for being trustworthy and law-abiding. Such cooperative tendencies on the part of states can be enhanced if cooperation is based on established norms and recognized principles. If those norms and principles become sufficiently well estab-lished, they provide the basis for regimes, or "sets of implicit or explicit principles, norms, rules and decision-making procedures around which actors' expectations converge in a given area of international relations" (Krasner, 1982, p. 186). The impact of regimes is at least potentially substantial. An antislavery regime in the nineteenth century, for exam-ple, eliminated a practice long thought to be an indestructible human phenomenon. There are some signs, such as the absence of war among democratic states, the absence of war between major powers since the

Second World War, and the demise of formal colonialism, that norms against the use of violence in international politics are becoming more effective.

KEY TERMS

ethical standards
norms
legal principles
international law
regimes
morality
anarchic
moral skepticism
moral relativists
just wars
proportionality
deontological theories
utilitarians
poverty
starvation
inequality in the distribution of the
   world's wealth
gap in per capita income
ratio of the per capita GNP figures
quality-of-life indicators
life expectancy
Human Development Index
reparations
productivity
nongovernmental organizations
  (NGOs)
CARE

Save the Children
female genital mutilation
female deficit
Convention on the Elimination of
   All Forms of Discrimination
   Against Women
International Court of Justice
World Court
Article 38 of the Statute of the
   International Court of Justice
international treaties
international custom
general principles of law
previous judicial decisions
writings of recognized legal scholars
sovereignty
clausula rebus sic stantibus
Kellogg-Briand Pact
diplomatic immunity
tit-for-tat strategy
regime
Nuclear Nonproliferation Treaty
International Atomic Energy Agency
neoliberal institutionalism
slave trade
slavery

SOURCES

Adler, Mortimer. *Ten Philosophical Mistakes.* New York: Macmillan, 1985.
"After the Withdrawal." *World Press Review,* April 29, 1989, p. 25.
Aron, Raymond. *Peace and War.* New York: Praeger, 1966.
Axelrod, Robert. *The Evolution of Cooperation.* New York: Basic Books, 1984.
Axelrod, Robert. "An Evolutionary Approach to Norms." *American Political Science Review,* 80 (December 1986), 1095–1111.
Bauer, P. T. "The Vicious Circle of Poverty." In Mitchell A. Seligson, ed., *The Gap Between Rich and Poor.* Boulder, Colo.: Westview Press, 1984.

Beitz, Charles R. "Justice and International Relations." In Charles R. Beitz, Marshall Cohen, Thomas A. Scanlon, and A. John Simmons, eds., *International Ethics.* Princeton, N.J.: Princeton University Press, 1985.

Beitz, Charles R. *Political Theory and International Relations.* Princeton, N.J.: Princeton University Press, 1979.

Brierly, J. L. *The Law of Nations.* 6th ed. New York: Oxford University Press, 1963.

Broad, Robin, and John Cavanaugh. "Don't Neglect the Impoverished South." *Foreign Policy,* No. 101 (Winter 1995–96), 18–36.

Bunch, Charlotte, and Roxanna Carrillo. "Global Violence Against Women: The Challenge to Human Rights." In Michael T. Klass and Daniel C. Thomas, eds., *World Security.* 2nd ed. New York: St. Martin's Press, 1994.

"Canada Will Offer Refuge to Women." *Washington Post,* circa March 3, 1993. Published in the *Tampa Tribune,* March 3, 1993, Nation/World, p. 3.

Chayes, Abram, and Antonia Handler Chayes. "On Compliance." *International Organization,* 47 (Spring 1993), 175–206.

Davis, David Brion. *Slavery and Human Progress.* New York: Oxford University Press, 1984.

Dawit, Seble, and Salem Mekuria. "The West Just Doesn't Get It." *New York Times,* December 7, 1993, Section A, p. 11.

Downs, George W., David M. Rocke, and Peter N. Barsoom. "Is the Good News About Compliance Good News About Cooperation?" *International Organization,* 50 (Summer 1996), 379–406.

Dougherty, James E., and Robert L. Pfaltzgraff, Jr. *Contending Theories of International Relations.* 3rd ed. New York: Harper & Row, 1990.

Drescher, Seymour. *Econocide: British Slavery in the Era of Abolition.* Pittsburgh: University of Pittsburgh Press, 1977.

Eltis, David. *Economic Growth and the Ending of the Transatlantic Slave Trade.* New York: Oxford University Press, 1987.

"Emerging Africa." *Economist,* June 14, 1997, pp. 13–14.

Finnis, John, Joseph M. Boyle, Jr., and Germain Grisez. *Nuclear Deterrence, Morality and Realism.* Oxford: Clarendon Press, 1987.

Fisher, Roger. "Law and Legal Institutions May Help." In Frederick H. Hartmann, ed., *World in Crisis.* 4th ed. New York: Macmillan, 1973.

Franck, Thomas M. "The Emerging Right to Democratic Governance." *American Journal of International Law,* 86 (January 1992), 46–91.

Frankena, William. *Ethics.* 2nd ed. Englewood Cliffs, N.J.: Prentice-Hall, 1973.

Goodman, Ellen. "Global Mistreatment of Women No Longer a Cultural Issue." *Boston Globe,* circa March 5, 1993. Published in the *Tallahassee Democrat,* March 5, 1993, Section A, p. 15.

Hare, J. E., and Carey B. Joynt. *Ethics and International Affairs.* New York: St. Martin's Press, 1982.

Hayter, Teresa. *Aid as Imperialism.* Baltimore, Md.: Penguin Books, 1971.

Heidenreich, John G. "The Gulf War: How Many Iraqis Died?" *Foreign Policy,* No. 90 (Spring 1993), 108–125.

Holsti, K. J. "The Horsemen of the Apocalypse: At the Gate, Detoured, or Retreating?" *International Studies Quarterly,* 30 (December 1986), 355–372.

Jervis, Robert. "The Political Effects of Nuclear Weapons." *International Security,* 13 (Fall 1988), 80–90.

Kausikan, Bilahari. "Asia's Different Standard." *Foreign Policy*, No. 92 (Fall 1993), 24–41.

Keegan, John. *A History of Warfare.* New York: Knopf, 1993.

Keohane, Robert. "The Diplomacy of Structural Change: Multilateral Institutions and State Strategies." In Helga Haftendorn and Christian Tuschhoff, eds., *America and Europe in the Era of Change.* Boulder, Colo.: Westview Press, 1993.

Keohane, Robert O., and Lisa L. Martin. "The Promise of Institutionalist Theory." *International Security*, 20 (Summer 1995), 39–51.

Krasner, Stephen. "Structural Causes and Regime Consequences: Regimes as Intervening Variables." *International Organization*, 36 (Spring 1982), 186.

Kratochwil, Friedrich V. *Rules, Norms, and Decisions.* New York: Cambridge University Press, 1989.

Kristoff, Nicholas D. "Peasants of China Discover New Way to Weed Out Girls." *New York Times*, July 21, 1993, Section A, pp. 1–4.

Kristol, Irving. "Human Rights: The Hidden Agenda." *National Interest*, 6 (Winter 1986–87), 3–11.

Legro, Jeffrey W. "Which Norms Matter? Revisiting the 'Failure' of Internationalism." *International Organization*, 51 (Winter 1997), 31–63.

Lerche, Charles O., and Abdul A. Said. *Concepts of International Politics.* Englewood Cliffs, N.J.: Prentice-Hall, 1963.

Linden, Eugene. "The Exploding Cities of the World." *Foreign Affairs*, 75 (January/February 1996), 52–65.

Long, Dianne. "The Other World." In Joseph Weatherby, Dianne Long, Randal L. Cruikshanks, Reginald Gooden, Earl D. Huff, Richard Kranzdorf, and Emmit B. Evans, Jr., *The Other World.* New York: Longman, 1994.

Long, Dianne, and Emmitt B. Evans, Jr. "Development." In Joseph N. Weatherby, Dianne Long, Randal L. Cruikshanks, Reginald Gooden, Earl D. Huff, Richard Kranzdorf, and Emmit B. Evans, Jr., *The Other World.* 2nd ed. New York: Longman, 1994.

Luard, Evan. *War in International Society.* London: Taurus, 1986.

Mandelbaum, Michael. "The Reluctance to Intervene." In Robert C. Art and Robert Jervis, eds., *International Politics: Enduring Concepts and Contemporary Issues.* New York: HarperCollins, 1996.

Maren, Michael. *The Road to Hell: The Ravaging Effects of Foreign Aid and International Charity.* New York: Free Press, 1997.

Margolis, Howard. *Selfishness, Altruism, and Rationality.* Cambridge, U.K.: Cambridge University Press, 1982.

Martin, Laurence. "Peacekeeping as a Growth Industry." *The National Interest*, No. 32 (Summer 1993), 3–11.

Marx, Karl, and Friedrich Engels. "The German Ideology." In Lewis S. Feuer, ed., *Marx and Engels.* Garden City, N.Y.: Anchor Books, 1959.

McCalla, Robert B. "NATO's Persistence After the Cold War." *International Organization*, 50 (Summer 1996), 445–475.

McMahan, Jefferson. "The Ethics of International Intervention." In Kenneth Kipnis and Diana T. Meyers, eds., *Political Realism and International Morality.* Boulder, Colo.: Westview Press, 1987.

Mearsheimer, John J. "The False Promise of International Institutions." *International Security*, 19 (Winter 1994/95), 5–49.

Morgenthau, Hans. *Politics Among Nations.* 4th ed. New York: Knopf, 1967.

Morgenthau, Hans, and Kenneth W. Thompson. *Politics Among Nations.* 6th ed. New York: Knopf, 1985.

Nadelmann, Ethan A. "Global Prohibition Regimes: The Evolution of Norms in International Society." *International Organization,* 44 (Autumn 1990), 479–526.

Neier, Aryeh. "Asia's Unacceptable Standard." *Foreign Policy,* No. 92 (Fall 1993), 42–51.

Nelson, William. "Introduction: Moral Principles and Moral Theory." In Kenneth Kipnis and Diana T. Meyers, eds., *Political Realism and International Morality.* Boulder, Colo.: Westview Press, 1987.

"The New-Bathed Stars Emerge." *Economist,* January 8, 1994, p. 16.

Nye, Joseph S., Jr. "Nuclear Learning and U.S.-Soviet Security Regimes." *International Organization,* 41 (Summer 1987), 371–402.

O'Brien, Patrick. "European Economic Development: The Contribution of the Periphery." *The Economic History Review,* 35 (February 1982), 1–18.

Olson, Mancur. *The Rise and Decline of Nations.* New Haven, Conn.: Yale University Press, 1982.

Ray, James Lee. "The Abolition of Slavery and the End of International War." *International Organization,* 43 (Summer 1989), 405–440.

Riding, Alan. "Rights Forum Ends in Call for a Greater Role by U.N." *New York Times,* June 26, 1993, Section A, p. 2.

Rieff, David. "Charity on the Rampage: The Business of Foreign Aid." *Foreign Affairs,* 76 (January/February 1997), 132–138.

Rochester, J. Martin. "The Rise and Fall of International Organization as a Field of Study." *International Organization,* 40 (Autumn 1986), 777–813.

Rosenberg, Nathan, and L. E. Birdzell, Jr. *How the West Grew Rich.* New York: Basic Books, 1986.

Rosenthal, A. M. "A Challenge to the Clintons and the Doles." *New York Times,* May 30, 1996a. Published in the *Tampa Tribune,* May 30, 1996, Nation/World, p. 13.

Rosenthal, A. M. "Fighting Female Mutilation." *New York Times,* April 12, 1996b, Section A, p. 15.

Russett, Bruce. "A Neo-Kantian Perspective: Democracy, Interdependence, and International Organizations in Building Security Communities." In Emanual Adler and Michael Barnett, eds., *Security Communities in Comparative and Historical Perspective.* New York: Cambridge University Press, 1997.

Russett, Bruce, and John Oneal. "The Third Leg of the Kantian Tripod for Peace: International Organizations Also Matter." Manuscript, Yale University Department of Political Science, 1996.

Seligson, Mitchell A. "Inequality in a Global Perspective: Directions for Further Research." In Mitchell A. Seligson, ed., *The Gap Between Rich and Poor.* Boulder, Colo.: Westview Press, 1984.

Sen, Amartya. "The Economics of Life and Death." *Scientific American,* 268 (May 1993), 40–47.

Singer, Max. *Passage to a Human World.* Indianapolis, Ind.: Hudson Institute, 1987.

Singer, Peter. "Famine, Affluence, and Morality." In Charles R. Beitz, Marshall Cohen, Thomas A. Scanlon, and A. John Simmons, eds., *International Ethics.* Princeton, N.J.: Princeton University Press, 1985.

Sivard, Ruth Leger. *World Military and Social Expenditures 1976.* Leesburg, Va.: WMSE Publications, 1976.

Sivard, Ruth Leger. *World Military and Social Expenditures 1991.* 14th ed. Washington, D.C.: World Priorities, 1991.

Stein, Arthur. "Coordination and Collaboration: Regimes in an Anarchic World." *International Organization,* 36 (Spring 1982), 299–324.

Stephens, Beth. "Hypocrisy on Rights." *New York Times,* June 24, 1993, Section A, p. 13.

Stern, Geoffrey. "Morality and International Order." In Alan James, ed., *The Bases of International Order.* New York: Oxford University Press, 1973.

Thompson, Kenneth W. *The Moral Issue in Statecraft.* Baton Rouge: Louisiana State University Press, 1966.

Thomson, Janice E. "State Practices, International Norms, and the Decline of Mercenarism." *International Studies Quarterly,* 34 (March 1990), 23–47.

Trotsky, Leon. *Their Morals and Ours.* New York: Pathfinder Press, 1973.

Tucker, Robert W. *The Nuclear Debate.* New York: Holmes & Meier, 1985.

United Nations Development Programme. *Human Development Report.* New York: Oxford University Press, 1996.

"The Wealth of Nations." *Economist,* May 15, 1993, p. 15.

Walzer, Michael. *Just and Unjust Wars.* 2nd ed. New York: Basic Books, 1992.

Williams, Eric. *Capitalism and Slavery.* Chapel Hill, N.C.: University of North Carolina Press, 1944.

World Bank. *World Development Report 1992.* New York: Oxford University Press, 1992.

Young, Oran. "International Regimes: Problems of Concept Formation." *World Politics,* 32 (April 1980), 331–356.

PART VI

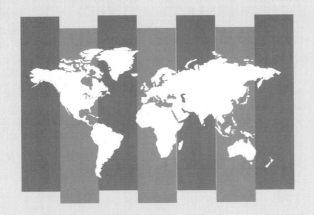

Global Problems

CHAPTER 13

Transnational Actors:
The Wave of the Future?

Nation-states, and groups or organizations of states, have been the primary focus of attention so far. Although they will not be entirely ignored here, this chapter concentrates instead on actors of a different kind in global politics, referred to variously as transnational, nongovernmental, or multinational actors. Their distinguishing feature is that although they are involved in activities that include people and objects in different states, they are not formally associated with the governments of states.

These organizations began to get the concerted attention of scholars of international politics in the early 1970s, with the onset of détente between the United States and the former Soviet Union, which helped to decrease the pressing importance of national security problems. Détente, in turn, increased the salience of economic issues and other problems outside the area of national security, which *nongovernmental* actors could address on a more equal footing with states. For instance the dramatic increase in the price of oil engineered by the Organization of Petroleum Exporting Countries (OPEC) reinforced the feeling among scholars in the early 1970s that issues outside the area of national security and potential military conflict were coming more and more to dominate the international agenda. They realized that international actors without formal, organized military forces would play an increasingly important role in international politics.

The rebirth of the Cold War toward the end of the 1970s and early 1980s refocused attention on national security problems and reduced the attention being given to nongovernmental transnational organizations. But now in the early 1990s, the Cold War has apparently died again, and the stage seems set for transnational organizations to play a corresponding larger role on the global political stage.

**Table 13.1   Number of International Nongovernmental Organizations,
1909–1996**

Year	Number	Year	Number	Year	Number
1909	176	1972	2173	1986	4649
1956	973	1976	2502	1988	4518
1960	1255	1978	2420	1990	4620
1964	1470	1981	4265	1993	4830
1968	1899	1984	4615	1996	5121

SOURCE: Union of International Associations, ed., *Yearbook of International Organizations,
1995/96.* New York: K. G. Saur, 1996, p. 1670.

Transnational organizations have increased in number quite rapidly
in recent decades (see Table 13.1). The organizations in this table,
compiled by the *Yearbook of International Organizations,* must have
aims that are "genuinely international in character, with . . . operations
in at least 3 countries," must contain members from at least three
countries, and must have a constitution giving members the right
periodically to elect a governing body and officers (Union of International Associations, 1993/94, p. 1691). They include such diverse organizations as the International League of Antiquarian Booksellers, the
International Committee for Mini-Basketball, the International Federation of Manufacturers of Gummed Paper, and the International Feminist Network Against Forced Prostitution and Other Forms of Female
Sexual Slavery. More rapid and inexpensive communications and transportation have allowed them to organize more effectively and thus to
have a bigger impact on the international system. The existence of
many small, poor, and badly integrated nation-states in the global
political system makes many of these transnational organizations—
multinational corporations (MNCs) in particular—look relatively
strong and effective by comparison. Even the larger and more important
states, which dominate an anarchic and politically decentralized global
political system, seem ill equipped today to deal with a growing variety
of problems such as global environmental issues. As a result, it seems
increasingly reasonable to argue that states need to give way to some
extent to nongovernmental political entities. According to one analyst
of these **nonstate entities,** "national governments are sharing powers
. . . with businesses, with international organizations, and with a multitude of citizens groups, known as **nongovernmental organizations
(NGOs).** The steady concentration of power in the hands of states that

began in 1648 with the Peace of Westphalia is over, at least for a while"
(Mathews, 1997, p. 50).

MULTINATIONAL CORPORATIONS

Probably the most important type of nonstate actor to emerge in the
last two or three decades is the multinational corporation. But
corporations that do business in more than one state are not new. As
early as the fifteenth century, the Fuggers operated on a multinational
basis in several parts of Europe (Clausen, 1972, p. 21). Many companies,
among them Singer, Herz, Unilever, and Nestlé, have been active in
several countries for most of this century (Walters and Blake, 1992, p.
104). The Krupp organization in Germany sold arms to countries in
remote areas of the world before this century began (Manchester, 1968).

Today's transnational corporations differ from those in the past in
three basic ways. First, in the past, companies that did business in
several countries were headquartered in one state, and all or most of
their production was centered there. This has changed. International
commerce is no longer dominated by international trade. Today, if a

Multinational corporations treat the entire world as their marketplace. The largest
McDonald's restaurant in the world, shown above, is in Beijing, China. SOURCE:
AP/Wide World Photos.

company wants to sell its products in another country, it may set up a subsidiary for manufacturing there. "American firms' revenues from manufacturing abroad are now twice their export earnings" (*Economist*, July 30, 1994, p. 57). Private capital flows have been growing twice as fast as trade flows for years. By 1993 the value of world exports was somewhat less than $4 trillion (Spero and Hart, 1997, p. 57), but one current estimate suggests that by the turn of the century the global financial market will grow to $83 trillion (Mathews, 1997, p. 57).

Second, there are many of these companies, and those involved on an international scale have dramatically increased the number of their foreign subsidiaries. A combination of opportunities presented by improved and inexpensive communication and transportation, the threat of being closed out of new markets, and a desire to take advantage of cheap labor in some developing countries has led to a rapid increase in MNC activity. From 1971 to 1992, the total value of **foreign direct investment (FDI)** by U.S. companies rose from $86.2 billion in 1971 to $423.2 billion (Spero and Hart, 1997, p. 103). The value of all FDI in the entire world rose from $12 billion in 1970 to over $171 billion in 1992 (see Figure 13.1). "The number of [MNCs] in the world's 14 richest countries has more than tripled in the past 25 years, from 7,000 in 1969 to 24,000 today. . . . The world now boasts a total of 37,000 [multinational] companies" (*Economist*, July 30, 1994, p. 57). Figure 13.1 shows that FDI declined in the early 1990s, but that has proven to be a temporary trend. "Global investment inflows rose 40% in 1995, to $315 billion" (*Economist*, October 26, 1997, p. 128).

The third reason that multinational corporations have become so visible is that they have been spectacularly successful. One of the more dramatic ways to demonstrate their degree of success is to compare annual revenues for corporations with gross domestic products of nation-states. As Table 13.2 (beginning on page 467) shows, many of the largest economic units in the world are corporations, not states. By these measures Japan's Mitsubishi Corporation is larger than Indonesia, and the U.S. Exxon Corporation is larger than Finland or Poland.

In rising to new importance and visibility, MNCs became controversial partly because most of them were American. In the 1970s, seven out of the ten largest corporations in the world were American. By 1994, though, according to *Fortune* (August 7, 1995, p. F-1), out of the ten corporations in the world with the largest annual revenues, only three were American. Clearly, multinational corporations in countries other than the United States are becoming increasingly important, but it is also clear that the United States is still by many measures preeminent in FDI competition among global corporations. Seven out of the top ten most profitable corporations in the world in 1993 were American-based firms (Holyoke, Dwyer, Toy, and Power, 1993, p. 53).

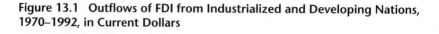

Figure 13.1 Outflows of FDI from Industrialized and Developing Nations, 1970–1992, in Current Dollars

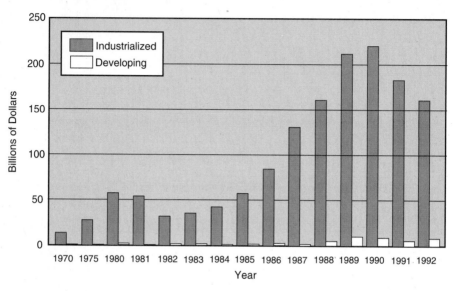

SOURCES: Center on Transnational Corporations, *Transnational Corporations in World Development: Trends and Prospects* (New York: United Nations, 1988), 503–510; UNCTAD, *World Investment Report, 1993: Transnational Corporations and Integrated International Production* (New York: United Nations, 1993), 234–247; UNCTAD, *World Investment Report, 1994: Transnational Corporations, Employment and the Workplace* (New York: United Nations, 1994), 409.

In 1992, the book value of all U.S.-owned direct investment abroad was $432 billion, while the next most important investors—Great Britain, Japan, and Germany—had stocks of investment abroad worth $259 billion, $251 billion, and $186 billion respectively (Spero and Hart, 1997, p. 104). Finally, if the corporations of the world are ranked according to their market value (instead of their annual revenues), currently six out of the top ten corporations are based in the United States (*Business Week*, July 8, 1996, p. 47).

MNCs in Their Home Countries

Interestingly, multinational corporations are viewed as a threat in both rich and poor countries, that is, both in the countries that serve as their home bases and in those developing countries where they place subsidiaries. In the United States, for example, they are accused of causing a variety of economic problems. American labor unions are particularly

Table 13.2   The Hundred Largest Economic Units in the Global System: GDP for Countries, Annual Revenues for Corporations, 1994

States/Corporations, with Country of Origin	GNP, or Annual Revenues $U.S. millions	States/Corporations, with Country of Origin	GNP, or Annual Revenues $U.S. millions
1. USA	6,648,013	17. Switzerland	260,352
2. Japan	4,590,971	18. Belgium	227,550
3. Germany	2,045,991	19. Austria	196,546
4. France	1,330,381	20. Sweden	196,441
5. Italy	1,024,634	21. Mitsubishi, Japan	175,836
6. United Kingdom	1,017,306	22. Indonesia	174,640
7. Brazil	554,587	23. Mitsui, Japan	171,491
8. Canada	542,954	24. Itochu, Japan	167,825
9. China	522,172	25. Sumitomo, Japan	162,476
10. Spain	482,841	26. General Motors, USA	154,951
11. Mexico	377,115	27. Marubeni, Japan	150,187
12. Russian Federation	376,555	28. Denmark	146,076
13. South Korea	376,505	29. Thailand	143,209
14. Australia	331,990	30. Turkey	131,014
15. India	293,606	31. Ford Motor, USA	128,439
16. Argentina	281,922	32. South Africa	121,888

Continued on page 468

Table 13.2 Continued

States/Corporations, with Country of Origin	GNP, or Annual Revenues $U.S. millions	States/Corporations, with Country of Origin	GNP, or Annual Revenues $U.S. millions
33. Saudi Arabia	117,236	51. Matsushita Electric, Japan	69,947
34. Norway	109,568	52. Tomen, Japan	69,902
35. Exxon, USA	101,459	53. Singapore	68,949
36. Nissho Iwai, Japan	100,876	54. Colombia	67,266
37. Finland	97,961	55. General Electric, USA	64,687
38. Royal Dutch/Shell, UK/Netherlands	94,881	56. Daimler-Benz, Germany	64,169
39. Poland	92,580	57. Philippines	64,162
40. Ukraine	91,307	58. IBM, USA	64,052
41. Toyota Motor, Japan	88,159	59. Iran	63,716
42. Portugal	87,257	60. Mobil, USA	59,621
43. Wal-Mart Stores, USA	83,412	61. Nissan, Japan	58,732
44. Israel	77,777	62. Venezuela	58,257
45. Greece	77,721	63. Nichimen, Japan	56,203
46. Hitachi, Japan	76,430	64. Kanematsu, Japan	55,856
47. Nippon Life Insurance, Japan	75,350	65. Dai-Ichi Life Insurance, Japan	54,900
48. AT&T, USA	75,094	66. Sears Roebuck, USA	54,825
49. Nippon Telephone & Telegraph, Japan	70,844	67. Philip Morris, USA	53,776
50. Malaysia	70,626	68. Chrysler, USA	52,224

#		Value	#		Value
69.	Ireland	52,060	85.	Nestlé, Switzerland	41,625
70.	Pakistan	52,011	86.	Hungary	41,374
71.	Chile	51,957	87.	Deutsche Telekom, Germany	41,071
72.	Siemens, Germany	51,054	88.	Fiat, Italy	40,851
73.	New Zealand	50,777	89.	Allianz Holding, Germany	40,415
74.	British Petroleum, UK	50,737	90.	Sony, Japan	40,101
75.	Tokyo Electric, Japan	50,359	91.	Veba Group, Germany	40,071
76.	Peru	50,077	92.	Honda, Japan	39,927
77.	U.S. Postal Service, USA	49,383	93.	Elf Aquitaine, France	39,459
78.	Volkswagen, Germany	49,350	94.	State Farm Group, USA	38,850
79.	Sumitomo Life Insurance, Japan	49,063	95.	NEC, Japan	37,945
80.	Toshiba, Japan	48,228	96.	Prudential Insurance, USA	36,945
81.	Unilever, UK/Netherlands	45,451	97.	Oesterreichische Post, Austria	36,766
82.	IRI, Italy	45,388	98.	Meiji Life Insurance, Japan	36,344
83.	Egypt	42,923	99.	Daewoo, Japan	35,707
84.	Algeria	41,941	100.	United Arab Emirates	35,405

Sources: World Bank, 1996, pp. 210–211; *Fortune*, August 7, 1995, pp. F1–F2.

concerned about the contribution of MNCs to U.S. unemployment. Repeatedly, MNCs shut down factories in the United States and set up new ones in **export platforms** where labor is cheap—for example, Taiwan, Hong Kong, or Mexico—as many critics of the North American Free Trade Agreement (NAFTA), discussed in Chapter 10, point out. According to labor union leaders, American jobs are thus lost directly to the laborers in the export platforms, and even more jobs are then lost indirectly because the foreign subsidiaries monopolize export markets that otherwise could be served by American factories with American workers. In this view, by exporting jobs, investing money overseas, and having subsidiaries overseas that make it impossible for products made in the home country to be exported, MNCs exacerbate balance-of-trade and balance-of-payments problems for industrialized countries. In addition, goods made by American companies are made by overseas subsidiaries, and these products must be imported into the United States, adding further to its balance-of-trade and balance-of-payments deficits.

It can also be argued (as noted in Chapter 7) that MNCs are exacerbating the unequal distribution of wealth in industrialized societies such as the United States by moving a variety of productive jobs out of the country, leaving nothing but highly specialized occupations for which only their wealthy and highly educated citizens can qualify.

Similarly, a study of nine industries in the United States reveals that "multinationals create . . . jobs but that many of the jobs created [are] in the white-collar and managerial areas whereas the jobs lost [come] from the blue-collar ranks" (Walters and Blake, 1992, p. 128).

Perhaps all these complaints about MNCs can be summarized as suspicions that these corporations no longer have any loyalty to the countries that serve as their home bases. They are so intent, according to these suspicions, on serving and taking advantage of the global marketplace that national boundaries, and the political entities they define, are viewed primarily as inefficient nuisances. This attitude is summed up nicely in an article by Robert Reich, a former secretary of labor in the Clinton administration. According to Reich, corporations have lost their national identity. He points to such corporations as International Business Machines (IBM), where 40 percent of the employees are foreigners, and Du Pont, which currently employs 180 Japanese research and development scientists in Yokohama, Japan. Reich's conclusion is that "American-owned corporation[s] . . . have no special relationship with Americans" (Reich, 1990, p. 59). Although this is not exactly tantamount to an accusation of treason, it certainly does suggest that the lack of national loyalty in MNCs makes their motives, and their activities, highly suspect from the point of view of the governments and the citizens of the in-home countries.

MNCs and their defenders do not take these criticisms lying down, and in some cases their counterarguments are convincing. The contribution of foreign investment activity by MNCs to unemployment is direct and visible, but foreign investment also makes substantial, less direct, and less visible contributions to the number of jobs in an industrialized country like the United States. The wages MNCs pay to workers overseas, for example, create increased demands for American products in the countries where they operate. And these subsidiaries need parts and capital equipment from the United States, adding again to the number of jobs in the American economy. The fact that videocassette recorders can be made more cheaply in South Korea than in the United States saves American consumers thousands (or millions) of dollars a year, and since those machines are available to them at these lower prices, they can spend the money they saved on additional American products. It is also important not to overlook the fact that imports create jobs. When the United States imports automobiles from Japan, for example, *people* must transport them to dealerships, advertise them, sell them, and service them—and most of these people are Americans.

In any case, defenders of MNCs argue that if they were somehow prohibited from setting up subsidiaries in export platforms, it would not mean more jobs for Americans. MNCs from other countries would simply use such platforms to full advantage instead. Production facilities in the United States would not be economically viable, because they could not compete with those foreign MNC subsidiaries in places with lower costs, either in the United States or elsewhere. Of course, the United States could forbid American-based corporations from investing overseas (or tax such activity so heavily that it would not be feasible) *and* prevent the import of products made by foreign MNCs taking advantage of conditions in Taiwan or South Korea. But this would surely be the beginning of an escalatory process involving tariffs and countertariffs, quotas and counterquotas, that would be disastrous for the entire industrialized world.

The extent to which MNCs are inclined to export jobs to states with lower wages may also be somewhat exaggerated in the minds of their critics. Low wages are obviously only one consideration these corporations take into account when they decide where to set up a subsidiary, and the available evidence suggests that it is far from the most important consideration. Developing countries have attracted an increasing share of FDI in the mid-1990s, but it is still true that "industrialized nations [are] by far the main sources and destinations of FDI outflows" (Spero and Hart, 1997, p. 103). In 1995, developing countries received $100 billion of FDI, an increase of 14.5 percent over the previous year, and an all-time record. Still, even in that year, almost 70 percent (68.3 percent, to be exact) of FDI went into wealthy countries (*Economist*, October 26, 1996, p. 128). Another important fact to keep in mind in evaluating the impact of FDI on job opportunities is that the United States has now become the largest *recipient* of FDI in the world.

"From 1973 to 1990, foreign direct investment in the United States increased from $20.5 billion to $403.7 billion" (Walters and Blake, 1992, p. 107).[1] Most of this investment comes from Great Britain, Japan, the Netherlands, Canada, Germany, and Switzerland; that is, like most FDI, it originates in a rich industrialized country and is transferred to another rich industrialized country. And if the United States tried to restrict its own firms from investing in other rich industrialized countries, surely those countries would retaliate at some point, and the jobs those investments create would be lost to Americans.

It is also possible to counter suggestions that MNCs based in the United States have become so cosmopolitan and so tied to foreign economies that they are no longer really "American." "American" investors have invested a total equivalent to about 7 percent of the U.S. gross national product (GNP) in countries outside the United States, but that is the same proportion of the GNP that was so invested in 1900. The proportion of foreign to domestic employees in American MNCs has actually declined, from 25 percent in 1977 to the present 23 percent. Some American MNCs do earn most of their profits overseas, but they are exceptions to a very different rule. A look at the one hundred largest corporations in the United States reveals that their foreign sales as a percentage of total sales peaked at 33 percent in 1980, and have since declined to about 25 percent. In short, it is possible to mount a plausible argument that "the power of the home country over the multinational [corporation] has not diminished; if anything, it has continued to increase. Corporations have not become anational, multinational, or transnational; they remain wedded to their home governments for both political and economic reasons" (Kapstein, 1991/92, p. 56).[2]

More recently, analysis of MNCs in the United States, Japan, and Germany have found that they remain quite distinct from one another, with "a tendency for MNCs based in those countries to maintain an overwhelming share of the R&D [Research and Development] spending at home" (Pauly and Reich, 1997, p. 22). These same analysts, address-

---

[1] "By the late 1980s, the flow of FDI into the United States exceeded the outflow for the first time in U.S. history" (Spero and Hart, 1997, p. 107).

[2] Kapstein, the codirector of the Economics and National Security Program at Harvard University's John M. Olin Institute for Strategic Studies, concludes his analysis of the data presented above by declaring that "only the most xenophobic among us would find cause for concern in the aggregate data on multinational corporations" (p. 58).

ing the concern that MNCs have so loosened their ties to their home bases that they can no longer be controlled by national governments, conclude that "power, as distinct from legitimate authority, may indeed be shifting within those societies, but it is not obviously shifting away from them and into the boardrooms of supranational business entities."[3] In short, they argue, "durable national institutions and distinctive ideological traditions still seem to shape crucial corporate decisions[;] . . . markets in this sense are not replacing political leadership" (Pauly and Reich, 1997, p. 25, Abstract).

MNCs in Host States: Criticisms and Counterarguments

Of course, to the extent that MNCs *are* wedded to their home governments, they look increasingly suspicious to many of their most enthusiastic critics in developing countries. It is safe to say that the impact of MNCs on developing states has been even more controversial than the effects on their home states. Despite the fact that MNCs are more visible in the smaller economies of the developing states, there is passionate disagreement about whether or not that impact is beneficial. Controversy extends to the most basic questions, such as whether or not MNCs supply needed capital to poor countries. Some defenders of MNCs argue that they do perform this needed function and that, in addition to the investment money they bring in, they also serve to improve the balance of payments of those poor countries by adding to their exports and by manufacturing products locally that would otherwise have to be imported.

One of the most vigorous replies to such arguments by critics of MNCs focuses on comparisons of the inflows and outflows of capital associated with the activities of MNCs in developing countries. These comparisons show that MNCs actually take more money out of developing countries than they put into them, a fact even some defenders of the corporations acknowledge. Raymond Vernon, for example, a professor of international management at Harvard University and certainly no stern critic of MNCs, acknowledged in his well-known book *Sovereignty at Bay* that during the 1960s, when approximately $1 billion of capital was transferred to U.S.-controlled subsidiaries in developing countries, about $2.5 billion was being withdrawn annually from those same subsidiaries (Vernon, 1971, p. 172). More recently, a U.S. Depart-

---

[3] Not all analysts of the relationship between nation-states and MNCs agree, of course. One recent analysis, for example, asserts that "nowadays governments have only the appearance of free choice when they set out to make rules" (Mathews, 1997, p. 57).

ment of Commerce study estimated that in 1989 foreign investment in general generated income of $53.6 billion, while the flow of capital out of the United States in that year was only $31.7 billion, thus confirming the suspicions of those in developing countries who believe that MNCs generate a net flow of money *out of,* instead of into, their countries (Walters and Blake, 1992, p. 122).

In addition, critics of MNCs point out that these companies do not bring much money into developing countries in the first place. They borrow from local sources or reinvest profits that they have earned in other foreign countries. "Over the 1966 to 1976 period, 49 percent of all net new investment funds of U.S. transnational corporations in the less developed countries were reinvested earnings, 50 percent were funds acquired locally, *and only 1 percent were funds newly transferred from the United States*" (Szymanski, 1984, p. 152; emphasis added). In short, in other words, "the financing of foreign investment is done largely with host-country, not foreign, capital" (Spero and Hart, 1997, p. 256).

Defenders of MNCs claim that most of these arguments are based on misunderstandings or misinformation, or both. Consider the comparison of **inflow of investments** by MNCs and **outflows of repatriated profits** for a given period of time. It is true, MNC defenders concede, that these comparisons typically show that the global companies take more money out of a country than they put into it. But such comparisons are irrelevant or misleading. The fact that corporations took more money out of a country in, say, 1997, than they put into that country in the same year does not prove that country X is being **decapitalized,** or otherwise impoverished, by the activities of the MNCs, because what comes out of a country in the form of repatriated profits in a particular year is not a function of the direct investments that went into that country during that time. Rather, the profits of 1997 are the result of corporate investments over *several* previous years. Such comparisons also ignore the fact that once capital is invested in a country, it forms the basis of a capital stock that can grow and produce more with each passing year.

For example, imagine that the Apex Corporation invests $1 million in the developing country of Fredonia in 1997. After one year of operation, Apex sends half of its profits back home to the United States and uses the other half to expand and improve its production facilities—and to pay taxes—in Fredonia. Every year after that, Apex again sends half of its profits home and again uses the other half to expand its production facilities in Fredonia and to pay taxes. This means that every year after its first year of operation, Apex brings in no dollars and sends home many. Does this mean that Fredonia is being decapitalized, ripped off, or exploited? Every year, the productive capacity of Apex's plant in Fredonia is expanded, and so every year Apex hires more people, pays more in wages and salaries, and pays more in Fredonian taxes. The fact that the amount of money it sends back to the United States every year is much greater than the amount it brings into Fredonia from outside the country, which in this example is zero, is not a true indication of the impact that Apex has on Fredonia.

In addition, the comparison of inflows and outflows of capital ignores the multiplier effect of the original investments. Each dollar invested expands the economy by some factor greater than one. A dollar paid in wages is used by the worker who earns it to buy groceries, the grocery store owner buys a pair of shoes, the shoe store owner invests the dollar in some new furniture, and so on.

This is certainly not the end of the controversy surrounding MNCs. Corporate spokespersons argue that their companies transfer technology and management techniques necessary for economic development to developing countries. Critics respond that, on the contrary, the technology introduced by MNCs is capital intensive and thus inappropriate for the economies of developing countries for two basic reasons. First, although these states have an abundance of labor, the technologically sophisticated equipment MNCs use limits the need for a large labor force. Second, "in countries where the overall key legal institution governing economic relations is the private ownership of productive resources . . . it follows that the larger the proportion of total output due to capital-technology resources, the greater the amount of income going to the owners of those resources" (Muller, 1975, pp. 61–62). So, in addition to creating unemployment, this capital-intensive technology can exacerbate the already unequal distribution of wealth in developing countries.

Supporters of MNCs argue that they make products available to consumers in poor countries that would otherwise be impossible to purchase there. But, skeptics ask, is it not true that the Coca-Cola MNCs supply to the poor and the large cars they provide for the few rich people there are products that a developing country would be better off without? Surely it would be better if the poor invested their meager economic resources in milk for their children and if the rich diverted their wealth from the wasteful conspicuous consumption encouraged by MNCs to the creation of domestically owned productive capacities vital to long-term economic development.

Critics of MNCs also argue that any developing country that attempts meaningful political reforms may find such efforts stifled by the formidable opposition of MNCs. The spectacular example supporting this argument involves the activities of International Telephone and Telegraph (ITT) and Kennecott in Chile when Salvador Allende was in power in the early 1970s. It has been established that ITT offered the CIA funds to carry out subversive activities in Chile and that the CIA later did engage in such activities (although it has never been definitively established that the CIA accepted ITT financial support for those ventures). Allende's overthrow by the Chilean military on September 1, 1973, is just an extreme example, MNC opponents contend, of the preference of MNCs for right-wing regimes that can ensure "stability" through political oppression and their willingness to take active measures to install or maintain such regimes in power.

A recent analysis of cash flows from MNCs to developing countries from 1975 to 1986 set out to determine whether MNCs prefer to invest in countries with high degrees of repression and violations of human rights, or in countries with less repressive governments and relatively vigorous programs devoted to strengthening human rights. What the analysis reveals is that "MNCs in general [forgo] locating larger amounts of [foreign investments] in those [developing countries] that consistently implement fewer human rights reforms" (Billet, 1991, p. 184). The general conclusion of this study, based on patterns found in MNC investments, is that "it does not appear that MNCs view a lack of human rights reforms and the high use of repression in [developing countries] as acceptable" (p. 171).[4]

Dilemmas Faced by MNCs

Perhaps one of the strongest arguments that can be made in defense of MNCs is that when they invest in developing countries, in the long run they are destined to get caught in dilemmas from which there is no obvious escape. Take, for example, the focus by critics on the enormous profits that they repatriate. If MNCs respond to this criticism by keeping that money in the host country and reinvesting it there, they are unlikely to boost their own popularity. Continuous reinvestment will eventually become very threatening to the host country as MNCs expand and take over a larger share of its domestic markets. If MNCs avoid capital-intensive technology and turn to more labor-intensive production techniques, critics will then complain that they are using poor countries as a dumping ground for obsolete technology. In general, the longer MNCs stay in a developing country, the more unpopular they become. When they first arrive, they create jobs and face the risk of failure. But after they have become established, the risks are minimal, and they seem to be doing nothing but raking in enormous profits. If an

---

[4] Another article on this topic concludes that "extensive ties with capitalist states did not in themselves detract from or contribute to the levels of human rights violations in the nations of [the] dataset" (Mitchell and McCormick, 1988, p. 497). Foreign investment was one of the types of ties to capitalist states whose impact on human rights violations was investigated.

MNC hires many local people for important positions of responsibility, the locals are soon likely to believe that they can run the subsidiary on their own. If, on the other hand, the MNC keeps citizens of the host country out of management positions, that policy may lead to antagonism even more quickly, with local citizens arguing that the MNC's employment policies are designed to keep them in a position of permanent subordination and dependence.

Evaluating the Evidence

That subsidiaries of MNCs in developing countries risk becoming unpopular seems all but inevitable, but that unpopularity is not necessarily deserved. The companies may serve as engines of development even as they provoke antagonism and opposition. Many researchers have tried to determine the overall impact of MNCs on developing economies by statistically analyzing the relationship between foreign investment and economic performance.[5] Some have found that foreign investment in less developed countries (LDCs) retards economic growth; additional analyses reveal correlations between foreign investment and inequalities in the distribution of wealth (Bornschier and Chase-Dunn, 1985; Chan, 1989; Boswell and Dixon, 1990). But the weight of contrary evidence is such that conclusions regarding these controversies must be even more than normally tentative.[6] One analyst concludes that much of the empirical work reporting deleterious effects of foreign investment "in reality . . . demonstrates nothing more than how easy it is to produce just about any conceivable results with multivariate computer analysis—if one is willing to throw in enough control variables and utilize enough different sets of countries" (Szymanski, 1984, p. 152). Although this comment may be insensitive to the many complex problems that can make simpler, seemingly more straightforward analyses even more misleading, it does voice what seems to be an increasingly common opinion about the impact of MNC investment in developing countries: the nature of the impact depends on how the government of a given country deals with it. (And how it is dealt with is not inevitably determined by the presence of the investment.) In other words, MNC investments can have bad effects, but handled effectively, they also can bring substantial benefits. As one

---

[5] For a review of a large number of these analyses (from a time when they were much more common than they are now), see Bornschier, Chase-Dunn, and Rubinson (1978).

[6] Some of the more prominent examples are Robert Jackman (1982), Edward Muller (1984), and John Rothgeb (1989). Another analysis of the relationship between foreign capital penetration and economic development in sub-Saharan Africa reports a result that "sharply contradicts dependency theory." See Bradshaw and Tshandu (1990).

POLICY CHOICES

Preserving Autonomy, or Encouraging Investments by MNCs

ISSUE: MNC investments in developing countries can provide potential benefits but at the cost of depending on corporations whose home bases are elsewhere and whose long-term interests are more congruent with those of rich, industrialized countries.

Option #1: Discourage foreign direct investment and provide political and economic protection for corporations owned and operated by local interests.

Advantages: (a) Local talent may take a while to develop a viable corporation, but in the long run, they will better serve the economy of the country than subsidiaries of foreign corporations. (b) Foreign subsidiaries are more difficult than local firms to control; they can always threaten to shut down the local subsidiary and move production to countries with more pliant governments. (c) Reliance on foreign investment makes a poor country more vulnerable to the negative impact of economic setbacks in rich countries.

Disadvantages: (a) Local firms will produce more expensive goods for local consumers who will have to pay higher prices for many years until the domestic firms become as efficient as giant MNCs. (b) Local firms face severe disadvantages in their attempts to export their products. MNCs already have vast, international networks

noted scholar of international political economy concludes, MNCs are "neither as positive nor as negative in their impact on development as liberals or their critics suggest. Foreign direct investment can help or hinder, but the major determinants of economic development lie within LDCs themselves" (Gilpin, 1987). More recently, two additional well-known scholars of international political economy conclude that "FDI flows have a more strongly positive effect on economic growth in countries that have made significant investments in education and worker training than in countries that have not done this" (Spero and Hart, 1997, p. 258).

Figure 13.2 shows which countries in the developing world have received the most foreign investment in recent years. Note that the largest recipient has been China. By far the most important Communist country in the world has received by far the most FDI, symbolizing the fact that virtually all LDCs in the post–Cold War era seek investment, usually rather ardently, from the world's MNCs.

of contacts and familiarity with numerous markets in different regions of the world. (c) Few countries have achieved economic success utilizing policies of autonomy or self-reliance. Many countries that have tried such policies so far, such as North Korea, have instead brought on economic disaster.

Option #2: Foreign direct investment can be actively encouraged by providing tax breaks to MNCs that establish subsidiaries.

Advantages: (a) Competition between foreign and domestic firms, as well as the typical higher levels of efficiency achieved by MNCs, will result in lower prices for consumer goods in countries encouraging foreign investment. (b) Subsidiaries of foreign firms will achieve greater success than local firms would by exploiting export markets around the world. (c) Foreign firms will bring with them technological and administrative know-how that will bring benefits to the countries in which they establish subsidiaries.

Disadvantages: (a) Reliance on foreign subsidiaries will make the country vulnerable to decisions made by corporations with foreign headquarters. (b) Increased integration with recent globalizing forces in the worldwide economy often seems to exacerbate economic inequality. (c) Foreign subsidiaries may engage in harmful practices to the environment of the country in which they are established; any attempt to curb those practices will be met with threats to close down that subsidiary.

Of course, that does not necessarily prove that such investment is generally beneficial. It could mean that national leaders in poor or developing countries have reached a unanimous consensus about FDI that is mistaken, or perhaps that the investments help them and/or a small group of favored constituents rather than the country as a whole. It is also apparent that at least some MNCs in some places may currently be taking unfair advantage of their power and influential position in the global economy in undesirable ways. **Nike,** for example, has been accused of a wide variety of abuses, especially in such countries as China, Vietnam, and Indonesia, including "wretchedly low wages, enforced overtime, harsh and sometimes brutal discipline, and corporal punishment" (Herbert, 1997, Section A, p. 21).[7] Another, simi-

---

[7] Herbert (1997, Section A, p. 21) goes on to point out that "[i]n Ho Chi Minh City . . . Nike workers are paid the equivalent of $1.50 a day, which is not enough to cover the cost of food, shelter, and transportation to and from work."

Figure 13.2   Inward Foreign Direct Investment Stock

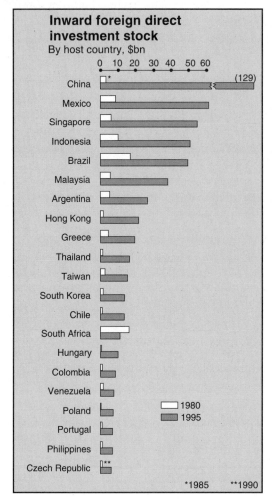

SOURCE: © 1996 The Economist Newspaper Group, Inc. Reprinted with permission. Further reproduction prohibited.

lar report points out that "a worker making Nike running shoes in Jakarta, Indonesia, for example, makes $2.28 a day. . . . The wage paid in Indonesia is not sufficient to live on. The Indonesian government admits that an individual needs no less than $4 a day to pay for basic human needs in an urban area such as Jakarta" (Stokes, 1997, p. 80). And Nike is of course only one example. It has been reported that "in the world of Asian laborers, which makes goods that line the shelves of American, European, and Japanese stores, workers get fired for leaving their machines to go to the bathroom. Bosses punish tardy workers by making them stand in the sun for hours" (Goozner, 1994, Section 1, p. 12). The use of **child labor** by MNCs in Asia and elsewhere has also been widely documented.

> Studies in India have found that adult unemployment is often highest in areas of the greatest use of child labor, suggesting that adult workers are frequently displaced by children. This phenomenon is part of a vicious cycle, in which jobless parents are forced to send their own children to work, displacing even more adults. Thus child labor is not simply a consequence of poverty, but one of its causes (Stokes, 1997, p. 82).

It is quite clear that as the new millennium approaches, "the globalization of the world economy [has] reached a point where few countries in the South [can] afford to say no to the multinationals" (Spero and Hart, 1997, p. 270). And it should not be forgotten that several countries have received substantial foreign investment and have subsequently experienced substantial improvements in the quality of life of significant numbers of their citizens. In Indonesia, for example, where abuses by MNCs undoubtedly take place, it is also true that per capita GNP is now ten times what it was in 1966, and "infant mortality rates and illiteracy rates are going down. The average [life expectancy] has risen to 61 (from 41 three decades ago)" (Goozner, 1997, Section 1, p. 13).

MNCs are currently riding high in the global economy as a whole, and in most developing countries. Their overall impact may well be beneficial, but there is also substantial evidence indicating that at least some of them exploit their dominant position to abuse their workers.

COMPUTERS, TRANSNATIONAL ORGANIZATIONS, AND INTERNATIONAL POLITICS

Nation-states are inherently territorial units, and nation-states still predominate in the global political system. **Modern means of communication and transportation** make geographic distance less of a barrier to interaction among people who are geographically dispersed, and as this barrier is removed, groups of people, even social entities that are not geographically based, can grow and become more important. The day when nongeographically-based social entities will become more important than **territorial units** like nation-states is a long way off. But it has perhaps been brought significantly closer, mostly in just the last ten or fifteen years, by the impact of computers on communications.

Computers and Computer-Mediated Communication

In 1980 there were probably fewer than 2 million **computers** in the entire world, and most of them were "mainframes," or very large computers. By 1993, there were about 150 million computers in the world, and about 135 million of those, or 90 percent, were **personal computers (PCs),** many of them small enough to be carried around like briefcases (see Figure 13.3). Eighteen million computers were added to the world's total in 1992 alone. "More than one-third of American families have [computers] in their homes. In 1995, for the first time, the amount of money spent on PCs exceeded that spent on televisions" (Burton, 1997, p. 32).

As computers have been getting much smaller, they have also been getting much more powerful, able to process more information in less

Figure 13.3   World Computers and Total Processing Power, 1987–1993

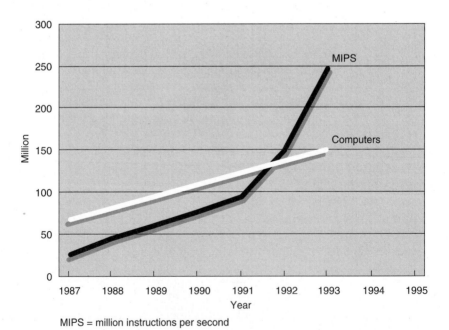

MIPS = million instructions per second

SOURCE: From John E. Young, *Global Network: Computers in a Sustainable Society,* Worldwatch Institute, 1993, p. 11. Reprinted by permission of Worldwatch Institute.

and less time. That power can be measured in "millions of instructions per second," or MIPS. Today's small PCs are about three thousand times as powerful as the large, mainframe computers of the early 1980s. In terms of MIPS, the world's computing power increased 1,100 percent from 1988 to 1993 (Young, 1993, p. 10). The first computer, the Electronic Numerical Integrator and Calculator (ENIAC), produced in 1946, weighed thirty tons, and was capable of processing what was then considered an astonishing five thousand instructions per second. Today, Pentium processors that can be placed on a piece of silicon about the size of a thumbnail are placed inside small portable computers capable of dealing with 200 million instructions per second (Burton, 1997, p. 26).

These computers have acquired the ability to transform the way the people of the planet communicate and interact with one another because they are increasingly connected to one another like telephones—in **electronic communication networks.** The launching of sputniks by the Soviet Union may have been indirectly responsible for initiating this process. "In October 1957, when the Soviet Union launched Sputnik, the people who were responsible for maintaining the state of the art in U.S. military technology were shocked into action. To keep up with the pace of technical developments, the Department of Defense created the Advanced Research Projects Agency with a specific mandate to leapfrog over existing technology" (Rheingold, 1993, p. 71). The Advanced Research Projects Agency, or ARPA, soon developed ARPANET, connecting computers around the country into a communications network. They created "cyberspace," a term used to describe "the conceptual space where words, human relations, data, wealth and power are manifested by people using **CMC [Computer-Mediated Communication]** technology." ARPANET, which had about one thousand users in the late 1960s, evolved into INTERNET in the 1980s. Thanks in part to the development of the **World Wide Web,** the number of people connected to the **Internet** has since expanded explosively. The World Wide Web (developed by Tim Berners-Lee at the European Particle Physics Laboratory in Switzerland in 1989)

> is a collection of documents residing on *servers* and viewers run from *clients*. Special documents link various information sources. The glue of the Web is a document language known as **HyperText Markup Language,** or **HTML** for short. HTML allows clients to jump from site to site. . . . This is just the beginning, though, because clients interpret HTML in a way that is user friendly, providing formatted texts, pictures, sounds, and even animation, in the same document. . . . One might view the WWW as an all-inclusive encyclopedia, where the pages have been strewn all over the world, yet linked with a magic thread that masks the fact that pages are no longer collated ("Introduction to the World Wide Web," 1997, p. 1).

In somewhat plainer, less technical language, the Web is the "part of the Internet that enables even neophytes to embark on digital tours of the world's computers" (Levy, 1996, p. 26), or a technological break-through that "makes it easy for someone using a computer connected to the Internet to grasp information across the Network [of computers] merely by clicking on little symbols displayed on the computer screen." Thanks in large part to this technological development, the number of people connected to the Internet has reached about 60 million, and is estimated to reach 250 million by the turn of the century (Burton, 1997, p. 25).

Those 60 million people can communicate with one another by typing messages into their computers that are then sent via the Internet to the computers of other people, literally around the world (although admittedly computers are concentrated in the industrialized world). These messages have come to be known as **electronic mail (e-mail).**

> E-mail is cheaper than international phone calls, faxes, or express package services, and allows its users to bypass busy signals, unpredictable postal service, and schedule conflicts created by different time zones. The rapidly growing international web of computer systems has made it easy for many people to keep in touch with friends or colleagues on the other side of the world (Young, 1993, p. 21).

This kind of computer-based communication network has already had an immense impact on the business world. "Because so much of business now depends on getting and sending information, companies around the world have been rushing to link their employees through electronic networks. These networks form the key infrastructure of the 21st century" (Toffler, 1990, p. 102).

Computer-based communication promises also to have profound political significance, because it allows people to communicate with one another as groups. In other words, it is a simple matter, technologically, to organize the e-mail addresses of whole groups of people in such a way that one person can send out a message that will reach all of these people simultaneously. These "e-mail lists" can involve "as few as two people or as many as thousands. There are approximately 2,600 different mailing lists [on the Internet] on subjects ranging from cooking to etymology, from music to genealogy" (Laquey with Ryer, 1993, p. 54).[8]

---

[8] Such estimates about the growth of the Internet and the World Wide Web are obsolete by the time they are published. As *Newsweek* pointed out in January 1996, the number of home pages on the World Wide Web expanded by 600 percent in just the first six months of 1995, and Yahoo!, one of the Web's more popular "search engines," was at that time receiving three thousand submissions for new Web sites every day (Levy, 1996, p. 26).

SOURCE: Reprinted with permission of A. Raeside.

This author sent a message to a "LISTSERV" e-mail address and received in response a document of 114 pages listing the names and addresses of e-mail groups that discuss continuously topics ranging from teaching effectiveness and the philosophy of Ayn Rand to the meaning of life and backgammon strategy.

The potential impact of the World Wide Web, e-mail, and e-mail-based groups is difficult to estimate, but it clearly could be profound. "This is a new dimension—an electronic, virtual world where time and space have almost no meaning. . . . The implications of this new global communication and information system are staggering" (LaQuey and Ryer, 1993, p. 2). Howard Rheingold, author of *The Virtual Community: Homesteading on the Electronic Frontier*, asserts that "the political significance of CMC lies in its capacity to challenge the existing political hierarchy's monopoly on powerful communications media, and perhaps thus revitalize citizen based democracy" (p. 14). Rheingold here most likely refers to the possible impact of CMC on politics within a given nation-state. One intriguing indicator of possibilities along these lines is that both President Bill Clinton and Vice President Al Gore have publicly available e-mail addresses.[9]

CMC might have a dramatic impact on politics among nation-states, too. Or perhaps not. PCs in great numbers, the Internet, and the Web have been around for such a short time that it is difficult to estimate their impact. There are skeptics who believe that the impact of computers and CMC have been "hyped" beyond their actual potential.

> The cliché of the information age is that instantaneous global telecommunications, television and computer networks will soon overthrow the ancient tyrannies of time and space. Companies will need no headquarters, workers will toil as effectively from home, car, or beach as they could in the offices that need no longer exist, and events half a world away will be seen, heard, and felt with the same immediacy as events across the street—if indeed streets still have any point (*Economist*, July 30, 1994, p. 13).

But the *Economist* goes on to point out that American multinationals have found that they cannot in fact manage their Asian operations from New York City. "Global strengths must be matched by a local feel—and a jet-lagged visit of a few days every so often does not provide one" (*Economist*, July 30, 1994, p. 13). In addition, it turns out that by examining "newspapers or news broadcasts anywhere on earth . . . you find them overwhelmingly dominated by stories about what is going on in the vicinity of their place of publication" (*Economist*, July 30, 1994, p. 13).

This domination of news sources by local stories has probably always existed, but curiously—and paradoxically—it seems to have become more pervasive following the end of the Cold War. At the same time that new communication technologies have made it far easier to link events and people separated by large geographic distances, people in many countries seem to have become less interested in that available information. "The amazing increase in the capacity to produce and distribute news from distant lands has been met by an obvious decrease in its consumption." This seems particularly true of the United States (see Table 13.3). "The number and length of foreign topics in the evening [television] news have declined far below Cold War levels. . . . While the networks devoted an average more than 40 percent of total news time to foreign items in the 1970s, that share had been cut to 13.5 per cent of news time by 1995" (Moisy, 1997, pp. 79, 82).

---

[9] Those addresses are PRESIDENT@WHITEHOUSE.GOV and VICE.PRESIDENT@ WHITEHOUSE.GOV. "Bill Clinton receives thousands of e-mail messages a day. . . . Does the President see any of this fan mail? Yes, but not much. On a given issue, only a few letters representing both sides reach Clinton's eyes. And of those, only a fraction receive a personal reply" (Kantor and Berlin, 1995, p. 17).

Table 13.3   Continuing Decline of Foreign News on Network Television

	1970s	1990–91	1993	1995
Percent of foreign stories	35	41	24	23
Percent of time	45	n/a	10	13.5
Average length of foreign story (min.)	1.7	2.2	1.6	1.2

SOURCE: Reprinted with permission from *Foreign Policy* 107, June 1997. Copyright 1997 by the Carnegie Endowment for International Peace.

Still, the U.S. Defense Department is increasingly convinced that the electronic age has had a profound impact on international politics in the area of "national security," broadly as well as traditionally defined. "About 95% of the Pentagon's communications travel along the same telephone lines that the public uses for chattering" (*Economist*, January 13, 1996, p. 77). And computer hackers have increasingly targeted the computer systems relied on by the defense establishment. "Hackers have occasionally broken into the Pentagon's network and last year defaced the CIA's home page" (Burton, 1997, p. 34). In fact, attempts by hackers to disrupt computer systems have reached astonishing levels. "Defense Information Systems Agency (DISA) data implies that Defense may have experienced as many as 250,000 attacks last year. [These] attacks are successful 65 percent of the time, and . . . the number of attacks is doubling each year" (Stillman et al., 1996, p. 3).

What could these hackers do that might pose a threat to the national security of the United States? According to a report issued by the General Accounting Office in Washington:

> At a minimum, these attacks are a multimillion dollar nuisance to Defense. At worst they are a serious threat to national security. Attackers have seized control of entire Defense systems, many of which support critical functions, such as weapons system research, and development, logistics, and finance.[10]

The potential for catastrophic damage is great. Organized foreign nationals or terrorists could use **"information warfare"** techniques to

---

[10] "Rome Laboratory, New York, is the air force's premier command and control research facility. The facility's research projects include artificial intelligence systems, radar guidance systems, and target detection and tracking systems. . . . During March and April 1994, more than 150 Internet intrusions were made on the Laboratory by a British hacker . . . the attackers were able to seize control of Rome's support systems for several days and establish links to foreign Internet sites" (Stillman et al., 1996, p. 14).

disrupt military operations by harming command and control systems (Stillman et al., 1996, p. 3).

Perhaps the potential for damage done by "information warfare" is even greater in the broader civilian society. The Defense Department has devised test scenarios in which ATMs are disabled, freight trains misrouted, telephone service disrupted, airplanes downed, and military attempts to respond to this chaos met by "weapons systems designed to pinpoint enemy tanks and troop formations [that] begin to malfunction due to electronic infections" (Stillman et al., 1996, p. 29). A civilian analyst (Schwartau, 1994) suggests that an "electromagnetic bomb" could be used to disable ATMs and to cause airplanes to crash.[11] What is needed to counter this threat, according to another observer, is "a fourth service, what some people have called a cyberforce. The army handles the land, the navy handles the water—we need a force to handle cyberspace" (Venzke, 1996, p. 137).

But on the happier side, other analysts are convinced that computer-modified communication will transform international politics in predominantly beneficial ways. One of the most optimistic analysts asserts that "the Internet is a tangible expression of the world coming together. If regionalism was the intermediate step toward a true global community, the World Wide Web is its consummation. . . . The Internet has already overrun geographic borders, making possible the creation of virtual communities of shared interests that transcend national boundaries" (Burton, 1997, pp. 33, 36). Another, similarly inclined observer argues that "the most powerful engine of change in the relative decline of states and the rise of nonstate actors is the computer and telecommunications revolution. . . . By drastically reducing the importance of proximity, the new technologies change people's perceptions of community. Fax machines, satellite hookups, and the Internet connect people across borders with exponentially growing ease while separating them from natural and historical associations [forming] . . . a powerful globalizing force" (Mathews, 1997, p. 52).

Transnational Organizations and the Future of International Politics

The relative independence of transnational organizations from national governments gives them the potential to play beneficial roles in the global political system, and some organizations, at least, take advantage of that opportunity. The **Red Cross,** for example, was started by citizens

---

[11] "An unnamed U.S. intelligence official has boasted that with $1 billion and 20 capable hackers, he could shut down America" (Laqueur, 1996, p. 35).

of Switzerland in 1860, and at present comprises more than 120 national Red Cross societies. The Red Cross, which has a secretariat in Geneva, is charged with the coordination of assistance in natural disasters and promoting the development of national societies. In addition to providing relief in case of natural disasters, the Red Cross has carved out a role for itself in situations such as war and other conflicts that result in administrative detention, summary executions, secret military trials, and so on. Since its inception, the organization has helped to bring into existence a series of multilateral treaties designed to humanize war and political conflict. These treaties deal with the rights and treatment of sick and wounded military personnel, prisoners of war, civilians in a war zone or occupied territory, and persons affected by internal war (Forsythe, 1976, pp. 610, 626). In addition, "today NGOs (nongovernmental organizations) deliver more official development assistance than the entire U.N. system (excluding the World Bank and the International Monetary Fund). In many countries they are delivering the services—in urban and rural community development, education, and health care—that faltering governments can no longer manage" (Mathews, 1997, p. 53).[12]

One of the more intriguing transnational groups to appear in the last twenty-five years is **Amnesty International.** This organization dedicates itself to the release of political prisoners all over the world, as well as securing humane treatment for political prisoners that it cannot get released. The organization works for the release of such prisoners "provided that [they have] not used or advocated violence" (*Amnesty International Report*, 1993, p. 327).

There is little doubt of the need for such an organization. Governments now have many sophisticated methods for apprehending political dissidents and abusing them while they are in custody. Miniaturized electronic surveillance equipment to gather information and computerized systems to process information make it difficult for dissidents to escape the clutches of repressive governments. Injections, tranquilizers, cattle prods, electroshock, sleep deprivation, noise bombardment, psychosurgery, and sensory deprivation chambers are among the instruments available to governments bent on torture and behavior modification.

Amnesty International's drive to curb human rights violations began in 1961. A London lawyer, Peter Benenson, noticed a newspaper story about Portuguese students who had been imprisoned for taking part in a peaceful demonstration. Benenson organized some friends and ac-

---

[12] Mathews (1997, p. 53) also points out that one of these NGOs engaged in such activities is CARE, with an annual budget of $400 billion. As noted in Chapter 12, sometimes, at least, the activities and impact of such NGOs may be less than beneficial.

quaintances to agitate for the release of these students. It was presumed to be a temporary campaign, but by the end of the year, the need for a continuing organization had become evident. In 1962, the movement adopted the name Amnesty International, and in 1963, an international secretariat was set up in London. The group today claims a membership of over 1,100,000 members in over 150 countries. "Amnesty International . . . has been using its Urgent Action Network on PeaceNet to mobilize its members to pressure government officials to release political prisoners. It may come as no surprise that dictators and tyrants don't appreciate their actions being made public through this democratic tool" (LaQuey with Ryer, 1993, p. 12).

Not all nongovernmental or nonstate actors with international dimensions engage in such benign or beneficial activities. The U.N. estimates that **"globally integrated crime"** is a kind of "transnational business" worth some $750 billion a year, $400 to $500 billion of it in narcotics (Mathews, 1997, pp. 57–58). Early in 1990, Italy's parliamentary Anti-Mafia Commission sent a message to the U.N. General Assembly to the effect that organized crime was "taking on the characteristics of an extremely dangerous world calamity." According to *Thieves' World: The Threat of the New Global Network of Organized Crime* (Sterling, 1994, p. 244):

> Modern criminal power has surpassed the ability of governments to contain it. International organized crime is too big; nobody knows how to deal with it. Perhaps it cannot be dealt with as long as the world is divided into nearly two hundred sovereign states. While the big crime syndicates simply go where the money is, sovereign states cannot do anything simply. . . . Obviously the mafias of the world cannot be fought on these terms. The question is how far sovereign states can go toward a planetwide defense against this planetwide assault.[13]

One can logically argue that the global political system needs to have an organization that operates outside or possibly above the nation-state framework to deal with organized crime, or to put pressure on states to respect human rights. Similar arguments can be made for analogous organizations, such as Greenpeace, regarding environmental issues. For these and other reasons, probably a growing number of observers of the global political system feel that "the relative power of states will continue to decline. . . . Both in numbers and in impact, nonstate actors

---

[13] Mathews (1997, p. 58) expresses a similar opinion: "Globalized crime is a security threat that neither police nor the military—the state's traditional responses—can meet. . . . If criminal groups can continue to take advantage of porous borders and transnational financial spaces while governments are limited to acting within their own territory, crime will have the winning edge."

have never before approached their current strength. And a still larger role likely lies ahead" (Mathews, 1997, pp. 52, 65).

TERRORISM AND TERRORIST GROUPS

"Terrorist" groups typically see themselves as combating tyranny and oppression. They often act in a "transnational" fashion across national boundaries. Operating in many parts of the world, they include the Basque separatists in Spain, the Sikhs in India, the Irish Republican Army in Northern Ireland, and the Shining Path in Peru.

Any useful discussion of terrorist groups or **terrorism** must first deal with the question "What is terrorism?" As is the case with most questions on this subject, the answers are both numerous and controversial.[14] The standard summary of this controversy asserts that "one person's terrorist is another person's freedom fighter." *Terrorism* is a highly charged political term used by most people to refer to political violence (or any other political tactic) of which they disapprove.

For example, Paul Johnson (1984, p. 50) says that "terrorism is the deliberate, systematic murder, maiming, and menacing of the innocent to inspire fear in order to gain political ends. . . . Terrorism . . . is intrinsically evil, necessarily evil, and wholly evil." Less judgmentally, Thomas Schelling (1982, p. 66) points out that the dictionary defines the term as "the use of terror, violence, and intimidation to achieve an end." Peter Sederberg (1989, p. 27) notes that a CIA-sponsored study has defined international terror as "the threat or use of violence for political purposes when (1) such action is intended to influence the attitude and behavior of a target group wider than its immediate victim, and (2) its ramifications transcend national boundaries."

The main problem with these definitions is that they are far too broad. They would include under the same rubric an incredibly diverse array of phenomena. According to these definitions, terrorism includes more than the hijacking of airplanes or the random machine-gunning of people in airports. The bombing of civilian populations in cities by both sides in the Second World War, the invasion of Germany by Allied troops, the nuclear bombing of Hiroshima and Nagasaki, the policy of nuclear deterrence,[15] the arrest and torture of political prisoners, the execution of criminals (or imprisonment of criminals, for that matter),

---

[14] Alex Schmid (1983, pp. 119–152), for example, provides more than one hundred definitions.

[15] In fact, Schelling (1982, pp. 66–67) explicitly labels the atomic bombings of Japan and nuclear deterrence as "terrorism."

and threats by parents to spank naughty children would all qualify as "terrorism."[16]

For the purpose of useful social scientific analysis, concepts should be defined simply, in a way that is **unidimensional.** Multidimensional concepts lead to confusing theories (Shively, 1980, p. 31).[17] A definition of terrorism that includes such diverse phenomena as nuclear war, airplane hijacking, capital punishment, and child spanking is multidimensional. Analyses of terrorism's origins, effects, and morality based on such a definition are bound to be hopelessly muddled. A more useful, unidimensional definition might stipulate that terrorism is "the use of violence for political purposes by nongovernmental actors."

Such a definition is not free of problems and troubling ambiguities. Some would insist, for example, that the essence of terrorism is random violence against innocent victims. But by this definition, violence that is purposely aimed at, say, Americans and Israelis, and so not randomly distributed, is not terrorism.

A more tenable distinction, perhaps, is offered by Peter Sederberg (1989, p. 33), who argues that "in terrorism, the perpetrators *deliberately* choose **noncombatant targets** and relatively indiscriminate means." It is probably easier to discriminate between combatants and noncombatants than between those who are innocent and those who are not. Even that distinction, though, is not free of ambiguities. President Reagan denounced as terrorism the 1983 attack that killed 241 marines in Beirut. He had argued previously that "freedom fighters" act against military targets, while "terrorists" attack innocent civilians. Can soldiers be classified as noncombatants? According to Sederberg, Reagan's answer to that question with respect to the bombing of the marines' barracks in Lebanon was yes. He argued that those troops were on a peace-keeping mission and that they were asleep when they were attacked. As Sederberg demonstrates (and as is obvious in any case), this argument is not likely to receive widespread acceptance even among those determined to conduct a relatively dispassionate analysis of terrorism. Still, some analysts feel that guerrilla fighters who restrict their

---

[16] Admittedly, this last type of threat would need to be made across an international boundary or by a parent against an adopted child from a foreign country to qualify as *international* terrorism.

[17] Shively discusses an example contrasting the unidimensional concept of temperature with the multidimensional concept of weather. A theory stating that temperatures below 30 degrees cause a spotted ibex to stop breeding is more easily understood than a theory asserting that bad weather causes such a change in the behavior of the ibex. The meaning of the second theory "would be left to the readers' judgment. Is it rain that discourages the ibexes' ardor? Or do high winds make them think of other things? Is it the heat? the humidity?" (Shively, 1980, p. 31).

targets to the military forces of the government they are trying to overthrow should not be labeled terrorists, and this does seem a reasonable objection to a definition of terrorism that does not include some reference to the characteristics of the target of the violence in question.

Title 22 of the United States Legal Code (Section 2656[d]) defines terrorism as "premeditated, politically motivated violence perpetrated against noncombatant targets by subnational groups or clandestine agents. . . . The term 'international terrorism' means terrorism involving citizens or the territory of more than one country" (Wilcox, 1997).[18]

This definition is reasonably specific and avoids many or even most of the problems posed by the definitions discussed above. The only possibly questionable phrase is "clandestine agents," which opens the door to the idea that nation-states can commit terrorism through such agents. Of course, it is certainly true that states can sponsor terrorism and terrorist agents. The State Department currently designates seven countries as sponsors of terrorism: Cuba, Iran, Iraq, Libya, North Korea, Sudan, and Syria (Wilcox, 1997). "Definition does not involve the discovery of some transcendent ideal; rather it reflects particular historical eras, intellectual professions, and partisan positions. The definition of terms, like other human actions, reflects the interests of those doing the defining" (Sederberg, 1989, p. 3). States should not necessarily be let off the hook, so to speak, even though perhaps the definition currently encoded into U.S. law does not draw a sufficiently clear line between terrorism and violent acts committed by states. In an attempt to alleviate any suspicions that the definition of terrorism preferred here is implicitly designed as an apology for the actions of states, it must be stated explicitly that in this author's opinion, violence perpetrated by governments is a problem incomparably greater in scope and intensity than terrorism, and one that is routinely more despicable. But by any definition sufficiently precise and unidimensional to be useful, such violence is not terrorism. An act of unjustifiable violence by a government should be called an atrocity, but not terrorism.

The Origins of Terrorism

It is probably a mistake to believe that terrorism is mindless violence, without purpose other than a release for pent-up frustration, although

---

[18] This is a quote from the U.S. State Department's annual report entitled "Patterns of Global Terrorism." In a footnote the report goes on to stipulate that "for the purposes of this definition, the term noncombatant is interpreted to include, in addition to civilians, military personnel who at the time of the incident are unarmed and/or not on duty" (Wilcox, 1997). In effect, apparently, President Reagan's argument that the marines in Lebanon who were asleep at the time of the attack has been incorporated into U.S. law.

some psychologically oriented analysts would disagree.[19] Terrorism can have several tactical aims for resistance groups like the Palestine Liberation Organization (PLO), such as publicizing their activities, "provoking Israel to adopt repressive measures against innocent, uncommitted Arabs in the hope that such measures will lead the latter to join or support the resistance . . . provoking Israel to retaliate severely against Arab states and thereby undermine diplomatic efforts to achieve peace, . . . dissuading moderate Arab regimes from making concessions to Israel" (O'Neil, 1978, pp. 34–35), and so on.

Two additional misconceptions about terrorism involve its history and its reliance on modern communications media. It is easy to get the impression that terrorism is a quite recent phenomenon, almost entirely dependent on, and so to a great extent a result of, modern communications media, especially television. But terrorist acts were quite common a hundred years ago:

> As the nineteenth century ended, it seemed no one was safe from terrorist attack. In 1894 an Italian anarchist assassinated French President Sadi Carnot. In 1897 anarchists fatally stabbed Empress Elizabeth of Austria and killed Antonio Canovas, the Spanish prime minister. In 1900 Umberto I, the Italian king, fell in yet another anarchist attack; in 1901 an American anarchist killed William McKinley, president of the United States (Laqueur, 1997, p. 24).[20]

One analysis of three groups of religious terrorists that existed centuries ago—the Thugs (Hindu), the Assassins (Islam), and the Zealots (Jewish)—makes it clear that terrorist activity on a significant scale has occurred at least since the days of the Roman Empire. Clearly, terrorism is not a phenomenon produced solely by excessive attention from modern media. The Assassins, for example, "did not need mass media to reach interested audiences, because their prominent victims were murdered in venerated sites and royal courts, usually on holy days when many witnesses were present." In general, the idea that "terrorist operations require modern technology to be significant" is a "misconception[;] . . . every society has weapon, transport, and communication facilities" (Rapoport, 1984, pp. 659, 672, 673, 675).

---

[19] As one specialist on terrorism has noted, according to "the psychological approach . . . terrorists are . . . people acting out their emotions, not rational calculators" (Crenshaw, 1985, p. 472).

[20] Laqueur (1997, p. 24) goes on to point out that "If in the year 1900 the leaders of the main industrial powers had assembled, most of them would have insisted on giving terrorism top priority on their agenda, as President Clinton did at the Group of Seven meeting after the June bombing of the U.S. military compound in Dhahran, Saudi Arabia.

Still, terrorists in the modern age have been more successful, perhaps, in acquiring substantial support from state governments. There were reports in 1979, for example, that Libya maintained camps within its borders capable of training five thousand men at a time (Dobson and Payne, 1979, p. 71). In 1984, another report claimed that "an ever-increasing flow of arms and ammunition, manufactured in the Soviet Union, Czechoslovakia, and East Germany, have been shipped to the PLO via East Germany and Hungary" (Cline and Alexander, 1984, p. 49). In addition, of course, the United States has funneled millions of dollars in support of such "nongovernmental perpetrators of violence for political purposes" (that is, terrorists) as the rebels in Afghanistan and the Contras in Central America.

One disturbing result of this trend toward state-supported terrorism is that terrorists acquire access to increasingly sophisticated military technology. Even in the 1970s, terrorists were arrested in Rome, Paris, and Kenya with antiaircraft missiles and portable rocket launchers (Dobson and Payne, 1979, p. 115). When the Israelis attacked the PLO camps in Lebanon in 1982, they found that the Soviets had supplied that organization with BM-21 rocket launchers and ZSU-4 radar-guided antiaircraft cannon (Cline and Alexander, 1984, p. 51). The ultimate fear along these lines used to be that some state at some time would supply nuclear weapons to a terrorist group. In April 1996, however, the Defense Department reported that most terrorist groups do not have the financial and technical resources to acquire nuclear weapons but *could* acquire and effectively use biological or chemical weapons (Laqueur, 1997, p. 29). As discussed in Chapter 9, the **Aum Shinrikyo** group in Japan used poison gas in an attack on the Tokyo subway system in March 1995, killing ten people and injuring five thousand. The United States had until recently remained relatively unscathed by international terrorism, but in February 1993 New York's **World Trade Center** was bombed by Islamic fundamentalists from Middle Eastern countries, who were subsequently tried and convicted. As is also discussed in Chapter 9, the intent of that attack was to "topple the city's tallest tower onto its twin, amid a cloud of cyanide gas" (Mylroie, 1995/96).[21]

Dealing with Terrorism

One approach to terrorism relies on conventional military attacks launched against the states that support it, such as the raid staged by the United States against Libya in April 1986 in retaliation against

---

[21] "Had the attack gone as planned, tens of thousands of Americans would have died" (Mylroie, 1995/96, p. 3).

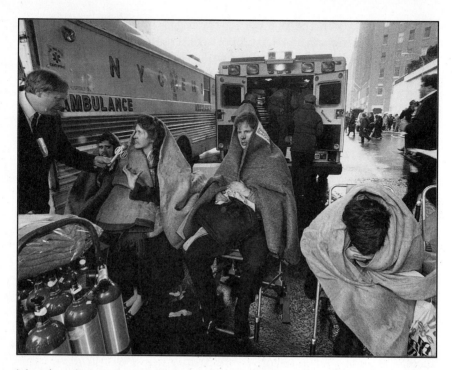

Injured workers in the triage area wait to be transported to area hospitals after a terrorist bombing of the World Trade Center in New York City in 1993. SOURCE: Stacy Rosenstock/Impact Visuals.

terrorist activities believed to be sponsored by Libya.\This attack caused a transatlantic maelstrom of controversy. Most Americans approved the action, whereas most Europeans did not. Only the British government cooperated with the attack. The controversy regarding the U.S. attack focused first on its effectiveness and second on its morality. The two issues are interdependent, according to the Catholic doctrine of a "just war," one criterion for which is that it must have a reasonable chance of success. Even officials in the Reagan administration acknowledged initially that the raid on Libya might cause an increase in terrorism in the short run. They also argued, however, that it would decrease terrorism in the long run. Another criterion for ethical military operations, according to Catholic doctrine, argues for discrimination—that is, immunity for noncombatants. Unfortunately, U.S. bombs in Libya killed civilians. Finally, the Catholic just-war doctrine stipulates that "the harm done by an act, even unintentionally, may not be disproportionate to the good intended to be achieved or to the evil to be avoided" (Russett, 1984, p. 44). One critic addressed the idea of using conventional military attacks as a response to terrorist activities even before President Reagan's retaliation against Khadafy's Libya. He said that such attacks would "substitute the greater evil of full-scale war, with all its attendant death and devastation and dangers of escalation, for the lesser evil of terrorism" (Wilkinson, 1984, p. 298).

The short-term impact of the U.S. raid on Libya, at least, confounded most of its critics; the number of terrorist incidents seemed to decrease. But then in December 1988, possibly in response to the 1986 raid, a Pan American flight en route from London to New York exploded over Lockerbie, Scotland, killing all 259 passengers and eleven more people on the ground. The tragedy provoked an intense investigation by British authorities, as well as U.S. intelligence officials. Investigations have led to the conclusion that those responsible currently reside in Libya, and U.N. sanctions were imposed on Libya in an attempt to get the Libyan government to extradite the suspects. Libya has so far refused to do that, but the U.S. State Department argues that the sanctions have served a useful purpose even so. "Terrorism by Libya has been sharply reduced," in the view of the State Department, "by U.N. sanctions imposed after the bombings of the Pan Am flight 103" (Wilcox, 1997). Some academic analysts agree: "The 1986 U.S. air strike against Libya and the various boycotts against Libya . . . had an effect" (Laqueur, 1997, p. 27).[22]

Many Americans, as well as some Europeans, feared that Saddam Hussein might use terrorism as a weapon in response to the concerted military attack on Iraq after it occupied Kuwait in 1990. But for some reason, those Iraqi-sponsored terrorist attacks never materialized. One study concludes that counterterrorist measures by the allies were effective, that the Iraqis' lack of precrisis preparation handicapped their efforts to mount terrorist actions once the Persian Gulf War was under way, and that "a number of other nations with terrorist linkages pressured their terrorist clients to refrain from helping Saddam Hussein" (Terrill, 1993, p. 219).

Another approach to dealing with terrorism is to address the grievances of the terrorists. Many of the most spectacular terrorist incidents, especially those involving Americans and Israelis, have been carried out by Palestinians or groups sympathetic to Palestinians. Providing Palestinians with some relief from their currently stateless condition might deprive at least some terrorist organizations of an important source of volunteers for their plans and projects. At this writing, the Israelis are negotiating with the Palestine Liberation Organization, and implementation of a peace agreement signed in 1993 seems a real possibility. But

---

[22] Laqueur (1997, p. 27) further observes that "no government today boasts about surrogate warfare it instigates and backs."

the process has been accompanied by, and has perhaps even provoked, several terrorist incidents.[23]

It seems clear by now that the end of the Cold War and the disappearance of Communist governments in Eastern Europe and the Soviet Union have had an effect on international terrorism. For years, several writers (Cline and Alexander, 1984; Sterling, 1981), as well as U.S. government officials, accused those Communist governments of providing support and places of refuge for terrorists. In late May 1992, "Sergei Shakhrai, an aide to Boris Yeltsin, announced to reporters that a cache of thousands of Communist Party documents had been discovered that detailed the Kremlin's financing of terrorism since the mid 1970s. Some \$20 million a year, as well as weapons, went to organizations . . . to carry out operations against American and Israeli personnel in third countries" (National Review, 1992, p. 18).

The Soviet Union disbanded in December 1991, thus presumably bringing to an end this flow of support to terrorist groups. It is at least curious that in 1992, according to a U.S. State Department report, "the number of international terrorist incidents dropped sharply [36 percent] . . . falling to its lowest level in 17 years." State Department officials claimed that this decline was attributable to "the disappearance of the Communist governments in Eastern Europe and the Soviet Union that provided support and safe haven for terrorist groups" (Holmes, 1993, p. 4). Even more recently, "during 1996, there were 296 actions of international terrorism, the lowest annual total in 25 years" (Wilcox, 1996). Figure 13.4 gives data on terrorist incidents over the last twenty years. And "left-wing terrorist groups . . . down through the Red Armies that operated in Germany, Italy, and Japan in the 1970s, have vanished" (Laqueur, 1997, p. 25). In addition, during the entire year of 1996 there was not a single incident of international terrorism in the United States (Wilcox, 1997).

Of course, the World Trade Center bombing demonstrated that the demise of the Communist governments in the Soviet Union and Eastern Europe will not be sufficient to rid the world entirely of terrorism. And in fact, one observer argues that "most international . . . terrorism these days . . . is neither left nor right, but ethnic-separatist in inspiration. Ethnic terrorists have more staying power than ideologically motivated ones, since they draw on a larger reservoir of public support" (Laqueur, 1997, p. 25). In addition while the number of terrorist incidents in 1996 was at a twenty-five-year low, "in contrast, the total number of casualties was one of the highest ever recorded: 311 persons killed, and 2,652 wounded." Nineteen Americans were killed by a terrorist attack out-

---

[23] In 1996, "there were several deadly bombings in Tel Aviv and Jerusalem by the Islamic Resistance Movement (HAMAS)" (Wilcox, 1997).

Figure 13.4 International Terrorist Incidents over Time, 1977–1996

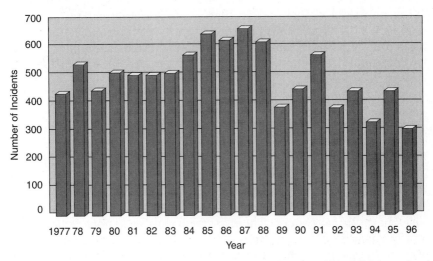

side a U.S. military installation in Saudi Arabia in 1996; overall, twenty-four American citizens died in international terrorist attacks in 1996, more than twice the number who died in 1995 (Wilcox, 1997). The higher number of deaths seems to have been caused by more attacks on large numbers of civilians, and the use of more powerful bombs.[24]

Still, in light of the actual amount of suffering and death international terrorism causes, it might be argued that it is an overpublicized phenomenon. In 1985, for example, twenty-three American lives were lost to terrorism overseas. In contrast, there were roughly eighteen thousand murders in the United States that year (Kegley, 190, p. 14). The *Economist* (March 2, 1996, p. 25) points out that the "State Department has totted up the deaths due to international terrorism from 1968 through 1995. Its total, and it defines terrorism broadly, is 8,700." That is a tragically large number, of course, but not all that large compared with the numbers killed by international wars, civil wars, government-sponsored policies of oppression, and so on.

In the end, perhaps, what is most worrisome about international terrorism in the contemporary era is its *potential* for wreaking massive havoc and suffering with nuclear weapons, biological and chemical

---

[24] Laqueur (1997, p. 25) argues that "the trend now seems to be away from attacking specific targets like the other side's officials and toward more indiscriminate killing."

weapons, or "information warfare" techniques that could result in massive dislocations in banking records, airline traffic, and communication networks. "Chances are that of 100 attempts at terrorist superviolence, 99 would fail. But the single successful one could claim many more victims, do more material damage, and unleash far greater panic than anything the world has yet experienced" (Laqueur, 1997, p. 36).

SUMMARY

Do multinational corporations, CARE, the Red Cross and Amnesty International, organized crime on a global scale, or terrorist groups represent the wave of the future, or are they simply aberrations and exceptions proving the rule that nation-states are the primary actors in the global political system? There are good reasons to hope that at least some transnational organizations do become increasingly important. (More influential and effective transnational criminal or terrorist groups are not, in this author's view, to be hoped for.) Certainly one of the points of this chapter is to highlight the extent to which they are already having an impact.

MNCs have proliferated in the last twenty or thirty years and have been very successful. Still, they have created suspicions both in their home countries and in the countries in which they set up transnational operations. They are capable of "exporting jobs" from rich countries to poor countries, and even in recent times they have been known to abuse their influence and power in developing countries by mistreating their workers. Certainly most current governments, though, in rich as well as developing countries, feel that FDI is beneficial. The nature of its impact seems to depend heavily on how the recipient country handles it.

Computers and computer-mediated networks seem to have the potential to transform the global political system. The phenomena of computers, people interconnected by the Internet, e-mail, and the World Wide Web have all exploded in recent years. Some skeptics feel that the potential impact of CMC has been exaggerated. Other analysts are convinced that "virtual communities" have the potential to revolutionize the global system, and that computer-based networks of communication are one of the reasons that nonstate actors are increasingly important in the contemporary global political system

Terrorism might most usefully be defined as the use of violence by nonstate actors for political purposes, typically against noncombatants. Terrorist groups are not new, but they do have new potential to wreak havoc in the international system, thanks to weapons of mass destruction such as nuclear, biological, and chemical weapons and the possibility that information warfare could disrupt communication networks that keep track of amounts in almost everybody's bank accounts, as well as the routes of airplanes and trains.

It would be premature to bury the so-called state-centric approach to global politics. Much of the current transnational activity is only marginally important for global politics. Such groups as the International Federation of Manufacturers of Gummed Paper, the International League of Antiquarian Booksellers, the International Society of Money Box Collectors, and the International Organization for the Study of the Endurance of Wire Ropes seem unlikely to transform international politics even in the aggregate.

It is also important to remember that passionately committed people have been trying to bury the state-dominated global political system almost from the time of its emergence in 1648. "Transnational relations . . . fits neatly into the anti-State centric position. . . . This position thus contains elements of anti-State integrative functionalism of the 1930s, which in turn owed much of its anti-State strain to 19th century economic liberalism" (Harrod, 1976, p. 103).

The global political system today faces numerous problems that a state-dominated system may find impossible to resolve. Transnational organizations have become increasingly visible in recent decades, and they can conceivably play a key role in the resolution of such problems as human rights violations, environmental problems, and economic disasters. And in the current era, they can rely on CMC and e-mail networks, phenomena with revolutionary potential to produce effective political organizations and unimpeded to an unprecedented extent by the geographical dispersion of their members. Whatever the outcome of the current contest for influence between states and transnational organizations, it is unlikely that the latter will lose out entirely; they will almost certainly win an increasingly important place in the global political system, even if it is not the predominant position.

KEY TERMS

transnational organizations
multinational corporations (MNCs)
nonstate entities
nongovernmental organizations
  (NGOs)
foreign direct investment (FDI)
export platforms
inflow of investments

outflows of repatriated profits
decapitalized
Nike
child labor
modern means of communication
  and transportation
territorial units
computers

personal computers (PCs)
electronic communication networks
CMC (Computer-Mediated
    Communication)
World Wide Web
Internet
HyperText Markup Language
    (HTML)
electronic mail (e-mail)

information warfare
Red Cross
Amnesty International
globally integrated crime
terrorism
unidimensional
noncombatant targets
Aum Shinrikyo
World Trade Center

SOURCES

Billet, Bret L. "Safeguarding or International Morality? The Behavior of Multi-national Corporations in Less Developed Countries, 1975–86." *International Interactions*, 17 (No. 2), 1991, 171–190.

Bornschier, Volker, and Christopher Chase-Dunn. *Transnational Corporations and Underdevelopment*. New York: Praeger, 1985.

Bornschier, Volker, Christopher Chase-Dunn, and Richard Rubinson, "Cross-National Evidence of the Effects of Foreign Investment and Aid on Economic Growth and Inequality." *American Journal of Sociology*, 84 (November 1978), 651–683.

Boswell, Terry, and William J. Dixon. "Dependency and Rebellion: A Cross-National Analysis." *American Sociological Review*, 55 (August 1990), 540–559.

Bradshaw, York W., and Zwelakhe Tshandu. "Foreign Capital Penetration, State Intervention, and Development in Sub-Saharan Africa." *International Studies Quarterly*, 34 (June 1990), 229–251.

Burton, Daniel F., Jr. "The Brave New Wired World." *Foreign Policy*, No. 106 (Spring 1997), 23–37.

Chan, Steve. "Income Inequality Among LDCs: A Comparative Analysis of Alternative Perspectives." *International Studies Quarterly*, 33 (March 1989), 45–65.

Clausen, A. W. "The Internationalized Corporation: An Executive's View." *Annals*, 403 (September 1972), 12–21.

Cline, Ray S., and Yonah Alexander. *Terrorism: The Soviet Connection*. New York: Crane Russak, 1984.

Crenshaw, Martha. "An Organizational Approach to the Analysis of Political Terrorism." *Orbis*, 29 (Fall 1985), 465–489.

"Cyber Wars." *Economist*, January 13, 1996, 77–78.

"The Discreet Charm of the Multicultural Multinational." *Economist*, July 30, 1994, 57–58.

Dobson, Christopher, and Ronald Payne. *The Terrorists: Their Weapons, Leaders and Tactics*. New York: Facts on File, 1979.

"Does It Matter Where You Are?" *Economist*, July 30, 1994, pp. 13–14.

Edington, Mark W. "Suddenly, America Is a World Trade Center." *New York Times*, March 2, 1993, Section A, p. 21.

"Emerging Market Indicators." *Economist*, October 26, 1996, p. 128.

Forsythe, David P. "The Red Cross as a Transnational Movement: Conserving and Changing the Nation-State System." *International Organization*, 30 (Autumn 1976), 607–630.

"*Fortune's* Global 500: The World's Largest Corporations." *Fortune*, August 7, 1995, F1–F10.

Gilpin, Robert. *The Political Economy of International Relations*. Princeton, N.J.: Princeton University Press, 1987.

Goozner, Merrill. "Asian Labor: Wages of Shame." *Chicago Tribune*, November 6, 1994, Section 1, 12–13.

Herbert, Bob. "Mr. Young Gets It Wrong." *New York Times*, June 27, 1996, Section A, p. 21.

Holmes, Steven A. "US Says Terrorist Attacks Dropped Sharply in 1992." *New York Times*, May 1, 1993, Section A, p. 4.

Holyoke, Larry, Paula Dwyer, Stewart Toy, and Christopher Power. "A Topsy-Turvy Year for Giants." *Business Week*, July 12, 1993, pp. 52–107.

Human Rights Watch. New York: Human Rights Watch, 1993.

"Introduction to the World Wide Web." http://www.ece.jhu/dept/local/wwwintro/section2.html#RTFToC7, 1997.

Jackman, Robert. "Dependence on Foreign Investment and Economic Growth in the Third World." *World Politics*, 34 (January 1982), 175–196.

Johnson, Paul. "The Seven Deadly Sins of Terrorism." In Henry Hyunwook Han, ed., *Terrorism, Political Violence, and World Order*. New York: University Press of America, 1984.

Kantor, Andrew, and Eric Berlin. "The Surfboard," *Internet: The Magazine for Internet Users*, February 1995, pp. 16–18.

Kapstein, Ethan B. "The Myth of the Multinational." *The National Interest*, No. 26 (Winter 1991/92), 55–70.

Kegley, Charles W. "The Characteristics of Contemporary International Terrorism." In Charles W. Kegley, Jr. ed., *International Terrorism: Characteristics, Causes, Control*. New York: St. Martin's Press, 1990.

LaQuey, Tracy, with Jeanne C. Ryer. *Internet Companion: A Beginner's Guide to Global Networking*. Reading, Mass.: Addison-Wesley, 1993.

Laqueur, Walter. "Postmodern Terrorism." *Foreign Affairs*, 75 (September/October 1996), 24–36.

Levy, Steven. "The Year of the Internet." *Newsweek*, January 1, 1996, pp. 21–30.

Manchester, William. *The Arms of Krupp*. Boston: Little, Brown, 1968.

Mathews, Jessica T. "Power Shift." *Foreign Affairs*, 76 (January/February 1997), 50–66.

Mitchell, Neil J., and James M. McCormick. "Economic and Political Explanations of Human Rights Violations." *World Politics*, 40 (July 1988), 476–498.

Muller, Edward N. "Financial Dependence in the Capitalist Economy and the Distribution of Income Within Nations." In Mitchell A. Seligson, ed., *The Gap Between Rich and Poor*. Boulder, Colo.: Westview Press, 1984.

Muller, Ronald. "The MNC and the Exercise of Power: Latin America." In Abdul Aziz Said and Luiz R. Simmons, eds., *The New Sovereigns: Multinational Corporations as World Powers*. Englewood Cliffs, N.J.: Prentice-Hall, 1975.

Mylroie, Laurie. "The World Trade Center Bomb." *National Interest*, No. 42 (Winter 1995/96), 3–15.

O'Neil, Bard E. "Towards a Typology of Terrorism: The Palestinian Resistance Movement." *Journal of International Affairs*, 32 (Spring–Summer 1978), 17–42.

Pauly, Louis W., and Simon Reich. "National Structures and Multinational Corporate Behavior: Enduring Differences in the Age of Globalization." *International Organization*, 51 (Winter 1997), 1–30.

"Pravda Will Out." *National Review*, June 22, 1992, pp. 18–19.

Rapoport, David C. "Fear and Trembling: Terrorism in Three Religious Traditions." *American Political Science Review*, 78 (September 1984), 658–677.

Reich, Robert B. "Who Is Us?" *Harvard Business Review*, 90 (January–February), 53–64.

Rheingold, Howard. *The Virtual Community: Homesteading on the Electronic Frontier.* Reading, Mass.: Addison-Wesley, 1993.

Rothgeb, John. *The Modern Leviathan in the Third World: The Myths and Realities of Foreign Investment in the Third World.* New York: Praeger, 1989.

Russett, Bruce M. "Ethical Dilemmas of Nuclear Deterrence." *International Security*, 8 (Spring 1984), 36–84.

Schelling, Thomas C. "Thinking About Nuclear Terrorism." *International Security*, 6 (Spring 1982), 61–77.

Schmid, Alex. *Political Terrorism.* New Brunswick, N.J.: Transaction Books, 1983.

Schwartau, Winn. *Information Warfare: Chaos on the Electronic Superhighway.* New York: Thunder's Mouth Press, 1994.

Sederberg, Peter C. *Terrorist Myths: Illusion, Rhetoric, and Reality.* Englewood Cliffs, N.J.: Prentice-Hall, 1989.

Shively, W. Phillips. *The Craft of Political Research.* 2nd ed. Englewood Cliffs, N.J.: Prentice-Hall, 1980, p. 31.

Spero, Joan Edelman, and Jeffrey A. Hart. *The Politics of International Economic Relations.* New York: St. Martin's Press, 1997.

Stephenson, Hugh. *The Coming Clash.* New York: Saturday Review Press, 1972.

Sterling, Claire. *The Terror Network: The Secret War of International Terrorism.* New York: Holt, Rinehart & Winston, 1981.

Sterling, Claire. *Thieves' World: The Threat of the New Global Network of Organized Crime.* New York: Simon & Schuster, 1994.

Stillman, Rona B., et al. "Information Security—Computer Attacks at Department of Defense Pose Increasing Risks." http://www.epic.org/computer_crime/gao_dod_security.html, October 3, 1996.

Stokes, Bruce. "Globalization: Workplace Winners and Losers." In Nancy Hoepli, ed., *Great Decisions 1997.* New York: Foreign Policy Association, 1997.

Szymanski, Albert. "Comment on Bornschier." *Journal of Conflict Resolution*, 28 (March 1984), 149–156.

Terrill, W. Andrew. "Saddam's Failed Counterstrike: Terrorism and the Gulf War." *Studies in Conflict and Terrorism*, 16 (September 1993), 219–232.

Toffler, Alvin. *Powershift.* New York: Bantam Books, 1990.

"The Top 100 Companies." *Business Week,* July 8, 1996, p. 47.

Union of International Associations (ed.). *Yearbook of International Organizations.* Munich: K. G. Lauer, 1995/96.

Venzke, Ben. "Information Warrior." *Wired,* August 1996, 137.

Vernon, Raymond. *Sovereignty at Bay.* New York: Basic Books, 1971.

Walters, Robert S., and David H. Blake. *The Politics of Global Economic Relations.* 4th ed. Englewood Cliffs, N.J.: Prentice-Hall, 1992.

"What Is Terrorism?" *Economist,* March 2, 1996, pp. 23–25.

Wilkinson, Paul. "State-Sponsored International Terrorism: The Problem of Response." *World Today,* 40 (July 1984), 292–298.

Wilcox, Philip, C., Jr. "Patterns of Global Terrorism" (Annual Report by the U.S. Department of State). http://dns.usis-israel.org.il/publish/terrorism/, 1997.

World Bank. *World Development Report 1996.* New York: Oxford University Press, 1996.

Young, John E. *Global Network: Computers in a Sustainable Society.* Washington, D.C.: Worldwatch Institute, 1993.

CHAPTER 14

The International System, the Balance of Power, and War

The preceding chapters have adopted progressively more comprehensive viewpoints. After starting with a focus on individuals and groups within states (Chapters 3 and 4), they next looked at states as entities (Chapters 5 and 6) and then analyzed interaction within and between different categories and groups of states (Chapters 7 through 11). Chapter 12 considered the impact of ethical norms, international law, and "regimes," which might be loosely defined as the bases for the informal (and sometimes formal) organizations that emerge within the community of nation-states in the global system. Chapter 13 discussed transnational organizations comprising members or activities in several states but without any formal affiliations with national governments. This chapter begins with a discussion of the virtues and problems associated with analyses that focus on the **international system** as a whole. It then analyzes the validity of one of the best-known theories in the annals of international politics, the **balance-of-power theory,** and its contemporary version emphasizing the **polarity** of the international system.

ANALYZING WHOLES AND PARTS

Some of the most vigorous and mystifying debates in this century over how best to analyze politics focus on the relationship between entire social systems and their components. Some analysts believe passionately that all valid explanations of political behavior must ultimately deal with individuals. These **individualists** "insist that no social laws operate independently of human understanding; all explanations can be reduced to the level of the individual and couched in terms of the nature and intentions of these actors" (Little, 1985, p. 74). For example, one school of thought suggests that understanding international war is not difficult; wars occur because human beings are evil. "Our miseries are ineluctably the product of our natures. The root of all evil is man, and thus he is himself the root of the specific evil, war" (Waltz, 1959, p. 3).[1]

The alternative viewpoint is that explanations of human behavior, and of problems such as war, must focus not on individuals or human nature but on the **social structures** that emerge as people interact with each other. In international politics, this idea leads to the conclusion that "bad" states cause wars or that the structure of the international system is at fault. One of the most persistent versions of this idea asserts that dictatorships are bad states. But according to **structuralists,** the blame for war should be placed not on the internal structure of *some* states (be they dictatorships or capitalistic) but on the structure of the international system in which all states must operate. That system is **anarchic;** each state must look out for itself or risk losing out in the war of "all against all." In such a system, "it is not only that a state, becoming too fond of peace, may thereby perish; but also that the seeming somnolence of one state may invite a war of aggression that a more aggressive pose by the peace-loving state might have avoided altogether" (Waltz, 1959, p. 221). Since, given the nature of the international system, even "peace-loving" states need to strike "aggressive poses" for their own protection, all states are aggressive (or strive to appear so). Under these conditions, wars are bound to break out periodically, and it is the anarchic structure of the international system that is the root cause of those wars.

One important initial step toward resolving this controversy between individualists and structuralists is appreciating the limitations of theories that emphasize human evil as *the* cause of war. For if people were more consistently self-centered and lacking in altruism (that is, even more thoroughly evil than they are), international wars might occur considerably *less* often than they actually do. In a more evil world, nobody could be found to engage in that brave, self-sacrificing behavior that soldiers characteristically exhibit on the battlefield, usually for very little in terms of personal gain and often at the cost of their lives. War might be at least as much a function of humankind's virtues as of its vices.

Even more important from a theoretical viewpoint, humankind's propensity for evil does not vary, at least not much, and only then over eons. Logically, this means that the evil nature of human beings cannot account for variations in international war over time and across space. For example, the international system was relatively peaceful in 1910 but engulfed in war in 1914. What accounts for this difference in the war

---

[1] Waltz is merely describing this kind of theory here, not advocating or defending it.

proneness of the system in those two different years? Surely humankind was not significantly more or less evil in 1910 than in 1914, so the passage of time could not account for the onset of the First World War (or any other war).

The Level-of-Analysis Problem in International Politics

Another crucial step toward forming an educated opinion about the "whole versus parts" controversy, or what has become known in the field of international politics as the **level-of-analysis problem,** involves clearly understanding that the differences at issue here are real. Proponents of the different approaches are not simply using different words to talk about the same things. Despite possible appearances to the contrary, disputes about the level-of-analysis problem are not silly word games amusing only to pedantic academics.

One of the most common disputes focuses on what exactly the level-of-analysis problem is. In one of the best-known (and earliest) articles on this problem, J. David Singer (1961, p. 77) asserts that he is concerned about the question of "whether . . . the observer . . . [chooses] to focus upon the parts or upon the whole, upon the components, or upon the system." That is, the level of an analysis is determined by the type of social entity (either individual states, for example, or the whole international system) whose behavior or operation the analyst seeks to explain. This criterion suggests that the level-of-analysis problem has to do with what kinds of *questions* are most useful. One can ask, for example, why some states are more war prone than other states or why individual states are more war prone at some times than at other times. These questions pertain to the national level of analysis. Or one can ask, "Why was the international system less war prone in the nineteenth century than in the twentieth century? Are bipolar international systems more or less war prone than multipolar systems?" These questions pertain to the international-system level of analysis. In recent years, partly due to the interest in the historical absence of wars between democratic states and the democratic peace proposition, renewed interest has focused on pairs of states and on the question "Why are some pairs of states more war prone than other pairs of states?"

Clearly, though, some writers in the field believe that the level-of-analysis problem has to do not only with the type of questions that are asked but also with the *answers* that are given—in other words, with the type of factors relied on to explain foreign policy decisions or political events. Some analysts, for example, stipulate that *level of analysis* "may refer to the actors themselves, to the states or individuals whose behavior we are trying to explain, or . . . to different kinds of influences on those actors" (Russett and Starr, 1996, p. 11). In this view, the level-of-analysis problem deals not only with which units one asks questions about but also with which units or social entities should be observed to find out why actors behave as they do.

For example, an analyst might feel that foreign policy makers are more often influenced by attributes of the particular states whose governments they serve (whether democratic or dictatorial, capitalist or socialist) than by, say, structural characteristics of the international system (the balance of power, perhaps). If so, he or she can be described as theoretically biased in favor of explanatory factors found on the national, rather than the international-system, level of analysis.

Both level-of-analysis problems, or issues, are worthy of attention. This book has already addressed the controversy regarding which kinds of factors have the greatest impact on foreign policy decisions and events. Recall the discussion in Chapter 4 on the relative potency of idiosyncratic personality traits of decision makers versus structural characteristics of states, or of the international system, within the "funnel of causality." An individual's preferences in that controversy can affect his or her attitude toward the other level-of-analysis problem, namely, which kind of social entity it is more fruitful to investigate. A person who feels that the balance of power in the international system is the most fundamental cause of international war (that is, the most potent explanatory factor) is likely also to feel that the causal impact of that system-level factor will be most visible in the incidence of war in the entire international system. That is, a theoretical bias in favor of a system-level causal factor will lead to a similar inclination to focus on the international system, as opposed to nation-states or individual decision makers, as the entity whose behavior or operation is to be explained.

Related though they are in this way, the two level-of-analysis problems are not identical. A preference for systemic explanatory factors does not necessarily lead to a corresponding bias in favor of analyses of the entire international system. One might believe, for example (as explained in Chapter 4), that system-level attributes or the environment provided by the international system are the most potent causal factors to be considered in explaining the behavior of individual states, or decisions by individual decision makers, as well as patterns that appear in the international system as a whole.[2] In other words, systemic explanatory factors can be included in analyses of individual states or

[2] For example, Bueno de Mesquita and Lalman (1988) investigate the effect of systemic-level factors on individual decision makers.

decision makers, as well as in those analyses that focus on the system as a whole.

It is argued here that the fuzzy consensus among researchers in the field makes it necessary, awkward as it is, to define the level-of-analysis problem as an issue involving the social entity whose behavior is explained *or* the social entity whose characteristics are used as explanatory factors. Such a definition may obscure (even though it specifically mentions) the difference between two different issues, and it may also contribute to the obviously widespread impression that there is really only one problem. If it were possible to have power over the terminology of international politics, this author would decree that the phrase "level-of-analysis problem" be reserved for *either* the question focusing on the location of **explanatory factors** *or* the issue of the **type of social entity** whose behavior or operation is to be explained. In the absence of that power, it may be more useful to point out that many, perhaps most, writers in the field perceive the level-of-analysis problem as involving one or both of the two issues discussed here. And many (unfortunately) tend to see the problems as identical or interchangeable.

The Relationship Between Analyses on Different Levels

For the sake of the following discussion only, then, the level-of-analysis problem involves the distinction between (1) analyses of different social entities (such as states or pairs of states) and (2) analyses of the entire international system, rather than the issue regarding the location of the most potent explanatory factors. The most vital point to be made is that analyses on different levels are relatively independent of each other— relative, that is, to what common sense or uninstructed intuition might indicate. In other words, the answers to questions addressed to one level of analysis (those focusing on pairs of nation-states, for example) may be so different from apparently similar questions addressed to another level (such as the international-system level) that it is crucial to keep the level-of-analysis distinction in mind to avoid serious confusion. The implication of this point is not that one kind of analysis is better than another but that analyses on different levels can lead to distinctly different conclusions regarding the relationship between the explanatory factors and behaviors or events being analyzed. Those conclusions, though apparently contradictory, may be equally valid. The contradictions are only apparent, and a function of the relative independence of the different levels of analysis.

Imagine, for the sake of simplicity, that there are only three pairs of states (pairs A, B, and C) in a hypothetical international system we want to investigate. Imagine further that we are interested in the relationship between the extent to which these pairs of states are democratic and the amount of war involving those same pairs of states. Looking first at Pair A and considering three successive time periods (t_0, t_1, and t_2), we find that when Pair A's democracy scores go up, it experiences more war, and when they go down, it becomes involved in less war. In other words, in this *imaginary* system (and its imaginary nature should be emphasized) we find, contrary to the democratic peace proposition, that war is positively related to democracy, that as the pair of states becomes more democratic, it gets involved in more military conflict.

Inferring a causal connection from this covariation would be risky. First, only three time periods have been considered; the degree of democracy within this pair of states and instances of war between them might have gone up and down together that many times just by chance. Also, perhaps some third factor, such as the amount of unrest in the state, has an impact on both democracy and war that causes them to covary. (In principle, it could also be true that war has a positive impact on democracy, rather than democracy having a positive impact on war.) But suppose, for the sake of this example, that investigations of all those possibilities reveal that none of them applies. For Pair A, the positive correlation between democracy and war indicates that the former causes the latter.

Suppose further that analyses of Pairs B and C in the same hypothetical system reveal the same pattern between democracy and war. In other words, we find that for each pair of states in the system, the greater its degree of democracy, the more war it experiences. It might then seem logical to conclude that the higher the average level of democracy in the system, the greater the amount of war that will occur. But such a conclusion would constitute a level-of-analysis error. Consider Table 14.1, showing the relationship between the level of democracy and war experience of pairs of states A, B, and C. Notice that, as the democracy scores for the three time periods for each pair of states go up, the numbers representing the amount of war experienced go up, too. Similarly, as the democracy scores go down (for example, for Pair A from t_1 to t_2), so, too, does the amount of war it experiences. For every pair of states, there is a positive relationship between democracy and war.

But now consider the data pertaining to the entire system, obtained by adding up the numbers on democracy and war for the separate pairs of states. In the international system as a whole, there is a *negative* relationship between the level of democracy and the amount of war. On the system level of analysis, as the level of democracy in the system increases, the amount of war *decreases*. And conversely, when democracy on the system level goes down, the amount of war *increases*.

Table 14.1 An Imaginary Systemwide Profile Showing Pairwise- and System-Level Relationships

	t_0	t_1	t_2
Pair A			
Democracy	10	40	20
War	5	10	5
Pair B			
Democracy	15	10	20
War	20	15	40
Pair C			
Democracy	30	15	20
War	40	10	30
Total system			
Democracy	55	65	60
War	65	35	75

This system-level negative correlation may or may not reflect a causal connection between democracy and war. The point is that one cannot safely infer that a pattern existing on a lower level of analysis necessarily also exists on a higher level, or vice versa. That is, it would be a logical mistake (a level-of-analysis error) to infer the system-level relationship from the patterns revealed on the lower, pairwise level of analysis. It would also be a mistake to focus on the negative system-level relationship between democracy and war depicted in Table 14.1 and to conclude that the democratic pairs of states (or individual democratic states) are likely to experience less war.

Similarly, if one finds a positive relationship between the number of alliances in the international system and the amount of war that occurs, it would be a mistake to conclude that states with many alliances are more likely to become involved in wars. The system-level correlation might occur because "smart" states form protective alliances, whereas "dumb" states avoid alliances and fight the wars. Even though, in such a case, there would be a positive correlation between the number of alliances and the amount of war in the international system, the relationship between alliances and war on the national level of analysis might be negative in every single case.

It does seem natural enough that the democratic peace proposition discussed at length in Chapter 6 would lead to an interest in the relationship between the prevalence of democracy in the international system and the war proneness (or conflict proneness) of the system; it is equally natural for this theory to create an assumption that higher levels of democracy in the international system should reduce the incidence of war. And in fact, system-level analyses of the relationship between levels of democracy and the incidence of war or conflict in the system are beginning to appear (see, for example, Gleditsch and Hegre, 1997; Senese, 1997). One of the earliest extensive analyses of the relationship between democracy in pairs of states and their war proneness also included a system-level analysis of the relationship between democracy and war (Maoz and Abdolali, 1989). As natural and straightforward as that interest and the assumption about the system-level relationship might seem, though, the problems involved in drawing inferences across different levels of analysis make it difficult to evaluate the significance of results produced by such system-level analyses.

THE BALANCE-OF-POWER THEORY

Level-of-analysis errors and other types of confusion and controversies often arise in discussions of one of the most venerable concepts in international relations, the *balance of power*. Despite this concept's longevity, its definition is subject to considerable controversy. One well-known analysis of this concept (Haas, 1953), for example, points out the following meanings of the term in scholarly writings on the subject: (1) distribution of power, (2) equilibrium, (3) hegemony, (4) stability and peace, (5) instability and war, (6) universal law of history, and (7) system and guide to policymaking.

Even though the concept has thus been used in a confusing variety of ways, in its essentials it is quite simple, according to perhaps its best-known advocate in the last ten or fifteen years, Kenneth Waltz (1979, p. 121). A balance-of-power system is one that emerges among any set of political units as long as two conditions are met. The first is that the system be anarchic, that is, have no central authority or government. The second condition is that the units in the system wish to survive.

One system that met these criteria was the set of European states from roughly 1700 up to the First World War. What might be referred to as the theory of **Classical Balance of Power** was developed by European foreign policy makers in that era. This Classical Balance of Power operated according to a rather elaborate set of rules, which were consciously adhered to by culturally homogeneous European elites dedicated to the preservation of the system.

The most basic assumption on which this theory rested was that the loosely integrated set of states in Europe should adopt policies that would preserve their individual existence and independence. This assumption pointed the way to the most fundamental premise of the Classical Balance of Power as it came to be applied in Europe, namely, that power ought to be distributed throughout the community of states in a such a way that no single state would ever become strong enough to dominate all the rest (Wight, 1973, p. 100).

Preserving such a distribution of power meant first that the states supporting the Classical Balance of Power needed constantly to be watching and evaluating one another. Thus, exchanging ambassadors became standard practice. The key type of information on which ambassadors (and spies) concentrated had to do with the power of the other states in the system. Obviously, if the independence of states was to be ensured by preventing any single state in the system from becoming powerful enough to dominate it, each state needed to monitor continually the **power** of others that threatened to become dominating, as well as the power of those states seeking to counterbalance that threat. This need in turn implied that power could be measured. "The power of individual states was conceived to be susceptible of measurement by certain well-defined factors: their population, their territories, their finances, i.e., the balance of trade—and by the state of their armies and navies" (Gulick, 1955, p. 24).

If the Classical Balance of Power were to work as intended, power had to be not only measurable but, within limits, also manipulable. States could help themselves by internal means—for example, by increasing military budgets or the size of their armies, or by augmenting industrial capacity and encouraging population growth. But the most rapid and flexible means of manipulating power within the system of the Classical Balance of Power was the formation of **alliances.** To maintain the balance of power required flexibility of alliances. Every member of the states system had to be prepared to cooperate with any other member of the states system, as circumstances demanded. Ultimately, if one state, or coalition of states, threatened the entire system, a "grand alliance" involving all the rest could be formed, preserving the equilibrium and the independence of each member state (Wight, 1973, pp. 104–105, 108).

This tendency for alliances to form against states or coalitions that threaten to dominate the system has been clearly visible, at least to advocates of the balance-of-power theory, in the history of international politics in the nineteenth and twentieth centuries. Napoleonic France posed just such a threat in the first decades of the nineteenth century, and that threat produced a coalition of virtually all the other Great Powers in the international system at that time (Britain, Austria-Hungary, Prussia, and Russia).[3] In the first decades of the twentieth century, Germany, aided by Austria-Hungary, posed a similar threat to the independence of the states of Europe, and the Dual Alliance between the Germans and the Austrians brought forth the Triple Entente—established by Russia, France, and Britain and ultimately joined by the United States—which managed to preserve the balance of power by winning the First World War. Similarly, when Hitler's Germany and its allies threatened to become a predominating force in the global system, the Soviet Union, France, Britain, and the United States united in opposition to that threat, fighting it off in the course of the Second World War.

Classical Balance of Power theorists also commonly assumed that it was important for one state, the so-called **holder of the balance,** to keep a watchful eye on the rest of the system and to step in at the appropriate moment to ally with a weaker coalition about to be crushed by a too powerful state or coalition. (In Europe, Great Britain usually played the role of holder of the balance.) Finally, players in this game of Classical Balance of Power typically felt it important to be moderate in victory; losers of wars, at least on most occasions, would not be humiliated or eliminated. In Europe, "wars . . . were ended by treaties which more often than not, represented a compromise, and in their forms studiously respected the dignity of the defeated party" (Gulick, 1955, p. 76).

The Balance of Power and the Preservation of Peace

How well did this Classical Balance of Power, and the theory on which it was based, work? The theory was certainly influential. "For two hundred years, the balance of power was generally accepted among diplomats and statesmen as the constituent principle of Europe's international society" (Wight, 1973, p. 98). The era of Classical Balance of Power in Europe was also marked by some notable successes. "In the period from 1648 to 1792, there were, generally speaking, no great territorial changes in continental Europe" (Gulick, 1955, p. 39). For a system whose basic purpose was the preservation of the states within it, this period of 144 years with virtually no important changes in

---

[3] One recent analysis insists, though, that "while actors balanced against the USSR, they did not balance against Napoleonic France, at least until the end (1813–1815)" (Rosecrance and Lo, 1996, p. 479).

boundaries should not pass unnoted. Perhaps even more important, though, was the absence of system-shattering wars throughout the nineteenth century (after 1815). From the viewpoint of the twentieth century, with its two world wars, the nineteenth century looks almost idyllic, even though there were several rather extensive conflicts, especially in the latter half.[4]

One of the more intriguing contemporary controversies regarding the Classical Balance of Power focuses on this relative stability of the nineteenth century and the role of the balance of power in maintaining that stability. According to A. F. K. Organski (1968, p. 292), the idea that peace was maintained in the nineteenth century by a balance of power is fundamentally wrong:

> In the nineteenth century, after the Napoleonic Wars, there was almost continuous peace. The balance of power is usually given a good share of the credit for this peaceful century, but . . . there was no balance at all, but rather a vast preponderance of power in the hands of England and France.

In contrast, Hans Morgenthau (1967, p. 213) looks at the nineteenth century and asserts:

> Of the temperance and indecisiveness of the political contests . . . from 1815 to 1914, the balance of power is not only the cause but also the metaphorical and symbolic expression as well as the technique of realization.

How could two well-known scholars of international politics look at the same century and come to such different conclusions about whether a balance of power existed *and* whether or not it made the system peaceful? One reason involves the ambiguity in the concept of power. But probably the most important reason involves both the variety of popular definitions of the balance of power and level-of-analysis confusion. For some, like Organski, the balance of power refers to the distribution of power among individual states. Organski also assumes that the balance-of-power theory stipulates that a more or less equal distribution of power among states is a prerequisite for peace. For others, like Morgenthau, the balance of power refers to the preferably equal distribution of power among *coalitions* of states. In terms of the definition preferred by Organski, there was no balance of power in the nineteenth century. Great Britain was clearly dominant, certainly in terms of the

---

[4] "The popular image of the post-Napoleonic nineteenth century as an era of basic international peace between the great powers is surely wrong, especially for the last half of the century (witness the Crimean War of 1854 between Britain and Russia, the Italian War of 1859 between Austria and France, the war between Denmark and the German states of 1864, the Austro-Prussian War of 1866, and the Franco-Prussian War of 1870)" (Brown, 1980, p. 24).

military-industrial indicators discussed in Chapter 6. But if we look instead at coalitions of states (that is, at a different level of analysis), the picture is less clear. Great Britain was very powerful, but it was often counterbalanced by coalitions of states. In the 1880s, for example, Austria-Hungary, Germany, and Russia were allied with each other, as were Austria-Hungary, Germany, and Italy. Compared with such alliances, Great Britain was quite powerful, but not overwhelmingly so, and one could plausibly argue that a balance of power (in the sense of an equal distribution of power among states and/or coalitions) existed in the 1880s and, for similar reasons, throughout much of the nineteenth century.

Even assuming that it would be possible to sort out this level-of-analysis confusion in the debate between Organski and Morgenthau, the two would probably still disagree about the cause of the relative peace among the major powers in the nineteenth century, because they have apparently opposite views on the relationship between the balance of power and peace. Organski believes that states are unlikely to go to war unless they have a good chance of winning and that this opportunity is unlikely to arise unless there is relative equality—that is, a balance of power—between the prospective opponents. Defenders of a balance of power, like Morgenthau, disagree. They argue that, on the contrary, as long as a balance is maintained, no state will feel confident that it can win a war, and so all states will be reluctant to start one (Haas and Whiting, 1956, p. 50). But if there is a preponderance of power in the system, the stronger states will constantly be tempted to take advantage of their superiority and repeatedly initiate wars against their weaker counterparts.

Both arguments are reasonable, but J. David Singer, Stuart Bremer, and John Stuckey (1972) decided to find out which one is more accurate. They collected data on the power of all the major powers in the international system from 1820 to 1965, using the indicators discussed in Chapter 6. They obtained these data for every fifth year in the time span and then calculated an index, called CON (Ray and Singer, 1973), that reflected the extent to which power or military-industrial capability was unequally distributed at each five-year observation point. The measure of concentration was used to predict the amount of war experienced by the major powers in the five-year periods following each observation. To count as a war for the purposes of this study, a conflict had to have resulted in at least one thousand battle deaths (Small and Singer, 1982).

What Singer, Bremer, and Stuckey found is that, generally speaking, the impact of the distribution of power in the international system on the war proneness of the system is minimal. When power was equally distributed, the major powers experienced a large amount of war 50 percent of the time. When power was *unequally* distributed, they experienced a large amount of war 46 percent of the time. In short, the probability of war involving the major powers was just about the same whether the concentration of power in the system was low or high.

Why does the distribution of power in the international system seemingly have no impact on its war proneness despite literally centuries of speculation to the contrary? One possibility is that Singer, Bremer, and Stuckey did not really test the balance-of-power theory in an appropriate manner. If we analyze their ideas closely, we can see that their logic applies most convincingly to conflicts between two states or two coalitions of states. One version of this central idea asserts that two *evenly* matched states or coalitions are more likely to become involved in war because in such a situation, each opponent can believe that it is likely to win. The contrary view is that two states or coalitions that are *unevenly* matched are more likely to become involved in war, because the more powerful state or coalition will find the weaker state or coalition an irresistible target for attack. It might seem logical to test these opposing ideas by analyzing the relationship between the distribution of power in the international system and the amount of war that occurs within it, but it is not.

Consider Table 14.2, which shows two imaginary international systems, with the states assigned power scores similar to those discussed in Chapter 6. In System 1, power is very unevenly distributed. State A possesses 80 percent of the military-industrial capabilities. The occurrence of war in such a system would seem to indicate that power disparity is likely to lead to war. But what if the war breaks out between States B and D, which are evenly matched in power, in spite of the unequal distribution of power in the entire system? In that situation, we can see that the co-occurrence of high power concentration and war in the *system* presents a misleading picture of the relationship between (1) the distribution of power within the system, and (2) the war proneness of *states*. In System 2, in a similar fashion, the co-occurrence of low power concentration and war in the *system* creates the misleading impression that equality between *states* leads to war, when in fact the opponents in the war were two very unequally matched *coalitions* of states. In general, then, analyses of entire systems are only loosely related to ideas about the relationship between the power equality and war proneness of states or coalitions of states.[5]

---

[5] Bremer (1992, p. 337) analyzes the relationship between power disparities and war proneness for all pairs of states in the international system from 1816 to 1965. He notes that "power preponderance is more conducive to peace in a dyad [a pair of states] than the lack thereof. . . . The existence of overwhelming preponderance is . . . a pacifying condition."

Table 14.2 Relationship Between (1) Equality and Disparity in Power and (2) the Incidence of War in Imaginary International Systems

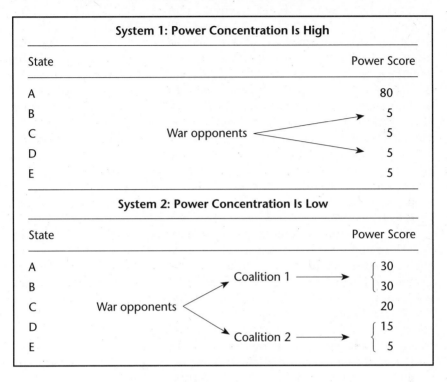

Singer, Bremer, and Stuckey also may have failed to find a significant, consistent relationship between the balance of power in the international system and the amount of war within it, because they (along with many others) misinterpreted balance-of-power theory. This is understandable, because the theory has been explained in a confusing variety of ways. But according to some apparently authoritative exponents of the theory, war is to a balance-of-power system as apple pie is to the American way. In other words, war, not peace, is unavoidably associated with the workings of a balance-of-power system. War, in this view, is one of the principal means of adjusting and/or preserving the balance of power. "We may say that survival, a degree of cooperation, and the prevention of a hostile predominance were all germane to the balance of power theory. We may also say that peace was not germane. . . . The clearest-headed theorists of equilibrium have not only not claimed peace as the principal aim, but have actually envisaged war as an instrument for balancing power" (Gulick, 1955, pp. 35–36). According to this view, Singer, Bremer, and Stuckey had no good reason to expect a systematic relationship between the distribution of power in the international system and its war proneness.

Another possible problem in the research by Singer, Bremer, and Stuckey (but only initially, as we shall see) involved lumping the nineteenth and twentieth centuries together in their analyses. The balance-of-power theory was developed in a world dominated by European states. That domination was undermined by the First World War and destroyed entirely by the Second World War, after which the United States and the Soviet Union emerged as superpowers. The leaders of the pre–First World War, European-dominated system shared not only a conscious commitment to the balance of power but also a certain amount of cultural homogeneity. "Europe was an in-group of states which excluded non-European countries. . . . [This] homogeneity was a necessary condition of the balance-of-power system" (Gulick, 1955, pp. 19–20).

But after the First World War, and particularly after the Second World War, the globe came to be dominated by the United States and the Soviet Union, joined eventually by such important non-European states as China and Japan. The elites in these non-European states had distinct world views, reinforced (especially in the cases of the United States and the Soviet Union) by opposing ideological principles to which they zealously adhered. Also, in the nineteenth century there was a relative lack of democratic pressure on foreign policy elites, which (along with the cultural homogeneity) allowed them to pursue flexible balance-of-power policies unencumbered by the necessity to explain them to "the people." That democratic pressure, combined with the ideological fervor of the Cold War, has (in theory, anyway) robbed the elites in the major powers of the contemporary international system of the ability continually to arrange and rearrange alliances as necessary to maintain the balance-of-power system.

In light of all these differences between the current system and that of Europe before the First World War, it is not surprising that when Singer, Bremer, and Stuckey analyzed the nineteenth and twentieth centuries *separately*, they found different relationships. In the nineteenth century, but not in the twentieth, greater amounts of war were more likely when power concentration was high—that is, when the distribution of power was *unequal*. A related analysis of the major powers that focused on the distribution of power among *blocs*, or coalitions of states, found that the concentration of power among those blocs correlated with war in the period from 1830 to 1914, but not in the period from 1919 to 1965 (Stoll, 1984b).

Thus, an intuitive consideration of differences between the nineteenth and twentieth centuries, along with some empirical evidence, suggests that the European Classical Balance of Power is quite different from the contemporary international system. Since the Second World War, many analysts have assumed that this difference exists and have argued accordingly that the Classical Balance of Power is an outmoded theory. They have developed a new theory about the relationship between the structure of the international system and the policies and interactions of the major powers. This theory focuses on the domination of the contemporary system by the superpowers and on the resulting bipolarity in that system.

Polarity and War in the International System

Until the demise of the Soviet Union in 1991, the United States and the Soviet Union were not only far superior to all other states in orthodox indicators of military power; they also possessed by far the largest stockpiles of nuclear weapons and far outranked any other states in the size and range of delivery systems they possessed. Soon after the Second World War, analysts came to refer to this domination of the system by those two states, coupled with the tendency of other states in the system to align themselves with one or the other, as **bipolarity.** Observers naturally wondered whether this bipolarity made international war more or less likely.

Some analysts concluded that bipolarity is inherently unstable and prone to disastrous collapse and that any trend toward **multipolarity**—that is, away from the domination of the international system by only two states and toward multiple groupings based on several of the most powerful states in the system—is desirable. One of the best-known analyses of this question, for example, argues that if there are only two really important actors, and if those two disagree on every important issue and virtually every other state in the system lines up with one of the "Big Two," conflict within the international system is bound to be exacerbated. But if there are several important actors in the system, no single issue will be likely to divide the system into two groups of states unremittingly hostile to each other, because some states on one side of one issue will agree with a number of states on the opposing side when another issue arises. Advocates of multipolarity also argue that states must devote considerable attention to one another before they become hostile enough to start a war. In a bipolar system, this is likely to happen. In a multipolar system, no state can devote full energy to concentrating on the dastardly deeds of any other single state, because every state must also worry about several *other* potential enemies (Deutsch and Singer, 1969, pp. 317–318).

"*Gentlemen, being a superpower is no longer enough. We must become a super-duper power.*"

Kenneth Waltz, widely recognized as the founder of **neorealism,** disagrees. He believed even during the tense days of the Cold War (and, as we shall see, continues to believe now that the Cold War has subsided) that the bipolar system that emerged after the Second World War was quite stable, especially in comparison with the multipolar system of the past:

> In a world of three or more powers the possibility of making and breaking alliances exists. . . . Flexibility of alignment then makes for rigidity of national strategies: a state's strategy must satisfy its partner lest that partner defect from the alliance. . . . The alliance diplomacy of Europe in the years before the First World War is rich in examples of this. Because the defection or defeat of a major state would have shaken the balance of power, each state was constrained to adjust its strategy, and the deployment of its forces to the aims and fears of its partners (Waltz, 1969, p. 306).

In short, Waltz argues that the multipolar system of the early 1900s resulted in the First World War because the major powers were inflexible in defense of their allies. The bipolar system, in contrast, has been (or was) relatively stable since the Second World War because the superpowers could afford to lose allies (they both "lost" China, for example) without feeling that a war was necessary to prevent such a loss.

The alert reader might have noticed that Waltz makes his point about the superior stability of bipolarity with the benefit of a type of levels-of-analysis switch. It is true, as Waltz contends, that if we focus on the relationship among states, the international system before the First World War was multipolar. But if we focus instead on the relationship between *coalitions* of states, then it was bipolar, with two major alliances confronting each other. Thus, the First World War can be attributed to bipolarity or multipolarity, depending on which kind of social entity or actor one chooses to concentrate on, as well as which particular ax one wants to grind.

So whether bipolarity should be absolved of blame for the First World War or given credit for the lack of major wars during the Cold War are both debatable questions. It does seem beyond contention, though, that neorealism has fairly clear implications regarding the end of the Cold War. If bipolarity and the **nuclear confrontation** between the United States and the Soviet Union were stabilizing factors, then it is virtually impossible to avoid the conclusion that the disappearance of both should be destabilizing. Logically enough, then, some neorealists hark back nostalgically to what they see as the relative calm of the Cold War. One such analyst, for example, argues that the end of Cold War "is likely to increase the chances that war and major crises will occur in Europe. Many observers now suggest that a new age of peace is dawning; in fact, the opposite is true" (Mearsheimer, 1990, p. 52).[6]

This same analyst has admitted more recently that "it is true that the great powers have been rather tame in their behavior toward each other over the past five years." But in the neorealist view, "five years is much too short a period to determine whether international relations has been fundamentally transformed by the end of the Cold War" (Mearsheimer, 1994/95, p. 45).

If the bipolar structure of the international system continues to dissolve, Europe, and to some extent the entire world, will be an interesting "laboratory" within which different ideas about the impact of the structure of the international system on its stability can be tested.

---

[6] Rather curiously, Mearsheimer asserts (p. 18) that "lacking a comprehensive survey of history, we cannot progress beyond offering examples pro and con" regarding the controversy about the relative merits of bipolar and multipolar international systems. In fact, there are several "surveys of history" regarding this controversy, typically accompanied by systematic analyses of data generated by those surveys. See, for example, Haas (1970); Bueno de Mesquita (1978); Levy (1985); Thompson (1988); Brecher, James, and Wilkenfeld (1990); and Kegley and Raymond (1994). It does need to be acknowledged, though, that these surveys and analyses do not consistently support one side or other regarding this controversy.

Within Europe in particular, will the spread of democracy to Eastern Europe and disarmament pacts between the erstwhile superpowers make it a more peaceful continent? Or, as the neorealistic advocates of bipolarity would have it, will Europe be a much more contentious and violent place in the absence of the nuclear confrontation between the United States and the Soviet Union?

At the moment, the withdrawal of the Soviet troops from Eastern Europe and the subsequent disintegration of the Soviet Union have seemingly brought to the surface a whole range of issues that could increase tension in Europe. "A tour of the map of Eastern Europe reveals at least nine potential border disputes, and at least thirteen significant ethnic pockets that may either seek independence or be claimed by other countries" (Van Evera, 1990/91, p. 48).[7] In fact, the early returns so to speak, from Europe in the post–Cold War era might have been interpreted as a trend toward confirmation of the neorealists' gloomy predictions about the baneful effects of the termination of the nuclear confrontation between the United States and the Soviet Union in that continent. One can certainly see the foreshadowings of a grim future in Europe in the internal unrest involving right-wing fanaticism in Germany, the demise of Czechoslovakia, ominous statements by Hungarian government officials regarding Hungarian minorities in neighboring states, Romanian irredentism involving Moldova, reversals in the movement toward unity within the European Union, and murderous wars among the republics that used to make up Yugoslavia (to cite only some examples). On the other side of the coin, though, the violence in Yugoslavia has been brought under control, and an exceedingly long list of potential border conflicts and ethnic problems (see footnote) has yet to produce the international conflict, strife, or interstate wars that neorealists predicted.

---

[7] Van Evera identifies the following as frontiers that may be disputed: Romanian-Soviet, Romanian-Hungarian, Polish-Soviet, Polish-German, Polish-Czechoslovakian, Hungarian-Czechoslovakian, Yugoslav-Albanian, Greek-Albanian, Greek-Turkish, and Greek-Yugoslav-Bulgarian. Van Evera foresaw potential problems involving ethnic groups with respect to Romanians in Soviet Bessarabia; Hungarians in Romania, Czechoslovakia, and the Soviet Union; Poles in the Soviet Union and Czechoslovakia; Germans in Poland, Czechoslovakia, and Romania; Macedonians in Bulgaria and Greece; Turks in Bulgaria; Greeks in Albania; and Albanians in Yugoslavia. Since Van Evera compiled this list, Czechoslovakia and the Soviet Union have ceased to exist; ethnic tensions, in part, have led Slovakia to break away from what is now known as the Czech Republic. Ethnic differences also obviously played a role in the demise of the Soviet Union. It might be noted, though, that the dissolution of both the Soviet Union and Czechoslovakia was accomplished in a basically peaceful way (at least so far), and that the reunification of Germany has so far been accomplished in a similarly peaceful manner.

Integrating Balance-of-Power Theory and Theories About Polarity

The controversies about balance-of-power theory and the effects of polarity may be a source of confusion, but it is still possible to find some coherence in ideas and the historical record concerning the relationship between the structure of the international system and the behavior of states. There is also a similarity of views regarding the impact of system structure on the probability of international war. One possible way to clarify the relationship between **system structure** on the one hand and the behavior of states and the probability of war on the other is to integrate the balance-of-power theory and theories that focus on polarity. According to prevailing conventional wisdom, balance-of-power theory (and the balance-of-power system associated with it) died in 1918 and was buried by 1945. The bipolar system of the post–Second World War era, dominated by the United States and the Soviet Union, allegedly operated according to a different set of rules and norms. Some evidence supports this view. (Otherwise, it would not be so widely accepted.) The Secret Treaty of London among the Allied Powers in 1915 was "the last international treaty to appeal to the principle of the balance of power" (Wight, 1973, p. 103). And perhaps the most important change in the international system that resulted from the two world wars was the subsequent domination of the system by only two major powers. These two were not European, flexibility of alliance configurations decreased dramatically, and the leading makers of foreign policy no longer adhered so consciously and publicly to the tenets of the Classical Balance of Power.

It is no wonder, then, that so many people regard the post–Second World War system as drastically different. But those differences may have been exaggerated by those who treat balance-of-power theory as entirely irrelevant to the present, and the bipolar system of post–Second World War era as unrecognizably different from the international system of the past. Both the Classical Balance of Power adhered to in eighteenth- and nineteenth-century Europe and the bipolar system of the post–Second World War era might usefully be classified as balance-of-power systems according to the broad definition of such systems offered by Waltz. To repeat, Waltz argues that a set of interacting political entities (such as nation-states) qualifies as a balance-of-power system if those entities wish to survive, and if the system does not have a central authority or government that rules over it, that is, if it is *anarchic*. By that definition, both the European Classical Balance of Power and the more recent bipolar system are balance-of-power systems. In Waltz's neorealistic version of the balance-of-power theory, anarchy does not imply a lack of order, or violence. Anarchy refers only to an absence of government (Waltz, 1979, p. 121).

Most political systems, such as that in the United States, are hierarchically ordered. The different political units within that system— the federal government; the governments of Alabama, Ohio, and Wyoming; and the governments of Cook County, Cleveland, and Miami—are *different* in structure and function, interdependent, and ordered from top to bottom. In the *global* political system, the different political units—that is, the nation-states—are basically the *same* in structure and function, relatively independent, and (in theory at least) all sovereign and equal.

Although anarchic systems in which each political unit must ultimately rely on itself (rather than appeal to a government for protection) can be violent, it would be a mistake to assume that such systems are inherently more violent than the hierarchically ordered systems in which governments exist. Civil wars and domestic political strife may in fact kill more people than international wars (Denton, 1969; Rummel, 1994). It may be impossible to determine definitively whether international violence is more deadly than domestic political violence; the next international war, if it is nuclear, would make any such data immediately obsolete. But, as R. J. Rummel (1991, p. 352) has pointed out, "whereas 36 million people have been killed in battle in all foreign and domestic wars in our century, at least 119 million more people have been killed by government genocide, massacres, and other mass killing." Waltz (1979, p. 103) makes a similar point when he asserts that the most destructive wars of the nineteenth century were civil wars; as many as 20 million people may have died in China's Taiping Rebellion (1851–1864), and 600,000 died in the U.S. Civil War. "We easily lose sight of the fact that struggles to achieve and maintain power . . . within states may be bloodier than wars among them."

We tend to lose sight of that fact because the international system is anarchic, and the connotation of "anarchy" is virtually synonymous with "disorder" and "violence." We also lose sight of the relatively peaceful and orderly nature of international politics because there is no overarching entity whose purpose it is to maintain peace and order in the international system, while every domestic political system possesses such an authoritative entity—that is, a government—composed of people who intend to achieve order. What could be more natural, remarks Waltz (1979, p. 121), than a belief that "if a result is to be produced, someone must want it, and must work for it"?

But it is an essential contention of neorealists such as Waltz and others who advocate analysis of entire social systems that this natural belief may be wrong, that the results of *interactions* among units in a system may be quite different from, even directly contrary to, the *intentions* behind the actions of the individual units within them. In competitive systems, for example, players who adopt rational strategies thrive; all the rest emulate those strategies, or they are eliminated. In a free market, all the firms strive to maximize their profits. To increase their profits, they must increase their sales. To augment their sales, they lower their prices so that their products are more attractive to consumers. Pressed to the limit, firms in such a competitive free-market system, intending to maximize profits, might in principle lower their profit rates to zero. In theory, at least (and the theoretical point here is valid, even if there never has been a perfectly competitive free market in the world, and even if no firm in the history of the world has ever been perfectly rational), before this limit is reached and all firms are eliminated, some will survive and continue to produce at a price high enough to allow them to make a profit and low enough to entice a sufficient number of consumers to buy their product. "Patterns emerge and endure without anyone arranging the parts to form patterns or striving to maintain them. . . . Order may prevail without an orderer; adjustments may be made without an adjuster; tasks may be allocated without an allocator" (Waltz, 1979, p. 76).

The Classical Balance of Power that obtained in eighteenth- and nineteenth-century Europe may have worked relatively well because foreign policy makers in the European states were conscious of the rules of the system and consciously adhered to them. But in principle at least, a balance-of-power system may develop, and consistent patterns may appear, even if no one consciously conforms to the rules of such a system or intends to preserve it.

Inis Claude is one of the most cogent critics of balance-of-power theory, and he effectively exposes many of its ambiguities and problems in *Power and International Relations*. But he concludes that balance-of-power theory "should be taken seriously, despite the prejudicial confusion in which advocates have enveloped it." Claude clearly perceives a balance-of-power system as one in which the participants need not (even though they did in Europe during the era of the Classical Balance of Power) consciously adopt balance-of-power policies. A balance-of-power system, according to Claude, "does not require that any state deliberately set out to put power relations into equilibrium." On the contrary, all the states in such a system may intend to acquire more power than their competitors (much as firms in a free market intend to maximize their profits). But a balance-of-power system need not necessarily be instituted by deliberate choice, even though it can be, and was in the case of the Classical Balance of Power in Europe. "Rather, it is the system which exists unless and until superseded by a consciously created alternative" (Claude, 1962, pp. 43, 47, 93).

Niccolo Machiavelli is one of many political thinkers in history to devise a "balance-of-power" theory. SOURCE: Alinari/Art Resource/NY.

So it is true, as many observers have pointed out, that the Classical Balance of Power is dead. There is no "holder of the balance." Contemporary foreign policy elites no longer constitute a culturally homogeneous aristocratic community. Ideological fervor, at least during the Cold War, robbed states of flexibility in forming alliances. Democracy creates irrational pressures on foreign policies. The number of true "major powers" during the Cold War was reduced to two (and now, perhaps, has been reduced to one). But the generically defined balance-of-power theory may still be worthy of attention. Claude (1962, p. 93) insists that "twentieth century efforts to replace the system have [failed] . . . today, the [balance-of-power] system exists by default." Quincy Wright (1955,

p. 488) points out that balance-of-power theory was discussed by "Lord Shang in ancient China, Kautilya in ancient India, Polybius in ancient Rome, and Machiavelli in sixteenth-century Italy." He might also have mentioned Thucydides of ancient Greece and many others. Why has this theory evoked such sustained interest over so many centuries, and is it in fact worthy of that interest in the twentieth century?

The Balance-of-Power Theory: Making Sense of International Politics?

As Waltz (1979, p. 66) notes, "The texture of international politics remains highly constant, patterns recur, and events repeat themselves endlessly." There is a "striking sameness in the quality of international life through the millennia." The balance-of-power theory elicits such persistent interest and support because it *seems* to account for a number of these enduring patterns and repeated events in international politics. In this writer's view, the presence of these patterns in so many diverse historical settings is rather powerfully persuasive evidence against some critics' claims that the arguments made by realists and neorealists about the impact of system structure are "philosophically arbitrary" (Vasquez, 1993, p. 118). One such critic asserts, for example, that "self-help and power politics do not follow either logically or causally from anarchy. . . . Anarchy is what states make of it" (Wendt, 1992, pp. 394–395). This idea that "anarchy is what states make of it" is central to what has become known as **critical theory** in the field of international politics. "Critical theorists take ideas very seriously. In fact, they believe that discourse, how we think and talk about the world, largely shapes practice" (Mearsheimer, 1994/95, p. 37).[8] Ultimately, what critical theorists seem to believe is that "we can if we think we can"; that is, if only states would stop thinking of themselves as isolated in a self-help system in which bloodthirsty competition predominates, then the system would be altered in character in a fundamental and beneficial way. In other words, in the view of critical theorists, we, the people of the world, can live in peace, without war, if we think differently than statesmen and political leaders have thought in the past and come to believe that it is possible to change the international political system in profoundly important ways.

But as one neorealist points out in response to the argument that international politics might cease to operate in its traditional manner and become based instead on revolutionary new ideas and practices,

---

[8] This is not an impartial description of "critical theory"; Mearsheimer is a critic of critical theory, and a neorealist.

"Seven centuries of security competition and war represents an impressive span of time, especially when you consider the tremendous political and economic changes that have taken place across the world during that lengthy period" (Mearsheimer, 1994/95, p. 45). Seven hundred years is indeed a long time, but one of the points made by critical theorists is that the "modern" international political system was preceded by one that was very different, and one that cannot be accounted for (they argue) by "balance-of-power," realist, or neorealist theoretical approaches. Neorealism, according to one critical theorist, "provides no means by which to account for, or even to describe, the most important contextual change in international politics in this millennium: the shift from the medieval to the modern international system" (Ruggie, 1983, p. 273). According to this view, the medieval international system was not anarchic, and was based on a very different **discourse,** with an emphasis on communal and cooperative norms and principles.

One recent analysis of international politics in medieval times (A.D. 800–1300) does find in fact that "feudal discourse" did emphasize norms of a communal and cooperative character. However, this analysis also concludes that

> the actual practices of feudal actors stood in stark contrast to the norms they professed, notwithstanding some adherence on the level of formal appearances. In essence, like modern states, feudal actors had to arm themselves to remain independent, sought to conquer one another, concluded alliances, formed spheres of influence, and resolved their conflicts by force. The results of this investigation cast grave doubts on the twin arguments of critical theorists that discourse shapes practice and that the international system undergoes fundamental change. Conversely, the results support the neorealist view that international politics is permanently conflictual because of the structural constraint that arises from the enduring absence of central authority (Fischer, 1992, Abstract).

It is certainly true that anarchy does not determine the behavior of states and produce the patterns pointed out by realists and neorealists in the same way that adding two plus two always results in four. But the recurrence of those behaviors and patterns in anarchical systems scattered all over the globe through several centuries, perhaps even in medieval times, in a system that was not based on sovereign states as the contemporary global political system is, does suggest rather persuasively that the deductions and hypotheses of realists and neorealists are neither as philosophically arbitrary, nor as contingent upon particular cultural attitudes or specific social practices, as some of their critics suggest.

So, for example, it may be significant, and supportive of balance-of-power theory, that there has been no world empire since that of the

Romans; and even they did not rule the entire world. Also, when certain states have threatened to become "too strong"—that is, preponderant—the other major states have engaged in the kind of "balancing" behavior predicted by balance-of-power theory. To repeat, Napoleon's France was eventually constrained by a coalition of all the other major powers, and Germany provoked counterbalancing coalitions twice in this century. The Soviet Union, as seen in Chapter 6, became the most powerful state in the world, according to some aggregate indicators. A balance-of-power theorist would be inclined to argue that perhaps it was no accident that the Soviet Union had no major-power allies in the world. In effect, all the other major powers of the world ganged up on it.

If the balance-of-power system has operated in such a way as to prevent a world empire from being established, it may also deserve some credit for safeguarding the existence of states within the system. The partitioning of Poland right out of existence (albeit temporarily) near the end of the eighteenth century is a prominent exception to the rule, but states defeated in war, and thus vulnerable to obliteration, regularly tend to be treated as valuable allies in the competition that typically emerges within the victorious coalition. And so, as pointed out in Chapter 10 (though the event was interpreted within a different theoretical framework), France after the Napoleonic Wars and Germany (as well as Japan) after both world wars were not destroyed. Instead, they were revived (although divided, in Germany's case) and soon came to play important roles in preserving the newly constituted balance of power. Even small states, perhaps, benefit from this tendency for the balance-of-power system to preserve the constituent units. The number of states in the contemporary system has expanded dramatically since the Second World War, and very few, such as Estonia, Latvia, Lithuania (now revived), and Tibet, have been destroyed. South Vietnam could be added to that list, but its demise may be instructive. South Vietnam no longer exists, but it disappeared only after the United States, motivated in part by balance-of-power considerations, waged a prolonged campaign to preserve it.

Perhaps, then, balance-of-power theory deserves credit for explaining why states collectively prevent total domination by one of their peers and only rarely completely destroy one another. But a social theory from which it is possible to deduce the prediction that, say, the majority of the population of a given country is unlikely to commit suicide on a single day, while overwhelmingly supported by empirical evidence, would be neither interesting nor useful. Some predictions based on the balance-of-power theory tend toward the exceedingly obvious in a roughly similar manner.

Still, the prediction that no predominating state will emerge may not be as blatantly commonsensical as it seems on the surface. It presumes that weaker states will band together to avoid domination. But why would it not make equal sense for those states to "jump on the bandwagon," so to speak, and join in an alliance *with* the prospective leader of the world empire so that they will be safely on the winning side and share the fruits of victory?

And if some predictions based on balance-of-power theory are too broad and obvious to be very interesting, it is important to keep in mind that more specific predictions face the clear danger of being wrong. In its simplest form, balance-of-power theory stipulates that the major states will tend, through distribution and redistribution of territory and population, to be equal in power. Because this kind of equality among all the major states has rarely, if ever, occurred, a more subtle kind of balancing, based on alliances, has been posited instead. Emerich de Vattel, in his eighteenth-century work *Law of Nations,* argued for "a kind of equality of power, but an equality which was based on blocs of allied power and not on a hoped-for redistribution of land along the lines of equal shares" (quoted in Gulick, 1955, p. 61).

Unfortunately for this version of balance-of-power theory, it is rather clear that the major powers do not arrange themselves with dependable regularity into coalitions that are equal in power. Even before the breakup of the Warsaw Pact, the United States and its allies were far superior to the Soviet Union and its allies in terms of aggregate indicators. The advantage was three to one in gross national product (GNP) and nearly two to one in population. "If states were solely concerned with balancing power, America's predominant position after the Second World War should have led the nations of Western Europe to align with the Soviet Union against the United States. Instead, they chose to balance the Soviet Union by aligning with the United States . . . and this *imbalance* of power has remained remarkably constant for nearly four decades" (Walt, 1988, p. 280).

One way of dealing with this problem is to modify balance-of-power theory so that it predicts an *imbalance* of power between existing coalitions in the system. And that version of the balance-of-power theory has been quite common, perhaps even most usual. Claude (1962, p. 59) argues that "balance of power theorists tend to put more stock in defeating aggressors by *preponderant* power than in deterring them by equivalent power." Another theorist deals with essentially the same point by arguing that states in the international system seek **allies** to balance **threats,** not power, and that threats are evaluated in terms of the population, economic capacity, location, and *intentions* of potential enemies. Thus, for example, the nations of Western Europe allied against the Soviets after the Second World War rather than against the more powerful Americans "because the former's proximity, its impressive military power, and its apparently aggressive aims, made it appear more threatening" (Walt, 1988, p. 280).

This theory, stipulating that a balance will emerge against perceived threats rather than against excessive power, is plausibly appealing. But it also demonstrates one obvious weakness: it is a little too flexible for its own good. Almost anything that happens, short of the destruction of all but one state and the emergence of a world empire, can be accommodated by the theory. For example, a focus on *intentions* gives that particular version of balance-of-power theory a loophole that is useful for saving it in the face of almost any conceivable evidence. Because intentions are difficult to assess, much less measure, one can always find some that will make any given distribution of power fit in with the theory.

This is not to say that balance-of-power theory is bereft of potentially interesting insights into the dynamics of contemporary international politics. For example, it provides an interesting explanation for the principle of alliance formation based on the assertion **"My enemy's enemy is my friend,"** which was discussed in Chapter 10. The explanation provided by Waltz's neorealistic theory (1979, p. 166) is that "it is important to notice that states will ally with the devil to avoid the hell of military defeat." Geography often plays a fundamental role in such balance-of-power calculations. Neighbors are more dangerous, and states located on the other side of neighbors are natural allies. "As your neighbor is your natural enemy, so the Power in your enemy's rear is your natural ally. . . . These . . . rules of international alignment [are] the most rudimentary stage of the balance of power" (Wight, 1973, pp. 89–90).

Thus, France and Russia, on opposite sides of Germany, found themselves allied with each other in both world wars, despite ideological differences. India and the Soviet Union (while it existed), on opposite sides of China, enjoyed consistently friendly relations, while China was and still is routinely sympathetic to Pakistan, on the other side of India. Such **checkerboard patterns** are common in international politics now and throughout history.

Absent most of the geographic considerations, this flexibility of alignment resulting from balance-of-power pressures may account in part for the cozy relationship between the United States and a series of right-wing dictatorships in the decades after the Second World War. An alternative explanation emphasizes the advantages for U.S. businesses that operate in countries where reactionary governments suppress labor unions. But the United States was perfectly capable even during the Cold War of friendly, supportive relationships with Communist governments with which it shared common enemies, as evidenced by its good relations with the Soviet Union during the Second World War, with the People's Republic of China since 1970, and with Yugoslavia since the 1950s (against the Soviet Union). Balance-of-power theory, unlike the alternative explanation stressing economic considerations, can account for the willingness of the United States to align itself with both reactionary military dictatorships and Communist governments, thus displaying the kind of flexibility that virtually all states exhibit in balance-of-power systems.

Balance-of-power competition also may explain the drive for reform in the Soviet Union in the 1980s and all the developments that flowed from that effort. Waltz (1979, p. 127) argues that in balance-of-power systems "competition produces a tendency toward the sameness of the competitors." In 1950, the GNP of the United States was sixteen times larger than that of Japan, while the GNP of the Soviet Union was six times larger. Even as late as 1965, the ratio of GNPs was ten to one in favor of the United States and four to one in favor of the Soviets over Japan. By 1986 or 1987, by most accounts Japan had a larger GNP than the Soviet Union, even though its population was less than half that of the Soviet Union.

One can easily surmise that it must have been a shock for the Soviet leaders to go from brave (and at the time, credible) talk about "burying" the United States economically in the 1950s to the point in the late 1980s where they had not only failed to narrow the gap between themselves and the United States but had been surpassed by the Japanese in terms of GNP. Could not *glasnost* (political opening or reform) and especially *perestroika* (economic restructuring) seen in this light be correctly interpreted as emulating the United States as well as Japan in the manner "predicted" by balance-of-power theory?[9] Clearly, Waltz (1993, p. 50) believes this to be the case:

> The political and economic reconstruction attempted by the Soviet Union followed in part from external causes. Gorbachev's expressed wish to see the Soviet Union "enter the new millennium as a great and flourishing state" suggests this. . . . [He] realized that the Soviet Union could no longer support a first-rate military establishment on the basis of a third-rate economy. . . . Soviet leaders tried to reverse their country's precipitous fall in international standing but did not succeed.

Waltz also makes a point, based on his neorealist view of the world, that is relevant to the question posed earlier about states making a

---

[9] In earlier decades, such as the 1930s or even the 1960s, it could be argued that the United States and other capitalist powers emulated, up to a point, social welfare programs in the Soviet Union, perhaps in part to keep the Soviet Union from appearing too much, from their point of view, like the "wave of the future" and from reaping the international political benefits associated with that image.

choice between joining alliances to counterbalance a potential predominant power and "jumping on the bandwagon" and allying with the potential winner. In domestic political systems, Waltz argues, politicians will engage in balancing behavior in preelection competition until someone looks like a winner. At that point, **bandwagoning** begins. This process is unlikely to occur, though, in political competition within anarchic international systems. A winner is bound to emerge according to the rules of the game in domestic political competition, and the winner will not, subsequent to its victory, physically eliminate or dominate the losers. In the anarchic international system, it is not necessarily the case that a "winner" (that is, one ruling, predominant state) will prevail. And if states engaged in "bandwagoning" do allow such a winner to emerge, there is nothing to prevent that winner from eliminating or annexing all its erstwhile allies after its original competitors have been subdued.

This point about the greater likelihood of "balancing" rather than "bandwagoning" in the anarchic international system has clear implications for the near future of international politics. The United States has emerged as the only superpower. From the point of view of balance-of-power theory, one can expect the other states in the system to react negatively to this situation and ultimately to form a coalition to resist domination of the system by the United States. As Waltz explains, "Balance-of-power theory leads one to expect that states, if they are free to do so, will flock to the weaker side. The stronger, not the weaker side, threatens them" (Waltz, 1993, p. 74). "In international politics," Waltz (1991, p. 670) concludes, "unbalanced power constitutes a danger even when it is American power that is out of balance."

From the point of view of analysts (such as those mentioned in Chapter 6) who believe that democratic states have never fought and are unlikely to fight international wars against each other, this kind of thinking is "deeply anachronistic." Such "neoliberals" believe that "the real world order in the democratic part of the world will be fundamentally different from any past world order" (Singer and Wildavsky, 1993, pp. 4–5).[10]

Another critic of realist or balance-of-power thinking argues that historically "states tend to bandwagon for profit rather than security and that contemporary realist theory, because of its status quo bias, has underestimated the extent of bandwagoning behavior." In this view,

---

[10] Singer and Wildavsky (1993, p. 4) go on to explain that "never in history have there been large diverse areas, containing most of the world's power, in which no country faced substantial military danger to its independence or survival. Since [that] fundamental fact underlying international relations . . . [has] never existed before, the nature of international order in these zones will be new."

"states across the globe have recently abandoned communism in favor of the newest wave of the future, liberal democracy," and this kind of bandwagoning behavior is historically quite common (Schweller, 1994, pp. 96, 99).[11]

But Waltz counters by pointing out that the prime minister of France asserted in 1992 that "it's unhealthy to have a single superpower in the world." He concludes that the prime minister of France felt this way "not because the one superpower is undemocratic, but simply because it is super. The stronger get their way—not always, but more often than the weaker. Democratic countries, like others, are concerned with losing or gaining more in the competition among nations" (Waltz, 1993, pp. 77–78).[12]

The Utility of Neorealism and the Balance-of-Power Theory

Some of Waltz's arguments about the stability of bipolar systems are persuasive. Balance-of-power theory in general may help us to understand phenomena such as the absence in recent centuries of world empires, the balancing behavior that prevents them from appearing, the apparent reluctance by victors in wars to eliminate the vanquished, alliances between states of sharply contrasting ideological persuasions, and the tendency for competition among the major powers to evoke emulation of the apparently more successful among them. And its warning about the world's potential reaction against overwhelming and overbearing American power in the wake of the Soviet Union's demise certainly has historical examples to support it.

These quite broad general patterns and predictions are obviously the kind of patterns and predictions in which Waltz is most interested. In his well-known work *Man, the State, and War,* he argues that "with many sovereign states, with no system of law enforceable among them, with each state judging its grievances and ambitions according to the dictates of its own reason or desire—conflict, sometimes leading to war, is bound to occur" (Waltz, 1959, p. 159). As an "explanation" of war, this is an answer to the question, "Why is this the kind of world in which wars continually occur?" It is not an answer to more specific questions about *variation* in war across time and space; questions about why,

---

[11] Schweller (1994, p. 107) also argues that "states pile on to the winning coalition at the end of large-scale wars to claim shares of the spoils or to escape the wrath of the victors." If we again consider the Cold War to be the equivalent of a "large-scale war," this statement might be applicable to the current era.

[12] Christopher Layne (1993) makes a more detailed neorealist argument on this same point.

when, and where—*specifically* in this world where wars periodically take place—they will actually occur. Those specific questions are of greater interest to researchers such as Singer, Bremer, and Stuckey (1972), who, as noted earlier in this chapter, have analyzed the relationship between the distribution of power and the amount of war in the international system.[13]

One reviewer of the difference between the approaches of analysts such as Waltz on the one hand and Singer on the other has pointed out that "one can see that the fundamental difference between Singer and Waltz . . . is that Singer does not profess to know what regularities of behavior pervade world politics. . . . Waltz, on the other hand, knows what the regularities are (indeed, he may find them obvious)" (Vasquez, 1987, p. 113). Singer knows as well as Waltz that wars continually recur, that world empires are rare, and that alliances between "strange bedfellows" are quite common. Singer, though, is looking for different kinds of regularities. Waltz views "regularities" as behaviors that recur with consistency, such as wars, emulation of "successful" states, and counterbalancing alliances. Singer, in contrast, sees as regularities systematic contemporaneity or covariation between different variables, such as the distribution of power and the incidence of international war. That is, he wants to know not just why, generally speaking, this is the kind of world in which wars occur but also which factors make war more likely to occur at some times than at others, or more likely to involve certain types of states but not others.

The balance-of-power theory as developed by Waltz and others suggests some answers to such specific questions, which, as noted earlier in this chapter, are offered in the work of Singer, Bremer, and Stuckey (1972). Related work (arguably more closely and logically structured along guidelines provided by balance-of-power theory) reveals that extremely unequal distributions of power among major powers and among alliances of major powers from 1816 to 1965 tend to be counterbalanced in a relatively short time (Stoll, 1984a), and that the initially weaker side in militarized interstate disputes between 1816 and 1976 has been more likely than the stronger side to attract support from third parties (Cusack and Stoll, 1991).

But the balance-of-power theory in which Waltz and other advocates have so much confidence is not really designed to provide answers to

---

[13] Waltz, in his *Theory of International Politics*, comments on Singer, Bremer, and Stuckey's work in some detail. One indication of these different approaches to the study of world politics is the following comment by Waltz (1979, p. 15) on the work by Singer, Bremer, and Stuckey discussed earlier in this chapter: "As their key independent variable they choose concentration of power or of capabilities. They mention no theory that in fact employs such a variable, and I know of none that does."

specific questions about covariation between variables. As Waltz acknowledges, "Because only a loosely defined and inconstant condition of balance is predicted, it is difficult to say that any given distribution of power falsifies the theory. . . . The theory does not give precise answers." Instead, balance-of-power theory serves as a framework for an understanding of regularly recurring behavior patterns, such as international wars, emulation of successful states, and coalitions against potentially predominating states.

Waltz's theory, and neorealism in general, do provide reasonably specific predictions about the **post–Cold War era.** The **demise of bipolarity,** according to Waltz, will have a negative effect on the stability of the international system. But "with the end of the cold war, the concept of polarity seemingly has become even more confused" (Kapstein, 1995, p. 772).[14] Charles Kegley and Gregory Raymond (1994) analyze the history of "multipolar" systems going back to 1495. Their general position seems to be that while the bipolar system after the Second World War may not have broken down into disastrous warfare between the superpowers, "the claims that (1) alliances deterred warfare, (2) preparations for war preserved the peace, or that (3) nuclear weapons made war obsolete rest on rather dubious premises" (Kegley and Raymond, 1994, p. 41). They argue further that while some past multipolar systems have been war prone, others have been peaceful and stable, and it will be possible to cope with the coming multipolar international system in a way that can make it peaceful, stable, and orderly.

Perhaps they underestimate the extent to which the international system will be quite **unipolar** for some time to come. They support their argument that "what we see unfolding before our eyes is . . . a new multipolar phase of history" (Kegley and Raymond, 1994, p. 175) by focusing on the **U.S. share of the gross world product** over the decades since 1948 (see Figure 14.1). That share has been falling steadily. But the last year shown in that chart is 1992, a time of relative stagnation for the American economy. In *The Rise and Fall of the Great Powers,* Paul Kennedy (1987, p. 436) tries to make the same point emphasized by Kegley and Raymond by providing data showing that the U.S. share of the gross world product fell from 25.9 percent in 1960 to 23 percent in 1970 to 21.5 percent in 1980. But more recent data show that the U.S. share of the world's economic product was a little over 26 percent in 1994 (World Bank, 1996, p. 211), a percentage remarkably similar to its share in 1960, considering all the economic growth that has occurred

---

[14] Kapstein (1995, p. 772) points out that "a significant debate has erupted about the definition of polarity, as exemplified by a set of recent articles that take contending views." (He cites Lynn-Jones and Miller, 1995.) This debate has been going on since the 1960s at least.

Figure 14.1   The Rise and Fall of the Great Powers' Financial Fortunes

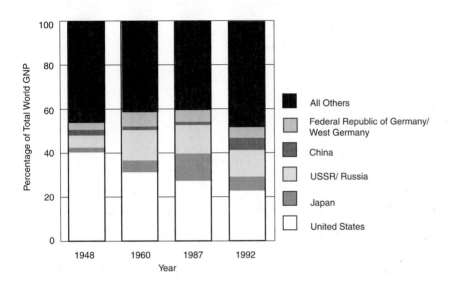

SOURCE: From Charles W. Kigley, Jr. and Gregory A. Raymond, *A Multipolar Peace? Great-Power Politics in the Twenty-first Century* (New York: St. Martin's Press, 1994), p. 174.

since that time in Western Europe, Japan, the four Asian Tigers, and most recently the People's Republic of China. In addition, on the more specifically military front, a recent article on "The Future of Warfare" (*Economist,* March 8, 1997, p. 15) argues that "this latest revolution is based on the application of information technology to weapons. It involves gathering huge amounts of data; processing them so that relevant information is displayed on a screen; and then destroying targets." It concludes that "all this is bad news for America's potential foes[;] . . . the Americans' mastery of the new warfare will make it increasingly foolish to take them on in a high-intensity shooting war."

Now defining and measuring "polarity" in a way that is widely agreed upon and accepted is a difficult task. Nevertheless, William Thompson's (1988, p. 219) review of the history of international politics from 1494 to 1983 leads him to conclude that "destabilizing warfare is least common in unipolar conditions" (see Table 14.3). But Thompson also provides a convenient example of the dangers confronting any analyst who cares to speculate about the future of polarity (or the distribution of power) in the international system, as well as its impact on the stability of that system. In 1988 (not all that long ago, and just about a year before the fall of the Berlin Wall), he observed that "the

Table 14.3 Polarity and Global Power Warfare, 1494–1983

Polarity Type	Number of Years	Per-centage	Weighted Warfare	Per-centage	Weighted Warfare Mean
Unipolar	144	29.4	26.442	20.6	.184
Near unipolar	61	12.4	10.944	8.5	.179
Bipolar	171	34.9	34.461	26.8	.202
Multipolar	114	23.3	56.809	44.2	.498
·	490	100.0	128.656	100.1	

SOURCE: From *On Global War: Historical-Structural Approaches to World Politics* by William R. Thompson (Columbia, S.C.: University of South Carolina Press, 1988), p. 219. Reprinted by permission of the publisher.

current bipolarity . . . seems permanent and, in some respects, even desirable (at least in comparison to multipolarity or Soviet unipolarity)" (Thompson, 1988, p. 222).

SUMMARY

Studies of international politics can focus on a variety of social entities, such as individual leaders, states, groups of states, or the entire international system. Confusion among these different kinds of studies leads to the level-of-analysis problem. Analyses on different levels do not simply use different words to describe the same things; rather, they are distinct in their purposes, and patterns found on one level of analysis do not provide a sound basis for inferring that analogous patterns exist on other levels. For example, it would be a mistake to infer from the fact that pairs of democratic states are less war prone than pairs of undemocratic states that there will necessarily be a negative relationship between the predominance of democracy in the international system and the amount of war or international conflict in that system. Similarly, large numbers of alliances in the international system may be consistently related to large amounts of war in the system. But this relationship does not necessarily mean that states in alliances are more likely to find themselves involved in wars. It could be that "smart" states join together in alliances while "dumb" states fight all the wars.

One of the most influential system-level theories of international politics is the balance-of-power theory. The concept of a balance of power has a confusing variety of meanings, but the concept of a Classical Balance of Power was well developed in Europe from about 1700 to the First World War. Its fundamental premise was that no single state should be allowed to dominate the system. Several techniques were used to deal with any state that became too powerful. The most important involved the formation of a counterbalancing alliance among the rest of the states in the system. The idea of the classical balance of power worked well in some respects within Europe. For example, during the nineteenth century, system-shattering wars similar to the world wars of the twentieth century were avoided.

But some scholars, such as A. F. K. Organski (1968), say that relative peace in the nineteenth century was preserved not by the balance of power but by the overwhelming *imbalance* in favor of some states, especially Great Britain. Others, such as Hans Morgenthau, disagree. To some extent, this disagreement is caused by level-of-analysis confusion. Organski focuses on the distribution of power among individual states in the nineteenth century, while Morgenthau (1967) and other balance-of-power theorists emphasize the distribution of power among groups or coalitions of states.

Singer, Bremer, and Stuckey (1972) investigated the relationship between the distribution of power and the amount of war in the international system by analyzing data on both factors (among the major powers) from 1820 to 1965. They found that there was no consistent relationship between the two. Perhaps the logic of the ideas they tested applies most convincingly to conflict between two states, or two coalitions of states, rather than conflict within the entire system. Also, some versions of balance-of-power theory do *not* stipulate that the distribution of power will affect the amount of war in the system; rather, war is presumed to be an important balancing mechanism that will occur however power is distributed. Finally, some analysts believe that the classical balance of power operated in eighteenth- and nineteenth-century Europe but has not worked since the First World War, when European states (which had developed the theory) lost control of the international system.

Since the Second World War, scholars have developed new ideas about the relationship between system structure and international conflict focusing on the *polarity* of the system. If two states dominate, as the United States and the Soviet Union did after the Second World War, the system is *bipolar*. Before the Second World War, when there were typically four or five major powers of roughly equal strength, the system was *multipolar*. Many scholars believe that multipolar systems are more stable, but Waltz argues that bipolar systems are preferable.

The lack of war between major powers since 1945 and additional research focusing on relationships among major powers over the past several centuries support his argument.

It may be a mistake, though, to view the bipolar system in the decades immediately after the Second World War as entirely different from the system of the Classical Balance of Power. That eighteenth- and nineteenth-century European system is dead, but generic balance-of-power systems emerge among sets of political units as long as the system is anarchic and the units strive to survive, even if policymaking elites within the units are not aware of balance-of-power theory. Generally speaking, the results of interactions among units in a system may be different from, even contrary to, the intentions of the individual units.

The theory that focuses on generic balance-of-power systems may help us to understand several continuing features of international politics, such as the constant failure of states to establish world empires, the low death rate of states, alliances by "strange bedfellows" in the international system, and a tendency for major powers to resemble each other because they each emulate the more powerful and successful among them. Also, the apparent demise of bipolarity in the current era may give us some insight into the increased instability in the international system, especially in Europe. Balance-of-power theory does not provide specific answers to questions about variation and covariation between variables, and it is so flexible that a suspiciously broad range of behaviors *seem* to correspond with it. Yet it may help us understand some of the regularly recurring behaviors discussed in this chapter. The form of balance-of-power theory advocated by neorealism does suggest that the end of bipolarity will have a destabilizing effect on the international system. Critics of neorealism suggest that multipolar systems can be peaceful. Some data suggest, though, that the current system may be unipolar for some time to come, and that unipolar systems have been relatively stable compared with both bipolar or multipolar systems. Polarity is a difficult concept to measure or define, though, and predictions about it and its relationship to stability in the international system are risky.

KEY TERMS

international system	anarchic
balance-of-power theory	level-of-analysis problem
polarity	explanatory factors
individualists	type of social entity
social structures	Classical Balance of Power
structuralists	power

alliances
holder of the balance
bipolarity
multipolarity
neorealism
nuclear confrontation
system structure
critical theory
discourse

allies
threats
"My enemy's enemy is my friend."
checkerboard patterns
bandwagoning
post–Cold War era
demise of bipolarity
unipolar
U.S. share of gross world product

SOURCES

Brecher, Michael, Patrick James, and Jonathan Wilkenfeld. "Polarity and Stability: New Concepts, Indicators, and Evidence." *International Interactions*, 16, No. 1 (1990), 49–80.

Bremer, Stuart. "Dangerous Dyads: Conditions Affecting the Likelihood of Interstate War, 1816–1965." *Journal of Conflict Resolution*, 36 (June 1992), 309–341.

Brown, Seyom. *New Faces, Old Forces, and the Future of World Politics.* Glenview, Ill.: Scott, Foresman, 1980.

Bueno de Mesquita, Bruce. "Systemic Polarization and the Occurrence and Duration of War." *Journal of Conflict Resolution*, 22 (June 1978), 241–267.

Bueno de Mesquita, Bruce, and David Lalman. "Empirical Support for Systemic and Dyadic Explanations of International Conflict." *World Politics*, 41 (October 1988), 1–20.

Claude, Inis L. *Power and International Relations.* New York: Random House, 1962.

Cusack, Thomas R., and Richard J. Stoll. "Balancing Behavior in the Interstate System, 1816–1976." *International Interactions*, 16, No. 4 (1991), 255–270.

Denton, F. H. *Factors in International System Violence, 1750 to 1960.* Santa Monica, Calif.: Rand Corporation, 1969.

Deutsch, Karl W., and J. David Singer. "Multipolar Power Systems and International Stability." In James N. Rosenau, ed., *International Politics and Foreign Policy.* 2nd ed. New York: Free Press, 1969.

Fischer, Markus. "Feudal Europe, 800–1300: Communal Discourse and Conflictual Practices." *International Organization*, 46 (Spring 1992), 427–466.

"The Future of Warfare." *Economist*, March 8, 1997, pp. 15–16.

Gledtisch, Nils Petter. "Peace and Democracy: Three Levels of Analysis." *Journal of Conflict Resolution*, 41 (April 1997) 283–310.

Gulick, Edward V. *Europe's Classical Balance of Power.* Ithaca, N.Y.: Cornell University Press, 1955.

Haas, Ernst B. "Balance of Power: Prescription, Concept, and Propaganda." *World Politics*, 5 (July 1953), 442–477.

Haas, Ernst B., and Allen S. Whiting. *Dynamics of International Relations.* New York: McGraw-Hill, 1956.

Haas, Michael. "International Systems: Stability and Polarity." *American Political Science Review*, 64 (March 1970), 98–123.

Kapstein, Ethan B. "Is Realism Dead? The Domestic Sources of International Politics." *International Organization*, 49 (Autumn 1995), 751–774.

Kegley, Charles W., Jr., and Gregory Raymond. *A Multipolar Peace?* New York: St. Martin's Press, 1994.

Layne, Christopher. "The Unipolar Illusion: Why New Great Powers Will Rise." *International Security*, 17 (Spring 1993), 5–51.

Levy, Jack S. "The Polarity of the System and International Stability: An Empirical Analysis." In Alan Ned Sabrosky, ed., *Polarity and War: The Changing Structure of International Conflict*. Boulder, Colo.: Westview Press, 1985.

Little, Richard. "Structuralism and Neo-Realism." In Margot Light and A. J. R. Groom, eds., *International Relations: A Handbook of Current Theory*. London: Pinter, 1985.

Lynn-Jones, Sean, and Steven Miller, eds. *The Cold War and After: Prospects for Peace*. Cambridge, Mass.: MIT Press, 1995.

Maoz, Zeev, and Nasrin Abdolali. "Regime Types and International Conflict, 1816–1976." *Journal of Conflict Resolution*, 33 (March 1989), 3–35.

Mearsheimer, John J. "Back to the Future: Instability in Europe After the Cold War." *International Security*, 15 (Summer 1990), 5–56.

Mearsheimer, John J. "The False Promise of International Institutions." *International Security*, 19 (Winter 1994/95), 5–49.

Morgenthau, Hans. *Politics Among Nations*. 4th ed. New York: Knopf, 1967.

Organski, A. F. K. *World Politics*. 2nd ed. New York: Knopf, 1968.

Ray, James Lee, and J. David Singer. "Measuring the Concentration of Power in the International System." *Sociological Methods and Research*, 1 (May 1973), 403–436.

Rosecrance, Richard, and Chih-Cheng Lo. "Balancing, Stability, and War: The Mysterious Case of the Napoleonic International System." *International Studies Quarterly*, 40 (December 1996), 479–500.

Ruggie, John Gerard. "Continuity and Transformation in the World Polity: Toward a Neorealist Synthesis." *World Politics*, 35 (January 1983), 261–285.

Rummel, R. J. *Death by Government: Genocide and Mass Murder Since 1900*. New Brunswick, N.J.: Transaction Publishers(forthcoming, 1994).

Rummel, R. J. "Political Systems, Violence, and War." In W. Scott Thompson and Kenneth M. Jensen, eds., *Approaches to Peace: An Intellectual Map*. Washington, D.C.: United States Institute of Peace, 1991.

Russett, Bruce, and Harvey Starr. *World Politics: The Menu for Choice*. 5th ed. New York: Freeman, 1996.

Schweller, Randall L. "Bandwagoning for Profit: Bringing the Revisionist State Back In." *International Security*, 19 (Summer 1994), 72–107.

Senese, Paul D. "Costs and Demands: International Sources of Dispute Challenges and Reciprocation." *Journal of Conflict Resolution*, 41 (June 1997), 407–427.

Singer, J. David. "The Level-of-Analysis Problem in International Relations." In Klaus Knorr and Sidney Verba, eds., *The International System*. Princeton, N.J.: Princeton University Press, 1961.

Singer, J. David, Stuart Bremer, and John Stuckey. "Capability Distribution, Uncertainty, and Major Power War, 1820–1965." In Bruce M. Russett, ed., *Peace, War, and Numbers.* Beverly Hills, Calif.: Sage Publications, 1972.

Singer, Max and Aaron Wildavsky. *The Real World Order.* Chatham, N.J.: Chatham House Publishers, 1993.

Small, Melvin, and J. David Singer. *Resort to Arms: International and Civil Wars, 1816–1980.* Beverly Hills, Calif.: Sage Publications, 1982.

Stoll, Richard J. "Bloc Concentration and the Balance of Power." *Journal of Conflict Resolution,* 28 (March 1984a), 25–50.

Stoll, Richard J. "Bloc Concentration and Dispute Escalation Among the Major Powers, 1830–1965." *Social Science Quarterly,* 65 (March 1984b), 48–59.

Thompson, William R. *On Global War: Historical-Structural Approaches to World Politics.* Columbia, S.C.: University of South Carolina Press, 1988.

Van Evera, Stephen. "Primed for Peace: Europe After the Cold War." *International Security,* 15 (Winter 1990/91), 7–57.

Vasquez, John A. "The Steps to War: Toward a Scientific Explanation of Correlates of War Findings." *World Politics,* 40 (October 1987), 108–145.

Vasquez, John A. *The War Puzzle.* Cambridge, U.K.: Cambridge University Press, 1993.

Walt, Stephen A. "Testing Theories of Alliance Formation: The Case of Southeast Asia." *International Organization,* 42 (Spring 1988), 275–316.

Waltz, Kenneth. "America as a Model for the World? A Foreign Policy Perspective." *PS: Political Science and Politics,* 24 (March 1991), 667–670.

Waltz, Kenneth. *Man, the State, and War.* New York: Columbia University Press, 1959.

Waltz, Kenneth. "International Structure, National Force, and the Balance of World Power." In James N. Rosenau, ed., *International Politics and Foreign Policy.* 2nd ed. New York: Free Press, 1969.

Waltz, Kenneth. *Theory of International Politics.* New York: Random House, 1979.

Waltz, Kenneth N. "The Emerging Structure of International Politics." *International Security,* 18 (Fall 1993), 44–79.

Wendt, Alexander. "Anarchy Is What States Make of It." *International Organization,* 46 (Spring 1992), 391–426.

Wight, Martin. "The Balance of Power and International Order." In Alan James, ed., *The Bases of International Order.* London: Oxford University Press, 1973.

World Bank. *World Development Report 1996.* New York: Oxford University Press, 1996.

Wright, Quincy. *A Study of International Relations.* New York: Appleton, 1955.

CHAPTER 15

The Future of
the Global Community

It is possible to analyze global politics from a viewpoint that is different from the international systemic level in the sense that it emphasizes the extent to which a **global community,** as opposed to a set of interrelated but still separate nation-states, exists. Such a viewpoint has become increasingly relevant partly because better methods of communication and transportation have led some individuals from different states to interact so intensively as to blur national boundaries. This kind of interaction is perhaps of special importance in the realm of economics, in which, as discussed in Chapter 13, multinational corporations have tried to treat the globe as a single market rather than a set of distinct national markets. There is a lively controversy about the good and bad effects of these corporations, but most would agree that they have served to unify the international economic system, transforming it into a nascent global market. Finally, the global community has emerged as a real entity, at least in the minds of some scholars, because a set of interrelated problems, continually threatening to reach crisis proportions, has served to highlight the extent to which people everywhere, of whatever nationality, are passengers on the spaceship *Earth.* **Poverty** and **starvation,** the **population explosion, deterioration of the ozone layer** in the upper atmosphere, and **global warming** resulting from the **greenhouse effect** all seem to be problems that cannot be solved on a state-by-state basis, and they all make the common fate of people in the global community dramatically visible.

This chapter focuses on the future of the global community. It describes some of the most important problems faced by the community and analyzes the current controversy over how best to deal with these problems. The controversy rages in large part because of widely disparate estimates of how serious the problems will become in the next few decades. The chapter considers starkly different predictions and examines their bases in such a way as to allow at least tentative assertions about which predictions are most likely to prove accurate and in what direction the most promising solutions lie.

FOUR CRISES

Poverty and Starvation

Certainly one of the most dismal facts about the world today is that so many people are poor and starving. The exact number is difficult to calculate because "no one officially dies of starvation—people die of dysentery, pneumonia, or other conditions associated with a weakened condition resulting from inadequate food—so there are no national or UN statistics on it" (Hughes, 1985, p. 124). This lack of data makes the number of seriously hungry people in the world difficult to estimate, and so the guesses range from a few tens of millions to as many as a billion. That the problem is enormous is not really in dispute.

One recent estimate suggests that there are 800 million people in the world who are chronically malnourished (*Economist*, November 16, 1996, p. 18). Worse, "children are the real victims of world hunger: at least 70% of the malnourished people of the world are children. By best estimate forty thousand children a day die of starvation" (Lafollete and May, 1996).

Equally distressing are some signs that the problem is likely to get worse. From 1950 to 1975, world food production outpaced world population growth. But growth in food production slowed in the decade after 1975, raising doubts about how long adequate food supplies can be maintained (Brown, 1985). Between 1950 and 1984, the **world's production of grain** grew at the rate of 3 percent a year, increasing the availability of grain on the global level by 40 percent. But during the 1990s the growth in world grain production has slowed down substantially. At the same time, demand has increased steadily because of the addition of 90 million people a year, and because of dramatically increasing affluence in much of Asia, especially China, which has a population of over one billion. "Part of this widening gap has been filled in recent years by drawing down carryover stocks—the amount left in the world's grain bins at the start of each new harvest. By 1996, these had fallen to 50 days of consumption, the lowest level on record" (Brown, 1997, p. 24).[1]

---

[1] Brown (1997, p. 35) concludes that "the growth in food production is slowing while the growth in demand, driven by both population growth and rising affluence, continues strong. The politics of surpluses that dominated the world food economy during the half-century following World War II is being replaced by the politics of scarcity."

Poverty leads to starvation in many poor countries. Here a mother in Somalia gives her starving daughter a drink of water. SOURCE: Reuters/Bettmann Newsphotos.

One of the problems producing this transition to food scarcity is the reduced **availability of cropland.** The amount of land under cultivation peaked in 1981 (at 732 million hectares). Between 1981 and 1995, cropland devoted to the production of grain fell by 7.6 percent. "Given projected increases in population in coming decades, the amount of cropland per person will certainly continue to fall. . . . The current area per person of 0.12 hectares will drop to 0.09 hectares by 2020 as global population climbs" (Gardner, 1997, pp. 43, 54).

The Population Explosion

The potential for food shortages and starvation (as well as many other global problems) on a massive scale seems to stem in important part from the rapid growth of the earth's population. It took from the beginning of the human species until 1804 for the world's population to reach one billion. The second billion was added in a little over 120 years (in 1927), and the third billion took only a little over thirty years (1960). By 1974, the world's population reached four billion, and the fifth billion was added in only thirteen more years (by 1987). If the current growth rate of 1.48 percent a year continues, the **globe's total population** will be six billion by the year 1999 (Crossette, 1996, Section 1, p. 3; see Figure 15.1). What makes the situation even more problematic is that population tends to grow fastest in those areas of the world where poverty is most stark. "World population increased by 80 million people in 1996. . . . Most of this growth—about 98 percent—occurred in developing countries" (Mitchell, 1997, p. 80).

Population experts agree that the population explosion has been brought about by two major factors. One is the success of medical science. In 1650, the average life expectancy was only about thirty years. In 1968 it was about fifty-three years, but by 1993 it had increased to sixty-three (Meadows, Meadows, Randers, and Behrens, 1972, p. 8; United Nations Development Programme, 1996, p. 137). "Population growth is assumed to be caused by more people being born: Actually,

Figure 15.1 World Population, 1950–1996

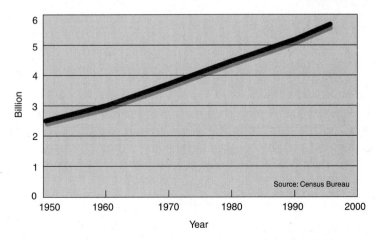

Year

the operative factor is fewer people dying—specifically, later death" (Easterbrook, 1995b, p. 485).

Nevertheless, great numbers of children still die at an early age, and this too adds pressure to the upward trend in population. Large families serve as a form of social security in many developing countries. Parents want to have several children around to support them in their old age. And since the **infant mortality rate** is so high in so many developing countries, they are likely to want to play it safe, adding more children to the family in anticipation of the early loss of several of them. Also, in some rural settings especially, children can be economic assets as agricultural laborers even before the parents reach old age, providing an added incentive for large families (Commoner, 1977).

Shrinking Natural Resources

In the 1970s, the view that the world would soon run out of several important **natural resources** gained widespread acceptance (Kahn, Brown, and Martel, 1976, p. 84). The **energy crises** of that decade were the major force making that idea so popular. By the middle of the 1980s, the world had recovered from the shock of the second major increase in the price of oil in 1979, and the glut of oil on the world market had driven prices down and threatened the unity of the Organization of Petroleum Exporting Countries (OPEC). Thus, the notion that supplies of natural resources were running dangerously low for the entire world fell from favor.

Still, many analysts feel that the oil glut has brought about a false sense of security. Indications are that the demand for energy will increase dramatically in the coming decades, spurred in part by the steady and lowering prices for oil that resulted from the glut of the mid-1980s. "Energy is the 'master resource' [because] the extraction of all other resources depends on availability and prices of energy" (Chandler, 1985, pp. 147–148). In other words, if increasing demand does deplete supplies of energy resources, all the other natural resources will become more difficult to obtain, and widespread shortages of many of them might develop. And in the 1990s, **fresh water** seems to be on the verge of becoming a scarce commodity. According to an environmental vice president of the World Bank, "The wars of the next century will be over water" instead of oil or politics (Robinson and Sweet 1997, p. 58).

Pollution

Starvation is not new. In the nineteenth century, economist Thomas Malthus worried about a population explosion. And fears that one or more natural resources will be entirely depleted have occurred before.

The only crisis of the present era that seems almost unprecedented involves the extent to which human beings are polluting the environment. Perhaps the most notorious pollution results from the world's reliance on **fossil fuels** (coal, oil, and natural gas) to generate most of its industrial energy. Carbon dioxide is released into the atmosphere when these fuels are burned.

In 1996, 6.25 billion tons of carbon were added to the atmosphere through fossil fuel combustion. If current trends continue, that number could be 9 billion by the year 2010, which would be almost 50 percent higher than 1990 levels. As Figure 15.2 illustrates, "**Global carbon emissions** have now nearly quadrupled since 1950" (Dunn, 1997a, p. 58). These emissions have a rather dramatic effect on the **concentration of carbon dioxide** in the atmosphere. "At the end of 1994, the atmosphere contained 4 billion tons more carbon than 12 months earlier. This lifted the overall concentration of carbon dioxide from 357.0 parts per million to 358.9, the biggest jump in six years" (Roodman, 1995, p. 66). Since the middle of the nineteenth century, the levels of carbon dioxide in the world's atmosphere have increased by 29 percent, to "their highest point in the last 150,000 years" (Dunn, 1997a, p. 58).[2] This rise in carbon emissions and in the concentration of carbon dioxide in the

---

[2] Roodman (1995, p. 66) also points out that "since 1860, people have added about 350 billion tons of carbon to the air; roughly 150 billion tons of it remain there."

Figure 15.2 World Carbon Emissions from Fossil Fuel Burning, 1950–1996

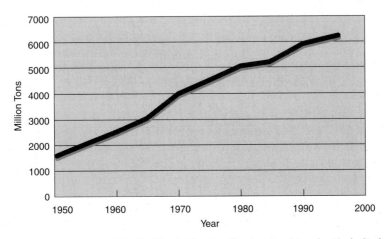

SOURCE: From *Vital Signs 1997: The Trends That Are Shaping Our Future* by Linda Starke, ed. Copyright © 1997 by W. W. Norton & Company, Inc. Reprinted by permission of the publisher.

atmosphere is worrisome, because it could dramatically change climate throughout the world. "Top scientists now believe that the earth's average temperature might go up by 1.5–2.0 degrees centigrade in the next half century, and conclude that would be enough to cause major disruptions: violent and unpredictable weather, more or less drastic shifts in the areas most suitable for agriculture, coastal erosion, deleterious health effects, and so on" (Robinson and Sweet, 1997, p. 60). One analyst of the impact of this global warming warns:

> Warm weather speeds up insect metabolism: in warm years, insects often grow quicker, breed more frequently, and migrate sooner. . . . Many of the world's most dangerous insects—for agriculture, forestry, and public health—are tropical or subtropical in origin; almost by definition they are poised to follow the retreat of temperature barriers (Bright, 1997, pp. 80, 87).

AN INTEGRATED VIEW OF WORLD CRISES

These crises are familiar to most people. Poverty and starvation, the population explosion, resource depletion, and pollution have been making news for many years. Starting in 1972, the media also paid a lot of attention to an analysis of all these problems based on a **computer simulation** of the world. The results of this simulation were published in a report titled ***The Limits to Growth*** (Meadows, Meadows, Randers, and Behrens, 1972), which has provoked a torrent of both praise and criticism that continues to this day; it sold nine million copies in twenty-nine languages.

Computer simulations of social systems allow social scientists a form of experimentation that would not otherwise be possible.[3] Once a simulation is operational, it can be used to obtain answers to a multitude of questions such as "What would happen if the world were this way?" The answers are quite often surprising, because social systems can behave in a counterintuitive manner. Actions designed to solve problems may have no effect or may make the problems worse (Forrester, 1975, pp. 216–217).

The world system, according to the designers of *The Limits to Growth* simulation, operates in just such a counterintuitive fashion. Measures that seem designed to alleviate problems actually make them worse or have an impact on other parts of the system that creates even worse problems. Given the rampant poverty and starvation in the global

---

[3] For a global simulation that, unlike *The Limits to Growth* and most of its successor models, explicitly takes into account political variables, see Stuart Bremer (1987).

system, for example, a seemingly logical solution would involve substantially increased food production and economic development. But *The Limits to Growth* simulation shows that the ultimate result of accelerated food production and economic development on a global basis would be disastrous. Increased economic growth would of course help alleviate poverty and starvation in the short run, but in the long run (over the next hundred years or so), it would exacerbate all the other problems in the system. Since more food would be available, the population would grow faster. In time, increases in per capita gross national product (GNP) would help bring the population under control, but the same rising GNP would accelerate depletion of natural resources and dramatically increase levels of pollution.

Part of the problem with the economic growth solution is that it depletes the earth's natural resources. What if, through intensified exploration, the amount of available natural resources doubled? According to *The Limits to Growth*, a rise in available resources would allow industrialization to accelerate until pollution reached dangerous levels. And even if the amount of natural resources doubled, growth would be so rapid that these reserves would be used up in a few years. If one becomes more optimistic and assumes that nuclear energy will permanently satisfy the world's energy needs, and if one allows recycling programs to conserve supplies of natural resources effectively, the world's population is still doomed to a sad end. Pollution, again, will lead the system to collapse within a hundred years.

At the root of many of these dilemmas, it seems, is the population explosion. But in the simulated world of *The Limits to Growth*, the ultimate impact of zero population growth would be disastrous. Industrial growth would accelerate as capital accumulation was facilitated by the decreased pressure of the population explosion. "Eventual depletion of nonrenewable resources brings a sudden collapse of the industrial system" (Meadows et al., 1972, p. 160).

There is just one problem left unattacked. Surely pollution control can have only good results? In the simulation, pollution controls would allow industrialization levels to reach new heights, unattainable in a world that would otherwise have choked to death. But people would no longer die of emphysema, cancer, lead poisoning, birth defects, and other pollution-related diseases, and so population growth would continue. Ultimately, food production would not be able to keep up with the population growth, arable land would be depleted, and within the next hundred years the system would collapse.

Is there no escape? There is, according to the authors of *The Limits to Growth*, but the path entails a drastically new and comprehensive approach to the world's problems. Pollution controls must be implemented. Population control is necessary. Natural resources should be conserved. But even if all these measures are successfully implemented, ultimately "industrial growth is halted, and the death rate rises as resources are depleted, pollution accumulates, and food production declines" (Meadows et al., 1972, p. 140). If the world is to avoid disaster, conservation and pollution control must be combined with a **halt in economic growth.** There are limits to growth, and the world is on the verge of reaching those limits. If economic growth is not checked, disaster is inevitable.

The Limits to Growth simulation has attracted imitators and critics since it appeared about twenty-five years ago. The Club of Rome, which sponsored the original work, also sponsored *Mankind at the Turning Point* (Mesarovic and Pestel, 1974), which was more optimistic about the world's future. Even more optimistic conclusions can be found in *Catastrophe or New Society,* developed by Argentine researchers who rejected the necessity to curb growth in developing countries for the sake of the global environment (Herrera et al., 1976). *The Limits to Growth* also inspired more optimistic rebuttals by American analysts, such as *The Next 200 Years* (Kahn, Brown, and Martel, 1976), *The Ultimate Resource* (Simon, 1981), and *The Resourceful Earth* (Simon and Kahn, 1984), a crescendo of optimism culminating in *Passage to a Human World* (Singer, 1987). Two important documents offering optimistic assessments of the globe's future published in the 1990s are *The Ultimate Resource 2* by **Julian Simon** (1996) and *A Moment on the Earth* by Gregg Easterbrook (1995). The main message of *The Limits to Growth* has been most visibly adopted in a series of annual (always quite pessimistic) reports entitled *The State of the World,* produced by the **Worldwatch Institute** in Washington, D.C., headed by **Lester Brown.**[4] By the 1990s, *The State of the World* was being used in more than one thousand courses in almost five hundred U.S. colleges and universities. The thirteenth edition, published in 1997, was published in twenty-seven languages, in virtually every country with a substantial publishing industry. The directors of the Worldwatch Institute can legitimately claim that "the public, environmental activists, national governments, United Nations Organizations, and the development community look to the *The State of the World* for current, authoritative and reasoned environmental policy analysis and information" (Starke, 1997).

---

[4] The Worldwatch Institute does not represent the extreme end of a continuum. Pennti Linkola, a "celebrated author" in Finland, advocates the following measures to deal with global ecological problems: "End Third World aid and asylum for refugees . . . so millions die. Try mandatory abortions for women who already have two children. And then find some way to get rid of the extra billions of people." Another world war, he says, would be "a happy occasion for the planet," given a population 2.5 times greater than the earth can support (Milbank, May 20, 1994, Section A, p. 1).

The disparity of opinions in the various analyses of the future of the globe is disconcerting. "It appears," one informed analyst of such work concludes, "that highly intelligent individuals, who presumably read each other's work and who appear to respond to one another, are not convincing one another, and perhaps are not even communicating" (Hughes, 1985, p. 25). What is a concerned citizen of the world to believe?

OPTIMISTS VERSUS PESSIMISTS ON THE FUTURE OF THE WORLD

Predicting the future of the world over the next twenty, fifty, or one hundred years is obviously a tricky business. No one knows for sure what the rest of this century or the beginning of the next will bring. Also, for many forecasters, ideology, or a world view based on preferences and emotions that are probably at least partially subconscious, takes over when the facts run out. And universally accepted facts soon become inadequate as a basis for valid predictions in many debates between those who espouse positive viewpoints and those who espouse negative viewpoints on the future of the world.

The debate between the **optimists** and the **pessimists,** though, is not necessarily a typical conflict between "liberals" and "conservatives," at least not as Americans use the terms. The ideological criticism of *The Limits to Growth,* for example, has come from widely separated points of the political spectrum. Many radicals and spokespersons for developing countries accused its authors of defending a reactionary status quo, condemning poor countries to permanent poverty while supporting the opulence of the industrialized world. But the political Right was not happy with the book's predictions either. In particular, defenders of the free-enterprise system have been highly suspicious of the "no-growth" idea. Also, liberals, in typical parlance, are more fervent advocates of change and progress, but in the environmental movement, they are suspicious of progress in the form of economic development, industrialization, and technological innovations such as nuclear power. Conservatives are usually thought of as more respectful of tradition and more cautious about changes, but within the context of this debate, they have little patience with the call for putting the brakes on current technological innovations.[5]

---

[5] And Gregg Easterbrook (1995, p. xviii), clearly among the more optimistic analysts of the globe's future, is a professed political liberal.

In any case, it would be a mistake to brush off the debate between optimists and pessimists about the future of the world's political, economic, and social systems as nothing more than arguments between equally ignorant factions regarding questions entirely beyond the understanding of humankind. The discussion need not be based completely on emotions, biases, and wild, uninformed guesses. On the contrary, mountains of data are available to any seriously interested person. Choices must be made, and these choices should be based in part on estimates about the future impact of current trends, as well as on the probable effects of the different options that are available. It is incumbent on all those who are responsible for these choices and concerned about the fate of the planet to reduce to a minimum the extent to which these choices are based on ignorance or uninformed guesswork, even if it is also advisable for everyone involved in the debate to remember that he or she could be wrong. With that in mind, let us turn to an evaluation of the arguments made by the optimists and the pessimists.

Food Supplies

It would be easy, considering the headlines in recent years concerning famine in Africa, to conclude that the pessimistic predictions made in the 1970s about food supplies are beginning to come true. *The Limits to Growth* predicted that land for agricultural use would be intolerably scarce by the year 2050[6] and perhaps we are seeing the beginnings of the problem in Africa.

But Lester Brown of the Worldwatch Institute feels that the real source of the current problem is China. In *Who Will Feed China: A Wakeup Call for a Small Planet* (Brown, 1995), he argues that as China's economy continues to grow, it will quite soon reach the point at which its increasingly necessary imports of wheat will create shortages and high prices around the globe.

> If China holds together as a country, and if its rapid modernization continues . . . its import needs may soon far exceed the exportable supply of grain at recent prices, converting the world grain economy from a buyer's market to a seller's market. . . . In an integrated world economy,

---

[6] Barry Hughes (1985, p. 137) points out that this projection is flawed because it is based on research in forty-four western U.S. counties, which are notorious for their sprawl, or inefficient use of land.

China's rising food prices will become the world's rising food prices. China's land scarcity will become everyone's land scarcity (p. 32).[7]

Brown may be correct. The world may be on the verge of food shortages, escalating food prices, and massive famines. But one of the main points of this chapter is that estimates and predictions of such crises vary widely. "For every headline-grabbing prediction of doom, there are sober reports predicting the opposite. A forthcoming study from the UN's Food and Agricultural Organization, for example, argues that Mr. Brown has miscalculated" (*Economist*, June 10, 1995, p. 39). Another report concludes:

> Researchers have not reached a consensus on just what China's grain balances are likely to be. . . . Some researchers predict that the country's demand for grain imports is likely to shoot up well beyond its capacity to grow its own food, draining international markets and inflating world food prices. Others project that China will become an exporter of grain (2020 Vision News and Views, 1997).

Another main point argued here will be that one seemingly underused criterion for evaluating such conflicting reports is the ability of the source in question to make **accurate predictions.** This is not the only criterion by which to evaluate competing sources, and it should be kept in mind that any single accurate prediction may be based on dumb luck, and conversely, that one inaccurate prediction does not establish that the predictor is incompetent, or deserves no further attention.

But it is only fair to evaluate Lester Brown's prediction regarding imminent food shortages and escalating prices, for example, by looking at his recent track record in making such predictions. Lester Brown predicted in 1981 that "the period of global food security is over." Unexpectedly, at least for Brown, grain prices promptly fell to historic lows during the 1980s. As the 1990s approached, Brown predicted that "the first concrete economic indication of broad-based environmental deterioration now seems likely to be rising grain prices." But "Brown's poor track record is intact. Grain prices have plummeted since he published his prediction. . . . The price of wheat has fallen by more than 40 percent" (Tierney, 1990, p. 78). Most recently, Brown's Worldwatch Institute noted that "a combination of strong prices at planting time,

---

[7] It is perhaps an interesting indication and measure of Brown's visibility and influence that when his Worldwatch Institute published this report in 1995, "On August 29, in Beijing, the Chinese government called a press conference at which it sharply denounced the . . . report. . . . Deputy Agriculture Minister Wan Baorui huffed to reporters that . . . his enormous country of 1.2 billion people [would] reach self-sufficiency by the year 2000" (Ayres, 1995, p. 3).

expanded area in grain, and unusually good weather helped make the 1996 grain harvest the largest ever" (Brown, 1997, p. 26). But Brown continues to be pessimistic. "All the basic indicators of food security" he asserts, "signal a tightening situation during the nineties" (Brown, 1997, p. 24).

Such predictions have by now a rather lengthy history among those who are pessimistic about the future with respect to these problems. Even before the publication of *The Limits to Growth*, **Paul Ehrlich** made an international reputation for himself with the publication of ***The Population Bomb*** (1968), in which he predicted that "the battle to feed humanity is already lost, in the sense that we will not be able to prevent large-scale famines in the next decade." He claimed that general famine was certain to strike even the United States by the 1980s, and that millions or even billions would have starved to death in developing countries by that time. "Somehow," an optimistic critic of Ehrlich points out, "Ehrlich maintains a reputation as an environmental seer despite having been miles wide of the mark on seemingly every major prediction he has ever made" (Easterbrook, 1995b, p. 479).[8]

On the optimistic side of coin, one estimate suggests that "we [meaning we, the people of the earth] can grow nine or ten times as much food as we do now, using only conventional agriculture—without damaging the environment and without spending more than a percent or two of our income. . . . It is quite reasonable to believe that we could grow . . . enough food for high quality diets for 100 billion people" (Singer, 1987, p. 118). A study by the U.N. Food and Agriculture Organization is less optimistic, although it does conclude that "[u]sing modern agriculture methods the Third World could support more than 30 billion people" (Mann, 1993, p. 50). Similarly, the well-known "optimist" in these matters, Julian Simon (1996, p. 101), argues that at current, already achieved levels of agricultural efficiency, "the entire present population of the world can be supplied from a square area about 140 miles on a side—about the area of Massachusetts and Vermont combined, and less than a tenth of Texas." He also points out, less speculatively, that "the record of food production entirely contradicts the scary forecasts. The world trend in recent decades shows unmistakably an increase in food production per person" (Simon, 1996, p. 87; see Figure 15.3).

Perhaps the "optimists" on this point are and have been too optimistic. But any evaluation of contrasting opinions on this point should take into account that during the most recent decades, when "pessimists"

---

[8] Easterbrook (1995, p. 479) goes on to point out that "[i]n the 1960s Ehrlich predicted mass starvations for the 1970s; in the 1970s, for the 1980s; now in the 1990s, he predicts them for the first decade of the twenty-first century."

Figure 15.3   Per Capita Food Production in the World

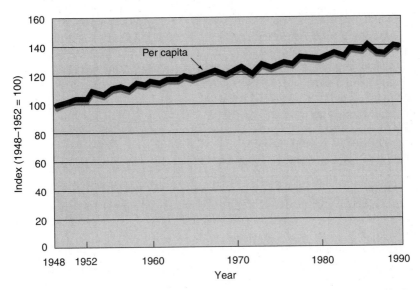

Source: Julian Simon, *The Ultimate Resource 2*. Copyright © 1996 by Princeton University Press. Reprinted by permission of Princeton University Press.

have consistently been predicting disaster, "what the United Nations defines as 'chronic malnutrition' has declined 16 percent" since the 1960s (Easterbrook, 1995b, p. 478). In addition, "a smaller percentage of the world's people are hungry than was the case a few decades ago. . . . Fewer than one in five people goes hungry today compared to one in three in 1969" (Robinson and Sweet, 1997, p. 59). Perhaps the optimists are unjustifiably optimistic, but their evaluations have served as a more accurate guide to developments in the last two or three decades, and there is a lot of room for error in their predictions about the future, since no one expects a world population of anywhere near 100 billion, or even 30 billion. (Most estimates fall somewhere between 10 and 20 billion.) Even quite gross "optimistic" errors would not undermine the basic conclusion that the world will, in the coming decades, be able to produce enough food to prevent massive famines or catastrophically escalating food prices.

The Population Explosion

The history of demographic predictions is replete with errors and marked by continuing modifications. The predictions of Thomas

Malthus in the nineteenth century, for example, proved to be very misleading. One recent analysis of Cassandras (those who predict disaster) among population experts notes that

> *The Population Bomb* appeared twenty-five years ago. . . . Written by the biologist Paul Ehrlich . . . it was a gloomy book for a gloomy time. A new Dark Age would [according to Ehrlich] cloud the world, and 'men [would] have to kill and eat one another.' A well-regarded book, *Famine 1975!* predicted that hunger would wipe out the Third World that year. . . . In 1972 a group of researchers at MIT . . . [issued] *The Limits to Growth,* which used advanced computer models to project that the world would run out of gold in 1981, oil in 1992, and arable land in 2000. Civilization itself would collapse by 2070 (Mann, 1993, p. 48).

In 1975, the U.N. Population Division, for the first time in its history, revised its estimate of future population growth *downward,* basing its conclusions on data from 1973. Previously it had predicted that by the year 2000, the world's population would be about 6.5 billion. In 1975, it pointed out that recent trends indicated that the figure would be closer to 6.3 billion (Panati and Lord, 1976, p. 58). In 1990, the U.N. Population Division again projected that the world's population in the year 2000 would be 6.3 billion (*Population Today,* 1990, p. 4). "The evidence from the late 1970s and 1980s seems to clinch [the] idea . . . that world population growth rates peaked in the 1960s" (Singer, 1987, p. 70). In fact, from 1965–1970 to 1980–1985, fertility in poor countries decreased by 30 percent. "If the decrease continues, it will surely be the most astonishing demographic shift in history" (Mann, 1993, p. 53). Most recently, the United Nations has reported that the world's population is growing virtually everywhere at a slower rate than expected even just a few years ago. From 1990 to 1995, the population growth rate worldwide was 1.48 percent a year, "significantly lower than the 1.57 percent projected by the previous report in 1994. The world already has 29 million fewer people than expected." The report goes on to point out that in that same 1990–1995 period, fertility declined to 2.96 children per woman, although the United Nations had projected 3.1 children per woman just a few years ago. And for the year 2050 the U.N. projection was a half billion people fewer than it had been just three years before. (The 1997 U.N. world population estimate is about 5.77 billion people; see Crossette, *New York Times,* Section 1, p. 3.)

Population estimates have often been wrong in the past, and these latest predictions may be wrong again. But even if the population of the world grows much faster than expected, disaster, in terms of food supplies or other aspects of the quality of life, will not necessarily result. It is quite commonly pointed out that "the parts of the world that have done most poorly economically are also those where projected population growth rates are the highest" (Robinson and Sweet, 1997, p. 57). But it is quite possible that poverty leads to population growth, not the opposite. Radical economists have typically been suspicious of efforts by rich countries to persuade poor countries to initiate programs of population control. One such radical economist, for example, argues that "the racist solution is that the poor, mostly black, should be pressured into having less babies. . . . The primary problem of these countries is not population, but imperialism" (Sherman, 1972, p. 80).

Radicals are not the only skeptics of the need to make vigorous efforts to reduce population growth rates. More orthodox students of the impact of population growth on standards of living argue that "dozens of studies . . . have found no association between the population growth rate and per capita income growth rate" and that "the empirical evidence thus indicates no negative correlation between the rate of population growth and the standard of living" (Perlman, 1984, p. 62). One of the better-known optimists on these matters, Julian Simon (1996, p. 493), insists that population "density has a *positive* effect on the rate of economic growth," and that, more fundamentally:

> the standard of living has risen along with the size of the world's population since the beginning of recorded time. And with increases in . . . population have come less severe shortages, lower costs, and an increased availability of resources, including a cleaner environment, and greater access to natural recreational areas. And there is no convincing reason why these trends toward a better life . . . should not continue indefinitely (Simon, 1996, p. 596).[9]

None of the preceding discussion should be taken to mean that all population control programs are outmoded. In many developing countries, such as Mexico, Egypt, and India (and possibly China), rapid population growth continues, and bringing it under control is almost certainly a desirable goal. But at this writing, the predictions made during the 1960s and 1970s about impending planetwide disasters resulting from population growth outstripping the world's food production capabilities seem unduly alarmist.

Reserves of Natural Resources

Even if these predictions prove false, it does not follow that all the warnings by pessimists can be ignored. Even if the world's population does not grow to disastrously high levels and the world's farmers can

---

[9] Simon (1996, p. 579) also observes that "such institutions as the World Bank and the National Academy of Sciences have recanted their former views that population growth is a crucial obstacle to economic development."

produce plenty of food for everybody, there still might be catastrophic shortages of oil and other energy sources, as well as of metals and other commodities needed for manufacturing.

But dire warnings about energy resources in the 1970s confronted overwhelmingly contrary evidence in the 1980s. Consider first the most publicized warnings of the 1970s—those regarding oil and other energy sources. After OPEC successfully quadrupled the price of oil in the winter of 1973, no-growth advocates used the price increase as proof that the world's supply of energy resources was running low. But in fact, the increase proved no such thing. The members of OPEC were not running out of oil; they were just charging more for it. Their cost of production was still about $.10 a barrel, even though they were charging $10 a barrel. The world production of oil actually increased by 8 percent in 1973 (Beckerman, 1974, p. 250).

OPEC raised the price of oil again in 1979, from about $12 a barrel to nearly $40 a barrel. Shortages again developed, and panic spread. But in the mid-1980s, Saudi Arabia and other OPEC members, as well as non-OPEC countries, were flooding the world with cheap oil in attempts to gain larger shares of the market. As a result, in the early 1980s the price of a barrel of oil fell from a high of around $39 to around $10. Although the price shot up again to almost $40 a barrel during the Persian Gulf crisis, oil is now (1997) selling on the world market for around $20 a barrel or less.

Oil was not the only natural resource that went from shortages in the 1970s to a global glut in the 1980s. In 1985, the *New York Times* reported that "in London, an eerie silence hangs over the tin trading ring at the Metal Exchange; trading has been halted because there are simply not enough buyers for the vast quantities of tin that producers . . . keep turning out." The same story presents evidence of precipitous declines in the prices of aluminum and copper in the first half of the 1980s. "Overabundance has replaced the chronic shortages of the 1970s" (*New York Times*, December 8, 1985, p. 1). And in 1992 the World Bank noted that "whereas fears that the world would run out of metals and other minerals were fashionable even fifteen years ago, the potential supply of these resources is now outstripping demand. Prices of minerals have shown a fairly consistent downward trend over the past hundred years. They fell sharply in the 1980s, leading to gluts that threatened to impoverish countries dependent on commodity exports" (World Bank, 1992, p. 9).

One reason that pessimistic predictions of long-term shortages made in the 1970s look rather ridiculous in the 1990s is that they were based on estimates of **known reserves** of the various raw materials in question. Estimates of known reserves provide a misleading basis for such predictions. For example, we now know that for resource after resource, estimates of known reserves made in the 1950s proved by 1970 to be drastically low (Kahn, Brown, and Martel, 1976, p. 203). This degree of underestimation happens with regularity, in part because of the economic incentives operating on those who gather data on known reserves. Usually, the original sources of such data are companies interested in the commercial exploitation of a given resource. Once a company has located reserves that are projected to last, say, thirty years, it is unlikely even to attempt to find additional reserves, for at least two important reasons. First, since the company will not be able to sell those reserves for thirty years, there is little incentive to spend time and energy locating them. Second, if known reserves become too abundant, they exert a strong downward pressure on the price of that resource.

The strength of this pattern was, arguably at least, revealed in the outcome of an interesting public wager in the 1980s between economist Julian Simon and ecologist Paul Ehrlich, well known for their optimistic and pessimistic viewpoints, respectively.

> In 1980 an ecologist and an economist chose a refreshingly unacademic way to resolve their differences. They bet $1000. Specifically the bet was over the future price of five metals, but at stake was much more—a view of the planet's ultimate limits, a vision of humanity's destiny (Tierney, 1990, p. 52).

Ehrlich selected five metals—chrome, copper, nickel, tin, and tungsten—and bet $1,000 that in ten years, the prices of those metals would be higher. Simon bet $1,000 that they would be lower. By 1990, "each of the five metals chosen by Ehrlich . . . had declined in price" (Tierney, 1990, p. 81). Ehrlich mailed a check to Simon.[10]

Thus, time after time, for resource after resource, dire predictions have emanated from various quarters about the imminent depletion of some vital commodity. But typically, by the time the resource is supposed to have been entirely depleted, even after many years of rapid depletion of that resource, there is still plenty of it around, and the known reserves have become larger than at the time of the original, gloomy prediction.

Table 15.1 shows an interesting series of predictions about the depletion of oil reserves in the United States. Although the table covers only the period from 1866 to 1949, it could easily be extended. For example, the CIA issued a well-publicized study in 1977 predicting that

---

[10] Ehrlich insisted at the time that "the bet doesn't mean anything." Simon's retort was that "Paul Ehrlich has never been able to learn from past experience." He has also offered to raise the wager to as much as $20,000 with regard to any other resource and for any year in the future (Tierney, 1990, p. 81).

Table 15.1 A Short History of Predictions About U.S. Oil Supplies, 1866–1949

Date	Prediction	What Actually Happened
1866	Synthetics available if oil production should end (U.S. Revenue Commission)	In next 82 years the U.S. produced 37 billion barrels with no need for synthetics
1885	Little or no chance of oil in California (U.S. Geological Survey)	8 billion barrels produced in California since that date with important new findings in 1948
1891	Little or no chance of oil in Kansas or Texas (U.S. Geological Survey)	14 billion barrels produced in these two states since 1891
1908	Maximum future supply of 22.5 billion barrels (officials of U.S. Geological Survey)	35 billion barrels produced since 1908, with 26.8-billion-barrel reserve proven and available on January 1, 1949
1914	Total future production only 5.7 billion barrels (official of U.S. Bureau of Mines)	34 billion barrels produced since 1914, or six times this prediction
1920	U.S. needs foreign oil and synthetics: peak domestic production almost reached (director of U.S. Geological Survey)	1948 U.S. production in excess of U.S. consumption and more than four times 1920 output
1931	Must import as much foreign oil as possible to save domestic supply (secretary of the interior)	During the next 8 years imports were discouraged and 14 billion barrels were found in the United States
1939	U.S. oil supplies will last only 13 years (radio broadcasts by Department of the Interior)	New oil found since 1939 exceeds the 13-year supply known at that time
1947	Sufficient oil cannot be found in United States (chief of Petroleum Division, State Department)	4.3 billion barrels found in 1948, the largest volume in history and twice our consumption
1949	End of oil supply almost in sight (secretary of the interior)	Petroleum industry demonstrated ability to increase U.S. production by more than a million barrels daily in the next 5 years

Source: Presidential Energy Program, Hearings Before the Subcommittee on Energy and Power of the Committee on Interstate and Foreign Commerce, House of Representatives. First sessions on the implication of the President's proposals on the Energy Independence Act of 1975. Serial no. 94-20, p. 643. Washington, D.C.: U.S. Government Printing Office, February 17, 18, 20, 21, 1975.

the global supply of fuel would fall noticeably below projected demand by 1985 (Central Intelligence Agency, 1977).

There was yet another energy crisis (albeit of mercifully short duration) when Iraq attacked Kuwait and indirectly threatened Saudi Arabia and its oil wells in August 1990. Why that attack had such an impact on the world's oil prices (sending them up briefly from about $18 a barrel to almost $40 a barrel) is hinted at strongly in Figure 15.4. That figure shows that as of 1989, the three countries in the world with the largest crude petroleum reserves were Saudi Arabia, Iraq, and Kuwait. Saddam Hussein threatened to take control of all that oil (not to mention that of the United Arab Emirates, another Persian Gulf country listed in the top ten in Figure 15.4).[11]

---

[11] Another interesting indication of the impact of developments in that part of the world on the oil market became visible the day after the first U.S. air attack on Iraq at the beginning of the Persian Gulf War. When that attack established that Iraq was unable to retaliate effectively against Saudi oilfields, or anything else, the price of oil fell $10 in one day, the largest absolute price drop on record.

Figure 15.4 The World's Crude Petroleum Reserves, 1989

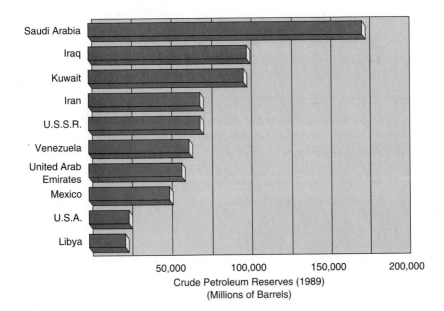

Crude Petroleum Reserves (1989)
(Millions of Barrels)

In the early 1990s, cheap oil was bringing the earlier trends toward global energy conservation to a halt (Flavin and Lenssen, 1991, p. 23). In addition, the United States had become even more dependent on imported oil, much of which came from the Persian Gulf, and the world's long-term dependence on Persian Gulf oil was becoming more marked. For example, in 1980, 55 percent of the proven global reserves of petroleum were in the Persian Gulf. By 1997, that share had increased to 67 percent (TOTAL, 1997).

The forecasts of the 1970s and early 1980s that oil prices would soon reach $50 to $100 a barrel and that oil and energy sources would soon be physically depleted look drastically premature at best. In 1993, the *New York Times* reported that "world reserves [of oil] now are nearly 50 times annual consumption, the highest ratio ever" (Wald, 1993, p. 4).[12] In the light of these data, even most pessimists no longer argue that the world is in imminent danger of running short of oil. Consider Figures 15.5 and 15.6, which depict respectively the surge in the world's fossil fuel use in the years from 1950 to 1996 and the world's proven reserves of oil for almost exactly the same years. Paradoxically (but as we have, seen, actually quite predictably), both fossil fuel consumption *and*

[12] Wald also notes that "the world's largest producer, the Soviet Union, collapsed in the early 1990s with barely a ripple in the market. In the early 1990s the world was also doing without oil, for the most part, from the country with the second largest reserves in the world, namely Iraq, whose exports of oil were embargoed."

Figure 15.5 World Fossil Fuel Use, 1950–1996

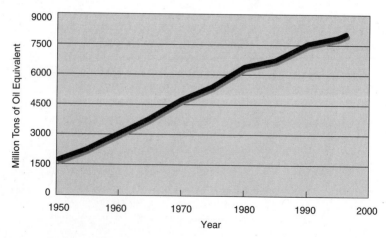

SOURCE: From *Vital Signs 1997: The Trends That Are Shaping Our Future* by Linda Starke, ed. Copyright © 1997 by W. W. Norton & Company, Inc. Reprinted by permission of the publisher.

Figure 15.6   World's Proven Oil Reserves as of the End of 1996

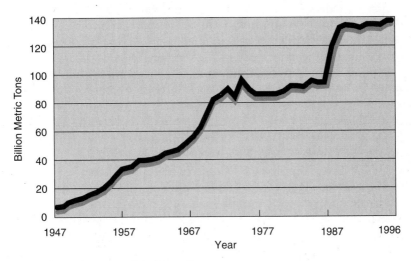

SOURCE: Reprinted courtesy of the Neste Group.

proven reserves have steadily increased through the last fifty years or so. Toward the end of that period in the United States "in 1994, gasoline was selling for less in real terms than in 1940" (Easterbrook, 1995b, p. 349). In 1996, the *Washington Post* reported that "known crude oil reserves amount to 1 trillion barrels—enough for 45 to 50 years at current world production rates, and estimated reserves are at least 1 trillion barrels more" (see Washingtonpost.com, 1996). And in general, "optimists" seem on fairly firm ground when they assert that "the potential supplies of all the important minerals are sufficient for many lifetimes" (Simon, 1996, p. 51).[13]

Still, "pessimists" here have a valid point when they emphasize the "two-thirds of the world's current reserves [are] in the Persian Gulf region" (Flavin and Lenssen, 1992, p. 22). It is possible that market forces will ultimately solve this problem, that the concentration of current known reserves will spark the discovery of huge reserves outside the politically unstable Persian Gulf, and that the world's supply of inexpensive, readily accessible oil will continue well into the twenty-first century. But it might be prudent to develop alternative sources of energy, even if the world is not about to run out of oil.

---

[13] Simon (1996, p. 51) adds that "this material-technical assessment is entirely consistent with the historical economic evidence of falling prices relative to wages for all raw materials, showing a trend of increasing availability and declining scarcity."

Pollution and Economic Growth

Pessimistic predictions about the impact of various forms of pollution on the global atmosphere are difficult to ignore, even though they are based on scanty evidence. That evidence is often weak because pollution is a relatively recent concern, and data on relevant problems rarely go back more than twenty to thirty years. But just because hard evidence is so hard to come by, the most cataclysmic predictions cannot be discounted or discredited. The predictions could turn out to be true.

As discussed above, rising levels of carbon dioxide in the air, leading to the possible greenhouse effect, could drastically modify the climate in various parts of the world. The greenhouse effect could also cause the polar ice caps to melt, which would result in the flooding of coastal cities. When trees die, carbon dioxide is added to the atmosphere in two ways. As the dead trees rot, carbon dioxide is released into the air. Also, trees consume carbon dioxide in the process of photosynthesis. When they die, less photosynthesis occurs, and so less carbon dioxide is absorbed.

Trees are also reduced in number when they are cut down for lumber or to clear areas for development, as in Brazil's rain forest. According to satellite data, in 1987, deforestation in Brazil was so extreme that the **Amazon rain forest** was reduced in size by 8 million hectares, or an area about the size of Austria (Brown, Flavin, and Postel, 1989, p. 4); by 1989 the deforested area was larger than the size of Japan (Postel and Flavin, 1991, p. 178). "Satellite monitoring indicates that the pace of deforestation in the Amazon actually increased 34 percent between 1991 and 1994" (Flavin, 1997b, p. 15). Combined with the destruction of tropical rain forests in Africa, Indonesia, and elsewhere, the deforestation in Brazil could mean that by the year 2000, the tropical rain forests of the world will have been largely destroyed. Over a recent ten-year period, destruction of tropical rain forests equaled an area the size of Malaysia, the Philippines, Ghana, the Congo, Ecuador, El Salvador, and Nicaragua combined (Brown, 1993, pp. 5–6).

Constant emissions of large amounts of carbon dioxide into the atmosphere through fossil fuel combustion and deforestation combine with the pollution of the atmosphere by volatile chemicals known as **chlorofluorocarbons (CFCs)** to produce the hypothesized greenhouse effect and a global warming trend (see Figure 15.7). There is still some debate about this trend (discussed in more detail below) but there does seem to be a growing consensus in the world's scientific community that a warming trend is in place on a global scale, and that human activities are making an important contribution to this trend. In 1995, the *New York Times* reported that "in an important shift of scientific judgment, experts advising the world's governments on climate change

Figure 15.7 Global Surface Air Temperature, Annual Average

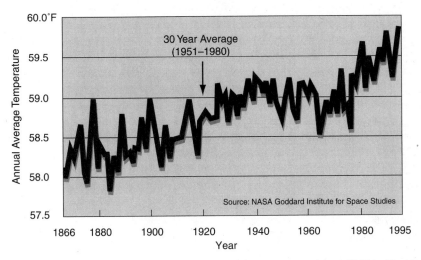

SOURCE: From *The New York Times*, September 10, 1995, p. A6. Copyright © 1995 by The New York Times Company. Reprinted by permission.

are saying for the first time that human activity is a likely cause of the warming of the global atmosphere" (Stevens, 1995, p. 1). The story refers to a report published in 1996 (a preliminary version of which became available on the Internet in 1995) by the **Intergovernmental Panel on Climate Change (IPCC),** consisting of more than two thousand scientists assembled by the United Nations to advise the world's governments on climate policy. According to an analyst from the Worldwatch Institute:

> Sophisticated computer modeling and actual measurements of the atmosphere are now converging with uncanny accuracy . . . increasingly the computer answers are corroborated by direct observation. By 1995, the fit looked too close to be pure coincidence; the . . . IPCC . . . concluded that human activity is warming the earth (Bright, 1997, p. 79).

In addition to their possible role in the process leading to global warming, CFCs may have helped to destroy the ozone layer in the upper atmosphere over the polar regions and, lately, over the entire world. The ozone layer screens out a portion of the ultraviolet radiation from the sun. Because that layer decreased by about 2 percent worldwide between 1969 and 1986, allowing 4 percent more radiation to reach the earth, an increase in skin cancer can be expected (Shea, 1989, p. 28). In 1991, new data from U.S. satellites showed that the protective ozone layer over the United States had been depleted by about 5 percent, at a

The bitter winter of 1993–1994 on the East Coast of the
United States caused some doubts about the theory of
global warming. Twenty years ago there was an "Ice
Age Scare" in the United States. SOURCE: AP/Wide World
Photos.

rate three times faster than previous studies had indicated. The Environmental Protection Agency estimates that ozone depletion will result
in an additional 11 million cases of skin cancer and that about 200,000
of those who get the disease will die (Laszewski, 1991, pp. 1, 5).

CFCs also prevent infrared radiation from escaping the earth's atmosphere, thus making their own contribution to the global warming effect.
CFCs are estimated to have caused 15 to 20 percent of global warming
thus far (Wirth, 1989, p. 5). Once released into the atmosphere, CFCs
can be expected to stay there for a hundred years, so it is especially
disturbing that they may have already had a disruptive effect on the
global climate.

By 1995, the concentration of carbon dioxide had reached the highest levels on record for the past 160,000 years (Bright, 1997, p. 79). And until the 1990s, the five warmest years of this century for the entire globe occurred during the 1980s (Brown, Flavin and Postel, 1989, p. 9). Then 1990 was reported to have been the warmest year for the entire globe in the history of temperature records (*New York Times*, circa January 10, 1991). But 1995 was warmer still, worldwide, than 1990, and "the 1990s are already the warmest decade on record—averaging 0.1 degrees Celsius above the 1980s" (Dunn, 1997b, p. 62).

If this trend continues, global warming could have catastrophic effects all over the world, mostly because of rising sea levels (due to melting polar ice caps), as well as permanently lower levels of rainfall in once fertile croplands. In Bangladesh, for example, a rising sea level might put 18 percent of the country's habitable land under water, making 17 million people "environmental refugees." "Sea level rise . . . may wreak so much damage that Bangladesh as it is known today may virtually cease to exist" (Jacobson, 1989, p. 24). It is also estimated that already, during the last fifty years, an area of ice the size of Delaware has disappeared from Antarctica. "Average **global sea level** has probably risen about 18 centimeters over the past century, and is currently rising at 0.1–0.3 centimeters per year" (Bright, 1997, p. 83). Climate models also suggest that global warming may permanently reduce rainfall in the U.S. Midwest, thus also permanently reducing crop yields in an area that produces 50 percent of the world's corn and 60 percent of its soybeans (Wirth, 1989, p. 25). But the United States is only one country that might be affected. "One possible result of disrupted climate is more frequent droughts. Chronic water shortages already plague 80 countries with 40 percent of the world's population" (Flavin, 1996, p. 25).

The continual stream of newspaper headlines and television newscasts about the greenhouse effect may have created an aura of inevitability about environmental trends and imminent disasters that is not warranted by the evidence. In the first place, it is not entirely clear that industrialization on a worldwide scale will have a warming effect on the global climate. Climatologists (like alarmists in other matters) do not have a particularly impressive record of prognostication in recent decades. Apparently, they were predominantly of the opinion in the 1930s that there was a global warming trend.[14] Spencer Weart, a specialist in the history of physics, asserts that the greenhouse effect rhetoric of the

---

[14] There were data to support this opinion (see Figure 15.6). But skeptics about global warming argue that if such a trend is in place, according to the theory, the warming process should be accelerating. Some data, at least, suggest that it is not. "The greatest increase in temperature in this century occurred between 1920 and 1940" (Associated Press, February 20, 1995).

1930s was virtually identical to that of the 1980s and 1990s, "of irreversible damage, of humankind overstepping its bounds in horrifying fashion" (Easterbrook, 1995b, p. 217).

Unfortunately (for the credibility of the forecasts in the 1930s), the world immediately got colder. The global temperature declined from the 1940s to the 1970s, with the winter of 1977 being the coldest in a century in North America. These data, too, had an apparent impact on forecasts about the future of the globe's climate. In 1971 (in a book edited by Paul Ehrlich), one analyst expressed his opinion that "global air pollution, through its effect on the reflectivity of the earth, is currently dominant and is responsible for the temperature decline of the past decade or two" (Bryson, 1971; cited by Simon, 1996, p. 267). An article in *International Wildlife* in 1975 suggested that "the threat of a **new ice age** must now stand alongside nuclear war as a likely source of wholesale death and misery for mankind" (Calder, 1975; cited by Simon, 1996, p. 267). About twenty years ago, the *New York Times* (August 14, 1975) reported that there were "many signs pointing to the possibility that the Earth may be heading for another ice age." *Science* magazine (March 1, 1975) warned that the globe faced "the approach of a full-blown 10,000-year ice age." Likewise, *Science Digest* (February 1973) suggested that "the world's climatologists are agreed" that the world must "prepare for the next ice age." *Newsweek* (April 28, 1975) reported that there were "ominous signs" that "the Earth's climate seems to be cooling down," and that meteorologists at that time were "almost unanimous" that "the trend will reduce agricultural productivity for the rest of the century" (Will, 1992, p. 5).

Lester Brown (1972, p. 25), currently one of the more influential writers on global warming (and other future catastrophes), pointed out in 1972 that "the earth's average temperature . . . since 1940 . . . has begun to decline, dropping 0.5 degrees Fahrenheit." He explained that this cooling trend might be a result of "the consumption of energy [that] . . . can . . . contribute to a cooling of the earth by discharging dust particles in the atmosphere which in turn reduces the inflow of solar energy." In general, it does seem that "many of the same persons who [warned] about global *cooling* are the same climatologists who are now warning of global *warming*" (Simon, 1996, p. 267).

This is not the context in which to attempt to sort out or evaluate comprehensively the opposing arguments about global warming. Let us instead examine here a couple of reasons why the issue is so difficult to resolve. First, global climate processes are so complex, and affected by so many countervailing factors, that making predictions about their future course is risky. Tropical deforestation, for example, continues at an alarming rate and may make an important contribution to global warming. Less noted is the fact that in North America and Eurasia, forests are growing larger. "The expanding boreal forests of North America and Eurasia are much larger than the rainforests of the tropics . . . growing trees absorb substantial amounts of carbon dioxide" (Easterbrook, 1995b, p. 297).[15]

Then, too, humankind's activities and impacts on the global climate may be dwarfed or minimized by natural processes. About 200 billion tons of carbon are emitted into the atmosphere by natural processes like volcanic eruptions, plant decay, or forest fires. Almost exactly that same amount is removed from the atmosphere every year, also by natural processes—"breathed in" by trees, or taken from the air by ocean plankton, for example. Human activities contribute about 7 billion tons of carbon annually (see Figure 15.2). That is only about 3.3 percent of the amount produced by natural processes. Can such a relatively insignificant amount have the substantial impact on global climate that global warming theorists suggest? Skeptics, at least, wonder.

They wonder also because not all available data suggest that there is a global warming trend. In fact, arguably the best data available fail to reveal such a trend. "The studies that find a global warming trend . . . rely on surface-temperatures readings taken near cities" (Easterbrook, 1995b, p. 279), which may not be representative of global conditions. The National Aeronautics and Space Administration records data from satellites. "Satellites, their enthusiasts claim, can provide a truly global picture since they measure temperatures uniformly across the earth's surface. Unlike their terrestrial counterparts, satellite thermometers show no warming trend" (*Economist*, March 23, 1996, p. 83; see Figure 15.8).[16]

Even assuming that some human activities are creating ecological problems of global scope, it is not entirely clear what should be done about these problems. It is clear that some pessimists' suggestions on how to address these problems are based on a questionable idea of the relationship between pollution and economic growth. Economic growth is perceived to be part of the problem, but it may be nearer to the truth that growth is an important part of the solution. "In the early stages of industrialization, countries and people are not yet ready to pay for clean-up operations" (Simon and Kahn, 1984, p. 9). As a result, although it is difficult to prove that things were worse in the "good old days," because there are virtually no precise measures of pollution from

---

[15] Easterbrook (1995, p. 297) adds that a couple of researchers from Harvard have concluded a study suggesting that trees in North America pull from the air "about 50 percent more CO_2 than assumed by standard studies."

[16] John Christy, a scientist who heads the NASA air temperature study, says, "We don't see any global warming in our data, and our satellites monitor the entire world, not just urban areas like the ground-temperature studies" (Easterbrook, 1995, p. 280).

Figure 15.8 Blowing Hot and Cold

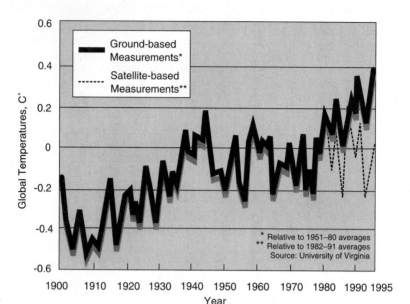

the nineteenth century, pollution was a serious problem even then. Charles Dickens, for example, in his novel *Hard Times*, describes nineteenth-century Coketown (actually Preston, England) in these terms:

> It was a town of machinery and tall chimneys, out of which interminable serpents of smoke trailed themselves for ever and ever, and never got uncoiled. It had a black canal in it, and a river that ran purple with ill-smelling dye, and vast piles of buildings full of windows, where there was a rattling and a trembling all day long (quoted in Sinclair, 1973, p. 182).

Meanwhile, things were unpleasant in another budding nineteenth-century industrial power, the United States. Its largest industrial center was New York City, with some 300 foundries and machine shops and a printing industry powered by 125 steam engines, bone mills, refineries, and tanneries.

> The crux of New York's filthy air was Hunter's Point, on the rim of the Bronx. Grievous odors from the Point poured over Manhattan, affecting all who lived there regardless of rank or address" (Bettman, 1974, pp. 5–6).

There apparently was a lively controversy in those days about whether New York was more grievously afflicted with pollution than Chicago. The Chicago River was reportedly polluted with "grease so thick on its surface it seemed a liquid rainbow."

Nineteenth-century Chicago and New York could not have been worse than Pittsburgh, with its 14,000 chimneys (belonging mostly to iron and steel mills) bombarding the city with smoke and soot twenty-four hours a day, "a noisome vomit, killing everything that grows— trees, grass, and flowers" (Bettman, 1974, p. 16).

A comparison of contemporary developing societies with industrialized countries provides additional support for the assertion that economic growth and environmental deterioration do not necessarily go hand in hand. For example, developing states typically have water pollution problems, brought about by poor sanitation systems, that are more serious than those of industrialized societies. Fatal illnesses related to the consumption of impure water are extremely rare in richer countries, whereas dysentery and more serious diseases are common in most poor states. And the crowding in the slums of major cities in many poor countries creates additional serious pollution problems. Economic growth may exacerbate some pollution problems for poor countries in the short run, but ultimately such growth is likely to be a necessary condition for the alleviation of pollution.[17]

In 1992, the World Bank published a study of the relationship between economic growth and pollution, and it revealed that "some problems decline as income increases" (World Bank, 1992, p. 10). It is also true that as per capita income increases, "some problems initially worsen but then improve as incomes rise" (World Bank, 1992, p. 10). One of these is urban concentrations of particulate matter. An interesting example demonstrating that burgeoning economic growth even in very large cities need not mean ever-increasing air pollution is Los Angeles, the American city that has become almost synonymous with smog. An article in *Scientific American* reports the following:

> [A]ir quality [in Los Angeles] has improved dramatically since the 1970s. From 1955 to 1992 the peak level of ozone—one of the best indicators of air pollution—declined from 680 parts per billion to 300 parts per billion. . . . Furthermore, the smog levels measured during each of the past three years have been the lowest on record. All these improvements were achieved at a time when human activity in the Los Angeles area was increasing at a rapid rate. Since the 1950s the population has

---

[17] "If you have any doubt that increases in income are associated with a decrease in pollution, examine the levels of street cleanliness in the richer versus the poorer countries of the world, [or] the mortality rates of richer versus poorer countries" (Simon, 1996, p. 432).

almost tripled . . . the number of motor vehicles on the road has more than quadrupled . . . and the city has grown into one of the most prosperous regions of the world (Lents and Kelly, 1993, p. 32).

Another report in *Scientific American* points out that a study by two researchers at Princeton University found that "in cities around the world sulfur dioxide pollution fell as per capita income rose" (Bhagwati, 1993, p. 43).

The World Bank data do show that municipal wastes per capita and carbon dioxide emissions per capita are two kinds of pollution that increase as per capita income increases. There is no question that disposal of solid wastes can be a serious problem for any economy, and it probably gets more serious as the economy gets larger and more prosperous. But in the United States, which certainly has the largest and one of the most prosperous economies in the world, all of the solid waste produced in the country for the next thousand years could fit into a landfill accounting for less than one-tenth of one percent of the territory of the country. Although recycling and other steps to reduce the bulk of solid wastes are usually advisable, the United States is certainly a long way from having to apply draconian brakes on economic expansion because it is on the verge of running out of room to dispose of its wastes (Adler, 1992, p. 3). In addition, in the United States, since 1970

> smog is down by more than 30 percent, even as the number of cars has soared. In 1970, one-third of rivers and lakes were safe for fishing and swimming; today, two-thirds are. Most forested areas have been expanding, not contracting. Municipal wastes going to landfills peaked in 1988 and have been declining since then, as recycling has taken hold. Ocean dumping of sludge has ended; land-filling of untreated chemical wastes has ended; most emissions of chlorofluorocarbons . . . have ended; endangered species such as the bald eagle and gray whale have made spectacular recoveries; pesticide use is declining (Easterbrook, 1995a, p. 31).[18]

And, of course, all this has occurred at a time of substantial economic growth and expansion in the United States. There is probably no way to eliminate future increases in carbon dioxide emissions into the global atmosphere without drastically curtailing future economic growth. But whether such a step would be wise is at least debatable. It is debatable partly because the impact of those emissions on the globe's meteorological system is not clear, and partly because it is absolutely clear that poverty is a deadly killer on a massive scale right now. As the World

---

[18] And yet "polls show that people believe the environment is getting worse" (Easterbrook, 1995, p. xviii). Simon (1996, p. 215) also observes that "people's answers to poll questions about whether environmental conditions have been getting better or worse during (say) the past twenty years shows that many more people believe that there has been deterioration than believe that there has been an improvement."

Bank has pointed out, nearly two billion people in the world currently live without clean water or sewers. Cholera, typhus, and other diseases kill some two million children every year. One billion people live in cities with dangerously high sulfur dioxide levels where coal-fired factories spread lung disease. Leaded gasoline fumes in many countries cause children to be retarded. "Poverty is already a worse killer than any foreseeable environmental distress," according to the chief economist of the World Bank. "Nobody should kid themselves that they are doing Bangladesh a favor when they worry about global warming" (Nasar, 1992, p. 6).

Economic growth, then, while certainly capable of damaging the environment, also can lead to environmental improvements. And even rather stringent steps to protect the environment need not stifle economic growth. In fact, energy conservation, which can, for example, decrease the amount of carbon dioxide emitted into the atmosphere, can also increase the efficiency of an economy and even speed up growth. In 1974, in the wake of the first OPEC-induced energy crisis, a Ford Foundation study predicted that if current trends continued, energy use in the United States would double between 1970 and 1987. It also predicted that even if the United States adopted a "zero-growth" policy option, energy use would still increase about 20 percent. Instead, energy consumption actually decreased from 1970 to 1987, while the economy grew more than 35 percent.

Population Control, Conservation, and Pollution Control

None of these arguments should be interpreted as condemning efforts aimed at **population control, conservation of natural resources,** and **pollution control.** All three goals are desirable, if not exactly for the reasons suggested by some pessimists. In purely physical terms, the world in the coming decades will probably be able to produce enough food for the population. But getting food to the people who need it may be difficult, to say the least. Population control in Pakistan, Bangladesh, Indonesia, and Mexico may not, as some economists argue, provide an important stimulus to economic growth and may not even be a necessary condition for such growth. Still, barring a series of unlikely economic miracles, these countries will not be able to feed themselves in the coming years, and disasters that loom there can only be made worse if their populations continue to grow at the present pace.

Similarly, in purely physical terms, the earth's supply of natural resources may be much farther from exhaustion than pessimists suggest. But disaster sparked by natural resource shortages brought about by political instability could still occur, as the Persian Gulf crisis of 1990–91 made clear. Economic growth may not logically lead to a deterioration of the environment. Even so, economic and political pressures can push economic growth in that direction, as suggested by the oil spill from the *Exxon Valdez* that ruined the Alaskan coast in 1989. Worldwide, nation-states are caught in a kind of prisoners' dilemma with respect to pollution. To put it another way, the nations of the world face the **"tragedy of the commons"** in attempts to deal with the global pollution problem. This tragedy, as described by Garrett Hardin, might be thought of as a multilateral prisoners' dilemma—that is, a game with many players rather than just two, as in Chapter 9. As Hardin explains, the tragedy of the commons develops when there is a pasture in a community open to all and each herder must decide whether to add one more animal to his or her herd of cattle. All the gain from a decision to do so will go to that herder. But the cost of that decision, in overgrazing on the pasture, is shared by all the herders. Because the gain all goes to one herder and the costs are shared by all, each herder is tempted to add to the herd. If each herder makes that decision, which is rational on the individual level, collectively they will ruin the pasture for everybody by overgrazing (Hardin, 1977).

Similarly, all states would be better off if pollution-creating activities were curbed. But each state individually can manufacture a product in a manner unrestricted by expensive pollution controls and thus put the product on the international market at a low price. All the profits from the sales of that product will go to the polluting nation, but the cost— that is, the increasingly polluted atmosphere—is shared by all. Because each country can see a clear profit for itself from manufacturing a product without pollution controls, all nations are tempted, rationally, to take steps that collectively will ruin the atmosphere for the entire globe. That temptation reaches nearly irresistible proportions in light of the fact that no one nation (with possible exceptions such as the huge economies of the United States and Japan) can by itself do enough harm to really matter—or enough good, by restraining its polluting activities.

These **collective action problems** perhaps help to explain why the world's nations are having a difficult time cooperating in a way that might effectively deal with the dangers of the global warming problem. The U.N. Conference on Environment and Development in 1992, attended by 106 national leaders and participants from 154 countries, did produce a climate treaty that recognized global warming as a serious problem. The richer countries of the world adopted a target of reducing greenhouse gas emissions to 1990 levels by the year 2000. However, only two of those countries (Great Britain and Germany) are likely to meet that goal. Currently, it looks as if the United States will produce

13 percent more such emissions by the year 2000. In addition, rich countries and poor countries cannot agree on who should make cuts in those emissions in the future. "By 2010 the developing countries are expected to be producing more greenhouse gases than the rich ones. Yet they are refusing to sign up to any targets" (*Economist*, June 14, 1997, p. 89).

Evaluating the Contending Arguments

Another reason, on top of the collective action problems, that the governments of the world have not moved with great effectiveness against the global warming problem has to do with doubts about whether the problem is as serious as some forecasts suggest. The IPCC is an august body, certainly deserving of serious attention. But it is not beyond criticism, nor without detractors. Some critics suggest that the IPCC has a vested interest in promoting fears of global warming, that it wants to keep the billions of dollars flowing into climate research (*Economist*, March 23, 1997, p. 84).[19]

Not being in a position to deny or support that accusation, this author believes that no source (including himself, of course) writing on these issues can be counted on to be either disinterested or entirely objective. Paul Ehrlich has recently acknowledged, with astounding candor, one reason for this. In a 1996 interview with a reporter from the *New York Times*, he admits that his influential book *The Population Bomb* was a "polemic" from start to finish. He goes on in this candid fashion to point out:

> It would be intellectually satisfying to say the real impact is through reasoned discourse . . . but in my view the real impact isn't in reasoned discourse. Media attention, press coverage, and, if necessary, alarmism at least set an agenda. And that way you can have a debate (Paul Ehrlich in Wines, 1997, p. 10).

In other words, Ehrlich comes quite close to admitting that he feels it is necessary to exaggerate in order to get attention and to have an impact on the policy process. And he is probably correct.[20] But that is

---

[19] H. Sterling Bennet, an environmental policy analyst for the National Center for Policy Analysis, asserts that "polling done by Greenpeace and Gallup shows that climatologists reject by a wide margin the notion that humans are causing cataclysmic global warming" (*New York Times*, June 27, 1997, Section A, p. 20).

[20] Interestingly, according to Julian Simon (1996, p. 49), the Club of Rome, which sponsored the publication of *The Limits to Growth* discussed above, disavowed the publication four years after it appeared, claiming that the authors had "purposely misled the public in order to 'awaken' public concern."

another reason (in addition to the desire that analysts might have to attract funding support) to be dubious about the objectivity of *any* source providing information on these issues. There simply are no neutral, objective sources that can be relied upon to arbitrate disputes over these issues authoritatively.

That is one reason this chapter has stressed the accuracy of these different "experts'" predictions as an important criterion for evaluating their expertise. Nobody is objective. But the future can serve as a kind of impartial arbiter of these debates (Ray and Russett, 1996). It can provide evidence regarding the extent to which the various competing sources of information and arguments deserve credence, by providing data on the accuracy of their predictions about the various global environmental issues discussed in this chapter. And it seems reasonable to argue (although, to repeat, no source is neutral or objective) that the pessimists and alarmists have made consistently inaccurate predictions about food shortages, the population explosion, the energy crisis in particular, the depletion of natural resources in general, and trends in the global climate. At least some skeptics and pessimists can claim with some justification that their predictions, "publicly stated in 1970 . . . have stood the test of time" (Simon, 1996, p. 578).[21]

But the pessimists and the alarmists are not necessarily always wrong. When F. Sherwood Rowland started arguing in the 1980s that spray deodorants and leaky car air conditioners posed a menacing threat to the ozone layer in the upper reaches of the atmosphere, his argument was greeted with great skepticism. But by 1987, agreement on the dangers posed to the ozone layer had developed to the point that international negotiations produced the Montreal Protocol on Substances That Deplete the Ozone Layer. International cooperation on this issue has been more effective than that aimed at the elimination of the threat of global warming, partly because the evidence was more convincing and, perhaps even more important, because the economic sacrifices involved in dealing with this threat are considerably less substantial. The results of that cooperation are clear. "By 1995, global production of the most significant ozone-depleting substance . . . CFCs . . . was down 76 percent from its peak in 1988" (French, 1997a, p. 151). Their production has been phased out almost entirely in industrialized countries. And "58 developing countries have stated a commitment to phase CFC's out earlier than required" (French, 1997b, p.

---

[21] The predictions in question here are: "Raw materials and energy are getting less scarce. The world's food supply is improving. Pollution in developed countries has been decreasing. . . . Most important, fewer people are dying young. . . . These benign trends have continued" (Simon, 1996, p. 578).

102).[22] In 1995, F. Sherwood Rowland won a Nobel Prize (see Wines, 1996, p. 10). And there may well be other warnings from the pessimists and alarmists that deserve attention. The generally rather optimistic *Economist*, for example, observes that while environmental panics are not usually to be taken too seriously, "on two issues, however, environmentalists' warnings deserve to be taken seriously: fish and water" (*Economist*, November 16, 1996, p. 23). Something like 70 percent of the world's fish stocks are being fished beyond (or nearly beyond) what is sustainable. Yet many governments persist in subsidizing fishing fleets that plunder these waters.[23] The amount of water diverted from lakes, rivers, springs, and aquifers has increased thirty-fivefold in the past three hundred years, with over half that increase occurring just since 1950 (Abramovitz, 1996, p. 31). "Worldwide demand for water is doubling every 21 years and even faster in some regions. Supply can't keep pace with growth in demand as populations soar and cities explode" (Vidal, 1995, p. 8).[24] Yet in most countries, farmers are provided with water at rates subsidized by the government.

Finally, it needs to be stressed that many initiatives and responses advocated by "pessimists" and "alarmists" in recent decades have by most accounts proved beneficial. Even the prominent "optimist" Gregg

---

[22] Satisfaction over this international achievement might reasonably be tempered by at least two considerations. First, "it takes years for CFCs . . . to reach the stratosphere, and some last for centuries once there. . . . The ozone layer will . . . mend gradually, though a full recovery is not expected until about 2050" (French, 1997b, p. 103). The other, quite contrasting consideration is that it is not entirely clear that this was a problem requiring an international response of any kind. "The long-run data on ozone show no trends that square with public scares. . . . Banning CFCs . . . runs the risk of raising the cost of refrigeration enough to put it out of the reach of some people in poor countries. . . . There is also the possibility that increased ultra-violet radiation stemming from decreased ozone may have beneficial effects in reducing rickets disease, which results from too little sunlight and lack of vitamin D" (Simon, 1996, pp. 270–271).

[23] Elsewhere, the *Economist* (March 18, 1995, p. 48) describes in detail the kind of collective action, "tragedy of the commons" problem in place with respect to this issue: "If all fishermen restrained themselves, each would benefit from enlarged stocks in the future. But no individual boat or fleet sees any gain from holding back. . . . And, alas, just as with individual fishermen, each . . . country on its own can gain from delaying a deal even though all would gain were they to co-operate."

[24] This same source points out that "80 countries . . . now have [water] shortages that threaten health and economies . . . 40 percent of the world (more than 2 billion people) has no access to clean water or sanitation . . . the situation is deteriorating" (Vidal, 1995, p. 8) It will by this point in the discussion come as no surprise to readers that not all "experts" are alarmed about this problem. "The American hydrologist Robert Ambroggi says, 'The total quantity of freshwater on earth exceeds all conceivable needs of the human population'" (Robinson and Sweet, 1997, p. 58).

SOURCE: Copyright, 1970, Los Angeles Times. Reprinted by permission.

Easterbrook (1995b, p. xviii), having observed (as noted above) widespread improvements in the United States in air quality, water quality, ocean pollution levels, acid rain emissions, and so on, acknowledges that these improvements are in large measure the result of initiatives backed by those who early on became concerned about the deteriorating environment in that country. "On environmental affairs . . . public investments yield significant benefits within the lifetimes of the people who make the investment. The first round of environmental investments did not fail; they worked, which is a great reason to have more."

SUMMARY

The global community can be analyzed as an integrated entity rather than simply a group of interrelated but separate nation-states. Global environmental problems lend themselves to such analyses, because pollution, for example, does not respect international boundaries. An integrated analysis of such global problems as the population explosion, famine, depletion of natural resources, global warming, and threats to the ozone layer in the upper atmosphere reveals that ostensible solutions to any one of those problems might unexpectedly make related problems even more serious. Analysts of environmental issues tend either to be very pessimistic about the future of the global community or optimistic that admittedly serious problems can be dealt with. Pessimistic predictions from the 1960s and the 1970s about the population explosion, food shortages, and depletion of energy resources, for example, have proved premature at best. And economic growth, which tends to be distrusted by many pessimistic analysts, can create resources to devote to the solution of global environmental problems, even though there clearly are structural forces, summarized in the concept "tragedy of the commons," that can lead economic growth in environmentally destructive directions. Pessimistic predictions about future global environmental disasters cannot be discounted entirely, if only because they focus on unprecedented threats, about which human understanding is necessarily limited. Still, skepticism about such predictions has probably been warranted more often than not. Comparing the predictive capabilities of competing sources of information is one important basis for evaluating their relative credibility. Yet pessimists, alarmists, and environmental activists have made important contributions. Some of their warnings, past and (perhaps) present, have proved worthy of attention. And some of their initiatives and campaigns have produced beneficial reforms.

KEY TERMS

global community
poverty
starvation
population explosion
deterioration of the ozone layer
global warming
greenhouse effect
world's production of grain
availability of cropland

globe's total population
infant motality rate
natural resources
energy crises
fresh water
fossil fuels
global carbon emissions
concentration of carbon dioxide
computer simulation

The Limits to Growth
halt in economic growth
Julian Simon
Worldwatch Institute
Lester Brown
optimists
pessimists
accurate predictions
Paul Ehrlich
The Population Bomb
known reserves

Amazon rain forest
chlorofluorocarbons (CFCs)
Intergovernmental Panel on Climate
    Change (IPCC)
global sea level
new ice age
population control
conservation of natural resources
pollution control
"tragedy of the commons"
collective action problems

SOURCES

Abramowitz, Janet N. "Imperiled Waters, Impoverished Future: The Decline of Freshwater Ecosystems." *Worldwatch Paper 128*, March 1996.

Adler, Jonathan. "Schools Resort to Teaching Green Lies." *The Detroit News*, July 26, 1992, Section B, p. 3.

"Ancient Rome Helped Pollute Hemisphere." Associated Press, September 22, 1994. Reprinted in the *Tampa Tribune*, September 22, 1994, Nation/World, p. 8.

Ayres, Ed. "Note to Readers." *World Watch*, January–February 1995, p. 3.

Bennett, H. Sterling. "Not All Scientists Back Global Warming Treaty." Letter to the *New York Times*, June 27, 1997, Section A, p. 20.

Bhagwati, Jagdish. "The Case for Free Trade." *Scientific American*, November 1993, pp. 42–49.

Beckerman, Wilfred. *In Defence of Economic Growth*. London: Cape, 1974.

Bettman, Otto L. *The Good Old Days—They Were Terrible*. New York: Random House, 1974.

Bright, Chris. "Tracking the Ecology of Climate Change." In Linda Starke, ed., *State of the World 1997*. New York: Norton, 1997.

Brown, Lester R. "Facing the Prospect of Food Scarcity." In Linda Starke, ed., *State of the World 1997*. New York: Norton, 1997.

Brown, Lester R. " A New Era Unfolds." In Lester R. Brown et al., eds., *The State of the World 1993*. New York: Norton, 1993.

Brown, Lester R. "Reducing Hunger." In Lester R. Brown et al., eds., *The State of the World 1985*. New York: Norton, 1985.

Brown, Lester. *Who Will Feed China: Wake-Up Call for a Small Planet*. New York: Norton, 1995.

Brown, Lester. "World Grain Harvest Sets Record." In Linda Starke, ed., *Vital Signs 1997*. New York: Norton, 1997.

Brown, Lester R. *World Without Borders*. New York: Random House, Vintage Books, 1972.

Brown, Lester R., Christopher Flavin, and Sandra Postel. "A World at Risk." In Lester R. Brown et al., eds., *The State of the World 1989*. New York: Norton, 1989.

Central Intelligence Agency. *The International Energy Situation: An Outlook to 1985.* Washington, D.C.: U.S. Government Printing Office, 1977.

Chandler, William V. "Increasing Energy Efficiency." In Lester R. Brown et al., eds., *The State of the World 1985.* New York: Norton, 1985.

"China's Future Grain Needs Will Be an Opportunity for Grain-Exporting Nations." *2020 Vision News and Views,* March 1997. http://www.cgiar.org/IFPRI/2020/newslet/nv_0397/2nv0397.htm

Commoner, Barry. "How Poverty Breeds Overpopulation." In Steven C. Spiegel, ed., *At Issue: Politics in the World Arena.* New York: St. Martin's Press, 1977.

Crossette, Barbara. "World Is Less Crowded Than Expected, the U.N. Reports." *New York Times,* November 17, 1996, Section 1, p. 3.

Dunn, Seth. "Carbon Emissions Set New Record." In Linda Starke, ed., *Vital Signs 1997.* New York: Norton, 1997a.

Dunn, Seth. "Global Temperature Down Slightly." In Linda Starke, ed., *Vital Signs 1997.* New York: Norton, 1997b.

Easterbrook, Gregg. "The Good Earth Looks Better." *New York Times,* April 21, 1995a, Section A, p. 31.

Easterbrook, Gregg. *A Moment on the Earth: The Coming Age of Environmental Optimism.* New York: Viking, 1995b.

"The Economics of the Sea." *Economist,* March 18, 1995, 48.

Ehrlich, Paul. *The Population Bomb.* New York: Ballantine, 1968.

"Facts About Oil and Gas." *TOTAL: Oil and Gas Industry.* http://www.calvacom.fr/total/us/cahier/ressources.html, 1997.

"Feeding the World." *Economist,* November 16, 1996, 18.

Flavin, Christopher. "Facing Up to the Risks of Climate Change." In Linda Starke, ed., *State of the World 1996.* New York: Norton, 1996.

Flavin, Christopher. "Fossil Fuel Use Surges to New High." In Linda Starke, ed., *Vital Signs 1997.* New York: Norton, 1997a.

Flavin, Christopher. "The Legacy of Rio." In Linda Starke, ed., *State of the World 1997.* New York: Norton, 1997b.

Flavin, Christopher, and Nicholas Lenssen. "Designing a Sustainable Energy System." In Lester R. Brown et al., eds., *State of the World 1991.* New York: Norton, 1991.

Forrester, Jay. "Counterintuitive Behavior of Social Systems." In *Collected Papers of Jay W. Forrester.* Cambridge, Mass.: Wright-Allen Press, 1975.

French, Hilary. "Learning from the Ozone Experience." In Linda Starke, ed., *State of The World 1997.* New York: Norton, 1997a.

French, Hilary. "Ozone Response Accelerates." In Linda Starke, ed., *Vital Signs 1997.* New York: Norton, 1997b.

Gardner, Gary. "Preserving Global Cropland." In Linda Starke, ed., *State of the World 1997.* New York: Norton, 1997.

Hardin, Garrett. "The Tragedy of the Commons." In Garrett Hardin and John Baden, eds., *Managing the Commons.* San Francisco: Freeman, 1977.

Herrera, Amilcar O., et al. *Catastrophe or New Society?* Ottawa, Canada: International Development Research Centre, 1976.

"How Hot Was It? Earth Sizzled to a Record in 1990." A *New York Times* Report. *Tampa Tribune,* January 10, 1991, Section A, p. 1.

Hughes, Barry B. *World Futures.* Baltimore, Md.: Johns Hopkins University Press, 1985.

Jacobson, Jodi. "Swept Away." *World Watch,* January–February 1989, pp. 20–26.

"Just When You Thought It Was Safe." *Economist,* November 16, 1996, 23.

Kahn, Herman, William Brown, and Leon Martel. *The Next 200 Years.* New York: Morrow, 1976.

LaFollete, Hugh, and Larry May. "Suffer the Little Children." In William Aiken and Hugh Lafollete, eds., *World Hunger and Morality.* Prentice-Hall, http://www.etsu-tn.edu/philos/faculty/hugh/suffer.htm, 1996.

Laszewski, Charles. "Ozone Layer Getting Thinner—Faster." *Tallahassee Democrat,* April 5, 1991, Section A, pp. 1, 5.

Lents, James M., and William J. Kelly. "Clearing the Air in Los Angeles." *Scientific American,* October 1993, pp. 32–39.

Mann, Charles C. "How Many Is Too Many?" *Atlantic Monthly,* February 1993, pp. 47–67.

Meadows, Donella H., Dennis L. Meadows, Jorgen Randers, and William W. Behrens III. *The Limits to Growth: A Report for the Club of Rome's Project on the Predicament of Mankind.* New York: Universe Books, 1972.

Mesarovic, Mihajlo D., and Eduard C. Pestel. *Mankind at the Turning Point: The Second Report to the Club of Rome.* New York: New American Library, 1974.

Milbank, Dana. "In His Solitude, a Finnish Thinker Posits Cataclysms." *Wall Street Journal,* May 20, 1994, Section A, 1,7.

Mitchell, Jennifer. "Population Increase Slows Slightly." In Linda Starke, ed., *Vital Signs 1997.* New York: Norton, 1997.

"What on Earth: More in the Pipeline." *WashingtonPost*.com. http://www.washingtonpost.com/wp-srv/inatl/longterm.woe/archives/oil.htm, 1997.

Nasar, Sylvia. "Cooling the Globe Would Be Nice; But Saving Lives Now May Cost Less." *New York Times,* May 31, 1992, Section 4, p. 6.

Panati, Charles, and Mary Lord. "Population Implosion." *Newsweek,* December 6, 1976, p. 58.

Perlman, Mark. "The Role of Population Projections for the Year 2000." In Julian L. Simon and Herman Kahn, eds., *The Resourceful Earth.* New York: Blackwell, 1984.

Ray, James Lee, and Bruce Russett. "The Future as Arbiter of Theoretical Controversies." *British Journal of Political Science,* 26 (October 1996), 441–470.

Robinson, Gail, and William Sweet. "Environmental Threats to Stability: The Role of Population Growth." In Nancy Hoepli-Phalon, ed., *Great Decisions '97.* New York: Foreign Policy Association.

Roodman, David Malinl "Carbon Emissions Resume Rise." In Linda Starke, ed., *Vital Signs 1995.* New York: Norton, 1995.

Shea, Cynthia Pollock. "Mending the Earth's Shield." *World Watch,* January–February 1989, pp. 27–34.

Sherman, Howard. *Radical Political Economy.* New York: Basic Books, 1972.

Simon, Julian L. *The Ultimate Resource.* Princeton, N.J.: Princeton University Press, 1981.

Simon, Julian L. *The Ultimate Resource 2*. Princeton, N.J.: Princeton University Press, 1996.

Simon, Julian L., and Herman Kahn (eds.). *The Resourceful Earth*. New York: Blackwell, 1984.

Sinclair, T. C. "Environmentalism." In H. S. D. Cole, Christopher Freeman, Marie Jahoda, and K. L. R. Pavitt, eds., *Models of Doom*. New York: Universe Books, 1973.

Singer, Max. *Passage to a Human World*. Indianapolis, Ind.: Hudson Institute, 1987.

Stevens, William K. "Experts Confirm Human Role in Global Warming." *New York Times*, September 10, 1995, Section 1, pp. 1, 6.

"Stormy Weather Ahead." *Economist*, March 23, 1996, pp. 83–85.

Tierney, John. "Betting the Planet." *New York Times* magazine, December 2, 1990, pp. 52–53, 74–81.

United Nations Development Programme. *Human Development Report*. New York: Oxford University Press, 1996.

"U.N. Projections Rise Slightly Higher than 1989." *Population Today*, November 1990, p. 4.

Vidal, John. "Next Wars over Water?" *The Guardian*, August 20, 1995. Reprinted in *World Press Review*, November 1995, 8–10.

"Waking Up to the Glut Economy." *New York Times*, December 8, 1985, Section 3, p. 1.

"Warm Words." *Economist*, June 14, 1997, pp. 89–91.

Wald, Matthew L. "After 20 Years, America's Foot Is Still on the Gas." *New York Times*, October 17, 1993, Section 4, p. 4.

"Weather Wisdom: Scientists Say Warming May Be Natural." Associated Press, February 20, 1995. Published in the *Tampa Tribune*, February 20, 1995, Nation/World, p. 3.

Will, George. "Global Warming Panic Supplants Earlier Warnings of Catastrophe." *Tampa Tribune*, June 1, 1992, Marion/Alachua, p. 5.

"Will the World Starve?" *Economist*, June 10, 1995, pp. 39–40.

Wines, Michael. "The Sky Is Falling: Three Cheers for Chicken Little." *New York Times*, December 29, 1996, Section 4, pp. 1, 10.

Wirth, David A. "Climate Chaos." *Foreign Policy*, No. 74 (Spring 1989).

World Bank. *World Development Report*. New York: Oxford University Press, 1992.

"World's Proven Oil Reserves and Product." *NESTE Exporation and Production*, http://www.neste.com/default/htm, 1997.

PART VII

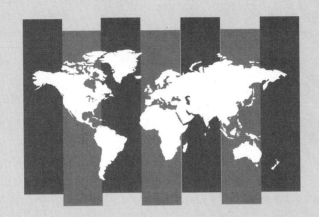

Conclusion

CHAPTER 16

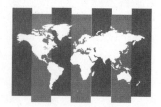

History, Science, and Values in the Study of Global Politics

This book has emphasized three themes of global politics: (1) its **history,** (2) its **scientific study,** and (3) its **future.** The historical theme was included in part because most important and influential people involved in global politics are generally familiar with the history of the global system, and their actions and decisions often bear the impact of this familiarity. Ignorance of history necessarily detracts from an understanding of those actions and decisions. The historical record of global politics also deserves emphasis because it provides a kind of laboratory within which generalizations about world politics can be tested.

THE LESSONS OF HISTORY

The impact of history on important decision makers emerges nicely from an analysis of the extent to which world leaders "learn from history to make the **opposite mistakes.**"[1] This aphorism applies neatly to many of the wars in the last one hundred years or so involving the major powers. We have already discussed, for example, how France's experience in the Franco-Prussian War in 1870 may have helped convince decision makers that it is vital to line up firmly committed **allies** before a crisis occurs. France did not do this before the clash with Prussia in 1870, and the absence of help from potential allies such as Austria and Italy contributed to its disastrous defeat. As a result, in the

---

[1] I believe that A. J. P. Taylor used this phrase, but I do not know if he coined it.

years leading up to the First World War, decision makers made the "opposite mistake" and set up a series of rigid alliances that helped turn that war into a catastrophe.

Another lesson learned from the Franco-Prussian War that helped precipitate the First World War stemmed from the rapidity with which Prussia mobilized for the prior war. Compared with France's **mobilization procedures,** those of Prussia were fantastically efficient, and Prussia went on to score a quick victory as a result. This is certainly one reason all the major powers in August 1914 were so intent on **rapid mobilization.** They thought that the most rapid mobilizer would emerge victorious in short order. They were terribly wrong, of course, but that lesson learned from the Franco-Prussian War provoked another "opposite mistake" that sparked the First World War.

After 1918, a whole series of lessons learned from the First World War led to "opposite mistakes" culminating in the Second World War. It has already been mentioned that the concept of alliances came into disrepute following the First World War. Partly as a result of this change, the Allied powers were reluctant to form a meaningful alliance with the Soviets and similarly reluctant to rely on and honor the alliance treaties they did have. (For example, the French did not honor their commitment to Czechoslovakia in 1938.) Another conclusion drawn by many historians and decision makers from the First World War was that the conflict had resulted in large measure from an **arms race,** especially between Great Britain and Germany. This conviction may explain why the British, in the 1930s, were determined not to get involved in another arms race with Germany and failed to meet the challenge posed by Hitler's rapid rearmament. Similarly, the French learned that the **offensive strategies** they had tried at the beginning of the First World War were tragically unsuccessful, whereas their defenses in that war had proved quite impenetrable. So they decided to rely on a quintessentially defensive strategy as the Second World War approached, based on the **Maginot Line.** Perhaps the most important lesson learned from the First World War, as mentioned in Chapter 1, was that patience in the face of provocation is an important virtue for political leaders during an international crisis. According to this lesson, if only those leaders in July and August 1914 had been more patient and conciliatory, the war might have been averted. So their successors in the 1930s patiently allowed the Japanese to take over in Manchuria; let the Italians annex Ethiopia and Albania; and permitted Hitler to rearm in violation of the Versailles treaty, send troops into the Rhineland, annex Austria, take over the Sudetenland, and obliterate Czechoslovakia.

If one accepts that the North Koreans launched the Korean War with an unprovoked attack on South Korea, then it is difficult to argue that the U.S. decision to enter that war was a mistake. It is much less difficult, though, to argue that the British and French attack on Egypt in 1956 was a mistake, and one that was clearly based on a lesson culled from the British and French experience in the Second World War. Leaders in both countries perceived Nasser as another Hitler, and having learned that it does not pay to appease the aggressor, they made the "opposite mistake" and stood up to Nasser's first assertive move immediately and forcefully. If they had done that to Hitler, chances are that he might have been forced to retire early and in disgrace. But when they did it to Nasser, they made him a hero in the Arab states and throughout most of the Third World. And it is equally clear that the U.S. stand in Vietnam was based, in part, on the **lesson of Munich,** in spite of the fact that Ho Chi Minh bore no more resemblance to Hitler than Nasser did.

Did the United States learn a lesson from the Vietnam War that led it into an "opposite mistake"? It seems fairly clear that the United States did not err, as many conservatives feared it might, by becoming so isolationist that it stood by while another Hitler or totalitarian regime acquired such strength that he or it could only be stopped by a world war. The United States does seem to have applied a lesson from Vietnam in its conflict with Iraq. President Bush and the military were evidently determined to avoid a long, drawn-out conflict, and as a result, quickly applied massive force against an Iraqi army that, it turned out, was no match for the coalition forces. It could be argued that in an effort to expunge the pain of Vietnam, the United States fought a war that did not need to be fought, since economic sanctions would eventually have forced Iraq out of Kuwait without all the destruction, suffering, and death caused by the war. It also might turn out that the devastation of Iraq created the basis for political instability in the region and other long-term problems that will, in retrospect, make the decision to destroy so much of Iraq's infrastructure look like an "opposite mistake." For now, all that can be safely concluded is that the kind of war the United States fought against Iraq again showed that historical precedents and analogies have a clear impact on foreign policy makers.

Historical Generalizations

The assertion that grand coalitions fall apart is an example of a generalization that can be (and was) evaluated by analyzing the experience of grand coalitions in the global system since the Napoleonic Wars. History, used in this way, blends into the scientific theme in *Global Politics.* The **scientific method** and **analysis of the historical record** can be used to develop and evaluate **generalizations** about world politics. Traditional, intuitive historical analysis certainly cannot provide as rigorous a test for generalizations as the scientific method. But if the generalization lacks specificity (such as the one that asserts that world leaders "learn from history to make the opposite mistakes"), the scientific method is inapplicable. Some statements about global politics are not specific enough to be tested scientifically but may still provide valuable insights that can be evaluated with a logical, intuitive, and philosophical analysis of the historical record. In other cases, the generalization in question may be sufficiently specific to be tested scientifically ("Grand coalitions fall apart" is reasonably specific), but the number of cases to which it applies may be too small to allow a rigorous application of the scientific method. If so, analysis of the historical record provides a useful alternative.

SCIENTIFIC GENERALIZATIONS

On many occasions, the scientific method *is* applicable to generalizations and hypotheses about world politics, as, it is hoped, the scientific theme in *Global Politics* has demonstrated. Here *scientific method* means a logical method of testing hypotheses (or generalizations) based on **reproducible, controlled comparisons.**[2] An implication of this definition is that scientific analyses of generalizations must include all relevant cases or a representative sample of those cases. Once the data on the cases have been assembled, they can be subjected to reproducible comparisons. Such comparisons (as in Chapter 2) are based on procedures so clearly defined that any qualified scientist, in addition to the original researcher, can carry them out.

Controlled comparisons regarding the impact of the external economic and political environment on the economic performance of

---

[2] This definition of the scientific method is admittedly controversial, and it has equally debatable implications for what constitutes science. In their comprehensive review of the field of international relations, James E. Dougherty and Robert L. Pfaltzgraff, Jr. (1990, p. 37) assert that "whatever satisfies intelligent human beings in any age as the optimum means of enlarging their intellectual frontiers will pass muster as 'scientific.'" This definition has the advantage of offending nobody because it includes everybody, from astrologers and readers of entrails to devotees of mind-expanding drugs. For a different view of this controversy, readers might consult Julian L. Simon (1969, pp. 473–474), who asserts that "by this time, it is unnecessary to discuss whether or not the social sciences are real sciences. What is more interesting now is whether or not the social sciences are more scientific than are the natural sciences; as far as methodology goes, I think there is good reason to think that social sciences are far ahead of the natural sciences."

developing countries have yielded inconsistent findings, with some researchers, for example, reporting that foreign investment has a deleterious impact on Third World economies, while others argue that it does not.[3] But these comparisons also reveal, contrary to some common impressions, that multinational corporations are more likely to invest in countries that implement human rights reforms than in those that avoid such reforms. Research into the relationship between a state's characteristics and its foreign policies has found that large states are more active participants than small states in the international system. Controlled comparisons have produced several interesting findings regarding international conflicts and wars. Personalist regimes (dictatorships) exhibit more conflictual behavior than do polyarchic (democratic) regimes; and generally speaking, states with more internal conflict do not become involved in more foreign conflict. There is, though, an apparent tendency for the United States to use military force during those times when its economy is performing badly. When involved in disputes, democratic states are more likely than autocratic states to allow mediating efforts by third parties, and those efforts are more likely to be successful when the parties to the disputes are democratic than when they are not. In times of international crisis, states that use "bullying" bargaining strategies end up fighting a war about two-thirds of the time, while states that adopt reciprocating strategies (that is, respond to coercive moves with coercion, and to cooperative moves with cooperation) achieve a diplomatic victory or a compromise solution about two-thirds of the time. When states form alliances, they tend to forge ties that decrease the probability that they will be attacked by other states. Democratic states are more likely than their autocratic counterparts to win the wars in which they participate, and (perhaps partly for that reason) no dispute between states has ever escalated to international war unless at least *one* of those states was *not* democratic.

---

[3] I might interject here that although findings in many physical sciences are clearly more consistent, and more widely accepted (for example, among scientists within many different countries), it is not true that only the social sciences are marked by controversies and contradictory findings. As noted in Chapter 15, meteorologists now disagree about the hypothesized greenhouse effect of carbon dioxide emissions in the global atmosphere on human beings (they also still have some difficulty agreeing on or predicting whether or not it will rain tomorrow). Controversies also occur even in the most advanced areas of inquiry. Astronomers have recently gone through a period of time when their best estimates as to the age of the universe conflicted with their estimates about the ages of various stars. (For some time, at least, some evidence indicated that the universe is younger than some of the oldest stars.) Einstein's theory of relativity is inconsistent with those theories of quantum mechanics that best predict the behavior of subatomic particles.

Scientific Control

In at least one important way, the discussion of many of these analyses in previous chapters has been misleading. For the sake of simplicity, the discussion has often been restricted to relationships involving only two variables, and the evidence examined has been based on analyses of the relationships, or the correlations, between those two variables. **Correlation,** the old saying goes, does not prove **causation,** that is, a correlation between Variables A and B may be brought about entirely by Variable C. For example, in most societies there is a positive correlation between an individual's level of education (Variable A) and yearly income (Variable B). Is that correlation brought about because a higher education causes increased earning power? Perhaps, but the correlation, at least in part, probably also exists because the social class of an individual's parents (Variable C) is causally connected to both the educational level and yearly income of that individual. That is, the higher the social class of the parents, the more likely the person is to attain a higher educational level *and* to earn a higher salary later in life. In that case, though, it is not more education that causes higher salaries; the correlation between educational and salary levels is **spurious.**

A similar criticism could be directed at the two-variable relationships discussed in this book. It is at least possible that each relationship has been brought about by some third factor and that none of the correlations discussed is evidence of causal relationships. It is important to understand, though, that the scientific methods used by social scientists do not ignore this problem. In fact, a crucial aspect of those methods—that is, **control**—is designed specifically to meet the problem of dealing with third variables that can affect relationships between the two factors of greatest interest. In this context, *control* can be defined as the elimination of the effect of **confounding variables.** Confounding variables are variables that can lead to confusion; for example, if Variable C (such as parents' social class) causes a correlation between Variables A (level of education) and B (yearly income), thus leading to the confusing notion that Variable A causes Variable B, then Variable C is a confounding variable.

Some scientists handle confounding variables with **experimental controls** in a laboratory. Social scientists usually must rely on another kind of control—that is, **statistical control.** For example, if a social scientist suspects that the correlation between educational level and yearly income is not causal but is brought about by the confounding variable of parents' social class, he or she can control the third variable (that is, eliminate its effect) in the manner demonstrated in Figure 16.1. The representative sample of individuals from, say, U.S. society can be divided into two groups. One group will include only people with

Figure 16.1 Hypothetical Analysis of the Relationship Between Educational Level and Yearly Income, with Parents' Social Class Controlled

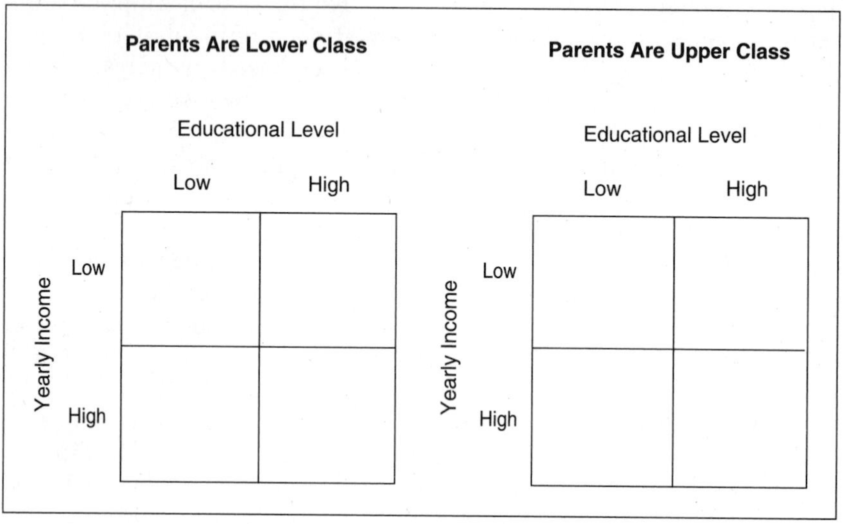

Third variables often influence apparently simple bivariate relationships.

lower-class parents, and the other will include people with upper-class parents. If it is discovered, even among individuals who all have lower-class parents (or all have upper-class parents), that those with higher levels of education have higher yearly incomes, then one can argue convincingly that education levels are causally connected to income levels. Controlling the potentially confounding variable of parents' social class provides evidence that the correlation between the other two variables is causal. Of course, some other variables can be controlled, too. The more often this is done, the more confidence one can have that the original correlation is causal.

The same kinds of procedures are applicable to variables of interest to scholars of global politics. Chapter 14, for example, discussed the correlation between the polarity of the international system and the intensity of wars. This correlation might not be causal but instead might be brought about by some prior third factor. It might be hypothesized that high levels of military expenditures cause both greater polarity and increased intensity of wars. This hypothesis can be tested using scientific control. That is, time periods can be divided into those when military expenditures were high and those when expenditures were low (see Figure 16.2). If it turns out that, in both groups, wars tended to be more intense during periods marked by greater polarity, then evidence

Figure 16.2 Hypothetical Analysis of the Relationship Between Changes in Polarity of the International System and Intensity of War, with Levels of Military Expenditure Controlled

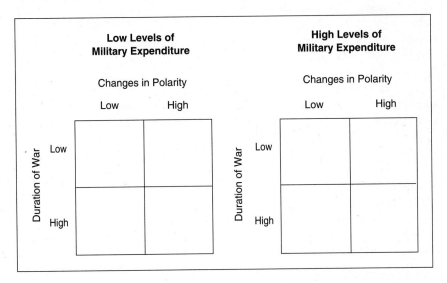

Chapter 14's discussion of the effect of polarity on the intensity of wars can be applied to this hypothetical analysis, which controls for the third factor of military expenditures.

will have been uncovered that the original correlation also reflects a causal relationship. Additional hypotheses to the contrary can be disposed of in a similar fashion.

The kind of statistical control demonstrated in Figures 16.1 and 16.2 is only one type available to social scientists. Other types of techniques are more amenable to controlling for three, four, or five variables at the same time. There are other reasons besides a desire for control for analyzing more than two variables at a time. The various phenomena of interest in global politics invariably have more than one cause. If the discussion of two-variable relationships created an impression that social scientists are unaware of this fact, then that is another way in which the discussion has been misleading. Multiple causes can certainly be dealt with by social scientific methods.

In short, the discussion of scientific analyses of global politics has been a preliminary one. Students who want to know more about these analyses should acquire the knowledge of the scientific method and analytical techniques (such as statistics) necessary to understand them fully.

HISTORY, SCIENCE, VALUES, AND
THE FUTURE

Serious students of global politics will want to develop several tools in addition to a competence in statistics. The discussion of the history of global politics in this book has been as preliminary as that dealing with its scientific study, and there are numerous excellent historical sources that can be consulted to increase one's knowledge about the history of the global political system. *A Diplomatic History of Europe Since the Congress of Vienna* by René Albrecht-Carrie (1958) is a good source of information about the Euro-centered international system up to the post–Second World War era, as is *The Rise and Fall of the Great Powers* by Paul Kennedy (1987). Both Charles L. Robertson's (1975) *International Politics Since World War II* and Peter Calvocoressi's (1991) *World Politics Since 1945* cover more recent events in a competent manner. For analyses of current events in more depth than one can usually find in newspapers or weekly magazines, the journals *Foreign Affairs* and *Foreign Policy* are widely respected and influential sources. Of the numerous additional scholarly journals with which serious students of global politics will want to become familiar, *World Politics, International Studies Quarterly, International Organization, International Interactions, International Security, Journal of Peace Research,* and *Journal of Conflict Resolution* are certainly among the most important.

As students become familiar with these and other sources, they should become aware that historical and scientific analyses should be combined in any fruitful attempt to predict the future of the global political system or any of its constituent elements. Conceptually, **future occurrences** can be divided into the unique and the recurrent. Historical intuitive analyses are well suited for understanding the former, while scientific studies are primarily aimed at comprehending the latter.

For example, imagine predicting the future foreign policies of Great Britain. To some extent, Great Britain has similarities with other states, and **scientific generalizations** about states like Great Britain (such as those about open societies) should help in formulating accurate predictions about its foreign policy. But in some ways, Great Britain is unique, having combinations of characteristics not shared by any other state in the global system, and these combinations of characteristics will probably have an important impact on Britain's foreign policy.

Scientific methods are not useless in the face of unique characteristics. The word *unique* does not necessarily imply *incomparable*. Britain is the only state in the world that was the most powerful in the global system throughout most of the nineteenth century, and this characteristic could conceivably have an impact on its current and future foreign policies. But Britain's uniqueness in this regard, from a scientific point of view, merely places it at the extreme end of a continuum, and thus Britain, even with respect to this unique characteristic, *is* comparable. The impact of this characteristic might be studied scientifically, with scientific methods being applied to the assertion that "the more powerful a state was in the nineteenth century, the more _____ its foreign policies will be in the future."

But the combinations of characteristics found in the British case may well make that country, to some extent, both unique and incomparable. Britain is the only modern, industrialized democracy on an island that was the most powerful state in the world in the nineteenth century and that evolved from a monarchy to its present democratic status. If the uniquely British constellation of characteristics will have an impact on Britain's future foreign policy, probably the only way to gain an appreciation of that impact will be to analyze British history in a traditional, intuitive, philosophical manner. Reproducible comparisons will not be possible, because the various combinations of characteristics exhibited by the British make their country (as well as every other country in the world) incomparable.

Similarly, the future of the global system can be divided into sectors consisting of **recurrent phenomena** and **unique events.** Scientific analyses allow one to identify relationships among recurrent phenomena (such as those between concentration of power and amounts of war, or between economic growth and pollution levels) and use the information to make predictions about the future of the global system. But in some ways, the global system of today is unique; it exhibits some characteristics (and combinations of characteristics) that did not exist in 1950 or 1900 or 1815. These characteristics (and combinations of characteristics), as well as relationships among recurrent phenomena, will make their mark on the future of the global political system. Without knowledge of the history of the global system, it would be impossible even to identify these unprecedented characteristics, much less apply one's logical and analytical abilities to the task of calculating what impact they may have on the future of global politics.

Finally, students of global politics (whether they are first-year college students or full professors) will be interested not only in how the global system *will* change but also in ways in which it *should* change. The two questions are obviously not unrelated. Changes that may be very desirable but are highly unlikely are necessarily less interesting than changes that combine some optimum amounts of desirability and feasibility. The ability to identify these latter kinds of changes and to formulate strategies that might bring them about must rest not only on a knowledge of the history of the global political system and on scientific evidence but also on one's **values.** To make coherent predictions about their preferred future world, students must combine their historical and scientific knowledge about global politics with an understanding of their own values, as well as make difficult decisions concerning the relative importance of those values.

KEY TERMS

history	reproducible, controlled comparisons
scientific study	correlation
future	causation
opposite mistakes	spurious
allies	control
mobilization procedures	confounding variables
rapid mobilization	experimental controls
arms race	statistical control
offensive strategies	future occurrences
Maginot Line	scientific generalizations
lesson of Munich	recurrent phenomena
scientific method	unique events
analysis of the historical record	values
generalizations	

SOURCES

Albrecht-Carrie, René. *A Diplomatic History of Europe Since the Congress of Vienna.* New York: Harper & Row, 1958.

Calvocoressi, Peter. *World Politics Since 1945.* London: Longman, 1991.

Dougherty, James E., and Robert L. Pfaltzgraff, Jr. *Contending Theories of International Relations.* 3rd ed. New York: Harper & Row, 1990.

Kennedy, Paul. *The Rise and Fall of the Great Powers.* New York: Random House, 1987.

Robertson, Charles L. *International Politics Since World War II.* New York: Wiley, 1975.

Simon, Julian L. *Basic Research Methods in Social Science.* New York: Random House, 1969.

Name Index

Abdolali, Nasrin, 213, 513
Abdollahian, Mark, 142
Abramovitz, Janet N., 581
Acheson, Dean, 44
Adams, Gordon, 98n
Adenauer, Konrad, 357
Adler, Jonathan, 576
Adler, Mortimer, 421
Albrecht-Carrie, René, 598
Albright, Madeleine, 147
Alexander, Yonah, 495, 498
Alexandre, Laurien, 73
Allende, Salvador, 217, 475–476
Allison, Graham T., 52, 127, 129, 130, 137
Allyn, Bruce J., 53, 127
Almond, Gabriel, 82, 83n, 88
Alperowitz, Gar, 41
Ambroggi, Robert, 581n
Ambrose, Stephen E., 59
Amuzegar, Jahangir, 283, 284
Anderson, George, 130n
Andropov, Yuri, 141
Apple, R. W., Jr., 365, 366, 368n
Aron, Raymond, 172n, 193, 207, 448
Axelrod, Robert, 448, 452
Axline, W. Andrew, 381
Ayres, Ed, 557n

Baker, James, 131
Balassa, Bela, 375
Baldwin, David, 173, 183, 184
Bamrud, Joachim, 385
Bandar bin Sultan, Prince, 131n
Barbieri, Katherine, 212
Barkin, J. Samuel, 161, 169, 171
Barnet, Richard J., 44, 85
Barsoom, Peter N., 450

Bauer, P. T., 427
Bauer, Raymond A., 95n
Bean, Richard, 165
Beck, Joan, 83
Beck, Robert J., 28n
Becker, Charles M., 290
Beckerman, Wilfred, 562
Behrens, William W., III, 549, 552
Beitz, Charles R., 420, 433, 434, 435, 438, 443, 452
Bello, Walden, 280, 286
Benenson, Peter, 489–490
Bennett, A. Leroy, 403
Bennett, H. Sterling, 579n
Benoit, Kenneth, 210
Bergsten, C. Fred, 237n
Berlin, Eric, 486n
Berners-Lee, Tim, 483
Bernstein, Aaron, 244, 246
Bernstein, Richard, 278, 340
Bettman, Otto L., 574, 575
Bhagwati, Jagdish, 576
Bialer, Seweryn, 313, 316
Bickers, Kenneth H., 209
Billet, Bret L., 476
Binyan, Liu, 295
Birdzell, L. E., Jr., 428
Bismarck, Otto von, 6, 23, 136n
Blake, David H., 273, 464, 470, 472, 474
Blaug, Mark, 265
Blight, James G., 53, 54, 127, 144n
Blum, Leon, 26
Bodin, Jean, 163, 445
Bornschier, Volker, 477
Boswell, Terry, 477
Boulding, Kenneth, 179
Boyle, Joseph M., Jr., 423n

601

Subject Index

Abkhazia, 116
Afghanistan, 90
  ethnic conflicts and, 109; loss-of-strength gradient and, 179; public opinion and, 84; resolve and, 181; Soviet Union and, 58, 59, 75, 84, 172–173, 175–177, 179, 181, 212, 268, 402, 453; United States and, 176–177, 178, 313, 495
Africa
  democracy and, 62, 293, 294–295, 297; economic integration and, 385–386; ethnic conflicts and, 107, 114, 115; European colonialism and, 23, 166; famine and food supply, 294–295, 556; female genital mutilation and, 439–440, 441; imperialism and, 262; urban bias and, 290
African Americans, 253–254, 255, 256
Aggression, collective security and, 400, 401, 411, 415
Agriculture; agrarian reform and, 289–290; European Union and, 379. *See also* Food supply
After Hegemony (Keohane), 242
Albania, 61, 443
  Italy and, 24, 407, 591; Macedonia and, 116
Algeria
  colonialism and, 170; democracy and, 62; Islamic fundamentalism and, 335, 336; nuclear weapons and, 329, 338
Alliances, 10, 352–369, 386
  balance of power and, 353–354, 520, 532, 535; Classical Balance of Power and, 514–515; Cold War and, 520; collective security and, 400–401; Eastern Europe

and, 366–368, 387; First World War and, 4, 6–8, 14, 35; game theory and, 353–354; makeup of, 359–361; power and, 175–178, 185, 202; rationality and war and, 139; threats versus power and, 532–533; unreliable, 178n; utility of formal theory and, 358–361; war and, 175–178, 185, 361–368, 540, 594. *See also specific alliances*
Allied Powers, 525, 591
Allies
  First World War, 8, 15, 16, 17, 18–19, 23, 25, 26, 97, 590–591; Second World War, 200, 396
Amazon rain forest, 568
American Revolution, 170
Amnesty International, 442, 489–490, 500
Analyses on different levels, 510–513
Anarchy, 72, 419, 444, 451, 507, 525–526, 529, 530, 535
Andean Common Market, 382
Angola, 57, 59, 170
  economy, 275, 276; ethnic conflicts and, 109; South Africa and, 276; United States and, 313
Antagonistic or hostile foreign policy, 207
Anti-Communist alliances, 212
ANZUS treaty, 363
Appeasement, 25–29, 35
Arab-Israeli confict, 47, 114, 181
  Intifada and, 113; Palestine and, 47; peace agreement of 1993, 59. *See also* Middle East; *and specific nations*
Argentina, 90, 102n
  economy, 286, 385; Great Britain and, 212; weapons and, 329, 332